Payroll Accounting

2023 Edition

Bernard J. Bieg
Bucks County Community College

Judith A. Toland
Bucks County Community College

Australia • Brazil • Canada • Mexico • Singapore • United Kingdom • United States

Payroll Accounting, 2023 Edition
Bernard J. Bieg and Judith A. Toland

SVP, Product: Erin Joyner

VP, Product: Thais Alencar

Portfolio Product Director: Joe Sabatino

Portfolio Product Manager: Jonathan Gross

Product Assistant: Flannery Cowan

Learning Designer: Kristen Meere

Content Manager: Ian Moeckel

Digital Project Manager: Brett Bachman

Director, Product Marketing: Danae April

Product Marketing Manager: Colin Kramer

Content Acquisition Analyst: Ashley Maynard

Production Service: Lumina Datamatics, Inc.

Designer: Chris Doughman

Cover Image Source: Govindanmarudhai /DigitalVision Vectors/Getty Images

For product information and technology assistance, contact us at
Cengage Customer & Sales Support, 1-800-354-9706 or support.cengage.com.

For permission to use material from this text or product, submit all requests online at **www.copyright.com.**

Library of Congress Control Number: 2022917279

Student Edition:
ISBN: 978-0-357-72227-5

Loose-Leaf Edition:
ISBN: 978-0-357-72230-5

Cengage
200 Pier 4 Boulevard
Boston, MA 02210
USA

Cengage is a leading provider of customized learning solutions. Our employees reside in nearly 40 different countries and serve digital learners in 165 countries around the world. Find your local representative at **www.cengage.com.**

To learn more about Cengage platforms and services, register or access your online learning solution, or purchase materials for your course, visit **www.cengage.com.**

Printed in the United States of America
Print Number: 03   Print Year: 2023

As We Go To Press...

For the most up-to-date information after publication of this textbook, please visit **www.cengage.com**. At the Cengage home page, enter the ISBN of your textbook (from the back cover of your book). This will take you to the product page where free companion resources can be found, along with a dedicated page of "As We Go To Press" updates. Unless otherwise noted, the source of this information is www.irs.gov.

Chapter 1

Job Posting

California Legislature passed a bill that mandates that all organizations with 15 or more employees include hourly pay or salary range on job listings in the state. A number of cities and states have also passed salary transparency laws.

Chapter 2

Minimum Wage

In 2022, 24 states have hiked their minimum wage for workers (in many cases the rates are indexed to inflation). There are now over 30 states that have minimum wage rates over $7.25, the current federal minimum.

Tipped Employees

Pennsylvania employers are no longer allowed to deduct processing fees associated with using a credit card for an employee's tip. Employers must also disclose that any automatic gratuities are not tips for employees and must proved a space on receipts to directly tip employees.

Chapter 3

FICA-OASDI Taxable Wage Base

In this edition of the textbook, we have used the 2022 wage base of $147,000, and current projections have projected the 2023 wage base to be $155,100. Actual annual increases to the FICA-OASDI taxable wage base are announced in October of the preceding year based on current economic conditions.

Federal Holiday

June 19 was officially established as a federal holiday. Juneteenth (also referred to as Freedom Day) commemorates the abolition of slavery on June 19, 1865.

Chapter 4

Tax Brackets

In 2023, income tax brackets will be wider as they are annually indexed to inflation. Other tax breaks (like standard deductions) will also increase.

Filing 1099 Forms

The IRS is developing a web portal that will allow taxpayers to electronically prepare and e-file 1099's.

Chapter 7

Philadelphia Wage Tax

Effective July 1, 2022, until June 30, 2023, the Philadelphia Wage Tax is 3.79 percent (resident) and 3.44 percent (nonresident).

Payroll Accounting and Today's Business Environment

Today's payroll accountant is a major player on a company's management team. Management's need for timely and accurate payroll cost data as a part of the total planning step has moved payroll from a disbursement and recording function to an integral part of the management process.

With constant changes in the legal environment, technology advancements in the administration of payroll functions, and with tax withholding responsibilities, the payroll accounting occupation has become proactive. During this time when the need for accurate information is so critical, *Payroll Accounting* has established a record of being the most thorough book on the market for over 20 years. Each edition has been updated with the most current data available.

The 2023 edition of *Payroll Accounting* continues to provide the most user-friendly payroll accounting coverage, in addition to significant resources that will aid instructors and students alike in their mastery of payroll accounting.

CNOWv2

Payroll Accounting 2023 is fully integrated with CNOWv2, a powerful course management and online homework tool that provides robust instructor control and customization to optimize the student learning experience and meet desired outcomes. Learn more at https://www.cengage.com/cnowv2/.

CNOWv2 Includes

- NEW! Automated General Ledger Software
- Integrated eBook
- End-of-chapter homework with static and algorithmic versions
- Continuing Payroll Problems (CPP)
- Adaptive Study Plan and multimedia study tools
- Test bank
- Excel Online
- Course management tools and flexible assignment options
- Gradebook Analytics
- Mastery Problems
- Tell Me More Lecture Activities with assignable questions
- Robust feedback, which now includes feedback for Forms 940 and 941
- Audit Tests in CNOWv2
- Show Me How Demonstrative Videos

Tell Me More Lecture Activities

Tell Me More Lecture Activities are available and correlate to each Learning Objective (LO). These Lecture Assignments review the material covered in each LO, giving students a way to review what is covered in each objective in a digestible video activity format so they come to class more prepared and ready to participate.

Cengage CNOWv2

"To students, it's quick feedback, and they can improve the grades by working on the questions multiple times; to instructors, it's less grading time, and easy to evaluate students' performance."

-Jack Wu,
Chemeketa Community College

Tell Me More

Audit Tests for Payroll Project

The Student Audit Tests are designed to help students as they work through the Payroll Project in Chapter 7, Appendix A, and new online Appendix B. These tests can be assigned specifically to the Payroll Dates inside CNOWv2, and students can answer them to ensure they are fully understanding the concept and process of the payroll project.

Show Me How Problem Demonstrative Videos

Show Me How

Show Me How Videos are available for all continuing payroll problems at the end of each chapter and the most commonly assigned end-of-chapter assignments in both the A Set and B Set. These Videos provide students with both a detailed walk-through of a similar problem and problem-solving strategies.

Going Further in Payroll Accounting

- **Updated:** Detailed Check My Work and Post-Submission feedback with explanations and tips for completing the problem

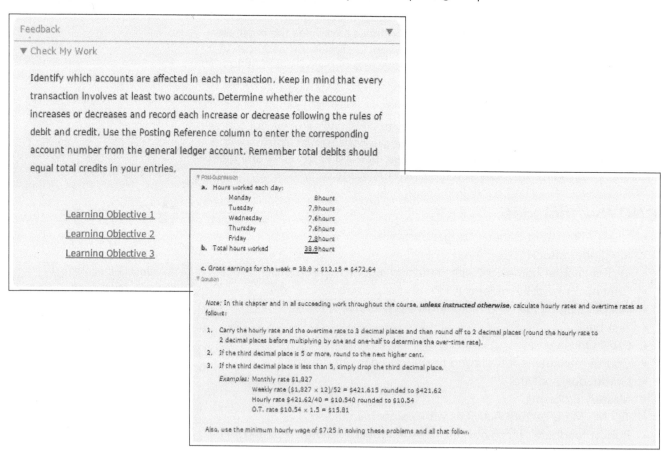

- **Mastery Problems** within CNOWv2 are designed to help students understand difficult topics in payroll accounting by breaking down the topic into smaller parts. Each part builds on other parts through a systematic problem-solving process. These problems address key chapter learning objectives and are algorithmic for versatile assignment options.

- CNOWv2 contains numerous algorithmic problems that allow instructors to have more flexibility and assurance that students are completing the projects on their own.

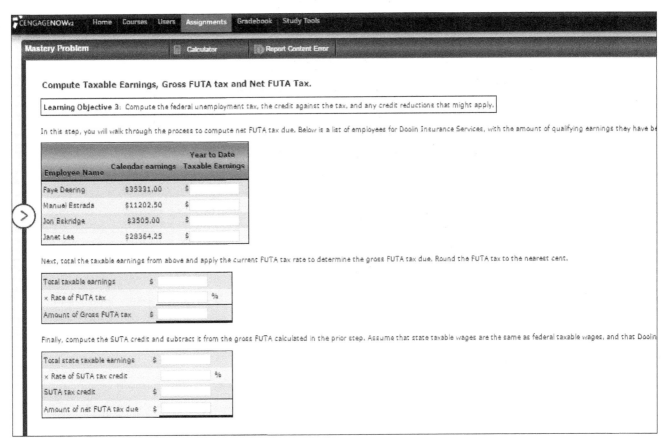

- Randomized Test Bank answers within CNOWv2 allow instructors to assign the same multiple-choice test problems, but CNOWv2 will randomize the selection choices. The selection order for each student changes, combating student cheating. See the following example.

The entry to deposit FICA taxes and federal income taxes withheld involves all of the following accounts *except*:	The entry to deposit FICA taxes and federal income taxes withheld involves all of the following accounts *except*:
a. Payroll Taxes.	a. Cash.
b. FICA Taxes Payable—OASDI.	b. Employees FIT.
c. Cash.	**c. Payroll Taxes.**
d. FICA Taxes Payable—HI.	d. FICA Taxes Payable—HI.
e. Employees FIT.	e. FICA Taxes Payable—OASDI.

Key Features

- **Motivation, Application, Mastery**—*Payroll Accounting 2023* and CNOWv2 help you elevate student thinking with unique content that addresses each stage of the learning process, prepares students to learn, provides practice opportunities that better prepare students for the exam, and helps students achieve mastery with tools that help them make connections and see the big picture.

- **The Washington Update**—The Washington Update, which appears within Chapters 1, 2, 3, 4, 5, and 7, advises the student of the tax code and tax laws that were used in the current edition. However, because tax code, tables, and laws may be changed by Congress after the

Washington Update

A number of states are evaluating changes to their overtime rules that will exceed the federal salary requirements. California has set its salary level for workers at large employers to $49,920 (set to change to $62,400 in 2023).[3]

text has been printed, the student is advised on how, in practice, they can find the most current tax code, tables, and laws.

- **Enhanced Excel Templates**—The Excel Templates include a feedback section giving instructors the option for adding a comment/grade and an area for students to show their work.

- **Excel Online**—Cengage and Microsoft have partnered in CNOWv2 to provide students with a uniform, authentic Excel experience. It provides instant feedback, built-in video tips, and easily accessible spreadsheet work. These features allow you to spend more time teaching college accounting applications, and less time troubleshooting Excel.

    These new algorithmic activities offer pre-populated data directly in Microsoft Excel Online. Each student receives his or her own version of the problem to perform the necessary data calculations in Excel Online. Their work is constantly saved in Cengage cloud storage as a part of homework assignments in CNOWv2. It's easily retrievable so students can review their answers without cumbersome file management and numerous downloads/uploads.

- **Superior Examples**—Examples are identified and numbered within the text. Various end-of-chapter problems are identified as a problem similar to an example within the text. See the examples below.

Ned Fromton, an employer, files his employment tax return 20 days after the due date of the return. The amount of tax that was unpaid is $6,000. Fromton's penalty is:
    Failure to file (5% × $6,000) = $300 *Note:* Any fraction of a month counts as a whole month.

Example 3-7

3-16A • LO 5   **See Example 3-6 on page 3-20, Example 3-8 on page 3-32, Example 3-9 on page 3-32**

Vulcan Company is a monthly depositor whose tax liability for March 20-- is $2,505.

1. What is the due date for the deposit of these taxes? _____
2. Assume that no deposit was made until April 29 (14 days late). Compute the following penalties:
    a. Penalty for failure to make timely deposit. $_____
    b. Penalty for failure to fully pay tax. $_____
    c. Interest on taxes due and unpaid (assume a 4% interest rate). $_____
    d. Total penalty imposed. $_____

Comprehensive Payroll Project

NEW! Comprehensive Payroll Project Overview

The Comprehensive Payroll Project Overview is a brand-new mini chapter, offering a clear and concise snapshot of the Payroll Project's 3 iterations. When assigning the Payroll Project, instructors can use this resource to make an informed decision about which Payroll Project option is best, both for them and for their students.

Chapter 7—The Payroll Project

Chapter 7 consists of a practice set or simulation. The student applies the knowledge acquired in the first six chapters to a practical payroll simulation as the payroll accountant for Glo-Brite Paint Company. The Payroll Project can be completed manually using fold-out Payroll Registers located at the back of the text, or by using Automated General Ledger Software, powered by CNOWv2, and the Appendix B. Payroll tax returns can now be completed manually using forms in the textbook or in CNOWv2.

Appendix A—Excel Template Instructions for the Glo-Brite Payroll Project (Chapter 7: Short Version)

Appendix A consists of an electronic version of the books of account and payroll records. It has specific instructions for using the Excel template, illustrative case demonstrating November 20 payroll, and complete instructions for the short version project. Students are encouraged to complete one manual payroll from Chapter 7 prior to using the Excel template. The Excel template is located on the Payroll Accounting Web site: **www.cengage.com**. Payroll tax returns can now be completed manually using forms in the textbook or in CNOWv2. Students may also complete the short version of the payroll project using Automated General Ledger Software, powered by CNOWv2, and Appendix B.

Appendix B—Payroll Project Using Online Automated General Ledger Software

Automated General Ledger Software gives your students hands on, real-world experience in processing a payroll on a computer. Students will maintain an employee database, process biweekly payrolls, and generate payroll entries and reports in a general ledger system, which is totally automated and graded in CNOWv2. In addition, the Appendix B walks students through the Payroll Project within the new online Automated General Ledger Software, providing screenshots of the system and Project Audit Tests for students to complete as they work through the Payroll Project.

Outstanding Pedagogy

Learning Objectives

Learning Objectives are enumerated at the beginning of each chapter, and the numbers are repeated next to the start of the applicable text coverage for easy navigation.

Tax Rates

The Social Security Act, as amended, imposes a separate tax on employees and employers for old-age, survivors, and disability insurance (OASDI) benefits and for hospital insurance (HI) benefits. The 2022 tax rates for both the employee and the employer portions of the tax follow:

> **LO 3**
>
> Apply the current tax rates and wage base for FICA and SECA purposes.

Self-Study Quizzes

Self-Study Quizzes appear throughout each chapter and test the understanding of major concepts. Answers to the quizzes are available within each chapter.

Self-Study Quiz 3-1

Which of the following are covered by FICA (indicate Yes or No)?
_____ 1. Andrian Mitchell, a full-time life insurance salesperson.
_____ 2. John Sain, a federal government employee, hired in 1990.
_____ 3. Bonnie Stone, a real estate agent.
_____ 4. Stuart Schuck, who offers lawn care service to homeowners in the neighborhood.

Note: Answers to Self-Study Quizzes are on page 3-34.

Over the Line Real-World Ethics Cases

The Over the Line feature illustrates cases of companies either intentionally or unintentionally crossing the boundaries of fairness in their interpretation of payroll laws.

Over the Line

In a recent lawsuit settlement, FedEx Ground Package System Inc. will distribute $2 million to an estimated 500 drivers who delivered packages for FedEx Ground and FedEx Home Delivery. The New York State Attorney General's Office filed the lawsuit alleging that drivers had been unlawfully misclassified as independent contractors, but were actually employees. This action sought restitution for violations of New York labor law, including unpaid overtime and unlawful deductions from wages.[2]

Check Figures Included at the End of This Text

Check figures provide help and assist users in staying on track as they learn the intricacies of payroll accounting.

Key Points Summary

This summary at the end of the chapter ties the key points in the chapter to the Learning Objectives.

Use of Marginal Icons

Use of marginal icons ("On the Net," "News Alert," "IRS Connection," and "On the Job") helps integrate the real-world applications of this facts-intensive area of study. "On the Net" icons allow optional integration of Internet research sites for learners. The icons in each chapter highlight the most current forms, instructions, and wage and tax laws available.

🌐 On the Net

http://www.ssa.gov
Social Security Online.
Maintained by the Social Security Administration, it contains general FICA information.
http://www.ssa.gov/employer/
"Employer W-2 Filing Instructions & Information."

Thorough End-of-Chapter Materials

End-of-chapter assignable materials include matching quizzes, review questions, discussion questions, practical problems, case problems, and continuing payroll problems, which can also be completed using Excel.

Continuing Payroll Problem • A [X] 🖥 Show Me How

Refer to the partially completed payroll register you started at the end of Chapter 2. You will now determine the amount of FICA taxes to be withheld from each employee's pay for the pay period ending January 8, 20--.

1. In the Taxable Earnings columns, record the amount of each employee's weekly earnings that is subject to FICA taxes. All wages are taxable for OASDI and HI taxes.

2. Using the amount recorded in step 1, compute the taxes for each employee and record in the appropriate column.

Note: Keep your partially completed payroll register for use at the end of Chapter 4.

Up-to-the-Minute Tax Law Changes

Up-to-date knowledge is especially important for today's payroll specialists. This edition has been completely updated to reflect the tax law changes that affect payroll accounting. Users can find these changes listed on the "As We Go To Press" page in the text and on www.cengage.com.

Instructor Resources

Instructor Web Site (login.cengage.com)

The instructor website contains password protected instructor resources, including:

- Solutions Manual, containing Learning Objectives, Chapter Outline, and solutions to end-of-chapter exercises and problems

- Comprehensive PowerPoint slides

- Achievement Tests and Keys for additional testing

- Excel solutions for all end-of-chapter problems

- Excel solutions for Payroll Project (Appendix A)

- Automated General Ledger Software solutions for Payroll Project (online Appendix B)

Test Bank Available With Cengage Learning Testing Powered by Cognero

What is Cognero?

- Full-featured, online-assessment system allows instructors to manage test bank content from multiple Cengage Learning solutions.

- Create multiple test versions in an instant.

- Deliver tests from your LMS, your classroom, or wherever you want.

- Works on any operating system or browser.

- No special installs or downloads needed.

- Create tests from school, home, the coffee shop—anywhere with Internet access.

"I am very satisfied with the ability to create a different version of a test at any given time."

-Vernon Bogan,
Brown Mackie College

How do I access it?

- Log into your Cengage Learning SSO account at login.cengage.com.

- Add *Payroll Accounting 2023* to your bookshelf (ISBN: 9780357722275).

- Once the book is added to your bookshelf, a link to access Cognero for *Payroll Accounting 2023* will appear, along with the link to the instructor and student companion sites.

How do I start?

- Online resources, user guides, and instructional videos are available on the instructor companion Web site at login.cengage.com.

- Please address any other technical questions to Cengage Learning Technical Support at support.cengage.com.

Student Resources

Student Companion Web Site (www.cengage.com)

Accessible through www.cengage.com with your Cengage Unlimited subscription or under the study tools tab of CNOWv2 course, the student Web site contains Check Figures, Web Links, and PowerPoint slides. The Excel templates are posted for the short version of the Glo-Brite Payroll Project, Continuing Payroll Problems A and B, and selected end-of-chapter problems designated by the Excel icon. In addition, the student has access to important information contained in Appendix C: Social Security Benefits and Appendix D: Unemployment Benefits.

Acknowledgments

Our sincere appreciation is extended to the many instructors and students who have contributed suggestions to make the textbook more interesting, understandable, and practical to those who pursue the study of payroll accounting. As a result of their very helpful recommendations, the textbook will better satisfy the learning needs of students and the teaching needs of instructors. We would like to thank the following instructors for their valuable comments and suggestions:

Victora Badura, *Metropolitan Community College*
Don Coleman, *Edmonds Community College*
Pamela Fack, *Santa Barbara City College*
Lauren Huskey, *Sampson Community College*
Sophia Ju, *Edmonds Community College*
Elida Kraja, *St. Louis Community College*
Carole Maske, *Southwestern Community College*
Howard Randall, *Mission College*
Barbara Rice, *Gateway Community and Technical College*
Teri Samo, *Del Mar College*

In addition, the authors would like to thank the following content providers and verifiers for the 2023 edition:

Bernie Hill, Spokane Falls Community College, retired instructor, for preparing the Excel templates, reviewing the Cognero test banks, verifying the text and Web site elements, verifying CNOWv2, verifying all end-of-chapter materials, and verification and work on the automated general ledger product.

Lisa Swallow, Missoula College, University of Montana Business and Accounting Technology, Program Director/Associate Professor, for aid in end-of-chapter verification, supplemental items, and CNOWv2 verification.

Molly McFadden-May, Penn State University, Lecturer, for aid in the CNOWv2 end-of-chapter feedback revisions.

Tracy Newman, M.S. Ed., for work on the Mastery Problems in CNOWv2, as well as review and verification of end-of-chapter and test bank content.

About the Authors

Bernard J. Bieg

Courtesy of Steve Bacher, Bucks County Community College

After receiving his Master's in Business Administration from the University of Notre Dame and passing the Certified Public Accountants' exam in the early 1970s, Bernard Bieg worked in both public and private accounting before turning his attention toward a career in teaching. He had been a professor at Bucks County Community College 50 years, before retiring in the summer of 2021 and earning his status as Professor Emeritus. During that time, he had taught the whole spectrum of accounting offerings, including payroll accounting. He had maintained strong connections with today's business world by serving as an internal auditor for a local nonprofit organization. His association with this textbook began in 1977 as a co-author with one of the originators of the book, Bill Keeling.

Judith A. Toland

Courtesy of Steve Bacher, Bucks County Community College

Judith Toland received her Master's Degree in Education from Temple University in 2002, her Bachelor's Degree in Business Administration—Accounting from Bloomsburg University in 1981, and her Associate's Degree from Bucks County Community College in Business Administration in 1979. Judy has taught Accounting courses at BCCC since 1989 and is currently a professor in the Business and Innovation Department. Judy earned the prestigious Certified Payroll Professional (CPP) designation in 2011. Her association with this textbook began in 2008 as a co-author with Bernard Bieg.

Contents

As We Go to Press — iii

Preface — v

Acknowledgments — xii

About the Authors — xiii

Chapter 1

The Need for Payroll and Personnel Records   1-1

The Payroll Profession   1-2

Fair Labor Standards Act   1-3

Federal Insurance Contributions Act   1-4

Income Tax Withholding Laws   1-4

Unemployment Tax Acts   1-4

Recordkeeping Requirements   1-5

Fair Employment Laws   1-5

Other Federal Laws Affecting the Need for Payroll and Personnel Records   1-8

Other State Laws Affecting the Need for Payroll and Personnel Records   1-13

Human Resources and Payroll Accounting Systems   1-14

Human Resources System   1-15

Recordkeeping System   1-23

Payroll Accounting System   1-23

Chapter 2

Computing Wages and Salaries   2-1

The Fair Labor Standards Act   2-1

Determining Employee's Work Time   2-16

Records Used for Timekeeping   2-21

Methods of Computing Wages and Salaries   2-24

Chapter 3

Social Security Taxes   3-1

Coverage Under FICA   3-1

A Self-Employed Person   3-13

Employer Identification Number   3-14

Employee's Application for Social Security Card (Form SS-5)   3-16

Returns Required for Social Security Purposes   3-17

Preparing Form 941 (Employer's QUARTERLY Federal Tax Return)   3-21

Failure-to-Comply Penalties   3-30

Chapter 4

Income Tax Withholding   4-1

Coverage Under Federal Income Tax Withholding Laws   4-2

Tax-Deferred Retirement Accounts   4-8

Revised Form W-4 and Withholding Calculations   4-10

Federal Income Tax Withholding   4-16

Other Methods of Withholding   4-18

Supplemental Wage Payments   4-20

Wage and Tax Statements   4-23

Returns Employers Must Complete   4-29

Information Returns   4-30

Independent Contractor Payments   4-31

Backup Withholding   4-31

Electronic Filing Form W-2 and Information Returns   4-32

Withholding State Income Tax   4-32

Chapter 4 Supplement   4-37
Withholding Allowances   4-37

Federal Income Tax Withholding   4-39

Chapter 5

Unemployment Compensation Taxes   5-1

Coverage Under FUTA and SUTA   5-2

Unemployment Compensation Taxes and Credits   5-9

Unemployment Compensation Reports Required of the Employer   5-21

Chapter 6

Analyzing and Journalizing Payroll

6-1

The Payroll Register   6-1

The Employee's Earnings Record   6-4

Recording the Gross Payroll and Withholdings   6-5

Methods of Paying Wages and Salaries   6-15

Recording Payroll Taxes   6-21

Recording Workers' Compensation Insurance Expense   6-25

Recording the Deposit or Payment of Payroll Taxes   6-26

Recording End-of-Period Adjustments   6-28

Summary of Accounts Used in Recording Payroll Transactions   6-29

Illustrative Case   6-30

Comprehensive Payroll Project Overview   PP-1

Chapter 7

Payroll Project

7-1

Books of Account and Payroll Records   7-2

General Information   7-3

Start of Payroll Project   7-6

End-of-Year Activities   7-19

Accounting Records and Reports   7-23

Project Audit Test   7-69

Appendix A: Excel Template Instructions for the Glo-Brite
Payroll Project (Chapter 7: Short Version)   A-1

I.   Getting to Know Excel   A-2

II.   Excel Templates for Payroll Project's Short Version   A-6

III.   Illustrative Case   A-12

IV.   Short Payroll Project   A-19

V.   End-of-Year Activities   A-22

VI.   Project Audit Tests   A-27

Appendix B: Payroll Project Using Online Automated General Ledger Software   B-1

I.   Payroll Project   B-1
II. Illustrative Case—Full Project   B-3
III. Payroll Project (Short Version)   B-23
IV. Illustrative Case—Short Project   B-25
V.   End-of-Year Activities   B-39
VI. Project Audit Test   B-43

Tax Table A: 2022 Percentage Method Tables For Manual Payroll Systems With Forms W-4 From 2020 Or Later   T-2

Tax Table B: 2022 Wage Bracket Method Tables For Manual Payroll Systems With Forms W-4 From 2020 Or Later   T-5

Table Of Allowance Values For Percentage Method Tables For Manual Payroll Systems With Forms W-4 From 2019 Or Earlier   T-14

Tax Table *C: 2022 Percentage Method Tables For Manual Payroll Systems With Forms W-4 From 2019 Or Earlier   T-15

Tax Table *D: 2022 Wage Bracket Method Tables For Manual Payroll Systems With Forms W-4 From 2019 Or Earlier   T-17

Check Figures   CF-1

Glossary   G-1

Index   I-1

Federal Payroll Taxes Calendar   PC-1

Online Web Appendices (cengage.com)

Controlling Costs: Payroll, Benefits, and Taxes   CC-1

Appendix C: Social Security Benefits   C-1

What Factors Are Used to Determine Social Security Benefits?   C-1
What Benefits Are Provided by Social Security?   C-2
What Are Reduced Benefits?   C-4
How Does Working After Retirement Affect Social Security Benefits?   C-5
How Do You Apply for Social Security Benefits?   C-6
What Is Medicare?   C-7

Appendix D: Unemployment Benefits   D-1

Unemployment Compensation Benefits   D-1

Chapter 1

The Need for Payroll and Personnel Records

Most of our exposure to payroll has been with the receipt of a paycheck. But there is so much in the payroll process that is done before each payday, and the process is always being changed and improved. Even the paycheck is being updated into direct deposits and even on-demand pay.

The process begins with hiring employees—applications, interviews, references, and credit reports. There are many legal do's and don'ts that must be followed. How far can we go in checking on the background of an individual applicant? What records should we keep on each employee? Where do we show the calculations that must be completed in order to give each employee a paycheck?

Get ready to experience the nuts and bolts of payroll operations.

Learning Objectives

After studying this chapter, you should be able to:

1. Identify the various laws that affect employers in their payroll operations.
2. Examine the recordkeeping requirements of these laws.
3. Describe the employment procedures generally followed in a Human Resources Department.
4. Identify the various personnel records used by businesses and the type of information shown on each form.
5. Identify the *payroll register* and the *employee's earnings record*.

No matter the size of the company, the profitability, the product or service being sold, or the type of organization, employees have to be paid. This task has become more difficult as numerous regulations have been enacted. Recent legislation has only added to the administrative burden, and future legislation will continue this trend. The payroll person is no longer the employee stuck in the corner who only appears on payday to distribute paychecks. The job responsibilities have multiplied and now require persons with advanced knowledge in the area of payroll to handle the position. In many cases, the payroll specialist has been on the leading edge of change and automation.

Photographee.eu/Shutterstock.com

Payroll professionals are responsible for processing over 4 billion pay statements each year to over 160 million people in the workforce of the United States. The processing of payrolls allows no margin for error. Employees, employers, and government agencies monitor the work performed by payroll professionals. A payroll accounting system is the only operation in a business that is almost completely governed by various federal, state, and local laws and regulations. Rules establish who is an employee, what is time worked, when overtime is to be paid, what deductions are made, when to pay an employee, what benefits have to be provided, and when taxes are paid. Local, state, federal, and international legislation must be monitored to follow the impact on payroll operations. Changes in legislation bring the potential for fraud and errors. Lack of compliance with these laws and regulations can result in both fines and back-pay awards.

Payroll professionals have risen in the ranks of the accounting profession and now demand salaries commensurate with their peers. The confidentiality of the payroll information from each employee's pay rate to the garnishments imposed on some employees has tightened the link to the upper management teams. The confidence and trust that must be placed in payroll professionals have made them an integral part of the "inner circle." This chapter briefly examines the various laws that affect employers in their payroll operations and the payroll and personnel records that they use to meet the requirements of the laws. First, however, let's take a brief look at payroll accounting as a profession.

The Payroll Profession

A 2022 payroll survey conducted by Robert Half Associates revealed an average of salaries for payroll managers of $78,500 and for payroll clerks of $41,750.

Typically, an entry-level payroll clerk collects, reviews, approves, and records time records. The clerk also updates attendance records, including vacation, sick, and personal days. Once a payroll is processed, the clerk reviews the information to ensure the accuracy of each employee's pay statement. Job responsibilities will include entering the following information into the payroll system:

1. Time-worked data.
2. Pay rate changes.
3. Tax rate changes.
4. Employee-authorized payroll deductions.
5. New employee information.
6. Marital and employee allowance changes.

Providing information to the Finance Department concerning the amounts to be paid for taxes, health insurance premiums, retirement plans, etc., may also be part of the evolving duties of the advancing payroll professional. One of the final stages involves the completion of payroll tax returns, employee information returns, federal and state census surveys, and fringe benefit and welfare plan returns.

Payroll professionals must keep abreast of the changes in their field so that they can remain technically proficient. This need has been met by an association of payroll practitioners—the American Payroll Association (APA). Membership in the association is open to anyone interested in or engaged in the support of payroll accounting. The APA offers professional training seminars and various publications to its members. Each year, the APA administers examinations for the payroll accountant and awards certificates to those who pass the exams, Fundamental Payroll Certification (to demonstrate a baseline of payroll competency) and Payroll Professional Certification (for the experienced professional to demonstrate the full-range of payroll competency). This testing and certification process has helped the payroll profession to gain recognition in the business community. The APA has also established guidelines for the conduct of the payroll professional. This "Code of Ethics," shown in Figure 1.1, sets the direction for the profession.[1]

One of a number of publications designed to provide current information to the practitioner is published by the Research Institute of America, Inc. This biweekly publication is entitled *Payroll Guide*, and it is a comprehensive review of changes in regulations affecting payroll reporting.[2]

---

1 For more information on the organization, write to American Payroll Association, 660 North Main Avenue, Suite 100, San Antonio, TX 78205-1217; Tel: 210-224-6406; APA@americanpayroll.org.
2 *Payroll Guide* is published by Thomson Reuters, 121 River Street, Hoboken, NJ 07030; Tel: 1-800-431-9025.

FIGURE 1.1
APA Code of Ethics

1. To be mindful of the personal aspect of the payroll relationship between employer and employee, and to ensure that harmony is maintained through constant concern for the Payroll Professional's fellow employees.
2. To strive for perfect compliance, accuracy, and timeliness of all payroll activities.
3. To keep abreast of the state of the payroll art with regard to developments in payroll technologies.
4. To be current with legislative developments and actions on the part of regulatory bodies, insofar as they affect payroll.
5. To maintain the absolute confidentiality of the payroll within the procedures of the employer.
6. To refrain from using Association activities for one's personal self-interest or financial gain.
7. To take as one's commitment the enhancement of one's professional abilities through the resources of the American Payroll Association.
8. To support one's fellow payroll professionals, both within and outside one's organization.

Source: For more information on the organization, contact the American Payroll Association, 660 North Main Avenue, Suite 100, San Antonio, TX 78205-1217; Tel: 210-224-6406; APA@americanpayroll.org.

Washington Update

In order to keep abreast of major changes in the laws concerning payroll activities, please refer to our online version of the textbook where these developing changes can be listed as they become law. The printed version will be as current as possible based on the information available to the authors at the time of the writing of the manuscript.

Fair Labor Standards Act

The Fair Labor Standards Act (FLSA), referred to as the Federal Wage and Hour Law, is covered in Chapter 2. The outline of the law deals with:

- Minimum wage ($7.25 per hour) and overtime pay requirements.
- In addition, equal pay for equal work, employment of child labor, public service contracts, and wage garnishment.
- Coverage of employers engaged in interstate commerce or in production of goods and services for interstate commerce.
- Maintaining records that explain the basis of wage differentials paid to employees of opposite sex for equal work.
- Displaying a poster (from the regional office of the Wage and Hour Division) informing employees of the provisions of the law.
- States' Minimum Wage and Maximum Hour Laws that also establish minimum wage rates for covered employees. Where both federal and state laws cover the same employee, the higher of two rates prevails (e.g., Rhode Island—$13.00 per hour, in 2023)
- The State's wage orders that also can affect pay periods, pay for call-in and waiting times, rest and meal periods, absences, meals and lodging, uniforms, etc.

LO 1
Identify the various laws that affect employers in their payroll operations.

On the Job

Up until July 24, 2009, the minimum wage was $6.55 per hour.

On the Net

http://www.dol.gov/whd/minwage/america.htm This Web site contains the minimum wage laws by state in map and text form.

Federal Insurance Contributions Act

Chapter 3 covers FICA (social security) in detail; however, the basic provisions of the act deal with:

- Tax on employees (set percent of their gross wages) and employers for the Federal Old-Age and Survivors' Trust Fund and the Federal Disability Insurance Trust Fund.
- Separate tax on employees and employers to finance the Health Insurance Plan—Medicare.
- Tax on net earnings of the self-employed individual (Self-Employment Contributions Act—SECA).
- Making payments to persons who are entitled to benefits under these social security taxes.

Income Tax Withholding Laws

Chapter 4 covers income tax withholding, but basically:

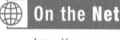

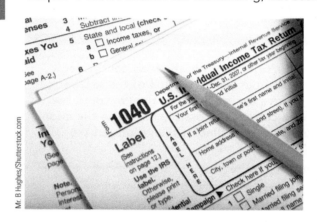

- **Income tax** is levied on the earnings of most employees and is deducted from their gross pay.
- Income taxes can be imposed by federal, state, and local governments.
- Federal Income Tax (FIT) employs a percentage formula or a wage bracket chart used by each employer to withhold a specified amount from each wage payment.
- State tax rates vary from state to state.

Unemployment Tax Acts

Chapter 5 covers unemployment taxes with a detailed discussion of:

- Tax levied on employers (Federal Unemployment Tax Act—FUTA) that is used to pay state and federal administrative expenses of the unemployment program.
- A credit granted against most of the FUTA tax if the employer pays a state unemployment tax. A smaller credit is granted to states that have not paid back borrowings from the federal government which were used to pay the cost of benefits to their eligible unemployed workers.
- State unemployment taxes (SUTA) on employers imposed by all states. These taxes are used to pay unemployment benefits.
- Standards set by the Social Security Act that result in a high degree of uniformity in the requirements of state unemployment laws.
- Employers' need to be aware of the SUTA laws in the states where they operate.

Recordkeeping Requirements

Although the laws do impose recordkeeping requirements on employers, no specific form of record is mandated. Figure 1.2, on page 1-6, lists the specific information needed and the retention time periods required.

Fair Employment Laws

Federal and state legislations have been enacted to enforce **fair employment practices**. Many of these laws deal with discrimination on the basis of age, race, color, religion, sex, or national origin.

Civil Rights Act of 1964

Title VII of the Civil Rights Act of 1964, entitled "Equal Employment Opportunity," provides for several fair employment practices. The act, as amended, forbids employers to discriminate in hiring, firing, promoting, compensating, or in any other condition of employment on the basis of race, color, religion, sex, or national origin. Guidelines, established by the Equal Employment Opportunity Commission (EEOC), also include physical characteristics in the definition of national origin discrimination. For example, unnecessary height or weight requirements could exclude some individuals on the basis of their national origin. The EEOC has also declared that sexual harassment violates the Civil Rights Act. Unwelcome sexual advances, requests for sexual favors, and other verbal or physical conduct of a sexual nature can constitute sexual harassment.

The EEOC consists of five members who administer the law. The commission is bipartisan and can have no more than three members of the same political party. A General Counsel of the Commission, appointed by the President for a period of four years, handles all EEOC litigations.

The EEOC prohibits unions from excluding or segregating their members on these bases, and employment agencies may not refer or refuse to refer applicants for employment on the basis of race, color, religion, sex, or national origin.

This act covers all employers who engage in an industry "affecting commerce" and who employ 15 or more workers for each working day in each of 20 or more weeks in the current or preceding calendar year. Employers specifically excluded from coverage of the fair employment practices include the U.S. government (state and local governments are covered), a corporation wholly owned by the United States, Native Americans, private membership clubs (other than labor unions) exempt from federal income tax, and religious societies in the employment of members of a particular religion to work on the societies' religious activities. Although the U.S. government is classified as an exempt employer, the act states that the policy of the U.S. government provides equal employment opportunities without discrimination and that the president should use his existing authority to implement this policy.

The act requires an employer information report (EEO-I) to be filed annually by employers with federal government contracts of $50,000 or more who have 50 or more employees, and employers without a government contract who have 100 or more employees.

Title VII does not protect an employee from arbitrary treatment or dismissal. As long as the employer applies these policies in a nondiscriminatory manner, Title VII requirements have not been violated.

To accomplish the purpose of eliminating discrimination, the EEOC tries to obtain voluntary compliance with the law before filing a court action for an injunction. It can institute court proceedings for an injunction if it believes that any person or group of persons is not complying with the law. Where a state or local law forbids discriminatory practices, relief must first be sought under the

On the Net

http://www.eeoc.gov/ This EEOC homepage overviews guidelines and services of the Equal Employment Opportunity Commission (EEOC).

On the Job

Title VII requires employers to reasonably accommodate workers' religious-based requests without causing an undue hardship to others.

FIGURE 1.2

Summary of Information Required by Major Federal Payroll Laws

	Item	Fair Labor Standards Act	Social Security	Income Tax Withholding	Unemployment Tax
EMPLOYEE DATA	Name	Yes	Yes	Yes	Yes
	Address	Yes	Yes	Yes	Yes
	Sex	Yes	….	….	….
	Date of birth	Yes	….	….	….
	Social security number	Yes	Yes	Yes	Yes
	Withholding allowances claimed	….	….	Yes	….
	Occupation	Yes	Yes	Yes	Yes
	Period employed	….	Yes	Yes	Yes
	State where services rendered	….	Yes	….	Yes
EMPLOYMENT DATA	Beginning and ending dates of employee's employment	….	Yes	Yes	….
	Day and time of day when workweek begins	Yes	….	….	….
	Regular hourly rate of pay	Yes	….	….	….
	Basis of wage payments; e.g., $9.25 per hour; $74.00 per day	Yes	….	….	….
	Hours worked each day	Yes	….	….	….
	Hours worked each week	Yes	….	….	….
	Daily or weekly straight-time pay, exclusive of overtime pay	Yes	….	….	….
	Amount and nature of exempt pay	Yes	….	….	….
	Weekly overtime pay	Yes	….	….	….
	Total additions to or deductions from wages	Yes	….	….	….
	Total remuneration for payroll period	Yes	Yes	Yes	….
	Total remuneration for calendar year	….	Yes	….	Yes
	Date of payment	Yes	Yes	Yes	Yes
	Payroll period	Yes	Yes	Yes	Yes
TAX DATA	Employee's wages subject to tax for payroll period	….	Yes	Yes	….
	Employee's wages subject to tax for calendar year	….	Yes	….	Yes
	Taxable remuneration—if different from total remuneration, reason for difference	….	Yes	Yes	Yes
	Tax deductions from employee's wages	….	Yes	Yes	Yes
	Date tax collected if other than date of payment	….	Yes	Yes	….
	Tax paid by employer but not deducted from employee's wages	….	Yes	Yes	Yes
GEN'L	Specific form of records	No	No	No	No
	Number of years records must be kept	2–3	4*	4*	4*

*Four years after the due date of the payment of the tax to which the records relate.

state or local law before a complaint is filed with the Commission. In most states, a special commission or the state Department of Labor administers the laws and may authorize cease-and-desist orders that are enforceable in the courts.

The Civil Rights Act of 1991 grants compensatory and punitive damages in cases where the discrimination is intentional. It also provides for the repayment of attorney fees and the possibility of a jury trial.

Executive Orders

Employers not subject to the Title VII coverage discussed above may come within the scope of the Civil Rights Act by reason of a contract or a subcontract involving federal funds. In a series of **executive orders**, the federal government has banned, in employment on government contracts, discrimination based on race, color, religion, sex, or national origin.

Age Discrimination in Employment Act

The Age Discrimination in Employment Act of 1967 (ADEA) prohibits employers, employment agencies, and labor unions from discriminating on the basis of age in their employment practices. The act covers employers engaged in an industry affecting interstate commerce (who employ 20 or more workers), employment agencies, and labor unions. The act also covers federal, state, and local government employees, other than elected officials and certain aides not covered by civil service. The ADEA provides protection for virtually all workers over 40. A key exception is executives who are 65 or older and who have held high policy-making positions during the two-year period prior to retirement. If such an employee is entitled to an annual retirement benefit from the employer of at least $44,000, the employee can be forcibly retired.

In order to prove compliance with the various fair employment laws, employers must keep accurate personnel and payroll records. All employment applications, along with notations as to their disposition and the reasons for the disposition, should be retained. All records pertaining to promotions, discharges, seniority plans, merit programs, incentive payment plans, etc., should also be retained.

On the Job

Court rulings have updated the regulations to state that favoring an older individual over a younger individual because of age is not unlawful discrimination under the ADEA.

Over the Line

Louisville-based Texas Roadhouse with more than 450 locations in the United States fought a lawsuit brought by 55 women and men charging discrimination against workers age 40 and older by refusing to employ them as hosts, bartenders, and servers. In legal filings, the company stated that even if its policies had an adverse impact on older workers, they were lawful, because they are job-related and consistent with business necessity (in that servers must line dance, wear jeans, and work evenings). The company had to pay $12 million to settle the Equal Employment Opportunity Commission's lawsuit.

Americans with Disabilities Act

The Americans with Disabilities Act of 1990 (ADA) prohibits employers with 15 or more employees, employment agencies, labor organizations, or joint labor-management committees from discriminating against qualified persons with disabilities because of their disability.

The prohibition of disability-based discrimination applies to job application procedures, hiring, advancement, termination, compensation, job training, and other conditions of employment. In addition, reasonable accommodations,

On the Job

Even though alcoholism is a disability under the ADA, employees can be disciplined for misconduct that occurred while under the influence.

such as wheelchair-accessible restrooms and ramps for qualified disabled job applicants and workers, must be provided.

Under the ADA, a person is considered "qualified" if the individual can perform the essential functions of the job with or without reasonable accommodation.

Other Federal Laws Affecting the Need for Payroll and Personnel Records

Generally, the payroll and personnel records and reports that a business prepares and retains to meet the requirements of the laws already discussed provide sufficient information needed under the laws outlined in Figure 1.3 and discussed below.

Federal Personal Responsibility and Work Opportunity Reconciliation Act of 1996

The Federal Personal Responsibility and Work Opportunity Reconciliation Act of 1996 (PRWORA) mandates that all states must establish new-hire reporting programs. Every employer is required to report the name, address, and social security number on each new employee and the employer's name, address, and federal employer identification number *within 20 days of hire* to the State Directory of New Hire Reporting. In many states, submission of a copy of the employee's W-4 form (Employee's Withholding Allowance Certificate) will satisfy the reporting requirement. This information must then be forwarded within 5 business days by the state to the federal Office of Child Support Enforcement (OCSE) for entry into the National Directory of New Hires. Employers with operations in more than one state may file one report with the state of their choice. That state is then to share the information with the other states.

New-hire reporting requirements in some states now also include information reporting on independent contractors. The main reason for this requirement is to help in the enforcement of child support obligations. In addition, it will reduce fraud in the unemployment, workers' compensation, and public assistance programs. Failure to report this information can result in fines of up to $25.00 per new hire. Even though under federal law employers do not have to report this same information on independent contractors, some states do require such reporting.

Immigration Reform and Control Act of 1986

The Immigration Reform and Control Act of 1986 (IRCA) bars employers from hiring and retaining persons unauthorized to work in the United States (an exception is non-immigrant aliens as temporary workers in occupations where an adequate domestic workforce cannot be recruited). It also requires all employers to verify employment eligibility for all individuals by examining the employee's verification documents and having the employee complete **Form I-9, Employment Eligibility Verification**. Form I-9 lists the documents that an employee can choose from to furnish to the employer. These documents identify the employee and, if an immigrant, verify authorization to work in the United States. The employer must examine the documents to verify their authenticity and then record the appropriate information on the employee's Form I-9. Employers must also follow up on documents (with an expiration date) that limit the employee's authorization to work. The employer cannot ask an applicant about the candidate's immigration status before a conditional job offer.

Photocopying new employees' I-9 documents is permitted but not required. If done, photocopying should apply to *all* new employees. Employers are not required to submit Forms I-9 to the U.S. Citizenship and Immigration Service.

FIGURE 1.3
Federal Laws Affecting the Need for Payroll and Personnel Records

Law	Coverage	Contract Dollar Minimum	Major Provisions
Davis-Bacon Act (1931)	Laborers for contractors or subcontractors on federal government contracts for construction, alteration, or repair of public buildings or works.	$ 2,000	Minimum wage set by secretary of labor (weight is given to union wage scale prevailing in the project area).
Walsh-Healey Public Contracts Act (1936)	Laborers for contractors who furnish materials, supplies, articles, and equipment to any agency of the United States.	$ 15,000	Single minimum wage determined by secretary of labor for all covered employees in a given industry.
McNamara-O'Hara Service Contract Act (1965)	Service employees on contracts with the United States or the District of Columbia for the furnishing of services.	$ 2,500	Minimum wage set by secretary of labor based on wages and fringe benefits found to be prevailing in that locality.
Occupational Safety and Health Act (OSHA) (1970)	Any business involved in interstate commerce.	$ 0	Sets specific occupational and health standards for employers; requires that records be kept of work-related injuries, illnesses, and deaths.
Vocational Rehabilitation Act (1973)	Companies with federal agency contracts.	$ 10,000	Must include in the contract an affirmative action clause requiring that the handicapped applicant or employee will be given appropriate consideration.
Vietnam Era Veterans' Readjustment Act (1974)	Government contractors with federal contracts or subcontracts.	$150,000	Requires contractors to take affirmative action to employ and advance in employment qualified veterans of the Vietnam era and disabled veterans.

Section 1 of the form must be signed by the employee no later than the first day of employment, but not before accepting a job offer. Section 2 must be signed by the employer or authorized representative within three business days of the employee's first day of employment. The person signing Section 2 must be the same person who examined the employee's documents.

Failure to produce the required documents can result in termination as long as the employer applies this rule uniformly to all employees. If it is confirmed that an employee is not legally authorized to work in this country, the employee must be fired immediately.

The process of collecting, filing, and retaining I-9 forms and supporting documentation should be a centralized function so that inconsistencies are eliminated. The forms (I-9) and supporting documentation should be filed separately from other personnel records so that the information contained in the forms is kept private. The form must be retained for three years after the date of hiring or for one year after the date the employment is terminated, whichever is later. Terminated employees who are rehired within three years of the date of the initially filed Form I-9 need only reverify the information to the employer.

The U.S. Citizenship and Immigration Services (USCIS) can levy fines if an audit uncovers hiring, recruiting, or referring violations.

The fines on employers are broken down as follows:

- First offense—$590 to $4,722 per undocumented employee.
- Second offense—$4,722 to $11,803 per undocumented employee.
- Third offense or more—$7,082 to $23,607 per undocumented employee.
- Pattern of violations—extra fines and up to six months in jail.
  There are also fines levied for document fraud.

Over the Line

One of the largest ever penalties in an immigration case ($95 million) was assessed to a Pennsylvania-based tree company for hiring workers whom company executives knew lacked proper immigration documents.

E-Verify

This is a government-run Internet-based system that allows employers to check the employment eligibility of new hires by comparing the information on an employee's Form I-9 with databases of the Social Security Administration and the Department of Homeland Security. E-Verify requires a social security number (SSN) for the employee, so even though a newly hired employee is not required to have applied for a SSN before completing Form I-9, the employee must apply for it as soon as possible.

For most employers, this is a voluntary program; however, all new federal employees must have their employment eligibility confirmed through E-Verify. Federal contractors and subcontractors are now required to use the E-Verify system to verify employees' eligibility (contracts for less than $100,000 are exempt). State laws can also require employers to E-Verify (mandatory in over 20 states for some or all employees).

If there is a record mismatch, a tentative nonconfirmation is issued to the employer who must then notify the affected employee. If the employee had voluntarily provided their e-mail address on Form I-9, E-Verify will inform the employee at the same time as the employer. In case of a mismatch, the employee has eight working days to correct the discrepancy or be fired.

> ### On the Job
>
> FMLA absenteeism is highest among health-care employees with 39 percent of their workforce with open FMLA leave (average length of 28 days).

Family and Medical Leave Act of 1993

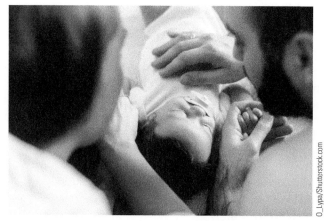
O_Lypa/Shutterstock.com

The Family and Medical Leave Act of 1993 (FMLA) requires employers that have 50 or more employees within a 75-mile radius, for at least 20 weeks in the current or preceding calendar year, to grant workers *unpaid leave* for a family or medical emergency. In cases of childbirth, adoption, serious illness of the employee or the employee's child, spouse, or parent, or emergency due to active duty in the Armed Forces, the employer must offer the worker as many as 12 weeks of unpaid leave. The leave may be used all at once, or in separate weeks, days, or hours. However, the leave must be taken within 12 months of the qualifying event. It is the employer's obligation to designate leave as an FMLA-qualifying event. Employees cannot pick and choose when they want to use FMLA time (even if they have accumulated sick leave); however, the FMLA time can run concurrently with paid sick time.

During the leave, employers must continue health-care coverage, and they must also guarantee that the employee will return to the same job or to a comparable position. The employer can substitute an employee's earned paid leave for any part of the 12-week family leave as long as notification is given to the employee within two business days of receiving the request for the leave and it does not violate an existing employment contract.

Employers that pay employees on family and medical leave at least 50 percent of their normal wages may take a general business tax credit equal to 12.5 percent of the wages paid. The credit increases (to a maximum of 25 percent) in increments of 0.25 percent for each percentage point over the 50 percent starting point. The credit applies to wages paid for up to 12 weeks of leave time and does not apply to employees with wages over $78,000.

An expansion of FMLA allowed employees to take leave (up to 12 weeks) when a family member is on active duty or when the employee cares for a family member with a serious injury or illness incurred in the line of duty (up to 26 weeks).

An employee who has used the 12-week allotment under FMLA may be entitled to additional time off as a reasonable accommodation under the Americans with Disabilities Act (see page 1-7) as long as the employee's condition qualifies as a disability.

Employers can exempt the following:

1. The highest-paid 10 percent of their workforce.
2. Those who have not worked at least one year and at least 1,250 hours in the previous 12 months for the company.

Current regulations allow employers to contact employees' doctors for clarification on the information on the employees' certification forms. This contact cannot be made by the employees' direct supervisors but must be done by human resources professionals, leave administrators, or management officials.[3]

The definition of "spouse" was revised to examine the law of the state in which the marriage was entered into instead of the law of the state in which the employee resides. This allows all legally married couples, including same-sex and common-law, to have consistent family leave rights regardless of where they live.

An organization that is below the limits of coverage could be courting an FMLA lawsuit if in its employee handbook or benefits materials there is a statement that it complies with the FMLA. An employee can sue an employer who violates the general leave requirements within two years of the violation or three years if it is a willful violation.

A few states (California, Massachusetts, New Jersey, New York, Rhode Island, Washington, and the District of Columbia) have implemented *paid* family leave plans. For example, New Jersey now allows workers 12 weeks' paid leave (at two-thirds of their salary up to $993/week) to care for family members with a serious health condition, or to be with a child during the first 12 months after the child's birth or adoption. The program is funded through payroll deductions that are estimated to have cost employees a maximum of $212.66 in 2022.

Uniformed Services Employment and Reemployment Rights Act of 1994

The Uniformed Services Employment and Reemployment Rights Act (USERRA) gives military personnel the right to take leaves of absences from their civilian jobs for active military service and to return to their jobs with accrued seniority. The reinstatement must be to the employee's original position or its equivalent, except for the dishonorably discharged. In addition, the return must be granted within two weeks of the job request, and health benefits must be started without any waiting period.

Employee Retirement Income Security Act of 1974

The Employee Retirement Income Security Act of 1974 (ERISA) covers employee pension and welfare plans established or maintained by any employer or employee organization representing employees engaged in commerce or in any industry or activity affecting commerce. The legislation safeguards pension funds by regulating how the funds are to be raised and disbursed, who controls them, and what is to be done when funds are insufficient to pay promised benefits. The law *does not* require every employer to establish a pension plan; however, if there is an employer pension plan, every employee is eligible *after reaching age 21 or completing one year of service*, whichever is later. The year of service is a 12-month period during which the employee works at least 1,000 hours.

---

3 "Compensation and Benefits," *HR Specialist*, March 2012, p. 2.

ERISA has different funding requirements on benefit plans depending on whether they are a:

- Defined benefit plan: Benefits to the employee or his/her beneficiary will be based on a definitive formula based on length of service, average compensation, or compensation during the final year of service.
- Defined contribution plan: Benefits are based solely on the contributions into the employee's account. There are no ERISA funding requirements on most defined contribution plans.

ERISA was designed primarily to ensure that workers covered by private pension plans receive benefits from those plans in accordance with their credited years of service with their employers. **Vesting** conveys to employees the right to share in a retirement fund if they are terminated before the normal retirement age. The vesting process is linked to the number of years needed for workers to earn an equity in their retirement plans and to become entitled to full or partial benefits at some future date if they leave the company before retirement. Once vested, a worker has the right to receive a pension at retirement age, based on years of covered service, even though the worker may not be working for the firm at that time. Currently, the law provides for two minimum vesting schedules on the employer's contributions:

- Zero vesting for the first five years of service, with 100% vesting at the end of the fifth year.
- Three-to-seven-year vesting provides for 20% vesting after three years of service and 20% annual increase until 100% vesting is reached after seven years.

The plan administrator must file an annual report (Form 5500) with the federal government by the end of the seventh month following the close of the plan year.

Benefit payouts must begin within 60 days of the latest of these events:

- When the employee reaches age 65,
- 10 years after participation began, or
- The plan year in which the employee leaves the company.

To protect against potential benefit losses because of a plan's termination, ERISA set up a government insurance program, the Pension Benefit Guaranty Corporation, to pay any benefits that could not be met with funds from the plan.

On the Job

Certain plans are exempt from ERISA: governmental plans; church plans; workers' compensation, disability and unemployment insurance plans.

Disclosure Requirements

Informational reports must be filed with the U.S. Department of Labor, the IRS, and the government insurance program. In general, the reports consist of descriptions of the plans and the annual financial data. The plan descriptions include the eligibility requirements for participation and for benefits; provisions for nonforfeitable pension benefits; circumstances that may result in disqualification, loss, or denial of benefits; and procedures for presenting claims. The annual reports include financial statements and schedules showing the current value of plan assets and liabilities, receipts and disbursements, and employer contributions; the assets held for investment purposes; insurance data; and an opinion by an independent qualified public accountant. Upon written request from the participants, the administrator must also furnish a statement, not more than once in a 12-month period, of the total benefits accrued, accrued benefits that are vested, if any, or the earliest date on which accrued benefits will become vested.

Affordable Care Act of 2010 (ACA)

The Affordable Care Act (Obamacare) consists of two pieces of legislation: Patient Protection and Affordable Care Act and Health Care and Education Reconciliation Act. The act was designed to expand health insurance coverage to more Americans while increasing benefits and lowering costs for consumers.

State-based health insurance exchanges are established for those who do not have access to employer-provided coverage or do not qualify for public programs like Medicaid. These will be marketplaces where individuals can comparison shop. Individuals and families with incomes between 100 percent and 400 percent of the federal poverty level will receive subsidies to buy coverage.

The Tax Overhaul Bill of 2017 repealed the requirement that all Americans obtain health insurance. This has caused a drop in the number of insurance companies on the states' insurance exchanges. It has also added to an uncertain future for the ACA.

Applicable Large Employers (ALEs)

Employers with 50 or more full-time employees during the previous year (**applicable large employers—ALEs**) are required to provide coverage for all full-time employees and their dependents. If an employer does not offer coverage, the employer will owe a penalty for each full-time employee who, under the health law, is eligible for and receives federally subsidized health-care coverage.

There are two information reporting obligations for applicable large employers (Form 1095-C):

- A return to be filed with the IRS for each employee with information about the health coverage offered, or not offered, to that employee during the previous year. This return is due to the IRS by February 28 on paper or March 31 if filed electronically.
- An information statement to each full-time employee containing certain health coverage facts. This statement is due by January 31.

Penalties for failing to comply with the information reporting requirements can result in fines of $280 for each return with a total maximum penalty of $3,426,000.

Small Employers

A sliding scale income tax credit is established for **small employers** (fewer than 50 full-time equivalent employees with average annual wages of less than $50,000) who offer health insurance coverage to their employees. Employers can purchase affordable insurance through the Small Business Health Options Program. If the employer pays at least 50 percent of the cost (the premium rate for an employee with single coverage), there is a 50 percent maximum credit of the employer's premium cost (35 percent for tax-exempt employers) against the employer's income tax liability.

The law also provides for a Medicare tax increase on wages over $200,000 for single filers and $250,000 for joint filers. This tax must be withheld by the employer of any worker whose wages exceed $200,000 (see page 3-9).

On the Job

According to the Kaiser Family Foundation, in 2021 the total average cost of employer-provided health insurance was over $7,739 for single coverage and over $22,221 for family coverage.

Other State Laws Affecting the Need for Payroll and Personnel Records

States have enacted other laws that have a direct bearing on the payroll and personnel records that an employer must maintain and on the rights that must be extended to employees.

Workers' Compensation Laws

Workers' compensation insurance protects employees and their dependents against losses due to work-related injury, illness, or death. Most states have passed laws that require

wavebreakmedia/Shutterstock.com

employers to provide workers' compensation insurance through one of the following plans:

1. Contribution to a state compensation insurance fund administered by an insurance department of the state.
2. Purchase of workers' compensation insurance from a private insurance company authorized by the state to issue this type of policy.
3. Establishment of a self-insurance plan, approved by the state, under which the company bears all risk itself.

Over the Line

A New Jersey plumbing company denied workers' compensation benefits to an employee who was in a car accident as he was driving to get coffee because his meeting at a work site was delayed. An appeals court awarded benefits, stating that off-site employees are covered during slight diversions from their normal activities.[4]

Benefits are paid to cover medical bills and also to provide a percentage of the worker's regular wages during the time that the employee is unable to work. The employer bears the cost of the workers' compensation insurance premiums, except in Montana, New Mexico, Oregon, and Washington, where both the employer and the employee contribute to the workers' compensation fund.

The insurance premiums are often based upon the total gross payroll of the business and may be stated in terms of an amount for each $100 of weekly wages paid to employees. The premium rates vary among types of jobs and the employers' accident experience rate.

Example 1-1

The rate for office workers of Volpe Parts Company is $0.75 per $100 of payroll, while the rate for machine-shop workers is $1.90 per $100 of payroll.

Disability Benefit Laws

The Social Security Disability Insurance (SSDI) and Supplemental Security Income (SSI) programs provide assistance to people with disabilities. The SSDI program pays benefits to workers and certain family members. The SSI program pays benefits to those disabled who have limited income.

Five states (California, Hawaii, New York, New Jersey, and Rhode Island) have **disability benefit laws** to provide benefits to employees absent from work because of illness, accident, or death. This coverage is different from Worker's Compensation because it covers injuries away from the worker's place of employment. Chapter 5 presents further discussion of state disability benefit laws.

Human Resources and Payroll Accounting Systems

Up to this point, we have seen that a business must keep human resources and payroll records to meet the requirements of the various laws under which it operates. In developing its human resources and payroll accounting systems, a business should design basic forms and records that satisfy the requirements

4 "Employment Law," *HR Specialist*, October 2019, p. 5.

of all the laws applicable to that organization. Properly designed forms and records, as described later in this chapter, not only supply the information required by the various laws but also provide management with information needed in its decision-making process. They also result in savings in both time and work because the necessary information is recorded, stored, retrieved, and distributed economically, efficiently, and quickly.

Before studying the employment process, it is important to examine the close relationship between the Payroll Department and the Human Resources Department. Some businesses consider payroll to be strictly an accounting function and, as such, place it under the direct control of the chief financial officer. However, because of the need for frequent interchange of information between the Payroll and Human Resources departments, the trend has been to place payroll under the control of the director of human resources. This movement toward centralization eliminates the duplication of many tasks. With the required information in one department, the process of completing these forms is shortened. Further, questions from employees concerning sick pay, vacation pay, and other benefits can be answered from one source.

Individual computer programs have been developed for the combined needs of payroll and human resources. Information concerning such diverse activities as attendance, retirement benefits, health insurance coverages, and bonus pay is now available to designated employees in the Human Resources Department through a computer terminal.

Human Resources System

LO 3
Describe the employment procedures generally followed in a Human Resources Department.

In many medium-size and large companies, the **human resources system** embodies all those procedures and methods related to recruiting, selecting, orienting, training, and terminating personnel. Extensive recordkeeping procedures are required in order to:

1. Provide data for considering promotions and changes in the status and earnings of workers.
2. Provide the information required by various federal, state, and local laws.
3. Justify company actions if investigated by national or state labor relations boards.
4. Justify company actions in discussions with local unions or plant committees.

Before the Payroll Department can pay newly hired employees, the Human Resources Department must process those employees. Figure 1.4 on page 1-16, charts the procedure that the Human Resources Department follows in this hiring process.

A number of companies that manufacture business forms have available standard personnel forms and records that may be successfully used if a business does not care to design its own special forms. In small companies, an application form or an employee history record may be the only document needed. Throughout the remainder of this chapter, several illustrations augment the discussion of the various human resources and payroll records. In these examples, we shall follow Cheryl Crowson from her initial application for employment with Palmero Maintenance Company to her entry onto the company's payroll records.

Job Descriptions

One way to protect companies from discrimination charges in hiring practices is to have true and clear job descriptions for every position in the organization. This is one of the items that courts examine in determining the validity of a discrimination charge. The descriptions must be accurate and must have been prepared before the job was advertised or the interviewing began.

FIGURE 1.4
Human Resources Department Procedure in the Hiring Process

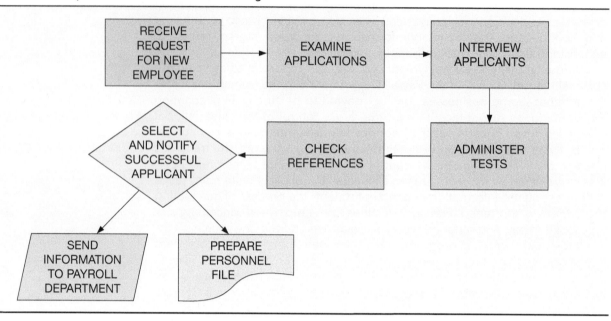

The descriptions should include:

- Job title.
- Essential and nonessential duties.
- Department/supervisor.
- Necessary skills.
- Needed experience.
- Education, credentials required.
- Working conditions.
- Results expected.[5]

> **In today's world, many of the paper forms presented in this chapter have been replaced with electronic substitutes. They are illustrated here to show the type of information that should be included no matter what format is used.**

Requisition for Personnel

The **requisition for personnel** form notifies the Human Resources Department of the need for additional or replacement employees. The requisition for new employees can be initiated in a number of ways. Some companies utilize a memo that is forwarded to the Human Resources Department stating the title of the position to be filled, a brief description of the duties of the job, and the salary range. Other companies may use preprinted forms. A preprinted form should indicate the type and number of persons needed, the position to be filled, the rate of pay for the job, the salary range, the date the employee is needed, a summary of any special qualifications, and whether the position is permanent or temporary. This process can also be completed electronically, through the use of a company's e-mail system.

Application for Employment

Every business, regardless of size, should have an application form (similar to that in Figure 1.5, on pages 1-18 and 1-19) to be filled out by a person seeking

---

employment. The **application form** gives the applicant an opportunity to provide complete information as to:

1. Personal information including the name, address, telephone number, and social security number of the applicant.
2. Educational background including a summary of the schools attended, whether the applicant graduated, and degrees conferred.
3. Employment and experience record.
4. Type of employment desired.
5. References.

> **LO 4**
> Identify the various personnel records used by businesses and the type of information shown on each form.

The application form also provides information for the checking of references, serves as a guide to effective interviewing, and provides information for correlation with data obtained from employment tests. It serves as a permanent record for the business. This form can also be set up to be completed electronically by the applicant.

Employers subject to fair employment laws must make certain that all aspects of the pre-hire inquiries are free of discrimination on the basis of race, color, religion, sex, national origin, or age. A number of states have instituted a "lifestyle discrimination law" that deals with discrimination based on employees' use of legal products on their own time, e.g., tobacco use. **Pre-hire inquiries** include questions asked in the employment interview and on application forms, résumés of experience or education required of an applicant, and any kind of written testing. None of the federal civil rights laws specifically outlaws questions concerning the race, color, religion, sex, national origin, or age of an applicant. However, if the employer can offer no logical explanation for asking such questions, the EEOC and the Wage and Hour Administrator view such questions as discriminatory. Of course, pre-hire questions pertaining to religion, sex, national origin, or age are allowed when these factors are bona fide occupational qualifications for a job. Many states have banned the use of a check box relating to an applicant's criminal past; however, employers can still ask about arrest records during the job interview. The EEOC has stated that criminal background checks can only be used if there is a solid business reason for them. Asking for arrest records is illegal.

Background checks must be in compliance with the rules established by the Fair Credit Reporting Act (FCRA). These steps must be closely followed where an **investigative consumer report** is being used:

- Notify the applicant in writing that the information obtained will be used in the employment decision.
- Have the applicant sign the notification.
- Give the applicant a notice and a copy of the report at least five days before making an adverse employment decision.
- Provide a copy of the government document "A Summary of Your Rights Under the FCRA."

Over the Line

Wells Fargo had to pay over $12 million to 6,255 unsuccessful job applicants due to background check violations. The lead plaintiff in the case stated that Wells Fargo ran an employment-purposed consumer report on him without telling him about the report, nor did the bank give him a copy of the report after being rejected for the job.[6]

---

6 "Employment Law," *HR Specialist*, April 2016, p. 6.

FIGURE 1.5
Application for Employment

APPLICATION FOR EMPLOYMENT
An Affirmative Action/Equal Opportunity Employer

POSITION APPLIED FOR ___*Payroll Specialist*___

This job application is valid only for the position you have listed above. If you wish to be considered for other positions, you will need to complete and/or submit a separate application for each position.

PERSONAL

Name ___*Cheryl Crowson*___

Address ___*1630 West End Ave.   Huntington, WV 25703*___
STREET   CITY   STATE   ZIP

Telephone ___*(304) 555-2192*___   ___*(304) 555-1618*___
WORK   HOME   OTHER

Social Security Number ___*000-00-6357*___

Have you worked for Palmero Maintenance Company before? YES ☐ NO ☑
If Yes, when? _____

If hired, can you provide proof of identity and eligibility to work in the U.S.? YES ☑ NO ☐

NAMES	ADDRESS	ACADEMIC MAJOR	NO. OF YEARS ATTENDED	DEGREE
HIGH SCHOOL *Centennial Senior*	*Stanford Road Huntington, WV*	*Business*	*4*	*Yes*
COLLEGE, JUNIOR COLLEGE, OR UNIVERSITY *Huntington Community College*	*Swamp Road Huntington, WV*	*Business— Occupational*	*2*	*Associate*
TECHNICAL OR VOCATIONAL				

Other details of training: _____ (Courses) _____ (Cert.)

FIGURE 1.5 (concluded)
Application for Employment

EMPLOYMENT HISTORY

List in sequence all employers, beginning with present/most recent employer, including military experience and apprenticeship. Explain any gaps in employment in comments section below. If additional space is needed, please attach sheet(s).

EMPLOYER	TELEPHONE	DATES EMPLOYED		Summarize the nature of the work performed and job responsibilities
		FROM Month Year	TO Month Year	
Brennan Shipping Co.	*(304) 555-1119*			
ADDRESS *193 Mountain Blvd., Huntington, WV*		*5/10*	*Present*	*Input time worked*
JOB TITLE *Payroll Assistant*				*information, checked*
IMMEDIATE SUPERVISOR AND TITLE *Helen Young—Payroll Manager*		Full-time ✔	Part-time	*payroll, distributed*
REASON FOR LEAVING *Want to have more responsibility*				*checks*
MAY WE CONTACT FOR REFERENCE? ☑ YES ☐ NO ☐ LATER				

EMPLOYER	TELEPHONE	DATES EMPLOYED		Summarize the nature of the work performed and job responsibilities
		FROM Month Year	TO Month Year	
AVS Drug	*(304) 555-0101*			
ADDRESS *Broad & Cherry Sts., Huntington, WV*		*9/08*	*5/10*	*Served as head cashier*
JOB TITLE *Clerk/Cashier*				*and maintained inventory*
IMMEDIATE SUPERVISOR AND TITLE *John Stumley—Manager*		Full-time	Part-time ✔	
REASON FOR LEAVING *Graduated college—Full-time position*				
MAY WE CONTACT FOR REFERENCE? ☑ YES ☐ NO ☐ LATER				

REFERENCES

Give names of persons we may contact to verify your qualifications for the position:

Edna White	*Instructor*	*Teacher*	*Huntington Community College*
Name	(Title)	(Occupation)	(Organization)

Swamp Road, Huntington, WV		Bus. No.: *(304) 555-8000*	Home No.: *(304) 555-2111*
(Address)			

Henry Stone	*Controller*	*Finance*	*Brennan Shipping Co.*
Name	(Title)	(Occupation)	(Organization)

193 Mountain Blvd., Huntington, WV		Bus. No.: *(304) 555-1119*	Home No.: *(304) 555-8710*
(Address)			

I hereby certify that all statements made in this application (and accompanying résumé, if any) are true and complete. I understand that any false or misleading statement on this application constitutes sufficient grounds for dismissal, if hired. I further certify that I may lawfully be employed in this country and, if employed, will provide required documentation to verify identity and employment eligibility. In addition, in making this application for employment, I understand that the Company may investigate my employment and educational records. I hereby authorize my current and/or former employer(s) and school(s) to furnish the information requested by the Palmero Maintenance Company.

Signature of Applicant   *Cheryl Crowson*   Date *June 10, 20--*

Testing applicants can also be an area fraught with legal ramifications. Aptitude and psychological testings are unlawful unless results can be related to job performance. The use of online personality tests has surged in the past decade. These tests are used to assess the personality, skills, cognitive abilities, and other traits of 60 to 70 percent of prospective workers in the United States. These types of tests must be approved by the EEOC. Lie detector tests are strictly illegal. With regard to drug testing, employers must consult their state's laws.

Asking an applicant's age or date of birth may tend to deter the older worker. Thus, if an application form calls for such information, a statement should appear on that form notifying the applicant that the ADEA prohibits discrimination on the basis of age with respect to individuals who are at least 40. Questions on the application and during the interview process should be used only to determine the applicant's ability to do the job.

Some of the safeguards to prevent lawsuits would be:

- Accept applications almost exclusively online.
- Have someone not involved in the interview process review applications.
- Screen applications with computer software that looks for experience, education, and training characteristics.[7]

Another recent development that will affect the job interviewing process concerns past salary information. In an effort to ensure pay equality for women, over half of the states have enacted salary history bans.

The final part of the application form should be a statement affirming the employer's right to:

- Verify the information on the application.
- Terminate the employee for providing false information on the application or during the interview process.
- Obtain authorization for any planned credit or background checks.

The application should then be signed by the applicant.

Federal antidiscrimination laws require employers to keep all applications for at least one year from the date of hiring decision, even those from unqualified candidates.

Reference Inquiry

Before employing an applicant, a company may check some of the references given on the application. Many businesses use a standard **reference inquiry form**, which can be mailed or e-mailed to the person or company given as a reference. Other companies prefer a telephone reference check because they feel that a more frank opinion of the candidate is received over the telephone. Some companies prefer not to check on personal references given by the job applicant, since these tend to be less objective than business references (e.g., prior employers).

Today, any type of reference checking has taken on new meaning—expensive litigation. In most cases, respondents to these inquiries will verify dates of employment and job titles only, with no information on former employees' work habits. To reduce the increasing number of "failure-to-warn" lawsuits, a number of states have passed laws providing protection from liability to employers who want to provide references. Recent court decisions have held the reference process to

---

7 "From the Courts," *The HR Law Weekly*, 2018 Special Education, p. 3.

be privileged.[8] Some companies have also made an "Employment Reference Release" part of the employment application.

Hiring Notice

After the successful applicant is notified of employment and the starting date, time, and to whom to report, a **hiring notice** is sent to the Payroll Department so that the new employee can be added properly to the payroll. A hiring notice, such as that shown in Figure 1.6, usually gives the name, address, and telephone number of the new employee, the department in which employed, the starting date, the rate of pay, and any other information pertaining to deductions that are to be made from the employee's wages.

Employee History Record

Although many businesses keep no personnel records other than the application, a more detailed record is needed to provide a continuous record of the relationship between the employer and the employee. The **employee history record** is such a record and, in addition to providing personal and other information usually found on an application, provides space to record the employee's progress, attendance, promotions, performance appraisals, and salary increases. As with most records, the individual employee must have access to the worker's human resource files.

On the Job

Jumping to a new job—an ADP study found that a 13 percent raise in salary is the turning point at which employees will change to a new job.

FIGURE 1.6
Hiring Notice

HIRING NOTICE		NO. 220		
SOCIAL SECURITY NO. 000 - 00 - 6357		**DATE** June 28, 20--		
NAME Cheryl Crowson		**CLOCK NO.** 418		
ADDRESS 1630 West End Ave., Huntington, WV	**ZIP** 25703	**PHONE NO.** 555-1618		
OCCUPATION Payroll Specialist	**DEPT.** Accounting	**GROUP NO.** – –		
STARTING DATE July 1, 20--	**TIME** 8:00	**A.M.** **P.M.**	**RATE** $48,000 yr.	
FILING STATUS Single		**BIRTH DATE** 8/1/--		
LAST EMPLOYMENT	Brennan Shipping Co.	**LOCATION** Huntington, WV		
	DATE LEFT June 30, 20--	**REASON** Advancement		
NO. OF WITHHOLDING ALLOWANCES N/A				
IN EMERGENCY NOTIFY Robert Crowson		**PHONE NO.** 555-5136		
EMPLOYEE'S SIGNATURE IN FULL *Cheryl Crowson*				
SUPERVISOR'S SIGNATURE *Margaret T. Johnson*				
EMPLOYMENT DEPARTMENT				
ORIGINAL TO PAYROLL DEPT. **DUPLICATE RETAINED BY HUMAN RESOURCES DEPT.**				

---

8 "HIRE AT WILL," HR *Specialist*, 2010, p. 28.

Change in Payroll Rate

The **change in payroll rate form** notifies the proper departments of a change in the employee's rate of remuneration. The change in rate may originate in the Human Resources Department or with the head of the department in which the employee works. In either event, the Payroll Department must be informed of the change for the employee so that the rate change is put into effect at the proper time and so that the records reflect the new rate. Figure 1.7 shows a form that may be used for this purpose.

Terminating an Employee

If an employee has an employee contract or if promises were made to the employee, termination can only be done with "good cause." This means the firing must be based on reasons related to business needs and goals. An "at-will" employee can be discharged for any reason as long as it is not a discriminatory reason, even if the employee just does not work well together with the staff. In cases where the company has made past mistakes in the handling of the employee, it would be wise to consult a lawyer before making the final decision. The lawyer can check all the angles in order to protect the company from lawsuit liability.

Sirtravelalot/Shutterstock.com

FIGURE 1.7
Change in Status Form

CHANGE OF STATUS

Please enter the following change(s) as of _____ January 1, 20 -- _____

Name _____ Cheryl Crowson _____ Clock or Payroll No. _____ 418 _____ Soc. Sec. Number _____ 000-00-6357 _____

FROM

Job	Dept.	Shift	Rate
Payroll Specialist	Acct.	—	$48,000

TO

Job	Dept.	Shift	Rate
Accounting Analyst	Acct.	—	$51,500

REASON FOR CHANGE:

☐ Hired	☐ Length of Serv. Increase
☐ Re-hired	☐ Re-eval. of Existing Job
☒ Promotion	☐ Resignation
☐ Demotion	☐ Retirement
☐ Transfer	☐ Layoff
☐ Merit Increase	☐ Discharge
☐ Leave of Absence to _____	
	Date

Other reason or explanation: _____

_____

_____

AUTHORIZED BY _____ *Margaret T. Johnson* _____ APPROVED BY _____ *E. J. Dunn* _____

Prepare in triplicate: (1) Human Resources (2) Payroll (3) Employee's Department

Recordkeeping System

Whether the system is paper-based or computer-based or records in the cloud, it is advantageous to have four separate sets of records for each employee:

- Personnel file—basic information (e.g., name, address, etc.).
- Payroll file—salary and benefits.
- Medical file—insurance and private medical data.
- I-9 file—copies of the forms and the appropriate documents.[9]

Employee Access—Personnel Files

Even though personnel files are the property of the employer, employees may have the right to view and receive a copy of their own files. Even though no federal law guarantees it, more than half of the states allow current employees access to their records.

Even with this right, some documents are considered confidential, and employers should not allow employees to view anything that would be considered an invasion of privacy (e.g., reference letters, investigative notes, etc.). Before granting access to personnel files, the payroll professional should check all applicable state laws and their own company's written policy.

Payroll Accounting System

A **payroll accounting system** embodies all those procedures and methods related to the disbursement of pay to employees. A typical payroll accounting system includes the procedures shown in Figure 1.8. The nature of the payroll records depends to a great extent on the size of the workforce and the degree

On the Job

Payroll schemes account for almost 10 percent of all reported business frauds. Companies become most vulnerable when employees have access to check-writing software and hardware and when outsiders have access to company checks that are distributed to employees.

LO 5

Identify the *payroll register* and the *employee's earnings record.*

FIGURE 1.8
Procedures in a Payroll Accounting System

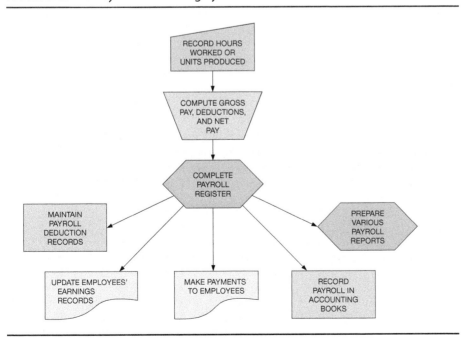

9 "Nuts & Bolts," *HR Specialist: Employment Law,* December 2012, p. 7.

to which the recordkeeping is automated. This course describes and illustrates manual payroll accounting systems. Appendix A describes a computerized payroll accounting system using Excel. In most payroll systems—manual or automated—the payroll register and the employee's earnings record are the two basic records that are utilized.

Payroll Register

The **payroll register** is a multicolumn form used to assemble and summarize the data needed at the end of each payroll period. It provides a detailed listing of a company's complete payroll for that particular pay period. Thus, the payroll register lists all the employees who earned remuneration, the amount of remuneration, the deductions, and the net amount paid. The information provided in the payroll register is used primarily to meet the requirements of the Fair Labor Standards Act. However, the register also provides information for recording the payroll entries and for preparing reports required by other federal, state, and local laws. Figure 1.9 shows one form of payroll register. Another form, used in the Continuing Payroll Problem at the end of Chapters 2 through 6, is shown in the fold-out at the back of this book.

FIGURE 1.9
Payroll Register   **Tell Me More**

PAYROLL REGISTER

FOR WEEK ENDING   *January 19*   20 - -

No.	Name	Total Hours Worked	Regular Earnings			Overtime Earnings			Total Earnings	Deductions				Net Paid	
			Hrs.	Rate	Amount	Hrs.	Rate	Amount		OASDI Tax	HI Tax	Fed. Income Tax	State Income Tax	Check No.	Amount
1 403	*Springs, Carl A.*	*40*	*40*	*10.75*	*430.00*				*430.00*	*26.66*	*6.24*	*18.00*	*15.00*	*504*	*364.10*
2 409	*Kadoba, Sue T.*	*42*	*40*	*10.50*	*420.00*	*2*	*15.75*	*31.50*	*451.50*	*27.99*	*6.55*	*0.00*	*13.00*	*505*	*403.96*
3 412	*O'Neill, John B.*	*38*	*38*	*11.10*	*421.80*				*421.80*	*26.15*	*6.12*	*0.00*	*13.00*	*506*	*376.53*
4 413	*Sanchez, Marie S.*	*44*	*40*	*10.80*	*432.00*	*4*	*16.20*	*64.80*	*496.80*	*30.80*	*7.20*	*26.00*	*20.00*	*507*	*412.80*
5 418	*Crowson, Cheryl*	*40*	*40*	*S*	*990.38*				*990.38*	*61.40*	*14.36*	*85.00*	*46.00*	*508*	*783.62*
47	*Totals*				*9,895.75*			*917.20*	*10,812.95*	*670.40*	*156.79*	*2,008.00*	*542.00*		*7,435.76*

Employee's Earnings Record

In addition to the information contained in the payroll register, businesses must provide more complete information about the accumulated earnings of each employee. For that reason, it is necessary to keep a separate payroll record on each employee—the **employee's earnings record**. Each payday, after the information has been recorded in the payroll register, the information for each employee is transferred, or posted, to the employee's earnings record. The employee's earnings record provides the information needed to prepare periodic reports required by the withholding tax laws, the FICA tax law, and state unemployment or disability laws. Employers also use the employee's earnings record in preparing **Form W-2, Wage and Tax Statement**. This form shows the amount of wages paid each worker in the course of the trade or business of the employer. Figure 1.10 shows an example of the employee's earnings record. Chapter 6 presents a more detailed discussion of the preparation and use of the payroll register and the earnings record.

On the Job

The retention requirements imposed on employers by various government agencies set a limit of seven years on payroll registers and eight years on employees' earnings records.

FIGURE 1.10
Employee's Earnings Record   Tell Me More

EMPLOYEE'S EARNINGS RECORD

Week	Week Ending	Total Hours Worked	Regular Earnings			Overtime Earnings			Total Earnings	Deductions				Net Paid		Cumulative Earnings
			Hrs.	Rate	Amount	Hrs.	Rate	Amount		OASDI Tax	HI Tax	Fed. Income Tax	State Income Tax	Check No.	Amount	
1	1/5	40	40	S	990.38				990.38	61.40	14.36	85.00	46.00	419	783.62	990.38
2	1/12	42	40	S	990.38	2	37.14	74.28	1,064.66	66.01	15.44	94.00	53.00	463	836.21	2,055.04
3	1/19	40	40	S	990.38				990.38	61.40	14.36	85.00	46.00	508	783.62	3,045.42

Department	Occupation	State Employed	S.S.No.	Name—Last First Middle	No.W/HAllow.
Accounting	*Accounting Analyst (A)*	*West Virginia*	*000-00-6357*	*Crowson, Cheryl*	*N/A*
					Marital Status *S*

Paycheck

When employees are paid by check, a check is written for each worker, using as the amount of net pay that figure appearing in the Net Paid column of the payroll register. Most paychecks, such as that depicted in Figure 1.11, on page 1-26, carry a stub, or voucher, that shows the earnings and deductions. Paying workers in cash, by check, by means of electronic transfer, or by pay cards is discussed in Chapter 6.

Many states (but not the FLSA) have laws that affect the frequency of wage payments. In Connecticut, for example, employees must be paid on a weekly basis unless the labor commission has approved an exception.

Outsourcing Payroll

With the increased need for up-to-the-minute information concerning changes in payroll tax laws, the trend toward outsourcing payroll operations has grown stronger. This is especially true with small to midsize companies. Many businesses have found that processing payroll by using an outside payroll company is more cost effective than doing the processing in-house. Other benefits realized are increased quality, improved efficiency, and a quicker release time, all of which enable the company to concentrate on its other operations.

Basically, the payroll operations at the company's site need only deal with the entry of new employee information and the number of hours worked by each employee. This information is sent to the payroll processing company electronically. The input is then processed by the outside firm. Once the processing is completed, the output package (paychecks, payroll, and management reports) is returned to the company.

These third-party payroll arrangements can range from just the cutting of paychecks and filing of tax returns to handling all aspects of employment from the hiring through the firing process.

Leading companies in the industry, such as ADP,[10] will custom-make a comprehensive and integrated program that will meet the needs of each individual business at a cost that many businesses find affordable.

On the Job

Surveys have found that 50 percent of mid-market companies (those with 500–4,999 employees) outsource their payrolls.

---

10 The ADP Logo is a registered trademark of ADP (Automatic Data Processing) of North America, Inc.

When outsourcing payroll, in order to reduce the risk of unpaid payroll taxes, the following steps should be followed:

- Hire only bonded service bureaus.
- Do not allow the service bureau to sign tax returns.
- Do not allow tax correspondence to be sent to the service bureau.
- Request regular IRS transcripts of the company accounts.[11]

FIGURE 1.11

Paycheck with Stub Showing Current and Year-to-Date Earnings and Deductions

REGULAR HOURS	O.T.B. HOURS	REGULAR EARNINGS	O.T.B. EARNINGS	GROSS EARNINGS	OASDI	HI	FIT	SIT		CODE	DEDUCTIONS
40		990.38		990.38	61.40	14.36	85.00	46.00			

DEDUCTIONS

1. MISC.	5. SPECIAL INSURANCE	9. TOOLS
2. BONDS	6. WELFARE FUND	10. RELIEF ASSOC.
3. CREDIT UNION	7. ADVANCES	11. SHOES
4. GROUP INSURANCE	8. UNIFORMS	12.

418	S	1	19	3,045.42	188.81	44.16	264.00	145.00			783.62
CLOCK NO.	RATE	PERIOD ENDING		GROSS EARNINGS	OASDI	HI	FIT	SIT			NET PAY ↑
					YEAR TO DATE						

RETAIN THIS STUB
IT IS A STATEMENT OF YOUR
EARNINGS AND DEDUCTIONS

Palmero Maintenance

- -

CLOCK NO.
418

Palmero Maintenance
Huntington, WV

DATE January 19, 20 – –

69-21
513

No. 508

PAYROLL ACCOUNT

PAY TO THE ORDER OF   Cheryl Crowson

	DOLLARS	CENTS
783.62	783	62

the 1st national bank
Huntington, WV

BY   *S. Hollis Stevenson*

⑈051300212⑈ 6139‴

Key Terms

applicable large employer (p. 1-13)	human resources system (p. 1-15)
application form (p. 1-17)	income tax (p. 1-4)
change in payroll rate form (p. 1-22)	investigative consumer report (p. 1-17)
disability benefit laws (p. 1-14)	payroll accounting system (p. 1-23)
employee history record (p. 1-21)	payroll register (p. 1-24)
employee's earnings record (p. 1-24)	pre-hire inquiries (p. 1-17)
executive orders (p. 1-7)	reference inquiry form (p. 1-20)
fair employment practices (p. 1-5)	requisition for personnel (p. 1-16)
Form I-9, Employment Eligibility Verification (p. 1-8)	small employer (p. 1-13)
Form W-2, Wage and Tax Statement (p. 1-24)	vesting (p. 1-12)
hiring notice (p. 1-21)	workers' compensation insurance (p. 1-13)

---

11 "Outsourcing Your Payroll May Not Be a Good Idea, After All" *Payroll Legal Alert*, June 2012, p. 1.

Key Points Summary

	Learning Objectives	Key Points	Problem Sets A & B
LO1	Identify the various laws that affect employers in their payroll operations.	• Fair Labor Standards Act—minimum wage and overtime. • Federal Insurance Contributions Act—social security taxes on employers and employees. • Income Tax Withholding Laws—deductions from employees' pays for federal and state income taxes. • Unemployment Tax Acts—federal tax on employers to pay administrative costs and state tax on employers to cover benefits.	N/A
LO2	Examine the recordkeeping requirements of these laws.	• No specific forms are mandated, but information to be collected and retention periods are. • Fair employment laws on the federal and state levels deal with discrimination on the basis of age, race, color, religion, sex, or national origin. • Laws requiring verification of employment eligibility of new hires.	N/A
LO3	Describe the employment procedures generally followed in a Human Resources Department.	• From the request for a new employee to applications and interviews, to administering tests, to checking references, to notifying payroll.	N/A
LO4	Identify the various personnel records used by businesses and the type of information shown on each form.	• Application form is used by most companies to get personal information, educational background, experience records, and references on each applicant. • Order forms that may be used—hiring notice, history record, change in payroll note.	N/A
LO5	Identify the *payroll register* and the *employee's earnings record*. ▶ **Tell Me More**	• Payroll register is a list of all employees for each pay period showing their gross pay, deductions, and net pay. • Employee's earnings record is a separate record for each employee showing the same information as the payroll register; used to prepare W-2s.	N/A

Matching Quiz

_____ 1. Employee's earnings record
_____ 2. Payroll register
_____ 3. Executive orders
_____ 4. Fair Labor Standards Act
_____ 5. Immigration Reform and Control Act
_____ 6. Unemployment insurance taxes
_____ 7. Vesting
_____ 8. Workers' compensation insurance
_____ 9. Family and Medical Leave Act
_____ 10. Affordable Care Act

A. Also known as the Federal Wage and Hour Law.
B. Record used in preparing employee's W-2.
C. Protection against losses due to work-related injuries.
D. Multicolumn form used to summarize data needed each pay date.
E. Highest-paid 10 percent of workforce can be exempted.
F. Antidiscrimination orders for employers with contracts involving federal funds.
G. Applicable large employers (ALE).
H. Form I-9 to be completed by all new employees.
I. Levied by both federal and state governments.
J. Conveys to employees the right to share in a retirement fund.

Questions For Review

1. Which act sets the minimum wage, and what is the current wage rate?
2. Under the FLSA, what information concerning employees' wages earned must be maintained by the employer?
3. Who pays the social security taxes that are levied by the Federal Insurance Contributions Act?
4. How are the funds used which are provided by FUTA and SUTA?

5. What types of unfair employment practices are prohibited by the Civil Rights Act of 1964 as amended?
6. What is the purpose of the Age Discrimination in Employment Act (ADEA)?
7. Are there any exceptions to the protection afforded older workers by the Age Discrimination in Employment Act?
8. Who is covered by the Walsh-Healey Public Contracts Act?
9. Under the Family and Medical Leave Act, what is the maximum number of weeks of unpaid leave that a covered employer is required to offer an employee whose spouse is seriously ill?
10. What is the primary purpose of the Employee Retirement Income Security Act (ERISA)?
11. Explain the concept of vesting.
12. Under ERISA, if requested in writing, what information must the administrator of the pension fund supply to the participants?
13. Under the Affordable Care Act, which employers are required to provide insurance coverage for all full-time employees and their dependents?
14. Summarize the procedure that may be followed by the Human Resources Department in hiring new employees.
15. What information is commonly provided by a job-seeker on the application for employment form?
16. What is the significance of the Civil Rights Act of 1964 and the Age Discrimination in Employment Act in the employer's use of pre-hire inquiries?
17. What obligations are imposed upon the employer by the Fair Credit Reporting Act of 1968?
18. What procedures are usually included in a typical payroll accounting system?
19. What two basic records are generated in most payroll accounting systems?
20. What uses are made of the information shown in the employee's earnings record?

Questions For Discussion

1. What personnel records would you suggest for a small retailer with three employees?
2. What kind of problem can be encountered when requesting references from previous employers of job applicants?
3. In staffing their offices, some firms encourage in-house referrals (recommendations of their present employees). What are some possible objections to this practice as a means of obtaining job applicants? What advantages may be realized by the firm that uses in-house referrals?
4. The main office of a large bank has an annual turnover of 500 office workers. As an employment officer of this bank, discuss the sources you would use in obtaining replacement employees.
5. Among the questions asked on the application for employment form of Horner Company are the following:

   a. What is the name of your church, and what religious holidays do you observe?
   b. Where is your birthplace?
   c. Are you a citizen of the United States?
   d. What foreign languages can you read, write, or speak fluently?

   In view of federal and state civil rights laws, do you believe that Horner Company is acting legally or illegally in asking each of the questions listed above?

Case Problem

C1. Paychecks Kept Coming. LO 3.

Ken, a salaried employee, was terminated from his company in April of this year. Business had been slow since the beginning of the year, and each of the operating plants had laid off workers.

Ken's dismissal was processed through the Human Resources Department, but the information was not relayed to the corporate payroll office.

As had been the policy, checks for workers at remote sites were mailed to the employees. The mailing of Ken's checks continued for the next four weekly paydays. It wasn't until the monthly payroll reports were sent to Ken's supervisor that the error was detected.

Ken refused to return the four extra checks. What actions should the company take?[12]

Chapter 2

Computing Wages and Salaries

So you are working at a pizza shop. Do you know if you are an employee? Are you paid a salary, or are you paid per delivery or by the hour? What about tips? How about a mileage allowance?

What's your work schedule? Do you work weekends or nights? Do you normally work overtime?

You should learn about the wonderful world of the FLSA.

Learning Objectives

After studying this chapter, you should be able to:

1. Explain the major provisions of the Fair Labor Standards Act.
2. Define *hours worked*.
3. Describe the main types of records used to collect payroll data.
4. Calculate regular and overtime pay.
5. Identify distinctive compensation plans.

This chapter examines the major provisions of the Fair Labor Standards Act, how to determine hours worked by employees, commonly used methods to record time worked, and the major methods of computing salaries and wages. Tracing its origin back to the 1930s, the Fair Labor Standards Act is the most encompassing of all the labor laws. However, it is also the one most violated.

Antoniodiaz/Shutterstock.com

The Fair Labor Standards Act

The Fair Labor Standards Act (FLSA), commonly known as the Federal Wage and Hour Law, contains provisions and standards concerning minimum wages, equal pay for equal work regardless of sex, overtime pay, recordkeeping, and child labor. The Wage and Hour Division of the U.S. Department of Labor (DOL) administers the act.

LO 1

Explain the major provisions of the Fair Labor Standards Act.

Coverage

The FLSA provides for two bases of coverage—enterprise coverage and individual employee coverage.

Enterprise Coverage

Enterprise coverage includes all employees of an enterprise if:

1. At least two employees engage in interstate commerce or produce goods for interstate commerce. Interstate commerce refers to the trade, transportation, or communication among several states or between a state and any place outside that state. The law also covers employees if they handle, sell, or otherwise work on goods or materials that have been moved in or produced for interstate commerce, and

2. The business has annual gross sales of at least $500,000.

On the Job

A National Call Center has been established by the Department of Labor to answer employees' and employers' questions on a range of employment issues. The toll-free number is 1-866-4-USA-DOL.

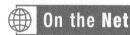

http://www.dol.gov/

U.S. Department of Labor Employment Standards Administration homepage. This site contains various sections of code, such as affirmative action and workers' compensation. To find the most useful information, choose the ESA program that interests you.

Coverage extends, *without regard to annual sales volume*, to those who operate:

1. A hospital.
2. A nursing home.
3. An institution for the mentally ill.
4. A school for mentally or physically handicapped or gifted children.
5. A preschool, elementary, or secondary school.
6. An institution of higher education.
7. A public agency.

The enterprise coverage under the FLSA does not apply to family establishments, often referred to as "mom and pop stores." Thus, if the only regular employees of an establishment include the owner, parent, spouse, child, or other immediate family members, the establishment is exempt from FLSA coverage.

Individual Employee Coverage

Under **individual employee coverage**, the FLSA covers a worker if the employee either engages in interstate commerce or produces goods for such commerce. Coverage also includes employment in a fringe occupation closely related and directly essential to the production of goods for interstate commerce. Coverage depends on the activities of the individual employee and not on the work of fellow employees, the nature of the employer's business, or the character of the industry as a whole. Thus, even though a business does not meet the enterprise coverage test, it must pay FLSA wages to those workers eligible for individual coverage.

Glenn Morris works for a small manufacturing firm that has an annual sales volume of $370,000. Although the firm does not meet the $500,000 volume-of-sales requirement for enterprise coverage, Morris is *individually* covered since he operates machinery used to produce goods for interstate commerce.

Employer

The FLSA defines an employer as "any person acting directly or indirectly in the interest of an employer" in relation to an employee. In order to protect employees, courts have defined "employers" in the broadest sense. Co-owners who control the day-to-day operations of the business are employers who are individually liable for violations of the law.

Employee

 IRS Connection

If you want the IRS to determine whether a worker is an employee, file **Form SS-8, Determination of Employee Work Status** for purposes of Federal Employment Taxes and Income Tax Withholding. Over 90 percent of these filed forms were determined to be for employees.

An individual is an **employee** if the individual performs services in a covered employment. As long as the common-law relationship of employer and employee exists and the employment is not exempt from the provisions of the law, both are covered and must observe its provisions. No differentiation is made between regular, temporary, substitute, or part-time workers.

A **common-law relationship** of employer and employee exists when the employer has the right to control both *what work will be done and how it will be done*. How the relationship is labeled is immaterial; it is the substance of the relationship that governs the worker's status.

To determine if a worker may be classified as an employee and if the employer has the right to control, the U.S. Department of Labor has reinstituted a new six-factor economic reality test:

1. Nature and degree of the employer's control.
2. Permanency of the worker's relationship with the employer.
3. Whether the worker or employer provides the means and instrumentalities of the work, such as investment in facilities, equipment, or assistants.

4. Amount of skill, initiative, judgment, or foresight required for the worker's services.

5. Whether the worker is at risk or benefit of profit or loss.

6. Degree of integration of the worker's services into the employer's business.

Employees of a Corporation

Managers, superintendents, supervisors, department heads, and other executives of a corporation are considered employees under the FICA tax law. All officers, such as the president, vice president, secretary, and treasurer, are also employees of the corporation. Their salaries are taxable the same as the wages paid to other employees. A *director of a corporation* who performs no services other than attending and participating in meetings of the board of directors is not an employee.

Partnerships

Partners generally are not employees of the partnership. In some cases, however, a partnership may operate as an association that may be classified as a corporation. In such situations, any partner who renders services similar to those of corporate officers would be an employee.

Domestics

Domestic workers also must be paid the minimum wage if:

1. They perform services in one or more homes for a total of eight hours or more in any workweek, *or if*

2. They earn wages of at least $2,400 from an employer in a calendar year.

Domestic service consists of services of a household nature performed in or about a private home of the person who employs the domestic. Some typical domestics include cooks, butlers, maids, caretakers, gardeners, and chauffeurs. The term also includes a baby sitter employed on other than a casual basis, such as a person who sits for a child five days a week. If the domestics do not live in the household, they must be paid overtime compensation as well as the minimum wage. However, live-in domestics do not have to be paid overtime. A casual baby sitter (one employed on an irregular or intermittent basis) or a companion for the aged or infirmed is not covered.

Direct care workers provide essential home care assistance to the elderly and people with injuries, illnesses, or disabilities. These workers if employed directly by a family or individual are not covered unless they are performing medically related duties or are providing more than a limited amount of care in addition to fellowship and protection. Direct care workers, employed by third-party employers, started to receive minimum wage and overtime coverage in 2015.

Statutory Employees

Workers who qualify as independent contractors under common law, but are taxed as employees for social security, are statutory employees. This status applies to agent or commission drivers, industrial home workers, full-time life insurance agents, and full-time traveling or city salespeople.

Statutory Nonemployees

There are two categories of statutory nonemployees—direct sellers and licensed real estate agents. For federal tax purposes, they are considered to be self-employed as long as their earnings are based on the amount of sales and their services are performed under a written contract stating that they will not be treated as employees for federal tax purposes.

On the Job

Today, nearly 25 percent of the workforce is made up of temporary workers, consultants, and independent contractors.

Interns

In the public and nonprofit sectors, volunteer interns who do not expect compensation are generally exempt from FLSA requirements. Interns in the for-profit sector may be exempt from the minimum wage and overtime requirements of the FLSA when they receive training for their own educational benefit.

Wages

Wages include the remuneration or compensation of paid employees. The terms wages and salaries are commonly used interchangeably. However, **wage** usually refers to remuneration paid on an hourly or a piecework basis. **Salary** usually refers to the remuneration paid on a weekly, **biweekly** (every two weeks), **semimonthly** (twice a month), monthly, or yearly basis.

The Minimum Wage

The FLSA of 1938 established a minimum wage of 25 cents per hour for a straight-time workweek of 44 hours. With the objective of improving the purchasing power of covered workers, succeeding amendments to the FLSA increased the minimum hourly rate and reduced the workweek. The Fair Minimum Wage Act of 2007 increased the minimum wage to $7.25 beginning on July 24, 2009.

Included in the regular rate of pay is all remuneration for employment paid to or on behalf of the employee. Some examples are:

1. Commission payments.
2. Earned bonuses (**nondiscretionary bonus**—which is a bonus normally based on hours worked, units produced, production efficiency, or work quality).
3. Severance pay.
4. On-call pay.
5. Shift or weekend differentials.

A **discretionary bonus**, which is a bonus not agreed upon, announced, or promised before payment, is not included in an employee's regular rate of pay. The employer retains discretion both to the granting and to the amount of the bonus until close to the end of the period for which the bonus is paid (discussion of nondiscretionary bonus, page 2-33).

The law also allows employers to credit the reasonable cost of housing, meals, and transportation to work that they provide toward payment of the minimum wage. To qualify, these facility credits must be furnished for the employee's benefit and must be accepted voluntarily by the employee.

Some other payments are not included in the regular rate of pay. Examples are:

1. Gifts made as a reward for service.
2. Payments for a bona fide profit-sharing or savings plan.
3. Payments for periods when no work is performed—vacations, holidays, sick days, or jury duty days.
4. Payments reported as part of a guaranteed minimum number of hours paid that are more than the actual hours worked.
5. Allowances for vehicles, tools, and uniforms that are considered an offset of employee expenses.
6. Call back pay that is infrequent and sporadic.
7. Certain sign-in and longevity bonuses.
8. Cost of providing certain parking benefits, wellness programs, gym access, employee discounts on retail goods or services, and certain tuition benefits.

On the Job

The minimum wage for employees paid for a 40 - hour week:
- a weekly basis is $290
- a semimonthly basis is $628.33
- a monthly basis is $1,256.67

News Alert

The country with the highest minimum wage is Australia, where the minimum hourly wage is set at the equivalent of $14.54 in U.S. dollars.

The exact wage rate, not the employee's "book rate," determines whether the statutory minimum is met. An employer who requires employees to live in company-provided housing and then deducts from their pay excessive rental charges may have reduced the wage rate below the FLSA minimum limit.

Paying Less Than the Minimum Wage

Under certain conditions, wages lower than the minimum wage may be paid to some employees.

1. Tipped employees (see page 2-6).
2. A training wage allows employers to pay $4.25 per hour to newly hired employees under 20 years of age (opportunity wage). This only applies to the first 90 consecutive calendar days of employment.
3. Retail or service establishments and farms may employ full-time students at 85 percent of the minimum wage ($6.1625 per hour, government rounds to $6.17 in favor of the employee).
4. Institutions of higher education may employ their own full-time students at 85 percent of the minimum wage.
5. Student-learners may be employed at 75 percent of the minimum wage if they are participating in a bona fide vocational training program conducted by an accredited school ($5.44 per hour).
6. Firms whose principal business is the delivery of letters and messages may employ messengers at not less than 95 percent of the minimum wage.
7. Persons whose earning capacity is impaired by age, physical or mental deficiency, or injury may be employed at special minimum wage rates. However, a certificate authorizing employment at such rates must first be obtained from the Department of Labor's Wage and Hour Division.

News Alert

The Department of Labor has ruled that undocumented immigrants must also be paid at least the minimum wage and overtime as stipulated in the FLSA.

Example 2-1

Jim Droghan, a full-time student, works at the Dollar Store. This week he worked 30 hours and earned $185.10. Retail establishments can pay full-time students less than the minimum wage (85 percent).

$$7.25 \times 85\% = \$6.17/\text{hour}$$
$$\$6.17 \times 30 \text{ hours} = \$185.10$$

Paying More Than the Minimum Wage

In some cases, wages higher than the minimum must be paid to some employees.

1. Effective January 30, 2022, employees of federal contractors must be paid at least $15.00 per hour. The rate will be increased every year by the Secretary of Labor based on increases in the Consumer Price Index.
2. Employees in states that have a higher minimum wage rate than the federal rate must be paid the higher rate.

On the Job

By February, 2022, the average hourly earnings of workers in the United States was $31.58, which represented an average annualized growth rate of 5.1 percent.

Self-Study Quiz 2-1

Indicate which of the following statements regarding the Fair Labor Standards Act are false.

_____ 1. Under the FLSA, wages include sales commissions and bonuses paid for employee performance.
_____ 2. Direct care workers must always be paid overtime compensation in addition to the minimum wage.
_____ 3. A son working for his parents in a family-owned business is not covered under the FLSA.

_____ 4. Individual employee coverage under the FLSA applies only if fellow employees are engaged in similar activities.

_____ 5. A college may pay its own full-time students less than the minimum wage.

Note: Answers to Self-Study Quizzes are on page 2-34.

State Laws

All states except for Alabama, Louisiana, Mississippi, South Carolina, and Tennessee have minimum wage and overtime rules that apply both to employees covered by the FLSA and to those not covered. Some states have created multiple rates based on region, employer size, and for urban versus nonurban counties. In Oregon, it is $12.50 per hour in nonurban counties, $13.5 in standard counties, and $14.75 per hour in Portland's service district. The FLSA requires payment of the higher wage standard if it is more than the federal $7.25 per hour.

Paying a "Living Wage"

Over 100 cities have enacted local ordinances to require employers who do business with the government to pay a "living wage" to their low-wage workers. The movement, started by local advocates, grew out of the failure to keep the national minimum wage on pace with the needs of the working poor. Recently, some living wage laws have been passed that also include private industry doing business within the cities' jurisdiction. In Miami, all city workers and workers for companies that have contracts (over $100,000) with the city after October 1, 1986, must be paid $14.03 per hour with health insurance coverage or $17.62 per hour without coverage (for contracts entered into before October 1, 2016, the rates are $14.25 and $16.31 respectively). In Santa Fe, New Mexico, the living wage rate is set at $12.95 per hour with the value of any employer-provided health benefits credited against this minimum.

News Alert

In 2007, Maryland became the first state to have a living wage law (covers contractors and subcontractors with a state contract for services at $100,000 or more).

Depending on the area of the state, in 2022 the wage rates ranged from $10.93 to $14.55 per hour.

Over the Line

In a lawsuit against Amazon, Inc., warehouse employees in Pennsylvania were required to clock out each workday and then wait for and undergo mandatory security checks, which were unpaid times. The Pennsylvania Supreme Court ruled against Amazon and defined "hours worked" to include "time during which an employee is required to be on the premises of the employer." The court stated that the state minimum wage laws' requirements are different from those under the federal FLSA.[1]

On the Job

The Department of Labor has stated that if tipped employees routinely spend more than 20 percent of their time on general preparation or maintenance work, the tip credit may not be claimed for the time spent performing those tasks, known as the "80/20 rule."

Tips

A **tip** (to ensure promptness) is a gift or gratuity given by a customer in recognition of some service performed. A **tipped employee** is one who engages in an occupation in which tips of more than $30 a month are customarily and regularly received. An employer may consider, within prescribed limits, the tips received by a tipped employee as part of the

---

1 *Payroll Currently*, February, 2022, Volume 30, Issue 2, p. 44.

employee's wages. In 1996, the Small Business Job Protection Act froze the minimum cash wage required for tipped employees at *$2.13* per hour. Tips received by the employee are credited toward the remainder ($5.12) of the total minimum wage ($7.25 − $2.13). The employee is required to report tips to the employer each month (if more than $20.00). If tips received do not amount to at least $5.12 per hour, the employer must increase the hourly rate of pay so that the hourly wage plus the equivalent hourly rate of tips received equal, at a minimum, $7.25 per hour. In 2022, the minimum wage for tipped employees of federal contractors was set at $10.50 per hour. Through a combination of tips and wages, these tipped employees must earn at least $15.00 per hour.

In order to take the tip credit, employers must notify the affected employees of the minimum wage requirements and of their intention to take the tip credit. This information can be provided orally to the employees.

Example 2-2

James Rudolph, a waiter, earns a weekly wage of $100.00 for a 40-hour workweek and receives tips of $100.00 each week. Even though the hourly rate paid to Rudolph ($100.00 ÷ 40 hours = $2.50) exceeds the minimum wage rate of $2.13, the employer must pay Rudolph an extra $90.00 so that the tips received plus the wages paid equal the minimum wage of $7.25 per hour.

$7.25 × 40 = ...	$290.00
Weekly wage..	(100.00)*
Tips received..	(100.00)
Extra weekly pay	$ 90.00

*$100.00 + $90.00 = $190.00; $190.00 ÷ 40 hours = $4.75/hour

All of the tips are the property of the employee and must be retained by the tipped employee unless there is a pooling of tips among the tipped employees. If employees are required to share the tips with employees not automatically tipped such as janitors, dishwashers, chefs, etc., the tip credit will be lost; however, voluntary arrangements among employees to pool tips will not eliminate the credit. The tip must be offered by the customer free from pressure, and the amount should not be based on a dictated employer policy. If any portion of the tips is turned over to the employer, no credit is allowed.

Service charges imposed on patrons by the employer do not count toward the tip credit. The IRS has begun to classify automatic gratuities (e.g., event fees, room service charges, and bottle service charges) as service charges which are treated as wages subject to tax withholdings. This will entail more paperwork and extra cost to the employer.

An alternative tip-reporting system can be used in which the employer and the IRS determine a predetermined tip rate for the employer's various occupations. At least 75 percent of the employees must sign agreements to report tips at or above the predetermined rate. The employer is then required to report any employee violations to the IRS.

In cases of two jobs performed by one worker, the tip credit can only be applied to the job that qualifies as tipped employment.

ProStockStudio/Shutterstock.com

On the Job

Companies that accept credit cards can deduct the amount of the credit card company's administrative fee that relates to the tip from the tip amount before giving it to the employee. These tips must be paid to the employee by the next regular payday.

Karl Marx worked for the Hilton Hotel in Las Vegas as a waiter. In addition, on his days off, he worked on Hilton's maintenance crew. Hilton can only claim the tip credit against Marx's wages on his waiter job.

Over the Line

Nevada-based Caesar's Entertainment Group must pay $175,128 in back wages and liquidated damages to 889 employees at two Indiana casinos that it operates. The casinos used deductions from employees' wages to cover the costs for individual employees' casino gaming licenses required by the Indiana Gaming Commission. These deductions brought employees' pay below $7.25 per hour.[2]

Under state laws, the states' tip credit percentage (different in each state) is applied to the federal minimum wage to calculate the actual tip credit and the resulting minimum wage required under state law. In states where the tip credit differs from the federal, employers must determine the credit and the resulting minimum wage under both federal and state law and pay their employees the higher cash wage.

Self-Study Quiz 2-2

Genna Harrison, a waitress, earns $85.20 a week for a 40-hour workweek. During one week, Harrison received tips of $90.
1. What hourly rate is being paid to Harrison?
    $ _____
2. How much must the employer pay Harrison in addition to her $85.20 weekly wage?
    $ _____

News Alert

The 4-day workweek is making inroads in Europe. Iceland has made the transition to shorter workweeks without pay cuts over several years. Belgium has just implemented a policy of allowing workers to request the compression of their work hours into four days.

News Alert

According to the U.S. Office of Personnel Management, the average American worker spends 261 days per year at work.

Workweek

The FLSA defines a **workweek** as a fixed and regularly recurring period of 168 hours—seven consecutive 24-hour periods. The individual employee's workweek is the statutory or contract number of hours to be worked regularly during that period. The workweek may begin on any day of the week and need not coincide with the calendar week. An employer may establish the same workweek for the business operations as a whole or assign different workweeks to individual workers or groups of workers.

An employer may change the day a workweek begins if intended to be a permanent change and not just to evade the overtime pay requirements of the FLSA. If, however, a union contract fixes the workweek, the employer's right to change the workweek depends upon the wording in the contract. Each workweek stands alone, and the overtime hours worked in one week may not be shifted to another workweek. Thus, each workweek is a separate unit for the purpose of computing overtime pay.

Overtime Hours and Overtime Pay

The FLSA requires overtime pay for all hours worked in excess of 40 in a workweek. The FLSA requires no overtime pay for daily hours worked in excess of any given number or for work on Saturdays, Sundays, holidays, or other special days. The law requires overtime pay to be *one and one-half times* the employee's regular hourly rate of pay, which must not be less than the statutory minimum. If the state's overtime rule is more generous than the FLSA's, the state law is followed. The payment for the overtime worked must generally be made on the regular payday for the time period in which the overtime work took place.

If an employee's regular rate of pay is $18.40 an hour, the overtime rate must be at least $18.40 $\times$ 1.5, or $27.60 an hour.

 Example 2-3

With some restrictions, employees covered under the FLSA can be required by their employers to work overtime. If they refuse, they can be fired under the law. There is also no limit on the overtime that can be required. However, in these cases, the state laws may be the governing force. On the other side, employees should only work overtime if authorized in advance by a supervisor and this should be a written policy. The consequences of unauthorized overtime must be communicated to all employees. Discipline for violating this policy must be administered equally, but payment must still be made for these non-approved hours. If reprimands do not work, suspension and even termination can legally result. In cases of disputed overtime work, courts have ruled that the employee bears the burden of proof. However, if the employer fails to keep proper and accurate records as required by the FLSA, the employer will bear the consequences of the failure.

If an hourly-rate employee works in pay periods of two weeks or longer, the employer can elect to give the employee 1.5 hours off for every overtime hour. However, the time off must be in the same pay period as the overtime hours worked, e.g., an employee works 44 hours the first week of a biweekly pay period; he works 34 hours in the second week and is paid for a total of 80 hours [40 + (4 O.T. $\times$ 1.5) + 34].

In the case of *tipped employees*, the same tip credit also applies to overtime hours. The regular rate of pay for a tipped employee is the current minimum wage—$2.13 plus $5.12 tip credit = $7.25/hour. Time and one-half of $7.25 is $10.88. Since the employer can use the same tip credit for overtime hours, the employee's overtime cash wages are $5.76/hour ($10.88 − $5.12).

On the Job

California defines overtime as any hours worked over 8 in one day, 40 in a workweek, and hours on the 7th consecutive day in a work week, and also provides for double-time pay for hours over 12 in one day and over 8 on the seventh consecutive day worked.

Alfred Sim is a tipped employee who normally works a 40-hour week and averages over $300 in tips each week. If his employer takes the maximum tip credit against the minimum wage ($5.12 per hour), in a week in which Sim worked 44 hours, the restaurant would pay him:

Example 2-4

Tell Me More

$$
\begin{array}{rr}
40 \text{ hours} \times \$2.13 = & \$\ 85.20 \\
4 \text{ hours} \times \$5.76 = & \underline{23.04} \\
\text{Gross pay} & \underline{\$108.24}
\end{array}
$$

Exceptions to Overtime Hours and Overtime Pay Provisions

An exception to overtime hours and overtime pay applies to *hospital employees who care for residents who are sick, aged, or mentally ill*. Hospitals may enter into an agreement with their employees under which a 14-day period, rather than a workweek, becomes the basis for computing overtime pay. Employees entering such an agreement must receive overtime pay at not less than one and one-half times their regular hourly rate for hours worked in excess of 8 hours in any workday or in excess of 80 hours in a 14-day period, whichever is the greater number of overtime hours (referred to as the 8 and 80 system). Although employers have the option of using the normal workweek or the 14-day period, they cannot change from one method to the other arbitrarily.

Donna Maloney, a lab technician, agreed that a 14-day period would be used to figure her overtime pay. Maloney works 12 hours in one day during the period and 8 hours in each of the 9 other days worked during the period, a total of 84 hours.

Maloney is entitled to 80 hours of straight-time pay and 4 hours of overtime pay for the 14-day period.

If Maloney worked only 7 hours in each of the 9 other days during the period, or a total of 75 hours, she would be entitled to 71 hours of straight-time pay and 4 hours of overtime pay for the 14-day period.

Employees in retail or service industries are exempt from the overtime provisions as long as their regular weekly rate of pay, including commissions, is at least one and one-half times the federal minimum wage rate ($10.88) and more than half of their pay over a monthly period comes from commissions. The overtime exemption is lost for any week in which the pay drops below $10.88 per hour.

Minimum wage legislation also provides an exception for *employees receiving remedial education*. Under this law, employees who receive remedial education offered by their employers are permitted to work up to 10 hours overtime each week without receiving overtime compensation. The remedial training, which does not include training for a specific job, must be designed to provide reading and other basic skills at an eighth-grade level or below.

Compensatory Time Off

A state, a political subdivision of a state, or an interstate governmental agency may grant employees (not covered by a collective bargaining agreement) compensatory time off in lieu of overtime compensation. Employees working in public safety, emergency response, or seasonal activities may accumulate compensatory time off up to 480 hours. (The 480-hour limit represents 320 hours of overtime actually worked at the one and one-half overtime rate.) Employees may "bank" their hours and use them later as time off at time and one-half during the course of their employment.

Employees whose work does not include the preceding activities may bank 240 hours for compensatory time off. Upon reaching the 480- or 240-hour limit, an employee must receive either cash for additional hours of overtime worked or use some compensatory time before receiving further overtime compensation in the form of compensatory time off. Note that not all 480 or 240 hours have to be accrued before compensatory time off may be used. The FLSA also provides for the payment of cash for unused comp time when the employee terminates employment.

Exemptions from FLSA Requirements

Exempt employees (see Figure 2.1) are those workers exempt from some, or all, of the FLSA requirements, such as minimum wages, equal pay, and overtime pay.

White-Collar Workers

The FLSA exempts some workers, such as executives, administrators, professional employees, highly compensated employees, computer professionals, and outside salespersons, from the minimum wage and overtime pay provisions if they satisfy certain tests.

Test of Exemption

To be eligible for this exemption, the employee must be paid on a *salary basis*, must be paid at least $684 per week, or $35,568 annually and must meet the "primary duty" requirements as listed in Figure 2.2, on page 2-12. This salary must be a predetermined amount that cannot be reduced because of fluctuations in

On the Job

For bona fide teachers, the salary level requirements for the white-collar exemption do not apply.

Fizkes/Shutterstock.com

FIGURE 2.1

Exemption Status of Workers Under FLSA

Employee Job Description	Minimum Wage Exemption	Equal-Pay Exemption	Full Overtime Exemption
Agricultural employees.			X
Agricultural workers who are members of the employer's immediate family.	X	X	X
Air carrier employees if the carrier is subject to Title II of the Railway Labor Act.			X
Amusement or recreational establishment employees, provided the business has seasonal peaks.	X	X	X
Announcers, news editors, and chief engineers of radio or television stations in small communities.			X
Baby sitters (casual) and companions to ill or aged persons unable to care for themselves.	X	X	X
Drivers and drivers' helpers who make local deliveries and are paid on a trip-rate or similar basis following a plan approved by the government.			X
Executive, administrative, and professional employees, including teachers and academic administrative personnel in schools.	X		X
Fruit and vegetable employees who are engaged in the local transportation of these items or of workers employed or to be employed in the harvesting of fruits or vegetables.			X
Household domestic service employees who reside in the household.			X
Motion picture theater employees.			X
Motor carrier employees if the carrier is subject to regulation by the secretary of transportation.			X
Newspaper employees if the newspaper is published on a weekly, semiweekly, or daily basis and if the circulation is less than 4,000 copies, with the major circulation in the county of publication or contiguous counties.	X	X	X
Railroad, express company, and water carrier employees if the companies are subject to Part I of the Interstate Commerce Act.			X
Salespersons for automobile, truck, or farm implement dealers; parts stock clerks or mechanics; salespersons for boat, trailer, or aircraft dealers.			X
Taxicab drivers.			X

the quantity or quality of the work performed. In addition, employers may use nondiscretionary bonus and incentive payments to satisfy up to 10 percent of the salary level, provided such payments are paid on at least a quarterly basis.

Washington Update

A number of states are evaluating changes to their overtime rules that will exceed the federal salary requirements. California has set its salary level for workers at large employers to $49,920 (set to change to $62,400 in 2023).[3]

In the case of executive, administrative, and professional employees, work not directly nor closely related to the employee's exempt duties cannot exceed 20 percent of their hours worked in a workweek.

---

3 "New Rule Opens Overtime to More Workers," *The Wall Street Journal*, September 25, 2019, p. A2.

FIGURE 2.2
Indications of Exempt Status

Executive	Administrative	Professional	Business Owner
1. Primary duty—managing 2. Supervises two or more employees 3. Authority to hire, fire, promote	1. Primary duty—performs office work 2. Regularly uses discretion and independent judgment	1. Work requires advanced knowledge (science or learning) 2. Knowledge acquired by prolonged course of instruction	1. Owns at least 20% of equity 2. Actively manages business operations
Highly Compensated	**Computer Professionals**	**Creative Professional**	**Outside Salespeople**
1. Earns $107,432 or more 2. Performs nonmanual work 3. Regularly performs one of the exempt duties of an executive, professional, or administrative employee	1. Salary of at least $684/week or $27.63/hour 2. Duties consist of system analysis techniques, design of computer systems or programs	1. Requires invention, imagination, originality, or talent in an artistic or a creative endeavor	1. Primary duty—makes sales or obtains orders for services or use of facilities 2. Regularly away from the employer's place of business 3. No salary test

The exemption is not lost if the wages are computed on an hourly, daily, or shift basis as long as the arrangement includes a guarantee of at least the minimum weekly required amount, paid on a salary basis. The guaranteed amount must be equivalent to the employee's usual earnings at the hourly, daily, or shift rate for the normal scheduled workweek. This would also apply to exempt employees paid on a fee basis for a single job.

Salary Basis

On the Job

The salary requirement does not apply in cases of law and medicine.

These white-collar employees must be paid their full salary in any week in which any work is performed without regard to the number of hours worked. However, deductions can be made from the salary if an exempt employee misses one or more full days of work for personal reasons, other than sickness or accident. If the employee does not qualify for the employer's sick pay plan or has used up all available sick time, deductions can also be made for these full-day absences. However, if there is not a bona fide sick-leave plan, an employer cannot make deductions from the salaries of exempt employees for absences due to sickness.

A proportionate share of an exempt employee's salary for the time actually worked is allowed only for the employee's first or last week of employment.

Example 2-5

Kurt Lopez began work this week for the Jaworski Company. Based on a 5-day workweek, his annual salary is $78,000, and he meets the test of an exempt white-collar employee. Since he started working on Tuesday, his first week's pay would be $1,200.

$$\$78,000/52 \text{ weeks} = \$1,500$$
$$\$1,500 \times 4/5 = \$1,200$$

Partial-day absences cannot be deducted from the exempt employee's salary. However, the Wage and Hour Division has stated that the employer can require the employee to use any accumulated leave time to offset the time absent. Employers should keep records that describe the workweek and the wages paid for that work time and can require exempt employees to record and track hours worked, to work a specified schedule, and to work as many hours as the employer desires as long as their salaries are paid.

Exempt status can be lost when employers make improper deductions from the pays of exempt employees. This loss of status only applies to the pay periods when the deductions were made.

An exception to the FLSA salary pay requirement is the use of FMLA leave. If an employee works half a day, the other half a day taken for FMLA can be unpaid (if personal time is not used to cover the FMLA part of the day).

Over the Line

A store manager at a Family Dollar store in Florida was paid on a weekly salary basis, and even though she spent 60 to 70 percent of her time doing nonexempt work, she did handle many exempt managerial duties—scheduling, directing employees' work, etc. When the employee sued for overtime, the court determined that time alone is not the sole test of an employee's primary duty, and recognized the concept of multitasking: concurrent performance of exempt and nonexempt duties. The court ruled against the employee stating that her managerial duties were more important than the other duties performed.[4]

Blue-Collar Workers

The exemption from overtime pay based on the duties and salary tests does not apply to blue-collar workers (manual workers). No matter how highly paid, these workers are still entitled to overtime pay. This also applies to police officers, firefighters, paramedics, emergency medical technicians, and licensed practical nurses.

Equal Pay Act

The Equal Pay Act amended the FLSA to require that men and women performing equal work must receive equal pay. The Equal Pay Act applies to any employer having workers subject to the minimum pay provisions of the Wage and Hour Law. The equal-pay requirements also apply to white-collar workers and outside salespersons, even though they are exempt from the minimum wage standards.

The Equal Pay Law prohibits an employer from discriminating by paying wages to employees of one sex at a lower rate than those paid the opposite sex for equal work on jobs that require equal skill, effort, and responsibility and that are performed under similar working conditions. However, wage differentials between sexes are allowable if based on a seniority system, a merit system, a payment plan that measures earnings by quantity or quality of production, or any factor other than sex. If an unlawful pay differential between men and women exists, the employer must raise the lower rate to equal the higher rate.

Child-Labor Restrictions

The FLSA prohibits a business from the interstate shipment of its goods or services if it employs child labor unlawfully. Under the FLSA, the secretary of labor issues regulations that restrict the employment of individuals under the age of 18. The restrictions divide child employment into nonfarm occupations and agricultural occupations.

Nonfarm Occupations

The basic minimum age for most jobs is 16 years. This is the minimum age for work in manufacturing and processing jobs or in any other occupations except those declared by the secretary of labor as hazardous for minors

On the Job

The Department of Labor prohibits occupational driving for minors except on an occasional or incidental basis. Permitted driving can only be done during daylight hours and in vehicles not exceeding 6,000 pounds. In New York state, 16- and 17-year-olds are prohibited from driving in Manhattan.

Sorbis/Shutterstock.com

under 18. The FLSA lists 17 occupations that are considered too dangerous. These include mining, forestry, excavation, roofing work, operation of certain power-driven tools, and most on-the-job driving. However, employees ages 16 and 17 may work an unlimited number of hours each week in non-hazardous jobs.

Within certain limits, 14- and 15-year-olds may be employed in retail, food service, and gasoline service establishments. For example, this age group may be employed in office and clerical work, including the operation of office machines; cashiering; selling; price marking and tagging by hand or by machine; errand and delivery work; kitchen work and other work involved in preparing and serving food and beverages; dispensing gasoline and oil; and car cleaning.

The employment of minors between the ages of 14 and 16 cannot interfere with their schooling, health, and well-being. In addition, the following conditions must be met:

1. All work must be performed outside school hours.
2. There is a maximum 3-hour day and 18-hour week when school is in session (8 hours and 40 hours when not in session).
3. All work must be performed between 7 A.M. and 7 P.M. (9 P.M. during the summer).

Over the Line

A Wendy's franchise owner in Michigan had to pay $258,000 in fines for allowing teen workers to operate deep fryers and permitting 14- and 15-year-olds to work more than three hours on school days and over eight hours on non-school days.[5]

Agricultural Occupations

The employment of children under age 12 is generally prohibited in agricultural occupations, as described below.

1. During hours when school is in session.
2. Outside school hours on farms, including conglomerates, that used more than 500 man-days of labor in any quarter of the preceding calendar year.
3. Outside school hours on noncovered farms without parental consent.

However, children may work on farms owned or operated by their parents or guardians. Children 10 and 11 years old can work as hand harvest laborers outside school hours for up to eight weeks between June 1 and October 15, with a number of strict conditions on the employer. Children aged 12 and 13 may be employed only during hours when school is not in session provided there is parental consent or the employment is on a farm where the parents are employed. Children aged 14 and 15 may be employed, but only during hours when school is not in session. No child under the age of 16 may be

---

5 "Employment Law," *HR Specialist*, May 2018, p. 5.

employed in a hazardous farm occupation, such as operating large tractors, corn pickers, cotton pickers, grain combines, and feed grinders.

Certificate of Age

Employers cannot be charged with having violated the child-labor restrictions of the law if they have on file an officially executed *certificate of age* which shows that the minor has reached the stipulated minimum age. In most states, a state employment or age certificate, issued by the Federal Wage and Hour Division or by a state agency, serves as proof of age. In some states, a state or federal certificate of age, a state employment certificate, or a work permit may not be available. In such cases, the employer may rely on any one of the following documents as evidence of age for minor employees:

1. Birth certificate (or attested transcript thereof) or a signed statement of the recorded date and place of birth issued by a registrar of vital statistics or other officer charged with the duty of recording births.

2. Record of baptism (or attested transcript thereof) showing the date of birth of the minor.

3. Statement on the census records of the Bureau of Indian Affairs and signed by an administrative representative thereof showing the name, date, and place of the minor's birth.

The employer should maintain a copy of the document or indicate in the payroll records which document verified the minor's age.

Wage Theft

Wage theft is a term that refers to situations when employers do not pay employees in accordance with statutory or contract requirements. This includes violations such as not paying minimum or agreed-upon wages, not paying the proper overtime rates, having employees working off of the clock or under the table, or misclassifying employees as consultants. States are now attacking this problem with increased costs of noncompliance. States' remedies include assessing higher fines and penalties, prohibiting companies from receiving state contracts, denying or canceling business licenses, or criminalizing the violations.[6]

Penalties

A number of remedies may be applied for violations of the FLSA:

- Backpay—to satisfy the requirements of the law.
- Liquidated damages—equal to the amount of backpay and overtime.
- Civil penalties (discussed below)—employees engaged in a "course of conduct."
- "Hot goods" injunction—bars shipment of any goods manufactured in violation of the FLSA.
- Attorney fees and court costs—if employees win a lawsuit.

The civil and criminal penalties that could result are:

Misclassified Workers

- Unintentional with a filed Form 1099 (showing nonemployee compensation)—1.5 percent of wages paid + 20 percent of the employee's social security tax.

IRS Connection

The IRS has recently issued guidance regarding same-sex marriage relating to retirement plans. If a couple is legally married in a jurisdiction that recognizes it, then they are married for federal tax purposes.

6 "States, Localities Crack Down on Wage Theft," *PAYTECH*, November 2015, p. 40.

- Unintentional without a filed Form 1099—above penalties are doubled.
- Intentional—100 percent of the worker's federal income tax and social security taxes.
- In addition to the above, the employer remains liable for any penalties for failure to withhold, to file returns, and to pay taxes.

Wage and Hour Provisions (Willful Violations)

- Fines of up to $2,203.
- Unpaid fines can result in court-ordered imprisonment.

Tip Retention Violations

- Penalties of up to $1,100 per violation against employers who retain tips earned by employees.

Providing False Data

- Fines up to $10,000 and imprisonment up to 10 years (Federal False Information Act).

Repeated Violations

- Fines up to $10,000 per violation resulting from a "continuous course of conduct"; second offenders can be imprisoned for up to six months.

Child-Labor Provisions Violations

- Maximum fine of $14,050 without serious injury or death of any employee under 18 years old ($63,855 if serious injury or death occurs).
- Minimum fine of $6,000 per violation for illegally employing 12–13 year olds ($8,000 for under 12 year olds).
- Willful or repeated violations will cause a maximum penalty of $127,710.

It is unlawful to discharge or discriminate against an employee because the individual has filed a wage-hour complaint. This could result in a lawsuit in which lost wages, liquidated damages, and even punitive damages are awarded.

Areas Not Covered by the FLSA

The FLSA does not require employers to:

1. Pay extra wages for work on Saturdays, Sundays, or holidays.
2. Pay for holidays, vacations, or severance.
3. Limit the number of hours or work for persons 16 years of age or over.
4. Give holidays off.
5. Grant vacation time.
6. Grant sick leave.

LO 2

Define hours worked.

Determining Employee's Work Time

To avoid paying for time not actually spent on the job and to eliminate payment for unnecessary overtime work, employers must know what types of employee activities count as working time under the law. Generally, the hours counted as working time include all the time that employees actually work or must be on duty. A distinction must be made between an employee's principal activities and the preliminary and postliminary activities.

Principal Activities

The **principal activities** of employees include those tasks employees must perform and include any work of consequence performed for the employer. Principal activities include those indispensable to the performance of productive work and those that are an integral part of a principal activity.

The test of compensability with respect to principal activities requires that there be physical or mental exertion, controlled or required by the employer and performed for the employer's benefit.

On the Job

Employees do not have the legal right to carry their cell phones at work. Employers can require employees to place their phones and other electronic devices in storage lockers.

Chad Cabrera is a lathe operator who oils and cleans his machines at the beginning of each workday and installs new cutting tools. These activities performed by Cabrera are part of his principal activity.

Clothes-Changing Time and Wash-Up

Because of the nature of their work, some employees change clothes or wash on the employer's premises. Statutes or ordinances may require clothes changing or washing. Employees who spend time changing clothes or washing on the employer's premises regard this time as part of their principal activities. However, even where the nature of the job or the law requires clothes changing or wash-up, it may be excluded from time worked either expressly or by custom and practice under a collective bargaining contract. The U.S. Supreme Court has ruled that time spent donning and doffing protective gear qualified as "clothes changing" under a collective bargaining agreement between the employer and the unionized workforce, and was noncompensable. This ruling affects all employers of a unionized workforce that have uniform or other dress requirements.

Sandyman/Shutterstock.com

Over the Line

A District of Columbia federal court ruled that time spent donning and doffing protective gear and firearms by police officers was compensable time unless the time was too short to monitor. However, changing into uniforms was not considered to be an integral nor indispensable part of their policing duties. Since the officers could change clothes at home, this time is not considered "time worked."[7]

Travel Time

The time spent by employees traveling to and from work needs to be counted as time worked only if contract, custom, or practice so requires. In some situations, however, travel time between home and work counts as time worked. If an employee who regularly works at a fixed location is given a special one-day work assignment in another city, time worked includes the travel time.

Areej MacAvoy receives an emergency call outside regular working hours and must travel a substantial distance to perform a job away from MacAvoy's usual work site for one of the employer's customers. The travel time counts as time worked.

When performed during the workday as part of an employee's principal activities, the travel time counts as time worked. In addition, when traveling between workdays from one city to another, the travel time counts as working

---

7 *Payroll Manager's Letter*, March 7, 2012, Volume 28, Issue 5, p. 8.

time when the hours correspond to regular working hours, even though the hours may occur on Saturday and Sunday.

Rena Thorpe travels throughout the city to various job sites during regular working hours, 9 A.M. to 5 P.M., Mondays through Fridays. Such travel time counts as work time.

   If Thorpe is sent on a trip requiring travel on Saturday and Sunday to be at a job the first thing Monday morning, the travel time on Saturday and Sunday between the hours of 9 A.M. and 5 P.M. counts as time worked, but travel time before 9 A.M. and after 5 P.M. does not count.

Idle Time

Readiness to serve can also be considered employment. If the time spent while idle was primarily for the benefit of the employer, this time must be compensated. However, even if workers are required to carry a beeper, pager, or cell phone, this on-call time is not compensable, provided they can use this time for their own purposes. Also, travel limitations during this on-call time does not make it work time.

Waiting Time

If an employee is "engaged to wait," this is work time. For example, workers required to be at a car wash at a scheduled time while waiting for cars to be washed are considered to be working. On the other hand, if an employee is "waiting to be engaged," this is not work time. An employee completely relieved from duty until a certain hour is not working during the time spent waiting for that hour.

Rest Periods and Coffee Breaks

The FLSA does not require that an employer give employees a rest period or a coffee break. However, the employer may grant such rest periods voluntarily; or the union contract or municipal or state legislation may require them. In these cases, the time spent on a rest period of 20 minutes or less counts as part of the hours worked. If longer than 20 minutes, the compensability for the time depends upon the employee's freedom during that time or upon the provisions of the union contract.

Over the Line

Progressive Business Publications (PBP) did not provide paid breaks to its sales representatives and paid them only for the time they were logged off their computers if logged off for less than 90 seconds—this even applied to time off to get coffee, use the bathroom, or prepare for the next sales call. The DOL filed suit (rest periods up to 20 minutes count as time worked) and a federal judge fined PBP $1.75 million.[8]

On the Job

Over 40 states have laws covering meals and rest periods. California requires a 30-minute break (unpaid) after five hours and a 10-minute rest period per four hours of work. If non-exempt employees do not get this break, they must be given an additional hour of pay.

Meal Periods

Bona fide meal periods (not including coffee breaks or snack times) during which the employee is completely relieved from duty are not considered working time. Lunch periods during which the employee must perform some duties while eating are not bona fide meal periods. The general rule sets a bona fide meal period at 30 minutes or longer.

---

8 www.bizjournals.com/philadelphia/news/2019/04/04/back-pay-american-future-systems-progressive-busin.html.

In cases where the employer and employee agree that it is sufficient, a 15-minute lunch period can be considered a bona fide meal period. However, the lunchroom facilities must be readily accessible.

Virginia Gomez, an office worker, must eat at her desk and operate the switchboard at lunch time. Gomez must be paid for the lunch period.

Taking Work Home

With more and more employees taking work home with them, it is important to understand that this is compensable time. Nonexempt employees must be paid for *all hours worked*, even those outside the regular workplace. This holds true whether the work was assigned or the employees took on the extra workload themselves. Even if told not to take work home, the employer must pay for the time worked. The only recourse for the employer would be future warnings and, if the practice continues, dismissal of the employee.

Another area of concern for employers would be employees sending work-related e-mails, even when they are technically off the clock. This time spent is considered work time and could trigger overtime pay. A clear statement on e-mail usage for hourly staff should be part of an employee policy manual.

Sleep Time

If required to be on duty for less than 24 hours, the employee is considered to be working even though the employee is sleeping or engaging in other personal activities. If over 24 hours, an agreement to exclude a sleeping period of not more than 8 hours from time worked is binding. Adequate sleeping facilities must be provided, and the employee must be permitted at least 5 hours of uninterrupted sleep.

News Alert

In a report by Osterman Research, 94 percent of office workers admitted to sending work-related e-mails on weekends.

Over the Line

Self Pride, a Maryland-based residential facilities operator, altered employees' records to reduce hours worked during the 48-hour weekend shift. Based on testimony from the employees, they were not able to sleep during these 48-hour shifts, breaks were routinely interrupted, calls had to be made each hour to the main office or pay was docked, and leaving the facility during breaks was not practical. After receiving all the testimony, the Fourth Circuit Court ruled that the entire 48 hours of the shift constituted work time as defined by the FLSA—break time was interrupted by duties carried out for Self Pride's benefit.[9]

Training Sessions

Generally, working time includes the time spent by employees in attending lectures and meetings for training purposes.

The working time spent by postal clerks in learning mail distribution practices and the operation of letter-sorting machines counts as compensable time because it is (a) controlled and required by the employer, (b) for the primary benefit of the employer, and (c) an integral and indispensable part of the employees' principal work activities.

Iakov Filimonov/Shutterstock.com

However, time spent in training sessions need not be counted as working time if ALL the following conditions are met:

1. Attendance by the employee is voluntary.
2. The employee does not produce any goods or perform any other productive work during the meeting or lecture.
3. The meeting or lecture takes place outside regular working hours.
4. The meeting or lecture is not directly related to the employee's work.

Doctor's Appointments

Time spent waiting for and receiving medical assistance on the employer's premises or at the employer's direction during the employee's normal working hours during the workweek is considered time worked. As such, it cannot be deducted from the employee's accrued leave.

Preliminary and Postliminary Activities

Preliminary and postliminary activities are compensated if one of the following conditions is met:

- There is a prior agreement between the employer and employee.
- It is customary in the industry.
- It is an integral and indispensable part of the employee's principal activity.

Under the Portal-to-Portal Act, unless one of the above conditions is met, these activities are not compensated.

Some examples of activities regarded as preliminary and postliminary include: walking, riding, or traveling to or from the actual place where employees engage in their principal activities; checking in and out at the plant or office and waiting in line to do so; changing clothes for the convenience of the employee, washing up and showering unless directly related to the specific type of work the employee is hired to perform; and waiting in line to receive paychecks.

Activities that qualify as "work time" but the time spent on them is so short that they are considered *de minimis* (insignificant) need not be compensated.

Fractional Parts of an Hour

The FLSA requires that employees be paid for *all* time worked, including fractional parts of an hour. An employer cannot use an arbitrary formula or an estimate as a substitute for determining precisely the compensable working time which is part of an employee's fixed or regular hours.

Uncertain and indefinite working periods beyond the scheduled working hours cannot be practicably determined. Therefore, a few seconds or minutes may be disregarded. Some courts have allowed from 10 to 20 minutes to be ignored, while other courts have refused to apply the law to periods as small as 10 minutes. Generally, a few minutes of time spent by employees on the company premises for their own convenience before or after their workdays are not included in the hours worked.

Employers using time clocks may round starting and stopping times of their employees to the nearest 5 minutes, or to the nearest 6 minutes (tenth of an hour), or 15 minutes (quarter of an hour). However, consistently rounding time *down* to the nearest 5 minutes or one-tenth or one-quarter of an hour would be a violation in that employees would not be properly compensated for all time worked. These rules must be administered fairly and consistently.

The Labor Department states that the rounding must not result, over a period of time, in a failure to compensate employees for time they have actually worked. Safe methods to use would be:

- Minute-based—in case of 15-minute intervals, pay for the full quarter hour if 7 minutes late; if 8 minutes late, do not pay for that quarter hour.
- Start-stop—round off in the employee's favor at all starting times, but to the employer's favor at all quitting times.
- Safe—always round to the employee's favor.[10]

In the case of union or other employment contracts, the method of computing regular and overtime rates may be prescribed in the contracts.

Absences

The FLSA does not require an employer to pay an employee for hours not worked because of illness. For employees on an hourly wage basis, the time card shows the exact hours worked. In addition, the time off for absences does not count toward the 40 hours for overtime pay purposes even if the employee is paid for the absences. In practice, most U.S. employers provide vacation days, sick days, and/or paid time off (PTO) days for full-time employees. Only one-third of employers offer paid leave to part-time employees.

Tardiness

Employers may handle tardiness in many ways. Frequently, when an employee is late or leaves early, the supervisor must OK the time card. Some companies require the employee to sign a special slip indicating the reason for being late or leaving early. Some companies keep time according to the decimal system, whereby each hour is divided into units of tens (6 minutes times 10 periods in each hour). An employee who is late one through 6 minutes is penalized or "docked" one-tenth of an hour. One who is 7 through 12 minutes late is "docked" one-fifth of an hour, etc.

Records Used for Timekeeping

The FLSA requires employers subject to the law to keep certain time and pay records. For example, employers must keep records that indicate the hours each employee worked each workday and each workweek.

How the employer chooses the methods of keeping time records depends on the size of the company and whether employees are paid on an hourly, weekly, biweekly, semimonthly, or monthly basis. Employees on a salary basis usually work a given number of hours each day and can be required to record and track their hours and to work a specified schedule. Employees on an hourly wage basis may work a varying number of hours with some "down time" and layoffs and some overtime work. All of this time must be recorded in some way.

Time Sheets

A **time sheet** provides the information required by law and the data used to compute the payroll. Many small businesses that must keep a record of time

On the Job

In the case of bad weather that prevents exempt employees from getting to work, a full day's pay can be deducted from their pay. However, the employees could be required to use their leave time to cover the missed day. If the business closes, the employer could require the use of leave time, but cannot deduct a day's pay.

LO 3

Describe the main types of records used to collect payroll data.

On the Job

The World Population Review reports that the average number of work hours per week in the United States is 41.5, with average annual wages in "international dollars" of $55,253.

---

10 "Employment Law," *HR Specialist*, December 2018, p. 4.

worked by each employee require each person to submit and sign a time sheet, indicating the times of arrival and departure from work. These time reports are approved by the appropriate supervisor or department head at the end of the pay period. They are then forwarded to the Payroll Department for entry into the payroll system. Time sheets offer a simple method of accumulating employees' working times.

Time Cards

Under this timekeeping system, each employee receives a **time card** on which the time worked is recorded manually by the employee or automatically by a time clock. The time card is designed to fit various lengths of pay periods. Figure 2.3 shows one type of time card frequently used for a weekly pay period. The card provides space to record the hours worked, the rate of pay, deductions, and net pay. The Payroll Department inserts the handwritten figures to be used in computing total earnings, deductions, and net pay for the payroll period.

Some time clocks use the **continental system** of recording time, where each day consists of one 24-hour period, instead of two 12-hour periods. The time runs from 12 midnight to 12 midnight. Eight o'clock in the morning is recorded as 800; eight o'clock in the evening, as 2000.

Computerized Time and Attendance Recording Systems

The main kinds of computerized time and attendance recording systems include:

1. *Card-generated systems*—employees use time cards similar to the traditional time cards illustrated earlier. Daily and weekly totals are calculated and printed on the time cards for data entry into the firm's computer system.

2. *Badge systems*—employees are issued plastic laminated badges containing punched holes or having magnetic strips or bar codes. The badges are used with electronic time clocks that collect and store data, which later become input to the computer system.

3. *Cardless and badgeless systems*—employees enter only their personal identification numbers (PIN) on a numerical or alphanumerical key pad. This system, like the badge system, uses time clocks to collect and store data for transmission to, and processing by, the firm's computer system.

4. *Personal computer-based systems*—employees swipe their identification cards across bar code readers connected to personal computers for easy recording of time worked.

For example, the Timekeeper, a self-contained, wall-mounted time clock, contains a computer system.[11] This time clock accepts time and attendance data from time cards and computes complex payroll and on-the-job information. Time-clock systems, such as the Timekeeper, eliminate most manual payroll processing operations. Employees receive their own time cards that show their daily attendance record, thus complying with federal, state, and union regulations. The Timekeeper also totals employee hours and rounds out employee time to fractions of an hour in accordance with the payroll practice of the firm.

The Timekeeper card, shown in Figure 2.4, is similar to the time card illustrated in Figure 2.3. The mark-sense field at the bottom of the card identifies each employee or supervisor and authorizes access to and use of the Timekeeper.

---

11 Information supplied by Kronos, Incorporated.

FIGURE 2.3
Time Card

	Hours	Rate	Amount			
				OASDI	32	66
Reg.	40	10.75	430 00	HI	7	64
O/T	6	16.13	96 78	FIT	63	00
				SIT	10	54
				Group Life Ins.	1	60
				Hospital Ins.	3	15
Total Earnings			526 78	U.S. Sav. Bonds	5	00
Less Deductions			123 59	Other		
NET PAY			403 19	Total	123	59

No. **312**   Pay Ending October 17, 20--

NAME GARY A. SCHNEIDER   000-00-7471

Days	MORNING IN	MORNING OUT	AFTERNOON IN	AFTERNOON OUT	OVERTIME IN	OVERTIME OUT	Daily Totals
1	M 7 59	M 12 03	M 1 00	M 5 05			8
2	TU 7 50	TU 12 04	TU 12 59	TU 5 07			8
3	W 7 51	W 12 01	W 12 50	W 5 04	W 5 29	W 7 35	10
4	TH 8 00	TH 12 02	TH 12 58	TH 5 03			8
5	FR 8 00	FR 12 05	FR 1 01	FR 5 06			8
6	SA 7 55	SA 12 04					4
7							

Signature _Gary A. Schneider_

FIGURE 2.4
Mark-Sense Time Card Used in the Timekeeper Computerized System

When an employee places the card in the time clock, the computer scans the card, optically verifies the employee's number, and locates the last print line on the card. The time of entry is then printed on the next line. Simultaneously, the computer stores the punch-in time in the system's memory. When an employee punches out, the Timekeeper again verifies the employee's identification number and computes and rounds off the daily and cumulative payroll hours. Next, the actual punch-out time and the computed cumulative hours are printed on the card and stored within the Timekeeper for transmission to a computer for payroll processing.

Next Generation

With more and more employees working outside the traditional office environment, the time clock has not been able to keep up with most companies' needs for time and attendance information. Many companies have been forced to acquire more automated systems. These systems allow for:

1. quicker and more accurate data assembly.
2. elimination of calculation errors.
3. easier tracking of labor cost to projects.
4. faster and more reliable scheduling.

Chinnapong/Shutterstock.com

The new generation systems can communicate key messages to employees. They allow employees to check their schedules, vacation and sick time balances, and the status of time-off requests.

Touch-Screen Technology

In this system, data can be collected and processed instantaneously. The system requires employees to punch in and out on touch-screen personal computers (PCs), which are connected to the company's main computer server. These touchscreen kiosks are also used to provide information back to the employee regarding the organization.

Internet

Some Web-based time accounting systems now allow employees to "clock" in and out via the Internet. Employees use passwords to log on to a secured Web site. This site can also be used by the employees to check their hours worked, vacation time accrued, and messages from the Human Resources Department. This can also be accomplished through the use of mobile and wireless data collection devices (cell phones, personal digital assistants, and Global Positioning Satellite—GPS—enabled smartphones). Without ever visiting their office, employees can enter time and labor information.

Biometrics

The need for greater security and precision has recently produced a more affordable alternative to companies that are searching for time and attendance systems. A biometric time system uses a time clock that reads an employee's unique fingerprint or hand geometry (size and shape) to validate the employee. This technology is also available in other forms—voice recognition, iris scan, and even whole-face recognition.

IVR

A telephone-based time system (Interactive Voice Response) allows employees to use a phone, cell phone, or app on a smartphone for time collection. Just as an employee's hand can be identified, so can an employee's voice tract. Employees call a toll-free number, say their pass code and press 1 to clock in, and repeat the procedure to clock out.[12]

Cloud-Based

These are online time clock software systems. Employees can use any computer or smart device to clock in and out. Employees can check their work schedules, can request time off, and can keep account of their upcoming shifts through a Web site or app. Employers can also use a computer or smart device to create work schedules, to see who is clocked in, and even track labor cost by comparing it to budgeted cost.

On the Net

http://www.timeclockeshop .com/ In this era of heightened attention to security, biometric time recording systems are becoming reasonably priced and more readily accepted.

LO 4
Calculate regular and overtime pay.

Methods of Computing Wages and Salaries

Employees are usually paid for time worked at a time rate, such as hourly, weekly, biweekly, semimonthly, or monthly. The employee may also be paid at a piece rate, incentive rate, commission basis, or a combination of these rates. Even though most payroll systems automatically calculate the payroll amounts, it is important to be able to understand how the amounts are figured.

---

12 "Time Collection for Remote, Mobile Field Employees with Biometric Employee Verification," *PAYTECH*, October 2009, p. 44.

Time Rate

To compute the wages of employees on an hourly basis, multiply the total regular hours worked by the regular hourly rate. If the employee works overtime, multiply the total overtime hours by the overtime rate. By adding the total regular earnings and the total overtime earnings, we obtain the **gross earnings**. (In the examples that follow, if needed, rates have been rounded to two decimal places.)

Example 2-7

Joanne French works a 40-hour week at $12.40 an hour with overtime hours paid at 1½ times the regular rate.

Regular weekly earnings are .... $496.00 (40 × $12.40)
The overtime rate is .... $18.60 ($12.40 × 1.5)
If French works 4 hours overtime, additional earnings for the 4 hours are .... $74.40 (4 × $18.60)
French's weekly gross earnings are... $570.40 ($496.00 + $74.40)
If paid only for time actually worked and she works only 36 hours during a week,
    French earns .... $446.40 (36 × $12.40)

The employee's regular rate of pay includes *all payments* given for working a particular job. This does not include discretionary bonuses, gifts on special occasions, and contributions to certain welfare plans (see page 2-4).

In the case of factory workers, many factories compute the actual time spent on a certain job so that amount can be charged to that job.

Example 2-8

Sonja Patel spent 100 minutes on a certain job. The wages chargeable to that job at the regular hourly rate of $11.58 would be computed as follows:

$$\$11.58 \times \frac{100}{60} = \$19.30$$

Calculating Overtime Pay

In calculating the gross pay of an employee who worked overtime, one of two methods can be used, both of which will result in the same total gross pay.

The most common method is to calculate the gross pay for the 40 hours and then calculate the overtime pay by multiplying the number of hours over 40 by a pay rate of one and one-half times the employee's regular rate of pay.

Example 2-9

John Escobar is paid an hourly rate of $18.50 per hour, and he worked 49 hours this week. His gross pay is:

40 hours × $18.50 = 740.00 regular earnings
9 hours × $27.75 ($18.50 × 1.5) = 249.75 overtime earnings
Total gross pay = $989.75

The other method is the **overtime premium** approach. In this case, the total hours worked (including overtime hours) are multiplied by the regular rate of pay. Then the overtime premium pay is calculated by multiplying the overtime hours by an overtime premium rate of one-half the regular hourly rate.

Example 2-10

John Escobar's (the prior example) pay would be calculated as follows:

49 hours × $18.50 = $906.50
9 hours × $9.25 ($18.50 × 0.5) = 83.25 overtime premium pay
Total gross pay = $989.75

By using the overtime premium approach, an employer could save on the calculation of workers' compensation insurance. Most states do not include the overtime premium in the determination of the workers' compensation insurance costs to employers.

Plans in which overtime is *paid in advance* do not violate the pay requirements of the FLSA. In these plans, in weeks in which an employee works less than the applicable statutory workweek (e.g., 40 hours), the employer will advance the difference in pay to raise it to the standard for the statutory workweek. When overtime is worked, the advances (computed at the time and one-half rate) will offset the overtime pay. A running account must be maintained for each employee, and if the prepayment credits are not sufficient to cover the overtime compensation, the difference must be paid on the following payday.

In cases where an employee works at *different rates for different jobs* during the same workweek, the employers can, at their option, calculate the overtime in one of three ways. (1) One could pay at the higher rate for the overtime hours. (2) One could calculate it by taking the total earnings for both jobs, dividing by the total hours worked, then taking one-half of this rate, and multiplying by the overtime hours. (3) One could use an overtime rate based on the rate for the job performed after the 40th hour (the employee must have agreed to this in advance).

Example 2-11

Yuri Timko worked at two different pay rates during the past week. His main job paid $17.30/hour, while the extra job rate was $20.50. He worked the first 36 hours at Job "A" and 8 hours at Job "B."

Method (1)

Regular earnings	$622.80 (36 × $17.30)
Job B	$164.00 (8 × $20.50)
Overtime rate (higher rate)	$ 10.25 (0.5 × $20.50)
Overtime pay	$ 41.00 (4 × $10.25)
Total pay	$827.80 ($622.80 + $164.00 + $41.00)

Method (2)

Job A	$622.80 (36 × $17.30)
Job B	$164.00 (8 × $20.50)
Overtime rate (1/2)	$ 8.94 ($786.80 ÷ 44 × 0.5)
Extra overtime pay	$ 35.76 (4 × $8.94)
Total pay	$822.56 ($622.80 + $164.00 + $35.76)

Method (3)

Job A	$622.80 (36 × $17.30)
Job B	$164.00 (8 × $20.50)
Overtime pay (Job B)	$ 41.00 (4 × $10.25)
Total pay	$827.80 ($622.80 + $164.00 + $41.00)

Converting Weekly Wage Rates to Hourly Rates

When paying on a weekly basis, sometimes employers must convert the weekly wage rate to an hourly rate, especially to figure overtime earnings. To do this, divide the weekly wage rate by the number of hours in the regular workweek.

Example 2-12

Samar Hazelton earns $412 a week for a workweek consisting of 40 hours. If Hazelton worked 43 hours in a particular week, compute gross pay as follows:

$$\$412.00 \div 40 \text{ hours} = \$10.30 \text{ hourly wage rate}$$
$$\$10.30 \text{ hourly wage rate} \times 1.5 = \$15.45 \text{ overtime wage rate}$$
$$\text{Gross pay} = \$412.00 + (3 \text{ hours} \times \$15.45) = \$458.35$$

Converting Biweekly Wage Rates to Hourly Rates

If paying employees biweekly, divide the biweekly earnings by 2 to arrive at the weekly rate, and divide the weekly rate by the standard number of hours.

> **Example 2-13**
>
> Glenda Rome earns $980 biweekly and works a standard 40-hour workweek. Compute Rome's hourly and overtime rates as follows:
>
> $$980.00 \div 2 = \$490.00 \text{ regular weekly earnings}$$
> $$\$490.00 \div 40 = \$12.25 \text{ regular hourly rate}$$
> $$\$12.25 \times 1.5 = \$18.38 \text{ overtime hourly rate}$$

Converting Monthly Salary Rates to Hourly Rates

If workers paid on a monthly basis earn overtime pay for work beyond a 40-hour week, compute the hourly overtime rate by converting the monthly salary rate to an hourly rate. To do this correctly, you must extend the monthly salary to an annual figure, divide by 52, and then divide by the regular number of hours worked each week.

Tell Me More

> **Example 2-14**
>
> Al Lee earns $5,200 per month and works a standard 40-hour week. During one week, Lee earned 6 hours of overtime.
>
> **Step 1**
> Convert the monthly salary rate to a weekly rate by first annualizing the monthly salary. Then divide the annual salary by 52 weeks.
>
> $5,200 monthly salary × 12 months = $62,400 annual salary
> $62,400 annual salary ÷ 52 weeks = $1,200 weekly salary
>
> **Step 2**
> Divide the weekly rate by the standard number of hours in the workweek.
>
> $1,200 weekly salary ÷ 40 hours = $30.00 hourly rate
>
> **Step 3**
> Compute the overtime rate by multiplying the hourly rate by 1.5.
>
> $30.00 hourly rate × 1.5 = $45.00 overtime rate
>
> **Step 4**
> Compute the *gross pay* for the week by adding the overtime earnings to the regular weekly earnings.
>
> | | |
> |---|---:|
> | Regular weekly earnings | $1,200.00 |
> | Overtime earnings (6 × $45.00) | 270.00 |
> | Gross pay | $1,470.00 |

Converting Semimonthly Salary Rates to Hourly Rates

Semimonthly salary rates are converted the same as monthly rates except semimonthly earnings are multiplied by 24 instead of by 12 to compute the annual earnings.

> **Example 2-15**
>
> Margaret Johnson earns $1,175 semimonthly.
>
> **Step 1**
> Annualize the salary.
>
> $1,175 × 24 = $28,200 annual rate
>
> **Step 2**
> Compute the weekly salary.
>
> $28,200 ÷ 52 = $542.31 weekly rate
>
> **Step 3**
> Compute the hourly rate.
>
> $542.31 ÷ 40 = $13.56 hourly rate
>
> **Step 4**
> Compute the overtime rate.
>
> 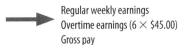 $13.56 × 1.5 = $20.34 overtime rate

Numerous tables of decimal equivalents, such as the one shown in Figure 2.5, on page 2-28, help in converting wages to an hourly rate.

> **Example 2-16**
>
> Weekly salary $550: $550 × 0.025 = $13.75 hourly rate; $550 × 0.0375 = $20.63 hourly overtime rate
> Monthly salary $1,800: $1,800 × 0.00577 = $10.39 hourly rate; $1,800 × 0.00866 = $15.59 hourly overtime rate

FIGURE 2.5
Table of Decimal Equivalents to Convert into Weekly, Hourly, and Hourly Overtime Salary Rates

To convert into:	Weekly Salary Rate	Hourly Salary Rate	Hourly Overtime Salary Rate
Multiply the:			
Weekly salary rate by	...	0.025	0.0375
Semimonthly salary rate by	0.4615	0.01154	0.0173
Monthly salary rate by	0.2308	0.00577	0.00866
Yearly salary rate by	0.01923	0.00048	0.000721

LO 5

Identify distinctive compensation plans.

Salaried Nonexempt Employees

In order to cut administrative costs, salaries can be paid to nonexempt employees; however, these employees are still subject to the FLSA's overtime rules. The employee's *regular rate* of pay is found by dividing the number of *hours expected to be worked* each week into the weekly salary. The employee is then entitled to be paid at the regular rate of pay for the first 40 hours and at one and one-half times the regular rate of pay for the hours over 40.

Example 2-17

Alex Seigle earns a monthly salary of $3,100 for a 35-hour week. For overtime, they receive their regular hourly rate of pay for the hours up to 40 and time and one-half beyond 40 hours in any week. For this semimonthly pay period, Seigle worked 8 hours overtime—only 1 hour was beyond 40 in any week, and they were paid $1,723.74 based on:

$$\$3,100 \times 12 = \$37,200 \text{ annual}$$
$$\$37,200/52 = \$715.38 \text{ weekly}$$
$$\$715.38/35 = \$20.44 \text{ hourly}$$
$$\$20.44 \times 1.5 = \$30.66 \text{ overtime}$$
$$\$1,550.00 \text{ (semimonthly pay)} + (7 \times \$20.44) + (1 \times \$30.66) = \$1,723.74$$

If an employee's normal workweek is less than 40 hours, as long as an agreement exists between the employee and the employer that the salary covers all hours worked up to and including 40 hours, the employer does not have to pay for the "overtime hours" up to the 40 hours.

Example 2-18

Rob Hau, a nonexempt employee, works a standard 35-hour week and is paid a salary of $1,080.00. Last week, Hau worked 39 hours and was paid his normal salary of $1,080.00 since he has an agreement with his employer that the salary covers all hours worked with the exception of the work hours over 40.

If he had worked 43 hours, his pay would have been:

$$\text{Regular (up to 40 hours)} = \$1,080.00$$
$$\text{Overtime pay:}$$
$$\$1,080.00 \div 35 = \$30.86 \text{ per hour}$$
$$\$30.86 \times 1.5 = \$46.29$$
$$\$46.29 \times 3 = \$138.87$$
$$\$1,080.00 + \$138.87 = \$1,218.87 \text{ gross pay}$$

Salaried with Fluctuating Workweek

Employers may pay employees who work fluctuating schedules a fixed salary, regardless of the number of hours worked.

Both parties must agree, prior to the workweek, that this pay calculation method will be used, and the salary must cover at least the minimum wage rate for the total hours worked each workweek. In such cases, overtime pay is found by dividing the normal salary by the total hours worked. An *extra half rate* is then paid for all hours worked over 40. Incentive payments, such as bonuses, premium payments, commissions, and hazard pay, must be included along with the fixed salary in the determination of the regular rate of pay.

Example 2-19

Matt Leonard earns $739.20 a week with fluctuating workweek hours. If he worked 48 hours in one week, his gross pay would be calculated as follows:

$$\$739.20 \div 48 \text{ hours} = \$15.40 \text{ regular rate}$$
$$\$15.40 \times 0.5 = \$7.70 \text{ extra half pay rate}$$
$$8 \text{ hours O.T.} \times \$7.70 = \$61.60 \text{ extra pay}$$
$$\$739.20 + \$61.60 = \$800.80 \text{ weekly gross pay}$$

This calculation also applies to employees who receive a day rate compensation. The total pay for the week would be divided by the hours worked. The extra half rate would then be applied to the hours worked over 40 to determine the overtime pay.

An alternative method of calculating the overtime is to use the fixed salary divided by 40 hours to determine the regular rate of pay. This way, the overtime premium will be the same no matter how many hours are worked. This method eliminates the need to recalculate the regular rate of pay each week as the number of hours worked changes.

Example 2-20

Same as the example above.

$$\$739.20 \div 40 \text{ hours} = \$18.48 \text{ regular rate}$$
$$\$18.48 \times 0.5 = \$9.24 \text{ extra half pay rate}$$
$$8 \text{ hours O.T.} \times \$9.24 = \$73.92 \text{ extra pay}$$
$$\$739.20 + \$73.92 = \$813.12 \text{ weekly gross pay}$$

As a true "fixed salary arrangement," employers cannot make deductions from the salary for absences occasioned by the employee. The exception would apply to disciplinary deductions.

BELO Plan An alternative salary method to compensate employees working fluctuating schedules is the BELO plan. It is more restrictive than the fluctuating workweek method, and the following conditions must be met:

- Irregular work hours are the nature of the job.
- There are large variations in weekly hours above and below 40 hours.
- Rate of pay cannot include additional forms of compensation—bonuses, commissions, etc.
- Guaranteed compensation cannot be for more than 60 hours—beyond 60 hours requires one and one-half times the regular rate.
- Agreement must exist between the employer and the employee.

Basically, the salary is figured by calculating the wages for the maximum number of hours at straight time and then adding 50 percent (one-half) of the regular rate for the overtime hours.

Example 2-21

The agreement between John Kalas and his employer provides for a pay rate of $14 per hour with a maximum of 48 hours per week.

48 hours × $14 = $672.00
8 hours × 0.5 × $14 = 56.00
John's weekly salary = $728.00

No matter how many hours John works each week (above and below 40), his gross pay would be $728.00. However, if John works beyond the agreed-upon maximum of 48 hours, he must be paid at one and one-half times his regular rate of pay (1.5 × $14 = $21) for the hours over 48.

Self-Study Quiz 2-3

Compute the hourly and overtime rates for a standard 40-hour workweek for the following amounts:

	Hourly Rate	Overtime Rate
1. $525.00 weekly	_____	_____
2. $892.00 biweekly	_____	_____
3. $1,450.00 semimonthly	_____	_____
4. $2,600.00 monthly	_____	_____

Piece Rate

Under the **piece-rate system**, the employer pays workers according to their output, such as an amount for each unit or piece produced. Thus, the wages increase as production increases. The employer keeps production records for each employee so that these records will be available when computing the wages earned by each employee. The Fair Labor Standards Act specifies that under a piece-rate system, the regular hourly rate of pay is computed as shown in the following example.

Example 2-22

Sally Choi produced 13,000 items during a 40-hour workweek. Choi is paid 4 cents per unit and receives a bonus of 2 cents for each unit over 12,000 in a week. Choi's weekly earnings are:

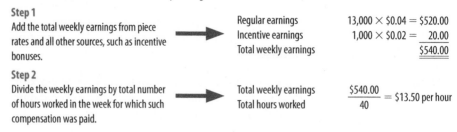

Step 1
Add the total weekly earnings from piece rates and all other sources, such as incentive bonuses.

Regular earnings	13,000 × $0.04 = $520.00
Incentive earnings	1,000 × $0.02 = 20.00
Total weekly earnings	$540.00

Step 2
Divide the weekly earnings by total number of hours worked in the week for which such compensation was paid.

$$\frac{\text{Total weekly earnings}}{\text{Total hours worked}} \qquad \frac{\$540.00}{40} = \$13.50 \text{ per hour}$$

The piece rate must at least equal the statutory minimum wage rate. In some instances, an employer may pay a worker an hourly rate for some hours and a piece rate for other hours during the week. In such cases, both the hourly rate and the piece-rate earnings must be at least the minimum rate.

> In these piece-rate calculations, when rounding is required (for weekly earnings, hourly rate, overtime rate, or total earnings), carry the calculation to three decimal places and then round off to two decimal places.

Bibiphoto/Shutterstock.com

Overtime Earnings for Pieceworkers—Method A

For overtime work, the pieceworker is entitled to be paid, in addition to piece-work earnings for the entire period, a sum equal to one-half the regular hourly rate of pay multiplied by the number of hours worked in excess of 40 in the week.

Example 2-23

Xavi Galmes produced 3,073 pieces in a 44-hour workweek and is paid 18¾ cents for every unit produced.

Step 1
Compute the total regular weekly earnings.

→ 3,073 × $0.1875 = $576.188 (rounded to $576.19) regular weekly earnings

Step 2
Compute the regular hourly rate of pay.

→ $576.19 ÷ 44 hours = $13.10 regular hourly rate of pay

Step 3
Compute the overtime rate of pay and compute the overtime earnings. The regular earnings include the pay for the overtime hours at the regular rate. This is for the extra one-half time.

→ 0.5 × $13.10 = $6.55 overtime rate of pay
4 hours ÷ $6.55 = $26.20 overtime earnings

Step 4
Compute the total regular and overtime earnings for the week.

→ $576.19 + $26.20 = $602.39 piecework and overtime earnings

Overtime Earnings for Pieceworkers—Method B

Another method of computing overtime payment for pieceworkers complies with the requirements of the FLSA. Before doing the work, piece-rate employ-ees may agree with their employer, in advance of the work being done, to be paid at a rate not less than one and one-half times the piece rate for each piece produced during the overtime hours. No additional overtime pay will be due to the employees.

Example 2-24

Assume that in the preceding example, Galmes earned overtime at a piece rate of one and one-half times the regular rate for all pieces produced during overtime hours. Of the total 3,073 pieces produced, 272 were produced in the 4 overtime hours. Galmes' total piecework and overtime earnings are as follows:

2,801 × $0.1875 = $525.19 piecework earnings
272 pieces × $0.2813 ($0.1875 × 1.5) = $76.51 overtime earnings
$525.19 + $76.51 = $601.70 piecework and overtime earnings

Self-Study Quiz 2-4

Bruce Eaton is paid 10 cents per unit under the piece-rate system. During one week, Eaton worked 46 hours and produced 5,520 units. Compute the following:

1. The piecework earnings $ _____
2. The regular hourly rate $ _____
3. The overtime hourly rate $ _____
4. The overtime earnings $ _____
5. The total earnings $ _____

On the Net

http://www.incentivelogic .com There are companies that specialize in setting up different forms of employee incentive plans.

Special Incentive Plans

Most wage systems involving special incentives are modifications of the piece-rate system described previously. Under many incentive plans, the company determines a standard for the quantity that an average worker can produce in a certain period of time. Workers failing to reach the standard earn a lower piece rate, while those who produce more than the standard receive a higher rate. With incentive plans, the computation of the payroll is usually more complicated than under the time-rate or piece-rate systems. Records of time worked as well as the production of each employee must be available in computing wages under most incentive plans.

Chu Wang, Inc., pays its blade polishers according to the following piece-rate incentive plan:

No. of Blades Polished per 8-Hour Workday	Earnings per Blade Polished
less than 1,850	0.0150
1,850 to 1,999	0.0165
2,000 (Daily Standard)	0.0180
2,001 to 2,100	0.0198
2,101 to 2,250	0.0217
over 2,250	0.0240

Commissions

The entire remuneration, or at least part of the remuneration, of certain employees may be on a commission basis. A **commission** is a stated percentage of revenue paid to an employee who transacts a piece of business or performs a service. Thus, a salesperson working in a certain territory may have a fixed salary each year plus a bonus for sales in excess of a certain amount.

Example 2-25

Kate Kline receives an annual $35,000 base salary for working a certain territory. A sales quota of $800,000 has been set for that territory for the current year. Kline will receive a 6 percent commission on all sales in excess of $800,000. For the current year, the sales in the territory are $1,030,000. The bonus paid Kline would be:

$13,800 (6% of $230,000)

Kline's total earnings for the year would be:

$48,800 ($35,000 + $13,800)

There are numerous variations of the commission method of remuneration. Some businesses offer special premiums or bonuses for selling certain merchandise. For example, to help move merchandise in a ready-to-wear department, a department store will frequently pay a premium or a bonus to the salesperson who sells specific items of merchandise. Commissions are considered to be payments for hours worked and must be included in determining the regular hourly rate. This applies regardless of whether the commission is the sole source of the employee's compensation or is paid in addition to a salary or hourly rate. It does not matter whether the commission earnings are computed daily, weekly, monthly, or at some other interval. However, in the case of outside salespeople who are exempt from the FLSA, commissions paid to them do not have to meet the minimum wage criteria.

Commissions are treated as straight-time pay. To calculate overtime, the weekly commission is divided by the *total hours* worked. This is the employee's regular rate of pay. The overtime pay would be one-half the regular rate of pay for all hours worked over 40 in the workweek.

Nondiscretionary Bonuses

A bonus that is part of employees' wage rates must be allocated to the wages for the period covered by the bonus. Bonuses that are known in advance, or that are set up as inducements to achieve goals, would fit into this category. The employer has only to add the bonus to the wages for the week and divide the sum by the total hours worked to determine the regular rate of pay. One-half of the regular rate would be the premium needed to apply to the overtime hours.

Example 2-26

Garrison Heard earns $12.00 per hour and has earned a production bonus this week of $27.60. Since Heard worked 46 hours this week, his gross pay would be:

$$46 \text{ hours} \times \$12.00 = \$552.00 + \$27.60 = \$579.60$$
$$\$579.60 \div 46 \text{ hours} = \$12.60 \text{ regular rate of pay}$$
$$\$12.60 \times 0.5 = \$6.30 \times 6 \text{ hours} = \$37.80$$
$$\$579.60 + \$37.80 = \$617.40 \text{ gross pay}$$

Example 2-27

Els Company instituted a perfect attendance program. The bonus ($2,184) is paid in January for the previous year. John Garcia worked 42 hours each week during the year and earned the bonus. The extra overtime pay due Garcia is:

$$\$2,184 \div 52 = \$42/\text{week}$$
$$\$42 \div 42 \text{ hours} = \$1.00 \text{ bonus for each hour}$$
$$\$1.00 \times 0.5 = \$0.50 \text{ extra overtime rate}$$
$$\$0.50 \times 2 \text{ overtime hours/week} \times 52 \text{ weeks} = \$52 \text{ extra earnings}$$

Profit-Sharing Plans

Many businesses have developed **profit-sharing plans** whereby the employer shares with the employees a portion of the profits of the business. Generally, profit-sharing plans include the following three types:

1. Cash payments based upon the earnings of a specified period.
2. Profits placed in a special fund or account to be drawn upon by employees at some future time. This plan may be in the form of a savings account, a pension fund, or an annuity.
3. Profits distributed to employees in the form of capital stock.

The payments made pursuant to a bona fide profit-sharing plan that meets the standards fixed by the secretary of labor's regulations are not deemed wages in determining the employee's regular rate of pay for overtime purposes.

Key Terms

biweekly (p. 2-4)

commission (p. 2-32)

common-law relationship (p. 2-2)

continental system (p. 2-22)

discretionary bonus (p. 2-4)

domestic service (p. 2-3)

employee (p. 2-2)

enterprise coverage (p. 2-1)

exempt employees (p. 2-10)

gross earnings (p. 2-25)

individual employee coverage (p. 2-2)

nondiscretionary bonus (p. 2-4)

overtime premium (p. 2-25)

piece-rate system (p. 2-30)

principal activities (p. 2-17)

profit-sharing plans (p. 2-33)

salary (p. 2-4)

semimonthly (p. 2-4)

time card (p. 2-22)

time sheet (p. 2-21)

tip (p. 2-6)

tipped employee (p. 2-6)

wage (p. 2-4)

wage theft (p. 2-15)

wages (p. 2-4)

workweek (p. 2-8)

Answers to Self-Study Quizzes

Self-Study Quiz 2-1

1. True.
2. False. Direct care workers employed by a family or individual are not covered if only performing fellowship and protection services.
3. True.
4. False. Individual employee coverage is not affected by the work of fellow employees.
5. True.

Self-Study Quiz 2-2

1. $ 2.13
2. $114.80 $ 290.00 ($7.25 × 40 hours)
   − 85.20 weekly wage
   − 90.00 tip credit claimed by employer
   $ 114.80

Self-Study Quiz 2-3

	Hourly Rate	Overtime Rate
1.	$13.13	$19.70
2.	$11.15	$16.73
3.	$16.73	$25.10
4.	$15.00	$22.50

Self-Study Quiz 2-4

1. $552.00
2. $12.00 ($552.00 ÷ 46)
3. $6.00 ($12.00 × 0.50)
4. $36.00 ($6.00 × 6)
5. $588.00

Key Points Summary

	Learning Objectives	Key Points	Problem Sets A & B
LO1	Explain the major provisions of the Fair Labor Standards Act.	• Minimum wage ($7.25/hour) but tipped employees ($2.13/hour).	2-1, 2-2
		• Overtime pay at time and one-half for hours over 40.	
		• Exemption for white-collar workers.	
		• Equal pay for equal work.	
		• Child-labor laws (basic minimum is 16 years).	
		• Penalties for violations.	

LO2	Define *hours worked*.	• Principal activities are indispensable to performance of productive work.	2-7
		• "Gray areas"—clothes-changing, travel, rest periods, meal periods, training.	
		• Preliminary/postliminary activities not counted unless by contract or custom.	
LO3	Describe the main types of records used to collect payroll data.	• From time sheets to time cards to computerized record systems.	2-9, 2-10
		• Next generation—biometrics.	
LO4	Calculate regular and overtime pay.	• Regular pay (hours worked $\times$ hourly rate of pay), overtime pay (hours over 40 $\times$ time and one-half the hourly rate).	2-3, 2-4, 2-5, 2-6, 2-8, 2-10, 2-11, 2-12, 2-13, 2-14, 2-15
(▶) Tell Me More		• Converting weekly $\dfrac{Salary}{regular\ hours\ worked}$ biweekly $\dfrac{Salary}{2}$ = weekly semimonthly $\dfrac{Salary \times 24}{52}$ = weekly monthly $\dfrac{Salary \times 12}{52}$ = weekly	
LO5	Identify distinctive compensation plans.	• Salaried nonexempt (salary $\div$ hours expected to be worked = regular rate of pay, then one and one-half that rate for hours over 40).	2-16, 2-17, 2-18, 2-19, 2-20, 2-21
		• Fluctuating workweek (salary $\div$ total hours worked with an extra half for hours over 40).	
		• piece-rate $\dfrac{Piece\text{-}rate\ total}{hours\ worked}$ = hourly rate of pay, then one-half rate for hours over 40.	
		• Commissions—treated as straight-time pay.	
		• Nondiscretionary bonuses—add to wages and divide total by hours worked to get regular rate of pay.	

Matching Quiz

_____ 1. Biweekly
_____ 2. Commission
_____ 3. Statutory nonemployee
_____ 4. Common-law relationship
_____ 5. Gross earnings
_____ 6. Individual employee coverage
_____ 7. Overtime premium
_____ 8. Statutory employee
_____ 9. Piece-rate system
_____ 10. Semimonthly

A. Remuneration paid twice a month
B. Full-time life insurance agents
C. Employee engages in interstate commerce or produces goods for such commerce
D. Remuneration paid every two weeks
E. Employer has the right to control both what work will be done and how it will be done
F. Licensed real estate agent
G. Payment to employee based on a stated percentage of revenue
H. Regular earnings plus overtime earnings
I. Pay system based on an amount paid to the employee per units produced
J. One-half the regular hourly rate

Questions for Review

1. Explain the two bases of coverage provided by the FLSA.
2. In determining the existence of an employer/employee relationship, what tests are applied by the U.S. Department of Labor?
3. What kinds of establishments may employ full-time students at 85 percent of the minimum wage?
4. What is Miami's living wage rate for contracts entered into on or after October 1, 2016?
5. To what extent are tips considered wages under the FLSA?
6. Explain how a state employee working in the area of public safety may use compensatory time off in lieu of overtime compensation.

7. Under what conditions would an employee of a state receive cash for compensatory time off?
8. The following employees are exempt from various requirements of the FLSA. Indicate from which requirement or requirements each of the following employees is exempt:
    a. Amusement park employee
    b. Taxicab driver
    c. Casual baby sitter
    d. Elementary school teacher
    e. Outside salesperson
9. What are the types of exempt white-collar employees?
10. What requirements need be met in order to be classified as a "highly compensated" employee?
11. In order not to interfere with the schooling and well-being of minors between the ages of 14 and 16, employers of these minors must satisfy what three conditions?
12. In determining the working time of employees, how are the principal activities of employees defined?
13. Under what conditions is travel time counted as time worked?
14. What is the difference between "engaged to wait" and "waiting to be engaged" as far as working time?
15. In order to get caught up, an employee takes work home. Must the employee be paid for this extra time?
16. When is time spent by employees in attending lectures and meetings for training purposes not counted as working time?
17. Under what conditions would preliminary and postliminary activities be counted as time worked?
18. How does a biometric time system identify an employee?
19. What is the Wage and Hour Division's position on the rounding off of fractional parts of an hour in determining an employee's time worked?
20. If the overtime premium approach is used, how is the overtime premium pay calculated?
21. Explain how to calculate the overtime hourly rate for employees who are paid biweekly.
22. In the case of a salaried nonexempt employee, how is the regular rate of pay determined?
23. How is overtime pay calculated for a nonexempt employee who works on fluctuating schedules and is paid a fixed salary?
24. Are commissions included in determining an employee's regular rate of pay?
25. What is a nondiscretionary bonus?

Questions for Discussion

1. Abreu Company allows employees the option of carrying over unused vacation days or "cashing" them out. If they cash out, does the employer count the time or earnings when calculating overtime for these nonexempt employees?[13]
2. Along with many other companies, Sanchez Printers observes the Friday after Thanksgiving as a paid holiday. The company requires each employee to make up Friday's lost hours in the following workweek by working extra hours without pay. Is Sanchez Printers proceeding legally by requiring its employees to work extra hours without compensation to make up for the hours lost on the Friday holiday? Explain.
3. Lidle Company needs time to calculate employees' overtime payments by the end of the pay period in which the overtime is worked. Can it pay the overtime payments with the following period's paycheck?
4. The Payroll Department of DuMont has a policy of waiting one full week before correcting any paycheck errors of $30 or less. However, any pay shortages that exceed $30 are made up the same day. Also, any amounts less than $30 are made up the same day when the particular circumstances of the employees indicate that it would place an undue hardship on them to wait until the next pay one week later.

    Denise Harris, an order checker in DuMont's Shipping Department, discovered an error of $28.34 in her weekly check. When Harris reported the error, a payroll clerk informed her that she would have to wait until the next week's paycheck to recover the amount, since the underpayment was less than $30.

    What is your reaction to DuMont's policy of providing for paycheck corrections? Assume that Harris protests the delay and in court argues that her earned wages should be paid on the date due. As the judge hearing the case, how would you decide?
5. Mack Banta, a nonexempt account representative, worked extra hours this week as a call operator. A number of operators were out for the week and Banta was asked to pick up some of their hours. Can the company pay Banta at a lower pay rate for the hours he worked as an operator? These extra hours also pushed Banta's work time over 40 hours. How should the company calculate Banta's overtime pay?

Problem Set • A

Special forms required to solve the problems are provided along with the problems in each chapter.

> *Note:* In this chapter and in all succeeding work throughout the course, *unless instructed otherwise,* calculate hourly rates and overtime rates as follows:
> 1. Carry the hourly rate and the overtime rate to 3 decimal places and then round off to 2 decimal places (round the hourly rate to 2 decimal places before multiplying by one and one-half to determine the overtime rate).
> 2. If the third decimal place is 5 or more, round to the next higher cent.
> 3. If the third decimal place is less than 5, simply drop the third decimal place.
>   *Examples:* Monthly rate $1,827
>   Weekly rate ($1,827 × 12)/52 = $421.615 rounded to $421.62
>   Hourly rate $421.62/40 = $10.540 rounded to $10.54
>   O.T. rate $10.54 × 1.5 = $15.81
> Also, use the minimum hourly wage of $7.25 in solving these problems and all that follow.

2-1A • LO 1   See Example 2-1 on page 2-5

Carson Beck works at the local Worst Buy Shop. As a full-time student at the local university, he is being paid an hourly rate of $4.20 an hour. One week, Beck worked 37 hours.

a. Beck's earnings for the week are .... $ _____

b. Is the hourly rate in violation of the FLSA? Explain.

_____

_____

c. If the hourly rate is in violation of the FLSA, the amount the shop should pay Beck is .... $ _____

2-2A • LO 1   See Example 2-2 on page 2-7

Ben Lieber is a waiter at Harbor House, where he receives a weekly wage of $80 plus tips for a 40-hour workweek. Lieber's weekly tips usually range from $280 to $400.

a. Under the Fair Labor Standards Act, the minimum amount of wages that Lieber must receive for a 40-hour workweek is .... $ _____

b. Since Harbor House is in violation of the FLSA, the additional amount it should pay Lieber each week to meet the minimum wage requirement for a tipped employee is .... $ _____

2-3A • LO 4   See Example 2-7 on page 2-25

The hours worked and the hourly wage rates for five employees of Ka Company for the week ended September 9 follow.

a. For each employee, compute the gross earnings.

b. Compute the total gross earnings for all employees.

2-3A (concluded)

Employee	Hours Worked	Regular Hourly Wage Rate	(a) Gross Earnings
Darley, R.	38	$11.70	$
Waxman, B.	40	12.35	
Isaac, J.	37	13.00	
Bruner, H.	40	10.75	
Kellogg, P.	32½	12.40	
		(b) Total gross earnings	$

2-4A • LO 4   See Example 2-9 on page 2-25

The wages and hours information for five employees of McNeese Enterprises for the week ended July 7 is given below. Employees work a standard 40-hour workweek and are paid time and one-half for all hours over 40 in each workweek.

a. For each employee, compute the regular earnings, overtime rate, overtime earnings, and total gross earnings.

b. Compute the total gross earnings for all employees.

Employee	Hours Worked	Regular Hourly Wage Rate	Regular Earnings	Overtime Rate	Overtime Earnings	Total Gross Earnings
Carman, T.	47	$12.45	$	$	$	$
Galasso, A.	42	11.90				
Jones, B.	48	10.85				
Rodna, G.	44	11.25				
Lee, W.	45½	13.40				
					(b) Total gross earnings ...	$

2-5A • LO 4   See Example 2-4 on page 2-9

Gabrielle Pavon, a waitress at the Hole-in-the-Wall restaurant, worked 42 hours this week and collected over $500 in tips. The restaurant uses the full tip credit against the minimum wage and pays Pavon the minimum required for tipped employees. Determine her gross pay from the restaurant.

a. Pay for the 40 hours.. $

b. Pay for the overtime hours... $

2-6A • LO 4   See Example 2-5 on page 2-12

Connie Duffy started working for Dexter Company on Thursday of this week. She worked 9 hours on Thursday and 8 hours on Friday. Her annual salary is $80,000, and she is an exempt white-collar employee. Determine her gross pay for her first partial week of work.

Gross pay .... $

2-7A • LO 2   **See Example 2-9 on page 2-25**

John Porter is an hourly employee of Motter Company located in New York City. This week, Porter had to travel to the company's regional office in Albany. He left Sunday at noon and arrived in Albany at 3:00 P.M. During the week, he worked his normal 40 hours in the Albany office (Monday through Friday—9 A.M. to 5 P.M.). In addition, he attended the company's mandatory 4-hour work training session on Wednesday evening. Porter's hourly rate of pay is $24.80 per hour.

   a. Porter's overtime earnings for the week are .... $ _____
   b. Porter's total earnings for the week are .... $ _____

2-8A • LO 4   **See Example 2-10 on page 2-25**

Joseph Cavato is paid $12.96 per hour. During the past week, he worked 46 hours, and he is a covered employee who must be paid for overtime. Calculate his gross pay using the overtime premium approach.

   a. Regular pay (46 hours) .... $ _____
   b. Overtime premium pay.. _____
   c. Gross pay .... $ _____

2-9A • LO 3   **See Figure 2.3 on page 2-23**

Under the decimal system of computing time worked at Timmerman Company, production workers who are tardy are "docked" according to the schedule shown below.

Minutes Late in Ringing in	Fractional Hour Deducted
1 through 6	1/10
7 through 12	2/10
13 through 18	3/10
19 through 24, etc.	4/10

   The regular hours of work, Monday through Friday, are from 7:30 to 11:30 A.M. and from 12:30 to 4:30 P.M. During one week, Henry Bjorn, who earns $12.15 an hour, reports in and checks out as shown below. Employees are not paid for ringing in a few minutes before 7:30 and 12:30 nor for ringing out a few minutes after 11:30 and 4:30.

(a)

DAY	AM		PM		HRS WORKED
	In	Out	In	Out	
M	7:28	11:31	12:29	4:31	
T	7:35	11:30	12:30	4:30	
W	7:50	11:33	12:27	4:32	
Th	7:27	11:31	12:50	4:33	
F	7:28	11:32	12:40	4:30	

2-9A (concluded)

Refer to the partial time card and compute:

a. The hours worked each day .... _____

b. The total hours worked .... _____

c. The gross earnings for the week .... $ _____

2-10A • LO 3, 4   See Figure 2.3 on page 2-23

Villegas, Inc., recently converted from a 5-day, 40-hour workweek to a 4-day, 40-hour workweek, with overtime continuing to be paid at one and one-half times the regular hourly rate for all hours worked beyond 40 in the week. In this company, time is recorded under the continental system, as shown on the time card below.

Sue Ellen Boggs is part of the Group B employees whose regular workweek is Tuesday through Friday. The working hours each day are 800 to 1200; 1230 to 1630; and 1800 to 2000. The company disregards any time before 800, between 1200 and 1230, and between 1630 and 1800, and permits employees to ring in up to 10 minutes late before any deduction is made for tardiness. Deductions are made to the nearest ¼ of an hour for workers who are more than 10 minutes late in ringing in.

Refer to the time card and compute:

a. The daily total hours .... _____

b. The total hours for the week .... _____

c. The regular weekly earnings .... $ _____

d. The overtime earnings (company rounds O.T. rate to 3 decimal places) .... _____

e. The total weekly earnings .... $ _____

| No. 160 | | | | | Hr. Rate $10.45 | | |
| Name Sue Ellen Boggs | | | | | O.T. Rate $15.675 | | |
Time		Mon	Tues	Wed	Thurs	Fri	Sat
Evening	Out		2002	2001	2005	2000	
	In		1801	1809	1802	1800	
Afternoon	Out		1630	1631	1630	1635	
	In		1230	1231	1230	1238	
Morning	Out		1200	1202	1200	1203	1201
	In		755	750	813	759	800	Total for Week
Daily Totals	(a)						(b)

Remarks *13 minutes late Thursday – deduct ¼ hr.*

2-11A • LO 4 See Example 2-11 on page 2-26

Kyle Forman worked 47 hours during the week for Erickson Company at two different jobs. His pay rate was $14.00 for the first 40 hours, and his pay rate was $11.80 for the other 7 hours. Determine his gross pay for that week if the company uses the one-half average rate method.

a. Gross pay .... $ _____

b. If prior agreement existed that overtime would be paid at the rate for the job
performed after the 40th hour, the gross pay would be .... $ _____

2-12A • LO 4 See Example 2-12 on page 2-26

Barbara Ripa receives $695 for a regular 40-hour week and time and one-half for overtime. For a workweek of 45 hours, compute:

a. The regular earnings .... $ _____

b. The overtime earnings .... _____

c. The total earnings .... $ _____

2-13A • LO 4 See Example 2-14 on page 2-27

Cal DiMangino earns $2,875 each month and works 40 hours each week. Compute:

a. The hourly rate .... $ _____

b. The overtime rate at time and one-half .... $ _____

2-14A • LO 4 See Example 2-17 on page 2-28

Sheila Williams, a medical secretary, earns $3,575 monthly for a 35-hour week. For overtime work, she receives extra pay at the regular hourly rate up to 40 hours and time and one-half beyond 40 hours in any week. During one semimonthly pay period, Williams worked 10 hours overtime. Only 2 hours of this overtime were beyond 40 hours in any one week. Compute:

a. The regular semimonthly earnings .... $ _____

b. The overtime earnings .... _____

c. The total earnings .... $ _____

2-15A • LO 4 See Example 2-18 on page 2-28

Kenneth Feng is a salaried employee who normally works a 37½-hour week and is paid a weekly salary of $675.00. The agreement that he has with his employer states that his salary is to cover all hours worked up to and including 40. This week, Feng worked 42 hours. Calculate his gross pay.

Gross pay .... $ _____

Show Me How

2-16A • LO 5   **See Examples 2-20 and 2-21 on pages 2-29 and 2-30**

Carrie Ortiz works fluctuating work schedules. Besides her fixed salary of $1,050 per week, her employment agreement provides for overtime pay at an extra half-rate for hours worked over 40. This week she worked 48 hours. Compute:

a. The overtime earnings .... $ _____

b. The total earnings .... $ _____

c. If this was a BELO plan with a pay rate of $22.00 per hour and a maximum of 53 hours, how much would Ortiz be paid for 48 hours? .... $ _____

2-17A • LO 5   **See Example 2-23 on page 2-31**

During the first week in November, Erin Mills worked 45½ hours and produced 1,275 units under a piece-rate system. The regular piece rate is $0.45 a unit. Mills is paid overtime according to the FLSA ruling for overtime work under a piece-rate system. Compute:

a. The piecework earnings .... $ _____

b. The regular hourly rate .... $ _____

The overtime hourly rate .... $ _____

c. The overtime earnings .... $ _____

d. The total earnings .... $ _____

2-18A • LO 5   **See Example 2-24 on page 2-31**

Refer to Problem 2-17A. Assume that Mills had agreed with her employer prior to the performance of the work that she would be paid one and one-half times the regular piece rate for all pieces produced during the overtime hours. Assume that her production totals for the week were 1,075 pieces during regular hours and 200 pieces during overtime hours. Compute:

a. The piecework earnings .... $ _____

b. The overtime earnings .... $ _____

c. The total earnings .... $ _____

2-19A • LO 5   **See Example 2-25 on page 2-32** X

Wendy Epstein, a sales representative, earns an annual salary of $29,500 and receives a commission on that portion of her annual sales that exceeds $150,000. The commission is 8.5% on all sales up to $50,000 above the quota. Beyond that amount, she receives a commission of 10%. Her total sales for the past year were $295,000. Compute:

a. The regular annual salary .... $ _____

b. The commission .... _____

c. The total annual earnings .... $ _____

2-20A • LO 5 **See Example 2-25 on page 2-32**

Jill Connor is employed as a salesperson in the men's department of Fashion Line. In addition to her weekly base salary of $440, Connor is paid a commission of 2% on her total net sales for the week (total gross sales less any customer returns). During the past week, to promote the sale of its fine cashmere sweaters, Fashion Line agreed to pay Connor an additional PM (push money) of 2% of the total net sales of cashmere sweaters. Connor's weekly sales tally is given below.

Item	Gross Sales	Customer Returns
Regular sweaters..	$400	$48
Cashmere sweaters	995	75
Ties	190	0
Dress shirts..	445	39
Sports shirts...	185	25

Compute Connor's total weekly earnings, showing her (a) weekly base salary, (b) commission, (c) PM, and (d) total weekly earnings.

a. Weekly base salary .... $ 440.00

Weekly gross sales .... $ _____

Less customer returns .... _____

Weekly net sales .... $ _____

b. Commission: $ _____ × 2% .... _____

Weekly gross sales of cashmere sweaters .... $ _____

Less customer returns .... _____

Weekly net sales of cashmere sweaters .... $ _____

c. PM: $ _____ × 2% .... _____

d. Total weekly earnings .... $ _____

2-21A • LO 5 **See Example 2-27 on page 2-33**

Casey Na's average workweek during the first quarter of the year (13 weeks) was 43 hours. As part of his company's perfect attendance program, he earned a bonus of $975. Determine the extra overtime pay due Na for the first quarter.

Extra overtime pay .... $ _____

Date _____ Name _____

Problem Set • B

Special forms required to solve the problems are provided along with the problems in each chapter.

Note: In this chapter and in all succeeding work throughout the course, *unless instructed otherwise,* calculate hourly rates and overtime rates as follows:
1. Carry the hourly rate and the overtime rate to 3 decimal places and then round off to 2 decimal places (round the hourly rate to 2 decimal places before multiplying by one and one-half to determine the overtime rate).
2. If the third decimal place is 5 or more, round to the next higher cent.
3. If the third decimal place is less than 5, simply drop the third decimal place.
    *Example*s: Monthly rate $1,827
    $\qquad$ Weekly rate ($1,827 × 12)/52 = $421.615 rounded to $421.62
    $\qquad$ Hourly rate $421.62/40 = $10.540 rounded to $10.54
    $\qquad$ O.T. rate $10.54 × 1.5 = $15.81
Also, use the minimum hourly wage of $7.25 in solving these problems and all that follow.

2-1B • LO 1 See Example 2-1 on page 2-5

Genna Cross, a full-time student at Kirby University, is employed by The Boot Shop as a salesperson. Her hourly rate is $5.25. One week, Cross worked 33¼ hours.

a. Cross's earnings for the week are .... $ _____

b. Is the hourly rate in violation of the FLSA? Explain.

_____

_____

c. If the hourly rate is in violation of the FLSA, the amount The Boot Shop should pay
Cross is .... $ _____

2-2B • LO 1 See Example 2-2 on page 2-7

Bert Garro is a waiter at La Bron House, where he receives a weekly wage of $75 plus tips for a 40-hour workweek. Garro's weekly tips usually range from $300 to $350.

a. Under the Fair Labor Standards Act, the minimum amount of wages that Garro must receive for a
40-hour workweek is .... $ _____

b. Since La Bron House is in violation of the FLSA, the additional amount it should pay
Garro each week to meet the minimum wage requirement for a tipped employee is .... $ _____

2-3B • LO 4 See Example 2-7 on page 2-25

The hours worked and the hourly wage rates for five employees of Koogel Company for the week ended June 10 follow.

a. For each employee, compute the gross earnings.

b. Compute the total gross earnings for all employees.

2-3B (concluded)

Employee	Hours Worked	Regular Hourly Wage Rate	(a) Gross Earnings
Campillo, M.	35	$11.90	$ _____
Hazelton, G.	28	14.15	_____
Inman, T.	39½	10.90	_____
Palmer, C.	24½	16.40	_____
Diaz, O.	31	12.90	_____
		(b) Total gross earnings	$ _____

2-4B • LO 4   See Example 2-9 on page 2-25

The wages and hours information for five employees of Somja Enterprises for the week ended April 7 is given below. Employees work a standard 40-hour workweek and are paid time and one-half for all hours over 40 in each workweek.

a. For each employee, compute the regular earnings, overtime rate, overtime earnings, and total gross earnings.

b. Compute the total gross earnings for all employees.

Employee	Hours Worked	Regular Hourly Wage Rate	Regular Earnings	Overtime Rate	Overtime Earnings	Total Gross Earnings
Kawamura, H.	43	$11.90	$ _____	$ _____	$ _____	$ _____
Aha, C.	42	14.20	_____	_____	_____	_____
Shoup, K.	47	13.90	_____	_____	_____	_____
Carlyn, D.	41½	10.70	_____	_____	_____	_____
McMurray, J.	45	17.10	_____	_____	_____	_____
					(b) Total gross earnings ...	$ _____

2-5B • LO 4   See Example 2-4 on page 2-9

Hunter Sobitson, a waiter at the Twentieth Hole restaurant, worked 43½ hours this week and collected over $650 in tips. The restaurant uses the full tip credit against the minimum wage and pays Sobitson the minimum required for tipped employees. Determine his gross pay from the restaurant.

a. Pay for the 40 hours... $ _____

b. Pay for overtime hours .... $ _____

2-6B • LO 4   See Example 2-5 on page 2-12

Cam Fitzer, a white-collar exempt employee, started working for Villan Company on Thursday of this week. He worked 9 hours on both Thursday and Friday. His annual salary is $77,000, and he is paid weekly for a 5-day week. Determine his gross pay for his first partial week of work.

Gross pay .... $ _____

2-7B • LO 2 **See Example 2-9 on page 2-25** Show Me How

Jamie Kerr is an hourly employee of Noonan Company located in Los Angeles. This week, Kerr had to travel to the company's regional office in Santa Fe. He left Sunday at noon and arrived in Santa Fe at 3:30 P.M. During the week, he worked his normal 40 hours in the Santa Fe office (Monday through Friday—9 A.M. to 5 P.M.). In addition, he attended the company's mandatory 3½-hour work training session on Wednesday evening. Kerr's hourly rate of pay is $26.90 per hour.

   a. Kerr's overtime earnings for the week are .... $ _____

   b. Kerr's total earnings for the week are .... $ _____

2-8B • LO 4 **See Example 2-10 on page 2-25**

Peter Jones is paid $13.76 per hour. During the past week, he worked 44 hours, and he is a covered employee who must be paid for overtime. Calculate his gross pay using the overtime premium approach.

   a. Regular pay (44 hours) .... $ _____

   b. Overtime premium pay .... _____

   c. Gross pay .... $ _____

2-9B • LO 3 **See Figure 2.3 on page 2-23**

Under the decimal system of computing time worked at Carman's Company, production workers who are tardy are "docked" according to the schedule shown below.

Minutes Late in Ringing in	Fractional Hour Deducted
1 through 6	1/10
7 through 12	2/10
13 through 18	3/10
19 through 24, etc.	4/10

The regular hours of work, Monday through Friday, are from 7:30 to 11:30 A.M. and from 12:30 to 4:30 P.M. During one week, Bernard Hoskins, who earns $12.95 an hour, reports in and checks out as shown below. Employees are not paid for ringing in a few minutes before 7:30 and 12:30 nor for ringing out a few minutes after 11:30 and 4:30.

(a)

DAY	AM		PM		HRS WORKED
	In	Out	In	Out	
M	7:28	11:31	12:50	4:31	
T	7:35	11:30	12:30	4:30	
W	7:44	11:33	12:27	4:32	
Th	7:27	11:31	12:32	4:33	
F	7:34	11:32	12:40	4:30	

Refer to the partial time card and compute:

   a. The hours worked each day.. _____

   b. The total hours worked.. _____

   c. The gross earnings for the week.. $ _____

2-10B • LO 3, 4   **See Figure 2.3 on page 2-23**

Costa, Inc., recently converted from a 5-day, 40-hour workweek to a 4-day, 40-hour workweek, with overtime continuing to be paid at one and one-half times the regular hourly rate for all hours worked beyond 40 in the week. In this company, time is recorded under the continental system, as shown on the time card below.

Barbara Bansta is part of the Group B employees whose regular workweek is Tuesday through Friday. The working hours each day are 800 to 1200; 1230 to 1630; and 1800 to 2000. The company disregards any time before 800, between 1200 and 1230, and between 1630 and 1800, and permits employees to ring in up to 10 minutes late before any deduction is made for tardiness. Deductions are made to the nearest ¼ of an hour for workers who are more than 10 minutes late in ringing in.

Refer to the time card and compute:

a. The daily total hours .... _____

b. The total hours for the week .... _____

c. The regular weekly earnings .... $ _____

d. The overtime earnings (company rounds O.T. rate to 3 decimal places) .... _____

e. The total weekly earnings .... $ _____

No. 160				Hr. Rate $13.85		
Name Barbara Bansta				O.T. Rate $20.775		

Time		Mon	Tues	Wed	Thurs	Fri	Sat	
Evening	Out		2002	2001	2005	2000		
	In		1801	1809	1802	1800		
Afternoon	Out		1630	1631	1630	1635		
	In		1230	1231	1230	1238		
Morning	Out		1200	1202	1200	1203	1201	
	In		755	750	825	759	800	Total for Week
Daily Totals		(a)						(b)

Remarks *25 minutes late Thursday – deduct ½ hr.*

2-11B • LO 4   **See Example 2-11 on page 2-26**   Show Me How

Kenneth Johanson worked 49 hours during the week for Luben Company at two different jobs. His pay rate was $15.00 for the first 40 hours, and his pay rate was $13.10 for the other 9 hours. Determine his gross pay for that week if the company uses the one-half average rate method.

a. Gross pay .... $ _____

b. If prior agreement existed that overtime would be paid at the rate for the job
performed after the 40th hour, the gross pay would be .... $ _____

2-12B • LO 4　　See Example 2-12 on page 2-26

Pat Kunz receives $725 for a regular 40-hour week and time and one-half for overtime. For a workweek of 44 hours, compute:

　a. The regular earnings .... $ _____

　b. The overtime earnings .... _____

　c. The total earnings .... $ _____

2-13B • LO 4　　See Example 2-14 on page 2-27　Show Me How

Carl La Duca earns $3,875 each month and works 40 hours each week. Compute:

　a. The hourly rate .... $ _____

　b. The overtime rate at time and one-half .... $ _____

2-14B • LO 4　　See Example 2-17 on page 2-28　Show Me How

Stefani Wilson, a medical secretary, earns $3,650 monthly for a 37½-hour week. For overtime work, she receives extra pay at the regular hourly rate up to 40 hours and time and one-half beyond 40 hours in any week. During one semimonthly pay period, Wilson worked 6 hours overtime. Only 2 hours of this overtime were beyond 40 hours in any one week. Compute:

　a. The regular semimonthly earnings .... $ _____

　b. The overtime earnings .... _____

　c. The total earnings .... $ _____

2-15B • LO 4　　See Example 2-18 page 2-28

Jody Baush is a salaried employee who normally works a 35-hour week and is paid a weekly salary of $735.00. The agreement that he has with his employer states that his salary is to cover all hours worked up to and including 40. This week, Baush worked 42 hours. Calculate his gross pay.

　　　Gross pay .... $ _____

2-16B • LO 5　　See Examples 2-20 and 2-21 on pages 2-29 and 2-30　Show Me How

Colleen Prescott is a salaried employee who works fluctuating work schedules. She is paid a fixed salary of $920 each week, with an agreement with her employer that overtime (over 40 hours) will be paid at an extra half-rate, based on the actual hours worked. This week she worked 42 hours. Compute:

　a. The overtime earnings .... $ _____

　b. The total earnings .... $ _____

　c. If this was a BELO plan with a pay rate of $21 per hour and a maximum of 45 hours, how much would Prescott be paid for 42 hours? .... $ _____

2-17B • LO 5 See Example 2-23 on page 2-31

During the first week in April, Courtney Nelson worked 46 hours and produced 1,450 units under a piece-rate system. The regular piece rate is $0.38 a unit. Nelson is paid overtime according to the FLSA ruling for overtime work under a piece-rate system. Compute:

a. The piecework earnings .... $ _____

b. The regular hourly rate .... $ _____

    The overtime hourly rate .... $ _____

c. The overtime earnings .... _____

d. The total earnings .... $ _____

2-18B • LO 5 See Example 2-24 on page 2-31

Refer to Problem 2-17B. Assume that Nelson had agreed with her employer prior to the performance of the work that she would be paid one and one-half times the regular piece rate for all pieces produced during the overtime hours. Assume that her production totals for the week were 1,120 pieces during regular hours and 330 pieces during overtime hours. Compute:

a. The piecework earnings .... $ _____

b. The overtime earnings .... _____

c. The total earnings .... $ _____

2-19B • LO 5 See Example 2-25 on page 2-32

Warrenda Spuhn, a sales representative, earns an annual salary of $34,500 and receives a commission on that portion of her annual sales that exceeds $150,000. The commission is 9.5% on all sales up to $50,000 above the quota. Beyond that amount, she receives a commission of 12%. Her total sales for the past year were $315,000. Compute:

a. The regular annual salary .... $ _____

b. The commission .... _____

c. The total annual earnings .... $ _____

2-20B • LO 5 See Example 2-25 on page 2-32

Maria Cohen is employed as a salesperson in the men's department of Lee's Fashions. In addition to her weekly base salary of $400 (35-hour week), Cohen is paid a commission of 1% on her total net sales for the week (total gross sales less any customer returns). During the past week, to promote the sale of its fine cashmere sweaters, Lee's agreed to pay Cohen an additional PM (push money) of 3% of the total net sales of cashmere sweaters. Cohen's weekly sales tally is given below.

Item	Gross Sales	Customer Returns
Regular sweaters	$600	$58
Cashmere sweaters	895	75
Ties	190	0
Dress shirts	445	39
Sports shirts	585	45

Compute Cohen's total weekly earnings, showing her (a) weekly base salary, (b) commission, (c) PM, and (d) total weekly earnings.

2-20B (concluded)

a. Weekly base salary.. $ 400.00

    Weekly gross sales... $ _____

       Less customer returns .... _____

    Weekly net sales .... $ _____

b. Commission: $ _____ × 1% .... _____

    Weekly gross sales of cashmere sweaters .... $ _____

       Less customer returns .... _____

    Weekly net sales of cashmere sweaters.............................. $ _____

c. PM: $ _____ × 3% .... _____

d. Total weekly earnings .... $ _____

2-21B • LO 5   See Example 2-27 on page 2-33

Connie Gibbs collected a $2,000 bonus for her department's safety record for the year (52 weeks). During that year, Gibbs worked an average of 44 hours each week. Calculate the extra overtime pay due Gibbs for that year.

    Extra overtime pay.. $ _____

Continuing Payroll Problem • A
Show Me How

In the Continuing Payroll Problem A, presented at the end of succeeding chapters, you will gain experience in computing wages and salaries and preparing a payroll register for Kipley Company, Inc., a newly formed corporation. At the end of subsequent chapters, information will be presented so that the payroll register can be completed step by step as you proceed through the discussion material relating to that particular section of the payroll register.

Kipley Company is a small manufacturing firm located in Pittsburgh, Pennsylvania. The company has a workforce of both hourly and salaried employees.

Each employee is paid for hours actually worked during each week, with the time worked being recorded in quarter-hour increments. The standard workweek consists of 40 hours, with all employees being paid time and one-half for any hours worked beyond the 40 regular hours.

Wages are paid every Friday, with one week's pay being held back by the company. Thus, the first payday for Kipley Company is January 14 for the workweek ending January 8 (Saturday).

The information below will be used in preparing the payroll for the pay period ending January 8, 20--.

Time Card No.	Employee Name	Hourly Wage or Salary	
11	Fran M. Carson	$ 17.50	per hour
12	William A. Wilson	17.25	per hour
13	Harry T. Utley	18.10	per hour
21	Lawrence R. Fife	17.90	per hour
22	Lucy K. Smith	19.75	per hour
31	Gretchen R. Fay	515	per week
32	Glenda B. Robey	2,700	per month
33	Thomas K. Schork	3,350	per month
51	Barbara T. Hardy	2,510	per month
99	Carson C. Kipley	52,000	per year

Glenda B. Robey prepares the time clerk's report for each pay period. The report for the first week of operations is given below.

TIME CLERK'S REPORT NO. 1											
For Period Ending January 8, 20--											

	Employee	**Time Record**						**Time Worked***	**Time Lost**
		M	**T**	**W**	**T**	**F**	**S**		
11	Fran M. Carson	8	8	8	8	8	—	40	
12	William A. Wilson	8	8	8	8	8	8	48	
13	Harry T. Utley	8	5½	8	8	8	—	37½	2½ hrs. tardy
21	Lawrence R. Fife	10	10	8	8	10	—	46	
22	Lucy K. Smith	8	8	8	8	8	—	40	
31	Gretchen R. Fay	9	8	8	8	8	1¼	41¼	
32	Glenda B. Robey	8	8	8	8	8	—	40	
33	Thomas K. Schork	8	8	8	8	8	—	40	
51	Barbara T. Hardy	8	8	8	8	8	4	44	
99	Carson C. Kipley	8	8	8	8	8	—	40	

* All employees, except for Carson Kipley, are paid for hours worked beyond 40 at one and one-half times their regular hourly rate of pay.

Using the payroll register for Kipley Company, which is reproduced on a fold-out at the back of the book (PR-1), proceed as follows:
1. Enter each employee's time card number and name in the appropriate columns.
2. Record the regular hours and the overtime hours worked for each employee, using the time clerk's report as your reference.
3. Complete the Regular Earnings columns (Rate per Hour and Amount) and the Overtime Earnings columns (Rate per Hour and Amount) for each hourly employee. For salaried workers, complete the Regular Earnings column and show the hourly overtime rate and earnings only if overtime was worked.
4. Record the Total Earnings for each employee by adding the Regular Earnings and the Overtime Earnings.

Note: Retain your partially completed payroll register for use at the end of Chapter 3.

Continuing Payroll Problem • B

Show Me How

In the Continuing Payroll Problem B, presented at the end of succeeding chapters, you will gain experience in computing wages and salaries and preparing a payroll register for Olney Company, Inc., a newly formed corporation. At the end of subsequent chapters, information will be presented so that the payroll register can be completed step by step as you proceed through the discussion material relating to that particular section of the payroll register.

Olney Company is a small manufacturing firm located in Newtown, Pennsylvania. The company has a workforce of both hourly and salaried employees. Each employee is paid for hours actually worked during each week, with the time worked being recorded in quarter-hour increments. The standard workweek consists of 40 hours, with all employees being paid time and one-half for any hours worked beyond the 40 regular hours.

Wages are paid every Friday, with one week's pay being held back by the company. Thus, the first payday for Olney Company is January 14 for the workweek ending January 8 (Saturday).

The information on the next page will be used in preparing the payroll for the pay period ending January 8, 20--.

Time Card No.	Employee Name	Hourly Wage or Salary
11	Rob A. Mangino	$ 18.50 per hour
12	Inga C. Flores	19.25 per hour
13	Carson S. Palmetto	17.80 per hour
21	Randy F. Waters	20.70 per hour
22	Cathy T. Kroll	23.80 per hour
31	Carmen V. Ruppert	800 per week
32	William M. Scott	780 per week
33	Sarah A. Wickman	3,500 per month
51	Lucas T. Foley	4,500 per month
99	Marshal W. Olney	78,000 per year

Carmen V. Ruppert prepares the time clerk's report for each pay period. The report for the first week of operations is given below.

Using the payroll register for Olney Company, which is reproduced on a fold-out at the back of the book (PR-1), proceed as follows:

1. Enter each employee's time card number and name in the appropriate columns.
2. Record the regular hours and the overtime hours worked for each employee, using the time clerk's report as your reference.

3. Complete the Regular Earnings columns (Rate per Hour and Amount) and the Overtime Earnings columns (Rate per Hour and Amount) for each hourly employee. For salaried workers, complete the Regular Earnings column and show the hourly overtime rate and earnings only if overtime was worked.
4. Record the Total Earnings for each employee by adding the Regular Earnings and the Overtime Earnings.

Note: Retain your partially completed payroll register for use at the end of Chapter 3.

TIME CLERK'S REPORT NO. 1 For Period Ending January 8, 20--									
	Employee	Time Record						Time Worked*	Time Lost
		M	T	W	T	F	S		
11	ROB A. MANGINO	8	8	8	8	8	—	40	
12	INGA C. FLORES	8	8	8	8	10	8	50	
13	CARSON S. PALMETTO	8	5½	8	8	9	—	38½	1½ hrs. tardy
21	RANDY F. WATERS	10	10	8	8	11	—	47	
22	CATHY T. KROLL	8	8	8	8	8	—	40	
31	CARMEN V. RUPPERT	8	8	8	8	8	1¼	41¼	
32	WILLIAM M. SCOTT	8	8	8	8	8	—	40	
33	SARAH A. WICKMAN	8	8	8	8	8	—	40	
51	LUCAS T. FOLEY	8	8	8	8	9	4	45	
99	MARSHAL W. OLNEY	8	8	8	8	8	—	40	

*All employees, except for Marshal Olney, are paid for hours worked beyond 40 at one and one-half times their regular hourly rate of pay.

Case Problems

C1. Reducing the Cost of Compensated Leave Time. LO 1.

For the past several weeks, Adele Delgado, payroll manager for Petrillo Packing Company, has been studying the mounting costs of accrued vacations and sick leave. Most of her firm's employees are entitled to two weeks' vacation each year and the privilege of accruing their vacation time for future use. Also, the workers have a generous sick-leave plan that reimburses them while they are ill at home or in the hospital.

Scanning the employees' accrued vacation times on the computer printout, Delgado notes the line entry for John Mannick. Mannick recently retired and cashed in 14 weeks of accrued vacation—all paid at his current wage, which was much more than when he originally earned the vacations. And, of course, the firm's payroll taxes for the accrued vacation payout were significantly increased.

Delgado also knows that some workers feel short-changed if they do not use their sick leave each year.

They realize that if the leave is not used, they lose it for that year. Probably, she thinks, this accounts for those who regularly become ill on Mondays or Fridays.

What solutions can you offer to limit the cost of and more effectively manage the firm's policies for compensated leave time?

C2. Payment of Personal Time Off at Year-End. LO 5.

Huche Company allows its employees to carry over unused personal time off (PTO) days (vacation, sick days, etc.) from year to year. In addition, employees have the option to "cash out" their unused days at the end of the year.

John Keevens was just paid $685 for his unused PTO days. Since he is a nonexempt employee, John has questioned the amount of his last paycheck (which includes the $685). The PTO days push the paid hours over 40, and he wants to be paid for his overtime hours.

What would you tell John?

Chapter 3

Social Security Taxes

So your grandparents are getting social security checks and are now covered by Medicare. Who is paying for these benefits? Part of it comes from your own paycheck. You pay it now and will collect your benefits later.

Your employer is the middleman—collects taxes from you, pays the employer's portion of the tax, remits the taxes to the federal government, and files quarterly tax returns.

Let's look at the who's, what's, when's, and where's of FICA taxes.

Learning Objectives

After studying this chapter, you should be able to:

1. Identify, for social security purposes, those persons covered under the law and those services that make up employment.
2. Identify the types of compensation that are defined as wages.
3. Apply the current tax rates and wage base for FICA and SECA purposes.
4. Describe the different requirements and procedures for depositing FICA taxes and income taxes withheld from employees' wages.
5. Complete Form 941, Employer's QUARTERLY Federal Tax Return.

This chapter covers the government's old-age, survivors, and disability insurance benefits program (OASDI) and the retirees' health insurance program (HI). These programs are funded by social security and Medicare taxes imposed on employees and their employers. The taxes are calculated at a standard flat rate for every employee and employer. The statutes that provide the taxes include:

Photographee.eu/Shutterstock.com

1. **Federal Insurance Contributions Act (FICA)**, which imposes two taxes on employees and two taxes on employers. One of the taxes finances the federal old-age, survivors, and disability insurance program (OASDI). The other finances the hospital insurance (HI), or Medicare, program.
2. **Self-Employment Contributions Act (SECA)**, which levies a tax upon the net earnings of the self-employed.

Coverage Under FICA

The retirement and disability parts of the social security program cover most workers in the United States. However, before an individual is considered to be "covered" for social security purposes, the following must be determined:

1. If the individual is an "employee," as defined by the common-law relationship of employer and employee.
2. If the service the individual renders is "employment," as defined by FICA tax law.
3. If the compensation the individual receives is "taxable wages," as defined by FICA tax law.

LO 1

Identify, for social security purposes, those persons covered under the law and those services that make up employment.

By identifying a "covered" employee and "covered" employment, it can then be determined who pays the tax and who will be entitled to benefits. An employee who is receiving social security benefits must pay the tax on their current earned wages. Part-time employees and seasonal employees are taxed in the same way as full-time employees.

Employer

Every **person** is an **employer** if the person employs one or more individuals for the performances of services in the United States, unless such services or employment are specifically exempted by the law. The term "person," as defined in the law, means an individual, a trust or estate, a partnership, or a corporation.

The term **employment** applies to any service performed by employees for their employer, regardless of the citizenship or residence of either. FICA covers most types of employment, but there are specific exclusions. Some types of employment are wholly exempt from coverage, and others are exempt only if the cash wages received are less than a stipulated dollar amount, as shown in Figure 3.1.

If an employee's services performed during one-half or more of any period constitute covered employment, then all the employee's services for that pay period must be counted as covered employment, and vice versa. In these cases, a pay period cannot exceed 31 consecutive days.

Employee

As explained in Chapter 2, the test used by the IRS to determine a worker's classification is the common-law test. Basically, if a business tells, or has a right to tell, a worker how, when, and where to work, then the worker is an employee.

Occupations Specifically Covered by FICA

In addition to the common-law test, FICA law also provides specific coverage for the following list of four occupations. Even though these workers are independent contractors under common law, they are treated by statute as employees.

FIGURE 3.1
Exempt Employment

Employment Type	Conditions of Exclusion
Agricultural services	Compensation of all farm workers is less than $2,500 in any calendar year, or compensation is less than $150 for each worker in a calendar year. Remuneration other than cash is not taxed.
Domestic service	Service performed in a local college club or a chapter of a college fraternity or sorority by a student who is *enrolled* and *regularly attending classes* at the school, college, or university.
Services performed by civilians for the U.S. government	Of any of its agencies if such agencies are specifically exempt from the employer portion of the FICA tax, or if such services are covered by a retirement system established by law.
Services performed by railroad workers	For employers covered by the Railroad Retirement Tax Act.
Services performed in the employment of foreign governments	Ambassadors, ministers, and other diplomatic officers and employees.
Services performed by an individual under the age of 18, as a newspaper distributor	Delivery or distribution of newspapers or shopping news, excluding delivery or distribution to a point for subsequent delivery or distribution.
Services performed by student nurses	In the employ of a hospital or a nurses' training school chartered or approved under state law, and the nurses are *enrolled* and *regularly attending classes* in that school. FICA exempts only the pay received by student nurses if the pay is nominal and their work is part time and an integral part of the curriculum.
Services performed by students for their public or private school, college, or university	Working as "noncareer" employees while enrolled academically at least half time (for undergraduates, at least six credit hours). This student FICA exception does not apply to an employee who regularly works 40 or more hours a week.

However, such persons are not covered by FICA if they have a substantial interest in the facilities used in connection with their jobs or if the services consist of a single transaction. The list includes:

1. *Agent-drivers* and *commission-drivers* who distribute food and beverage products or handle laundry or dry cleaning.
2. Full-time *life insurance salespersons* who sell primarily for one company.
3. Full-time *traveling or city salespersons* for one firm or person.
4. An individual who works *at home* on materials or goods that you supply and that must be returned to you or to a person you name if you also furnish specifications for the work to be done.

Government Employees

Different rules apply.

- Federal   Hired after 1983—full coverage.
                       Hired prior to 1984—only Medicare (HI) applies.
- State and local   Work done after July 1, 1991, and not in public retirement plan—full coverage.
                       Hired after March 31, 1986, and covered by a public retirement plan—Medicare (HI) only.
- Military   Basic pay—full FICA taxes.

                       Excess of basic pay—not subject to FICA tax.
                       Temporary service with National Guard—difference in pay covered by civilian employer—subject to FICA tax.

International Agreements

Totalization agreements with over 20 foreign countries have eliminated dual taxation and dual coverage. Inpatriates (employees transferred from a foreign country to company's home country) who are working in the United States from one of these countries will not have social security taxes withheld on U.S.-sourced income. If the worker is from a country that has no such agreement, social security tax must be withheld.

Expatriates (employees transferred from company's home country to foreign country) will be subject to U.S. social security tax and could also be subject to foreign social security taxes.

Family Employment

Work performed for a parent by a child under the age of 18 is exempt from FICA. If the work is not in the course of the parent's business and the child is under 21, the exemption also applies. However, if the child's services are done for a corporation, a partnership (unless each partner is a parent of the child), or an estate, the exemption does not apply.

Household Employee

If a worker performs household services in or around your home subject to your will and control, as to both what must be done and how it will be done, that worker is your household employee. It does not matter whether you exercise this control as long as you have the legal right to control the method and result of the work.

However, in order for the household employee and the employer to be liable for the FICA taxes, the household employee must receive **$2,400 or more in cash wages** from any one employer in the year.[1] Household employees do not include people (a) who work for you in your business; (b) who follow an independent trade, business, or profession in which they offer services to the general public; and (c) who are under the age of 18 unless their principal occupation is household employment.

---

1 For election workers, it is $2,000 or more.

IRS Connection

Foreign agricultural workers lawfully admitted to the United States on a temporary basis are exempt from social security taxes.

On the Job

Some examples of workers who may be household employees include:

- Baby sitters
- Caretakers
- Cooks
- Drivers
- Gardeners
- Nannies
- Housekeepers
- Maids

Exempt Employees

Employees of not-for-profit organizations are subject to FICA taxes. Some services, such as those performed by duly ordained ministers of churches, remain exempt from FICA taxes, but the individuals are then subject to self-employment tax on their net earnings. Ministers, certain members of religious orders, and Christian Science practitioners previously electing exemption from social security coverage may now be covered by filing a waiver form with the IRS. Once an election to be covered by social security is made, it is irrevocable.

The following are also exempt from both the OASDI and HI portions of the tax:

- Medical interns.
- Student nurses.
- Inmates of U.S. penal institutions.
- Those serving temporarily in case of emergency (storm, flood, etc.).

Voluntary Coverage

Coverage under FICA can be extended to certain classes of services that otherwise would be excluded. For example, service in the employ of a state or local government that began prior to April 1, 1986, is still exempt for the OASDI portion of the FICA tax. However, coverage can be extended to these employees by means of a voluntary agreement entered into by the state and secretary of health and human services. When a state elects voluntary coverage, it becomes responsible for the collection and payment of the FICA tax as if it were covered employment.

Self-Study Quiz 3-1

Which of the following are covered by FICA (indicate Yes or No)?

_____ 1. Andrian Mitchell, a full-time life insurance salesperson.
_____ 2. John Sain, a federal government employee, hired in 1990.
_____ 3. Bonnie Stone, a real estate agent.
_____ 4. Stuart Schuck, who offers lawn care service to homeowners in the neighborhood.

Note: Answers to Self-Study Quizzes are on page 3-34.

Independent Contractor

The FICA tax law identifies **independent contractors** as persons who follow an independent trade, business, or profession where they offer their services to the public. A recent study by the U.S. Bureau of Labor Statistics shows over 10 million workers are independent contractors. The test in Figure 3.2 determines independent contractor status.

Employers do not pay or withhold payroll taxes on payments made to independent contractors. However, the individual contractors are liable for social security taxes (self-employment taxes) on the net earnings of their businesses.

Misclassifying employees carries a penalty for the employer. Generally, the penalty will be the employer's share of FICA taxes plus the income and FICA taxes that were not withheld from the employee's earnings. If the employee did report the earnings on the federal tax return, the penalty is voided. If not reported, the employer may qualify for a reduced rate of 1.5 percent of the employee's wage if a Form 1099 (see Figure 4.14 on page 4-31) was filed (3.0 percent if not filed). A reduced rate might also apply to the employee's share of FICA taxes—20 percent of the full FICA tax if Form 1099 was filed (40 percent if not filed).

FIGURE 3.2
Test for Independent Contractor Status

Workers *may* be classified as independent contractors if they:
1. Hire, supervise, and pay assistants.
2. Determine the sequence of their work.
3. Set their own hours of work.
4. Work for as many employers as they wish.
5. Are paid by the job.
6. Make their services available to the public.
7. Have an opportunity for profit or loss.
8. Furnish their own tools.
9. Have a substantial investment in their trade.
10. May be dismissed only under terms of contract.

Over the Line

In a recent lawsuit settlement, FedEx Ground Package System Inc. will distribute $2 million to an estimated 500 drivers who delivered packages for FedEx Ground and FedEx Home Delivery. The New York State Attorney General's Office filed the lawsuit alleging that drivers had been unlawfully misclassified as independent contractors, but were actually employees. This action sought restitution for violations of New York labor law, including unpaid overtime and unlawful deductions from wages.[2]

Taxable Wages

The amount of wages paid by employers to their employees during the calendar year determines the amount of OASDI/HI taxes. The basis of payment may be hourly, daily, weekly, biweekly, semimonthly, monthly, annually, piece rate, or a percentage of profits. Wages include the following:

LO 2

Identify the types of compensation that are defined as wages.

1. Actual money received by employees, whether called wages or salaries.
2. Cash value of meals and lodging provided for the convenience of the *employees*.
3. Bonuses and commissions paid by the employer with respect to employment.

Other common types of payments that are considered wages under FICA are listed in Figure 3.3 (on page 3-6).

Tips

FICA considers cash tips of $20 or more in a calendar month to be taxable wages. Employees must report their tips in writing to their employers by the 10th of the month following the month in which the tips were received. Employers can require more frequent reporting. Rules for reporting tips by employees and employers are summarized as follows:

1. Employees can report tips on **Form 4070, Employee's Report of Tips to Employer**, shown in Figure 3.4 (on page 3-7).
2. Employees failing to report tips to their employers may be penalized 50 percent of the FICA tax due on the tips. The tax court may rule that the nonreporting of tip income constitutes fraud.

---

2 https://www.pressrepublican.com/news/local_news/lawsuit-against-fedex-settled/article_56f164d1-e6dc-5e50-af17-4c0ff859b386.html

FIGURE 3.3
Other Types of Taxable Wages

Type of Wage	Conditions
Advance payments	For future work to be done by the individual receiving the advance where the employer considers the work satisfaction for the advance.
Back-pay awards	Pay received in one period for employment in an earlier period, unless it is a settlement for failure to employ workers.
Bonuses	For services rendered by employees for an employer.
Cash and noncash prizes and awards	For outstanding work, exceeding sales quotas, contributing suggestions that increase productivity or efficiency.
Christmas gifts	Except noncash gifts of nominal value (such as a turkey or a ham).
Commissions	On sales or insurance premiums paid as compensation for services performed.
Death benefits	Wage payments (not gratuity) to an employee's beneficiaries or estate after the employee's death. Payments made after the calendar year in which the employee died and employer-provided death-benefit plans are not taxed.
Employees' federal income and social security taxes paid for by the employer	Payment of the employee portion of the FICA tax by the employer for domestics working in the employer's home and for agricultural laborers is an exception to this rule.
Fringe benefits—noncash	Personal use of company car, employer-provided vehicles for commuting, flights on employer-provided airplanes, and free or discounted flights on commercial airlines.
Guaranteed annual wage payments	Union contract agreements whereby an employer guarantees certain employees will either work during or be paid for each normal workweek in a calendar year.
Idle time or standby payments	Amounts paid workers who are at the beck and call of an employer but who are performing no work.
Insurance premiums paid by the employer for an employee's group-term life insurance coverage	Exceeding $50,000 of coverage. For retired workers, their group-term life insurance that exceeds $50,000 is also subject to FICA.
Jury duty pay	The difference between the employee's regular wages and the amount received for jury duty, paid by employers.
Moving expense reimbursements	Except active members of the U.S. Armed Forces.
Retroactive wage increases	Treated as wages in the period paid.
Severance pay	Severance payments are taxable wages for FICA.
Sick pay—first six months	For sickness or accident disability. Payments under a state temporary disability law are also subject to FICA taxes.
Stock payments	The fair market value of stock transferred by employers to employees as remuneration for services.
Vacation pay	Whether the leave is taken or not.

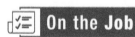

On the Job

Many restaurants now use software to help in tracking tips. Some programs add a "prompt" that freezes the computer screen as employees try to clock out if they have not entered their tips for the day.

3. Employers must collect the employee's FICA tax on the tips that each employee reports. The employer deducts the employee's FICA tax from the wages due the employee or from other funds the employee makes available. The employer should deduct the FICA taxes (on the reported tips plus the wage payment) from the first pay after the reporting of the previous month's tips.

4. Employers are also liable for their share of the FICA tax on any tips subject to the employee's FICA tax. Employers are allowed a business tax credit (Form 8846) on their income tax return for FICA taxes paid on their employees' tip income.

5. Large food and beverage establishments (11 or more employees where tipping is customary) are required to allocate to their tipped employees the excess of 8 percent of the establishment's gross receipts over the tips actually reported by their employees. However, employers withhold FICA taxes only on the tips reported by employees, not from tips that are allocated. The amount of allocated tip income is shown separately on the employee's *Wage and Tax Statement (Form W-2)*, as explained in Chapter 4.

6. Every large food or beverage establishment must report the amount of its receipts from food and beverage operations annually to the IRS and the amount of tips reported by its employees [*Form 8027, Employer's Annual Information Return of Tip Income and Allocated Tips* (not illustrated)].

FIGURE 3.4

Form 4070, Employee's Report of Tips to Employer

Form **4070** (Rev. August 2005) Department of the Treasury Internal Revenue Service	**Employee's Report of Tips to Employer**	OMB No. 1545-0074
Employee's name and address Carmen T. Perez 1704 Elm St., San Diego, CA 92121-8837	Social security number 000 ⋮ 00 ⋮ 7220	
Employer's name and address (include establishment name, if different) Holland House Inn 9 Fairway, San Diego, CA 92123-1369	**1** Cash tips received $389.10	
	2 Credit and debit card tips received —	
	3 Tips paid out —	
Month or shorter period in which tips were received from July 1 , 20-- , to July 31 , 20--	**4** Net tips (lines **1** + **2** - **3**) $389.10	
Signature *Carmen T. Perez*	Date August 10, 20--	
For Paperwork Reduction Act Notice, see the instructions on the back of this form.	Cat. No. 41320P	Form **4070** (Rev. 8-2005)

Source: Internal Revenue Service.

7. Employers can claim a credit for social security and Medicare taxes paid on certain employees' tips on **Form 8846, Credit for Employer Social Security and Medicare Taxes Paid on Certain Employee Tips**. The tips on which the credit is claimed is the amount of tips in excess of those treated as wages for purposes of satisfying the minimum wage.

An alternative tip reporting method (**The Attributed Tip Income Program—ATIP**) can be used. Under ATIP, a formula based on the employer's credit card sales determines the amount of tips that must be reported to the IRS. The employer then assigns the required amount of tips among all tipped employees. To be eligible to use ATIP, the employer must have at least 20 percent of its gross receipts from charged receipts that show charged tips and at least 75 percent of its tipped employees must sign a participation agreement.

Exempt Payments

FICA tax only applies to types of compensation considered taxable under the law. Examples of compensation that the law excludes from the tax follow.

Meals and Lodging FICA exempts the value of meals or lodging furnished to employees for the *convenience of the employer*. The value of meals or lodging not meeting this test will be subject to FICA tax. The IRS places no specific value on meals or lodging furnished by employers to employees. Instead, the IRS relies on state valuations. Where a state has no law or regulation on the subject, fair value is defined as the reasonable prevailing value of the meals or lodging.

Sick Pay The *first six months of sick pay* an employee receives is considered wages and is subject to FICA tax. Payments made *after* the expiration of the six consecutive calendar months following the last month in which the employee worked for the employer are not taxed. The period off the job must be continuous for six months. Any return to work starts a new six-month period. FICA defines sick pay as any payment made to individuals due to personal injury or sickness that does not constitute wages. **Sick pay** payments must be part of a plan to which the employer is a party. Sick pay must not include amounts paid to individuals who are permanently disabled.

Sick pay payments may also be made by a third party, including insurance companies, trusts providing sick and accident benefits, and employers' associations funded to pay sickness and accident benefits. The third party is treated as a separate employer and must withhold and deposit the employees' FICA taxes. However, the third party may be relieved of the liability for the employer's share of the FICA taxes if the third party fulfills each of these requirements:

1. Withholds and deposits the employee portion of the FICA tax.
2. Notifies the employer of the amount of wages or compensation involved.

The liability for that share of the taxes then reverts back to the employer. For convenience, an employer may contract to have the third-party deposit the employer portion of the tax as well as the employee portion.

Generally, payments made to employees or their dependents for medical or hospital expenses in connection with sickness or accident disability are not considered wages. However, these payments must be part of a plan established by the employer for all employees or for a particular class of employees. However, employer payments made directly to employees and their dependents in lieu of health insurance coverage are taxable wages.

Makeup Pay for Military Duty Wage supplements paid by employers to cover the difference between employees' salary and their military pay or payment of their full salary are exempt from FICA and Medicare taxes (though subject to income tax withholding). This applies to active-duty soldiers and reservists activated for *more than 30 days*.

Contributions to Deferred Compensation Plans

Employee pretax (federal income tax) contributions under a qualified cash or deferred compensation arrangement (*Tax-Deferred Retirement Plans*, as discussed in Chapter 4) are subject to FICA tax. However, the employers' matching contributions are tax free.

Payments for Educational Assistance

Educational assistance refers to the expenses that an employer pays for an employee's education, such as tuition, fees, and payments for books, supplies, and equipment. Also, educational assistance includes the cost of employer-provided courses of instruction (books, supplies, and equipment). Educational assistance excludes payment for tools or supplies that employees keep after they complete a course of instruction. Payments for job-related educational expenses are not subject to FICA taxes if the education maintains or improves skills required by the individual's employment. Payments for non-job-related educational expenses up to *$5,250* are also exempt from FICA taxes.

Monkey Business Images/Shutterstock.com

Self-Study Quiz 3-2

Which of the following are subject to FICA tax (indicate Yes or No)?

_____ 1. A $15 gift certificate for a local grocery store given to employees as a Christmas gift.

_____ 2. Sales representatives using their company cars for personal use on weeknights and weekends.

_____ 3. Employer's contributions to a Simplified Employee Pension Plan (SEP) for its employees.

_____ 4. A tuition reimbursement plan that pays tuition for employees successfully completing job-related courses.

_____ 5. Severance pay made to an employee discharged for theft.

Tax Rates

The Social Security Act, as amended, imposes a separate tax on employees and employers for old-age, survivors, and disability insurance (OASDI) benefits and for hospital insurance (HI) benefits. The 2022 tax rates for both the employee and the employer portions of the tax follow:

> **LO 3**
>
> Apply the current tax rates and wage base for FICA and SECA purposes.

	Rate	Wage Base	Maximum Tax
Employee and Employer OASDI:	6.20%	$147,000	$9,114.00
Employee* and Employer HI:	1.45%	No limit	No maximum

*Employee HI: Plus an additional 0.9% on wages over $200,000.

Taxable Wage Base

The employer must consider the **taxable wage base** when computing the OASDI portion of the FICA tax. The law exempts wages that exceed this base during the calendar year (*$147,000 for 2022, please see "As We Go to Press" on page iii* and our online *"As We Go to Press" for estimated 2023 OASDI*). Once the OASDI taxable wage base has been reached, all payments made to the employee during the remainder of the year are not taxable. The wage base applies to amounts *paid* employees in a calendar year and not to the time when the services were performed by the employees. The HI portion of the FICA tax is 1.45 percent withheld on total earnings plus an additional 0.9 percent on wages over $200,000. The employer does not "match" the Employee's Supplemental HI rate of 0.9 percent on wages in excess of $200,000. The employer HI rate is 1.45 percent on all wages. Just as social security benefits increase each year based on changes in the Consumer Price Index, the taxable wage base is increased also.

    This means that an employee who makes $34,000 would pay the FICA tax (6.2% + 1.45%) on the total earnings, while an employee who makes $1 million would pay the HI portion (1.45%) on the total earnings plus additional HI tax (0.9%) on wages in excess of $200,000, but only $147,000 of the $1 million would be taxed at 6.2 percent.

Washington Update

On March 27, 2020, then President Trump signed the Coronavirus Aid, Relief, and Economic Security (CARES) act into law. This legislation allowed employers to defer payment of their 6.2 percent employer share of social security taxes due between March 27, 2020, and before January 1, 2021. Employers were required to deposit 50 percent of the amount due by December 31, 2021, and the remaining 50 percent by December 31, 2022.

The legislation gave eligible employers a payroll tax credit against applicable employment taxes for each calendar quarter equal to 50 percent of the qualified wages paid to employees.

The American Rescue Plan Act (ARPA) of 2021 was signed into law by President Biden on March 11, 2021, to help recovery from the COVID-19 pandemic and the ongoing recession. The ARPA extended the date of the qualified wages from January 1, 2021, through June 30, 2021.

A credit for qualified sick and family leave wages, enacted under the Families First Coronavirus Response Act (FFCRA) and amended and extended by the COVID-related Tax Relief Act of 2020, for leave taken after March 31, 2020, and before April 1, 2021, and the credit for qualified sick and family leave wages as enacted under the American Rescue Plan Act of 2021 (the ARP), for leave taken after March 31, 2021, and before October 1, 2021, have expired. However, employers that pay qualified sick and family leave wages in 2022 for leave taken after March 31, 2020, and before October 1, 2021, are eligible to claim a credit for qualified sick and family leave wages in 2022.

Form 941 has been revised due to the CARES act. The new version of form 941 (Employer's QUARTERLY Federal Tax Return) reflects these updates. Please see "As We Go to Press" on page iii and our online "As We Go to Press" for the most current updates.

IRS Connection

In 1950, there were 16 workers paying into the social security system for every one person collecting benefits. By 2042, the projection is a ratio of 2 to 1.

Determining OASDI tax:

If:

Cumulative Wages + Current Wage Payment < OASDI Wage Base, then
$52,400 + $6,000 = $58,400

compute the OASDI tax on the entire wage payment. ($6,000 × 0.062 = $372.00)

If:

Cumulative Wages + Current Wage Payment > OASDI Wage Base, then
$134,800 + $26,000 = $160,800

compute the OASDI tax on the part of the current wage payment that brings the cumulative wages up to the OASDI taxable wage limit. ($134,800 + $12,200 = $147,000)

$$\$12,200 \times 0.062 = \$756.40$$

Employees' FICA (OASDI/HI) Taxes and Withholdings

FICA requires employers to collect the OASDI/HI taxes from their employees and pay the taxes to the IRS at the same time they pay their own tax. The employer deducts the tax from the wages at the time of payment. The amount of each tax to be withheld is computed by applying to the employee's taxable wages the tax rate in effect at the time that the wages are received. In calculating the amounts of FICA taxes to withhold from employees' pays, the employer may disregard any fractional part of a cent, unless it is one-half cent or more, which must be rounded up one cent.

Ruth Engle receives pay on January 4, 20--, for work done during the last week of the previous year. The wages would be taxed as income in the year received, using the current tax rates.

The liability for the tax extends to both the employee and the employer, but after the employer has collected the tax, the employee's liability ceases. The following examples illustrate the computation of the FICA taxes to be withheld.

> **On the Job**
>
> Cost of employer-provided group-term life insurance in excess of $50,000 is taxable and is subject to social security and Medicare tax withholding.

Example 3-1

1. Casey Berra, employed by Gobel Company, earned $460 during the week ended January 25, 20--. Prior to January 25, Berra's cumulative gross earnings for the year were $2,765.70. FICA taxes to be withheld on $460 are computed as follows:

   OASDI

Taxable Wages	$ 460
Tax Rate	× 6.2%
OASDI Tax to Be Withheld	$ 28.52

   HI

Taxable Wages	$ 460
Tax Rate	× 1.45%
HI Tax to Be Withheld	$ 6.67

2. Francis Aha, a salaried employee of Wilson Advertising Agency, is paid every Friday. She earned $1,925 for this pay. Prior to the pay of November 1, 20--, she had earned $146,550. The FICA taxes to be withheld from Aha's pay on November 1 are computed as follows:

   OASDI

Taxable Wage Limit	$147,000
Wages Paid to Date	146,550
Taxable Wages This Pay	$ 450
Tax Rate	× 6.2%
OASDI Tax to Be Withheld	$ 27.90

   HI

Taxable Wage Limit	NONE
Wages Paid to Date	$146,550
Taxable Wages This Pay	$ 1,925
Tax Rate	× 1.45%
HI Tax to Be Withheld	$ 27.91

3. Marc Garcia, president of Uni-Sight, Inc., is paid $5,200 semimonthly. Prior to his last pay on December 27, 20--, Todd had earned $150,000. The FICA taxes to be withheld from Garcia's pay on December 27 are computed as follows:

   OASDI

Taxable Wage Limit	
Wages Paid to Date	$147,000
Taxable Wages This Pay	150,000
OASDI Tax to Be Withheld	$ -0-
	$ -0-

   HI

Taxable Wage Limit	NONE
Wages Paid to Date	$150,000
Taxable Wage This Pay	$ 5,200
Tax Rate	× 1.45%
HI Tax to Be Withheld	$ 75.40

4. Senja Matthews employed by Quality Company is paid $5,000 weekly. Prior to the pay of September 27, 20--, she had earned $200,000. The FICA taxes to be withheld from Jennifer's pay on September 27 are computed as follows:

   OASDI

Taxable Wage Limit	$147,000
Wages Paid to Date	200,000
Taxable Wages This Pay	$ -0-
OASDI to Be Withheld	$ -0-

   HI

Taxable Wage Limit (Applicable on Wages at 1.45%)	NONE
Wages Paid to Date	$200,000
Taxable Wage This Pay	$ 5,000
Tax Rate	1.45%
HI Tax to Be Withheld	$ 72.50
Additional 0.9% HI Tax on Wages in Excess of $200,000 = $5,000 × 0.9 =	45.00
Total HI Tax to Be Withheld	$ 117.50

Sometimes an employee has paid FICA taxes on wages in excess of the taxable base because of having worked for more than one employer. If so, the employee is entitled to a refund for the overpayment. The amount of the overpayment is credited against the employee's federal income taxes for that year. Instructions are given on the **Individual Income Tax Return (Form 1040)** that explain how the overpayment should be treated.

Employer's FICA (OASDI) Taxes

In addition to withholding the correct amount of FICA tax from the employees' taxable earnings, the employer must make contributions to the program. The employer's portion of the tax is based on the wages paid to the employees. The employer's taxes, however, are not computed on the wages paid each employee, but on the total taxable wages paid all employees. As shown in Example 3-2 below, the calculation for employees' and employer FICA taxes may result in slightly different amounts. This difference is reconciled on Form 941 as current quarter's fractions of cents. As with employee withholdings, once the OASDI taxable wage base is reached, the employer no longer contributes for that

---

Example 3-2

Wallington Company has 100 employees, each earning $525.25 a week.

OASDI

Amount of OASDI tax withheld from each employee's paycheck each week:	$ 32.57	(6.2% × $525.25)
Total tax withheld from the 100 employees' wages:	$3,257.00	($32.57 × 100)
Tax on employer:	$3,256.55	[6.2% × ($525.25 × 100)]

HI

Amount of HI tax withheld from each employee's paycheck each week:	$ 7.62	(1.45% × $525.25)
Total tax withheld from the 100 employees' wages is:	$762.00	($7.62 × 100)
Tax on employer:	$761.61	[1.45% × ($525.25 × 100)]

particular employee. The employer's OASDI tax is 6.2 percent of total employees' wages paid, and the HI tax is 1.45 percent of total employees' wages paid.

Successor Employer

Wages paid by the prior employer can be counted towards the annual OASDI wage base by a successor employer if all the following criteria are met:

1. The successor has acquired all the property used in the prior employer's business.
2. The affected employees were employed immediately before and continued working right after the transfer of the business.
3. Wages were paid by the prior employer during the calendar year of acquisition.

Self-Study Quiz 3-3

Patrick's Fine Foods employs five people. For each person, compute the amount of OASDI and HI tax for the first week in January.

Employee	Weekly Wage	OASDI	HI
Tammy Wolf	$225.00		
Bill Young	300.00		

Employee	Weekly Wage	OASDI	HI
Howard Feldman	$ 175.00		
Carin Clever	1,000.00		
Bud McAvoy	3,100.00		

Compute the employer's portion of the FICA taxes, based on the payroll data above.

Will any of the employees exceed the taxable wage base during the year? If yes, on which payday will it occur?

A Self-Employed Person

The Self-Employment Contributions Act (SECA) extended coverage under the social security system to the self-employed in 1951. Over the years, most self-employed persons have become covered by the law.

Self-Employment Income

SECA uses an individual's **self-employment income** as the basis for levying taxes and for determining the amount of income to credit toward OASDI insurance benefits or HI coverage. Self-employment income generally consists of the net earnings derived by individuals from a business or profession carried on as a sole proprietorship or as a partnership. Self-employed persons determine their net earnings by finding the sum of the following:

1. The **gross income** derived by an individual from any business or profession carried on, less allowable deductions attributable to such a business or profession, and

2. The **individual's distributive** share (whether or not distributed) of the ordinary net income or loss from any business or profession carried on by a partnership of which the individual is a member.

Self-Employment OASDI/HI Taxes

The self-employed tax rate for 2022 on the net earnings is 15.3 percent—12.4 percent for OASDI and 2.9 percent for HI (double the employee rate). Self-employment income is subject to 0.9 percent additional HI tax on earned income in excess of $200,000.

On the Net

https://www.irs.gov/businesses/small-businesses-self-employed/independent-contractor-self-employed-or-employee

Lists IRS criteria for determining employee versus independent contractor status.

Svetlana Priosky's net self-employment earnings for the year were $63,210. Her self-employment tax would be:

$$\$63,210 \times 0.153 = \$9,671.13$$

> **Example 3-3**

Usually, the net business income of individuals, as shown in their income tax returns, makes up their net earnings from self-employment for the purpose of the Social Security Act.

Earnings of less than $400 from self-employment are ignored. For computing the OASDI taxes, the maximum self-employment taxable income of any individual is $147,000 (2022). For the HI taxes, however, the total self-employment income is taxable. If the individual is also an employee of another company, the wages received can reduce the amount of self-employment income that is taxed for OASDI (wages + self-employment income > $147,000)

Roberta Wurst receives wages of $150,000 from her job. She also earned $15,000 in net self-employment income during the year. In computing her OASDI taxes, none of her self-employment income is considered, since her wages exceed the taxable wage base of $147,000. However, in computing her HI taxes, all of her earnings from self-employment are taxed.

OASDI Taxable Wages < Wages Received = OASDI Taxable Wages
$147,000   < $150,000   = $-0-
HI Self-Employment Income $15,000 × 0.029   = $435.00 HI Tax Due

> **Example 3-4**

If the wages received amount to less than $147,000, any net self-employment earnings amounting to $400 or more must be counted as self-employment income up to an aggregate amount of $147,000 for OASDI taxes.

Example 3-5

Tell Me More

Taylor Talbot receives wages amounting to $116,600. Their net earnings from self-employment amount to $32,800. Talbot must count $30,400 of their earnings in determining taxable self-employment income for OASDI taxes.

OASDI Taxable Wage Base	−	Wages Received	=	OASDI Taxable Self-Employment Income
$147,000	−	$116,600	=	$30,400

Taxable Year

In computing the taxes on self-employment income, sole proprietors use the same taxable year as that used for income tax purposes. In the case of a partnership, the taxable year of the partners may not correspond with that of the partnership. In such instances, the partners are required to include in computing net earnings from self-employment their distributive share of the income or loss from the partnership for any taxable year ending with or within their taxable year.

Reporting Self-Employment Income

Sole proprietors report their self-employment income by transferring certain data from **Schedule C (Form 1040), Profit or Loss from Business to Schedule SE (Form 1040), Self-Employment Tax**. SECA requires self-employed persons to include SECA taxes in their quarterly payment of estimated income taxes. The taxpayer's estimated tax is the sum of the estimated income taxes and SECA taxes less any credits against the tax.

Self-Study Quiz 3-4

Lori Kinmark works as a jeweler for a local company. She earns $1,000 per week, plus a year-end bonus of $2,000. Kinmark also earns an additional net self-employment income of $28,000 per year.

$_____ 1. Compute Kinmark's annual earnings from employment.

$_____ 2. Compute Kinmark's total earnings from her job and from self-employment income.

$_____ 3. How much self-employment income should Kinmark include in computing taxable self-employment income for OASDI taxes?

$_____ 4. What are the total FICA taxes on her self-employment earnings?

Employer Identification Number

Every employer of one or more persons must file an application for an identification number (employer identification number—EIN). EINs can be obtained directly from the Internet (http://www.irs.gov). No preregistration is required, and the number that is issued is immediately recognized by IRS systems. The Internal Revenue Service also offers employers a toll-free number (800-829-4933) where they can request an employer identification number. Businesses can still obtain EINs by mailing or faxing Form SS-4. This form must be sent to the IRS service center where the employer's federal tax returns are filed. Figure 3.5 shows a filled-in copy of Form SS-4.

FIGURE 3.5

Form SS-4, Application for Employer Identification Number

Form **SS-4** (Rev. December 2019) Department of the Treasury Internal Revenue Service	**Application for Employer Identification Number** (For use by employers, corporations, partnerships, trusts, estates, churches, government agencies, Indian tribal entities, certain individuals, and others.) ▶ Go to *www.irs.gov/FormSS4* for instructions and the latest information. ▶ See separate instructions for each line. ▶ Keep a copy for your records.	OMB No. 1545-0003 EIN

Type or print clearly.

1	Legal name of entity (or individual) for whom the EIN is being requested
	Myers Payroll Services, Inc.

2 Trade name of business (if different from name on line 1)	**3** Executor, administrator, trustee, "care of" name
	Care of Martin Myers

4a Mailing address (room, apt., suite no. and street, or P.O. box)	**5a** Street address (if different) (Don't enter a P.O. box.)
P.O. Box 212	3401 Atrium Way
4b City, state, and ZIP code (if foreign, see instructions)	**5b** City, state, and ZIP code (if foreign, see instructions)
Sacramento, CA 95814-1212	Sacramento, CA 95814-0340

6	County and state where principal business is located
	Orange County, CA

7a Name of responsible party	**7b** SSN, ITIN, or EIN
Catherine Myers	000-00-6119

8a	Is this application for a limited liability company (LLC) (or a foreign equivalent)? . . . . ☐ Yes ☑ No	**8b** If 8a is "Yes," enter the number of LLC members . . . . . . ▶

8c	If 8a is "Yes," was the LLC organized in the United States? . . . . ☐ Yes ☐ No

9a Type of entity (check only one box). **Caution:** If 8a is "Yes," see the instructions for the correct box to check.

☐ Sole proprietor (SSN) _____
☐ Partnership
☑ Corporation (enter form number to be filed) ▶ _1120_
☐ Personal service corporation
☐ Church or church-controlled organization
☐ Other nonprofit organization (specify) ▶ _____
☐ Other (specify) ▶

☐ Estate (SSN of decedent) _____
☐ Plan administrator (TIN) _____
☐ Trust (TIN of grantor) _____
☐ Military/National Guard   ☐ State/local government
☐ Farmers' cooperative   ☐ Federal government
☐ REMIC   ☐ Indian tribal governments/enterprises
Group Exemption Number (GEN) if any ▶

9b If a corporation, name the state or foreign country (if applicable) where incorporated	State California	Foreign country

10 **Reason for applying** (check only one box)

☑ Started new business (specify type) ▶ _____
   Payroll Processing
☐ Hired employees (Check the box and see line 13.)
☐ Compliance with IRS withholding regulations
☐ Other (specify) ▶

☐ Banking purpose (specify purpose) ▶ _____
☐ Changed type of organization (specify new type) ▶ _____
☐ Purchased going business
☐ Created a trust (specify type) ▶ _____
☐ Created a pension plan (specify type) ▶ _____

11 Date business started or acquired (month, day, year). See instructions. July 3, 20--	**12** Closing month of accounting year December
13 Highest number of employees expected in the next 12 months (enter -0- if none). If no employees expected, skip line 14.	**14** If you expect your employment tax liability to be $1,000 or less in a full calendar year **and** want to file Form 944 annually instead of Forms 941 quarterly, check here. (Your employment tax liability generally will be $1,000 or less if you expect to pay $5,000 or less in total wages.) If you don't check this box, you must file Form 941 for every quarter. ☑

Agricultural	Household	Other
		1

15	First date wages or annuities were paid (month, day, year). **Note:** If applicant is a withholding agent, enter date income will first be paid to nonresident alien (month, day, year) . . . . ▶ July 15, 20--

16 Check **one** box that best describes the principal activity of your business.

☐ Construction   ☐ Rental & leasing   ☐ Transportation & warehousing
☐ Real estate   ☐ Manufacturing   ☐ Finance & insurance
☐ Health care & social assistance   ☐ Wholesale-agent/broker
☐ Accommodation & food service   ☐ Wholesale-other   ☐ Retail
☑ Other (specify) ▶ Payroll Services

17	Indicate principal line of merchandise sold, specific construction work done, products produced, or services provided.
	Payroll Processing

18	Has the applicant entity shown on line 1 ever applied for and received an EIN? ☐ Yes ☑ No If "Yes," write previous EIN here ▶

Third Party Designee	Complete this section **only** if you want to authorize the named individual to receive the entity's EIN and answer questions about the completion of this form.	
	Designee's name	Designee's telephone number (include area code)
	Address and ZIP code	Designee's fax number (include area code)

Under penalties of perjury, I declare that I have examined this application, and to the best of my knowledge and belief, it is true, correct, and complete.

Name and title (type or print clearly) ▶ Catherine Myers, President	Applicant's telephone number (include area code) 919-555-2111
Signature ▶ *Catherine Myers* Date ▶ 6/4/--	Applicant's fax number (include area code) 919-555-2119

For Privacy Act and Paperwork Reduction Act Notice, see separate instructions.   Cat. No. 16055N   Form **SS-4** (Rev. 12-2019)

Source: Internal Revenue Service.

The employer must enter this EIN on all returns, forms, and correspondence sent to the District Director of Internal Revenue that relate to the taxes imposed under FICA. The employer uses the EIN in any correspondence with the Social Security Administration (SSA) and enters the number on forms issued by the SSA. Regardless of how many different business locations are operated, the employer receives only one EIN. The penalty for failing to supply the identification number is discussed later in this chapter. If the owner sells or otherwise transfers a business, the new owner must file an application for a new identification number.

Employee's Application for Social Security Card (Form SS-5)

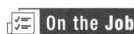

On the Job

The employer must obtain each employee's SSN to enter on Form W-2 (discussed in Chapter 4). If the employer does not provide the correct name and SSN, they may owe a penalty.

Under the Social Security Act, every employee and every self-employed person must have a social security number (SSN). The application for a SSN is available at any social security or IRS office. The **Application for a Social Security Card (Form SS-5)** can be filed with any field office of the SSA.

The Social Security Act requires applicants for a social security card to furnish evidence of their age, identity, and U.S. citizenship or lawful alien status. Applicants may either apply by mailing the required documents and forms to their nearest social security office or apply in person. If they are age 18 or older and have never had a social security card, or are aliens whose immigration documents should not be sent through the mail, they must apply in person.

Upon receipt of their SSN, employees should inform their employers of the number assigned them. If employees change positions, they must notify the new employer of their SSN when they begin employment. If an employee changes their name by court order or by marriage, the individual should request a new social security card by completing a new Form SS-5. Employees may have their SSN changed at any time by applying to the SSA and showing good reasons for a change. Otherwise, only one number is assigned to an employee, and the employee will continue to use that number regardless of the changes in positions or employers.

For aliens who must file U.S. tax returns but are not eligible to receive a social security number, the IRS has instituted **Form W-7, Application for IRS Individual Taxpayer Identification Number (ITIN)**. An ITIN (begins with the number 9) is intended for tax purposes only.

The secretary of health and human services is authorized to ensure that SSNs are issued to or on behalf of children who are below school age at the request of their parents or guardians and to children of school age when they first enroll in school. Further, SSNs must be obtained for children age one or over who are claimed as dependents on federal income tax returns.

Criminal penalties (of up to $5,000 or imprisonment of up to five years, or both) exist for persons involved in the following situations:

1. Knowingly and willfully using a SSN obtained with false information.
2. Using someone else's SSN.
3. Altering a social security card.
4. Buying or selling a card claimed to be issued by the secretary.
5. Possessing a card or counterfeit card with the intent to sell or alter it.

Verifying Social Security Numbers

The Social Security Administration offers employers an online system to check current and former employees' names and social security numbers. Employers can verify up to 10 names and SSNs per screen or upload files of up to 250,000 names and SSNs with verification results the next day (http://www.ssa.gov/employer/verifySSN.htm).

Returns Required for Social Security Purposes

Employers covered under FICA are liable for their own FICA taxes and their employees' FICA and income taxes withheld from wages. Withholding of income taxes is discussed in Chapter 4. Every employer (except those employing agricultural workers) who is required to withhold income taxes from wages or who is liable for social security taxes must file:

1. A *quarterly* or an *annual* tax and information return (Form 941 or 944). This return shows the total FICA wage paid and the total FICA taxes (employer and employee contributions) and federal income taxes withheld.

2. An *annual* return of withheld federal income taxes (Form 945). This return covers *nonpayroll* items such as backup withholding, withholding on gambling winnings, pensions, annuities, IRAs, and military retirement.

Generally, an employer must electronically transfer to the IRS the income taxes and social security taxes withheld and the employer's matching social security taxes.

Any employer who fails to pay the withheld income taxes and FICA taxes, fails to make deposits and payments, or does not file the tax returns as required by law may be required to deposit such taxes in a special trust account for the U.S. government and file monthly tax returns. Figure 3.6 lists and briefly describes the major forms used to prepare FICA tax returns and deposits.

FIGURE 3.6

Major Forms for Preparing FICA Tax Returns and Deposits

Form 941, Employer's QUARTERLY Federal Tax Return	Required of all covered employers, except employers of household and agricultural employees, who withhold income tax and social security taxes (see Figure 3.8 on pages 3-23 to 3-25).
Form 941-PR, Employer's QUARTERLY Federal Tax Return	Required of employers to report social security taxes for workers in Puerto Rico.
Form 941-SS, Employer's QUARTERLY Federal Tax Return	Required of employers to report social security taxes for workers in American Samoa, Guam, the Northern Mariana Islands, and the Virgin Islands.
Form 941-V, Form 941 Payment Voucher	Filled in by employers with a total tax liability of less than $2,500 for the quarter who are making payment with Form 941.
Form 941-X, Adjusted Employer's QUARTERLY Federal Tax Return or Claim for Refund	Use to correct previously filed Forms 941, 941-SS, 943, 944, and 945.
Form 943, Employer's ANNUAL Tax Return for Agricultural Employees	Used by employers of agricultural workers for reporting FICA and income taxes on wages paid.
Form 944, Employer's ANNUAL Federal Tax Return	Can be used by employers who owe $1,000 or less in employment taxes each year (in place of Form 941).
Form 945, ANNUAL Return of Withheld Federal Income Tax	Required of employers to report income tax withheld from nonpayroll payments.

LO 4

Describe the different requirements and procedures for depositing FICA taxes and income taxes withheld from employees' wages.

Deposit Requirements (Nonagricultural Workers)

The requirements for depositing *FICA taxes and income taxes withheld* from employees' wages vary according to the amount of such taxes reported during a **lookback period**. Depending on the total amount of taxes involved (federal income tax and FICA tax withheld from employees' earnings plus the employer's portion of the FICA tax), employers may have to pay their taxes several times a month or monthly. Some employers may not have to make any deposits but, instead, may pay their taxes at the time of filing their quarterly return, Form 941, discussed later in this chapter.

The amount of employment taxes that the employer reported on the quarterly returns for the *four quarters in the lookback period* determines if the employer is a monthly or a semiweekly depositor. A lookback period consists of four quarters beginning July 1 of the second preceding year and ending June 30 of the prior year. These four quarters are the employer's lookback period even if no taxes were reported for any of the quarters. Figure 3.7 shows the lookback period for 2023.

Each November, the IRS notifies employers whether they will be a monthly or a semiweekly depositor for the next calendar year.

FIGURE 3.7

Lookback Period for Calendar Year 2023

2021		2022	
July–Sept.	Oct.–Dec.	Jan.–Mar.	Apr.–June

% **IRS Connection**

At the end of the year, the IRS sends a notice to employers whose deposit schedules will change for the upcoming year.

Monthly Depositor	Reported—$50,000 or less in lookback period. Required deposits—By the 15th of the following month (if not a banking day, next banking day).
Semiweekly Depositor	Reported—More than $50,000 in lookback period. Required deposits—Within three business days of the semiweekly period (if any of the three weekdays is a nonbusiness day, add one additional business day to the due date). • Payday on Wednesday, Thursday, or Friday—due following Wednesday. • Payday on Saturday, Sunday, Monday, or Tuesday—due following Friday. Separate liabilities and deposits—When deposit period spans two separate quarters.
One-Day Rule	Reported—$100,000 or more in undeposited taxes on any day during a deposit period. Required deposit—Close of the next banking day. Semiweekly status—If an employer falls under the one-day rule at any time during this year or last year.
No Deposits	Reported—Accumulated employment taxes of less than $2,500 for the whole calendar quarter. Required deposit—Pay with the filing of quarterly Form 941 or deposit by the end of month following the calendar quarter. Unsure of $2,500 total—Use the appropriate rules above.

Monthly

1. Robart Company's deposit status for 2023 was determined by using the lookback period in Figure 3.7 as shown above. During the two quarters of 2021, Robart reported employment taxes (FICA & employees' income tax) of $16,000. For each of the two quarters in 2022, the company reported taxes of $10,000. Since the taxes reported by Robart during the lookback period do not exceed $50,000, the company is classed as a monthly depositor and follows the monthly rule for the current year, 2023.

2. Vu-Tu, Inc., is a monthly depositor. If July employment taxes are $11,000, Vu-Tu must deposit the $11,000 on or before August 15, 20--.

Semiweekly

1. Meyer Company's deposit status for 2023 was determined by using the lookback period shown in Figure 3.7. In the two quarters of 2021, Meyer reported taxes of $35,000. The taxes reported in the two quarters of 2022 totaled $30,000. Since the total taxes reported during the four quarters of the lookback period exceeded $50,000, Meyer is subject to the semiweekly rule for the current year, 2023.

2. The employees of Franchild, a semiweekly depositor, are paid every Monday. On payday, Franchild has accumulated taxes totaling $24,000. Franchild is required to deposit the $24,000 on or before the following Friday.

One-Day

1. On Wednesday, January 2, 20--, Wycheck Company accumulated $105,000 in employment taxes for wages paid on that day. Regardless of Wycheck's deposit status, the firm is required to deposit the $105,000 by the next banking day, Thursday, January 3. Note that if Wycheck was not subject to the semiweekly rule on January 3, 20--, the company would become subject to that rule as of January 4, 20--.

2. Blastein Company is subject to the semiweekly rule. On Monday, February 4, 20--, Blastein accumulated $120,000 in employment taxes. The firm is required to deposit the $120,000 by the next banking day, Tuesday, February 5.

   On Tuesday, February 5, Blastein accumulates $30,000 more in employment taxes. Even though Blastein had a previous $120,000 deposit obligation that occurred earlier in the semiweekly period, Blastein now has an additional and separate deposit obligation that must be met by the following Friday, February 8.

A ***new employer*** becomes a **monthly depositor** until a lookback period that can be used to determine deposit frequency is established. However, if an unsatisfied deposit of $100,000 or more triggers the $100,000 one-day rule (see Figure 3.7) at any time during the year, the new employer becomes a **semiweekly depositor** for the remainder of the current calendar year and the subsequent calendar year.

The Safe Harbor Rule (98 Percent Rule)

The amount deposited by an employer may be affected by the **safe harbor rule**. Under this rule, an employer satisfies the deposit obligations provided:

1. The amount of any shortfall (under deposit) does not exceed the greater of $100 or 2 percent of the amount of employment taxes required to be deposited.

2. The employer deposits the shortfall on or before the shortfall makeup date.

A **shortfall** is the excess of the amount of employment taxes required to be deposited over the amount deposited on or before the last date prescribed for the deposit. The shortfall makeup rules follow:

1. ***Monthly depositors***: The shortfall must be deposited or remitted by the quarterly return due date, in accordance with the applicable form and instruction.

2. *Semiweekly depositors and those subject to the $100,000 one-day rule*: The shortfall must be deposited on or before the first Wednesday or Friday, whichever is earlier, falling on or after the 15th day of the month following the month in which the deposit was required to be made.

3. *Shortfall over $100,000*: If the shortfall is more than $100,000, the one-day rule overrides the safe harbor rule.

Example 3-6

1. On Friday, May 24, 20--, Rogers, Ltd., a semiweekly depositor, pays wages and accumulates employment taxes. Rogers makes a deposit on Wednesday, May 29, in the amount of $4,000. Later it was determined that Rogers was actually required to deposit $4,080 by Wednesday.

   Rogers has a shortfall of $80. The shortfall is less than the greater of $100 or 2 percent of the amount required to be deposited. Therefore, Rogers satisfies the safe harbor rule so long as the $80 shortfall is deposited by Wednesday, June 19.

2. On Friday, October 4, 20--, Vargan Company, a semiweekly depositor, pays wages and accumulates employment taxes. Vargan makes a deposit of $30,000 but later finds that the amount of the deposit should have been $32,000.

   The $2,000 shortfall ($32,000 − $30,000) exceeds the greater of $100 or 2 percent of the amount required to be deposited (2% × $32,000 = $640). Thus, the safe harbor rule was not met. As a result, Vargan is subject to a failure-to-deposit penalty, as described later in this chapter.

Deposit Requirements for Employers of Agricultural Workers

The deposit-making rules that apply to employers of agricultural laborers resemble those for employers of nonagricultural workers. However, there are exceptions, explained in the instructions accompanying **Form 943, Employer's Annual Tax Return for Agricultural Employees**.

Deposit Requirements for Employers of Household Employees

Household or domestic employees are usually not subject to federal income tax withholding, but they may voluntarily request that federal income taxes be with-held from their wages. Even though federal income taxes are not withheld from their wages, they are subject to FICA taxes if each worker has been paid cash wages of $2,400 or more in a calendar year. Noncash items given to household employees are not subject to FICA tax.

Employers who withhold and pay FICA taxes and federal income taxes for household services must report these taxes on **Form W-2, Wage and Tax Statement**, for each household employee.

Deposit Requirements for State and Local Government Employers

Each state and local government employer must file its return on Form 941 with the IRS and deposit its FICA taxes through the federal deposit system. State and local government employers must make their tax deposits according to the same deposit schedule used by private employers.

Procedures for Making Deposits

The original paper-based system has been replaced by an electronic depositing system.

Electronic Deposits Most employers must now make their deposits via the Electronic Federal Tax Payment System (EFTPS). The major exception will be for businesses with $2,500 or less in quarterly tax liabilities that pay when they file their returns (see Form 941). A deposit using this system must be initiated at least one business day before it is due in order to be considered timely.

This system is a communications network that facilitates the direct transfer of funds from the employer's bank to the Treasury Department. Generally, these transfers are transacted by touch-tone phone, personal computer, or online.

To use the online option, the employer must have Internet access. Enrollment in EFTPS Online can be done at http://www.eftps.gov.

Once enrolled in the EFTPS program, an employer can switch between computer software or online methods anytime. The linkage on all the methods is provided by the company's employer identification number.

There are two electronic methods of deposit:

1. **EFTPS (direct)**—the employer can instruct the Treasury Financial Agent for the area to withdraw funds from the employer's bank account and route them to the Treasury's account at the Federal Reserve Bank (ACH debit method).

2. **EFTPS (through a financial institution)**—the employer could also instruct the bank to send each payment directly to the Treasury's account at the Federal Reserve Bank (ACH credit method).

To enroll, an employer must complete *Form 9779, EFTPS Business Enrollment Form*. Enrollment takes from three to six weeks, and a confirmation package will be sent by the IRS to the employer with a personal identification number (PIN) and payment instructions.

> **On the Job**
>
> If a deposit is required and the employer has not yet received the employer identification number, the deposit must be mailed directly to the Internal Revenue Service with an explanation attached.

Over the Line

A U.S. District Court ruled that a business that deposited withheld federal income taxes in full and on time, but not through the Electronic Federal Tax Payment System (EFTPS), was correctly assessed a failure-to-deposit penalty. Commonwealth Bank and Trust Co. erroneously used deposit forms instead of using EFTPS, resulting in the IRS assessing $252,842.87 in failure-to-deposit penalties.[3]

Self-Study Quiz 3-5

_____ 1. Johnson Industries, a semiweekly depositor, pays its employees every Friday. When should the company deposit the employment taxes for each weekly payday?

_____ 2. What rule should Bartlett Repair, a new company, follow in making its deposits for accumulated employment taxes?

_____ 3. Quail Hollow Motors (a semiweekly depositor) accumulates taxes of $105,000 on Monday and must deposit this amount on Tuesday, the next banking day. On Tuesday, the company accumulates additional taxes of $20,000. What deposit rule should Quail Hollow Motors follow for depositing the additional $20,000?

Preparing Form 941 (Employer's QUARTERLY Federal Tax Return)

Generally, the employer must make a quarterly return of FICA taxes and withheld income taxes for the three months of each calendar quarter, using *Form 941, Employer's QUARTERLY Federal Tax Return*. Figure 3.8 on pages 3-23

Tell Me More

> **LO 5**
>
> Complete Form 941, Employer's QUARTERLY Federal Tax Return.

3 *PAYTECH*, The Official Publication of the American Payroll Association, February 2015, p. 56.

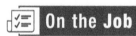

to 3-25 shows a completed copy of Form 941. Form 941 may be submitted electronically using the Form 941 e-file program.

All nonpayroll items (backup withholding and withholding from pensions, annuities, IRAs, military retirement, and gambling winnings) are reported on **Form 945, Annual Return of Withheld Federal Income Tax** (Chapter 4).

Completing the Return

In making entries on the form:

a. Dollar signs and decimal points—not used.

b. Zero value line item—leave blank.

c. Negative amounts—use "minus" sign.

d. No rounding to nearest dollar.

Part 1

Most of the entries required on this part are self-explanatory. Other sources of information are shown in Figure 3.9 on page 3-26. The tax adjustments and credits relate to:

5f. Employer's share of FICA taxes on tips reported on **Form 4137, Social Security and Medicare Tax on Unreported Tip Income**.

7. Fractions of cents—employees' share (one-half) of amounts on lines 5(a)–5(d) may differ slightly from amounts actually withheld (due to rounding).

8. Sick pay—adjustment for employees' share of FICA taxes that were withheld by third-party sick pay payer.

9. Tips and group-term life insurance—uncollected FICA taxes on tips and group-term life insurance premiums.

11a. Qualified small business payroll tax credit for increasing research activities.

11b. Nonrefundable portion of credit for qualified sick and family leave wages.

11d. Nonrefundable portion of credit for qualified sick and family leave wages for leave taken after March 31, 2021, and before October 1, 2021.

11e. Nonrefundable portion of COBRA premium assistance credit (see instructions for applicable quarter).

11f. Number of individuals provided COBRA premium assistance.

13c. Refundable portion of credit for qualified sick and family leave wages for leave taken before April 1, 2021.

13e. Refundable portion of credit for qualified sick and family leave wages for leave taken after March 31, 2021, and before October 1, 2021.

13f. Refundable portion of COBRA premium assistance credit (see instructions for applicable quarter).

Part 2

16. Check the appropriate box. If the monthly schedule applies, enter a summary of your **tax liability** by month.

In addition, semiweekly and next-day depositors must complete **Schedule B (Form 941), Report of Tax Liability for Semiweekly Schedule Depositors**, instead of Form 941, line 16 (if the tax liability for the quarter was $2,500 or more). The employer's tax liability is listed by each payday (see Figure 3.10 on page 3-27).

Part 3

17 to 28.   Complete if any situation applies.

Part 4

Complete if the employer wants to allow an employee, a paid tax preparer, or another person to discuss Form 941 with the IRS.

FIGURE 3.8
Form 941, Employer's QUARTERLY Federal Tax Return

Form **941 for 20--:** **Employer's QUARTERLY Federal Tax Return**
(Rev. March 2022)

Department of the Treasury — Internal Revenue Service   OMB No. 1545-0029

Employer identification number (EIN)   0 0 – 0 0 0 7 7 7 9

Name (not your trade name)   JUSTIN GRANATELLI

Trade name (if any)   GRANATELLI

Address   3709 FIFTH
Number   Street   Suite or room number

CHICAGO   IL   60605
City   State   ZIP code

Foreign country name   Foreign province/county   Foreign postal code

Report for this Quarter of 20--
(Check one.)

- [x] **1:** January, February, March
- [ ] **2:** April, May, June
- [ ] **3:** July, August, September
- [ ] **4:** October, November, December

Go to *www.irs.gov/Form941* for instructions and the latest information.

Read the separate instructions before you complete Form 941. Type or print within the boxes.

Part 1:   Answer these questions for this quarter.

1	Number of employees who received wages, tips, or other compensation for the pay period including: *Mar. 12 (Quarter 1)*	1	26
2	Wages, tips, and other compensation	2	74895 . 92
3	Federal income tax withheld from wages, tips, and other compensation	3	12372 . 13
4	If no wages, tips, and other compensation are subject to social security or Medicare tax [ ] Check and go to line 6.		

	Column 1		Column 2	
5a Taxable social security wages* . .	74895 . 92	× 0.124 =	9287 . 09	
5a (i) Qualified sick leave wages* .	.	× 0.062 =	.	
5a (ii) Qualified family leave wages* .	.	× 0.062 =	.	
5b Taxable social security tips . . .	.	× 0.124 =	.	
5c Taxable Medicare wages & tips . .	74895 . 92	× 0.029 =	2171 . 98	
5d Taxable wages & tips subject to Additional Medicare Tax withholding	.	× 0.009 =	.	

*Include taxable qualified sick and family leave wages paid in 2022 for leave taken after March 31, 2021, and before October 1, 2021, on line 5a. Use lines 5a(i) and 5a(ii) **only** for taxable qualified sick and family leave wages paid in 2022 for leave taken after March 31, 2020, and before April 1, 2021.*

5e	Total social security and Medicare taxes. Add Column 2 from lines 5a, 5a(i), 5a(ii), 5b, 5c, and 5d	5e	11459 . 07
5f	Section 3121(q) Notice and Demand—Tax due on unreported tips (see instructions) . .	5f	.
6	Total taxes before adjustments. Add lines 3, 5e, and 5f	6	23831 . 20
7	Current quarter's adjustment for fractions of cents	7	— . 15
8	Current quarter's adjustment for sick pay	8	.
9	Current quarter's adjustments for tips and group-term life insurance	9	.
10	Total taxes after adjustments. Combine lines 6 through 9	10	23831 . 05
11a	Qualified small business payroll tax credit for increasing research activities. Attach Form 8974	11a	.
11b	Nonrefundable portion of credit for qualified sick and family leave wages for leave taken before April 1, 2021	11b	.
11c	Reserved for future use	11c	.

▶ **You MUST complete all three pages of Form 941 and SIGN it.**   Next ▶

For Privacy Act and Paperwork Reduction Act Notice, see the back of the Payment Voucher.   Cat. No. 17001Z   Form **941** (Rev. 3-2022)

FIGURE 3.8 (continued)

Form 941, Employer's QUARTERLY Federal Tax Return

Name (not your trade name)	Employer identification number (EIN)
JUSTIN GRANATELLI	00-0007779

Part 1: Answer these questions for this quarter. (continued)

11d Nonrefundable portion of credit for qualified sick and family leave wages for leave taken after March 31, 2021, and before October 1, 2021 . . . . **11d** | ▪

11e Nonrefundable portion of COBRA premium assistance credit (see instructions for applicable quarter) . . . . **11e** | ▪

11f Number of individuals provided COBRA premium assistance | _____

11g Total nonrefundable credits. Add lines 11a, 11b, 11d, and 11e . . . . **11g** | ▪

12 Total taxes after adjustments and nonrefundable credits. Subtract line 11g from line 10 . **12** | 23831 ▪ 05

13a Total deposits for this quarter, including overpayment applied from a prior quarter and overpayments applied from Form 941-X, 941-X (PR), 944-X, or 944-X (SP) filed in the current quarter **13a** | 23831 ▪ 05

13b Reserved for future use . . . . **13b** | ▪

13c Refundable portion of credit for qualified sick and family leave wages for leave taken before April 1, 2021 . . . . **13c** | ▪

13d Reserved for future use . . . . **13d** | ▪

13e Refundable portion of credit for qualified sick and family leave wages for leave taken after March 31, 2021, and before October 1, 2021 . . . . **13e** | ▪

13f Refundable portion of COBRA premium assistance credit (see instructions for applicable quarter) . . . . **13f** | ▪

13g Total deposits and refundable credits. Add lines 13a, 13c, 13e, and 13f . . . . . . **13g** | 23831 ▪ 05

13h Reserved for future use . . . . **13h** | ▪

13i Reserved for future use . . . . **13i** | ▪

14 Balance due. If line 12 is more than line 13g, enter the difference and see instructions . . . **14** | ▪

15 Overpayment. If line 13g is more than line 12, enter the difference _____ ▪ Check one: ☐ Apply to next return. ☐ Send a refund.

Part 2: Tell us about your deposit schedule and tax liability for this quarter.

If you're unsure about whether you're a monthly schedule depositor or a semiweekly schedule depositor, see section 11 of Pub. 15.

16 Check one: ☐ Line 12 on this return is less than $2,500 or line 12 on the return for the prior quarter was less than $2,500, and you didn't incur a $100,000 next-day deposit obligation during the current quarter. If line 12 for the prior quarter was less than $2,500 but line 12 on this return is $100,000 or more, you must provide a record of your federal tax liability. If you're a monthly schedule depositor, complete the deposit schedule below; if you're a semiweekly schedule depositor, attach Schedule B (Form 941). Go to Part 3.

☐ You were a monthly schedule depositor for the entire quarter. Enter your tax liability for each month and total liability for the quarter, then go to Part 3.

Tax liability: Month 1 | _____ ▪

Month 2 | _____ ▪

Month 3 | _____ ▪

Total liability for quarter | _____ ▪ Total must equal line 12.

☒ You were a semiweekly schedule depositor for any part of this quarter. Complete Schedule B (Form 941), Report of Tax Liability for Semiweekly Schedule Depositors, and attach it to Form 941. Go to Part 3.

► You MUST complete all three pages of Form 941 and SIGN it. | Next ▶

FIGURE 3.8 (concluded)

Form 941, Employer's QUARTERLY Federal Tax Return

Name *(not your trade name)*	Employer identification number (EIN)
JUSTIN GRANATELLI	00-0007779

Part 3:	**Tell us about your business. If a question does NOT apply to your business, leave it blank.**

17 If your business has closed or you stopped paying wages . . . . ☐ Check here, and

enter the final date you paid wages [/   /   ] ; also attach a statement to your return. See instructions.

18 **If you're a seasonal employer and you don't have to file a return for every quarter of the year** . . . ☐ Check here.

19 Qualified health plan expenses allocable to qualified sick leave wages for leave taken before April 1, 2021 **19** [.]

20 Qualified health plan expenses allocable to qualified family leave wages for leave taken before April 1, 2021 **20** [.]

21 Reserved for future use . . . . **21** [.]

22 Reserved for future use . . . . **22** [.]

23 Qualified sick leave wages for leave taken after March 31, 2021, and before October 1, 2021 **23** [.]

24 Qualified health plan expenses allocable to qualified sick leave wages reported on line 23 **24** [.]

25 Amounts under certain collectively bargained agreements allocable to qualified sick leave wages reported on line 23 . . . . **25** [.]

26 Qualified family leave wages for leave taken after March 31, 2021, and before October 1, 2021 **26** [.]

27 Qualified health plan expenses allocable to qualified family leave wages reported on line 26 **27** [.]

28 Amounts under certain collectively bargained agreements allocable to qualified family leave wages reported on line 26 . . . . **28** [.]

Part 4:	**May we speak with your third-party designee?**

Do you want to allow an employee, a paid tax preparer, or another person to discuss this return with the IRS? See the instructions for details.

☐ Yes. Designee's name and phone number [   ] [   ]

Select a 5-digit personal identification number (PIN) to use when talking to the IRS. [ ] [ ] [ ] [ ] [ ]

☒ No.

Part 5:	**Sign here. You MUST complete all three pages of Form 941 and SIGN it.**

Under penalties of perjury, I declare that I have examined this return, including accompanying schedules and statements, and to the best of my knowledge and belief, it is true, correct, and complete. Declaration of preparer (other than taxpayer) is based on all information of which preparer has any knowledge.

X **Sign your name here** *Justin Granatelli*

Print your name here [JUSTIN GRANATELLI]

Print your title here [OWNER]

Date [04/30/--]

Best daytime phone [773-555-2119]

Paid Preparer Use Only

Check if you're self-employed . . . . ☐

Preparer's name	[ ]	PTIN	[ ]
Preparer's signature	[ ]	Date	[/ /]
Firm's name (or yours if self-employed)	[ ]	EIN	[ ]
Address	[ ]	Phone	[ ]
City	[ ] State [ ]	ZIP code	[ ]

Source: Internal Revenue Service.

FIGURE 3.9
Sources of Information for Completing Form 941

Line Number	Source of Information
1	Payroll register.
2	General ledger accounts for wages and salaries; Forms 4070, or employees' written statements reporting cash tips.
3	General ledger accounts.
4	General ledger balances.
5a	Payroll register; include any social security taxes (OASDI) paid for employees, sick pay, and taxable fringe benefits subject to OASDI. Do not include any tips. Do not report any employees' wages that exceed $147,000, the taxable wage base for 2022. 5a (i) Payroll Register 5a (ii) Payroll Register
5b	Forms 4070, or employees' written statements to report cash tips. Enter all tips reported until tips and wages for each employee reach $147,000. Report this information even if you are unable to withhold the employee OASDI tax. Do not include allocated tips, which should be reported on Form 8027.
5c	Payroll register; Forms 4070, or employees' written statements to report cash tips. Report amounts paid to certain federal, state, and local government employees who are subject only to the HI portion of the FICA tax.
5d	Payroll register; enter all wages, tips, sick pay, and taxable fringe benefits that are subject to additional Medicare tax withholding.
5f	Enter the tax due from Notice and Demand on line 5f. The IRS issues a Notice and Demand to advise an employer of the amount of tips received by employees who failed to report or underreported tips to the employer.
7	To adjust for fractions of cents: If there is a difference between the total tax on line 6 and the total deducted from your employees' wages or tips plus the employer's tax on those wages or tips (general ledger accounts) because of fractions of cents added or dropped in collecting the tax, report the difference. Enter this difference in the space for "Fractions of Cents." If a negative number is to be used, use a minus sign —.
8	To adjust for the tax on third-party sick pay: Deduct the social security tax on third-party sick pay for which you are not responsible. Enter the amount of the adjustment in the space for "Sick Pay."
9	To adjust for the tax on tips and group-term life insurance: Include the total uncollected employee social security tax for lines 5b and 5d.
11a	Form 8974, line 12.
11b	Worksheet 1, (not illustrated).
11d	Payroll Register
11e	Worksheet 3 (not illustrated)
11f	Payroll Register
13a	General ledger accounts, previous Form 941; record the total deposits for the quarter, including any overpayment applied from previous quarter.
13c	Worksheet 1 (not illustrated).
13e	Worksheet 1 (not illustrated)
13f	Worksheet 3 (not illustrated)
19 and 20	Worksheet 1 (not illustrated).
23	Payroll Register
24	General Ledger
25	Worksheet 2 (not illustrated)
26	Payroll Register
27 and 28	General Ledger

Source: Internal Revenue Service.

FIGURE 3.10
Report of Tax Liability for Semiweekly Schedule Depositors

Schedule B (Form 941):

Report of Tax Liability for Semiweekly Schedule Depositors

OMB No. 1545-0029

(Rev. January 2017) Department of the Treasury — Internal Revenue Service

Employer identification number (EIN) 0 0 — 0 0 0 7 7 7 9

Name *(not your trade name)* JUSTIN GRANATELLI

Calendar year 2 0 - -   (Also check quarter)

Report for this Quarter...
(Check one.)

[X] **1:** January, February, March

[ ] **2:** April, May, June

[ ] **3:** July, August, September

[ ] **4:** October, November, December

Use this schedule to show your **TAX LIABILITY** for the quarter; don't use it to show your deposits. When you file this form with Form 941 or Form 941-SS, don't change your tax liability by adjustments reported on any Forms 941-X or 944-X. You must fill out this form and attach it to Form 941 or Form 941-SS if you're a semiweekly schedule depositor or became one because your accumulated tax liability on any day was $100,000 or more. Write your daily tax liability on the numbered space that corresponds to the date wages were paid. See Section 11 in Pub. 15 for details.

Month 1

#		#		#		#		Tax liability for Month 1
1	.	9	.	17	.	25	.	
2	.	10	.	18	3189 . 34	26	.	6578 . 45
3	.	11	.	19	.	27	.	
4	3389 . 11	12	.	20	.	28	.	
5	.	13	.	21	.	29	.	
6	.	14	.	22	.	30	.	
7	.	15	.	23	.	31	.	
8	.	16	.	24	.			

Month 2

#		#		#		#		Tax liability for Month 2
1	3396 . 81	9	.	17	.	25	.	
2	.	10	.	18	.	26	.	6680 . 76
3	.	11	.	19	.	27	.	
4	.	12	.	20	.	28	.	
5	.	13	.	21	.	29	.	
6	.	14	.	22	.	30	.	
7	.	15	3283 . 95	23	.	31	.	
8	.	16	.	24	.			

Month 3

#		#		#		#		Tax liability for Month 3
1	3477 . 18	9	.	17	.	25	.	
2	.	10	.	18	.	26	.	10571 . 84
3	.	11	.	19	.	27	.	
4	.	12	.	20	.	28	.	
5	.	13	.	21	.	29	3780 . 06	
6	.	14	.	22	.	30	.	
7	.	15	3314 . 60	23	.	31	.	
8	.	16	.	24	.			

Fill in your total liability for the quarter (Month 1 + Month 2 + Month 3) ▶
Total must equal line 12 on Form 941 or Form 941-SS.

Total liability for the quarter

23831 . 05

For Paperwork Reduction Act Notice, see separate instructions. IRS.gov/form941 Cat. No. 11967Q Schedule B (Form 941) (Rev. 1-2017)

Source: Internal Revenue Service.

Part 5

The form must be signed by the employer or other person who is required to withhold and pay the tax. If the employer is:

1. An *individual*, the return should be signed by that person.

2. A *corporation*, the return should be signed by its president, vice president, or other principal officer authorized to sign the return. Corporate officers or duly authorized agents may use facsimile signatures under certain conditions.

3. A *partnership or other unincorporated organization*, a responsible and duly authorized partner or officer having knowledge of the firm's affairs should sign the return.

4. A *trust or estate*, the return should be signed by the fiduciary of the trust or estate.

5. A *political body*, such as a state or territory, the return should be signed by the officer or employee having control of the wage payments or officer properly designated for that purpose.

6. An *agent*, who pays the wages for the employer, may be authorized by the employer to sign the appropriate tax returns.

Employment tax forms can be signed by a facsimile-rubber stamp, mechanical device, or computer software program.

Employers can use credit cards to pay the balance due as shown on Form 941—this does not apply to tax deposits.

Filing Form 941

The law requires employers to file Form 941 on or before the last day of the month following the close of the calendar quarter for which the return applies. If an employer makes timely tax deposits for the quarter, the employer may file Form 941 on or before the 10th day of the second month following the close of the calendar quarter.

Payments can be made with Form 941 only if either the net taxes for the quarter (line 10) are less than $2,500 or the payment serves as a deposit for a monthly depositor in accordance with the accuracy of deposits rule (can be more than $2,500).

If the last day for filing a quarterly return falls on Saturday, Sunday, or a legal holiday, the employer may file the return on the next business day. If the return is filed by mailing, the employer should mail the return in sufficient time for it to reach the IRS Center no later than the next business day under ordinary handling of the mail.

---

1. An employer files a return by April 30 for the calendar quarter ending March 31.
2. An employer makes timely deposits for the quarter ending March 31. The form can be filed on or before May 10.
3. Pruit Company was not required to make any deposits for FICA taxes during the quarter ending March 31. The company makes its deposit for the first quarter taxes on April 15 for taxes due. Pruit can still file Form 941 on or before May 10 for the first quarter return.

Individual employers file quarterly returns with the IRS Center of the region in which the employer's principal place of business, office, or agency is located. The return may still be filed at the local office of the district director of the IRS if the taxpayer hand delivers the return.

After filing their first Form 941, employers must file returns for each quarter even if there were no taxes to report (unless they had checked box 17—business closed—in their last filing). The exception to this is for *seasonal employers* who do not have to file for quarters when they have no tax liability (they must check line 18 for every quarter that they do file).

Electronic Filing of Form 941

Several programs allow for the electronic filing of Form 941 information:

- 941 e-file programs: Business taxpayers, reporting agents, software developers, and transmitters can transmit the return electronically via an IRS-provided and certified secure Internet transport. The program sends electronic acknowledgements and builds records to be processed by IRS computer systems. An e-file application must be completed in order to participate in the program.
- 941 online filing programs: Taxpayers can file electronically through an authorized third-party transmitter using this Web-based system. To participate, businesses must apply for a PIN (personal identification number) by completing the PIN registration online at the IRS Web site.
- Electronic 941 filing for reporting agents: Reporting agents may directly file their clients' Forms 941 electronically under the 941 e-file program.

Undrey/Shutterstock.com

Non-Filers

Certain employers are not required to file this form.

- Seasonal employers—for quarters when they have no payroll tax liability because no wages were paid.
- Small employers—whose estimated annual tax liability is $2,500 or less.
- Employers of farmworkers—file an annual tax return, Form 943.
- Household employers—report and pay FICA taxes on their personal income tax return, Form 1040.

Form 941-X

Adjusted Employer's QUARTERLY Federal Tax Return or Claim for Refund is used to correct errors on previously filed Form 941s. It is a stand-alone form that is not attached to Form 941.

Form 944

Employer's ANNUAL Federal Tax Return can be used by employers who owe $1,000 or less in employment taxes per year and have not been late with any deposits for two years. These employers have to file the form and pay their employment taxes only once a year. Employers who believe they are eligible can contact the IRS and express their wish to file Form 944. The IRS will then send a notification letter to qualified Form 944 employers. A $2,500 threshold that

News Alert

Approximately 17 percent of tax filers are eligible to file Form 944.

triggers the federal tax deposit is different from the amount of the annual tax liability ($1,000 or less) that makes an employer eligible to file Form 944 for that year. However, they must start filing Form 941 at the beginning of the next year.

This return can also be used by new employers who expect to pay wages of $5,000 or less this year. Employers that are required to file Form 944 can notify the IRS if they want to file Form 941 quarterly instead.

The form (which is not illustrated) is basically the same as Form 941.

Failure-to-Comply Penalties

Employers act as collection agents for the government by collecting employment taxes and paying them to the appropriate government agency. Employers who fail to carry out their duties as collection agents are subject to civil and criminal penalties. The penalties may be additions to the tax, interest charges, and fines and imprisonment. Penalties also apply to federal income taxes (Chapter 4) and federal unemployment taxes (Chapter 5) and are imposed on employers who fail to do the following:

1. File employment tax returns.
2. Fully pay taxes when due.
3. Make timely deposits.
4. Furnish wage and tax statements.
5. File or provide information returns.
6. Supply identification numbers.

The penalty depends on the degree of willfulness present in the employer's conduct. Persons other than the employer who have the duty or responsibility for collecting, accounting for, and paying any taxes may also be assessed penalties. Passing bad checks in payment of any employment tax also carries a penalty.

Once Form 941 is received, it usually takes the IRS about five weeks to notify an employer of any tax delinquencies.

Failure to File Employment Tax Returns

If an employer fails to file an employment tax return on the date prescribed for filing, a certain percentage of the amount of tax required to be reported will be added to the tax. Employers may avoid this addition if they show to the satisfaction of the IRS that failure to file was due to reasonable cause and not willful conduct.

Additions to the Tax	5 percent combined penalty of the net amount of tax that should have been reported less any amounts timely paid; an additional 5 percent for each additional month or fraction of a month during which failure continues, not to exceed 25 percent.
	15 percent per month, not to exceed 75 percent, for fraudulent failure to file.
	Minimum penalty for failing to file within 60 days of its due date is the lesser of $435, or 100 percent of the amount required to be shown on the return.
Criminal Penalties	Not more than $25,000 ($100,000 for corporations), imprisonment of not more than one year, or both.
	Not more than $100,000, imprisonment of no more than three years, or both for willfully signing a return not true and correct as to every material statement.

Example 3-7

Ned Fromton, an employer, files his employment tax return 20 days after the due date of the return. The amount of tax that was unpaid is $6,000. Fromton's penalty is:

Failure to file (5% × $6,000) = $300 *Note:* Any fraction of a month counts as a whole month.

Failure to Fully Pay Employment Taxes

Employers who fail to pay the amount as shown on a return by the due date are faced with the following civil and criminal penalties:

IRS Connection %

Nearly one-third of small firms are hit with penalties for payroll mistakes, with the average fine being $848.

Additions to the Tax	0.5 percent of the amount shown as tax on a return per month or fraction of a month, not to exceed 25 percent. The amount on which the penalty is calculated can be reduced by payments made on or before the beginning of the month. If both penalties for filing a late return and for not fully paying the tax apply in the same month, the failure to file penalty is reduced by the amount of the failure to pay full penalty. There is also a separate 1.0 percent per month penalty for failing to pay a tax amount due that was not shown on the return within 21 days of the notice (10 days if the amount is $100,000 or greater) and demand from the IRS. The penalty is based on the amount in the IRS notice. In addition, any taxes due will bear *interest at the rate of 4 percent* per year. Large corporate underpayments ($100,000) will carry the rate of 6 percent.[4]
Additions to the Tax	20 percent of the underpayment for negligence (failure to make a reasonable attempt to comply) or intentional disregard (careless, reckless, or intentional disregard of the law) of the payment rules.
	75 percent of the underpayment if underpayment is due to fraud with the intent to evade the tax.
The 100% Penalty	100 percent of the tax due for willfully failing to collect, account for, or pay employment taxes or willfully attempting to evade or defeat the taxes.
Tax Levies	Levy on and seize any property and property rights held by the employer at the time of levy for failure of the employer to pay any taxes, 10 days after notice and demand for payment.
Criminal Penalties	Not more than $10,000, imprisonment of no more than five years, or both, for willful failure to pay the tax. These penalties are in addition to the 75 percent fraud penalty.

---

4 The IRS sets the interest rate each calendar quarter, based on the short-term Treasury bill rate for the first month in each calendar quarter, plus five percentage points, and applies it for the following calendar quarter. The rate stated is for the second quarter of 2022.

Example 3-8

Yeld Company failed to pay its employment taxes of $5,000 for March 20-- (due April 15) until May 20. The failure to pay penalty assessed against Yeld Company is:

Failure to Pay Tax ($5,000 × 0.5% × 2)	=	$50.00
Interest on Taxes Due, assume a 4% interest rate ($5,000 × 0.04 × 35/365)	=	19.18
Total Penalty		$69.18

Note: In addition, a penalty for failure to make a timely deposit will also be assessed.

On the Job

Deposits are applied to the most recent tax liabilities within the quarter; however, a depositor can designate to the IRS the period to which a deposit is to be applied. The employer has 90 days from the date of a penalty notice to make the designation.

Failure to Make Timely Deposits

Penalties may apply if employers do not make required deposits on time in an authorized government depository.

Deposits made 1 to 5 calendar days late	2 percent of the undeposited taxes
Deposits made 6 to 15 days late	5 percent of the undeposited taxes
Deposits made 16 or more days late	10 percent of the undeposited taxes
Deposits made at unauthorized financial institutions or directly to IRS	10 percent of the undeposited taxes
Deposits subject to electronic deposit requirements but not deposited by EFTPS	10 percent of the tax deposit required
Amounts unpaid more than 10 days after IRS notice	15 percent of the undeposited taxes

Example 3-9

Greerson Inc. must make a deposit of $1,800 on June 15, 20--. The deposit was made 11 days late. The penalty assessed against Greerson is:

Failure to make timely deposit ($1,800 × 5%) = $90

Failure to Furnish Payee Statements

If employers willfully fail to furnish their employees with properly executed wage and tax statements or willfully furnish false or fraudulent statements (employee's copy of W-2 or recipient's Form 1099—discussed in Chapter 4), the civil penalty is $290 for each statement.[5]

Maximum Penalty	$3,532,500 in any calendar year ($1,177,500 for small businesses).[6]
Intentional Disregard	$580 per statement with no limit on the maximum penalty for the calendar year.
Criminal Penalties	$5,000 or more, plus may be subject to criminal sanctions.

Failure to Furnish Information Returns

Employers who fail to timely file their information returns **with the government** (any 1099 series or Forms W-2) are subject to fines for each failure. These penalties also apply to failures to include all required information on

---

5 Penalties will be adjusted for annual inflation.

6 Small business is a concern whose average annual gross receipts for the three years before the year in question were $5 million or less. If less than three years, the entire period in existence is used.

the forms, to supply only correct information, to file magnetically if required, and to report correct taxpayer identification numbers. The penalty is based on when the correct information is filed.[7]

Correction within 30 days	$50 per failure, maximum fine of $588,500 ($206,000 for small businesses).
Correction after 30 days, before August 1	$110 per failure, maximum fine $1,766,000 ($588,500 for small businesses).
Not filed correctly by August 1	$290 per return, maximum fine $3,532,500 ($1,177,500 for small businesses).
Intentional disregard	$580 per statement with no limit on the maximum penalty for the calendar year.

Bad Checks

Checks or money orders not tendered in good faith	2 percent of the amount. If the check, money order, or electronic payment is less than $1,250, penalty is $25 or the amount of the check, whichever is less.

Crispy Fish Images/Shutterstock.com

Key Terms

educational assistance (p. 3-8)

employer (p. 3-2)

employment (p. 3-2)

independent contractors (p. 3-4)

lookback period (p. 3-18)

monthly depositor (p. 3-19)

person (p. 3-2)

safe harbor rule (p. 3-19)

self-employment income (p. 3-13)

semiweekly depositor (p. 3-19)

shortfall (p. 3-19)

sick pay (p. 3-8)

taxable wage base (p. 3-9)

---

7 Penalties will be adjusted for annual inflation.

Answers to Self-Study Quizzes

Self-Study Quiz 3-1

1. Yes. Full-time life insurance salespersons are covered as statutory employees for social security, Medicare, and FUTA tax purposes.
2. Yes. Federal government employees hired after 1983 are subject to full FICA coverage.
3. No. Real estate agents are considered independent contractors.
4. No. Schuck offers his services to the general public and is considered an independent contractor.

Self-Study Quiz 3-2

1. Yes. The gift certificates are considered cash equivalents.
2. Yes. Personal use of a company vehicle for nonbusiness-related activities constitutes a taxable fringe benefit.
3. No. An employer may contribute to an SEP setup by or on behalf of its employees. The employer's contributions are exempt from FICA taxes if reason to believe exists that employees will be entitled to deduct the employer contributions for federal income tax purposes.
4. No. Generally, employers do not have to include in wages or withhold on the value of payment made for job-related training for their employees.
5. Yes. Payments by employers for involuntary separation of an employee from the employer's service are taxable under FICA.

Self-Study Quiz 3-3

Employee	OASDI	HI
Tammy Wolf	$ 13.95	$ 3.26
Bill Young	18.60	4.35
Howard Feldman	10.85	2.54
Carin Clever	62.00	14.50
Bud McAvoy	192.20	44.95
Totals	$297.60	$69.60
Employer's taxes	$ 297.60	$ 69.60
(based on $4,800 gross wages)		

Bud McAvoy will earn an annual salary of $161,200, which exceeds the wage base for OASDI taxes ($147,000).

Through the 47th weekly payday, McAvoy will have cumulative wages of $145,700.

When the payment is made on the 48th payday, McAvoy will exceed the wage base for OASDI taxes:

Cumulative wages taxes	$145,700
Current wage payment	3,100
	$148,800

Therefore, only $1,300 is taxable ($147,000 − $145,700).

Self-Study Quiz 3-4

1. $54,000 [($1,000 per week × 52) + $2,000 bonus]
2. $82,000 ($54,000 + $28,000)
3. $28,000 (taxable wage base $147,000)
4. $4,284 [($28,000 × 0.124) + ($28,000 × 0.029)]

Self-Study Quiz 3-5

1. Johnson should pay its taxes by the following Wednesday.
2. During the first calendar year for a new business, the company is a monthly depositor. However, if during the year it has an undeposited tax liability of $100,000 (which triggers the one-banking-day rule), the company becomes a semiweekly depositor for the remainder of the year.
3. The additional taxes are not accumulated with the previous liability of $105,000. The company should follow the semiweekly deposit rules and pay the $20,000 by Friday.

Key Points Summary

	Learning Objectives	Key Points	Problem Sets A & B
LO1	Identify, for social security purposes, those persons covered under the law and those services that make up employment.	• Employer/employee relationship, service is employment and compensation is taxable wages. • Specific coverage—agent-drivers, life insurance salespersons, traveling salespersons, and home workers. • Independent contractors are not employees but are taxed for FICA on earnings of their business.	
LO2	Identify the types of compensation that are defined as wages.	• Wages, bonuses, and commissions are taxed. • Tips of $20 or more a month are taxable—employer collects tax from the wage payments to the tipped employee.	3-3, 3-4, 3-17
LO3	Apply the current tax rates and wage base for FICA and SECA purposes. ▶ Tell Me More	• Employer's OASDI—6.2 percent on first $147,000; HI—1.45 percent on total wages plus additional 0.9 percent on wages in excess of $200,000. • Employer's OASDI—6.2 percent on first $147,000. HI—1.45 percent on total wages. • Employer collects tax from the employees' wages and calculates the employer's share. • Rate for all self-employed is 12.4 percent and 2.9 percent, respectively. Self-employed also subject to supplemental 0.9 percent HI tax on earned income in excess of $200,000. • Employer ID number—Form SS-4. • Employee social security number—Form SS-5. • Form 941—employers' quarterly information return.	3-1, 3-2, 3-3, 3-4, 3-5, 3-6, 3-7, 3-8, 3-9, 3-10, 3-17
LO4	Describe the different requirements and procedures for depositing FICA taxes and income taxes withheld from employees' wages.	• Amount of taxes reported in the "lookback" period determines status. • Deposits—Employees' Withheld FICA Taxes + Employer's FICA Taxes + Employees' FIT Taxes. • Monthly depositors—15th of following month. • Semiweekly depositors—Wednesday, Thursday, or Friday payday (following Wednesday); Saturday, Sunday, Monday, or Tuesday payday (following Friday). • One-day rule—$100,000 or more in undeposited taxes on any day during a deposit period. • Deposits made electronically.	3-15
LO5	Complete Form 941, Employer's QUARTERLY Federal Tax Return. ▶ Tell Me More	• Form 941 due one month after the end of each quarter. • Semiweekly and one-day depositors must also complete Schedule B—Report of Tax Liability. • Penalties for failure to file returns and to pay employment taxes.	3-11, 3-12, 3-13, 3-14, 3-15, 3-16

Matching Quiz

_____ 1. Employee's FICA tax rates
_____ 2. Form SS-4
_____ 3. Semiweekly depositor
_____ 4. Taxable for FICA
_____ 5. Nontaxable for FICA
_____ 6. Self-employed's FICA tax rates
_____ 7. Form 941
_____ 8. Monthly depositor
_____ 9. OASDI taxable wage base
_____ 10. Form SS-5

A. Severance pay
B. By the 15th day of the following month
C. Employer's QUARTERLY Federal Tax Return
D. Application for Employer Identification Number
E. 6.2 percent and 1.45 percent
F. Employee's application for social security card
G. Cumulative wages of $147,000
H. More than $50,000 in employment taxes in the lookback period
I. 12.4 percent and 2.9 percent
J. Employer's matching contributions into employees' deferred compensation arrangements

Questions for Review

1. For social security purposes, what conditions must an individual meet to be classified as a "covered" employer?
2. For social security purposes, what conditions must an individual meet to be classified as a "covered" employee?
3. Under what conditions does a common-law relationship exist between an employee and an employer?
4. Summarize the test conditions under which a worker is classified as an independent contractor.
5. What are an employer's responsibilities for FICA taxes on:
   a. Tips reported by employees?
   b. Wages paid tipped employees?
6. What conditions exclude sick pay from the definition of wages for FICA tax purposes?
7. What is the FICA tax liability status of pretax contributions to a qualified deferred compensation arrangement?

8. John Luis receives wages from three employers during 20--. Is he entitled to a refund on the OASDI taxes paid on wages in excess of the taxable wage base? If so, how can he receive a refund?
9. What are the self-employment tax rates for 2022? Explain how the tax is computed.
10. How does an employer file an application for an employer identification number?
11. Summarize the deposit rules for nonagricultural employers.
12. Which employers must deposit their employment taxes electronically?
13. How are the electronic tax deposits transferred from the employer's account to the IRS?
14. How often must an employer file Form 941?
15. List the penalties imposed on the employer for the following:
    a. Filing Form 941 late.
    b. Seven days late making a deposit.
    c. Issuing a bad check to the IRS.

Questions for Discussion

1. During the year, employee Sean Matthews earned wages in the amount of $250,000. Discuss how the employee's HI tax will differ from the employer's HI tax for this employee.
2. In order to improve the cash flow of the company, Neal Emerald decided to postpone depositing all employment taxes a few months ago. He told his sales manager, "I'll pay up before the IRS catches up with me." What risks does Emerald face by not upholding his responsibility for the collection and payment of employment taxes?
3. Instead of being classified as an employee, Matthew McGinnis was misclassified as an independent contractor. How will Quality Company's employer FICA taxes be affected? What penalty will the employer face for this misclassification?
4. When employees of County Bank are summoned to serve on jury duty, the firm pays its workers the difference between their regular wages and the amount received for jury duty. One such employee has been receiving $365 per week. She just completed a five-day week of jury duty, for which she was paid $65 ($9 per day plus 20 cents per mile from her house to the courthouse, a 20-mile round trip). How much of the employee's earnings are subject to FICA tax?

Problem Set • A

Note: In this chapter and in all succeeding work throughout the course, *unless instructed otherwise*, use the following rates, ceiling, and maximum taxes.

Employee and Employer OASDI:	6.20%	$147,000	$9,114.00
Employee* and Employer HI:	1.45%	No limit	No maximum
Self-employed OASDI:	12.4%	$147,000	$18,228.00
Self-employed HI:	2.9%	No limit	No maximum

For rounding rules, refer to page 2-37.

*Employee HI: Plus an additional 0.9% on wages over $200,000. Also applicable to self-employed.

3-1A • LO 3   See Example 3-1 on page 3-11, Example 3-2 on page 3-12

The biweekly taxable wages for the employees of Rite-Shop follow. Compute the FICA taxes for each employee and the employer's FICA taxes.

			FICA Taxes	
Employee No.	Employee Name	Biweekly Taxable Wages	OASDI	HI
711	Castro, Manny	$1,000.00	$ _____	$ _____
512	Corrales, Pat	968.00	_____	_____
624	Guitar, Joseph	1,004.00	_____	_____
325	Moore, Connie	1,046.40	_____	_____
422	Morrison, Harry	1,200.00	_____	_____
210	Robertson, Catherine	1,044.80	_____	_____
111	Swarez, Joseph	1,122.00	_____	_____
		Totals	$ _____	$ _____

Employer's OASDI $ _____ $ _____
                  Total Taxable Wages   Employer's OASDI Tax

Employer's HI Tax $ _____ $ _____
                  Total Taxable Wages   Employer's HI Tax

3-2A • LO 3   See Example 3-1 on page 3-11
Show Me How

During 20--, Rachael Lopez, president of Mathieson Company, was paid a semimonthly salary of $9,000. Compute the amount of FICA taxes that should be withheld from her:

	OASDI	HI
a. 9th paycheck	$ _____	$ _____
b. 17th paycheck	$ _____	$ _____
c. 23rd paycheck	$ _____	$ _____
d. If Lopez's year-to-date earnings as of her 24th paycheck are $216,000, and her year-end bonus is $100,000, how much is the additional 0.9% HI tax?		$ _____

3-3A • LO 2, 3 See Example 3-1 on page 3-11

Ernie Gilmore began working as a part-time waiter on June 1, 20--, at Sporthouse Restaurant. The cash tips of $390 that he received during June were reported on Form 4070, which he submitted to his employer on July 3. During July, he was paid wages of $525 by the restaurant. Compute OASDI and HI:

		OASDI	HI
a.	The amount of FICA taxes that the employer should withhold from Gilmore's wages during July.	$ _____	$ _____
b.	The amount of the employer's FICA taxes on Gilmore's wages and tips during July.	$ _____	$ _____

3-4A • LO 2, 3 See Example 3-1 on page 3-11

Ken Gorman is a maitre d' at Carmel Dinner Club. On February 1, 20-- his gross pay was $800 (three days working, one paid vacation day, and one paid sick day). He also reported to his employer tips of $900 for the previous month (applicable taxes to be deducted out of this pay). Gorman belongs to the company's 401(k) plan and has 5% of his gross pay ($800) deducted each week (salary reduction). Carmel Dinner Club also provides a matching contribution ($40) into the plan for Gorman. This week's pay would have a:

a. Deduction for OASDI tax $ _____

b. Deduction for HI tax $ _____

3-5A • LO 3 See Example 3-1 on page 3-11

In 20--, the annual salaries paid each of the officers of Abrew, Inc., follow. The officers are paid semimonthly on the 15th and the last day of the month. Compute the FICA taxes to be withheld from each officer's pay on (a) November 15 and (b) December 31.

a.

Name and Title	Annual Salary	November 15			
		OASDI Taxable Earnings	OASDI Tax	HI Taxable Earnings	HI Tax
Hanks, Timothy, President	$174,000	_____	_____	_____	_____
Grath, John, VP Finance	148,800	_____	_____	_____	_____
James, Sally, VP Sales	69,600	_____	_____	_____	_____
Kimmel, Joan, VP Mfg.	54,000	_____	_____	_____	_____
Wie, Pam, VP Personnel	51,600	_____	_____	_____	_____
Grant, Mary, VP Secretary	49,200	_____	_____	_____	_____

b.

Name and Title	Annual Salary	December 31			
		OASDI Taxable Earnings	OASDI Tax	HI Taxable Earnings	HI Tax
Hanks, Timothy, President	$174,000	_____	_____	_____	_____
Grath, John, VP Finance	148,800	_____	_____	_____	_____
James, Sally, VP Sales	69,600	_____	_____	_____	_____
Kimmel, Joan, VP Mfg.	54,000	_____	_____	_____	_____
Wie, Pam, VP Personnel	51,600	_____	_____	_____	_____
Grant, Mary, VP Secretary	49,200	_____	_____	_____	_____

3-6A • LO 3 **See Example 3-1 on page 3-11, Example 3-2 on page 3-12**

Audrey Martin and Beth James are partners in the Country Gift Shop, which employs the individuals listed below. Paychecks are distributed every Friday to all employees. Based on the information given, compute the amounts listed below for a weekly payroll period.

Name and Position	Salary	OASDI Taxable Earnings	OASDI Tax	HI Taxable Earnings	HI Tax
Zena Vertin, Office	$ 700 per week	_____	_____	_____	_____
Nicole Norge, Sales	2,980 per month	_____	_____	_____	_____
Bob Mert, Delivery	650 per week	_____	_____	_____	_____
Audrey Martin, Partner	950 per week	_____	_____	_____	_____
Beth James, Partner	950 per week	_____	_____	_____	_____
Totals		$ _____	$ _____	$ _____	$ _____

Employer's OASDI Tax $ _____

Employer's HI Tax $ _____

3-7A • LO 3 **See Example 3-1 on page 3-11, Example 3-2 on page 3-12**

Volpe Corporation has only five employees who are all paid $850 per week. Compute the total FICA taxes that the employer would withhold from the five employees each week and the amount the company would pay as its own liability for the employer's share of the FICA taxes on the weekly wages of the five employees:

Employees' total OASDI......... $ _____

Employees' total HI .... $ _____

Employer's total OASDI.......... $ _____

Employer's total HI .... $ _____

3-8A • LO 3 **See Example 3-5 on page 3-14**

Ralph Henwood was paid a salary of $64,600 during 20-- by Odesto Company. In addition, during the year, Henwood started his own business as a public accountant and reported a net business income of $90,000 on his income tax return for 20--. Compute the following:

a. The amount of FICA taxes that was withheld from his earnings during 20-- by Odesto Company.

OASDI $ _____
HI $ _____

b. Henwood's self-employment taxes on the income derived from the public accounting business for 20--.

OASDI $ _____
HI $ _____

3-9A • LO 3 See Example 3-1 on page 3-11, Example 3-2 on page 3-12

Empty Fields Company pays its salaried employees monthly on the last day of each month. The annual salary payroll for 20-- follows. Compute the following for the payroll of December 31:

Employee	Annual Salary	OASDI Taxable Wages	OASDI Tax	HI Taxable Wages	HI Tax
Utley, Genna	$ 37,040				
Werth, Norm	48,900				
Bass, John	40,000				
Ruiz, Sam	150,000				
Compton, Sue	36,900				
Williams, Mary	48,500				
Patel, Raymond	106,080				
Carson, Abe	56,900				
Livinsky, Sarah	37,850				
Harper, Mark	51,200				
Totals		$	$	$	$

Employer's OASDI Tax $ _____

Employer's HI Tax $ _____

3-10A • LO 3 See Example 3-1 on page 3-11

The monthly and hourly wage schedule for the employees of Quirk, Inc., follows. No employees are due overtime pay. Compute the following for the last monthly pay of the year:

- **a.** The total wages of each part-time employee for December 20--.
- **b.** The OASDI and HI taxable wages for each employee.
- **c.** The FICA taxes withheld from each employee's wages for December.
- **d.** Totals of columns.
- **e.** The employer's FICA taxes for the month.

Employees	Total Monthly Payroll	OASDI Taxable Wages	OASDI Tax	HI Taxable Wages	HI Tax
Full-Time Office:					
Adaiar, Gene	$2,450.00				
Crup, Jason	2,800.00				
Essex, Joan	2,975.00				
Garza, Irma	2,985.00				
Leason, Mel	2,900.00				
Pruit, Marne	7,000.00				
Rubble, Deanne	2,400.00				
Simpson, Dick	3,985.00				
Truap, Ann	5,000.00				
Wilson, Trudy	2,440.00				

3-10A (concluded)

	Hours Worked	Hourly Rate	Total Monthly	OASDI Taxable Wages	OASDI Tax	HI Taxable Wages	HI Tax
Part-Time Office:							
Kyle, Judy	170	$16.50	_____	_____	_____	_____	_____
Laird, Sharon	170	16.60	_____	_____	_____	_____	_____
Maxwell, Sara	140	17.00	_____	_____	_____	_____	_____
Nelson, Donna	145	18.20	_____	_____	_____	_____	_____
Scott, Kim	162	16.00	_____	_____	_____	_____	_____
Totals for all employees			$ _____	$ _____	$ _____	$ _____	$ _____
Employer's FICA taxes				OASDI $ _____		HI $ _____	

3-11A • LO 5   See Figure 3.8 on pages 3-23 and 3-24

Cruz Company has gathered the information needed to complete its Form 941 for the quarter ended September 30, 20--. Using the information presented below, complete Part 1 of Form 941, reproduced on pages 3-42 and 3-43.

> # of employees for pay period that included September 12—14 employees
> Wages paid third quarter—$79,750.17
> Federal income tax withheld in the third quarter—$9,570.00
> Taxable social security and Medicare wages—$79,750.17
> Total tax deposits for the quarter—$21,771.83

3-12A • LO 5   See Figure 3.8 on pages 3-24 and 3-25

Refer to Problem 3-11A. Complete Parts 2, 4, and 5 of Form 941 (on pages 3-43 and 3-44) for Cruz Company for the third quarter of 20--. Cruz Company is a monthly depositor with the following monthly tax liabilities for this quarter:

July	$7,193.10
August	7,000.95
September	7,577.78

State unemployment taxes are only paid to California. The company does not use a third-party designee, the tax returns are signed by the president, Carlos Cruz (Phone: 916-555-9739), and the date filed is October 31, 20--.

3-11A (continued)

Form **941 for 20--:** **Employer's QUARTERLY Federal Tax Return**
(Rev. March 2022)   Department of the Treasury — Internal Revenue Service

OMB No. 1545-0029

Employer identification number (EIN) 0 0 – 0 0 0 6 5 0 9

Name (not your trade name) CARLOS CRUZ

Trade name (if any) CRUZ COMPANY

Address 901 KEYSTONE
Number   Street   Suite or room number

SACRAMENTO   CA   95919
City   State   ZIP code

Foreign country name   Foreign province/county   Foreign postal code

Report for this Quarter of 20--
(Check one.)

☐ **1:** January, February, March

☐ **2:** April, May, June

☐ **3:** July, August, September

☐ **4:** October, November, December

Go to *www.irs.gov/Form941* for instructions and the latest information.

Read the separate instructions before you complete Form 941. Type or print within the boxes.

Part 1:   Answer these questions for this quarter.

1   Number of employees who received wages, tips, or other compensation for the pay period including: *Mar. 12* (Quarter 1) . . . .   1 [   ]

2   Wages, tips, and other compensation . . . .   2 [.]

3   Federal income tax withheld from wages, tips, and other compensation . . . . . .   3 [.]

4   If no wages, tips, and other compensation are subject to social security or Medicare tax   ☐ Check and go to line 6.

		Column 1		Column 2	
5a	Taxable social security wages* . .	[.]	× 0.124 =	[.]	
5a	(i) Qualified sick leave wages* .	[.]	× 0.062 =	[.]	
5a	(ii) Qualified family leave wages* .	[.]	× 0.062 =	[.]	
5b	Taxable social security tips . . .	[.]	× 0.124 =	[.]	
5c	Taxable Medicare wages & tips. .	[.]	× 0.029 =	[.]	
5d	Taxable wages & tips subject to Additional Medicare Tax withholding	[.]	× 0.009 =	[.]	

*Include taxable qualified sick and family leave wages paid in 2022 for leave taken after March 31, 2021, and before October 1, 2021, on line 5a. Use lines 5a(i) and 5a(ii) only for taxable qualified sick and family leave wages paid in 2022 for leave taken after March 31, 2020, and before April 1, 2021.

5e   Total social security and Medicare taxes. Add Column 2 from lines 5a, 5a(i), 5a(ii), 5b, 5c, and 5d   5e [.]

5f   Section 3121(q) Notice and Demand—Tax due on unreported tips (see instructions) . .   5f [.]

6   Total taxes before adjustments. Add lines 3, 5e, and 5f . . . .   6 [.]

7   Current quarter's adjustment for fractions of cents . . . .   7 [.]

8   Current quarter's adjustment for sick pay . . . .   8 [.]

9   Current quarter's adjustments for tips and group-term life insurance . . . . . .   9 [.]

10   Total taxes after adjustments. Combine lines 6 through 9 . . . .   10 [.]

11a   Qualified small business payroll tax credit for increasing research activities. Attach Form 8974   11a [.]

11b   Nonrefundable portion of credit for qualified sick and family leave wages for leave taken before April 1, 2021 . . . .   11b [.]

11c   Reserved for future use . . . .   11c [.]

▶ **You MUST complete all three pages of Form 941 and SIGN it.**   Next ▶

For Privacy Act and Paperwork Reduction Act Notice, see the back of the Payment Voucher.   Cat. No. 17001Z   Form **941** (Rev. 3-2022)

3-11A (concluded) and 3-12A

Name *(not your trade name)*	Employer identification number (EIN)
CARLOS CRUZ	00-0006509

Part 1: Answer these questions for this quarter. *(continued)*

11d **Nonrefundable portion of credit for qualified sick and family leave wages for leave taken after March 31, 2021, and before October 1, 2021** . . . . **11d** [_____ . __]

11e **Nonrefundable portion of COBRA premium assistance credit (see instructions for applicable quarter)** . . . . **11e** [_____ . __]

11f **Number of individuals provided COBRA premium assistance** [_____]

11g **Total nonrefundable credits.** Add lines 11a, 11b, 11d, and 11e . . . . **11g** [_____ . __]

12 **Total taxes after adjustments and nonrefundable credits.** Subtract line 11g from line 10 . **12** [_____ . __]

13a **Total deposits for this quarter, including overpayment applied from a prior quarter and overpayments applied from Form 941-X, 941-X (PR), 944-X, or 944-X (SP) filed in the current quarter** **13a** [_____ . __]

13b **Reserved for future use** . . . . **13b** [_____ . __]

13c **Refundable portion of credit for qualified sick and family leave wages for leave taken before April 1, 2021** . . . . **13c** [_____ . __]

13d **Reserved for future use** . . . . **13d** [_____ . __]

13e **Refundable portion of credit for qualified sick and family leave wages for leave taken after March 31, 2021, and before October 1, 2021** . . . . **13e** [_____ . __]

13f **Refundable portion of COBRA premium assistance credit (see instructions for applicable quarter)** . . . . **13f** [_____ . __]

13g **Total deposits and refundable credits.** Add lines 13a, 13c, 13e, and 13f . . . . . . **13g** [_____ . __]

13h **Reserved for future use** . . . . **13h** [_____ . __]

13i **Reserved for future use** . . . . **13i** [_____ . __]

14 **Balance due.** If line 12 is more than line 13g, enter the difference and see instructions . . . **14** [_____ . __]

15 **Overpayment.** If line 13g is more than line 12, enter the difference [_____ . __] Check one: ☐ Apply to next return. ☐ Send a refund.

Part 2: Tell us about your deposit schedule and tax liability for this quarter.

If you're unsure about whether you're a monthly schedule depositor or a semiweekly schedule depositor, see section 11 of Pub. 15.

16 **Check one:** ☐ **Line 12 on this return is less than $2,500 or line 12 on the return for the prior quarter was less than $2,500, and you didn't incur a $100,000 next-day deposit obligation during the current quarter.** If line 12 for the prior quarter was less than $2,500 but line 12 on this return is $100,000 or more, you must provide a record of your federal tax liability. If you're a monthly schedule depositor, complete the deposit schedule below; if you're a semiweekly schedule depositor, attach Schedule B (Form 941). Go to Part 3.

☐ **You were a monthly schedule depositor for the entire quarter.** Enter your tax liability for each month and total liability for the quarter, then go to Part 3.

Tax liability: Month 1 [_____ . __]

Month 2 [_____ . __]

Month 3 [_____ . __]

Total liability for quarter [_____ . __] **Total must equal line 12.**

☐ **You were a semiweekly schedule depositor for any part of this quarter.** Complete Schedule B (Form 941), Report of Tax Liability for Semiweekly Schedule Depositors, and attach it to Form 941. Go to Part 3.

► **You MUST complete all three pages of Form 941 and SIGN it.** Next ▶

3-12A (concluded)

Name *(not your trade name)*	Employer identification number (EIN)
CARLOS CRUZ	00-0006509

Part 3: Tell us about your business. If a question does NOT apply to your business, leave it blank.

17 If your business has closed or you stopped paying wages . . . . ☐ Check here, and

enter the final date you paid wages [/   /   ] ; also attach a statement to your return. See instructions.

18 If you're a seasonal employer and you don't have to file a return for every quarter of the year . . . ☐ Check here.

19 Qualified health plan expenses allocable to qualified sick leave wages for leave taken before April 1, 2021   **19** [·]

20 Qualified health plan expenses allocable to qualified family leave wages for leave taken before April 1, 2021   **20** [·]

21 Reserved for future use . . . . **21** [·]

22 Reserved for future use . . . . **22** [·]

23 Qualified sick leave wages for leave taken after March 31, 2021, and before October 1, 2021   **23** [·]

24 Qualified health plan expenses allocable to qualified sick leave wages reported on line 23   **24** [·]

25 Amounts under certain collectively bargained agreements allocable to qualified sick leave wages reported on line 23 . . . . **25** [·]

26 Qualified family leave wages for leave taken after March 31, 2021, and before October 1, 2021   **26** [·]

27 Qualified health plan expenses allocable to qualified family leave wages reported on line 26   **27** [·]

28 Amounts under certain collectively bargained agreements allocable to qualified family leave wages reported on line 26 . . . . **28** [·]

Part 4: May we speak with your third-party designee?

Do you want to allow an employee, a paid tax preparer, or another person to discuss this return with the IRS? See the instructions for details.

☐ Yes. Designee's name and phone number [   ] [   ]

     Select a 5-digit personal identification number (PIN) to use when talking to the IRS. [ ] [ ] [ ] [ ] [ ]

☐ No.

Part 5: Sign here. You MUST complete all three pages of Form 941 and SIGN it.

Under penalties of perjury, I declare that I have examined this return, including accompanying schedules and statements, and to the best of my knowledge and belief, it is true, correct, and complete. Declaration of preparer (other than taxpayer) is based on all information of which preparer has any knowledge.

X   Sign your name here [   ]

Print your name here [   ]

Print your title here [   ]

Date [/   /   ]

Best daytime phone [   ]

Paid Preparer Use Only

Check if you're self-employed . . . ☐

Preparer's name	[ ]	PTIN	[ ]
Preparer's signature	[ ]	Date	[/ /]
Firm's name (or yours if self-employed)	[ ]	EIN	[ ]
Address	[ ]	Phone	[ ]
City	[ ] State [ ]	ZIP code	[ ]

Page **3**

Form **941** (Rev. 3-2022)

Source: Internal Revenue Service.

Date _____ Name _____

Show
Me How

3-13A • LO 5   **See Figure 3.8 on pages 3-23 to 3-25**

Karen Kluster opened Lube and Wash on January 2, 20--. The business is subject to FICA taxes. At the end of the first quarter of 20--, Kluster, as a president of the company, must file Form 941, Employer's QUARTERLY Federal Tax Return. Using Form 941 (Parts 1 through 5), reproduced on pages 3-46 to 3-48, prepare, sign, and date the return on the basis of the information shown below.

Employer's address:	234 Oak, Austin, TX 78711-0234
Employer's ID number:	00-0005874
Phone number:	(512)555-1111
Date filed:	April 30, 20--

Each employee is paid semimonthly on the 15th and last day of each month. Shown below is the payroll information for the first quarter of 20--. All pay periods were the same.

PAYROLL INFORMATION FOR JANUARY–MARCH

Employee	SSN	Quarterly Wage	OASDI Tax	HI Tax	Federal Income Tax	Total Deductions	Net Pay
Paul Purson	000-00-7233	$12,000.00	$ 744.00	$174.00	$1,260.00	$2,178.00	$ 9,822.00
Matt Dirkson	000-00-8451	12,600.00	781.20	182.70	1,200.00	2,163.90	10,436.10
Joan Howard	000-00-3668	12,500.00	775.02	181.26	1,080.00	2,036.28	10,463.72
Dorrie Smith	000-00-6527	10,800.00	669.60	156.60	1,140.00	1,966.20	8,833.80
Totals		$47,900.00	$2,969.82	$694.56	$4,680.00	$8,344.38	$39,555.62
Employer's FICA taxes for the quarter			$2,969.80 OASDI	$694.55 HI			

The total taxes per payday are:

Employees' FICA Tax—OASDI	$ 494.97
Employer's FICA Tax—OASDI	494.97
Employees' FICA Tax—HI	115.76
Employer's FICA Tax—HI	115.76
Employees' FIT	780.00
Total	$2,001.46 × 6 deposits = $12,008.76 for the quarter

None of the employees reported tips during the quarter.

Note: Lines 5a and 5c of Form 941, tax on total taxable wages, are computed by multiplying by the combined tax rate for both employer and employee. Small differences due to rounding may occur between this total and the total taxes withheld from employees each pay period and the amount of the employer's taxes calculated each pay period. This difference is reported on line 7 as a deduction or an addition as "Fractions of Cents."

3-13A (continued)

Form **941 for 20--:** **Employer's QUARTERLY Federal Tax Return**
(Rev. March 2022)   Department of the Treasury — Internal Revenue Service

OMB No. 1545-0029

Employer identification number (EIN)   0 0 – 0 0 0 5 8 7 4

Name (not your trade name)   KAREN KLUSTER

Trade name (if any)   LUBE AND WASH

Address   234 OAK
Number   Street   Suite or room number

AUSTIN   TX   78711-0234
City   State   ZIP code

Foreign country name   Foreign province/county   Foreign postal code

Report for this Quarter of 20--
(Check one.)

- ☐ **1:** January, February, March
- ☐ **2:** April, May, June
- ☐ **3:** July, August, September
- ☐ **4:** October, November, December

Go to *www.irs.gov/Form941* for instructions and the latest information.

Read the separate instructions before you complete Form 941. Type or print within the boxes.

Part 1:   Answer these questions for this quarter.

1   Number of employees who received wages, tips, or other compensation for the pay period including: *Mar. 12* (Quarter 1) . . . . **1** ☐

2   Wages, tips, and other compensation . . . . **2** ☐

3   Federal income tax withheld from wages, tips, and other compensation . . . . . . **3** ☐

4   If no wages, tips, and other compensation are subject to social security or Medicare tax ☐ **Check and go to line 6.**

		Column 1		Column 2	
5a	Taxable social security wages* . .	☐	× 0.124 =	☐	
5a (i)	Qualified sick leave wages* .	☐	× 0.062 =	☐	
5a (ii)	Qualified family leave wages* .	☐	× 0.062 =	☐	
5b	Taxable social security tips . . .	☐	× 0.124 =	☐	
5c	Taxable Medicare wages & tips. .	☐	× 0.029 =	☐	
5d	Taxable wages & tips subject to Additional Medicare Tax withholding	☐	× 0.009 =	☐	

*Include taxable qualified sick and family leave wages paid in 2022 for leave taken after March 31, 2021, and before October 1, 2021, on line 5a. Use lines 5a(i) and 5a(ii) **only** for taxable qualified sick and family leave wages paid in 2022 for leave taken after March 31, 2020, and before April 1, 2021.*

5e   Total social security and Medicare taxes. Add Column 2 from lines 5a, 5a(i), 5a(ii), 5b, 5c, and 5d   **5e** ☐

5f   Section 3121(q) Notice and Demand—Tax due on unreported tips (see instructions) . . **5f** ☐

6   Total taxes before adjustments. Add lines 3, 5e, and 5f . . . . **6** ☐

7   Current quarter's adjustment for fractions of cents . . . . **7** ☐

8   Current quarter's adjustment for sick pay . . . . **8** ☐

9   Current quarter's adjustments for tips and group-term life insurance . . . . . . **9** ☐

10   Total taxes after adjustments. Combine lines 6 through 9 . . . . **10** ☐

11a   Qualified small business payroll tax credit for increasing research activities. Attach Form 8974   **11a** ☐

11b   Nonrefundable portion of credit for qualified sick and family leave wages for leave taken before April 1, 2021 . . . . **11b** ☐

11c   Reserved for future use . . . . **11c** ☐

▶ **You MUST complete all three pages of Form 941 and SIGN it.**

Next ▶

For Privacy Act and Paperwork Reduction Act Notice, see the back of the Payment Voucher.   Cat. No. 17001Z   Form **941** (Rev. 3-2022)

3-13A (continued)

Name (not your trade name)	Employer identification number (EIN)
KAREN KLUSTER	00-0005874

Part 1: Answer these questions for this quarter. (continued)

11d Nonrefundable portion of credit for qualified sick and family leave wages for leave taken after March 31, 2021, and before October 1, 2021 . . . . 11d [.]

11e Nonrefundable portion of COBRA premium assistance credit (see instructions for applicable quarter) . . . . 11e [.]

11f Number of individuals provided COBRA premium assistance [   ]

11g Total nonrefundable credits. Add lines 11a, 11b, 11d, and 11e . . . . 11g [.]

12 Total taxes after adjustments and nonrefundable credits. Subtract line 11g from line 10 . 12 [.]

13a Total deposits for this quarter, including overpayment applied from a prior quarter and overpayments applied from Form 941-X, 941-X (PR), 944-X, or 944-X (SP) filed in the current quarter 13a [.]

13b Reserved for future use . . . . 13b [.]

13c Refundable portion of credit for qualified sick and family leave wages for leave taken before April 1, 2021 . . . . 13c [.]

13d Reserved for future use . . . . 13d [.]

13e Refundable portion of credit for qualified sick and family leave wages for leave taken after March 31, 2021, and before October 1, 2021 . . . . 13e [.]

13f Refundable portion of COBRA premium assistance credit (see instructions for applicable quarter) . . . . 13f [.]

13g Total deposits and refundable credits. Add lines 13a, 13c, 13e, and 13f . . . . . . 13g [.]

13h Reserved for future use . . . . 13h [.]

13i Reserved for future use . . . . 13i [.]

14 Balance due. If line 12 is more than line 13g, enter the difference and see instructions . . . 14 [.]

15 Overpayment. If line 13g is more than line 12, enter the difference [.] Check one: ☐ Apply to next return. ☐ Send a refund.

Part 2: Tell us about your deposit schedule and tax liability for this quarter.

If you're unsure about whether you're a monthly schedule depositor or a semiweekly schedule depositor, see section 11 of Pub. 15.

16 Check one: ☐ Line 12 on this return is less than $2,500 or line 12 on the return for the prior quarter was less than $2,500, and you didn't incur a $100,000 next-day deposit obligation during the current quarter. If line 12 for the prior quarter was less than $2,500 but line 12 on this return is $100,000 or more, you must provide a record of your federal tax liability. If you're a monthly schedule depositor, complete the deposit schedule below; if you're a semiweekly schedule depositor, attach Schedule B (Form 941). Go to Part 3.

☐ You were a monthly schedule depositor for the entire quarter. Enter your tax liability for each month and total liability for the quarter, then go to Part 3.

Tax liability: Month 1 [.]

Month 2 [.]

Month 3 [.]

Total liability for quarter [.] Total must equal line 12.

☐ You were a semiweekly schedule depositor for any part of this quarter. Complete Schedule B (Form 941), Report of Tax Liability for Semiweekly Schedule Depositors, and attach it to Form 941. Go to Part 3.

▶ You MUST complete all three pages of Form 941 and SIGN it. Next ▶

Page **2** Form **941** (Rev. 3-2022)

3-13A (concluded)

Name *(not your trade name)*	Employer identification number (EIN)
KAREN KLUSTER	00-0005874

Part 3:   Tell us about your business. If a question does NOT apply to your business, leave it blank.

17   If your business has closed or you stopped paying wages . . . . ☐ Check here, and

         enter the final date you paid wages   [/ /] ; also attach a statement to your return. See instructions.

18   If you're a seasonal employer and you don't have to file a return for every quarter of the year . . .   ☐ Check here.

19	Qualified health plan expenses allocable to qualified sick leave wages for leave taken before April 1, 2021	19	.
20	Qualified health plan expenses allocable to qualified family leave wages for leave taken before April 1, 2021	20	.
21	Reserved for future use	21	.
22	Reserved for future use	22	.
23	Qualified sick leave wages for leave taken after March 31, 2021, and before October 1, 2021	23	.
24	Qualified health plan expenses allocable to qualified sick leave wages reported on line 23	24	.
25	Amounts under certain collectively bargained agreements allocable to qualified sick leave wages reported on line 23	25	.
26	Qualified family leave wages for leave taken after March 31, 2021, and before October 1, 2021	26	.
27	Qualified health plan expenses allocable to qualified family leave wages reported on line 26	27	.
28	Amounts under certain collectively bargained agreements allocable to qualified family leave wages reported on line 26	28	.

Part 4:   May we speak with your third-party designee?

Do you want to allow an employee, a paid tax preparer, or another person to discuss this return with the IRS? See the instructions for details.

☐ Yes. Designee's name and phone number [   ] [   ]

          Select a 5-digit personal identification number (PIN) to use when talking to the IRS.   ☐ ☐ ☐ ☐ ☐

☐ No.

Part 5:   Sign here. You MUST complete all three pages of Form 941 and SIGN it.

Under penalties of perjury, I declare that I have examined this return, including accompanying schedules and statements, and to the best of my knowledge and belief, it is true, correct, and complete. Declaration of preparer (other than taxpayer) is based on all information of which preparer has any knowledge.

X   **Sign your name here** [   ]   Print your name here [   ]

                                                               Print your title here [   ]

            Date [/ /]   Best daytime phone [   ]

Paid Preparer Use Only   Check if you're self-employed . . . . ☐

Preparer's name	[ ]	PTIN	[ ]
Preparer's signature	[ ]	Date	[/ /]
Firm's name (or yours if self-employed)	[ ]	EIN	[ ]
Address	[ ]	Phone	[ ]
City	[ ] State [ ]	ZIP code	[ ]

Page **3**   Form **941** (Rev. 3-2022)

Source: Internal Revenue Service.

3-14A • LO 5   See Figure 3.8 on pages 3-23 to 3-25

During the third calendar quarter of 20--, Bayview Inn, owned by Diane R. Peters, employed the persons listed below. Also given are the employees' salaries or wages and the amount of tips reported to the owner. The tips were reported by the 10th of each month. The federal income tax and FICA tax to be withheld from the tips were estimated by the owner and withheld equally over the 13 weekly pay periods. The employer's portion of FICA tax on the tips was estimated as the same amount.

Employee	Salary or Wage	Quarter's Wages	Quarter's Tips	Quarter's OASDI	Quarter's HI	Quarter's FIT
Grant Frazier	$78,000/year	$ 19,500.00		$1,209.00	$ 282.75	$1,500.00
Joseph LaVange	52,000/year	13,000.00		806.00	188.50	1,100.00
Susanne Ayers	800/week	10,400.00	$ 2,240.90	783.77	183.30	750.00
Howard Cohen	650/week	8,450.00	2,493.10	678.47	158.73	740.00
Lee Soong	675/week	8,775.00	2,640.30	707.72	165.49	660.00
Mary Yee	750/week	9,750.00	2,704.00	772.20	180.70	900.00
Helen Woods	750/week	9,750.00		604.50	141.44	800.00
Koo Shin	600/week	7,800.00		483.60	113.10	1,100.00
Aaron Abalis	750/week	9,750.00		604.50	141.44	800.00
David Harad	600/week	7,800.00		483.60	113.10	750.00
		$104,975.00	$10,078.30	$7,133.36	$1,668.55	$9,100.00

Employees are paid weekly on Friday. The following paydays occurred during this quarter:

July	August	September
5 weekly paydays	4 weekly paydays	4 weekly paydays

Taxes withheld for the 13 paydays in the third quarter follow:

Employees' Federal Income Tax	Weekly FICA Taxes Withheld on Wages		Weekly FICA Taxes on Tips	
	OASDI	HI	OASDI	HI
$700 per week	Employees' $500.65	$ 117.11	Employees' $48.07	$11.24
	Employer's 500.65	117.09	Employer's 48.07	11.24

Based on the information given, complete Form 941 on pages 3-50 to 3-52 for Diane R. Peters.
Phone number: (901) 555-7959
Date filed: October 31, 20--

Form 941 for 20--: **Employer's QUARTERLY Federal Tax Return**
(Rev. March 2022)   Department of the Treasury — Internal Revenue Service

OMB No. 1545-0029

Employer identification number (EIN) 0 0 – 0 0 0 3 6 0 7

Name *(not your trade name)* DIANE R. PETERS

Trade name *(if any)* BAYVIEW INN

Address 404 UNION AVE.
Number   Street   Suite or room number

MEMPHIS   TN   38112
City   State   ZIP code

Foreign country name   Foreign province/county   Foreign postal code

Report for this Quarter of 20--
(Check one.)

☐ **1:** January, February, March
☐ **2:** April, May, June
☐ **3:** July, August, September
☐ **4:** October, November, December

Go to *www.irs.gov/Form941* for instructions and the latest information.

Read the separate instructions before you complete Form 941. Type or print within the boxes.

Part 1: Answer these questions for this quarter.

1 Number of employees who received wages, tips, or other compensation for the pay period including: *Mar. 12* (Quarter 1) **1**

2 Wages, tips, and other compensation **2**

3 Federal income tax withheld from wages, tips, and other compensation **3**

4 If no wages, tips, and other compensation are subject to social security or Medicare tax ☐ Check and go to line 6.

	Column 1		Column 2
5a Taxable social security wages* . .		× 0.124 =	
5a (i) Qualified sick leave wages* .		× 0.062 =	
5a (ii) Qualified family leave wages* .		× 0.062 =	
5b Taxable social security tips . . .		× 0.124 =	
5c Taxable Medicare wages & tips . .		× 0.029 =	
5d Taxable wages & tips subject to Additional Medicare Tax withholding		× 0.009 =	

*Include taxable qualified sick and family leave wages paid in 2022 for leave taken after March 31, 2021, and before October 1, 2021, on line 5a. Use lines 5a(i) and 5a(ii) only for taxable qualified sick and family leave wages paid in 2022 for leave taken after March 31, 2020, and before April 1, 2021.

5e Total social security and Medicare taxes. Add Column 2 from lines 5a, 5a(i), 5a(ii), 5b, 5c, and 5d **5e**

5f Section 3121(q) Notice and Demand—Tax due on unreported tips (see instructions) . . **5f**

6 Total taxes before adjustments. Add lines 3, 5e, and 5f **6**

7 Current quarter's adjustment for fractions of cents **7**

8 Current quarter's adjustment for sick pay **8**

9 Current quarter's adjustments for tips and group-term life insurance **9**

10 Total taxes after adjustments. Combine lines 6 through 9 . . . **10**

11a Qualified small business payroll tax credit for increasing research activities. Attach Form 8974 **11a**

11b Nonrefundable portion of credit for qualified sick and family leave wages for leave taken before April 1, 2021 . . . . **11b**

11c Reserved for future use **11c**

▶ You MUST complete all three pages of Form 941 and SIGN it.   Next ▶

For Privacy Act and Paperwork Reduction Act Notice, see the back of the Payment Voucher.   Cat. No. 17001Z   Form **941** (Rev. 3-2022)

3-14A (continued)

Name *(not your trade name)*	Employer identification number (EIN)
DIANE R. PETERS	00-0003607

Part 1: Answer these questions for this quarter. *(continued)*

11d Nonrefundable portion of credit for qualified sick and family leave wages for leave taken after March 31, 2021, and before October 1, 2021 . . . . **11d** [▪   ]

11e Nonrefundable portion of COBRA premium assistance credit (see instructions for applicable quarter) . . . . **11e** [▪   ]

11f Number of individuals provided COBRA premium assistance [   ]

11g Total nonrefundable credits. Add lines 11a, 11b, 11d, and 11e . . . . **11g** [▪   ]

12 Total taxes after adjustments and nonrefundable credits. Subtract line 11g from line 10 . **12** [▪   ]

13a Total deposits for this quarter, including overpayment applied from a prior quarter and overpayments applied from Form 941-X, 941-X (PR), 944-X, or 944-X (SP) filed in the current quarter **13a** [▪   ]

13b Reserved for future use . . . . **13b** [▪   ]

13c Refundable portion of credit for qualified sick and family leave wages for leave taken before April 1, 2021 . . . . **13c** [▪   ]

13d Reserved for future use . . . . **13d** [▪   ]

13e Refundable portion of credit for qualified sick and family leave wages for leave taken after March 31, 2021, and before October 1, 2021 . . . . **13e** [▪   ]

13f Refundable portion of COBRA premium assistance credit (see instructions for applicable quarter) . . . . **13f** [▪   ]

13g Total deposits and refundable credits. Add lines 13a, 13c, 13e, and 13f . . . . . . **13g** [▪   ]

13h Reserved for future use . . . . **13h** [▪   ]

13i Reserved for future use . . . . **13i** [▪   ]

14 Balance due. If line 12 is more than line 13g, enter the difference and see instructions . . . **14** [▪   ]

15 Overpayment. If line 13g is more than line 12, enter the difference [▪   ] Check one: ☐ Apply to next return. ☐ Send a refund.

Part 2: Tell us about your deposit schedule and tax liability for this quarter.

If you're unsure about whether you're a monthly schedule depositor or a semiweekly schedule depositor, see section 11 of Pub. 15.

16 Check one: ☐ **Line 12 on this return is less than $2,500 or line 12 on the return for the prior quarter was less than $2,500, and you didn't incur a $100,000 next-day deposit obligation during the current quarter.** If line 12 for the prior quarter was less than $2,500 but line 12 on this return is $100,000 or more, you must provide a record of your federal tax liability. If you're a monthly schedule depositor, complete the deposit schedule below; if you're a semiweekly schedule depositor, attach Schedule B (Form 941). Go to Part 3.

☐ **You were a monthly schedule depositor for the entire quarter.** Enter your tax liability for each month and total liability for the quarter, then go to Part 3.

Tax liability: Month 1 [▪   ]

Month 2 [▪   ]

Month 3 [▪   ]

Total liability for quarter [▪   ] **Total must equal line 12.**

☐ **You were a semiweekly schedule depositor for any part of this quarter.** Complete Schedule B (Form 941), Report of Tax Liability for Semiweekly Schedule Depositors, and attach it to Form 941. Go to Part 3.

▶ **You MUST complete all three pages of Form 941 and SIGN it.** **Next** ▶

3-14A (concluded)

Name *(not your trade name)*	Employer identification number (EIN)
DIANE R. PETERS	00-0003607

Part 3: Tell us about your business. If a question does NOT apply to your business, leave it blank.

17 If your business has closed or you stopped paying wages . . . . ☐ Check here, and

enter the final date you paid wages [/ /] ; also attach a statement to your return. See instructions.

18 If you're a seasonal employer and you don't have to file a return for every quarter of the year . . . ☐ Check here.

19	Qualified health plan expenses allocable to qualified sick leave wages for leave taken before April 1, 2021	19	▪
20	Qualified health plan expenses allocable to qualified family leave wages for leave taken before April 1, 2021	20	▪
21	Reserved for future use	21	▪
22	Reserved for future use	22	▪
23	Qualified sick leave wages for leave taken after March 31, 2021, and before October 1, 2021	23	▪
24	Qualified health plan expenses allocable to qualified sick leave wages reported on line 23	24	▪
25	Amounts under certain collectively bargained agreements allocable to qualified sick leave wages reported on line 23	25	▪
26	Qualified family leave wages for leave taken after March 31, 2021, and before October 1, 2021	26	▪
27	Qualified health plan expenses allocable to qualified family leave wages reported on line 26	27	▪
28	Amounts under certain collectively bargained agreements allocable to qualified family leave wages reported on line 26	28	▪

Part 4: May we speak with your third-party designee?

Do you want to allow an employee, a paid tax preparer, or another person to discuss this return with the IRS? See the instructions for details.

☐ Yes. Designee's name and phone number [ ] [ ]

Select a 5-digit personal identification number (PIN) to use when talking to the IRS. ☐ ☐ ☐ ☐ ☐

☐ No.

Part 5: Sign here. You MUST complete all three pages of Form 941 and SIGN it.

Under penalties of perjury, I declare that I have examined this return, including accompanying schedules and statements, and to the best of my knowledge and belief, it is true, correct, and complete. Declaration of preparer (other than taxpayer) is based on all information of which preparer has any knowledge.

X   Sign your name here [ ]   Print your name here [ ]

Print your title here [ ]

Date [/ /]   Best daytime phone [ ]

Paid Preparer Use Only   Check if you're self-employed . . . ☐

Preparer's name	[ ]	PTIN	[ ]
Preparer's signature	[ ]	Date	[/ /]
Firm's name (or yours if self-employed)	[ ]	EIN	[ ]
Address	[ ]	Phone	[ ]
City	[ ]	State [ ]	ZIP code	[ ]

Page **3**   Form **941** (Rev. 3-2022)

Source: Internal Revenue Service.

D a t e _____ N a m e _____

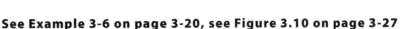

3-15A • LO 4, 5   **See Example 3-6 on page 3-20, see Figure 3.10 on page 3-27** *Show Me How*

The taxable wages and withheld taxes for Stafford Company (EIN 00-0001462), semiweekly depositor, for the first quarter of 20-- follow.

Semimonthly Paydays	Gross and Taxable Wages	FICA Withheld OASDI	FICA Withheld HI	Federal Income Tax Withheld
1/15	$ 24,500	$1,519.00	$ 355.25	$ 3,185.00
1/31	23,985	1,487.07	347.78	3,090.00
2/15	25,190	1,561.78	365.26	3,410.00
2/28	25,530	1,582.86	370.19	3,497.00
3/15	24,950	1,546.90	361.78	3,385.00
3/29	25,100	1,556.20	363.95	3,400.00
	$149,255	$9,253.81	$2,164.21	$19,967.00

a. Complete Schedule B of Form 941 on page 3-54 for the first quarter for Steve Hazelton, the owner of Stafford Company.

b. Using the calendar below, list the due dates of each deposit in the first quarter.

January							February							March							April						
Su	Mo	Tu	We	Th	Fr	Sa	Su	Mo	Tu	We	Th	Fr	Sa	Su	Mo	Tu	We	Th	Fr	Sa	Su	Mo	Tu	We	Th	Fr	Sa
		1	2	3	4	5						1	2						1	2		1	2	3	4	5	6
6	7	8	9	10	11	12	3	4	5	6	7	8	9	3	4	5	6	7	8	9	7	8	9	10	11	12	13
13	14	15	16	17	18	19	10	11	12	13	14	15	16	10	11	12	13	14	15	16	14	15	16	17	18	19	20
20	21	22	23	24	25	26	17	18	19	20	21	22	23	17	18	19	20	21	22	23	21	22	23	24	25	26	27
27	28	29	30	31			24	25	26	27	28			24	25	26	27	28	29	30	28	29	30				
														31													

Paydays	Deposit Due Dates
January 15	1. _____
January 31	2. _____
February 15	3. _____
February 28	4. _____
March 15	5. _____
March 29	6. _____

3-16A • LO 5   **See Example 3-6 on page 3-20, Example 3-8 on page 3-32,**
Example 3-9 on page 3-32

Vulcan Company is a monthly depositor whose tax liability for March 20-- is $2,505.

1. What is the due date for the deposit of these taxes? _____

2. Assume that no deposit was made until April 29 (14 days late). Compute the following penalties:

a. Penalty for failure to make timely deposit. $ _____

b. Penalty for failure to fully pay tax. $ _____

c. Interest on taxes due and unpaid (assume a 4% interest rate). $ _____

d. Total penalty imposed. $ _____

3-15A (concluded)

Schedule B (Form 941):
Report of Tax Liability for Semiweekly Schedule Depositors

(Rev. January 2017)   Department of the Treasury — Internal Revenue Service

OMB No. 1545-0029

Employer identification number (EIN)   0 0 – 0 0 0 1 4 6 2

Name *(not your trade name)*   STEVE HAZELTON

Calendar year   *(Also check quarter)*

Report for this Quarter...
(Check one.)

☐ **1:** January, February, March

☐ **2:** April, May, June

☐ **3:** July, August, September

☐ **4:** October, November, December

Use this schedule to show your **TAX LIABILITY** for the quarter; don't use it to show your deposits. When you file this form with Form 941 or Form 941-SS, don't change your tax liability by adjustments reported on any Forms 941-X or 944-X. You must fill out this form and attach it to Form 941 or Form 941-SS if you're a semiweekly schedule depositor or became one because your accumulated tax liability on any day was $100,000 or more. Write your daily tax liability on the numbered space that corresponds to the date wages were paid. See Section 11 in Pub. 15 for details.

Month 1

1		9		17		25		**Tax liability for Month 1**
2		10		18		26		
3		11		19		27		
4		12		20		28		
5		13		21		29		
6		14		22		30		
7		15		23		31		
8		16		24				

Month 2

1		9		17		25		**Tax liability for Month 2**
2		10		18		26		
3		11		19		27		
4		12		20		28		
5		13		21		29		
6		14		22		30		
7		15		23		31		
8		16		24				

Month 3

1		9		17		25		**Tax liability for Month 3**
2		10		18		26		
3		11		19		27		
4		12		20		28		
5		13		21		29		
6		14		22		30		
7		15		23		31		
8		16		24				

Fill in your total liability for the quarter (Month 1 + Month 2 + Month 3) ▶

Total must equal line 12 on Form 941 or Form 941-SS.

Total liability for the quarter

For Paperwork Reduction Act Notice, see separate instructions.   IRS.gov/form941   Cat. No. 11967Q   **Schedule B (Form 941)** (Rev. 1-2017)

Source: Internal Revenue Service.

Date _____ Name _____

3-17A • LO 2, 3 See Example 3-1 on page 3-11

At Vision Club Company, office workers are employed for a 40-hour workweek on either an annual or a monthly salary basis.

Given on the form below are the current annual and monthly salary rates for five office workers for the week ended December 13, 20-- (50th payday of the year). In addition, with this pay, these employees are paid their sliding- scale annual bonuses. The bonuses are listed on the register.

For each worker, compute:

1. Regular earnings for the weekly payroll ended December 13, 20--.
2. Overtime earnings (if applicable).
3. Total regular, overtime earnings, and bonus.
4. FICA taxable wages for this pay period.
5. FICA taxes to be withheld for this pay period.

VISION CLUB COMPANY

Employee	Salary	Hours Worked	Annual Bonus	Regular Earnings	Overtime Earnings	Total Earnings
Marx, A.	$97,240/yr.	40	$60,000	_____	_____	_____
Boxer, C.	91,000/yr.	40	25,000	_____	_____	_____
Lundy, R.	6,240/mo.	40	20,000	_____	_____	_____
Ruth, B.	4,680/mo.	40	15,000	_____	_____	_____
Gehrig, L.	4,900/mo.	48	8,000	_____	_____	_____
Totals				_____	_____	_____

(left side)

VISION CLUB COMPANY

Cumulative Earnings as of Last Pay Period	FICA Taxable Wages This Pay Period		FICA Taxes to Be Withheld		Employee
	OASDI	HI	OASDI	HI	
$91,630.00	_____	_____	_____	_____	Marx, A.
85,750.00	_____	_____	_____	_____	Boxer, C.
70,560.00	_____	_____	_____	_____	Lundy, R.
52,920.00	_____	_____	_____	_____	Ruth, B.
34,890.00	_____	_____	_____	_____	Gehrig, L.
	_____	_____	_____	_____	Totals

(right side)

Employer's FICA taxes for week ended December 13, 20--: $ _____ $ _____

OASDI   HI

Date_____ Name_____

Problem Set · B

Note: In this chapter and in all succeeding work throughout the course, *unless instructed otherwise,* use the following rates, ceiling, and maximum taxes.

Employee and Employer OASDI:	6.20%	$147,000	$9,114.00
Employee* and Employer HI:	1.45%	No limit	No maximum
Self-employed OASDI:	12.4%	$147,000	$18,228.00
Self-employed HI:	2.9%	No limit	No maximum

For rounding rules, refer to page 2-37.

*Employee HI: Plus an additional 0.9% on wages over $200,000. Also applicable to self-employed.

3-1B · LO 3 See Example 3-1 on page 3-11, Example 3-2 on page 3-12

The biweekly taxable wages for the employees of Wee-Ones Foods follow. Compute the FICA taxes for each employee and the employer's FICA taxes.

		Biweekly Taxable	FICA Taxes	
Employee No.	Employee Name	Wages	OASDI	HI
711	Adams, Jane	$1,100.00	$ _____	$ _____
512	Candy, James	1,000.00	_____	_____
624	Guiterrez, Roberta	1,050.00	_____	_____
325	Harrison, Ken	1,250.00	_____	_____
422	Lowland, Harriet	1,600.00	_____	_____
210	Ranger, Ralph	1,310.50	_____	_____
111	Sweat, Rudy	1,419.45	_____	_____
		Totals	$ _____	$ _____

Employer's OASDI	$ _____	$ _____	
	Total Taxable Wages	Employer's OASDI Tax	
Employer's HI Tax	$ _____	$ _____	
	Total Taxable Wages	Employer's HI Tax	

3-2B · LO 3 See Example 3-1 on page 3-11

During 20--, Matti Perez, president of Maggert Company, was paid a semimonthly salary of $6,700. Compute the amount of FICA taxes that should be withheld from her:

	OASDI	HI
a. 9th paycheck	$ _____	$ _____
b. 22nd paycheck	$ _____	$ _____
c. 24th paycheck	$ _____	$ _____
d. If Perez's year-to-date earnings as of her 24th paycheck are $160,800 and her year-end bonus is $100,000, how much is the additional 0.9% HI tax?	$ _____	

3-3B • LO 2, 3 See Example 3-1 on page 3-11

Eric Sherm began working as a part-time waiter on April 1, 20--, at Yardville Restaurant. The cash tips of $475 that he received during April were reported on Form 4070, which he submitted to his employer on May 1. During May, he was paid wages of $630 by the restaurant. Compute OASDI and HI:

	OASDI	HI
a. The amount of FICA taxes that the employer should withhold from Sherm's wages during May.	$ _____	$ _____
b. The amount of the employer's FICA taxes on Sherm's wages and tips during May.	$ _____	$ _____

3-4B • LO 2, 3 See Example 3-1 on page 3-11

Moisa Evans is a maitre d' at Red Rock Club. On September 6, 20--, his gross pay was $900 (three days working, one paid vacation day, and one paid sick day). He also reported to his employer tips of $860 for the previous month (applicable taxes to be deducted out of this pay). Evans belongs to the company's 401(k) plan and has 5 percent of his gross pay ($900) deducted each week (salary reduction). Red Rock Club also provides a matching contribution ($45) into the plan for Evans. This week's pay would have a:

a. Deduction for OASDI tax $ _____

b. Deduction for HI tax $ _____

3-5B • LO 3 See Example 3-1 on page 3-11

In 20--, the annual salaries paid each of the officers of Perez, Inc., follow. The officers are paid semimonthly on the 15th and the last day of the month. Compute the FICA taxes to be withheld from each officer's pay on (a) November 15 and (b) December 31.

a.

		November 15			
Name and Title	Annual Salary	OASDI Taxable Earnings	OASDI Tax	HI Taxable Earnings	HI Tax
Perez, Paul, President	$172,800				
Donald, Donna, VP Finance	148,800				
Funke, Jack, VP Sales	76,800				
Weis, Al, VP Mfg.	92,400				
Lang, Hope, VP Personnel	78,000				
Lee, Amy, VP Secretary	52,800				

b.

		December 31			
Name and Title	Annual Salary	OASDI Taxable Earnings	OASDI Tax	HI Taxable Earnings	HI Tax
Perez, Paul, President	$172,800				
Donald, Donna, VP Finance	148,800				
Funke, Jack, VP Sales	76,800				
Weis, Al, VP Mfg.	92,400				
Lang, Hope, VP Personnel	78,000				
Lee, Amy, VP Secretary	52,800				

3-6B • LO 3 See Example 3-1 on page 3-11, Example 3-2 on page 3-12

Amanda Autry and Carley Wilson are partners in A & W Gift Shop, which employs the individuals listed below. Pay-checks are distributed every Friday to all employees. Based on the information given, compute the amounts listed below for a weekly payroll period.

Name and Position	Salary	OASDI Taxable Earnings	OASDI Tax	HI Taxable Earnings	HI Tax
Kelly Simon, Office	$ 750 per week	_____	_____	_____	_____
Jim Tress, Sales	3,450 per month	_____	_____	_____	_____
May Aha, Delivery	720 per week	_____	_____	_____	_____
Amanda Autry, Partner	1,900 per week	_____	_____	_____	_____
Carley Wilson, Partner	1,900 per week	_____	_____	_____	_____
	Totals	$ _____	$ _____	$ _____	$ _____

Employer's OASDI Tax $ _____

Employer's HI Tax $ _____

3-7B • LO 3 See Example 3-1 on page 3-11, Example 3-2 on page 3-12

Montalvo Corporation has only five employees who are all paid $1,050 per week. Compute the total FICA taxes that the employer would withhold from the five employees each week and the amount the company would pay as its own liability for the employer's share of the FICA taxes on the weekly wages of the five employees:

Employees' total OASDI .... $ _____

Employees' total HI .... $ _____

Employer's total OASDI .... $ _____

Employer's total HI .... $ _____

3-8B • LO 3 See Example 3-5 on page 3-14

George Parker was paid a salary of $74,700 during 20-- by Umberger Company. In addition, during the year, Parker started his own business as a public accountant and reported a net business income of $80,000 on his income tax return for 20--. Compute the following:

a. The amount of FICA taxes that was withheld from his earnings during 20-- by Umberger Company.   OASDI $ _____   HI $ _____

b. Parker's self-employment taxes on the income derived from the public accounting business for 20--.   OASDI $ _____   HI $ _____

3-9B • LO 3 **See Example 3-1 on page 3-11, Example 3-2 on page 3-12**

Haggerty Company pays its salaried employees monthly on the last day of each month. The annual salary payroll for 20-- follows. Compute the following for the payroll of December 31:

Employee	Annual Salary	OASDI Taxable Wages	OASDI Tax	HI Taxable Wages	HI Tax
Stern, Myra	$ 42,150				
Lundy, Hal	39,500				
Franks, Rob	46,000				
Haggerty, Alan	161,280				
Ward, Randy	40,800				
Hoskin, Al	39,600				
Wee, Pam	156,000				
Prince, Harry	76,800				
Maven, Mary	52,000				
Harley, David	68,960				
Totals		$	$	$	$

Employer's OASDI Tax $ _____

Employer's HI Tax $ _____

3-10B • LO 3 **See Example 3-1 on page 3-11**

The monthly and hourly wage schedule for the employees of Quincy, Inc., follows. No employees are due over-time pay. Compute the following for the last monthly pay of the year:

a. The total wages of each part-time employee for December 20--.

b. The OASDI and HI taxable wages for each employee.

c. The FICA taxes withheld from each employee's wages for December.

d. Totals of columns.

e. The employer's FICA taxes for the month.

Employees	Total Monthly Payroll	OASDI Taxable Wages	OASDI Tax	HI Taxable Wages	HI Tax
Full-Time Office:					
Hutchings, Jean	$3,250.00				
Florio, Anne	4,000.00				
Trabert, Judy	3,500.00				
Williams, Justin	3,100.00				
Galzano, Jared	4,250.00				
Sussex, Jude	8,000.00				
Robinson, Dave	6,300.00				
Prender, Hank	4,985.00				
Sorenson, Deb	5,600.00				
Hutchinson, Wendy	5,200.00				

3-10B (concluded)

	Hours Worked	Hourly Rate	Total Monthly	OASDI Taxable Wages	OASDI Tax	HI Taxable Wages	HI Tax
Part-Time Office:							
Fox, Mandy	180	$15.50					
Billings, Clara	160	16.00					
Nau, Kevin	170	19.75					
Millis, Toby	142	15.00					
Cummings, Cheryl	162	17.50					
Totals for all employees			$	$	$	$	$
Employer's FICA taxes				OASDI $		HI $	

3-11B • LO 5   See Figure 3.8 on pages 3-23 and 3-24

Gallagher Company has gathered the information needed to complete its Form 941 for the quarter ended September 30, 20--. Using the information presented below, complete Part 1 of Form 941, reproduced on pages 3-62 and 3-63.

> # of employees for pay period that included September 12—15 employees
> Wages paid third quarter—$89,352.18
> Federal income tax withheld in the third quarter—$10,195.00
> Taxable social security and Medicare wages—$89,352.18
> Total tax deposits for the quarter—$23,865.92

3-12B • LO 5   See Figure 3.8 on pages 3-24 and 3-25

Refer to Problem 3-11B. Complete Parts 2, 4, and 5 of Form 941 (on pages 3-63 and 3-64) for Gallagher Company for the third quarter of 20--. Gallagher Company is a monthly depositor with the following monthly tax liabilities for this quarter:

July	$7,891.75
August	7,984.90
September	7,989.27

State unemployment taxes are only paid to California. The company does not use a third-party designee, the tax returns are signed by the president, James Gallagher (Phone: 916-555-9739), and the date filed is October 31, 20--.

3-11B (continued)

Form **941 for 20--:** **Employer's QUARTERLY Federal Tax Return**
(Rev. March 2022)   Department of the Treasury — Internal Revenue Service

OMB No. 1545-0029

Employer identification number (EIN)   0 0 – 0 0 0 6 5 0 9

Name *(not your trade name)*   JAMES GALLAGHER

Trade name *(if any)*   GALLAGHER COMPANY

Address   901 KEYSTONE
Number   Street   Suite or room number

SACRAMENTO   CA   95919
City   State   ZIP code

Foreign country name   Foreign province/county   Foreign postal code

Report for this Quarter of 20--
(Check one.)

☐ **1:** January, February, March

☐ **2:** April, May, June

☐ **3:** July, August, September

☐ **4:** October, November, December

Go to *www.irs.gov/Form941* for instructions and the latest information.

Read the separate instructions before you complete Form 941. Type or print within the boxes.

Part 1:   **Answer these questions for this quarter.**

1   Number of employees who received wages, tips, or other compensation for the pay period including: *Mar. 12 (Quarter 1)* . . . .   **1** [   ]

2   Wages, tips, and other compensation   . . . .   **2** [.]

3   Federal income tax withheld from wages, tips, and other compensation . . . . . .   **3** [.]

4   If no wages, tips, and other compensation are subject to social security or Medicare tax   ☐ Check and go to line 6.

		Column 1		Column 2	
5a	Taxable social security wages* .	[.]	× 0.124 =	[.]	
5a	(i) Qualified sick leave wages* .	[.]	× 0.062 =	[.]	
5a	(ii) Qualified family leave wages* .	[.]	× 0.062 =	[.]	
5b	Taxable social security tips . . .	[.]	× 0.124 =	[.]	
5c	Taxable Medicare wages & tips. .	[.]	× 0.029 =	[.]	
5d	Taxable wages & tips subject to Additional Medicare Tax withholding	[.]	× 0.009 =	[.]	

*Include taxable qualified sick and family leave wages paid in 2022 for leave taken after March 31, 2021, and before October 1, 2021, on line 5a. Use lines 5a(i) and 5a(ii) **only** for taxable qualified sick and family leave wages paid in 2022 for leave taken after March 31, 2020, and before April 1, 2021.*

5e   Total social security and Medicare taxes. Add Column 2 from lines 5a, 5a(i), 5a(ii), 5b, 5c, and 5d   **5e** [.]

5f   Section 3121(q) Notice and Demand—Tax due on unreported tips (see instructions)   . .   **5f** [.]

6   Total taxes before adjustments. Add lines 3, 5e, and 5f . . . .   **6** [.]

7   Current quarter's adjustment for fractions of cents . . . .   **7** [.]

8   Current quarter's adjustment for sick pay . . . .   **8** [.]

9   Current quarter's adjustments for tips and group-term life insurance . . . . . .   **9** [.]

10   Total taxes after adjustments. Combine lines 6 through 9 . . . . .   **10** [.]

11a   Qualified small business payroll tax credit for increasing research activities. Attach Form 8974   **11a** [.]

11b   Nonrefundable portion of credit for qualified sick and family leave wages for leave taken before April 1, 2021 . . . . .   **11b** [.]

11c   Reserved for future use . . . .   **11c** [.]

▶ **You MUST complete all three pages of Form 941 and SIGN it.**   Next ▶

For Privacy Act and Paperwork Reduction Act Notice, see the back of the Payment Voucher.   Cat. No. 17001Z   Form **941** (Rev. 3-2022)

Date _____ Name _____

3-11B (concluded) and 3-12B

Name (not your trade name)	Employer identification number (EIN)
JAMES GALLAGHER	00-0006509

Part 1: Answer these questions for this quarter. *(continued)*

11d Nonrefundable portion of credit for qualified sick and family leave wages for leave taken after March 31, 2021, and before October 1, 2021 . . . . **11d** [_____ . __]

11e Nonrefundable portion of COBRA premium assistance credit (see instructions for applicable quarter) . . . . **11e** [_____ . __]

11f Number of individuals provided COBRA premium assistance [_____]

11g Total nonrefundable credits. Add lines 11a, 11b, 11d, and 11e . . . . **11g** [_____ . __]

12 Total taxes after adjustments and nonrefundable credits. Subtract line 11g from line 10 . **12** [_____ . __]

13a Total deposits for this quarter, including overpayment applied from a prior quarter and overpayments applied from Form 941-X, 941-X (PR), 944-X, or 944-X (SP) filed in the current quarter **13a** [_____ . __]

13b Reserved for future use . . . . **13b** [_____ . __]

13c Refundable portion of credit for qualified sick and family leave wages for leave taken before April 1, 2021 . . . . **13c** [_____ . __]

13d Reserved for future use . . . . **13d** [_____ . __]

13e Refundable portion of credit for qualified sick and family leave wages for leave taken after March 31, 2021, and before October 1, 2021 . . . . **13e** [_____ . __]

13f Refundable portion of COBRA premium assistance credit (see instructions for applicable quarter) . . . . **13f** [_____ . __]

13g Total deposits and refundable credits. Add lines 13a, 13c, 13e, and 13f . . . . . . **13g** [_____ . __]

13h Reserved for future use . . . . **13h** [_____ . __]

13i Reserved for future use . . . . **13i** [_____ . __]

14 Balance due. If line 12 is more than line 13g, enter the difference and see instructions . . . **14** [_____ . __]

15 Overpayment. If line 13g is more than line 12, enter the difference [_____ . __] Check one: ☐ Apply to next return. ☐ Send a refund.

Part 2: Tell us about your deposit schedule and tax liability for this quarter.

If you're unsure about whether you're a monthly schedule depositor or a semiweekly schedule depositor, see section 11 of Pub. 15.

16 Check one: ☐ Line 12 on this return is less than $2,500 or line 12 on the return for the prior quarter was less than $2,500, and you didn't incur a $100,000 next-day deposit obligation during the current quarter. If line 12 for the prior quarter was less than $2,500 but line 12 on this return is $100,000 or more, you must provide a record of your federal tax liability. If you're a monthly schedule depositor, complete the deposit schedule below; if you're a semiweekly schedule depositor, attach Schedule B (Form 941). Go to Part 3.

☐ You were a monthly schedule depositor for the entire quarter. Enter your tax liability for each month and total liability for the quarter, then go to Part 3.

Tax liability: Month 1 [_____ . __]

Month 2 [_____ . __]

Month 3 [_____ . __]

Total liability for quarter [_____ . __] Total must equal line 12.

☐ You were a semiweekly schedule depositor for any part of this quarter. Complete Schedule B (Form 941), Report of Tax Liability for Semiweekly Schedule Depositors, and attach it to Form 941. Go to Part 3.

▶ You MUST complete all three pages of Form 941 and SIGN it. Next ▶

3-12B (concluded)

Name *(not your trade name)*	Employer identification number (EIN)
JAMES GALLAGHER	00-0006509

Part 3: **Tell us about your business. If a question does NOT apply to your business, leave it blank.**

17 If your business has closed or you stopped paying wages . . . . ☐ Check here, and

enter the final date you paid wages [/ /] ; also attach a statement to your return. See instructions.

18 If you're a seasonal employer and you don't have to file a return for every quarter of the year . . . ☐ Check here.

19	Qualified health plan expenses allocable to qualified sick leave wages for leave taken before April 1, 2021	19	.
20	Qualified health plan expenses allocable to qualified family leave wages for leave taken before April 1, 2021	20	.
21	Reserved for future use	21	.
22	Reserved for future use	22	.
23	Qualified sick leave wages for leave taken after March 31, 2021, and before October 1, 2021	23	.
24	Qualified health plan expenses allocable to qualified sick leave wages reported on line 23	24	.
25	Amounts under certain collectively bargained agreements allocable to qualified sick leave wages reported on line 23	25	.
26	Qualified family leave wages for leave taken after March 31, 2021, and before October 1, 2021	26	.
27	Qualified health plan expenses allocable to qualified family leave wages reported on line 26	27	.
28	Amounts under certain collectively bargained agreements allocable to qualified family leave wages reported on line 26	28	.

Part 4: **May we speak with your third-party designee?**

Do you want to allow an employee, a paid tax preparer, or another person to discuss this return with the IRS? See the instructions for details.

☐ Yes. Designee's name and phone number [　　　　　] [　　　　　]

Select a 5-digit personal identification number (PIN) to use when talking to the IRS. ☐ ☐ ☐ ☐ ☐

☐ No.

Part 5: **Sign here. You MUST complete all three pages of Form 941 and SIGN it.**

Under penalties of perjury, I declare that I have examined this return, including accompanying schedules and statements, and to the best of my knowledge and belief, it is true, correct, and complete. Declaration of preparer (other than taxpayer) is based on all information of which preparer has any knowledge.

X **Sign your name here** [　　　　　]

Print your name here [　　　　　]
Print your title here [　　　　　]

Date [/ /]

Best daytime phone [　　　　　]

Paid Preparer Use Only

Check if you're self-employed . . . ☐

Preparer's name	[　]	PTIN	[　]
Preparer's signature	[　]	Date	[/ /]
Firm's name (or yours if self-employed)	[　]	EIN	[　]
Address	[　]	Phone	[　]
City	[　] State [　]	ZIP code	[　]

Form **941** (Rev. 3-2022)

Source: Internal Revenue Service.

Show
Me How

3-13B • LO 5   See Figure 3.8 on pages 3-23 to 3-25

Stan Barker opened Quik-Stop Market on January 2, 20--. The business is subject to FICA taxes. At the end of the first quarter of 20--, Barker, as president of the company, must file Form 941, Employer's QUARTERLY Federal Tax Return. Using Form 941 (Parts 1 through 5), reproduced on pages 3-66 to 3-68, prepare, sign, and date the return on the basis of the information shown below.

Employer's address:	**234 Oak, Austin, TX 78711-0234**
Employer's ID number:	**00-0005874**
Phone number:	**(512)555-1111**
Date filed:	**April 30, 20--**

Each employee is paid semimonthly on the 15th and last day of each month. Shown below is the payroll information for the first quarter of 20--. All pay periods were the same.

PAYROLL INFORMATION FOR JANUARY–MARCH

Employee	SSN	Quarterly Wage	OASDI Tax	HI Tax	Federal Income Tax	Total Deductions	Net Pay
Albert Greer	000-00-7233	$10,440	$ 647.28	$151.38	$1,260.00	$2,058.66	$ 8,381.34
Patty Dilts	000-00-8451	10,530	652.86	152.70	1,200.00	2,005.56	8,524.44
Jerod Hughs	000-00-3668	23,220	1,439.64	336.72	1,080.00	2,856.36	20,363.64
Denise Eaton	000-00-6527	11,700	725.40	169.68	1,140.00	2,035.08	9,664.92
Totals		$55,890	$3,465.18	$810.48	$4,680.00	$8,955.66	$46,934.34

Employer's FICA taxes	$3,465.18	$810.41
for the Quarter	OASDI	HI

The total taxes per payday are:

Employees' FICA Tax—OASDI	$ 577.53
Employer's FICA Tax—OASDI	577.53
Employees' FICA Tax—HI	135.08
Employer's FICA Tax—HI	135.07
Employees' FIT Tax	780.00
Total	$2,205.21 × 6 deposits = $13,231.26 for the quarter

None of the employees reported tips during the quarter.

_____

Note: Lines 5a and 5c of Form 941, tax on total taxable wages, are computed by multiplying by the combined tax rate for both employer and employee. Small differences due to rounding may occur between this total and the total taxes withheld from employees each pay period and the amount of the employer's taxes calculated each pay period. This difference is reported on line 7 as a deduction or an addition as "Fractions of Cents."

3-13B (continued)

Form **941 for 20--:** **Employer's QUARTERLY Federal Tax Return**
(Rev. March 2022)   Department of the Treasury — Internal Revenue Service

OMB No. 1545-0029

Employer identification number (EIN) 0 0 – 0 0 0 5 8 7 4

Name (not your trade name) STAN BARKER

Trade name (if any) QUIK-STOP MARKET

Address 234 OAK
Number   Street   Suite or room number

AUSTIN   TX   78711-0234
City   State   ZIP code

Foreign country name   Foreign province/county   Foreign postal code

Report for this Quarter of 20--
(Check one.)

☐ **1:** January, February, March

☐ **2:** April, May, June

☐ **3:** July, August, September

☐ **4:** October, November, December

Go to *www.irs.gov/Form941* for instructions and the latest information.

Read the separate instructions before you complete Form 941. Type or print within the boxes.

Part 1:   Answer these questions for this quarter.

1 Number of employees who received wages, tips, or other compensation for the pay period including: *Mar. 12* (Quarter 1) . . . . **1** ☐

2 Wages, tips, and other compensation . . . . **2** ☐

3 Federal income tax withheld from wages, tips, and other compensation . . . . **3** ☐

4 If no wages, tips, and other compensation are subject to social security or Medicare tax   ☐ Check and go to line 6.

	Column 1		Column 2	
5a Taxable social security wages* . .	☐	× 0.124 =	☐	
5a (i) Qualified sick leave wages* .	☐	× 0.062 =	☐	
5a (ii) Qualified family leave wages* .	☐	× 0.062 =	☐	
5b Taxable social security tips . . .	☐	× 0.124 =	☐	
5c Taxable Medicare wages & tips. .	☐	× 0.029 =	☐	
5d Taxable wages & tips subject to Additional Medicare Tax withholding	☐	× 0.009 =	☐	

*Include taxable qualified sick and family leave wages paid in 2022 for leave taken after March 31, 2021, and before October 1, 2021, on line 5a. Use lines 5a(i) and 5a(ii) **only** for taxable qualified sick and family leave wages paid in 2022 for leave taken after March 31, 2020, and before April 1, 2021.

5e Total social security and Medicare taxes. Add Column 2 from lines 5a, 5a(i), 5a(ii), 5b, 5c, and 5d   **5e** ☐

5f Section 3121(q) Notice and Demand—Tax due on unreported tips (see instructions) . .   **5f** ☐

6 Total taxes before adjustments. Add lines 3, 5e, and 5f . . . .   **6** ☐

7 Current quarter's adjustment for fractions of cents . . . .   **7** ☐

8 Current quarter's adjustment for sick pay . . . .   **8** ☐

9 Current quarter's adjustments for tips and group-term life insurance . . . . . .   **9** ☐

10 Total taxes after adjustments. Combine lines 6 through 9 . . . .   **10** ☐

11a Qualified small business payroll tax credit for increasing research activities. Attach Form 8974   **11a** ☐

11b Nonrefundable portion of credit for qualified sick and family leave wages for leave taken before April 1, 2021 . . . .   **11b** ☐

11c Reserved for future use . . . .   **11c** ☐

▶ **You MUST complete all three pages of Form 941 and SIGN it.**

Next ▶

For Privacy Act and Paperwork Reduction Act Notice, see the back of the Payment Voucher.   Cat. No. 17001Z   Form **941** (Rev. 3-2022)

3-13B (continued)

Name (not your trade name)	Employer identification number (EIN)
STAN BARKER	00-0005874

Part 1: Answer these questions for this quarter. *(continued)*

11d Nonrefundable portion of credit for qualified sick and family leave wages for leave taken after March 31, 2021, and before October 1, 2021 . . . . **11d** [.   ]

11e Nonrefundable portion of COBRA premium assistance credit (see instructions for applicable quarter) . . . . **11e** [.   ]

11f Number of individuals provided COBRA premium assistance [   ]

11g Total nonrefundable credits. Add lines 11a, 11b, 11d, and 11e . . . . **11g** [.   ]

12 Total taxes after adjustments and nonrefundable credits. Subtract line 11g from line 10 . **12** [.   ]

13a Total deposits for this quarter, including overpayment applied from a prior quarter and overpayments applied from Form 941-X, 941-X (PR), 944-X, or 944-X (SP) filed in the current quarter **13a** [.   ]

13b Reserved for future use . . . . **13b** [.   ]

13c Refundable portion of credit for qualified sick and family leave wages for leave taken before April 1, 2021 . . . . **13c** [.   ]

13d Reserved for future use . . . . **13d** [.   ]

13e Refundable portion of credit for qualified sick and family leave wages for leave taken after March 31, 2021, and before October 1, 2021 . . . . **13e** [.   ]

13f Refundable portion of COBRA premium assistance credit (see instructions for applicable quarter) . . . . **13f** [.   ]

13g Total deposits and refundable credits. Add lines 13a, 13c, 13e, and 13f . . . . . . **13g** [.   ]

13h Reserved for future use . . . . **13h** [.   ]

13i Reserved for future use . . . . **13i** [.   ]

14 Balance due. If line 12 is more than line 13g, enter the difference and see instructions . . . **14** [.   ]

15 Overpayment. If line 13g is more than line 12, enter the difference [.   ] Check one: ☐ Apply to next return. ☐ Send a refund.

Part 2: Tell us about your deposit schedule and tax liability for this quarter.

If you're unsure about whether you're a monthly schedule depositor or a semiweekly schedule depositor, see section 11 of Pub. 15.

16 Check one: ☐ **Line 12 on this return is less than $2,500 or line 12 on the return for the prior quarter was less than $2,500, and you didn't incur a $100,000 next-day deposit obligation during the current quarter.** If line 12 for the prior quarter was less than $2,500 but line 12 on this return is $100,000 or more, you must provide a record of your federal tax liability. If you're a monthly schedule depositor, complete the deposit schedule below; if you're a semiweekly schedule depositor, attach Schedule B (Form 941). Go to Part 3.

☐ **You were a monthly schedule depositor for the entire quarter.** Enter your tax liability for each month and total liability for the quarter, then go to Part 3.

Tax liability: Month 1 [.   ]

Month 2 [.   ]

Month 3 [.   ]

Total liability for quarter [.   ] Total must equal line 12.

☐ **You were a semiweekly schedule depositor for any part of this quarter.** Complete Schedule B (Form 941), Report of Tax Liability for Semiweekly Schedule Depositors, and attach it to Form 941. Go to Part 3.

▶ **You MUST complete all three pages of Form 941 and SIGN it.** Next ▶

3-13B (concluded)

Name *(not your trade name)*	Employer identification number (EIN)
STAN BARKER	00-0005874

Part 3: Tell us about your business. If a question does NOT apply to your business, leave it blank.

17 If your business has closed or you stopped paying wages . . . . ☐ Check here, and

enter the final date you paid wages [/   /] ; also attach a statement to your return. See instructions.

18 If you're a seasonal employer and you don't have to file a return for every quarter of the year . . . ☐ Check here.

19	Qualified health plan expenses allocable to qualified sick leave wages for leave taken before April 1, 2021	19	.
20	Qualified health plan expenses allocable to qualified family leave wages for leave taken before April 1, 2021	20	.
21	Reserved for future use	21	.
22	Reserved for future use	22	.
23	Qualified sick leave wages for leave taken after March 31, 2021, and before October 1, 2021	23	.
24	Qualified health plan expenses allocable to qualified sick leave wages reported on line 23	24	.
25	Amounts under certain collectively bargained agreements allocable to qualified sick leave wages reported on line 23	25	.
26	Qualified family leave wages for leave taken after March 31, 2021, and before October 1, 2021	26	.
27	Qualified health plan expenses allocable to qualified family leave wages reported on line 26	27	.
28	Amounts under certain collectively bargained agreements allocable to qualified family leave wages reported on line 26	28	.

Part 4: May we speak with your third-party designee?

Do you want to allow an employee, a paid tax preparer, or another person to discuss this return with the IRS? See the instructions for details.

☐ Yes. Designee's name and phone number [   ] [   ]

Select a 5-digit personal identification number (PIN) to use when talking to the IRS. ☐ ☐ ☐ ☐ ☐

☐ No.

Part 5: Sign here. You MUST complete all three pages of Form 941 and SIGN it.

Under penalties of perjury, I declare that I have examined this return, including accompanying schedules and statements, and to the best of my knowledge and belief, it is true, correct, and complete. Declaration of preparer (other than taxpayer) is based on all information of which preparer has any knowledge.

X   **Sign your name here** [   ]   Print your name here [   ]

Print your title here [   ]

Date [/   /]   Best daytime phone [   ]

Paid Preparer Use Only   Check if you're self-employed . . . ☐

Preparer's name		PTIN	
Preparer's signature		Date	/ /
Firm's name (or yours if self-employed)		EIN	
Address		Phone	
City		State	ZIP code	

Page **3**   Form **941** (Rev. 3-2022)

3-14B • LO 5   See Figure 3.8 on pages 3-23 to 3-25

During the third calendar quarter of 20--, the Beechtree Inn, owned by Dawn Smedley, employed the persons listed below. Also given are the employees' salaries or wages and the amount of tips reported to the owner. The tips were reported by the 10th of each month. The federal income tax and FICA tax to be withheld from the tips were estimated by the owner and withheld equally over the 13 weekly pay periods. The employer's portion of FICA tax on the tips was estimated as the same amount.

Employee	Salary or Wage	Quarter's Wages	Quarter's Tips	Quarter's OASDI	Quarter's HI	Quarter's FIT
Jennifer Pasco	$104,000/year	$ 26,000.00		$1,612.00	$ 337.00	$1,980.00
Shelby Toland	78,000/year	19,500.00		1,209.00	282.75	1,290.00
Casey Riordan	800/week	10,400.00	$ 3,240.90	845.78	197.73	600.00
Howard Cohen	650/week	8,450.00	3,493.10	740.48	173.29	630.00
Rebecca Somerville	675/week	8,775.00	3,640.30	769.73	180.05	690.00
Matthew Chalfont	750/week	9,750.00	3,704.00	834.21	195.13	540.00
Sean Matthews	750/week	9,750.00		604.50	141.44	910.00
Holly Perry	600/week	7,800.00		483.60	113.10	653.00
Margaret Levine	750/week	9,750.00		604.50	141.44	364.00
Mary Bullen	600/week	7,800.00		483.60	113.10	559.00
		$117,975.00	$14,078.30	$8,187.40	$1,915.03	$8,216.00

Employees are paid weekly on Friday. The following paydays occurred during this quarter:

July	August	September
5 weekly paydays	4 weekly paydays	4 weekly paydays

Taxes withheld for the 13 paydays in the third quarter follow:

Employees' Federal Income Tax	Weekly FICA Taxes Withheld on Wages		Weekly FICA Taxes on Tips	
	OASDI	HI	OASDI	HI
$632 per week	Employees' $562.65	$131.61	Employees' $67.15	$15.70
	Employer's 562.65	131.59	Employer's 67.14	15.70

Based on the information given, complete Form 941 on pages 3-70 to 3-72 for Dawn Smedley.
Phone number: (901) 555-7959
Date filed: October 31, 20--

3-14B (continued)

Form **941 for 20--:** **Employer's QUARTERLY Federal Tax Return**
(Rev. March 2022)   Department of the Treasury — Internal Revenue Service

OMB No. 1545-0029

Employer identification number (EIN)   0 0 – 0 0 0 3 6 0 7

Name (not your trade name)   DAWN SMEDLEY

Trade name (if any)   BEECHTREE INN

Address   404 UNION AVE.
Number   Street   Suite or room number

MEMPHIS   TN   38112
City   State   ZIP code

Foreign country name   Foreign province/county   Foreign postal code

Report for this Quarter of 20--
(Check one.)

☐ **1:** January, February, March

☐ **2:** April, May, June

☐ **3:** July, August, September

☐ **4:** October, November, December

Go to *www.irs.gov/Form941* for instructions and the latest information.

Read the separate instructions before you complete Form 941. Type or print within the boxes.

Part 1:   Answer these questions for this quarter.

1 Number of employees who received wages, tips, or other compensation for the pay period including: *Mar. 12* (Quarter 1) . . . . **1** [   ]

2 Wages, tips, and other compensation . . . . **2** [.   ]

3 Federal income tax withheld from wages, tips, and other compensation . . . . . . **3** [.   ]

4 If no wages, tips, and other compensation are subject to social security or Medicare tax   ☐ Check and go to line 6.

		Column 1		Column 2	
5a	Taxable social security wages* . .	[.]	× 0.124 =	[.]	
5a	**(i)** Qualified sick leave wages* .	[.]	× 0.062 =	[.]	
5a	**(ii)** Qualified family leave wages* .	[.]	× 0.062 =	[.]	
5b	Taxable social security tips . . .	[.]	× 0.124 =	[.]	
5c	Taxable Medicare wages & tips. .	[.]	× 0.029 =	[.]	
5d	Taxable wages & tips subject to Additional Medicare Tax withholding	[.]	× 0.009 =	[.]	

*Include taxable qualified sick and family leave wages paid in 2022 for leave taken after March 31, 2021, and before October 1, 2021, on line 5a. Use lines 5a(i) and 5a(ii) **only** for taxable qualified sick and family leave wages paid in 2022 for leave taken after March 31, 2020, and before April 1, 2021.

5e Total social security and Medicare taxes. Add Column 2 from lines 5a, 5a(i), 5a(ii), 5b, 5c, and 5d   **5e** [.   ]

5f Section 3121(q) Notice and Demand—Tax due on unreported tips (see instructions) . .   **5f** [.   ]

6 Total taxes before adjustments. Add lines 3, 5e, and 5f . . . .   **6** [.   ]

7 Current quarter's adjustment for fractions of cents . . . .   **7** [.   ]

8 Current quarter's adjustment for sick pay . . . .   **8** [.   ]

9 Current quarter's adjustments for tips and group-term life insurance . . . . . .   **9** [.   ]

10 Total taxes after adjustments. Combine lines 6 through 9 . . . .   **10** [.   ]

11a Qualified small business payroll tax credit for increasing research activities. Attach Form 8974   **11a** [.   ]

11b Nonrefundable portion of credit for qualified sick and family leave wages for leave taken before April 1, 2021 . . . .   **11b** [.   ]

11c Reserved for future use . . . .   **11c** [.   ]

▶ You MUST complete all three pages of Form 941 and SIGN it.   Next ▶

For Privacy Act and Paperwork Reduction Act Notice, see the back of the Payment Voucher.   Cat. No. 17001Z   Form **941** (Rev. 3-2022)

3-14B (continued)

Name *(not your trade name)* DAWN SMEDLEY	Employer identification number (EIN) 00-0003607

Part 1: Answer these questions for this quarter. *(continued)*

11d Nonrefundable portion of credit for qualified sick and family leave wages for leave taken after March 31, 2021, and before October 1, 2021 . . . . 11d [＿＿＿＿＿＿. ▪]

11e Nonrefundable portion of COBRA premium assistance credit (see instructions for applicable quarter) . . . . 11e [＿＿＿＿＿＿. ▪]

11f Number of individuals provided COBRA premium assistance [＿＿＿＿＿＿]

11g Total nonrefundable credits. Add lines 11a, 11b, 11d, and 11e . . . . 11g [＿＿＿＿＿＿. ▪]

12 Total taxes after adjustments and nonrefundable credits. Subtract line 11g from line 10 . 12 [＿＿＿＿＿＿. ▪]

13a Total deposits for this quarter, including overpayment applied from a prior quarter and overpayments applied from Form 941-X, 941-X (PR), 944-X, or 944-X (SP) filed in the current quarter 13a [＿＿＿＿＿＿. ▪]

13b Reserved for future use . . . . 13b [＿＿＿＿＿＿. ▪]

13c Refundable portion of credit for qualified sick and family leave wages for leave taken before April 1, 2021 . . . . 13c [＿＿＿＿＿＿. ▪]

13d Reserved for future use . . . . 13d [＿＿＿＿＿＿. ▪]

13e Refundable portion of credit for qualified sick and family leave wages for leave taken after March 31, 2021, and before October 1, 2021 . . . . 13e [＿＿＿＿＿＿. ▪]

13f Refundable portion of COBRA premium assistance credit (see instructions for applicable quarter) . . . . 13f [＿＿＿＿＿＿. ▪]

13g Total deposits and refundable credits. Add lines 13a, 13c, 13e, and 13f . . . . . . 13g [＿＿＿＿＿＿. ▪]

13h Reserved for future use . . . . 13h [＿＿＿＿＿＿. ▪]

13i Reserved for future use . . . . 13i [＿＿＿＿＿＿. ▪]

14 Balance due. If line 12 is more than line 13g, enter the difference and see instructions . . . 14 [＿＿＿＿＿＿. ▪]

15 Overpayment. If line 13g is more than line 12, enter the difference [＿＿＿＿. ▪] Check one: ☐ Apply to next return. ☐ Send a refund.

Part 2: Tell us about your deposit schedule and tax liability for this quarter.

If you're unsure about whether you're a monthly schedule depositor or a semiweekly schedule depositor, see section 11 of Pub. 15.

16 Check one: ☐ Line 12 on this return is less than $2,500 or line 12 on the return for the prior quarter was less than $2,500, **and you didn't incur a $100,000 next-day deposit obligation during the current quarter.** If line 12 for the prior quarter was less than $2,500 but line 12 on this return is $100,000 or more, you must provide a record of your federal tax liability. If you're a monthly schedule depositor, complete the deposit schedule below; if you're a semiweekly schedule depositor, attach Schedule B (Form 941). Go to Part 3.

☐ **You were a monthly schedule depositor for the entire quarter.** Enter your tax liability for each month and total liability for the quarter, then go to Part 3.

Tax liability: Month 1 [＿＿＿＿＿. ▪]

Month 2 [＿＿＿＿＿. ▪]

Month 3 [＿＿＿＿＿. ▪]

Total liability for quarter [＿＿＿＿＿. ▪] Total must equal line 12.

☐ **You were a semiweekly schedule depositor for any part of this quarter.** Complete Schedule B (Form 941), Report of Tax Liability for Semiweekly Schedule Depositors, and attach it to Form 941. Go to Part 3.

▶ **You MUST complete all three pages of Form 941 and SIGN it.** [Next ▶]

Page **2** Form **941** (Rev. 3-2022)

3-14B (concluded)

Name *(not your trade name)*	Employer identification number (EIN)
DAWN SMEDLEY	00-0003607

Part 3: Tell us about your business. If a question does NOT apply to your business, leave it blank.

17 If your business has closed or you stopped paying wages . . . . ☐ Check here, and

enter the final date you paid wages ⬚ / / ⬚ ; also attach a statement to your return. See instructions.

18 If you're a seasonal employer and you don't have to file a return for every quarter of the year . . . ☐ Check here.

19	Qualified health plan expenses allocable to qualified sick leave wages for leave taken before April 1, 2021	19	▪
20	Qualified health plan expenses allocable to qualified family leave wages for leave taken before April 1, 2021	20	▪
21	Reserved for future use	21	▪
22	Reserved for future use	22	▪
23	Qualified sick leave wages for leave taken after March 31, 2021, and before October 1, 2021	23	▪
24	Qualified health plan expenses allocable to qualified sick leave wages reported on line 23	24	▪
25	Amounts under certain collectively bargained agreements allocable to qualified sick leave wages reported on line 23	25	▪
26	Qualified family leave wages for leave taken after March 31, 2021, and before October 1, 2021	26	▪
27	Qualified health plan expenses allocable to qualified family leave wages reported on line 26	27	▪
28	Amounts under certain collectively bargained agreements allocable to qualified family leave wages reported on line 26	28	▪

Part 4: May we speak with your third-party designee?

Do you want to allow an employee, a paid tax preparer, or another person to discuss this return with the IRS? See the instructions for details.

☐ Yes. Designee's name and phone number

Select a 5-digit personal identification number (PIN) to use when talking to the IRS. ☐ ☐ ☐ ☐ ☐

☐ No.

Part 5: Sign here. You MUST complete all three pages of Form 941 and SIGN it.

Under penalties of perjury, I declare that I have examined this return, including accompanying schedules and statements, and to the best of my knowledge and belief, it is true, correct, and complete. Declaration of preparer (other than taxpayer) is based on all information of which preparer has any knowledge.

X **Sign your name here**

Print your name here

Print your title here

Date / /

Best daytime phone

Paid Preparer Use Only

Check if you're self-employed . . . ☐

Preparer's name		PTIN	
Preparer's signature		Date	/ /
Firm's name (or yours if self-employed)		EIN	
Address		Phone	
City		State	ZIP code

Form **941** (Rev. 3-2022)

Source: Internal Revenue Service.

3-15B • LO 4, 5    **See Example 3-6 on page 3-20, see Figure 3.10 on page 3-27**
Show Me How

The taxable wages and withheld taxes for Hamilton Company (EIN 00-0001462), semiweekly depositor, for the first quarter of 20-- follow.

Semimonthly Paydays	Gross and Taxable Wages	FICA Withheld OASDI	FICA Withheld HI	Federal Income Tax Withheld
1/15	$ 34,200	$ 2,120.40	$ 495.90	$ 4,180.00
1/31	32,900	2,039.80	477.05	4,090.00
2/15	31,750	1,968.50	460.38	3,996.00
2/28	28,970	1,796.14	420.07	3,797.00
3/15	28,800	1,785.60	417.60	3,790.00
3/29	29,400	1,822.80	426.30	3,999.00
	$186,020	$11,533.24	$2,697.30	$23,852.00

a. Complete Schedule B of Form 941 on page 3-74 for the first quarter for Harry Conway, the owner of Hamilton Company.

b. Using the calendar below, list the due dates of each deposit in the first quarter.

January							February							March							April						
Su	Mo	Tu	We	Th	Fr	Sa	Su	Mo	Tu	We	Th	Fr	Sa	Su	Mo	Tu	We	Th	Fr	Sa	Su	Mo	Tu	We	Th	Fr	Sa
	1	2	3	4	5							1	2						1	2		1	2	3	4	5	6
6	7	8	9	10	11	12	3	4	5	6	7	8	9	3	4	5	6	7	8	9	7	8	9	10	11	12	13
13	14	15	16	17	18	19	10	11	12	13	14	15	16	10	11	12	13	14	15	16	14	15	16	17	18	19	20
20	21	22	23	24	25	26	17	18	19	20	21	22	23	17	18	19	20	21	22	23	21	22	23	24	25	26	27
27	28	29	30	31			24	25	26	27	28			24	25	26	27	28	29	30	28	29	30				
														31													

Paydays	Deposit Due Dates
January 15	1. _____
January 31	2. _____
February 15	3. _____
February 28	4. _____
March 15	5. _____
March 29	6. _____

3-16B • LO 5   **See Example 3-6 on page 3-20, Example 3-8 on page 3-32,**
Example 3-9 on page 3-32

Yelman Company is a monthly depositor whose tax liability for June 20-- is $3,930.

1. What is the due date for the deposit of these taxes?   _____

2. Assume that no deposit was made until August 2 (18 days late). Compute the following penalties:

    a. Penalty for failure to make timely deposit. $ _____

    b. Penalty for failure to fully pay tax. $ _____

    c. Interest on taxes due and unpaid (assume a 4% interest rate). $ _____

    d. Total penalty imposed. $ _____

3-15B (concluded)

Schedule B (Form 941):

Report of Tax Liability for Semiweekly Schedule Depositors

(Rev. January 2017)   Department of the Treasury — Internal Revenue Service

OMB No. 1545-0029

Employer identification number (EIN)   0 0 – 0 0 0 1 4 6 2

Name (not your trade name)   HARRY CONWAY

Calendar year   ☐ ☐ ☐ ☐   (Also check quarter)

Report for this Quarter...
(Check one.)

☐ **1:** January, February, March

☐ **2:** April, May, June

☐ **3:** July, August, September

☐ **4:** October, November, December

Use this schedule to show your TAX LIABILITY for the quarter; don't use it to show your deposits. When you file this form with Form 941 or Form 941-SS, don't change your tax liability by adjustments reported on any Forms 941-X or 944-X. You must fill out this form and attach it to Form 941 or Form 941-SS if you're a semiweekly schedule depositor or became one because your accumulated tax liability on any day was $100,000 or more. Write your daily tax liability on the numbered space that corresponds to the date wages were paid. See Section 11 in Pub. 15 for details.

Month 1

Tax liability for Month 1

Month 2

Tax liability for Month 2

Month 3

Tax liability for Month 3

Total liability for the quarter

Fill in your total liability for the quarter (Month 1 + Month 2 + Month 3) ▶

Total must equal line 12 on Form 941 or Form 941-SS.

For Paperwork Reduction Act Notice, see separate instructions.   IRS.gov/form941   Cat. No. 11967Q   **Schedule B (Form 941)** (Rev. 1-2017)

Source: Internal Revenue Service.

Date _____ Name _____

3-17B • LO 2, 3 See Example 3-1 on page 3-11

At Gleeson Brewing Company, office workers are employed for a 40-hour workweek on either an annual or a monthly salary basis.

Given on the form below are the current annual and monthly salary rates for five office workers for the week ended December 13, 20-- (50th payday of the year). In addition, with this pay, these employees are paid their sliding scale annual bonuses. The bonuses are listed on the register.

For each worker, compute:

1. Regular earnings for the weekly payroll ended December 13, 20--.
2. Overtime earnings (if applicable).
3. Total regular, overtime earnings, and bonus.
4. FICA taxable wages for this pay period.
5. FICA taxes to be withheld for this pay period.

GLEESON BREWING COMPANY

Employee	Salary	Hours Worked	Annual Bonus	Regular Earnings	Overtime Earnings	Total Earnings
Won, H.	$99,840/yr.	40	$55,000			
Park, B.	96,200/yr.	40	25,000			
James, R.	7,280/mo.	40	20,000			
Oho, J.	5,265/mo.	40	15,000			
Mack, K.	3,400/mo.	46	8,000			
Totals						

(left side)

GLEESON BREWING COMPANY

Cumulative Earnings as of Last Pay Period	FICA Taxable Wages This Pay Period		FICA Taxes to Be Withheld		Employee
	OASDI	HI	OASDI	HI	
$94,080.00					Won, H.
90,650.00					Park, B.
82,320.00					James, R.
59,535.00					Oho, J.
38,446.38					Mack, K.
					Totals

(right side)

Employer's FICA taxes for week ended December 13, 20--: $ _____ (OASDI) $ _____ (HI)

Continuing Payroll Problem • A

Refer to the partially completed payroll register you started at the end of Chapter 2. You will now determine the amount of FICA taxes to be withheld from each employee's pay for the pay period ending January 8, 20--.

1. In the Taxable Earnings columns, record the amount of each employee's weekly earnings that is subject to FICA taxes. All wages are taxable for OASDI and HI taxes.

2. Using the amount recorded in step 1, compute the taxes for each employee and record in the appropriate column.

Note: Keep your partially completed payroll register for use at the end of Chapter 4.

Continuing Payroll Problem • B

Refer to the partially completed payroll register you started at the end of Chapter 2. You will now determine the amount of FICA taxes to be withheld from each employee's pay for the pay period ending January 8, 20--.

1. In the Taxable Earnings columns, record the amount of each employee's weekly earnings that is subject to FICA taxes. All wages are taxable for OASDI and HI taxes.

2. Using the amount recorded in step 1, compute the taxes for each employee and record in the appropriate column.

Note: Keep your partially completed payroll register for use at the end of Chapter 4.

Case Problems

C1. Auditing Form 941. LO 4, 5.

Your assistant has just completed a rough draft of Form 941, shown on pages 3-79 to 3-81, for the quarter ending March 31, 20--. As the supervisor and authorized signer, you are auditing the form before it is mailed to ensure its accuracy.

Four of the company's general ledger accounts are shown on the following two pages. The company's 17 employees are paid on the 15th and last day of each month. The company is a semiweekly depositor. Indicate any changes that should be made on the form before it is signed, dated, and mailed.

C1 (continued)

FICA TAXES PAYABLE—OASDI				Account No. 214	
				Balance	
Date	Debit	Credit	Debit	Debit	Credit
20--					
Jan. 15		773.94			773.94
15		773.96			1,547.90
19	1,547.90				—
31		843.78			843.78
31		843.78			1,687.56
Feb. 2	1,687.56				—
15		833.74			833.74
15		833.72			1,667.46
22	1,667.46				—
28		803.79			803.79
28		803.79			1,607.58
Mar. 3	1,607.58				—
15		786.73			786.73
15		786.72			1,573.45
20	1,573.45				—
31		787.87			787.87
31		787.88			1,575.75
Apr. 5	1,575.75				—

FICA TAXES PAYABLE—HI				Account No. 215	
				Balance	
Date	Debit	Credit	Debit	Debit	Credit
20--					
Jan. 15		181.01			181.01
15		181.01			362.02
19	362.02				—
31		197.32			197.32
31		197.34			394.66
Feb. 2	394.66				—
15		194.98			194.98
15		194.98			389.96
22	389.96				—
28		187.98			187.98
28		187.98			375.96
Mar. 3	375.96				—
15		183.99			183.99
15		184.01			368.00
20	368.00				—
31		184.24			184.24
31		184.26			368.50
Apr. 5	368.50				—

C1 (continued)

EMPLOYEES FEDERAL INCOME TAX PAYABLE   Account No. 216

Date		Debit	Credit	Balance Debit	Balance Credit
20--					
Jan.	15		1,980.00		1,980.00
	19	1,980.00			—
	31		2,217.00		2,217.00
Feb.	2	2,217.00			—
	15		2,016.00		2,016.00
	22	2,016.00			—
	28		2,007.00		2,007.00
Mar.	3	2,007.00			—
	15		1,970.00		1,970.00
	20	1,970.00			—
	31		1,887.00		1,887.00
Apr.	5	1,887.00			—

WAGES AND SALARIES   Account No. 511

Date		Debit	Credit	Balance Debit	Balance Credit
20--					
Jan.	15	12,483.16		12,483.16	
	31	13,609.40		26,092.56	
Feb.	15	13,447.13		39,539.69	
	28	12,964.43		52,504.12	
Mar.	15	12,689.02		65,193.14	
	31	12,707.69		77,900.83	

C1 (continued)

Form **941 for 20--:** **Employer's QUARTERLY Federal Tax Return**
(Rev. March 2022)   Department of the Treasury — Internal Revenue Service

OMB No. 1545-0029

Employer identification number (EIN) `0 0 - 0 0 0 0 7 1 4 2`

Name (not your trade name)

Trade name (if any)   COASTAL COMPANY

Address   77 CASTRO
Number   Street   Suite or room number

SAN FRANCISCO   CA   94117
City   State   ZIP code

Foreign country name   Foreign province/county   Foreign postal code

Report for this Quarter of 20--
(Check one.)

☐ **1:** January, February, March
☐ **2:** April, May, June
☐ **3:** July, August, September
☐ **4:** October, November, December

Go to *www.irs.gov/Form941* for instructions and the latest information.

Read the separate instructions before you complete Form 941. Type or print within the boxes.

Part 1: Answer these questions for this quarter.

1	Number of employees who received wages, tips, or other compensation for the pay period including: *Mar. 12* (Quarter 1)	1	17
2	Wages, tips, and other compensation	2	77900 . 38
3	Federal income tax withheld from wages, tips, and other compensation	3	12077 . 00

4   If no wages, tips, and other compensation are subject to social security or Medicare tax   ☐ Check and go to line 6.

		Column 1		Column 2	
5a	Taxable social security wages* . .	77900 . 38	× 0.124 =	9659 . 65	
5a (i)	Qualified sick leave wages* .	.	× 0.062 =	.	
5a (ii)	Qualified family leave wages* .	.	× 0.062 =	.	
5b	Taxable social security tips . . .	.	× 0.124 =	.	
5c	Taxable Medicare wages & tips. .	77900 . 38	× 0.029 =	2259 . 11	
5d	Taxable wages & tips subject to Additional Medicare Tax withholding	.	× 0.009 =	.	

*Include taxable qualified sick and family leave wages paid in 2022 for leave taken after March 31, 2021, and before October 1, 2021, on line 5a. Use lines 5a(i) and 5a(ii) **only** for taxable qualified sick and family leave wages paid in 2022 for leave taken after March 31, 2020, and before April 1, 2021.*

5e	Total social security and Medicare taxes. Add Column 2 from lines 5a, 5a(i), 5a(ii), 5b, 5c, and 5d	5e	11918 . 76
5f	Section 3121(q) Notice and Demand—Tax due on unreported tips (see instructions) . .	5f	.
6	Total taxes before adjustments. Add lines 3, 5e, and 5f	6	23995 . 76
7	Current quarter's adjustment for fractions of cents	7	. 04
8	Current quarter's adjustment for sick pay	8	
9	Current quarter's adjustments for tips and group-term life insurance	9	
10	Total taxes after adjustments. Combine lines 6 through 9	10	23995 . 80
11a	Qualified small business payroll tax credit for increasing research activities. Attach Form 8974	11a	.
11b	Nonrefundable portion of credit for qualified sick and family leave wages for leave taken before April 1, 2021	11b	.
11c	Reserved for future use	11c	.

▶ **You MUST complete all three pages of Form 941 and SIGN it.**   Next ▶

For Privacy Act and Paperwork Reduction Act Notice, see the back of the Payment Voucher.   Cat. No. 17001Z   Form **941** (Rev. 3-2022)

C1 (continued)

Name *(not your trade name)*	Employer identification number (EIN)
COASTAL COMPANY	00-0007142

Part 1: Answer these questions for this quarter. *(continued)*

11d Nonrefundable portion of credit for qualified sick and family leave wages for leave taken after March 31, 2021, and before October 1, 2021 . . . . **11d** | ▢ . |

11e Nonrefundable portion of COBRA premium assistance credit (see instructions for applicable quarter) . . . . **11e** | ▢ . |

11f Number of individuals provided COBRA premium assistance [ ]

11g Total nonrefundable credits. Add lines 11a, 11b, 11d, and 11e . . . . **11g** | ▢ . |

12 Total taxes after adjustments and nonrefundable credits. Subtract line 11g from line 10 . **12** | 23995 . 80 |

13a Total deposits for this quarter, including overpayment applied from a prior quarter and overpayments applied from Form 941-X, 941-X (PR), 944-X, or 944-X (SP) filed in the current quarter **13a** | 23995 . 80 |

13b Reserved for future use . . . . **13b** | . |

13c Refundable portion of credit for qualified sick and family leave wages for leave taken before April 1, 2021 . . . . **13c** | . |

13d Reserved for future use . . . . **13d** | . |

13e Refundable portion of credit for qualified sick and family leave wages for leave taken after March 31, 2021, and before October 1, 2021 . . . . **13e** | . |

13f Refundable portion of COBRA premium assistance credit (see instructions for applicable quarter) . . . . **13f** | . |

13g Total deposits and refundable credits. Add lines 13a, 13c, 13e, and 13f . . . . **13g** | 23995 . 80 |

13h Reserved for future use . . . . **13h** | . |

13i Reserved for future use . . . . **13i** | . |

14 Balance due. If line 12 is more than line 13g, enter the difference and see instructions . . . **14** | 18 . 00 |

15 Overpayment. If line 13g is more than line 12, enter the difference [.] Check one: ▢ Apply to next return. ▢ Send a refund.

Part 2: Tell us about your deposit schedule and tax liability for this quarter.

If you're unsure about whether you're a monthly schedule depositor or a semiweekly schedule depositor, see section 11 of Pub. 15.

16 Check one: ▢ Line 12 on this return is less than $2,500 or line 12 on the return for the prior quarter was less than $2,500, and you didn't incur a $100,000 next-day deposit obligation during the current quarter. If line 12 for the prior quarter was less than $2,500 but line 12 on this return is $100,000 or more, you must provide a record of your federal tax liability. If you're a monthly schedule depositor, complete the deposit schedule below; if you're a semiweekly schedule depositor, attach Schedule B (Form 941). Go to Part 3.

▢ You were a monthly schedule depositor for the entire quarter. Enter your tax liability for each month and total liability for the quarter, then go to Part 3.

Tax liability:	Month 1	8189 . 14
	Month 2	8063 . 96
	Month 3	7742 . 70
Total liability for quarter		23995 . 80	Total must equal line 12.

▢ You were a semiweekly schedule depositor for any part of this quarter. Complete Schedule B (Form 941), Report of Tax Liability for Semiweekly Schedule Depositors, and attach it to Form 941. Go to Part 3.

▶ You MUST complete all three pages of Form 941 and SIGN it. Next ▶

Page **2** Form **941** (Rev. 3-2022)

C1 (concluded)

Name *(not your trade name)*	Employer identification number (EIN)
COASTAL COMPANY	00-0007142

Part 3: Tell us about your business. If a question does NOT apply to your business, leave it blank.

17 If your business has closed or you stopped paying wages . . . . ☐ Check here, and

    enter the final date you paid wages   └ / / ┘ ; also attach a statement to your return. See instructions.

18 If you're a seasonal employer and you don't have to file a return for every quarter of the year . . . ☐ Check here.

19	Qualified health plan expenses allocable to qualified sick leave wages for leave taken before April 1, 2021	19	▪
20	Qualified health plan expenses allocable to qualified family leave wages for leave taken before April 1, 2021	20	▪
21	Reserved for future use	21	▪
22	Reserved for future use	22	▪
23	Qualified sick leave wages for leave taken after March 31, 2021, and before October 1, 2021	23	▪
24	Qualified health plan expenses allocable to qualified sick leave wages reported on line 23	24	▪
25	Amounts under certain collectively bargained agreements allocable to qualified sick leave wages reported on line 23	25	▪
26	Qualified family leave wages for leave taken after March 31, 2021, and before October 1, 2021	26	▪
27	Qualified health plan expenses allocable to qualified family leave wages reported on line 26	27	▪
28	Amounts under certain collectively bargained agreements allocable to qualified family leave wages reported on line 26	28	▪

Part 4: May we speak with your third-party designee?

Do you want to allow an employee, a paid tax preparer, or another person to discuss this return with the IRS? See the instructions for details.

☐ Yes. Designee's name and phone number [_____] [_____]

    Select a 5-digit personal identification number (PIN) to use when talking to the IRS. ☐ ☐ ☐ ☐ ☐

☐ No.

Part 5: Sign here. You MUST complete all three pages of Form 941 and SIGN it.

Under penalties of perjury, I declare that I have examined this return, including accompanying schedules and statements, and to the best of my knowledge and belief, it is true, correct, and complete. Declaration of preparer (other than taxpayer) is based on all information of which preparer has any knowledge.

✗ **Sign your name here** [_____]

Print your name here [_____]

Print your title here [_____]

Date └ / / ┘

Best daytime phone [_____]

Paid Preparer Use Only   Check if you're self-employed . . . ☐

Preparer's name	[_____]	PTIN	[_____]
Preparer's signature	[_____]	Date	└ / / ┘
Firm's name (or yours if self-employed)	[_____]	EIN	[_____]
Address	[_____]	Phone	[_____]
City	[_____]	State [____]	ZIP code	[_____]

Form **941** (Rev. 3-2022)

Source: Internal Revenue Service.

C2. Household Employee? LO 1.

Nelson operates a placement service for companion sitting for the elderly. He placed Martha Jackson with Mrs. Mock, an elderly woman who needed a person to assist with her personal needs, household care, and companionship. Jackson is paid directly from Mrs. Mock. Jackson had to pay a placement fee of $50 to Nelson. Is Jackson an employee of Nelson or a household employee of Mrs. Mock? Explain.

Chapter 4

Income Tax Withholding

Now what do we take out of the employees' pay for federal income taxes? The IRS gives us charts to use! That should be easy! Some fringe benefits are taxed? Some deductions are pretax? What's an allowance? How about supplemental pays? Are tips going to be a problem again? And who gets copies of Form W-2 (Wage and Tax Statement)? It's bad enough filing an individual income tax return—being an employer is worse!

Learning Objectives

After studying this chapter, you should be able to:

1. Explain coverage under the Federal Income Tax Withholding Law by determining: (a) the employer-employee relationship, (b) the kinds of payments defined as wages, and (c) the kinds of pretax salary reductions.

2. Explain the purpose and use of Form W-4 from 2020 or later.

3. Compute the amount of federal income tax to be withheld using the appropriate tables for Manual Systems with Forms W-4 from 2020 or later for: (a) the percentage method; (b) the wage-bracket method; (c) alternative methods such as quarterly averaging, annualizing of wages, and part-year employment; and (d) withholding of federal income taxes on supplementary wage payments.

4. Explain the purpose and use of Form W-2.

5. Identify major types of information returns.

6. Discuss the impact of state and local income taxes on the payroll accounting process.

Supplement

7. Explain the purpose and use of Form W-4 from 2019 or earlier and the types of allowances that may be claimed by employees for income tax withholding.

8. Compute the amount of federal income tax to be withheld using the appropriate tables for Manual Systems with Forms W-4 from 2019 or earlier for: (a) the percentage method and (b) the wage-bracket method.

Due to printing schedules, the tax tables at the end of the book are the tables that were in effect until December 31, 2022.

At the beginning of World War II, the income tax became the principal source of revenue to finance government operations. The Ruml plan put the collection of this tax on a pay-as-you-go basis. This chapter describes the employer's responsibility for withholding income taxes from employees' wages and paying these taxes to the federal government. In addition, many employers must also comply with state, city, and county income tax withholding laws. Employers must be aware of these laws to avoid possible penalties.

D. Elmi/Shutterstock.com

Coverage Under Federal Income Tax Withholding Laws

Before an individual withholds any tax under the tax law, the following conditions must exist:

1. There must be, or have been, an employer-employee relationship.
2. The payments received by the employee must be defined as wages under the law.
3. The employment must not be exempted by the law.

Employer-Employee Relationship

As discussed in Chapter 3, establishing the correct relationship between the employer and employee is a very important factor in complying with the Social Security Tax Law. This also applies to the Federal Income Tax Withholding Law.

If a business has the right to control and direct the worker, it meets the definition of an employer under the common-law criteria.

Employers can be sole proprietorships, partners, corporations, not-for-profit corporations, and federal and state governments. No distinctions are made between classes or grades of employees—from executives to entry-level personnel. Directors of a corporation are not considered employees unless they perform services other than participation in board meetings. Partners are also eliminated from the definition of an employee.

If the employer-employee relationship exists, the pay is subject to federal income tax withholding.

Statutory Employees/Nonemployees

If a worker does not qualify as an employee under the common-law test, federal income taxes are not withheld. However, by statute, under certain conditions they may be considered **employees** for FICA and FUTA taxes. As discussed in Chapter 3, this applies to agent drivers, full-time life insurance salespersons, homeworkers, and traveling or city salespersons.

Direct sellers and qualified real estate agents are considered **nonemployees** by statute. They are treated as self-employed for *all* federal tax purposes.

Taxable Wages

For withholding purposes, the term **wages** includes the total compensation paid to employees for services. Employers withhold federal income taxes on the *gross amount* of wages before deductions such as state and local taxes, insurance premiums, savings bonds, profit-sharing contributions, and union dues. Examples of employee compensation subject to withholding include:

- Wages and salaries
- Vacation allowances
- Supplemental payments
- Bonuses and commissions
- Taxable fringe benefits
- Tips
- Cash awards

Employees may receive compensation in ways other than their regular wage payments. Figure 4.1 shows some special types of payments that are also subject to federal income tax withholding.

FIGURE 4.1

Taxable Payments to Employees

Disabled Worker's Wages	Withhold for wages paid after the year in which the worker became entitled to disability insurance under the Social Security Act.
Drawing Account Advances	Advance payments to salespersons against their commissions or unearned salaries for which they are to perform services, but for which they are not legally obligated to repay.
Gift Certificates (cards)	Considered cash equivalent, and therefore taxable.
Meals and Lodging	Unless furnished for the employer's convenience and on the employer's premises, as a condition of employment. Cash allowances for meals and lodging are taxable. If more than half of the meals provided to employees on the employer's premises are for the convenience of the employer, then these meals are treated as for the employer's convenience.
Moving Expenses	Nonqualified reimbursed and employer-paid expenses are subject to withholding. Nonqualified expenses include cost of sale of old residence, purchase of new residence, house hunting, temporary living expenses, and meals. See Figure 4.2 on page 4-6 for exempt reimbursements to members of U.S. Armed Forces.
Partially Exempt Employment	If the employee spends half or more time in a pay period performing services subject to employment taxes, all pay in that pay period is taxable.
Payments to Nonresident Aliens	Subject to withholding (unless excepted by regulations).
Scholarship	Cash or reduced tuition is taxable if paid for teaching, research, or other services as a condition of receiving the scholarship.
Sick Pay	Subject to withholding whether paid by the employer or third party (to the extent of the employer's contribution into the plan).
Supplemental Unemployment Compensation	To the extent it is includible in an employee's gross income. It does not include separation due to disciplinary problems or age.
Travel and Business Expenses (nonaccountable plans)	If (1) the employee is not required to or does not substantiate expenses with receipts or (2) the employee receives travel advances and does not or is not required to return any unused amount of the advance.

Payments to employees in a medium other than cash are also taxed. Payments in the form of goods, lodging, food, clothing, or services are taxed at their fair market value at the time that they are given.

If wages received in the same payroll period are in part subject to withholding and in part exempt, all wages received are treated alike. If one-half or more of the wages are subject to withholding, then withholding is required on all wages. If more than one-half of the pay is exempt from withholding, then no withholding is required for the total pay.

Fringe Benefits

Unless the law says otherwise, fringe benefits are subject to federal income tax withholding. In general, the taxable portion is the amount by which the fair market value of the benefits exceeds what the employee paid, plus any amount the law excludes. Fringe benefits include employer-provided items such as those listed here.

- Cars
- Free or discounted flights
- Discounts on property or services
- Vacations
- Memberships in social or country clubs
- Tickets for entertainment and sporting events

Frank Romeo/Shutterstock.com

Withholding on Fringe Benefits

Determination of the value of the fringe benefit must be made by January 31 of the following year. For withholding and depositing purposes, reasonable estimates may be used before that date. The employer may add the value of fringe benefits to regular wages for a payroll period and figure withholding taxes on the total or may withhold the tax on the value of the benefits at the *flat 22* percent supplemental wage rate.

The employer may choose not to withhold income tax on the value of an employee's personal use of a vehicle. The employer must, however, withhold social security, Medicare, or railroad retirement taxes on the use of the vehicle.

Flexible Reporting

With noncash fringe benefits, the employer has the option of treating the benefits as being paid on any basis (paying monthly, at year-end, etc.). As long as the benefits are treated as paid by December 31, the employer can choose any option.

Due to a *special period rule,* employers can even use October 31 as the cutoff date for valuing the noncash fringe benefit. This rule allows employers to treat noncash fringe benefits of November and December as being provided in the following year and therefore taxed in the next year.

If this special rule is applied to a particular benefit, it must apply to all employees who receive this benefit. Also, if applied, the employer must notify the employees of this special rule treatment prior to giving them their W-2 forms.

 On the Job

If you need to determine if a certain type of payment or individual is subject to income tax withholding, check **Circular E, Employer's Tax Guide**. Special classes of employment and payments are listed, along with their treatment under employment tax laws.

Employers may treat the value of a single fringe benefit as paid on one or more dates in the same calendar year even if the employee receives the entire benefit at one time.

A one-time receipt of a $1,000 fringe benefit in 2023 can be treated as four payments of $250, each in a different pay period of 2023.

News Alert

When an employer provides a cell phone to an employee "primarily for noncompensatory business reasons," the IRS will treat the employee's business use of the cell phone as a working condition fringe benefit, the value of which is excludable from the employee's income. Also, personal use of the employer-provided cell phone will be treated as a de minimis fringe benefit.[1]

Nontaxable Fringe Benefits

Fringe benefits that are nontaxable include:

- Services provided at no additional cost
- Qualified employee discounts
- Working condition fringes
- Qualified transportation fringes
- Use of on-premises athletic facilities
- Reduced tuition for education
- Job-placement assistance

Services the employer provides at no additional cost, qualified employee discounts, meals at employer-run eating establishments, and reduced tuition are excluded from their income only if the benefits are given to employees on a nondiscriminatory basis.

---

1 *Payroll Currently*, October 7, 2011, Issue 10, p. 3.

De Minimis Fringe Benefit

Any property or service the value of which is so small that accounting for it would be unreasonable or impractical is labeled a **de minimis fringe benefit** (i.e., coffee, dough-nuts, local telephone calls). There is no dollar cap on this type of nontaxable fringe benefit.

Iakov Filimonov/Shutterstock.com

Taxable Tips

As reported in Chapter 3, employees must report cash tips to the employer by the 10th of the month following the month they receive the tips. This report includes tips paid by the employer for charge customers and tips the employee receives directly from the customers. Tips of *less than $20* in a month and noncash tips need not be reported.

Withholding from Tips

The employer collects income tax, as well as social security taxes, on reported tips. The following procedures apply to withholding income tax on reported tips:

1. The employer collects the tax from the employee's wages or from other funds the employee makes available.

2. When tips are reported in connection with employment where the employee also receives a regular wage, compute the withholding tax on the aggregate—treat tips as a supplemental wage payment.

3. If the withholding tax exceeds the amount of wages paid to the employee, the employee must pay the uncollected portion of the taxes directly to the IRS when filing the annual income tax return (Form 1040).

4. The employer is not required to audit or verify the accuracy of the tip income reported.

WITHHOLDING ON WAGES AND TIPS Justin Miah, single, is a waiter at Metro American Bar and Grill. In his first week, he earned $350 for 20 hours and had $600 of reported tips. Justin's employer will withhold Federal Income tax based on the total of $950. Net pay is calculated by subtracting the withholding amounts from employer paid earnings of $350.

> **Example 4-1**

Allocated Tips

Large food and beverage establishments that have customary tipping and nor-mally had more than 10 employees on a typical business day in the preceding year may be required to allocate tips among employees if:

> *The total tips reported by the employees during any payroll period are less than 8 percent of the establishment's gross receipts for that period.*

The amount of allocated tips to employees equals:

> *The difference between tips reported and 8 percent of gross receipts, other than carryout sales and sales with at least a 10 percent service charge added.*

The tip allocation may be made using one of three methods: hours worked, gross receipts, good faith agreement. Federal income taxes are to be withheld only on the tips reported to the employer; no taxes are withheld on the tips that are merely allocated.

Traveling Expenses

Accountable Plan

Employee expense reimbursement amounts paid under an accountable plan are not subject to income tax withholding. An accountable plan requires the employer's reimbursement or allowance arrangement to meet all three of the following rules:

1. Business connected.
2. Adequate accounting within a reasonable time period (generally, 60 days).
3. Employee return of excess of substantiated amounts (generally, 120 days).

Nonaccountable Plan

A nonaccountable plan is an arrangement that does not meet all of the previous requirements. All amounts paid under this plan are considered wages and are subject to income tax withholding.

Payments Exempt from Withholding

The law excludes certain payments and payments to certain individuals from federal income tax withholding, as shown in Figure 4.2.

FIGURE 4.2
Exempt Payments

Type of Payment or Individual	Conditions
Advances	For travel and other business expenses reasonably expected to be incurred.
Accident and Health Insurance Payments	Exempt except 2% shareholder-employees of S corporations.
Deceased Person's Wages	Paid to the person's beneficiary or estate.
Dependent Care Assistance	To the extent it is reasonable to believe the amounts will be excludable from gross income. Up to $10,500 can be excluded from an employee's gross income without being subject to social security, Medicare, or income tax withholding.
Domestic Service	Private home, local college club, or local chapter of college fraternity or sorority.
Educational Assistance	If education maintains or improves employee's skills required by the job. For the non–job-related educational assistance, up to $5,250 per year of tax-exempt student loan repayment contributions or tuition assistance for undergraduate and graduate education is tax-free. Also applies to "downsized" employees and can be used after voluntary or involuntary termination.
Employee Business Expense Reimbursements	Accountable plans for amounts not exceeding specified government rates for mileage, lodging, meals, and incidental expenses.
Employee-Safety and Length-of-Service Awards	If merchandise costs $400 or less. Rises to $1,600 for a written nondiscriminatory plan.
Employer-Provided Parking	Up to $280 per month.
Foreign Service by U.S. Citizens	As employees for affiliates of American employers if entitled to exclusion under section 911 or required by law of foreign country to withhold income tax on such payment.
Group-Term Life Insurance Costs	The employer's cost of group-term life insurance less than $50,000.
Health Reimbursement Arrangements (HRA)	As long as no person has the right to receive cash or any other taxable or nontaxable benefit other than medical care reimbursement.
Individuals Under 18	For delivery or distribution of newspapers, shopping news, and vendors of newspapers and magazines where payment is the difference between the purchase and sales price.
Long-Term Care Insurance Premiums	Employer-paid premiums for long-term care insurance up to a limit. For example, for an employee age 40 or under, the first $450 of premiums are nontaxable.
Ministers of Churches, Members of Religious Orders	Performing services for the order agency of the supervising church or associated institution.
Moving Expense Reimbursements	No longer exempt, except for active military.
Public Officials	For fees only, not salaries.

FIGURE 4.2 (concluded)

Exempt Payments

Retirement and Pension Plans	• Employer contributions to a qualified plan. • Employer contributions to IRA accounts under an SEP [see section 402(g) for salary reduction limitation]. • Employer contributions to section 403(b) annuity contract [see section 402(g) for limitation]. • Elective contributions and deferrals to plans containing a qualified cash or deferred compensation arrangement, such as 401(k).
Sickness or Injury Payments	Payments made under workers' compensation law or contract of insurance.
Transportation in a Commuter Highway Vehicle and Transit Pass	Up to $280 per month.

Pretax Salary Reductions

An employee can authorize an employer to deduct certain withholdings from their pay on a pretax basis. These withholdings are taken from the gross pay and therefore reduce the amount of pay that is subject to federal income tax.

Cafeteria Plans

Some employers offer their employees a choice between cash (pay) or qualified (nontaxable) benefits. Employees can select various levels of health, accident, and life insurance coverage or choose to contribute to cash or deferred plans. The salary reductions are used to pay for the desired benefit, and these pretax contributions are not included in taxable wages for FIT. These salary reductions, which are allowed under a cafeteria plan, are also exempt from FICA and FUTA taxes and from most states' taxes.

Self-Study Quiz 4-1

Check any item of employee compensation not subject to withholding:

_____ 1.   Company-provided lunches at the plant to reduce tardiness by keeping employees on the premises.

_____ 2.   Year-end bonuses to managers and supervisors.

_____ 3.   Gym for employee use during lunch hours.

_____ 4.   Travel advances to salespersons for overnight sales calls out of town.

_____ 5.   Employer-paid sick pay.

_____ 6.   Memberships in the local country club for department managers.

_____ 7.   Meals provided by a local restaurant for its employees.

Note: Answers to Self-Study Quizzes are on page 4-42.

The following benefits may be included in the plan:

- Accident and health insurance
- Self-insured medical reimbursement plan
- Group-term life insurance (first $50,000 of coverage)
- Dependent care assistance (first $5,000)
- Health savings accounts (discussed below)

These benefits cannot be included in a cafeteria plan:

- Transportation fringe benefits
- Educational assistance
- Scholarships and fellowship grants
- Meals and lodging for the convenience of employer
- Dependent group-term life insurance
- Deferred compensation except for 401(k) contributions

On the Job

Children who have not reached age 27 as of the end of the tax year will qualify for health insurance, including cafeteria plans.

Flexible-Spending Accounts

These accounts allow employees to have money deducted from their paychecks to cover their out-of-pocket medical expenses. The deductions from the employees' pays are made with pretax dollars. Regulations now allow employers the carryover option in which the employee can carry over unused funds to the following plan year. Or the employer can offer the grace period option which extends the time period to spend the unused money in these accounts from the end of the year until March 15 of the following year. Employers can offer either option, but not both, or none at all. Reimbursements are made to employees from an employer-controlled account, and unused monies in these accounts are forfeited by the participants. In 2022, a limit on flexible spending arrangements in the amount of $2,850 per year was implemented.

Health Savings Accounts

These accounts are used by employees who have high-deductible health insurance (for 2023, $1,500 for self-only coverage and $3,000 for family coverage and with maximum out-of-pocket expenses of $7,500 and $15,000, respectively) to pay for medical expenses for themselves and their dependents. Contributions made into the plan by the employer are excluded from the employees' taxable income. For a single person in 2023, the maximum contribution is $3,850 or the amount of the annual deductible, if less (for family coverage—$7,750). Employees who are 55 or older by the end of the year can contribute an additional $1,000 to their HSA. If married and both are age 55 or older, both can contribute an additional $1,000. Employee contributions into the account (through payroll deductions) must be included in wages and are subject to withholding taxes. However, if these contributions are part of a salary reduction arrangement in a qualified cafeteria plan, they are not subject to withholding taxes.

Archer Medical Savings Accounts

These accounts are for employees of small businesses (50 or fewer employees) and are set up in conjunction with high-deductible insurance plans. Employees' payroll deductions are subject to federal income tax withholding (FICA also). However, employees can deduct the contributions on their tax returns, and they have full control over the account. Employer contributions are not subject to tax withholding. Unused monies in this type of account carry over from year to year.

Deferred Arrangements

Many deferred arrangements are usually set up as retirement plans. The most common of these is the **defined contribution plan** that provides future benefits based solely on the amount paid by each employee and employer into the account, plus investment gains. These plans are tax-deferred savings or stock accounts held in trust for employees. The most popular types of retirement accounts are the 401(k) and IRAs.

Example 4-2

Carl Jamison, an employee for the Scharman School, belongs to a tax-deferred retirement plan to which he contributes 3 percent of his pay which is matched by the school. His biweekly pay is $2,500. Because of the deferral (3% × $2,500 = $75), $2,425 is subject to federal income tax withholding.

Tax-Deferred Retirement Accounts

These types of accounts allow employees to contribute amounts from their wages into retirement accounts. These contributions reduce the amount of the employees' wages that are subject to federal income tax. These tax-deferred plans set limits on the amounts that employees can contribute tax-free and also provide for additional contributions to be made into the accounts by the employers. Upon retirement, the employees will receive their contributions back in the form of regular payments from their retirement plans. These payments are then subject to federal income tax. The advantage to tax-deferred retirement accounts is that the taxpayer may be in a lower tax bracket when the income is taxed.

- **401(k) Plan.** A standard tax-deferred retirement plan. A set percentage of an employee's wages is contributed on a pretax basis. Employers can limit the percentage of an employee's pay that can be contributed. This limit can be lower than the maximum set by law. Employees can add after-tax contributions to this total, and the employer can contribute to the employees' plan.
- **Section 403(b) Plan.** A plan for employees of tax-exempt organizations.
- **Section 457(b) Plan.** A plan for employees of state and local governments and of tax-exempt organizations other than churches.
- **Simple Plans.** A small company plan for a company with up to 100 employees. The employer can offer a SIMPLE plan as part of a 401(k) plan. This plan allows employees to contribute a percentage of their pay toward retirement.

The information for these plans shown in Figure 4.3 applies to 2022.

IRS Connection

The IRS has recently issued guidance regarding same-sex marriage relating to retirement plans. If a couple is legally married in a jurisdiction that recognizes it, then they are married for federal tax purposes.

FIGURE **4.3**
Tax Deferred Retirement Account Information

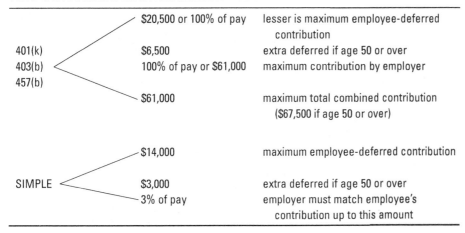

401(k) 403(b) 457(b)	$20,500 or 100% of pay	lesser is maximum employee-deferred contribution
	$6,500	extra deferred if age 50 or over
	100% of pay or $61,000	maximum contribution by employer
	$61,000	maximum total combined contribution ($67,500 if age 50 or over)
SIMPLE	$14,000	maximum employee-deferred contribution
	$3,000	extra deferred if age 50 or over
	3% of pay	employer must match employee's contribution up to this amount

Individual Retirement Accounts

Beyond the various payroll-related tax-deferred accounts, individuals can set up their own retirement accounts. In 2022, under certain conditions, an employee may put aside each year the lesser of $6,000 or 100 percent of their compensation without paying federal income taxes on their contributions. If an employee is age 50 or older before 2022, the most that can be contributed to a traditional IRA is the lesser of $7,000 or 100 percent of their compensation. Eligible employees may make an additional $6,000 contribution on behalf of a nonworking or low-earning spouse provided the combined compensation is at least equal to the total combined IRA contribution. To be eligible for such deductible (tax-free) contributions, either of the following two conditions must be met (for 2022):

1. The individual does not belong to a company-funded retirement plan.
2. The individual has modified adjusted gross income less than $68,000. (In the case of a married employee, the combined adjusted gross income must be less than $109,000.)

If the employee belongs to another qualified plan, full and partial tax-free deductions are allowed if:

1. The employee is single or head of household and has modified adjusted gross income less than $68,000 with phaseout at $78,000.
2. The employee is married, filing a joint return, and has modified adjusted gross income less than $109,000 with phaseout at $129,000.
3. The employee is married, filing separately, and has zero adjusted gross income with phaseout at $10,000.

If an employee's spouse belongs to a company-funded retirement plan, the employee is not considered an active participant in the plan. However, the nonactive spouse's tax-free IRA deduction ($6,000) will begin to phase out between $204,000 and $214,000 of their total adjusted gross income.

Even though these contributions can be made through payroll deductions, the employer is not considered a pension plan sponsor and is not subject to ERISA as long as the following guidelines are met:

1. The employer makes no matching contributions.
2. Participation is not mandatory.
3. The employer does not endorse any IRA sponsors.

Roth IRA

Another type of IRA that allows taxpayers and their spouses to make annual *nondeductible* contributions of up to $6,000 ($7,000 if age 50 or older) is the Roth IRA. The amount that may be contributed is reduced by the amount contributed into other IRAs. Allowable contributions are phased out for those with adjusted gross income of between $129,000 and $144,000 for single taxpayers, $204,000 and $214,000 for joint taxpayers, and $0 and $10,000 for married taxpayers filing separately.

The advantage of this type of IRA is that distributions made out of the fund at retirement are tax-free.

Revised Form W-4 and Withholding Calculations

Employees hired prior to 2020, with Form W-4 from 2019 or earlier on file, could exempt a portion of their earnings from withholdings by claiming a personal allowance and allowances for their dependents. Employees could also claim special allowances, allowances for itemized deductions, and tax credits. The Tax Cuts and Jobs Act (TCJA) eliminated personal withholding allowances.

Form W-4, *Employee's Withholding Certificate*, and tax withholding procedures were redesigned in 2020 to accommodate these changes. Current employees (hired prior to 2020) will not have to complete the Form W-4 from 2020 or later unless they wish to make a change to the latest Form W-4 on file with their employer. Employers-now have to withhold income tax based on either Form W-4 from 2019 or earlier and/or Form W-4 from 2020 or later (whichever is on file for the employee), which provide significantly different information. The IRS developed sets of withholding tables to accommodate each version of Forms W-4. The new tables for Forms W-4 from 2020 or later now include three filing statuses: married filing jointly, single or married filing separately, and head of household. *Publication* 15-T was created to contain all withholding procedures and tables. A list of updates is listed below.

- Employees hired prior to 2020 do not have to complete the Form W-4 from 2020 or later unless they wish to make a change to the latest Form W-4 on file with their employer.
- Employees who are hired in 2023 or wish to revise their W-4 information must use the current Form W-4. Publication 15-T allows employers to compute withholding based on the information from the employee's most recently submitted Form W-4, whether it is from a previous year.
- Employers have to withhold income tax based on either Form W-4 from 2019 or earlier and/or Form W-4 from 2020 or later. As previously mentioned, the IRS developed sets of withholding procedures and withholding tables to accommodate each version of Forms W-4.
- New filing status was added. The table for current Forms W-4 now includes three filing statuses: married filing jointly (MFJ), single (S) or married filing separately (MFS), and head of household (HOH).
- Five worksheets. There are five withholding tables, each with a corresponding worksheet. The worksheets guide the employer in determining the table and column to use.

Coverage of the Form W-4 from 2020 or later is included in this chapter, and the Form W-4 from 2019 or earlier is discussed in the supplement beginning on page 4-37.

News Alert

The Tax Cuts and Jobs Act (TCJA) eliminated personal withholding allowances and created the need for a redesigned Form W-4. Employers will now have to withhold income tax based on Forms W-4 from 2019 or earlier and/or Forms W-4 from 2020 or later, which provide significantly different information. The IRS developed separate sets of withholding tables to accommodate both versions of Forms W-4.

Form W-4 from 2020 or Later (Employee's Withholding Certificate)

The employer uses the information from the 2020 or later **Form W-4, Employee's Withholding Certificate,** to compute the amount of income tax to withhold from employees' wages. The employer must have Form W-4 on file for each employee. This form contains the withholding certificate (shown in Figure 4.4 on page 4-12), detailed instructions, and worksheets for employees to use in completing the certificate.

LO 2

Explain the purpose and use of Form W-4 from 2020 or later.

Completing Form W-4

The employee completes Form W-4 when they begin work for an employer. Employers must retain the withholding certificate as a supporting record of multiple jobs, dependents, and other adjustments used in deducting income taxes from the employees' salaries and wages.

Once filed, the certificate remains in effect until an amended certificate takes effect. Withholding certificates should be retained as long as they are in effect and for four years thereafter. A new employee who is first paid wages in 2023, including an employee who previously worked for you and rehired in 2023, and fails to furnish a Form W-4 will be treated as if they had checked the box for Single or Married filing separately in step 1(c) and made no entries in step 2, step 3, or step 4 of the current Form W-4. However, an employee who was first paid wages in 2019 and who failed to furnish a Form W-4 should continue to be treated as single and claiming zero allowances on a Form W-4 from 2019 or earlier (see Chapter 4 Supplement beginning on page 4-37).

Since the employers are required to get each employee's social security number on Form W-4, they can request to see the employee's social security card, and they can photocopy the card for their files.

On the Net

The IRS's online withholding calculator is available at http://www.irs.gov/individuals/irs-withholding-calculator. Employees can use the IRS's online withholding calculator to help complete Form W-4.

FIGURE 4.4

2022 Form W-4, Employee's Withholding Certificate

Form **W-4**	**Employee's Withholding Certificate**		OMB No. 1545-0074
Department of the Treasury Internal Revenue Service	► Complete Form W-4 so that your employer can withhold the correct federal income tax from your pay. ► Give Form W-4 to your employer. ► Your withholding is subject to review by the IRS.		20--

Step 1:

Enter Personal Information

(a) First name and middle initial — Mary Last name — Matthews

(b) Social security number — 000-00-2600

Address — 260 Cobalt Ridge Drive South

City or town, state, and ZIP code — New London, PA 19057

► **Does your name match the name on your social security card?** If not, to ensure you get credit for your earnings, contact SSA at 800-772-1213 or go to *www.ssa.gov*.

(c) ☐ Single or Married filing separately

☑ Married filing jointly (or Qualifying widow(er))

☐ Head of household (Check only if you're unmarried and pay more than half the costs of keeping up a home for yourself and a qualifying individual.)

Complete Steps 2–4 ONLY if they apply to you; otherwise, skip to Step 5. See page 2 for more information on each step, who can claim exemption from withholding, when to use the online estimator, and privacy.

Step 2:

Multiple Jobs or Spouse Works

Complete this step if you (1) hold more than one job at a time, or (2) are married filing jointly and your spouse also works. The correct amount of withholding depends on income earned from all of these jobs.

Do **only one** of the following.

(a) Use the estimator at *www.irs.gov/W4App* for most accurate withholding for this step (and Steps 3–4); **or**

(b) Use the Multiple Jobs Worksheet on page 3 and enter the result in Step 4(c) below for roughly accurate withholding; **or**

(c) If there are only two jobs total, you may check this box. Do the same on Form W-4 for the other job. This option is accurate for jobs with similar pay; otherwise, more tax than necessary may be withheld . . . . . ► ☐

TIP: To be accurate, submit a 20--. Form W-4 for all other jobs. If you (or your spouse) have self-employment income, including as an independent contractor, use the estimator.

Complete Steps 3–4(b) on Form W-4 for only ONE of these jobs. Leave those steps blank for the other jobs. (Your withholding will be most accurate if you complete Steps 3–4(b) on the Form W-4 for the highest paying job.)

Step 3:

Claim Dependents

If your income will be $200,000 or less ($400,000 or less if married filing jointly):

Multiply the number of qualifying children under age 17 by $2,000 ► $ _____

Multiply the number of other dependents by $500 . . . . ► $ _____

Add the amounts above and enter the total here . . . . | **3** | $ |

Step 4 (optional):

Other Adjustments

(a) **Other income (not from jobs).** If you want tax withheld for other income you expect this year that won't have withholding, enter the amount of other income here. This may include interest, dividends, and retirement income . . . . | **4(a)** | $ |

(b) **Deductions.** If you expect to claim deductions other than the standard deduction and want to reduce your withholding, use the Deductions Worksheet on page 3 and enter the result here . . . . | **4(b)** | $ |

(c) **Extra withholding.** Enter any additional tax you want withheld each **pay period** . | **4(c)** | $ |

Step 5:

Sign Here

Under penalties of perjury, I declare that this certificate, to the best of my knowledge and belief, is true, correct, and complete.

Mary Matthews

► Employee's signature (This form is not valid unless you sign it.)

► January 1, 20--

Date

Employers Only

Employer's name and address

First date of employment

Employer identification number (EIN)

For Privacy Act and Paperwork Reduction Act Notice, see page 3.

Cat. No. 10220Q

Form **W-4** (2022)

Source: Internal Revenue Service.

Changing Form W-4

If the status of an employee changes with respect to marital status, number of jobs, dependents, or other adjustments, the employee files an amended W-4.

The employer makes the certificate effective no later than the start of the first payroll period ending on or after the 30th day from the date the replacement Form W-4 is received. The employer may not repay or reimburse the employee for income taxes overwithheld before the effective date of the new certificate but may reimburse the employee after that date if the employer failed to implement the new certificate.

Exemption from Income Tax Withholding

Employees may claim exemption from income tax withholding if they had no income tax liability last year and expect none in the current year. The exemption is valid for one year and must be claimed on a new Form W-4 filed by February 15 of each succeeding year. If a new certificate is not filed, taxes are withheld at the single rate with zero withholding allowances.

> Single persons who made less than $12,950 in 2022 owed no federal income tax. Married couples filing jointly with combined wages up to $25,900 incurred no tax liability.

Employees may not claim exemption from withholding if (1) another person claims the employee as a dependent on that person's tax return, *and* (2) income exceeds $1,150 annually and includes more than $400 of unearned income (interest or dividends); or if unearned income is less than $400, but the total income exceeds $12,950.

Additional and Voluntary Withholding Agreements

A person with two or more jobs, or a married couple where both work, will complete Step 2 of Form W-4 from 2020 or later to have additional federal income taxes withheld. An employee may request that the employer withhold an additional amount from the employee's pay. This request must be done on Forms W-4 by filling in the additional amounts to be withheld in Step 4 part (c).

If an employee receives payments not classified as wages, or an employer-employee relationship does not exist, individuals can voluntarily request that the employer or the one making the payments withhold federal income taxes from their payments. These individuals need only furnish a Form W-4. Requests for additional and voluntary withholding become effective when the employer accepts them and begins to withhold tax. The agreements remain in effect until the specified termination date or until the termination is mutually agreed upon. Either party may terminate an agreement prior to a specified date or mutual agreement by furnishing the other party with a signed, written notice of termination.

> Individuals who may wish to request additional withholding or a voluntary agreement to withhold include:
> - Clergy
> - Two wage-earner married couples
> - Domestic workers in a private home
> - Individuals receiving significant amounts of interest or dividends
> - Individuals receiving self-employment income

Electronic Filing of Form W-4

Employers may establish a system that requires employees to file and make changes to their W-4s by using a computer network or interactive voice response technology. However, the employer must make available the paper W-4 option to any employee who objects to using the system or whose access to the system is limited.

On the Net

The IRS has created a page on its Web site (https://www.irs.gov/forms-pubs/about-form-w-4) for updates to Form W-4, Employee's Withholding Allowance Certificate.

Invalid Forms W-4

Employers are not required to verify the authenticity of the information on employees' W-4s. However, if the form is altered in any way or if the employee acknowledges that the information is false, the employer cannot accept the invalid W-4. The employer can ask for a new W-4. If the employee refuses to submit a new one, the employer can use the employee's most recent correct W-4 on file or, if a new hire, withhold as if the employee were single with no adjustments.

Requested Forms W-4

Regulations require employers to only submit copies of employees' Forms W-4 that are requested in a written notice from the IRS.

Figure 4.5 outlines the procedures to follow in submitting Forms W-4 to the IRS.

Employee Penalties

Employees who willfully file false information statements (Form W-4) are, in addition to any other penalty, subject to fines of up to $1,000 or imprisonment for up to one year or both.

Employees claiming excess deductions are subject to a $500 civil penalty for each offense.

Withholding on Nonresident Aliens

Resident aliens (those with green cards) are lawful citizens and are taxed similar to U.S. citizens. To avoid underwithholding, nonresident aliens (who cannot claim the standard exemption and are limited to one allowance when filing their personal U.S. income tax returns) should (1) not claim exemption from income tax withholding; (2) request withholding as single, regardless of actual status; (3) add an extra amount to wages, then determine withholding based on the total amount (e.g., $249.00 for a weekly payroll period); and (4) write "Nonresident Alien" or "NRA" in space below Step 4(c) on Form W-4.

Other Withholdings

Federal income taxes are also withheld from other kinds of payments made to current and former employees, as described below.

Withholding for Pension or Annuity Payments

Generally, the withholding of federal income taxes applies to payments made from pension, profit-sharing, stock bonus, annuity, and certain deferred compensation plans and individual retirement arrangements. You treat the payments from any of these sources as wages for the purpose of withholding.

FIGURE 4.5
Procedures for Submitting Forms W-4

- Send copies of Forms W-4 only after the IRS requests them in writing.
- The IRS can also issue "lock-in" letters to employers specifying the maximum number of withholding exemptions permitted for an employee without obtaining a copy of the employee's W-4.
- An "employee notice" is sent along with the lock-in letter. This notice must be given to the employee within 10 business days of the receipt. If no longer employed, the employer must notify the IRS in writing.
- Withhold federal income tax based on lock-in letter starting with the first pay period 60 days after the date of the letter, unless the IRS contacts the employer.
- Challenges to the lock-in letter must be sent in writing along with a new Form W-4 by the employee directly to the IRS.
- Employer should disregard any new W-4 (unless claiming fewer exemptions than the IRS notice) submitted by the employee until notified to do so by the IRS.

Unless the recipients of pension or annuity payments elect *not* to have federal income taxes withheld from such payments, the taxes will be withheld. Payers must withhold on monthly pension and annuity payments as married filing joint with three allowances, unless the payees elect otherwise. If the recipients do not instruct the payers to the contrary, the payers are required to withhold income taxes as if the recipients were single with no adjustments.

By completing Form W-4P, Withholding Certificate for Periodic Pension or Annuity Payments, or a substitute form furnished by the payer, an employee can elect to have no income tax withheld from the payments received. The form may also be used to change the amount of tax that would ordinarily be withheld by the payers. Once completed, Form W-4P remains in effect until the recipient changes or revokes the certificate. The payer must notify the recipients each year of their right to elect to have no taxes withheld or to revoke their election.

Starting in 2023, additional withholding on nonperiodic payments and eligible rollover distributions is requested on new Form W-4R, Withholding Certificate for Nonperiodic Payments and Eligible Rollover Distributions.

Withholding from Sick Pay

Form W-4S, Request for Federal Income Tax Withholding from Sick Pay, must be filed with the payer of sick pay if the employee wants federal income taxes to be withheld from the payments. Form W-4S is filed only if the payer is a third party, such as an insurance company. The form should not be filed with the worker's employer, who makes such payments, since employers already must withhold income taxes from sick pay.

Withholding on Government Payments

Form W-4V can be used to request federal income tax withholding on government payments (such as social security benefits or unemployment compensation). This request is voluntary.

Over the Line

The former owner of an employee leasing business, Excell Personnel, Inc., has been sentenced to 36 months in prison and ordered to pay $4,234,670.16 in restitution to the IRS. The company which "leased" employees made deductions for withholding of income taxes and FICA taxes; however, the owner admitted that he was aware of his legal obligations but deliberately chose not to remit the withheld taxes to the IRS.[2]

Self-Study Quiz 4-2

1. Grace Kyle submitted a new Form W-4 changing her filing status from single to married filing jointly. Kyle also requested to be reimbursed for the overwithholding prior to the change. How should the payroll manager respond to Kyle?

2. Bob Bradley is upset because his paycheck on February 8, 20--, has federal income tax withheld, even though he filed a W-4 claiming exemption from withholding earlier in the same year. What should the payroll manager say to Bradley?

3. Jack Matthews changed his filing status on his Form W-4 on April 4, 20--. How many days does the employer have to make the certificate effective?

---

2 Anne S. Lewis, "Employee Leasing Company Owner Sentenced to Prison, Ordered to Pay over $4 Million in Payroll Taxes," *PAYTECH*, June 2008, p. 57.

> ### Washington Update
>
> The 2023 federal income tax rates were not available during the production of this textbook. We have used the 2022 federal income tax rates, 2022 FICA tax rates, and 2022 OASDI tax base in this textbook. Please see "As We Go to Press" for the most current updates and our online version of "As We Go to Press" for updates subsequent to the printing deadline of this textbook.

LO 3

Compute the amount of federal income tax to be withheld using the appropriate tables for Manual Systems with Forms W-4 from 2020 or later for: (a) the percentage method; (b) the wage-bracket method; (c) alternative methods such as quarterly averaging, annualizing of wages, and part-year employment; and (d) withholding of federal income taxes on supplementary wage payments.

Federal Income Tax Withholding

After the employer learns from Form W-4 the filing status, dependents, and other adjustments for an employee, the employer selects a withholding method. Employers usually choose either the **percentage method** or the **wage-bracket method**. Both distinguish between married and unmarried persons, and both methods provide the full benefit of the information on Form W-4.

The choice of methods is usually based on the number of employees and the payroll accounting system used. The employer can change from one method to another at any time, and different methods may be used for different groups of employees.

Both methods take into account a **standard deduction**, an amount of money used to reduce an individual's adjusted gross income in arriving at the taxable income. For 2022, the following standard deductions apply:

Joint return filers and surviving spouses	$25,900
Married persons filing separately	12,950
Head of household filers	19,400
Single filers	12,950

The standard deduction increases by $1,400 if 65 or older or blind and by $1,750 for unmarried taxpayers. Each year, the standard deductions are adjusted for inflation.

Percentage Method

The IRS provides statutory percentage method tables for weekly, biweekly, semimonthly, monthly, and daily pay periods for married filing jointly, single or married filing separately, and head of household. Copies may be obtained from the District Director of Internal Revenue or online at www.irs.gov. Tax Table A on pages T-2 to T-4 at the end of the textbook provides the percentage method tables.

Tell Me More

On the Job

The basic income tax rates for 2022 are 10%, 12%, 22%, 24%, 32%, 35%, and 37%.

Example 4-3

To compute the tax using the percentage method for Manual Payroll Systems with Forms W-4 from 2020 or later using Standard Withholding Rate Schedules, follow the steps illustrated below.

Step 1
Determine the amount of gross wages earned, filing status, adjustments on Form W-4, and frequency of pay. *Note:* If the wage ends in a fractional dollar amount, the wage may be rounded to the nearest dollar. However, in this text, exact wages are used.

Wilson Goodman, single (S), has no adjustments on his Form W-4 and earns $915.60 semimonthly.

Step 2
Determine the withholding tax by referring to the appropriate Percentage Method Withholding Table (see Figure 4.6 below).

Compute tax from Tax Table A, Semimonthly, Standard Withholding Rate Schedule, page T-3.

($915.60 − $540.00 = $375.60 × 10% = $37.56 + $0) = $37.56

FIGURE 4.6

2022 Percentage Method Tables for Manual Payroll Systems
With Forms W-4 From 2020 or Later
SEMIMONTHLY Payroll Period

STANDARD Withholding Rate Schedules (Use these if the box in Step 2 of Form W-4 is **NOT** checked)					Form W-4, Step 2, Checkbox, Withholding Rate Schedules (Use these if the box in Step 2 of Form W-4 **IS** checked)				
If the Adjusted Wage Amount (line 1h) is:		The tentative amount to withhold is:	Plus this percentage—	of the amount that the Adjusted Wage exceeds—	If the Adjusted Wage Amount (line 1h) is:		The tentative amount to withhold is:	Plus this percentage—	of the amount that the Adjusted Wage exceeds—
At least—	But less than—				At least—	But less than—			
A	B	C	D	E	A	B	C	D	E
Single or Married Filing Separately					Single or Married Filing Separately				
$0	$540	$0.00	0%	$0	$0	$270	$0.00	0%	$0
540	968	0.00	10%	540	270	484	0.00	10%	270
968	2,280	42.80	12%	968	484	1,140	21.40	12%	484
2,280	4,251	200.24	22%	2,280	1,140	2,126	100.12	22%	1,140
4,251	7,625	633.86	24%	4,251	2,126	3,813	317.04	24%	2,126
7,625	9,538	1,443.62	32%	7,625	3,813	4,769	721.92	32%	3,813
9,538	23,035	2,055.78	35%	9,538	4,769	11,518	1,027.84	35%	4,769
23,035		6,779.73	37%	23,035	11,518		3,389.99	37%	11,518

Self-Study Quiz 4-3

Tiffany Moulder, married filing jointly (MFJ), has no adjustments on her Form W-4 and receives a semimonthly salary of $1,100.25. Compute the amount to withhold for federal income tax using Figure 4.6. Show the results of each step, as described for figuring withholding using the percentage method.

　　Step 1 Result ＿＿＿＿＿＿＿　　　　　Step 2 Result ＿＿＿＿＿＿＿

News Alert

The top 1 percent of taxpayers by income paid 38.5 percent of federal taxes collected, while the bottom half of taxpayers paid 3 percent.

Wage-Bracket Method

The IRS provides statutory wage tables for weekly, biweekly, semimonthly, monthly, or daily pay periods. Copies may be obtained from the District Director of Internal Revenue or online at www.irs.gov. Tax Table B on pages T-5 to T-13 at the end of the textbook provides the wage-bracket tables.

To use the wage-bracket method for Manual Payroll Systems with Forms W-4 from 2020 or later using Standard Withholding, follow the steps illustrated below.

Example 4-4

Step 1
Select the withholding table that applies to the employee's pay period.

Adrienne Huff is married filing jointly (MFJ). She is paid weekly at a rate of $815.

Step 2
Locate the wage bracket (the first two columns of the table) in which the employee's gross wages fall.

Locate the appropriate wage bracket (see Figure 4.7 on page 4-18):
　　　　　　At least $815 but less than $825

Step 3
Follow the line for the wage bracket across to the right to the column showing the appropriate filing status with standard withholding. Withhold this amount of tax.

Move across the line to the column showing Married Filing Jointly, Standard withholding.
　　　　　　The tax to withhold is $32

> If the employee's wages are higher than the last amount listed on the appropriate wage-bracket table, the percentage method must be used for that employee.

FIGURE 4.7

2022 Wage Bracket Method Tables for Manual Payroll Systems With Forms W-4 From 2020 or Later
WEEKLY Payroll Period

If the Adjusted Wage Amount (line 1h) is		Married Filing Jointly		Head of Household		Single or Married Filing Separately	
At Least	But less than	Standard withholding	Form W-4, Step 2, Checkbox withholding	Standard withholding	Form W-4, Step 2, Checkbox withholding	Standard withholding	Form W-4, Step 2, Checkbox withholding
				The Tentative Withholding Amount is:			
$765	$775	$27	$59	$42	$72	$59	$100
775	785	28	60	43	74	60	102
785	795	29	61	44	76	61	104
795	805	30	62	46	78	62	106
805	815	31	63	47	81	63	109
815	825	③②	65	48	83	65	111
825	835	33	66	49	85	66	113
835	845	34	67	50	87	67	115
845	855	35	68	52	89	68	117
855	865	36	69	53	92	69	120

Source: Internal Revenue Service.

Self-Study Quiz 4-4

Quirk Motors uses the wage-bracket method to withhold from the semi-monthly earnings of its employees. For each employee, compute the amount to be withheld from their earnings for the payroll period ending April 15, 20--.

Employee	Filing Status	No. of Allowances	Salary	Federal Income Tax Withheld
Kyle Lamb	S	N/A	$1,100	_____
Zed Nurin	S	N/A	850	_____
Carol Hogan	MFJ	N/A	975	_____
Marla Vick	MFJ	N/A	2,600	_____
Al Marks	S	N/A	1,200	_____

Other Methods of Withholding

In addition to the two principal methods of withholding previously described, employers may use other methods such as **quarterly averaging**, **annualizing wages**, and **part-year employment**.

QUARTERLY AVERAGING. Jackson, Inc., estimates that Cal Hudson will be paid $6,690 during the second quarter of the year. Hudson is married filing jointly with no adjustments on Form W-4 and is paid semimonthly.

Example 4-5

Step 1—Divide the estimated quarterly wages by 6 (the number of semimonthly pay periods in the quarter).

$$\$6,690 \div 6 = \$1,115$$

Step 2—Find the amount of federal income tax to withhold from each semimonthly payment.

MARRIED FILING JOINTLY Persons with Standard Withholding—SEMIMONTHLY Payroll Period

Wages at least $1,110 but not more than $1,125 = $4

The withholding is based on the average payment instead of the actual payment.

ANNUALIZING WAGES (Available for Automated Payroll Systems). Lucien Field, married filing jointly, receives $1,350 semimonthly. Under the annualizing method, do the following:

Example 4-6

Step 1—Multiply the semimonthly wage by 24 pay periods to compute his annual wage.

$$\$1,350 \times 24 = \$32,400$$

Step 2*—Subtract Pub. 15-T Worksheet 1, line 1g adjustment for married filing jointly of $12,900.

$$\$32,400 - \$12,900 = \$19,500 \text{ Adjusted Annual Wages}$$

Step 3—Using the 2022 Percentage Method Table for Automated Payrolls, married filing jointly and standard withholding.

$$\$19,500 - \$13,000 = \$6,500 \times 10\% = \$650$$

$$\$650 \div 24 \text{ semimonthly payrolls} = \$27.08 \text{ per paycheck}$$

* Tables and worksheet reference in problem are not included in text but can be found on pages 5 and 6 of Publication 15-T pages on the IRS website at www.irs.gov.

PART-YEAR EMPLOYMENT METHOD. Jack Matthews, previously unemployed for the calendar year, has agreed to begin temporary employment on September 9, 20--. He has made a written request for the part-year employment method of withholding. He is single and has no adjustments on his W-4. For the biweekly period from September 9 to September 20, he earns a total of $19,000.

Example 4-7

Step 1—Wages for the current payroll period are added to the wages paid previously.

$$\$19,000 + 0 = \$19,000$$

Step 2—The number of payroll periods worked in step 1 is added to the number of payroll periods between the employee's past and current employment.

$$1 + 18 = 19$$

Step 3—Divide the step 1 amount by the total number of payroll periods.

$$\$19,000 \div 19 = \$1,000$$

Step 4—Tax on the step 3 amount (from wage-bracket table B for single/biweekly, Standard Withholding).

$$\$52$$

Step 5—Total number of payroll periods from step 2 multiplied by step 4 equals the withholding for the pay period.

$$19 \times \$52 = \$988$$

On the Job

In order to reduce federal income tax withholding, a part-time employee who figures the federal income tax on a calendar-year basis can request in writing that the employer withhold tax by the part-year employment method.

Tell Me More

Supplemental Wage Payments

Supplemental wage payments include items such as vacation pay, bonuses, commissions, exercised nonqualified stock options, and dismissal pay. Since these types of payments may be paid at a different time from the regular payroll and not related to a particular payroll, the employer must decide whether to lump the regular wages and supplemental wages together or withhold from the supplemental wages separately. The first distinction is the treatment of vacation pays versus other types of supplemental pays.

Photostravellers/Shutterstock.com

Vacation Pay

Vacation pay is subject to withholding as though it were a regular payment made for the payroll period or periods occurring during the vacation. If the vacation pay is for a time longer than your usual payroll period, spread it over the pay period(s) for which you pay it. If an employee is paid weekly and is paid for two weeks of vacation, treat each vacation week separately and calculate the tax on each vacation week using the weekly tax tables or wage brackets.

However, if vacation pay is in lieu of taking vacation time, treat it as a regular supplemental wage payment and calculate the tax on the total as a single payment. A lump-sum vacation payment on termination of employment is also treated as a supplemental wage payment.

Supplemental Wages Paid with Regular Wages

If the employer pays supplemental wages with regular wages but does not specify the amount of each type of wage, the employer withholds as if the total were a single payment for a regular payroll period.

Example 4-8

Mandi Robinson, married filing jointly, earns a monthly salary of $2,400. She also receives a quarterly bonus on sales that exceeds her quota. For the first quarter, her bonus amounts to $4,600. Robinson's employer pays her the regular monthly salary and the bonus together on her March paycheck. The withholding for the March pay is computed on the total amount of $7,000 ($2,400 + $4,600). Using Wage Bracket Tax Table B, the amount to withhold is $546.

However, if the employer indicates specifically the amount of each payment, the employer may withhold at a ***flat 22 percent rate*** on the supplemental wages if the tax is withheld on the employee's regular wages at the appropriate rate.

Example 4-9

From the above example, if you indicate separately on Robinson's paycheck stub the amount of each payment, the amount of federal income tax to be withheld is computed as follows:

		Taxes Withheld	
Regular monthly earnings	$2,400	$ 24.00	(from wage-bracket tax tables*)
Quarterly bonus	4,600	1,012.00	($4,600 × 22%)
Totals	$7,000	$ 1,036.00	

The calculation of Robinson's federal income tax for the quarter would be computed as follows:

		Taxes Withheld		
Regular monthly earnings	$2,400	$24.00 × 3 months = $ 72.00	(from wage-bracket tax table B*)
Quarterly Bonus	4,600	1,012.00	($4,600 × 22%)
		$ 1,084.00	

* The percentage table could also be used.

Note: OASDI and HI withholdings are calculated on total earnings per pay period multiplied by number of pay periods and then added together to arrive at a quarter's total withholding. Quarterly and year-to-date information would appear on Robinson's employee earnings record.

If the employee has already received supplemental wages for the year in excess of $1 million, a **37 percent** withholding rate must be used for the amount above $1 million (the aggregate method cannot be used).

States that have income taxes usually set up their own flat rate for withholding on these supplemental pays. Some require that the supplemental pay be added to a regular pay and the total taxed.

Supplemental Wages Paid Separately from Regular Wages

If the supplemental wages are paid separately, the income tax withholding method depends on whether or not you withheld income tax from the employee's last regular wage payment. If you withheld income tax from the employee's regular wages, you can use either of the following methods for supplemental wages.

Method A

Add the supplemental wages and regular wages for the most recent payroll period. Then, figure the income tax as if the total were a single payment. Subtract the tax already withheld from the regular wage. Withhold the remaining tax from the supplemental wage.

Example 4-10

Louis Ernst, single, is paid $985 semimonthly. The tax to be withheld under the wage-bracket method on each semimonthly pay is $45. Ernst is paid his regular wage on June 14, 20--. On June 17, he receives a bonus of $500. The tax on the bonus is computed as follows:

Regular wage payment...	$ 985
Bonus..	500
Total..	$1,485
Tax on total from the wage-bracket table in Tax Table B....................................	$ 105
Less: Tax already withheld on $985	45
Tax to be withheld from $500 bonus...	$ 60

If you did not withhold income tax from the employee's regular wage payment, use Method A.

Method B

Withhold a flat 22 percent (37 percent if over $1 million) on the supplemental pay.

Example 4-11

The tax withheld on Louis Ernst's June 14, 20-- bonus of $500 is computed as follows:

Bonus...	$ 500
Tax rate	× 22%
Tax withheld on bonus..	$ 110

Self-Study Quiz 4-5

Fred Burdette, married filing jointly, received his regular semimonthly wage of $1,450 on June 14, 20--. On June 21, he received a semiannual bonus of $500. Compute the amount of federal income tax to be withheld on the bonus using each method for computing supplemental wage payments. The employer uses the wage-bracket tables.

Method A _____

Method B _____

If a supplemental payment is paid in a year where no regular wages are paid, the payment is treated as a regular wage payment, and withholding is determined by the rules that apply to a miscellaneous payroll period.

Gross-Up Supplemental

In order to give an employee the intended amount of a supplemental payment, the employer will need to gross up the payment so that after the appropriate payroll taxes are withheld, the net amount left is equal to the original intended payment.

A special "**gross-up**" formula can be applied in this situation:

$$\text{Grossed-Up Amount} = \frac{\text{Intended Payment}}{1 - \text{Applicable Tax Rates (FICA, 22\% federal income tax rate, and state tax rate)}}$$

Example 4-12

GROSSING-UP. Cotter Company wants to award a $4,000 bonus to Donna D'Amico. In addition, it wants the net bonus payment to equal $4,000. Assuming D'Amico is still under the OASDI/FICA limit, the calculation would be:

A. $\dfrac{\$4,000}{1 - 0.22 \text{ (Supplemental W/H rate)} - 0.062 \text{ (OASDI)} - 0.0145 \text{ (HI)}}$

B. $\dfrac{\$4,000}{0.7035} = \$5,685.86$ grossed-up bonus

C.
Gross bonus amount	$5,685.85*
Federal income tax withheld	1,250.89
OASDI tax withheld	352.52
HI tax withheld	82.44
Take-home bonus check	$4,000.00

If state or local taxes apply, they must also be included in the formula.

*Need to subtract $0.01 from $5,685.86 in order to arrive at $4,000.00 (due to rounding).

Wage and Tax Statements

> **LO 4**
> Explain the purpose and use of Form W-2.

Employers must furnish **wage and tax statements** to employees informing them of the wages paid during the calendar year and the amount of taxes withheld from those wages. The employer sends copies of these statements to the federal government and, in many cases, to state, city, and local governments.

Form W-2

Form W-2, Wage and Tax Statement (2022 version), shown in Figure 4.8, is prepared if any of the following items apply to an employee during the calendar year:

1. Income tax or social security taxes were withheld.
2. Income tax would have been withheld if the employee had not claimed more than one withholding allowance or had not claimed exemption from withholding on Form W-4.
3. Any amount was paid for services if the employer is in a trade or business. The cash value of any noncash payments made should be led.

Figure 4.9, on pages 4-24 and 4-25, summarizes the instructions for completing each of the boxes on Form W-2. Employees' names should appear exactly as shown on the employee's social security card (do not include titles or suffixes). If an entry does not apply to the firm or employee, leave the box blank. Employers must give employees Form W-2 on or before January 31 following the close of the calendar year.

FIGURE 4.8
Form W-2, Wage and Tax Statement **Tell Me More**

22222	Void ☐	a Employee's social security number 000-00-7478	For Official Use Only ▶ OMB No. 1545-0008
b Employer identification number (EIN) 00-0007221		1 Wages, tips, other compensation 29360.18	2 Federal income tax withheld 4610.00
c Employer's name, address, and ZIP code Keevey Motors 600 Third Avenue Philadelphia, PA 19103-5600		3 Social security wages 29360.18	4 Social security tax withheld 1820.33
		5 Medicare wages and tips 29360.18	6 Medicare tax withheld 425.72
		7 Social security tips	8 Allocated tips
d Control number		9	10 Dependent care benefits
e Employee's first name and initial Richard M.	Last name Cabor · Suff.	11 Nonqualified plans	12a See instructions for box 12 Code C 78.00
483 Monroe Street Philadelphia, PA 19119-4821		13 Statutory employee ☐ Retirement plan ☒ Third-party sick pay ☐	12b Code
f Employee's address and ZIP code		14 Other BC/BS Premium w/h 296.00 PA SUI 17.62	12c Code; 12d Code

15 State	Employer's state ID number	16 State wages, tips, etc.	17 State income tax	18 Local wages, tips, etc.	19 Local income tax	20 Locality name
PA	00-0-0013	29282.18	898.96	29282.18	1127.37	Phila.

Form **W-2** **Wage and Tax Statement** **20 - -**

Department of the Treasury—Internal Revenue Service

Copy A For Social Security Administration — Send this entire page with Form W-3 to the Social Security Administration; photocopies are **not** acceptable.

For Privacy Act and Paperwork Reduction Act Notice, see the separate instructions.

Cat. No. 10134D

Do Not Cut, Fold, or Staple Forms on This Page

Source: Internal Revenue Service.

FIGURE 4.9
How to Complete Form W-2

Box A—Employee's social security number: Filers may use truncated taxpayer identification numbers (TTINs) on electronically furnished payee statements.

An employee who does not have an SSN should apply for one by completing Form SS-5.

Void: Put an X in this box when an error has been made. Amounts shown on void forms should not be included in your subtotal Form W-2.

Box B—Employer identification number (EIN): Enter the number assigned to you by the IRS. Do not use a prior owner's EIN. If you do not have an EIN when filing Forms W-2, enter "Applied For." You can get an EIN by filing Form SS-4.

Box C—Employer's name, address, and ZIP code: This entry should be the same as shown on your Form 941 or 943.

Box D—Control number: For the employer to identify the individual Forms W-2. Up to 7 digits may be used to assign the number, which the employer uses when writing the Social Security Administration about the form. The employer does not have to use this box.

Box E—Employee's name: The name should be entered exactly as shown on the employee's social security card.

Box F—Employee's address and ZIP code: This box is combined with Box E on all copies except Copy A, to allow you to mail employee's copies in a window envelope or as a self-mailer.

Box 1—Wages, tips, other compensation: Record, before any payroll deductions, the total of (1) wages, prizes, and awards paid; (2) noncash payments (including certain fringe benefits); (3) tips reported by employee to employer (not allocated tips); (4) certain employee business expense reimbursements; (5) cost of accident and health insurance premiums paid on behalf of 2% or more shareholder employees by an S corporation; (6) taxable benefits made from a Section 125 (cafeteria plan); and (7) all other compensation including certain scholarships and fellowship grants and payments for moving expenses. Other compensation is an amount you pay your employee from which federal income tax is not withheld. You may show other compensation on a separate Form W-2. Do not include elective deferrals [i.e., 401(k)].

Box 2—Federal income tax withheld: Record the amount of federal income tax withheld from the employee's wages for the year.

Box 3—Social security wages: Enter the total wages paid (before payroll deductions) subject to employee social security (OASDI) tax. Do not include social security tips and allocated tips. Generally, noncash payments are considered wages. Include employee business expenses reported in Box 1. Include employer contributions to qualified cash or deferred compensation plans and to retirement arrangements described in Box 12 (Codes D, E, F, and G), even though the deferrals are not includible in Box 1 as wages, tips, and other compensation. Include any employee OASDI and HI taxes and employee state unemployment compensation taxes you paid for your employee rather than deducting it from wages. Report in this box the cost of group-term life insurance coverage over $50,000 that is taxable to former employees. Report the cost of accident and health insurance premiums paid on behalf of 2% or more shareholder-employees by an S corporation only if the exclusion under Section 312(a)(2)(B) is not satisfied. Do not enter more than the maximum OASDI taxable wage base for the year.

Box 4—Social security tax withheld: Record the total social security (OASDI) tax (not the employer's share) withheld or paid by the employer for the employee. Include only taxes withheld for the year's wages.

Box 5—Medicare wages and tips: Enter the Medicare (HI) wages and tips. Be sure to enter tips the employee reported even if you did not have enough employee funds to collect the HI tax for those tips. Report in this box the cost of group-term life insurance coverage over $50,000 that is taxable to former employees.

Box 6—Medicare tax withheld: Enter the total employee Medicare (HI) tax (not the employer's share) including the Additional Medicare Tax withheld or paid by the employer for the employee. Include only taxes withheld for the year's wages.

Box 7—Social security tips: Record the amount the employee reported even if you did not have enough employee funds to collect the social security (OASDI) tax for the tips. The total of Boxes 3 and 7 should not be more than the maximum OASDI wage base for the year. But report all tips in Box 1 along with wages and other compensation.

Box 8—Allocated tips: If you are a large food or beverage establishment, record the amount of tips allocated to the employee. Do not include this amount in Boxes 1, 3, 5, or 7.

Box 9—Currently not in use.

Box 10—Dependent care benefits: Record the total amount of dependent care benefits paid or incurred by you for your employee. This total should include any amount in excess of the exclusion ($5,000).

Box 11—Nonqualified plans: Enter the amount from a nonqualified deferred compensation plan or Section 457 plan that was distributed or became taxable because the substantial risk of forfeiture lapsed. Include this amount in Box 11 only if it is also includible in Boxes 1, 3, and 5. Report distributions to beneficiaries of deceased employees on Form 1099-R.

FIGURE 4.9 (concluded)

How to Complete Form W-2

Box 12—Complete and code this box for all applicable items listed in the Reference Guide. Additional information about any coded item may be found in the IRS's Instructions for Form W-2. Do not enter more than four codes in this box. If you are reporting more than four items, use a separate Form W-2 or a substitute Form W-2 to report the additional items. Use a capital letter when entering each code and enter the dollar amount on the same line. Use decimal points.

Box 13—Mark the boxes that apply.

    Statutory employee: Mark this box for statutory employees whose earnings are subject to social security (OASDI) and Medicare (HI) taxes but not subject to federal income tax withholding.

    Retirement plan: Mark this box if the employee was an active participant (for any part of the year) in a retirement plan such as 401(k) and SEP.

    Third-party sick plan: Mark this box only if you are a third-party, sick-pay payer filing a Form W-2 for an insured's employee.

Box 14—**Other:** Use this box for any other information you want to give your employee. Label each item. Examples are union dues, health insurance premiums deducted, moving expenses paid, nontaxable income, or educational assistance payments. Mandatory employee contributions to state unemployment taxes in AK, NJ, and PA are deductible for federal income tax purposes and therefore should be included in Box 14.

Boxes 15 through 20—**State or local income tax information:** You do not have to complete these boxes, but you may want to if you use copies of this form for your state and local returns. The ID number is assigned by each individual state. The state and local information boxes can be used to report wages and taxes on two states and two localities. Keep each state's and locality's information separated by the dotted line.

Reference Guide for Box 12 Codes

A—Uncollected social security (OASDI) tax on tips
B—Uncollected Medicare (HI) tax on tips
C—Group-term life insurance over $50,000
D—Elective deferrals to a Section 401(k) cash or deferred arrangement
E—Elective deferrals to a Section 403(b) salary reduction agreement
F—Elective deferrals to a Section 408(k)(6) salary reduction SEP
G—Elective and nonelective deferrals to a Section 457(b) deferred compensation plan (state and local government and tax-exempt employers)
H—Elective deferrals to a Section 501(c)(18)(D) tax-exempt organization plan
J—Nontaxable sick pay
K—20% excise tax on excess golden parachute payments
L—Substantiated employee business expense (federal rate)
M—Uncollected social security (OASDI) tax on group-term life insurance coverage
N—Uncollected Medicare (HI) tax on group-term life insurance coverage
P—Moving expense reimbursements paid directly to a member of the U.S. Armed Forces (not included in Box 1, 3, or 5)
Q—Nontaxable combat pay
R—Employer contributions to medical savings account
S—Employee salary reduction contributions to a 408(p) SIMPLE retirement plan
T—Employer-provided qualified adoption benefits
V—Exercise of nonstatutory stock options
W—Employer contributions to an employee's health savings account (HSA)
Y—Deferrals under a Section 409A nonqualified deferred compensation plan
Z—Income under a Section 409A nonqualified deferred compensation plan
AA—Designated Roth contributions to a 401(k) plan
BB—Designated Roth contributions under a 403(b) salary reduction agreement
DD—Cost of employer-sponsored health coverage. The amount reported with code DD is not taxable. This reporting requirement is for information purposes only.
EE—Designated Roth contributions under a governmental Section 457(b) plan. This amount does not apply to elective deferrals under Code G.
FF—Permitted benefits under a qualified small employer health reimbursement arrangement (QSEHRA). Maximum reimbursement for an eligible single employee is $5,450 ($11,050 maximum for a family), before indexing for inflation.
GG—Income from qualified grant under Section 83(i)
HH—Aggregate deferrals under Section 83(i) elections as of the close of the calendar year

Source: Internal Revenue Service.

The Affordable Care Act requires the reporting of the cost of employer-sponsored health coverage on Form W-2 in Box 12, coded as DD (see page 4-25, Figure 4.9). This includes coverage provided for domestic partners. The value of the employer's excludable contribution to health coverage continues to be excludable from an employee's income, and it is not taxable. This reporting is for informational purposes only. Employers that provide "applicable employer-sponsored coverage" under a group health plan are subject to the reporting requirement.

When employees leave the service of the employer, you may give them Form W-2 any time after employment ends. If employees ask for Form W-2, the employer should give it to them within 30 days of their request or the final wage payment, whichever is later. In instances where terminated workers may be rehired at some time before the year ends, the employer may delay furnishing the form until January 31 following the close of the calendar year. Employers distribute Form W-2 copies as follows:

Copy A—To the Social Security Administration **by the end of January** following the year for which Form W-2 is applicable.
Copy 1—To the state, city, or local tax department.
Copy B—To employees for filing with their federal income tax return.
Copy C—To employees for their personal records.
Copy 2—To employees for filing with their state, city, or local income tax returns.
Copy D—Retained by the employer.

If 250 or more Forms W-2 are being filed, reporting must be done electronically.

Employers that are going out of business must send W-2 forms to the employees by the date the final Form 941 is due. One month later, the W-2 forms are due at the Social Security Administration.

If Form W-2 has been lost or destroyed, employers are authorized to furnish substitute copies to the employee. The substitute form should be clearly marked **REISSUED STATEMENT**. Do not send Copy A of the substitute statement to the Social Security Administration. If, after a reasonable effort, the employer cannot deliver a Form W-2, the employer retains the employee's copies of the form for a four-year period. A "reasonable effort" means the forms were mailed to the last known address of the employee.

The IRS allows employers to put W-2s on a secure Web site and provide employees with passwords to access their individual W-2s. As long as an employee has affirmatively consented, their W-2 can be sent electronically. The consent by the employee must also be made electronically in a manner that indicates that the employee will be able to access the W-2. The W-2 must be posted on or before January 31 (kept until October 15), and the employee must be notified of its availability and must be given instructions on how to access and print the W-2.

Form W-2c

To correct errors in previously filed Forms W-2, employers file **Form W-2c, Corrected Wage and Tax Statement** shown in Figure 4.10. File Copy A with the Social Security Administration and the remaining copies as noted on the bottom of each form.

Form W-3c should accompany all corrected wage and tax statements unless the correction is for only one employee or to correct employees' names, addresses, or social security numbers. In the case of an incorrect address, the employer can mail the "incorrect" W-2 in an envelope bearing the corrected address.

FIGURE 4.10

Form W-2c, Corrected Wage and Tax Statement

DO NOT CUT, FOLD, OR STAPLE THIS FORM

44444	For Official Use Only ▶ OMB No. 1545-0008		

a Employer's name, address, and ZIP code	c Tax year/Form corrected	d Employee's correct SSN
Comcart Company 1600 Fourth Avenue Princeton, NJ 09109	20-- / **W-2**	000-00-6399

	e Corrected SSN and/or name (Check this box and complete boxes f and/or g if incorrect on form previously filed.) ☐

Complete boxes f and/or g only if incorrect on form **previously filed** ▶

f Employee's **previously reported** SSN

b Employer's Federal EIN 00-0007221	g Employee's **previously reported** name

h Employee's first name and initial	Last name	Suff.
Marge A.	Mangano	

8911 State Street
Trenton, NJ 08033

i Employee's address and ZIP code

Note. Only complete money fields that are being corrected (exception: for corrections involving MQGE, see the General Instructions for Forms W-2 and W-3, under Specific Instructions for Form W-2c, boxes 5 and 6).

Previously reported	Correct information	Previously reported	Correct information
1 Wages, tips, other compensation	1 Wages, tips, other compensation	2 Federal income tax withheld 3,293.00	2 Federal income tax withheld 3,923.00
3 Social security wages	3 Social security wages	4 Social security tax withheld	4 Social security tax withheld
5 Medicare wages and tips	5 Medicare wages and tips	6 Medicare tax withheld	6 Medicare tax withheld
7 Social security tips	7 Social security tips	8 Allocated tips	8 Allocated tips
9	9	10 Dependent care benefits	10 Dependent care benefits
11 Nonqualified plans	11 Nonqualified plans	12a See instructions for box 12 C o d e	12a See instructions for box 12 C o d e
13 Statutory employee Retirement plan Third-party sick pay ☐ ☐ ☐	13 Statutory employee Retirement plan Third-party sick pay ☐ ☐ ☐	12b C o d e	12b C o d e
14 Other (see instructions)	14 Other (see instructions)	12c C o d e	12c C o d e
		12d C o d e	12d C o d e

State Correction Information

Previously reported	Correct information	Previously reported	Correct information
15 State Employer's state ID number	15 State Employer's state ID number	15 State Employer's state ID number	15 State Employer's state ID number
16 State wages, tips, etc.	16 State wages, tips, etc.	16 State wages, tips, etc.	16 State wages, tips, etc.
17 State income tax	17 State income tax	17 State income tax	17 State income tax

Locality Correction Information

Previously reported	Correct information	Previously reported	Correct information
18 Local wages, tips, etc.	18 Local wages, tips, etc.	18 Local wages, tips, etc.	18 Local wages, tips, etc.
19 Local income tax	19 Local income tax	19 Local income tax	19 Local income tax
20 Locality name	20 Locality name	20 Locality name	20 Locality name

For Privacy Act and Paperwork Reduction Act Notice, see separate instructions.

Copy A—For Social Security Administration

Form **W-2c** (Rev. 8-2014)   **Corrected Wage and Tax Statement**   Cat. No. 61437D   Department of the Treasury Internal Revenue Service

Source: Internal Revenue Service.

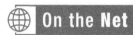

For access to all federal
tax forms, see the Forms
and Publications download
page: http://www.irs.gov/
formspubs/

Form W-3

Form W-3, Transmittal of Wage and Tax Statements, must be filed with the Social Security Administration by employers and other payers as a transmittal for Forms W-2. On Form W-3, the employer indicates the number of documents being transmitted. Form W-3 and the accompanying documents enable the Social Security Administration and the IRS to compare the totals to the amounts for the income tax withholdings, social security wages, social security tips, and Medicare wages and tips, as reported on the employer's 941s for the year. The IRS will require explanations of any differences and corrections to any errors. Figure 4.11 shows a completed Form W-3. The employer files all Forms W-2 with one W-3. Forms W-3 and the related documents are filed with the Social Security Administration by the end of January each year. Form W-3 is mailed to employers during the fourth quarter.

The information shown on Form W-3 is matched against the employer's Forms 941 for the year. If the totals do not match, the IRS notifies the employer of the discrepancy, and the employer is required to provide additional information.

FIGURE 4.11

Form W-3, Transmittal of Wage and Tax Statements

DO NOT STAPLE		
33333 a Control number	For Official Use Only ▶ OMB No. 1545-0008	

b Kind of Payer (Check one): 941 [X] · Military · 943 · 944 · CT-1 · Hshld. emp. · Medicare govt. emp.

Kind of Employer (Check one): None apply [X] · 501c non-govt. · State/local non-501c · State/local 501c · Federal govt. · Third-party sick pay (Check if applicable)

c Total number of Forms W-2 132	d Establishment number	1 Wages, tips, other compensation 2620736.40	2 Federal income tax withheld 330317.19
e Employer identification number (EIN) 00-0006281		3 Social security wages 2485210.05	4 Social security tax withheld 154083.02
f Employer's name Grove Electronics 33 Vista Road Vallejo, CA 94590-0033		5 Medicare wages and tips 2620736.40	6 Medicare tax withheld 38000.68
		7 Social security tips	8 Allocated tips
		9	10 Dependent care benefits
		11 Nonqualified plans	12a Deferred compensation
g Employer's address and ZIP code			
h Other EIN used this year	13 For third-party sick pay use only	12b
15 State CA Employer's state ID number 00-004132	14 Income tax withheld by payer of third-party sick pay	
16 State wages, tips, etc. 2620736.40	17 State income tax 111381.29	18 Local wages, tips, etc.	19 Local income tax
Employer's contact person Roger Damron	Employer's telephone number (415) 555-3200	For Official Use Only
Employer's fax number (415) 555-2229	Employer's email address RDamron@grove.com	

Under penalties of perjury, I declare that I have examined this return and accompanying documents and, to the best of my knowledge and belief, they are true, correct, and complete.

Signature ▶ *Carl W. Tolan* Title ▶ President Date ▶ 1/31/20--

Form **W-3** **Transmittal of Wage and Tax Statements** **20- -** Department of the Treasury Internal Revenue Service

Source: Internal Revenue Service.

Penalties

The following penalties are imposed for late or incorrect filing of W-2s:

1. If filed correctly within 30 days after the due date, $50 per return ($588,500 maximum penalty/$206,000 for small businesses).
2. If filed between 30 days after the due date and August 1, $110 per return ($1,766,000 maximum penalty/$588,500 for small businesses).

3. After August 1, $290 per return ($3,532,500 maximum penalty $1,177,500 for small businesses).
4. Penalties of $580 per return for intentional disregard of the requirements for filing, providing payee statements, and reporting incorrect information (no maximum penalty).
5. Filing W-2s with mismatched names and social security numbers, $290 per form.
6. Penalties of $290 per statement ($3,532,500 maximum) for failure to furnish the statements to *employees* on time, or furnishing incorrect information on the statements.

Forms W-2 with incorrect dollar amounts may qualify for a safe harbor for certain immaterial errors.

Form W-3c

The **Transmittal of Corrected Income and Tax Statements, Form W-3c,** not shown, is used to accompany copies of Form W-2c, sent to the Social Security Administration. This form can also be used to correct a previously filed Form W-3.

Privately Printed Forms

Employers may use their own forms by obtaining specifications for the private printing of Forms W-2 from any IRS center or district office. To the extent that the privately printed forms meet the specifications, the employer may use them without prior approval of the IRS.

On the Job

The Social Security Administration processes close to 240 million W-2s a year, and about 10 percent have names and numbers that do not match.

Self-Study Quiz 4-6

1. Marquat Company deducts union dues from its employees' paychecks each month during the year and sends them to the local union office. How should the company report this deduction on the employees' Forms W-2?
2. Gringle's terminated 10 of its employees on July 5, 20--. The company informed each employee that it may rehire them again during its peak season in September. When should the company furnish each employee with a W-2 statement?
3. While preparing her personal income tax return, Connie Becker, an employee of Trident Mills, discovered that she had lost her Form W-2. What procedures should the company follow to prepare a new Form W-2 for Becker?

Returns Employers Must Complete

Employers must file returns reporting the amount of wages paid and the amount of taxes withheld at designated times, beginning with the first quarter in which taxable wages are paid. Rules that require different returns for different types of employees further complicate the accounting tasks and payroll procedures. Figure 4.12 on page 30 briefly summarizes the major returns completed by employers.

The most recent information with regard to withholding, deposit, and payment and reporting of federal income taxes, FICA taxes, and FUTA taxes is available in **Circular E, Employer's Tax Guide.** This circular is sent to employers prior to the start of the new year and is also available at district offices of the IRS.

IRS Connection

The IRS recently created two forms to facilitate the e-filing of employment tax returns. Forms 8879-EMP and 8453-EMP facilitate a quicker method of electronically signing employment tax returns.

FIGURE 4.12
Major Returns Filed by Employers

Form 941, Employer's Quarterly Federal Tax Return	For reporting federal income taxes withheld during the calendar quarter and the employer and employee portions of the FICA taxes. Form 941 is illustrated in Chapter 3.
Form 943, Employer's Annual Tax Return for Agricultural Employees	For reporting the withholding of federal income taxes and FICA taxes on wages paid to agricultural workers. Form 943 is used for agricultural employees even though the employer may employ nonagricultural workers.
Form 944, Employer's Annual Federal Tax Return	Replaces Form 941 for employers who owe $1,000 or less in employment taxes for the year.
Form 945, Annual Return of Withheld Federal Income Tax	Used to report tax liability for nonpayroll items such as backup withholding and withholding on gambling winnings, pensions, and annuities, and deposits made for the year. **Backup withholding** occurs when an individual receives taxable interest, dividends, and certain other payments and fails to furnish the payer with the correct taxpayer identification numbers. Payers are then required to withhold 24% of those payments. Backup withholding does not apply to wages, pensions, annuities, or IRAs.

Information Returns

LO 5

Identify major types of information returns.

The IRS requires employers to file additional **information returns** to report compensation paid to certain individuals who are not employees. These returns allow the IRS to determine if taxpayers are reporting their true income. Figure 4.13 briefly summarizes the major information returns required by the IRS. The employer sends copies of the returns to the payee by the end of January. These forms can be sent to the contractors electronically as long as they agree in advance to this method of delivery. The payer's name, address, and phone number are led on the recipient's copy of Form 1099.

To transmit each type of Form 1099 to the IRS, the employer uses *Form 1096, Annual Summary and Transmittal of U.S. Information Returns*.

FIGURE 4.13
Major Returns Filed by Employers

Form 1099-DIV, Dividends and Distributions	For reporting dividends totaling $10 or more to any person; foreign tax withheld and paid on dividends and other distributions on stock for a person; distributions made by corporations and regulated investment companies (including money market funds) as part of liquidation.
Form 1099-G, Certain Government Payments	For reporting unemployment compensation payments, state and local income tax refunds of $10 or more, taxable grants, income tax refunds, and agricultural subsidy payments.
Form 1099-INT, Interest Income	For reporting payments of (a) interest of $10 or more paid or credited on earnings from savings and loans, credit unions, bank deposits, corporate bonds, etc.; (b) interest of $600 or more from other sources; (c) forfeited interest due on premature withdrawals of time deposits; (d) foreign tax eligible for the recipient's foreign tax credit withheld and paid on interest; (e) payments of any interest on bearer certificates of deposit.
Form 1099-MISC, Miscellaneous Income (See Figure 4.14)	For reporting miscellaneous income, such as rents, royalties, commissions, fees, prizes, and awards of at least $600 paid to nonemployees, and any backup withholding. Gross royalty payments of $10 or more must also be reported on this form. Life insurance companies may use either 1099-MISC or Form W-2 to report payments to full-time life insurance sales agents.
Form 1099-NEC, Nonemployee Compensation	For reporting payments made for (a) $600 or more paid to nonemployees for services performed, (b) cash paid for fish purchased from someone in the trade or business of fishing, (c) certain payments to an attorney, and (d) backup withholding.
Form 1099-PATR, Taxable Distributions Received from Cooperatives	For cooperatives to report patronage dividends paid and other distributions made that total $10 or more during the year.
Form 1099-R, Distributions from Pensions, Annuities, Retirement or Profit-Sharing Plans, IRAs, Insurance Contracts, etc.	For reporting all distributions that total $10 or more from pensions, annuities, profit-sharing and retirement plans, and individual retirement arrangements made by employees' trusts or funds; federal, state, or local government retirement system; life insurance companies.
Form 5498, IRA Contribution Information	For reporting contributions received from each person to an IRA or simplified employee pension plan (SEP) and qualified deductible voluntary employee contributions to a plan maintained by the employer.
Form 8027, Employer's Annual Information Return of Tip Income and Allocated Tips	For large food or beverage establishments to report to the IRS the receipts from food and beverage operations and tips reported by employees.

Employers use a separate Form 1096 to transmit each type of information return. For example, one Form 1096 is used to transmit all Forms 1099-MISC (see Figure 4.14) and another Form 1096 is used to transmit all Forms 1099-INT. The employer files Form 1096 and all accompanying forms to the IRS on or before the last day of February of the year following the payment. If box 7 is completed, the Form 1099-MISC due date is January 31. For returns filed electronically, the due date is March 31. Penalties previously listed for late submission of Forms W-2 also apply to the Form 1099 series (see page 4-28).

Independent Contractor Payments

Payments made to independent contractors (individuals or partnerships) of at least $600 must be reported on Form 1099-NEC Nonemployee Compensation. This does not apply to contractors who are incorporated unless the payments are medical or health-care related. Since payments to these independent contractors are not generated by payroll departments, the accounts payable departments usually complete the appropriate 1099 forms.

Form 1099-NEC can also be provided electronically to any recipient who has consented to receive the form in this manner.

Backup Withholding

Independent contractors must provide taxpayer identification numbers (TIN) to their employers (orally, in writing, or on Form W-9). If this is not done and the company anticipates paying the contractor $600 or more, the company

IRS Connection

The IRS estimates that self-employed taxpayers are underpaying their taxes by at least $81 billion. These nonwage workers are not caught because payers do not always report these payments to the IRS.

News Alert

Recipient's identification number is truncated on worker's copy of Form 1099-MISC.

FIGURE 4.14
Form 1099-MISC, Miscellaneous Income

	9595	☐ VOID	☐ CORRECTED		
PAYER'S name, street address, city or town, state or province, country, ZIP or foreign postal code, and telephone no.		**1** Rents $	OMB No. 1545-0115		Miscellaneous Information
Worldwide Publishing Co. 40 Fifth Avenue New York, NY 10011-4000 (212) 555-2000		**2** Royalties $ 34,970.65	Form **1099-MISC** (Rev. January 2022) For calendar year 20 ____		
		3 Other income $	**4** Federal income tax withheld $		Copy A For Internal Revenue Service Center
PAYER'S TIN 00-0003736	RECIPIENT'S TIN 000-00-4821	**5** Fishing boat proceeds $	**6** Medical and health care payments $		File with Form 1096.
RECIPIENT'S name Laurie T. Musberger		**7** Payer made direct sales totaling $5,000 or more of consumer products to recipient for resale ☐	**8** Substitute payments in lieu of dividends or interest $		For Privacy Act and Paperwork Reduction Act Notice, see the
Street address (including apt. no.) 1043 Maple Drive		**9** Crop insurance proceeds $	**10** Gross proceeds paid to an attorney $		current General Instructions for Certain
City or town, state or province, country, and ZIP or foreign postal code Chicago, IL 60615-3443		**11** Fish purchased for resale $	**12** Section 409A deferrals $		Information Returns.
	13 FATCA filing requirement ☐	**14** Excess golden parachute payments $	**15** Nonqualified deferred compensation $		
Account number (see instructions)	2nd TIN not. ☐	**16** State tax withheld $ $	**17** State/Payer's state no. 00-03378	**18** State income $ $	

Form **1099-MISC** (Rev. 1-2022)   Cat. No. 14425J   www.irs.gov/Form1099MISC   Department of the Treasury - Internal Revenue Service
Do Not Cut or Separate Forms on This Page — Do Not Cut or Separate Forms on This Page

Source: Internal Revenue Service.

must withhold federal income taxes of *24 percent* of the payments made. This **backup withholding** must continue until the number is reported. Failure to withhold will result in the payer being held liable by the IRS for the 24 percent withholding.

Nonpayroll Reporting

Payroll income tax withholdings are reported on Form 941, while nonpayroll items are reported on **Form 945, Annual Return of Withheld Federal Income Tax**. Nonpayroll items include backup withholdings and withholdings on pensions, IRAs, gambling winnings, and military retirement pay. Generally, all income tax withholdings that are reported on Form 1099 or Form W-2G belong on Form 945.

Over the Line

The IRS assessed employment taxes, penalties, and interest to Bruecher Foundation Services, Inc., in reference to workers that were misclassified as independent contractors. Section 530 of the Internal Revenue Code gives "safe harbor" for the misclassification of employees if the employer can show that it filed all federal tax and information returns. However, the IRS said Bruecher would not qualify for safe harbor because it did not file information returns (Forms 1099) on a timely basis.[3]

On the Net

For electronic filing of tax return and payment options, go to: **Electronic Filing for Businesses:** https://www.eftps.gov/eftps/

Electronic Filing Form W-2 and Information Returns

If employers file 250 or more Forms W-2 or other information returns (for each type of information return), they must use electronic filing instead of paper forms. Filing Forms W-2 does not require approval of the medium by the Social Security Administration. The employer must complete **Form 4419, Application for Filing Information Returns Electronically (FIRE)**, and file it with the IRS.

LO 6

Discuss the impact of state and local income taxes on the payroll accounting process.

Withholding State Income Tax

In addition to federal income taxes, many states also have income tax withholding requirements. The situation is further complicated if an employer has employees in several states. This requires employers to know how much tax to withhold, what types of employees and payments are exempt, and how to pay the tax.

In general, state income taxes should be withheld based on where the services are performed unless there is a reciprocal agreement between the states. If there is no such agreement and the employee works in one state and lives in another, the laws of both states must be considered.

3 Anne S. Lewis, "Employer That Failed to File Timely Information Returns for Misclassified Workers Was Not Entitled to Section 530 Relief," *PAYTECH*, October 2007, p. 73.

The three different methods of withholding are:

1. Full taxation—both resident's state and work state calculate the taxes without any credits.
2. Leftover taxation—pay the full tax to the work state, and then pay the rest to the resident state.
3. Reciprocity—withhold only for the work state or resident state depending on the reciprocal agreement between the states.[4]

Employers must also be informed about each state's regulations regarding:

1. The required frequency of making wage payments.
2. The acceptable media of payment.
3. The maximum interval between the end of a pay period and the payday for that period.
4. The time limits for making final wage payments to employees who are discharged, are laid off, quit, or go on strike.
5. How often to inform employees of the deductions made from their wages.
6. The maximum amount of unpaid wages to pay the surviving spouse or family of a deceased worker.

Wage-bracket tables and percentage method formulas are used in many states to determine the amount of state income taxes to withhold from their employees' wages. Each state also determines for state income tax purposes the taxability status of the various fringe benefits discussed in this chapter. Even though most states do not tax deductions made for cafeteria plans and 401(k) accounts, some states do not allow for the tax sheltering of these deductions from employees' wages. Once again, it is the employers' responsibility to know the laws of the states in which they conduct business.

Most states having income tax laws require employers to withhold tax from both nonresidents and residents, unless a **reciprocal agreement** exists with one or more states to the contrary. For example, a reciprocal agreement may exist between two states where both states grant an exemption to non-residents who work in each of those states.

Even though there is no law requiring an employer to withhold income tax from the employee's home state if the employer has no physical presence in that state, most employers do this as a courtesy to their out-of-state employees.

State Income Tax Returns and Reports

Payroll managers should be familiar with four main types of state income tax returns or reports:

1. **Periodic withholding returns** on which you report the wages paid and the state tax withheld during the reporting period. Figure 4.15, on page 4-34, shows the **Payroll Tax Deposit Coupon** used by employers in California. Depending on the amount of state income taxes withheld for each quarterly period, employers may be required to pay the taxes semi-monthly, monthly, or quarterly. Some states require employers to deposit their withheld income taxes through electronic funds transfer (EFT).

On the Job

Only nine states do not have a state income tax on wages—Alaska, Florida, Nevada, New Hampshire, South Dakota, Tennessee, Texas, Washington, and Wyoming.

---

[4] "State Tax Issues for Travelling and Telecommuting Employees," *Pay State Update,* American Payroll Association, May 30, 2002, Issue 11, p. 2.

FIGURE 4.15

Form DE 88ALL, California Payroll Tax Deposit (Submitted online)

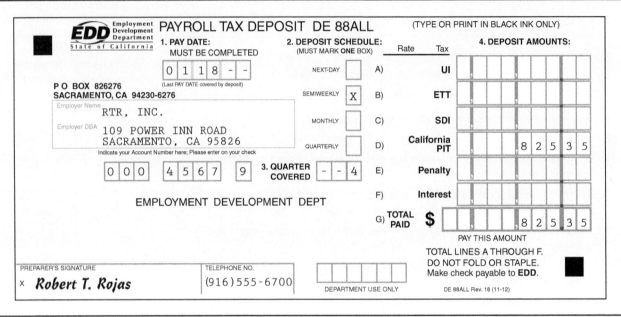

Source: CA Employment Development Department.

2. **Reconciliation returns** that compare the total amount of state tax paid as shown on the periodic returns with the amounts of state tax declared to have been withheld from employees' wages. Figure 4.16, shows the **Quarterly Contribution Return and Report of Wages (Continuation)** for use by employers in California. Employers may submit their information on magnetic media.

3. **Annual statements** to employees showing the amount of wages paid during the year and the state tax withheld from those wages.

4. **Information returns** used to report payments to individuals that are not subject to withholding and/or are not reported on the annual employee wage and tax statements. See Figure 4.13, on page 4-30, for a listing of the major information returns.

Since the requirements for transmitting returns and reports vary from state to state, employers should become familiar with the tax regulations of the state in which their business is located and of the state or states in which their employees reside. Because federal regulations require filing of information returns on magnetic media, many states permit employers to submit wage information on magnetic disk or tape. Also, many states take part in the Combined Federal/State Filing Program, which enables employers to file information returns with the federal government and authorize release of the information to the applicable state. To participate in this program, employers must first obtain permission from the IRS.

Withholding Local Income Taxes

In addition to state income tax laws, many cities and counties have passed local income tax legislation requiring employers to deduct and withhold income taxes or license fees on salaries or wages paid. In Alabama, several

FIGURE 4.16

Form DE 9c, California Quarterly Contribution Return and Report of Wages (continuation)

EDD Employment Development Department
State of California

QUARTERLY CONTRIBUTION RETURN AND REPORT OF WAGES (CONTINUATION)

REMINDER: File your DE 9 and DE 9C together.

009C0111

	YR	QTR
	- -	1

Page number _____ of _____

You must FILE this report even if you had no payroll. If you had no payroll, complete Items C and O.

QUARTER ENDED	DUE	DELINQUENT IF NOT POSTMARKED OR RECEIVED BY
03/31/20--	04/30/20--	04/30/20--

EMPLOYER ACCOUNT NO.
0 0 0 0 3 2 1 1

Vireng Company
1817 Kresson Road
Sacramento, CA 95826

DO NOT ALTER THIS AREA

P1 ☐ C ☐ T ☐ S ☐ W ☐ A ☐

EFFECTIVE DATE
Mo. Day Yr. WIC

A. **EMPLOYEES** full-time and part-time who worked during or received pay subject to UI for the payroll period which **includes the 12th** of the month.

1st Mo.	2nd Mo.	3rd Mo.
5	5	5

B. ☐ Check this box if you are reporting ONLY Voluntary Plan Disability Insurance wages on this page. Report Personal Income Tax (PIT) Wages and PIT Withheld, if appropriate. (See instructions for Item B.)

C. ☐ NO PAYROLL

D. SOCIAL SECURITY NUMBER	E. EMPLOYEE NAME (FIRST NAME)	(M.I.) (LAST NAME)	
000 00 6399	Maria	L Goshen	
F. TOTAL SUBJECT WAGES	G. PIT WAGES		H. PIT WITHHELD
5 0 0 9 2 5	5 0 0 9 2 5		5 5 2 5
000 00 7931	Carmen	M Rodgers	
F. TOTAL SUBJECT WAGES	G. PIT WAGES		H. PIT WITHHELD
7 1 9 5 0 0	7 1 9 5 0 0		9 5 0 3
000 00 8001	Joseph	N Nyugen	
F. TOTAL SUBJECT WAGES	G. PIT WAGES		H. PIT WITHHELD
1 0 3 1 9 0 0	1 0 3 1 9 0 0		1 2 0 7 7
000 00 9114	Elaine	M Schmidt	
F. TOTAL SUBJECT WAGES	G. PIT WAGES		H. PIT WITHHELD
1 5 9 1 0 0 0	1 5 9 1 0 0 0		7 2 4 6 2
000 00 4091	John	V Vireng	
F. TOTAL SUBJECT WAGES	G. PIT WAGES		H. PIT WITHHELD
2 8 3 5 0 0 0	2 8 3 5 0 0 0		1 3 8 3 9 8

I. TOTAL SUBJECT WAGES THIS PAGE	J. TOTAL PIT WAGES THIS PAGE	K. TOTAL PIT WITHHELD THIS PAGE
6 6 7 8 3 2 5	6 6 7 8 3 2 5	2 3 7 9 6 5

L. GRAND TOTAL SUBJECT WAGES	M. GRAND TOTAL PIT WAGES	N. GRAND TOTAL PIT WITHHELD
6 6 7 8 3 2 5	6 6 7 8 3 2 5	2 3 7 9 6 5

O. I declare that the information herein is true and correct to the best of my knowledge and belief.

Signature *Required* *John V Vireng* Title President (Owner, Accountant, Preparer, etc.) Phone ( ) 916 555-8121 Date 04/30/20--

SIGN AND MAIL TO: State of California / Employment Development Department / PO Box 989071 / West Sacramento CA 95798-9071

 DE 9C Rev. 3 (3-17) **(INTERNET)** Page 1 of 2

 File Online – It's Fast, Easy, and Secure! Visit **www.edd.ca.gov.** CU

Source: CA Employment Development Department.

cities have license fee ordinances that require the withholding of the fees from employees' wages. Certain employees in Denver, Colorado, are subject to the withholding of the Denver Occupational Privilege Tax from their compensation. In Kentucky, a number of cities and counties impose a license fee (payroll tax) or occupational tax.

Figure 4.17 shows the coupon that must be submitted online by employers in Philadelphia. All must withhold the city income tax from compensation paid their employees. Depending upon the amount of taxes withheld, employers may be required to make deposits weekly, monthly, or quarterly. Employers with more than 10 W-2s must remit electronically. For any late payments of the tax, the city imposes a penalty on the underpayment. Employers must file annual reconciliation returns by the end of February, reporting the amount of taxes deducted during the preceding calendar year.

FIGURE 4.17
Philadelphia Wage Tax Coupon

Monthly Wage Tax

Weiner, Inc.
820 Allen Drive
Ambler, PA 19002-0882

Use the Change Form to report any changes.

Signature: *Robert T. Rojas*
I hereby certify that I have examined this return and that it is correct to the best of my knowledge.

Phone #: (215) 555-6700

Account #: **0006301** From: **12/1/--**
Tax Type: **01** To: **12/31/--**
Period/Yr: **4/--** Due Date: **1/15/--**

Philadelphia Department of Revenue
P.O. Box 8040
Philadelphia, PA 19101-8040

1. TAX DUE PER WORKSHEET, *Line 8* $ 1,088 50
2. INTEREST AND PENALTY $ -0-
3. TOTAL DUE (LINE 1 & 2) $ 1,088 50

Make checks payable to:
CITY OF PHILADELPHIA

3330104309700000000061000440000000000000000000000000929780100000000002

Source: Philadelphia Department of Revenue.

Chapter 4 Supplement

Withholding Allowances

If an employee has a Form W-4 from 2019 or earlier on file with their employer, the law entitles employees to exempt a portion of their earnings from withholding by claiming a personal allowance and allowances for their dependents if they furnish their employers with a claim for the allowances. Employees may also claim special allowances and allowances for itemized deductions and tax credits. However, employees cannot claim the same withholding allowances with more than one employer at the same time.

Personal Allowances

Employees can claim a **personal allowance** for themselves and each qualified dependent, provided they are not claimed on another person's tax return. In 2022, the amount of the personal allowance was $4,300, and this was treated as a deduction in computing taxable income. A married employee may also claim one personal allowance for the employee's spouse if the spouse is not claimed as a dependent on another person's tax return.

If the employee has a second job or if the spouse also works, the personal allowances that the employee is entitled to should not also be claimed on the other job.

Allowances for Dependents

Employees may claim one allowance for each dependent (other than a spouse) who will be claimed on their federal income tax returns. To qualify as a dependent, the person must meet specific requirements that are listed in the instructions accompanying the individual's federal income tax return (six tests are involved— relationship, support, domicile, age, joint return, and citizenship).

Additional Withholding Allowance

Employees can also reduce the amount of withholding by claiming a **special withholding allowance**, whether or not they plan to itemize deductions on their tax returns. An additional withholding allowance can be claimed by a person under any one of the following situations:

Wavebreakmedia/Shutterstock.com

1. Single person who has only one job.
2. Married person who has only one job with nonworking spouse.
3. Person's wages from a second job or the spouse's wages (or both) equal $1,500 or less.

This allowance is only used to compute the employee's income tax withholding. The employee **cannot claim** this allowance on their income tax return.

Other Withholding Allowances

Withholding allowances reduce the overwithholding of income taxes on employees' wages. In addition to the allowances already discussed, employees may be entitled to withholding allowances based on estimated tax credits, such as child care, and itemized deductions for medical expenses, mortgage interest, and charitable contributions. Employees take these credits when filing their federal income tax returns. The number of withholding allowances is determined on the worksheet that accompanies **Form W-4, Employee's Withholding Allowance Certificate prepared in 2019 or earlier**, and is then reported on that form. The IRS has an online withholding calculator to help taxpayers with updating Form W-4.

Form W-4 from 2019 or Earlier (Employee's Withholding Allowance Certificate)

The employer uses the information from ***Form W-4, Employee's Withholding Allowance Certificate,*** from 2019 or earlier to compute the amount of income tax to withhold from employees' wages. The employer must have Form W-4 on file for each employee. This form contains the withholding allowance certificate (shown in Figure 4.18), detailed instructions, and worksheets for employees to use in completing the certificate. Employees hired in 2020 or later and employees with a change in their filing status or other adjustments will complete Form W-4 from 2020 or later. The tax table that the employer will use to determine the employees' federal tax withholding will depend on which Form W-4 the employer has on file.

Withholding Allowances

The process of determining the correct number of withholding allowances began with the number of personal exemptions the employee expected to claim on their tax return. The employee then increased or decreased this number based on the employee's eligibility and desire for a higher paycheck or a higher tax refund. The worksheets provided with Form W-4 enabled the employee to determine the exact number of allowances to enter on the certificate.

FIGURE 4.18

Form W-4 from 2019 or earlier, Employee's Withholding Allowance Certificate

Separate here and give Form W-4 to your employer. Keep the worksheet(s) for your records.

Form **W-4**
Department of the Treasury
Internal Revenue Service

Employee's Withholding Allowance Certificate

► **Whether you're entitled to claim a certain number of allowances or exemption from withholding is subject to review by the IRS. Your employer may be required to send a copy of this form to the IRS.**

OMB No. 1545-0074

2019

1 Your first name and middle initial: Harry M. | Last name: Weir | **2 Your social security number**: 000-00-6921

Home address (number and street or rural route): 421 Eastmont

3 ☑ Single ☐ Married ☐ Married, but withhold at higher Single rate.
Note: If married filing separately, check "Married, but withhold at higher Single rate."

City or town, state, and ZIP code: Richland, WA 99352

4 **If your last name differs from that shown on your social security card, check here. You must call 800-772-1213 for a replacement card.** ► ☐

5 Total number of allowances you're claiming (from the applicable worksheet on the following pages) . . . . | 5 | 4

6 Additional amount, if any, you want withheld from each paycheck . . . . | 6 | $ 0

7 I claim exemption from withholding for 2019, and I certify that I meet **both** of the following conditions for exemption.

- Last year I had a right to a refund of **all** federal income tax withheld because I had **no** tax liability, **and**
- This year I expect a refund of **all** federal income tax withheld because I expect to have **no** tax liability.

If you meet both conditions, write "Exempt" here . . . . ► | 7 |

Under penalties of perjury, I declare that I have examined this certificate and, to the best of my knowledge and belief, it is true, correct, and complete.

Employee's signature
(This form is not valid unless you sign it.) ► *Harry M. Weir* **Date ► January 1, 2019**

8 Employer's name and address (**Employer:** Complete boxes 8 and 10 if sending to IRS and complete boxes 8, 9, and 10 if sending to State Directory of New Hires.) | 9 First date of employment | 10 Employer identification number (EIN)

For Privacy Act and Paperwork Reduction Act Notice, see page 4. Cat. No. 10220Q Form **W-4** (2019)

Source: Internal Revenue Service.

Federal Income Tax Withholding

LO 8

Compute the amount of federal income tax to be withheld using the appropriate tables for Manual Systems with Forms W-4 from 2019 or earlier for: (a) the percentage method and (b) the wage-bracket method.

For employees with a Form W-4 from 2019 or earlier on file, the employer uses the number of withholding allowances and marital status found on Form W-4 to calculate the federal income tax withholding. Employers usually choose either the percentage method or the wage-bracket method using the tables for Forms W-4 from 2019 or earlier. Both distinguish between married and unmarried persons, and both methods provide the full benefit of the allowances claimed by the employee on Form W-4 from 2019 or earlier.

The choice of methods is usually based on the number of employees and the payroll accounting system used. The employer can change from one method to another at any time, and different methods may be used for different groups of employees.

Both methods take into account a standard deduction, an amount of money used to reduce an individual's adjusted gross income in arriving at the taxable income. For 2022, the following standard deductions apply:

Joint return filers and surviving spouses	$25,900
Married persons filing separately	12,950
Head of household filers	19,400
Single filers	12,950

The standard deduction increases by $1,400 if 65 or older or blind and by $1,750 for unmarried taxpayers. Each year, the standard deductions are adjusted for inflation.

Percentage Method for Manual Systems with Forms W-4 from 2019 or Earlier

The IRS provides statutory percentage method tables for weekly, biweekly, semimonthly, monthly, quarterly, semiannual, annual, and daily or miscellaneous pay periods for married and single persons. Copies may be obtained from the District Director of Internal Revenue or online at www.irs.gov. Tax Table C on pages T-15 and T-16 at the end of the textbook provides the percentage method tables.

Wage-Bracket Method

The IRS provides statutory wage tables for weekly, biweekly, semimonthly, monthly, daily or miscellaneous pay periods for married and single persons. Copies may be obtained from the District Director of Internal Revenue or online at www.irs.gov. Tax Table D on pages T-17 to T-34 at the end of the textbook provides the wage-bracket tables.

In cases where an employee claims more than 10 allowances, the employer has two methods for determining the amount to withhold when using the wage-bracket tables.

1. Withhold as if the employee claimed only 10 allowances, or
2. Multiply the value of one allowance for the applicable payroll period by the number of withholding allowances exceeding 10; subtract this amount from the employee's gross wage that is subject to federal income tax withholding. Use the resulting amount and column 10 for allowances in the wage-bracket table to determine the tax to withhold.

Example 4-13

Tell Me More

To compute the tax using the percentage method for Manual Payroll Systems with Forms W-4 or earlier, follow the steps illustrated below.

Step 1
Determine the amount of gross wages earned, marital status, number of allowances, and frequency of pay. *Note:* If the wage ends in a fractional dollar amount, the wage may be rounded to the nearest dollar. However, in this text, exact wages are used.

 Wilson Goodman, single, claims two allowances and earns $915.60 semimonthly.

Step 2
Multiply the number of allowances claimed by the amount of one allowance for the appropriate payroll period, as shown in the Table of Allowance Values in Figure 4.19.

Table of Allowance Values for semimonthly payroll period shows $179.00.

Multiply $179.00 × 2 = $358.00

Step 3
Subtract the amount for the number of allowances claimed from the employee's gross pay to find the excess of wages over allowances claimed.

Gross pay	$ 915.60
Less: Allowances	358.00
Excess wages	$ 557.60

Step 4
Determine the withholding tax on the excess of wages over allowances claimed by referring to the appropriate Percentage Method Withholding Table.

Compute tax from Tax Table C, pages T-15 and T-16.
($557.60 − $181.00 = $376.60 × 10% = $37.66 + $0) = $37.66

FIGURE 4.19
Table of Allowance Values for 2022

Weekly	83.00	Biweekly	165.00	Semimonthly	179.00	Monthly	358.00
Quarterly	1,075.00	Semiannual	2,150.00	Annual	4,300.00	Daily/Misc.	17.00

Example 4-14

To use the wage-bracket method tables for Manual Payroll Systems with Forms W-4 from 2019 or earlier, follow the steps illustrated below.

Step 1
Select the withholding table that applies to the employee's marital status and pay period.

 Adrienne Huff is married and claims 3 allowances. She is paid weekly at a rate of $815.

Step 2
Locate the wage bracket (the first two columns of the table) in which the employee's gross wages fall.

Locate the appropriate wage bracket (see Figure 4.20):

At least $815 but less than $830

Step 3
Follow the line for the wage bracket across to the right to the column showing the appropriate number of allowances. Withhold this amount of tax.

Move across the line to the column showing 3 allowances.

The tax to withhold is $32.

If the employee's wages are higher than the last amount listed on the appropriate wage-bracket table, the percentage method must be used for that employee.

FIGURE 4.20
Married Persons—Weekly Payroll Period

2022 Wage Bracket Method Tables for Manual Payroll Systems
With Forms W-4 From 2019 or Earlier
WEEKLY Payroll Period

If the **Wage Amount** (line 1a) is		MARRIED Persons										
		And the number of allowances is:										
At least	But less than	0	1	2	3	4	5	6	7	8	9	10
		The Tentative Withholding Amount is:										
$800	$815	$59	$49	$39	$31	$23	$14	$6	$0	$0	$0	$0
815	830	61	51	41	32	24	16	8	0	0	0	0
830	845	63	53	43	34	26	17	9	1	0	0	0
845	860	64	54	45	35	27	19	11	2	0	0	0
860	875	66	56	46	37	29	20	12	4	0	0	0
875	890	68	58	48	38	30	22	14	5	0	0	0
890	905	70	60	50	40	32	23	15	7	0	0	0
905	920	72	62	52	42	33	25	17	8	0	0	0
920	935	73	63	54	44	35	26	18	10	2	0	0

Source: Internal Revenue Service.

WITHHOLDING WITH OVER 10 ALLOWANCES. Genevieve Minster is married and claims 12 allowances. She is paid $3,000 semimonthly. To determine her federal tax withholding using the wage-bracket tables, do the following:

Example 4-15

Step 1—Multiply the amount of a withholding allowance for a semimonthly payroll period by 2.

$$\$179.00 \times 2 = \$358.00$$

Step 2—Subtract that number from the gross wages.

$$\$3,000 - \$358.00 = \$2,642.00$$

Step 3—Go to the wage-bracket table for a semimonthly pay period for a married person under the column for 10 allowances. (Page T-26)

$$\$29$$

Key Terms

annualizing wages (p. 4-18)

backup withholding (p. 4-32)

de minimis fringe benefit (p. 4-5)

defined contribution plan (p. 4-8)

gross-up (p. 4-22)

information returns (p. 4-30)

part-year employment (p. 4-18)

percentage method (p. 4-16)

personal allowance (p. 4-37)

quarterly averaging (p. 4-18)

reciprocal agreement (p. 4-33)

special withholding allowance (p. 4-37)

standard deduction (p. 4-16)

supplemental wage payments (p. 4-20)

wage and tax statements (p. 4-23)

wage-bracket method (p. 4-16)

wages (p. 4-2)

Answers to Self-Study Quizzes

Self-Study Quiz 4-1

✓	1.	Meals provided to employees for the convenience of the employer on the employer's premises.
_____	2.	Bonuses to managers and supervisors are considered compensation for services rendered as employees and are subject to withholding.
✓	3.	The use of on-site athletic facilities by employees is considered a nontaxable fringe benefit.
✓	4.	Advances for business expenses reasonably expected to be incurred.
_____	5.	Sick pay is subject to withholding.
_____	6.	Memberships in social or country clubs are taxable fringe benefits and are subject to withholding.
✓	7.	No-additional-cost meals provided to employees at an employer-operated eating establishment.

Self-Study Quiz 4-2

1. The payroll manager should inform Kyle that the company cannot reimburse her for any over-withholding that may have occurred prior to her submitting a new W-4. The only circumstances that allow the employer to reimburse an employee for overwithholding is if the employer failed to put a new W-4 into effect that resulted in overwithholding.

2. The payroll manager must inform Bradley that an employee may claim exemption from withholding for only one tax year at a time. The exemption must be claimed each year by February 15. If a new certificate is not filed, the employer must withhold at the single rate with zero withholding allowances.

3. Jack Matthews's employer has to make the certificate effective no later than the start of the first payroll period ending on or after the 30th day from the date the replacement Form W-4 was received.

Self-Study Quiz 4-3

Step 1—Determine gross wages, filing status, adjustments on Form W-4, and frequency of pay. $1,100.25, married filing jointly, has no adjustments on her Form W-4, paid semimonthly

Step 2—Compute the tax from the percentage tax table for Manual Payroll Systems With Forms W-4 From 2020 or Later, Standard Withholding Rate Schedules, SEMIMONTHLY MARRIED FILING JOINTLY person:

Over $1,079.00 But not over $1,935.......... 10% of excess over $1,079 plus $0

$1,100.25 − $1,079.00 = $21.25 × 10% = $2.13

Total tax to be withheld = $2.13

Self-Study Quiz 4-4

Employee	Tax	Employee	Tax
Lamb	$59	Vick	$166
Nurin	$31	Marks	$72
Hogan	$0		

Self-Study Quiz 4-5

Method A: Tax previously withheld on semimonthly wage of $1,450 = $37

Tax on wage and bonus ($1,950):	$ 87
Less tax previously withheld:	37
Withholding on bonus:	$ 50

Method B: 22% × $500 = $110

Self-Study Quiz 4-6

1. The company should report the total amount deducted from each employee in Box 14 of Form W-2. This box is to provide "other" information the company wants to give the employees. The company should label the amount as "union dues" in Box 14.

2. If an employee leaves the service of the employer, the employer may furnish Form W-2 any time after employment ends. If the employee requests Form W-2, the employer should give it to him/her within 30 days of the request or final wage payment, whichever is later. If there is a reasonable expectation that the employees may be rehired before the end of the year, the employer may delay providing Form W-2 until January following the close of the calendar year.

3. If Form W-2 has been destroyed or lost, employers are authorized to furnish substitute copies to the employee. Trident should provide a substitute form to Becker. The form should be clearly marked "Reissued Statement," and the company should not send the substitute statement to the Social Security Administration.

Key Points Summary

	Learning Objectives	Key Points	Problem Sets A & B Problems with asterisk (*) relate to Supplement.
L01	Explain coverage under the Federal Income Tax Withholding Law by determining: (a) the employer-employee relationship, (b) the kinds of payments defined as wages, and (c) the kinds of pretax salary reductions.	• Statutory employees/nonemployees. • Fringe benefit is added to regular wages—W/H taxes on total or 22 percent of fringe benefit. • Tips—tax on tips taken from regular wage payments. • Pretax salary reductions—from cafeteria plans to retirement contributions.	4-1, 4-7, 4-11
L02	Explain the purpose and use of Form W-4 from 2020 or later.	• Three filing statuses available for use are single or married filing separately, married filing jointly and head of household. • Adjustments are available for multiple jobs, qualifying dependents, other income/deductions, and extra withholding requests. • Can claim exemption from W/H if no tax last year and none expected this year.	
L03	Compute the amount of federal income tax to be withheld using the appropriate tables for Manual Systems with Forms W-4 from 2020 or later for: (a) the percentage method; (b) the wage-bracket method; (c) alternative methods such as quarterly averaging, annualizing of wages, and part-year employment; and (d) withholding of federal income taxes on supplementary wage payments.	• Use *Percentage Method W/H* table or *Wage-Bracket* table for Manual Payroll Systems with Forms W-4 from 2020 or later to determine federal tax withholding. • Supplemental—vacation (tax as separate wage payment) versus nonvacation (added to regular pay and total taxed or 22 percent of supplemental). • Gross-up formula.	4-2, 4-3, 4-4, 4-5, 4-6, 4-8, 4-9, 4-10, 4-13
L04	Explain the purpose and use of Form W-2.	• *Wage and Tax Statement* (W-2)—give to employees with copies to taxing authorities.	4-13
L05	Identify major types of information returns.	• *Form 1099-MISC Miscellaneous Income*—i.e., rents and royalties. • *Form 1099-NEC Nonemployee Compensation*—payment to non-employees for services.	
L06	Discuss the impact of state and local income taxes on the payroll accounting process.	• State and local filing and depositing requirements. • Impact on Form W-2.	4-12, 4-13
SUPPLEMENT **L07**	Explain the purpose and use of Form W-4 from 2019 or earlier and the types of allowances that may be claimed by employees for income tax withholding.	• Allowances claimed on W-4 for personal (themselves and spouse), dependents, special withholding, tax credits, and itemized deductions on personal tax return.	
L08	Compute the amount of federal income tax to be withheld using the appropriate tables for Manual Systems with Forms W-4 from 2019 or earlier for: (a) the percentage method and (b) the wage-bracket method.	• Use *Percentage Method W/H* or *Wage Bracket table for Manual Systems with Forms W-4 from 2019 or earlier*.	*4-14, *4-15, *4-16, *4-17

Matching Quiz

_____ 1. Taxable tips
_____ 2. Form W-4
_____ 3. Backup withholding
_____ 4. Form 1099-MISC
_____ 5. Roth IRA
_____ 6. Standard deduction
_____ 7. Pretax salary reductions
_____ 8. Form 1096
_____ 9. Nontaxable fringe benefits
_____ 10. Flexible reporting

A. Payments of at least $600 to independent contractors
B. Annual nondeductible contributions of up to $6,000
C. Annual summary and transmittal of U.S. information returns
D. Allows employers to use any basis as the time period for payment of noncash fringe benefits
E. Employee's Withholding Certificate
F. Withholdings from gross pay that reduce the amount of pay subject to federal income tax
G. Qualified employee discounts
H. Amount of money used to reduce an individual's adjusted gross income to taxable income
I. Withhold federal income taxes of 24 percent of payments made
J. $20 or more in a month

Questions for Review

Note: Use Tax Tables A, B, *C, and *D at the back of this text-book and the tax regulations presented in this chapter to answer all questions and solve all problems. Questions with an asterisk (*) refer to the Chapter 4 Supplement.

1. How is the amount of a fringe benefit that is tax-able to an employee determined?
2. To what extent are cash tips treated as remuneration subject to federal income tax withholding?
3. For each of the following kinds of wage payments, indicate whether or not the wages are exempt from the withholding of federal income taxes:
   a. Three weeks' vacation pay.
   b. Weekly advance to a sales representative for traveling expenses to be incurred.
   c. Weekly wages paid the housekeeper in a college fraternity.
   d. Monthly salary received by Rev. Cole Carpenter.
   e. Payments under a workers' compensation law for sickness or injury.
4. What is the maximum contribution that an employer can make to an employee's SIMPLE account?
5. What is the maximum amount that an employee can shelter into a 401(k) plan?
6. What was the standard deduction for a single filer for 2022?
7. Orrin D'Amato, single, participates in his firm's pension retirement plan. This year, his modified adjusted gross income will be about $74,000. How much of his compensation may D'Amato contribute to an IRA this year without paying federal income taxes on the contribution?

8. Are employer contributions into employees' health savings accounts taxed as earnings of the employees?
9. Under what conditions may employees be exempt from the withholding of federal income taxes during 2022? How do such employees indicate their no-tax-liability status?
10. How is the *special period rule* for the reporting of fringe benefits applied?
11. Commencing in June, Alan Oldt is eligible to receive monthly payments from a pension fund. What procedure should Oldt follow if he does not wish to have federal income taxes withheld from his periodic pension payments?
12. What formula is used to "gross-up" supplemental payments in order to cover the taxes on the supplemental payments?
13. Trowbridge Company has just completed the processing of its year-end payroll and distributed all the weekly paychecks. The payroll department is now computing the amount of the annual bonus to be given each worker. What methods may be used by the company in determining the amount of federal income taxes to be withheld from the annual bonus payments?
14. What is Form 944?
15. Why must some employers file Form 1096?
16. What is the penalty for filing W-2s with mismatched names and social security numbers?
17. What are the penalties imposed on employees for filing false information on Form W-4?
18. Under what conditions must employers submit copies of Form W-4 to the IRS?

19. Besides the name and address of the payer, what other information should be listed in the address box of the payer on the recipient's copy of Form 1099-MISC?

*20. Rhonda Gramm is single, and her wages are paid weekly. Under the percentage method, what is the amount of Gramm's one weekly withholding allowance? Howard Heinz, married, claims two withholding allowances, and his wages are paid semimonthly. What is the total amount of his semimonthly withholding allowances?

Questions for Discussion

1. Alex Oberstar, a cook in the Lagomarsino Company cafeteria, is furnished two meals each day during his eight-hour shift. Oberstar's duties require him to have his meals on the company's premises. Should the cash value of Oberstar's meals be included as part of his taxable wages? Explain.

2. Barbri Company ordinarily pays its employees on a weekly basis. Recently, one of the employees, Bernard Nagle, was sent from the home office on a three-week trip. Nagle has now returned to the office, and you are preparing a single check covering his three-week services. Should you withhold federal income taxes on the total gross earnings for the three-week period, or should you compute the federal income taxes as if Nagle were receiving three separate weekly wage payments?

3. Investigate your state's income tax withholding law (or that of some other state assigned by your instructor), and find the answers to the following questions:
   a. Who must withhold the tax?
   b. How are covered employers and covered employees defined?
   c. Are there any reciprocal agreements into which the state has entered? If so, describe them.
   d. How is the withholding rate determined?
   e. What payments are subject to withholding?
   f. What payments are not subject to withholding?
   g. Are there any employee withholding exemptions?
   h. What methods of withholding are permitted?
   i. Describe each of the returns required by the state.

   j. *What kinds of information must be retained by employers in their withholding tax records?*
   k. *What penalties are imposed for failure to comply with the withholding law?*
   l. *Are any employers required to deposit their withheld income taxes through electronic funds transfer (EFT)? If so, what requirements does the state impose?*

4. Rena Reynolds, one of your firm's workers, has just come into the payroll department and says to you: "I am thinking of amending my Form W-4 so that an additional $10 is withheld each week. That way I will get a fat refund next year. What do you think of my idea?" How would you reply to Reynolds?

5. Anita Leland, a waitress in Atlantis Casino, reported tips of $467 to her employer last year. Two months after she filed her federal income tax return, Leland received a letter from the IRS informing her that she had earned $5,260 in tips rather than the $467 reported and that she owed the government $1,872.94 in back taxes.
   a. *How is the IRS able to determine the amount of tips received by a waitress in a casino?*
   b. *If the IRS is correct in its determination of the tips received, is Atlantis subject to a penalty for not having withheld payroll taxes on all the tips Leland received during the year?*

6. Justin Holmes, an ex-employee, is entitled to a tax-able fringe benefit during the first part of this year. Because he wasn't paid any wages this year, can his employer report the taxable fringe benefit on Form 1099?

Problem Set • A

As we go to press, the federal income tax rates for 2023 are being determined by budget talks in Washington and not available for publication. For this edition, the 2022 federal income tax tables for Manual Systems with Forms W-4 from 2020 or later with Standard Withholding and 2022 FICA rates have been used.

4-1A • LO 3   See Example 4-1 on page 4-5, Example 4-4 on page 4-17

Justin Matthews is a waiter at the Duluxe Lounge. In his first weekly pay in March, he earned $300.00 for the 40 hours he worked. In addition, he reports his tips for February to his employer ($500.00), and the employer withholds the appropriate taxes for the tips from this first pay in March.

Calculate his net take-home pay assuming the employer withheld federal income tax (**wage-bracket,** married filing jointly), social security taxes, and state income tax (2%) .... $ _____

4-2A • LO 3   See Example 4-3 on page 4-16

Use the **percentage method** to compute the federal income taxes to withhold from the wages or salaries of each employee.

Employee No.	Employee Name	Filing Status	No. of Withholding Allowances	Gross Wage or Salary	Amount to Be Withheld
1	James, A.	MFJ	N/A	$1,610 weekly	_____
2	Lake, R.	S	N/A	825 biweekly	_____
3	Walls, S.	MFJ	N/A	925 semimonthly	_____
4	Free, Y.	MFJ	N/A	2,875 monthly	_____

4-3A • LO 3   See Example 4-3 on page 4-16, Example 4-4 on page 4-17

Use (a) the percentage method and (b) the wage-bracket method to compute the federal income taxes to withhold from the wages or salaries of each employee.

Employee	Filing Status	No. of Withholding Allowances	Gross Wage or Salary	Amount to Be Withheld	
				Percentage Method	Wage-Bracket Method
Lennon, A.	S	N/A	$ 675 weekly	_____	_____
Starr, P.	S	N/A	1,365 weekly	_____	_____
McNeil, S.	MFJ	N/A	1,775 biweekly	_____	_____
Harrison, W.	MFJ	N/A	2,480 semimonthly	_____	_____
Smythe, M.	MFJ	N/A	5,380 monthly	_____	_____

4-4A • LO 3   See Example 4-4 on page 4-17

Eaton Enterprises uses the **wage-bracket method** to determine federal income tax withholding on its employees. Find the amount to withhold from the wages paid each employee.

Employee	Filing Status	No. of Withholding Allowances	Payroll Period W = Weekly S = Semimonthly M = Monthly D = Daily	Wage	Amount to Be Withheld
Tarra James	MFJ	N/A	W	$1,350	_____
Mike Cramden	S	N/A	W	590	_____
Jim Jones	S	N/A	W	675	_____
Joan Kern	MFJ	N/A	M	3,100	_____
Mary Long	MFJ	N/A	M	2,730	_____
Cathy Luis	MFJ	N/A	S	955	_____
Josie Martin	S	N/A	D	108	_____
Terri Singer	S	N/A	S	2,500	_____
Shelby Torres	MFJ	N/A	M	3,215	_____

4-5A • LO 3   See Figure 1.9 on page 1-24, Example 4-4 on page 4-17

The names of the employees of Hogan Thrift Shop are listed on the following payroll register. Employees are paid weekly. The filing status is shown on the payroll register, along with each employee's weekly salary, which has remained the same all year. Complete the payroll register for the payroll period ending December 20, 20--, the 51st weekly payday. The state income tax rate is 2% of total earnings, the city income tax rate is 1.5% of the total gross earnings, and the *wage-bracket method* is used for federal income taxes.

HOGAN THRIFT SHOP
PAYROLL REGISTER

FOR PERIOD ENDING _____ 20___

EMPLOYEE NAME	FILING STATUS	NO. OF W/H ALLOW.	TOTAL EARNINGS	DEDUCTIONS (a) FICA OASDI	HI	(b) FIT	(c) SIT	(d) CIT	(e) NET PAY
John, Matthew	MFJ	N/A	2 9 0 0 00						
Smith, Jennifer	S	N/A	2 7 5 00						
Bullen, Catherine	MFJ	N/A	2 5 0 00						
Matthews, Mary	S	N/A	3 2 0 25						
Hadt, Bonnie	S	N/A	4 5 0 00						
Camp, Sean	S	N/A	5 6 0 50						
Aarav, Helen	S	N/A	4 7 5 50						
Gleason, Josie	MFJ	N/A	8 9 0 00						
Totals			6 1 2 5 25						

Compute the employer's FICA taxes for the pay period ending December 20, 20--.

OASDI Taxes		HI Taxes	
OASDI taxable earnings	$ _____	HI taxable earnings	$ _____
OASDI taxes	$ _____	HI taxes	$ _____

4-6A • LO 3   See Example 4-12 on page 4-22

Damerly Company (a Utah employer) wants to give a holiday bonus check of $250 to each employee. Since it wants the check amount to be $250, it will need to gross-up the amount of the bonus. Calculate the withholding taxes and the gross amount of the bonus to be made to John Rolen if his cumulative earnings for the year are $46,910. Besides being subject to social security taxes and federal income tax (supplemental rate), a 4.95% Utah income tax must be withheld on supplemental payments............ $ _____

4-7A • LO 1   See Example 4-2 on page 4-8

Julie Whiteweiler made $930 this week. Only social security (fully taxable) and federal income taxes attach to her pay. Whiteweiler contributes $100 each week to her company's 401(k) plan and has $25 put into her health savings account (nonqualified) each week. Her employer matches this $25 each week. Determine Whiteweiler's take-home pay if she is single (use the wage-bracket method).............. $ ____

4-8A • LO 3   See Figure 1.9 on page 1-24, Example 4-9 on page 4-21

The names of the employees of Cox Security Systems and their regular salaries are shown in the following payroll register. Note that Hall and Short are paid **monthly** on the last payday, while all others are paid **weekly**.

In addition to the regular salaries, the company pays an annual bonus based on the amount of earnings for the year. For the current year, the bonus amounts to 8% of the annual salary paid to each employee. The bonus is to be paid along with the regular salaries on December 27, 20--, but the amount of the bonus and the amount of the regular salary will be shown separately on each employee's earnings statement. Assume that all employees received their regular salary during the entire year.

Prepare the payroll for the pay period ending December 27, 20--, showing the following for each employee:

• Use the **wage-bracket method** to withhold federal income tax from the regular salaries.
• Withhold a flat 22% on the annual bonus.
• Total salaries and bonuses are subject to a 2% state income tax and a 1% city income tax.

20--

FOR PERIOD ENDING

EMPLOYEE NAME	FILING STATUS	NO. OF W/H ALLOW.	EARNINGS REGULAR	(a) SUPP'L	(b) TOTAL	(c) FICA OASDI	HI	(d) FIT	(e) SIT	(f) CIT	(g) NET PAY
Hall, Michael	MFJ	N/A	3 5 0 0 00 *								
Short, Joy T.	MFJ	N/A	2 7 5 0 00 *								
Abbott, Linda	S	N/A	5 2 0 00								
Smith, Joseph	MFJ	N/A	4 6 5 00								
Tols, Sean M.	MFJ	N/A	3 8 0 00								
Gillespie, Michelle	S	N/A	3 5 0 00								
Smart, Jennifer	MFJ	N/A	5 7 5 00								
White, Matthew J.	S	N/A	4 2 5 00								
Totals			8 9 6 5 00								

*Monthly

Compute the employer's FICA taxes for the pay period ending December 27, 20--.

OASDI Taxes		HI Taxes	
OASDI taxable earnings	$ ____	HI taxable earnings	$ ____
OASDI taxes	$ ____	HI taxes	$ ____

4-9A • LO 3   See Figure 1.9 on page 1-24, Examples 4-8 and 4-9 on page 4-21

Lake Community College gives its faculty the option of receiving the balance of their contract at the end of the semester on May 17, 20--. The faculty can receive one lump-sum payment instead of receiving the remaining seven biweekly pays over the summer. Use the data given below to complete the Payroll Register on May 17. No employee has reached the OASDI ceiling, and all employees are taking the lump-sum payment. The state withholding rate is 2.0% of total earnings; the city withholding rate is 1.0% of total earnings. The biweekly wage bracket is used for federal income taxes.

To calculate the tax withholdings, you must calculate the rounded tax for each pay and multiply by the number of pays in the lump-sum payment.

FOR PERIOD ENDING _____ 20

EMPLOYEE NAME	FILING STATUS	NO. OF W/H ALLOW.	BIWEEKLY EARNINGS	(a) TOTAL LUMP-SUM PAYMENT	(b) FICA OASDI	(b) FICA HI	(c) FIT	(d) SIT	(e) CIT	(f) NET PAY
Kinnery, Thomas	S	N/A	2 0 0 0 00							
Matthews, Mary	MFJ	N/A	2 6 0 0 00							
Grace, Catherine	S	N/A	2 2 0 0 00							
Michael, Sean	S	N/A	2 0 6 0 00							
Totals			8 8 6 0 00							

Compute the employer's FICA taxes for the pay period ending May 17, 20--.

OASDI Taxes		HI Taxes	
OASDI taxable earnings	$ _____	HI taxable earnings	$ _____
OASDI taxes	$ _____	HI taxes	$ _____

4-10A • LO 3 **See Example 4-12 on page 4-22**

Mattola Company is giving each of its employees a holiday bonus of $100 on December 13, 20-- (a nonpayday). The company wants each employee's check to be $100. The supplemental tax percent is used.

    a. What will be the gross amount of each bonus if each employee pays a state income tax of 2.8% (besides the other payroll taxes)? $ _____

    b. What would the net amount of each bonus check be if the company did not gross-up the bonus? $ _____

4-11A • LO 1 **See Figure 4.3 on page 4-9, Example 4-2 on page 4-8**

George Clausen (age 48) is employed by Kline Company and is paid an annual salary of $42,640. He has just decided to join the company's Simple Retirement Account (IRA form) and has a few questions. Answer the following for Clausen:

    a. What is the maximum that he can contribute into this retirement fund? $ _____

    b. What would be the company's contribution? $ _____

    c. What would be his weekly take-home pay with the retirement contribution deducted (married filing jointly, **wage-bracket method**, and a 2.3% state income tax on total wages)? $ _____

    d. What would be his weekly take-home pay without the retirement contribution deduction? $ _____

4-12A • LO 4 **See Figure 3.8 on pages 3-23 to 3-25**

During the fourth quarter of 20--, there were seven biweekly paydays on Friday (October 4, 18; November 1, 15, 29; December 13, 27) for Quality Repairs. Using the forms supplied on pages 4-52 to 4-56, complete the following for the fourth quarter:

    a. Complete the Federal Deposit Information Worksheets reflecting electronic deposits (monthly depositor). The employer's phone number is (501) 555-7331. Federal deposit liability each pay, 677.68.

    b. Employer's Quarterly Federal Tax Return, Form 941. The form is signed by you as president on January 31, 20--.

    c. Employer's Report of State Income Tax Withheld for the quarter, due on or before January 31, 20--.

Quarterly Payroll Data

Total Earnings 5 Employees	OASDI	HI	FIT	SIT
$18,750.00	$1,162.50	$271.88	$1,875.00	$1,312.50
Employer's OASDI	$1,162.50			
Employer's HI	271.88			
Federal deposit liability each pay	677.68			

4-12A (continued)

```
EMPLOYER'S REPORT
OF STATE INCOME TAX WITHHELD                    ( DO NOT WRITE IN THIS SPACE )

IMPORTANT: PLEASE REFER     WITHHOLDING IDENTIFICATION NUMBER   MONTH OF OR QUARTER ENDING
TO THIS NUMBER IN ANY
CORRESPONDENCE →              00-0-3301          DEC 20--      1. GROSS PAYROLL THIS
                                                                  PERIOD .........   $
IF YOU ARE A SEA-
SONAL    EMPLOYER                                             2. STATE INCOME TAX
AND THIS IS YOUR            QUALITY REPAIRS                       WITHHELD .........  $
FINAL REPORT FOR           10 SUMMIT SQUARE
THIS SEASON, CHECK         CITY, STATE 00000-0000             3. ADJUSTMENT FOR PREVIOUS
HERE                                                             PERIOD(S). (ATTACH STATEMENT) $
☐  AND SHOW THE
NEXT  MONTH  IN                                              4. TOTAL ADJUSTED TAX
WHICH  YOU  WILL                                                (LINE 2 PLUS OR MINUS LINE 3) $
PAY WAGES.
                                                             5. PENALTY (38% OF LINE 4)
         IF NAME OR ADDRESS IS INCORRECT, PLEASE MAKE CORRECTIONS.
         THIS REPORT MUST BE RETURNED EVEN IF NO AMOUNT HAS BEEN WITHHELD   6. INTEREST ..........

                                                             7. TOTAL AMOUNT DUE
Under penalties prescribed by law, I hereby affirm...           AND PAYABLE ......  $

                                                             MAIL THIS REPORT WITH CHECK OR MONEY ORDER PAYABLE TO
SIGNATURE:              TITLE:             DATE:              THE DEPT. OF REVENUE ON OR BEFORE DUE DATE TO AVOID
                                                             PENALTY.
```

FEDERAL DEPOSIT INFORMATION WORKSHEET

Employer Identification Number 00-0004701   Name QUALITY REPAIRS

Month Tax Year Ends 12   Amount of Deposit _____

Type of Tax (Form) _____   Tax Period _____

Address 10 SUMMIT SQUARE   Phone Number _____

City, State, Zip CITY, STATE 00000-0000

To be deposited on or before _____

4-12A (continued)

FEDERAL DEPOSIT INFORMATION WORKSHEET

Employer Identification Number	00-0004701	Name	QUALITY REPAIRS
Month Tax Year Ends	12	Amount of Deposit	_____
Type of Tax (Form)	_____	Tax Period	_____
Address	10 SUMMIT SQUARE	Phone Number	_____
City, State, Zip	CITY, STATE 00000-0000		

To be deposited on or before _____

FEDERAL DEPOSIT INFORMATION WORKSHEET

Employer Identification Number	00-0004701	Name	QUALITY REPAIRS
Month Tax Year Ends	12	Amount of Deposit	_____
Type of Tax (Form)	_____	Tax Period	_____
Address	10 SUMMIT SQUARE	Phone Number	_____
City, State, Zip	CITY, STATE 00000-0000		

To be deposited on or before _____

4-12A (continued)

Form **941 for 20--:** **Employer's QUARTERLY Federal Tax Return**
(Rev. March 2022)
Department of the Treasury — Internal Revenue Service

OMB No. 1545-0029

Employer identification number (EIN) `0 0 - 0 0 0 4 7 0 1`

Name *(not your trade name)* QUALITY REPAIRS

Trade name *(if any)*

Address 10 SUMMIT SQUARE
Number   Street   Suite or room number

CITY   ST   00000-0000
City   State   ZIP code

Foreign country name   Foreign province/county   Foreign postal code

Report for this Quarter of 20--
(Check one.)

☐ **1:** January, February, March

☐ **2:** April, May, June

☐ **3:** July, August, September

☐ **4:** October, November, December

Go to *www.irs.gov/Form941* for instructions and the latest information.

Read the separate instructions before you complete Form 941. Type or print within the boxes.

Part 1:   Answer these questions for this quarter.

1   Number of employees who received wages, tips, or other compensation for the pay period including: *Mar. 12* (Quarter 1) . . . .   **1** [   ]

2   Wages, tips, and other compensation . . . .   **2** [   ]

3   Federal income tax withheld from wages, tips, and other compensation . . . . . .   **3** [   ]

4   If no wages, tips, and other compensation are subject to social security or Medicare tax   ☐ Check and go to line 6.

	Column 1		Column 2
5a Taxable social security wages* . .	[ ]	× 0.124 =	[ ]
5a (i) Qualified sick leave wages* .	[ ]	× 0.062 =	[ ]
5a (ii) Qualified family leave wages* .	[ ]	× 0.062 =	[ ]
5b Taxable social security tips . . .	[ ]	× 0.124 =	[ ]
5c Taxable Medicare wages & tips . .	[ ]	× 0.029 =	[ ]
5d Taxable wages & tips subject to Additional Medicare Tax withholding	[ ]	× 0.009 =	[ ]

*Include taxable qualified sick and family leave wages paid in 2022 for leave taken after March 31, 2021, and before October 1, 2021, on line 5a. Use lines 5a(i) and 5a(ii) **only** for taxable qualified sick and family leave wages paid in 2022 for leave taken after March 31, 2020, and before April 1, 2021.*

5e   Total social security and Medicare taxes. Add Column 2 from lines 5a, 5a(i), 5a(ii), 5b, 5c, and 5d   **5e** [   ]

5f   Section 3121(q) Notice and Demand—Tax due on unreported tips (see instructions) . .   **5f** [   ]

6   Total taxes before adjustments. Add lines 3, 5e, and 5f . . . .   **6** [   ]

7   Current quarter's adjustment for fractions of cents . . . .   **7** [   ]

8   Current quarter's adjustment for sick pay . . . .   **8** [   ]

9   Current quarter's adjustments for tips and group-term life insurance . . . . . .   **9** [   ]

10   Total taxes after adjustments. Combine lines 6 through 9 . . . . .   **10** [   ]

11a   Qualified small business payroll tax credit for increasing research activities. Attach Form 8974   **11a** [   ]

11b   Nonrefundable portion of credit for qualified sick and family leave wages for leave taken before April 1, 2021 . . . .   **11b** [   ]

11c   Reserved for future use . . . .   **11c** [   ]

▶ **You MUST complete all three pages of Form 941 and SIGN it.**   Next ▶

For Privacy Act and Paperwork Reduction Act Notice, see the back of the Payment Voucher.   Cat. No. 17001Z   Form **941** (Rev. 3-2022)

Name *(not your trade name)*	Employer identification number (EIN)
QUALITY REPAIRS	00-0004701

Part 1: Answer these questions for this quarter. *(continued)*

11d Nonrefundable portion of credit for qualified sick and family leave wages for leave taken after March 31, 2021, and before October 1, 2021 . . . . **11d** [___ . ___]

11e Nonrefundable portion of COBRA premium assistance credit (see instructions for applicable quarter) . . . . **11e** [___ . ___]

11f Number of individuals provided COBRA premium assistance [___]

11g Total nonrefundable credits. Add lines 11a, 11b, 11d, and 11e . . . . **11g** [___ . ___]

12 Total taxes after adjustments and nonrefundable credits. Subtract line 11g from line 10 . **12** [___ . ___]

13a Total deposits for this quarter, including overpayment applied from a prior quarter and overpayments applied from Form 941-X, 941-X (PR), 944-X, or 944-X (SP) filed in the current quarter **13a** [___ . ___]

13b Reserved for future use . . . . **13b** [___ . ___]

13c Refundable portion of credit for qualified sick and family leave wages for leave taken before April 1, 2021 . . . . **13c** [___ . ___]

13d Reserved for future use . . . . **13d** [___ . ___]

13e Refundable portion of credit for qualified sick and family leave wages for leave taken after March 31, 2021, and before October 1, 2021 . . . . **13e** [___ . ___]

13f Refundable portion of COBRA premium assistance credit (see instructions for applicable quarter) . . . . **13f** [___ . ___]

13g Total deposits and refundable credits. Add lines 13a, 13c, 13e, and 13f . . . . **13g** [___ . ___]

13h Reserved for future use . . . . **13h** [___ . ___]

13i Reserved for future use . . . . **13i** [___ . ___]

14 Balance due. If line 12 is more than line 13g, enter the difference and see instructions . . . **14** [___ . ___]

15 Overpayment. If line 13g is more than line 12, enter the difference [___ . ___] Check one: ☐ Apply to next return. ☐ Send a refund.

Part 2: Tell us about your deposit schedule and tax liability for this quarter.

If you're unsure about whether you're a monthly schedule depositor or a semiweekly schedule depositor, see section 11 of Pub. 15.

16 Check one: ☐ **Line 12 on this return is less than $2,500 or line 12 on the return for the prior quarter was less than $2,500, and you didn't incur a $100,000 next-day deposit obligation during the current quarter.** If line 12 for the prior quarter was less than $2,500 but line 12 on this return is $100,000 or more, you must provide a record of your federal tax liability. If you're a monthly schedule depositor, complete the deposit schedule below; if you're a semiweekly schedule depositor, attach Schedule B (Form 941). Go to Part 3.

☐ **You were a monthly schedule depositor for the entire quarter.** Enter your tax liability for each month and total liability for the quarter, then go to Part 3.

      Tax liability: Month 1 [___ . ___]

                Month 2 [___ . ___]

                Month 3 [___ . ___]

      Total liability for quarter [___ . ___] Total must equal line 12.

☐ **You were a semiweekly schedule depositor for any part of this quarter.** Complete Schedule B (Form 941), Report of Tax Liability for Semiweekly Schedule Depositors, and attach it to Form 941. Go to Part 3.

▶ **You MUST complete all three pages of Form 941 and SIGN it.** Next ▶

4-12A (continued)

Name *(not your trade name)*	Employer identification number (EIN)
QUALITY REPAIRS	00-0004701

Part 3: Tell us about your business. If a question does NOT apply to your business, leave it blank.

17 If your business has closed or you stopped paying wages . . . . ☐ Check here, and

enter the final date you paid wages [/   /   ] ; also attach a statement to your return. See instructions.

18 If you're a seasonal employer and you don't have to file a return for every quarter of the year . . . ☐ Check here.

19 Qualified health plan expenses allocable to qualified sick leave wages for leave taken before April 1, 2021 — 19 [.]

20 Qualified health plan expenses allocable to qualified family leave wages for leave taken before April 1, 2021 — 20 [.]

21 Reserved for future use . . . . 21 [.]

22 Reserved for future use . . . . 22 [.]

23 Qualified sick leave wages for leave taken after March 31, 2021, and before October 1, 2021 — 23 [.]

24 Qualified health plan expenses allocable to qualified sick leave wages reported on line 23 — 24 [.]

25 Amounts under certain collectively bargained agreements allocable to qualified sick leave wages reported on line 23 . . . . 25 [.]

26 Qualified family leave wages for leave taken after March 31, 2021, and before October 1, 2021 — 26 [.]

27 Qualified health plan expenses allocable to qualified family leave wages reported on line 26 — 27 [.]

28 Amounts under certain collectively bargained agreements allocable to qualified family leave wages reported on line 26 . . . . 28 [.]

Part 4: May we speak with your third-party designee?

Do you want to allow an employee, a paid tax preparer, or another person to discuss this return with the IRS? See the instructions for details.

☐ Yes. Designee's name and phone number [   ] [   ]

Select a 5-digit personal identification number (PIN) to use when talking to the IRS. [ ] [ ] [ ] [ ] [ ]

☐ No.

Part 5: Sign here. You MUST complete all three pages of Form 941 and SIGN it.

Under penalties of perjury, I declare that I have examined this return, including accompanying schedules and statements, and to the best of my knowledge and belief, it is true, correct, and complete. Declaration of preparer (other than taxpayer) is based on all information of which preparer has any knowledge.

X Sign your name here [   ]

Print your name here [   ]

Print your title here [   ]

Date [/   /   ]

Best daytime phone [   ]

Paid Preparer Use Only

Check if you're self-employed . . . ☐

Preparer's name [ ]	PTIN [ ]
Preparer's signature [ ]	Date [/ /]
Firm's name (or yours if self-employed) [ ]	EIN [ ]
Address [ ]	Phone [ ]
City [ ] State [ ]	ZIP code [ ]

Page **3**   Form **941** (Rev. 3-2022)

Source: Internal Revenue Service.

Date _____ Name _____

4-13A • LO 3, 4   See Figure 4.8 on page 4-23, Figure 4.11 on page 4-28

During the first full week of 20--, the Payroll Department of Quigley Corporation is preparing the Forms W-2 for distribution to its employees along with their payroll checks on January 10. In this problem, you will complete six of the forms in order to gain some experience in recording the different kinds of information required.

Assume each employee earned the same weekly salary for each of the 52 paydays in 20-- (the previous year). Using the following information obtained from the personnel and payroll records of the firm, complete Copy A of the six Forms W-2 reproduced on the following pages. Also complete Form W-3. The form is to be signed by the president, Kenneth T. Ford, and is prepared by Ralph I. Volpe.

Company Information:

Address: 4800 River Road
Philadelphia, PA 19113-5548

Telephone number: (215) 555-0017
Fax number: (215) 555-0010

Pennsylvania state identification number: 00-0-1066
Federal identification number: 00-0000972
Philadelphia identification number: 0001895

Income Tax Information:

The wage-bracket method is used to determine federal income tax withholding. Calculate the annual federal income tax withheld by using the weekly wage-bracket table and multiply the answer by 52. The other taxes withheld are shown below.

Employee Data	Payroll Data	Annual Taxes Withheld	
See example of Kelly B. Roach's completed Form W-2 on next page.			
Kelly B. Roach 54 Gradison Place Philadelphia, PA 19113-4054	Single $715 per week SS#: 000-00-4310 Deduction for 401(k) plan: $50/week	Social security tax withheld Medicare tax withheld State income tax withheld Local income tax withheld State unemployment tax withheld**	2,305.16 539.24 1,141.40 1,427.40 22.36
Ralph I. Volpe 56 Andrews Court, Apt. 7 Philadelphia, PA 19103-3356	Married filing jointly $785 per week SS#: 000-00-8804 Dependent care payment: $950 $70/week—401(k)	Social security tax withheld Medicare tax withheld State income tax withheld Local income tax withheld State unemployment tax withheld**	2,530.84 591.76 1,253.20 1,567.28 24.44
Randi A. Myer 770 Camac Street Philadelphia, PA 19101-3770	Single $885 per week SS#: 000-00-3316 Union dues withheld: $102	Social security tax withheld Medicare tax withheld State income tax withheld Local income tax withheld State unemployment tax withheld**	2,853.24 667.16 1,412.84 1,766.96 27.56
Kenneth T. Ford 338 North Side Avenue Philadelphia, PA 19130-6638	Married filing jointly $1,350 per week SS#: 000-00-6839 Cost of group-term life insurance exceeding $50,000: $262.75 * $100/week—401(k)	Social security tax withheld Medicare tax withheld State income tax withheld Local income tax withheld State unemployment tax withheld**	4,368.69 1,021.97 2,155.40 2,695.68 42.12
Chrissy C. Carman 4900 Gladwynne Terrace Philadelphia, PA 19127-0049	Married filing jointly $820 per week SS#: 000-00-5771 Union dues withheld: $102	Social security tax withheld Medicare tax withheld State income tax withheld Local income tax withheld State unemployment tax withheld**	2,643.68 618.28 1,308.84 1,637.48 25.48
Hal B. Zuber 480-A Hopkinson Tower Philadelphia, PA 19101-3301	Single $790 per week SS#: 000-00-8703 Educational assistance payments (job-required): $675 $50/week—401(k)	Social security tax withheld Medicare tax withheld State income tax withheld Local income tax withheld State unemployment tax withheld**	2,546.96 595.92 1,261.00 1,577.16 24.44

*The cost of excess group-term life insurance is added to gross wages for federal income tax, Social Security, and Medicare. Employers withhold OASDI and HI tax on these amounts but are not required to withhold federal income tax. The cost is not added to gross wages for state and local taxes; therefore, it is not subject to those taxes (see Figure 4.8 on page 4-28).

**State unemployment tax withheld for Pennsylvania labeled as PA SUI on Form W-2 Box 14.

4-13A (continued)

22222	Void ☐	**a** Employee's social security number 000-00-4310	For Official Use Only ► OMB No. 1545-0008		

b Employer identification number (EIN) 00-0000972		**1** Wages, tips, other compensation 34580.00*	**2** Federal income tax withheld 2444.00**

c Employer's name, address, and ZIP code Quigley Corporation 4800 River Road Philadelphia, PA 19113-5548	**3** Social security wages 37180.00	**4** Social security tax withheld 2305.16

	5 Medicare wages and tips 37180.00	**6** Medicare tax withheld 539.24

	7 Social security tips	**8** Allocated tips

d Control number	**9**	**10** Dependent care benefits

e Employee's first name and initial Kelly B.	Last name Roach	Suff.	**11** Nonqualified plans	**12a** See instructions for box 12 D 2600.00

54 Gradison Place Philadelphia, PA 19113-4054	**13** Statutory employee ☐ Retirement plan ☒ Third-party sick pay ☐	**12b**

	14 Other PA SUI 22.36	**12c**

		12d

f Employee's address and ZIP code					

15 State PA	Employer's state ID number 00-0-1066	**16** State wages, tips, etc. 37180.00	**17** State income tax 1141.40	**18** Local wages, tips, etc. 37180.00	**19** Local income tax 1427.40	**20** Locality name Phila.

Form W-2 Wage and Tax Statement **20 - -**
Copy A For Social Security Administration — Send this entire page with Form W-3 to the Social Security Administration; photocopies are **not** acceptable.

Department of the Treasury—Internal Revenue Service
For Privacy Act and Paperwork Reduction Act Notice, see the separate instructions.
Cat. No. 10134D

*[Weekly salary $715.00 − $50.00 Contribution for 401(k)] × 52 weeks
**Federal income tax withheld $47.00 × 52 weeks

Do Not Cut, Fold, or Staple Forms on This Page

22222	Void ☐	**a** Employee's social security number	For Official Use Only ► OMB No. 1545-0008		

b Employer identification number (EIN)		**1** Wages, tips, other compensation	**2** Federal income tax withheld

c Employer's name, address, and ZIP code	**3** Social security wages	**4** Social security tax withheld

	5 Medicare wages and tips	**6** Medicare tax withheld

	7 Social security tips	**8** Allocated tips

d Control number	**9**	**10** Dependent care benefits

e Employee's first name and initial	Last name	Suff.	**11** Nonqualified plans	**12a** See instructions for box 12

	13 Statutory employee ☐ Retirement plan ☐ Third-party sick pay ☐	**12b**

	14 Other	**12c**

		12d

f Employee's address and ZIP code					

15 State	Employer's state ID number	**16** State wages, tips, etc.	**17** State income tax	**18** Local wages, tips, etc.	**19** Local income tax	**20** Locality name

Form W-2 Wage and Tax Statement **20 - -**
Copy A For Social Security Administration — Send this entire page with Form W-3 to the Social Security Administration; photocopies are **not** acceptable.

Department of the Treasury—Internal Revenue Service
For Privacy Act and Paperwork Reduction Act Notice, see the separate instructions.
Cat. No. 10134D

Do Not Cut, Fold, or Staple Forms on This Page

22222	Void ☐	**a** Employee's social security number	For Official Use Only ▶ OMB No. 1545-0008	
b Employer identification number (EIN)			**1** Wages, tips, other compensation	**2** Federal income tax withheld
c Employer's name, address, and ZIP code			**3** Social security wages	**4** Social security tax withheld
			5 Medicare wages and tips	**6** Medicare tax withheld
			7 Social security tips	**8** Allocated tips
d Control number			**9**	**10** Dependent care benefits
e Employee's first name and initial	Last name	Suff.	**11** Nonqualified plans	**12a** See instructions for box 12
			13 Statutory employee ☐ Retirement plan ☐ Third-party sick pay ☐	**12b**
			14 Other	**12c**
				12d
f Employee's address and ZIP code				

15 State Employer's state ID number	**16** State wages, tips, etc.	**17** State income tax	**18** Local wages, tips, etc.	**19** Local income tax	**20** Locality name

Form **W-2** Wage and Tax Statement 20 - -

Department of the Treasury—Internal Revenue Service

Copy A For Social Security Administration — Send this entire page with Form W-3 to the Social Security Administration; photocopies are **not** acceptable.

For Privacy Act and Paperwork Reduction Act Notice, see the separate instructions.

Cat. No. 10134D

Do Not Cut, Fold, or Staple Forms on This Page

22222	Void ☐	**a** Employee's social security number	For Official Use Only ▶ OMB No. 1545-0008	
b Employer identification number (EIN)			**1** Wages, tips, other compensation	**2** Federal income tax withheld
c Employer's name, address, and ZIP code			**3** Social security wages	**4** Social security tax withheld
			5 Medicare wages and tips	**6** Medicare tax withheld
			7 Social security tips	**8** Allocated tips
d Control number			**9**	**10** Dependent care benefits
e Employee's first name and initial	Last name	Suff.	**11** Nonqualified plans	**12a** See instructions for box 12
			13 Statutory employee ☐ Retirement plan ☐ Third-party sick pay ☐	**12b**
			14 Other	**12c**
				12d
f Employee's address and ZIP code				

15 State Employer's state ID number	**16** State wages, tips, etc.	**17** State income tax	**18** Local wages, tips, etc.	**19** Local income tax	**20** Locality name

Form **W-2** Wage and Tax Statement 20 - -

Department of the Treasury—Internal Revenue Service

Copy A For Social Security Administration — Send this entire page with Form W-3 to the Social Security Administration; photocopies are **not** acceptable.

For Privacy Act and Paperwork Reduction Act Notice, see the separate instructions.

Cat. No. 10134D

Do Not Cut, Fold, or Staple Forms on This Page

4-13A (continued)

22222	Void ☐	**a** Employee's social security number	For Official Use Only ▶ OMB No. 1545-0008		
b Employer identification number (EIN)			**1** Wages, tips, other compensation		**2** Federal income tax withheld
c Employer's name, address, and ZIP code			**3** Social security wages		**4** Social security tax withheld
			5 Medicare wages and tips		**6** Medicare tax withheld
			7 Social security tips		**8** Allocated tips
d Control number			**9**		**10** Dependent care benefits
e Employee's first name and initial	Last name	Suff.	**11** Nonqualified plans		**12a** See instructions for box 12
			13 Statutory employee ☐ Retirement plan ☐ Third-party sick pay ☐		**12b**
			14 Other		**12c**
					12d
f Employee's address and ZIP code					
15 State Employer's state ID number	**16** State wages, tips, etc.	**17** State income tax	**18** Local wages, tips, etc.	**19** Local income tax	**20** Locality name

Form **W-2** **Wage and Tax Statement** **20 - -**

Department of the Treasury—Internal Revenue Service

Copy A For Social Security Administration — Send this entire page with Form W-3 to the Social Security Administration; photocopies are **not** acceptable.

For Privacy Act and Paperwork Reduction Act Notice, see the separate instructions.

Cat. No. 10134D

Do Not Cut, Fold, or Staple Forms on This Page

22222	Void ☐	**a** Employee's social security number	For Official Use Only ▶ OMB No. 1545-0008		
b Employer identification number (EIN)			**1** Wages, tips, other compensation		**2** Federal income tax withheld
c Employer's name, address, and ZIP code			**3** Social security wages		**4** Social security tax withheld
			5 Medicare wages and tips		**6** Medicare tax withheld
			7 Social security tips		**8** Allocated tips
d Control number			**9**		**10** Dependent care benefits
e Employee's first name and initial	Last name	Suff.	**11** Nonqualified plans		**12a** See instructions for box 12
			13 Statutory employee ☐ Retirement plan ☐ Third-party sick pay ☐		**12b**
			14 Other		**12c**
					12d
f Employee's address and ZIP code					
15 State Employer's state ID number	**16** State wages, tips, etc.	**17** State income tax	**18** Local wages, tips, etc.	**19** Local income tax	**20** Locality name

Form **W-2** **Wage and Tax Statement** **20 - -**

Department of the Treasury—Internal Revenue Service

Copy A For Social Security Administration — Send this entire page with Form W-3 to the Social Security Administration; photocopies are **not** acceptable.

For Privacy Act and Paperwork Reduction Act Notice, see the separate instructions.

Cat. No. 10134D

Do Not Cut, Fold, or Staple Forms on This Page

Source: Internal Revenue Service.

4-13A (continued)

DO NOT STAPLE

33333	a Control number	For Official Use Only ▶ OMB No. 1545-0008		

| b **Kind of Payer** (Check one) ▶ | 941 ☐   Military ☐   943 ☐   944 ☐
 CT-1 ☐   Hshld. emp. ☐   Medicare govt. emp. ☐ | **Kind of Employer** (Check one) ▶ | None apply ☐   501c non-govt. ☐
 State/local non-501c ☐   State/local 501c ☐   Federal govt. ☐ | Third-party sick pay (Check if applicable) ☐ |

c Total number of Forms W-2	d Establishment number	1 Wages, tips, other compensation	2 Federal income tax withheld
e Employer identification number (EIN)		3 Social security wages	4 Social security tax withheld
f Employer's name		5 Medicare wages and tips	6 Medicare tax withheld
		7 Social security tips	8 Allocated tips
		9	10 Dependent care benefits
		11 Nonqualified plans	12a Deferred compensation
g Employer's address and ZIP code			
h Other EIN used this year		13 For third-party sick pay use only	12b
15 State Employer's state ID number		14 Income tax withheld by payer of third-party sick pay	
16 State wages, tips, etc.	**17** State income tax	18 Local wages, tips, etc.	19 Local income tax
Employer's contact person		Employer's telephone number	For Official Use Only
Employer's fax number		Employer's email address	

Under penalties of perjury, I declare that I have examined this return and accompanying documents and, to the best of my knowledge and belief, they are true, correct, and complete.

Signature ▶ _____   Title ▶ _____   Date ▶ _____

Form **W-3** **Transmittal of Wage and Tax Statements**   **20 - -**   Department of the Treasury Internal Revenue Service

Source: Internal Revenue Service.

Supplement Problem Set • A

As we go to press, the federal income tax rates for 2023 are being determined by budget talks in Washington and not available for publication. For this edition, the 2022 federal income tax tables for Manual Payroll Systems with Forms W-4 from 2019 or earlier and 2022 FICA rates have been used.

*4-14A • LO 3   See Example 4-1 on page 4-5, Example 4-14 on page 4-40

Sean Matthews is a waiter at the Duluxe Lounge. In his first weekly pay in March, he earned $300.00 for the 40 hours he worked. In addition, he reports his tips for February to his employer ($500.00), and the employer withholds the appropriate taxes for the tips from this first pay in March.

Calculate his net take-home pay assuming the employer withheld federal income tax (***wage-bracket,*** married, 2 allowances), social security taxes, and state income tax (2%) .... $ _____

*4-15A • LO 3 **See Example 4-13 on page 4-39**

Use the ***percentage method*** to compute the federal income taxes to withhold from the wages or salaries of each employee.

Employee No.	Employee Name	Marital Status	No. of Withholding Allowances	Gross Wage or Salary	Amount to Be Withheld
1	Amoroso, A.	M	4	$1,610 weekly	_____
2	Finley, R.	S	0	825 biweekly	_____
3	Gluck, E.	S	5	9,630 quarterly	_____
4	Quinn, S.	M	8	925 semimonthly	_____
5	Treave, Y.	M	3	2,875 monthly	_____

*4-16A • LO 3 **See Example 4-13 on page 4-39, Example 4-14 on page 4-40**

Use (a) the percentage method and (b) the wage-bracket method to compute the federal income taxes to withhold from the wages or salaries of each employee.

Employee	Marital Status	No. of Withholding Allowances	Gross Wage or Salary	Amount to Be Withheld Percentage Method	Amount to Be Withheld Wage-Bracket Method
Corn, A.	S	2	$ 675 weekly	_____	_____
Fogge, P.	S	1	1,365 weekly	_____	_____
Felps, S.	M	6	1,775 biweekly	_____	_____
Carson, W.	M	4	2,480 semimonthly	_____	_____
Gupta, M.	M	9	5,380 monthly	_____	_____

*4-17A • LO 3 **See Example 4-14 on page 4-40**

Eaton Enterprises uses the ***wage-bracket method*** to determine federal income tax withholding on its employees. Find the amount to withhold from the wages paid each employee.

Employee	Marital Status	No. of Withholding Allowances	Payroll Period W = Weekly S = Semimonthly M = Monthly D = Daily	Wage	Amount to Be Withheld
Hal Bower	M	1	W	$1,350	_____
Ruth Cramden	S	1	W	590	_____
Gil Jones	S	3	W	675	_____
Teresa Kern	M	4	M	3,100	_____
Ruby Long	M	2	M	2,730	_____
Katie Luis	M	8	S	955	_____
Susan Martin	S	1	D	108	_____
Jim Singer	S	4	S	2,500	_____
Martin Torres	M	4	M	3,215	_____

Problem Set • B

As we go to press, the federal income tax rates for 2023 are being determined by budget talks in Washington and not available for publication. For this edition, the 2022 federal income tax tables for Manual Systems with Forms W-4 from 2020 or later with Standard Withholding and 2022 FICA rates have been used.

4-1B • LO 3 See Example 4-1 on page 4-5, Example 4-4 on page 4-17

Mike Mays is a waiter at the Dixie Hotel. In his first weekly pay in March, he earned $360.00 for the 40 hours he worked. In addition, he reports his tips for February to his employer ($700.00), and the employer withholds the appropriate taxes for the tips from this first pay in March.

Calculate his net take-home pay assuming the employer withheld federal income tax (**wage-bracket,** married filing jointly), social security taxes, and state income tax (2%) .... $_____

4-2B • LO 3 See Example 4-3 on page 4-16

Use the **percentage method** to compute the federal income taxes to withhold from the wages or salaries of each employee.

Employee No.	Employee Name	Filing Status	No. of Withholding Allowances	Gross Wage or Salary	Amount to Be Withheld
1	Fox, A.	MFJ	N/A	$ 1,575 weekly	_____
2	Aiken, T.	S	N/A	1,200 biweekly	_____
3	Larey, P.	MFJ	N/A	1,090 semimonthly	_____
4	Wolf, M.	MFJ	N/A	8,120 monthly	_____

4-3B • LO 3 See Example 4-3 on page 4-16, Example 4-4 on page 4-17

Use (a) the percentage method and (b) the wage-bracket method to compute the federal income taxes to withhold from the wages or salaries of each employee.

Employee	Filing Status	No. of Withholding Allowances	Gross Wage or Salary	Amount to Be Withheld Percentage Method	Wage-Bracket Method
Louis, S.	S	N/A	$ 1,040 weekly	_____	_____
Hanks, X.	S	N/A	1,910 weekly	_____	_____
Gillespie, H.	MFJ	N/A	1,890 biweekly	_____	_____
Tromley, P.	MFJ	N/A	2,315 semimonthly	_____	_____
Farley, R.	MFJ	N/A	3,200 monthly	_____	_____

4-4B • LO 3 See Example 4-4 on page 4-17

Ernesto Enterprises uses the **wage-bracket method** to determine federal income tax withholding on its employees. Find the amount to withhold from the wages paid each employee.

Employee	Filing Status	No. of Withholding Allowances	Payroll Period W = Weekly S = Semimonthly M = Monthly D = Daily	Wage	Amount to Be Withheld
Lily Troon	MFJ	N/A	W	$1,250	_____
Barry Ortega	S	N/A	W	695	_____
Pat Lopez	S	N/A	W	915	_____
Rex Kim	MFJ	N/A	M	3,070	_____
Ruth Horace	MFJ	N/A	M	2,730	_____
Mike Gleam	MFJ	N/A	S	1,200	_____
Tom Abreu	S	N/A	D	115	_____
Holly Sanchez	S	N/A	S	2,040	_____
Kathy Nee	MFJ	N/A	M	3,500	_____

4-5B • LO 3   See Figure 1.9 on page 1-24, Example 4-4 on page 4-17

The names of the employees of Hogan Thrift Shop are listed on the following payroll register. Employees are paid weekly. The filing status is shown on the payroll register, along with each employee's weekly salary, which has remained the same all year. Complete the payroll register for the payroll period ending December 20, 20--, the 51st weekly payday. The state income tax rate is 3.1% of total earnings, the city income tax rate is 1% of the total gross earnings, and the **wage-bracket method** is used for federal income taxes.

HOGAN THRIFT SHOP

PAYROLL REGISTER

FOR PERIOD ENDING _____ 20___

EMPLOYEE NAME	FILING STATUS	NO. OF W/H ALLOW.	TOTAL EARNINGS	(a) FICA OASDI	(a) FICA HI	(b) FIT	(c) SIT	(d) CIT	(e) NET PAY
Gold, Ken	MFJ	N/A	1 9 0 0 00						
Morton, Cam	S	N/A	6 9 0 00						
Wendal, Hal	MFJ	N/A	6 7 5 00						
Cox, Debbie	S	N/A	5 1 0 00						
Hurley, Don	S	N/A	1 0 1 0 00						
Hand, Cheryl	S	N/A	8 5 0 00						
Welsh, Ronda	S	N/A	5 9 0 90						
Ruiz, Stacy	MFJ	N/A	6 1 1 15						
Totals			6 8 3 7 05						

Compute the employer's FICA taxes for the pay period ending December 20, 20--.

OASDI Taxes		HI Taxes	
OASDI taxable earnings	$ _____	HI taxable earnings	$ _____
OASDI taxes	$ _____	HI taxes	$ _____

4-6B • LO 3   See Example 4-12 on page 4-22

Youngston Company (a Massachusetts employer) wants to give a holiday bonus check of $750 to each employee. Since it wants the check amount to be $750, it will need to gross-up the amount of the bonus. Calculate the withholding taxes and the gross amount of the bonus to be made to Genna Fredrich if her earnings for the year are $55,920. Besides being subject to social security taxes and federal income tax (supplemental rate), a 5.00% Massachusetts income tax must be withheld on supplemental payments.......................... $ _____

4-7B • LO 1   See Example 4-2 on page 4-8

Jen Miller made $1,090 this week. Only social security (fully taxable) and federal income taxes attach to her pay. Miller contributes $125 each week to her company's 401(k) plan and has $40 put into her health savings account (nonqualified) each week. Her employer matches this $40 each week. Determine Miller's take-home pay if she is married filing jointly (use the wage-bracket method)............... $ _____

Show Me How

4-8B • LO 3   See Figure 1.9 on page 1-24, Example 4-9 on page 4-21

The names of the employees of Matson Office Systems and their regular salaries are shown in the following payroll register. Note that Wayne and Young are paid **monthly** on the last payday, while all others are paid **weekly**.

In addition to the regular salaries, the company pays an annual bonus based on the amount of earnings for the year. For the current year, the bonus amounts to 8% of the annual salary paid to each employee. The bonus is to be paid along with the regular salaries on December 27, 20--, but the amount of the bonus and the amount of the regular salary will be shown separately on each employee's earnings statement. Assume that all employees received their regular salary during the entire year.

Prepare the payroll for the pay period ending December 27, 20--, showing the following for each employee:

• Use the **wage-bracket method** to withhold federal income tax from the regular salaries.
• Withhold a flat 22% on the annual bonus.
• Total salaries and bonuses are subject to a 2% state income tax and a 1% city income tax.

FOR PERIOD ENDING _____ 20

EMPLOYEE NAME	FILING STATUS	NO. OF W/H ALLOW.	REGULAR	EARNINGS (a) SUPPL.	(b) TOTAL	(c) FICA OASDI	HI	(d) FIT	(e) SIT	(f) CIT	(g) NET PAY
Wayne, Bret	MFJ	N/A	3 0 0 0 00*								
Young, Gina	MFJ	N/A	2 5 0 0 00*								
Course, Rudy	S	N/A	8 1 0 00								
Dickson, Emile	MFJ	N/A	7 1 5 00								
Woodrow, Walt	MFJ	N/A	6 9 5 00								
Noblet, Jim	S	N/A	5 2 5 00								
Ono, Joan	MFJ	N/A	8 0 0 00								
Jones, Carrie	S	N/A	6 4 5 00								
Totals			9 6 9 0 00								

*Monthly

Compute the employer's FICA taxes for the pay period ending December 27, 20--.

OASDI Taxes		HI Taxes	
OASDI taxable earnings	$ _____	HI taxable earnings	$ _____
OASDI taxes	$ _____	HI taxes	$ _____

4-9B • LO 3   See Figure 1.9 on page 1-24, Examples 4-8 and 4-9 on page 4-21

Ocean City College gives its faculty the option of receiving the balance of their contract at the end of the semester on May 17, 20--. The faculty can receive one lump-sum payment instead of receiving the remaining seven biweekly pays over the summer. Use the data given below to complete the Payroll Register on May 17. No employee has reached the OASDI ceiling, and all employees are taking the lump-sum payment. The state withholding rate is 2.0% of total earnings; the city withholding rate is 1.0% of total earnings. The biweekly wage bracket is used for federal income taxes.

To calculate the tax withholdings, you must calculate the rounded tax for each pay and multiply by the number of pays in the lump-sum payment.

FOR PERIOD ENDING _____ 20___

EMPLOYEE NAME	FILING STATUS	NO. OF W/H ALLOW.	BIWEEKLY EARNINGS	(a) TOTAL LUMP-SUM PAYMENT	(b) FICA OASDI	(b) FICA HI	(c) FIT	(d) SIT	(e) CIT	(f) NET PAY
John, Matthew	MFJ	N/A	3 0 1 0 00							
Kuna, Mary	MFJ	N/A	2 5 0 0 00							
Timber, Bruce	S	N/A	1 9 0 0 00							
Ruce, Greg	MFJ	N/A	3 0 0 0 00							
Totals			1 0 4 1 0 00							

Compute the employer's FICA taxes for the pay period ending May 17, 20--.

OASDI Taxes		HI Taxes	
OASDI taxable earnings	$ _____	HI taxable earnings	$ _____
OASDI taxes	$ _____	HI taxes	$ _____

4-10B • LO 3 **See Example 4-12 on page 4-22** Show Me How

Harrington Company is giving each of its employees a holiday bonus of $250 on December 13, 20-- (a nonpay-day). The company wants each employee's check to be $250. The supplemental tax percent is used.

a. What will be the gross amount of each bonus if each employee pays a state income tax of 3.01% (besides the other payroll taxes)? $ _____

b. What would the net amount of each bonus check be if the company did not gross-up the bonus? $ _____

4-11B • LO 1 **See Figure 4.3 on page 4-9, Example 4-2 on page 4-8**

Samantha Montgomery (age 42) is employed by Canon Company and is paid an annual salary of $62,430. She has just decided to join the company's Simple Retirement Account (IRA form) and has a few questions. Answer the following for Montgomery:

a. What is the maximum that she can contribute into this retirement fund? $ _____

b. What would be the company's contribution? $ _____

c. What would be her weekly take-home pay with the retirement contribution deducted (married filing jointly, *wage-bracket method*, and a 2.3% state income tax on total wages)? $ _____

d. What would be her weekly take-home pay without the retirement contribution deduction? $ _____

4-12B • LO 4 **See Figure 3.8 on pages 3-23 to 3-25** Show Me How

During the fourth quarter of 20--, there were seven biweekly paydays on Friday (October 4, 18; November 1, 15, 29; December 13, 27) for Clarke's Roofing. Using the forms supplied on pages 4-68 to 4-72, complete the following for the fourth quarter:

a. Complete the Federal Deposit Information Worksheets, reflecting electronic deposits (monthly depositor). The employer's phone number is (501) 555-1212. Federal deposit liability each pay, $1,304.56.

b. Employer's Quarterly Federal Tax Return, Form 941. The form is signed by you as president on January 31, 20--.

c. Employer's Report of State Income Tax Withheld for the quarter, due on or before January 31, 20--.

Quarterly Payroll Data

Total Earnings 5 Employees	OASDI	HI	FIT	SIT
$37,450.00	$2,321.90	$543.06	$3,402.00	$2,621.50
Employer's OASDI	$2,321.90			
Employer's HI	543.06			
Federal deposit liability each pay	1,304.56			

4-12B (continued)

```
              EMPLOYER'S  REPORT
          OF STATE INCOME TAX WITHHELD                        ( DO NOT WRITE IN THIS SPACE )

IMPORTANT: PLEASE REFER    WITHHOLDING IDENTIFICATION NUMBER    MONTH OF OR QUARTER ENDING
TO THIS NUMBER IN ANY
CORRESPONDENCE              00-0-8787          DEC 20--     1. GROSS PAYROLL THIS
                                                              PERIOD . . . . . . . . .  $
IF YOU ARE A SEA-
SONAL    EMPLOYER                                          2. STATE INCOME TAX
AND THIS IS YOUR                                              WITHHELD . . . . . . . .  $
FINAL  REPORT  FOR       CLARKE'S ROOFING
THIS SEASON, CHECK       20 SUMMIT SQUARE                  3. ADJUSTMENT FOR PREVIOUS
HERE                     CITY, STATE 00000-0000               PERIOD(S). (ATTACH STATEMENT) $
☐  AND  SHOW  THE
NEXT   MONTH   IN                                          4. TOTAL ADJUSTED TAX
WHICH  YOU   WILL                                             (LINE 2 PLUS OR MINUS LINE 3) $
PAY WAGES.
                                                           5. PENALTY (35% OF LINE 4)
        IF NAME OR ADDRESS IS INCORRECT, PLEASE MAKE CORRECTIONS.
     THIS REPORT MUST BE RETURNED EVEN IF NO AMOUNT HAS BEEN WITHHELD   6. INTEREST . . . . . . . . . .

Under penalties prescribed by law, I hereby affirm that to the best of my knowledge  7. TOTAL AMOUNT DUE
and belief this return, including any accompanying schedules and                        AND PAYABLE . . . . . . . .  $
statements, is true and complete. If prepared by a person other than taxpayer, his
affirmation is based on all information of which he has any knowledge.           MAIL THIS REPORT WITH CHECK OR MONEY ORDER PAYABLE TO
                                                                                THE DEPT. OF REVENUE ON OR BEFORE DUE DATE TO AVOID
SIGNATURE:              TITLE:              DATE:                                PENALTY.
```

FEDERAL DEPOSIT INFORMATION WORKSHEET

Employer
Identification Number   00-0004701   Name   CLARKE'S ROOFING

Month Tax Year Ends   12   Amount of Deposit   _____

Type of Tax (Form)   _____   Tax Period   _____

Address   20 SUMMIT SQUARE   Phone Number   _____

City, State, Zip   CITY, STATE 00000-0000

To be deposited on or before _____

4-12B (continued)

FEDERAL DEPOSIT INFORMATION WORKSHEET

Employer
Identification Number   00-0004701   Name   CLARKE'S ROOFING

Month Tax Year Ends   12   Amount of Deposit   _____

Type of Tax (Form)   _____   Tax Period   _____

Address   20 SUMMIT SQUARE   Phone Number   _____

City, State, Zip   CITY, STATE 00000-0000

To be deposited on or before _____

FEDERAL DEPOSIT INFORMATION WORKSHEET

Employer
Identification Number   00-0004701   Name   CLARKE'S ROOFING

Month Tax Year Ends   12   Amount of Deposit   _____

Type of Tax (Form)   _____   Tax Period   _____

Address   20 SUMMIT SQUARE   Phone Number   _____

City, State, Zip   CITY, STATE 00000-0000

To be deposited on or before _____

4-12B (continued)

Form **941 for 20--:** **Employer's QUARTERLY Federal Tax Return**
(Rev. March 2022)   Department of the Treasury — Internal Revenue Service

OMB No. 1545-0029

Employer identification number (EIN) 0 0 – 0 0 0 4 7 0 1

Name (not your trade name)   CLARKE'S ROOFING

Trade name (if any)

Address   20 SUMMIT SQUARE
Number   Street   Suite or room number

CITY   ST   00000-0000
City   State   ZIP code

Foreign country name   Foreign province/county   Foreign postal code

Report for this Quarter of 20--
(Check one.)

☐ **1:** January, February, March

☐ **2:** April, May, June

☐ **3:** July, August, September

☐ **4:** October, November, December

Go to *www.irs.gov/Form941* for instructions and the latest information.

Read the separate instructions before you complete Form 941. Type or print within the boxes.

Part 1:   Answer these questions for this quarter.

1 Number of employees who received wages, tips, or other compensation for the pay period including: *Mar. 12* (Quarter 1) **1**

2 Wages, tips, and other compensation **2**

3 Federal income tax withheld from wages, tips, and other compensation **3**

4 If no wages, tips, and other compensation are subject to social security or Medicare tax   ☐ Check and go to line 6.

		Column 1		Column 2	
5a	Taxable social security wages* . .		× 0.124 =		*Include taxable qualified sick and family leave wages paid in 2022 for leave taken after March 31, 2021, and before October 1, 2021, on line 5a. Use lines 5a(i) and 5a(ii) **only** for taxable qualified sick and family leave wages paid in 2022 for leave taken after March 31, 2020, and before April 1, 2021.*
5a	(i) Qualified sick leave wages* . .		× 0.062 =		
5a	(ii) Qualified family leave wages* . .		× 0.062 =		
5b	Taxable social security tips . . .		× 0.124 =		
5c	Taxable Medicare wages & tips. .		× 0.029 =		
5d	Taxable wages & tips subject to Additional Medicare Tax withholding		× 0.009 =		

5e Total social security and Medicare taxes. Add Column 2 from lines 5a, 5a(i), 5a(ii), 5b, 5c, and 5d   **5e**

5f Section 3121(q) Notice and Demand—Tax due on unreported tips (see instructions) . .   **5f**

6 Total taxes before adjustments. Add lines 3, 5e, and 5f **6**

7 Current quarter's adjustment for fractions of cents **7**

8 Current quarter's adjustment for sick pay **8**

9 Current quarter's adjustments for tips and group-term life insurance **9**

10 Total taxes after adjustments. Combine lines 6 through 9 . . . .   **10**

11a Qualified small business payroll tax credit for increasing research activities. Attach Form 8974   **11a**

11b Nonrefundable portion of credit for qualified sick and family leave wages for leave taken before April 1, 2021 . . . .   **11b**

11c Reserved for future use **11c**

▶ **You MUST complete all three pages of Form 941 and SIGN it.**   Next ▶

For Privacy Act and Paperwork Reduction Act Notice, see the back of the Payment Voucher.   Cat. No. 17001Z   Form **941** (Rev. 3-2022)

4-12B (continued)

Name *(not your trade name)*	**Employer identification number (EIN)**
CLARKE'S ROOFING	00-0004701

Part 1: Answer these questions for this quarter. *(continued)*

11d Nonrefundable portion of credit for qualified sick and family leave wages for leave taken after March 31, 2021, and before October 1, 2021 . . . . 11d [_____ . __]

11e Nonrefundable portion of COBRA premium assistance credit (see instructions for applicable quarter) . . . . 11e [_____ . __]

11f Number of individuals provided COBRA premium assistance [_____]

11g Total nonrefundable credits. Add lines 11a, 11b, 11d, and 11e . . . . 11g [_____ . __]

12 Total taxes after adjustments and nonrefundable credits. Subtract line 11g from line 10 . 12 [_____ . __]

13a Total deposits for this quarter, including overpayment applied from a prior quarter and overpayments applied from Form 941-X, 941-X (PR), 944-X, or 944-X (SP) filed in the current quarter 13a [_____ . __]

13b Reserved for future use . . . . 13b [_____ . __]

13c Refundable portion of credit for qualified sick and family leave wages for leave taken before April 1, 2021 . . . . 13c [_____ . __]

13d Reserved for future use . . . . 13d [_____ . __]

13e Refundable portion of credit for qualified sick and family leave wages for leave taken after March 31, 2021, and before October 1, 2021 . . . . 13e [_____ . __]

13f Refundable portion of COBRA premium assistance credit (see instructions for applicable quarter) . . . . 13f [_____ . __]

13g Total deposits and refundable credits. Add lines 13a, 13c, 13e, and 13f . . . . 13g [_____ . __]

13h Reserved for future use . . . . 13h [_____ . __]

13i Reserved for future use . . . . 13i [_____ . __]

14 Balance due. If line 12 is more than line 13g, enter the difference and see instructions . . . 14 [_____ . __]

15 Overpayment. If line 13g is more than line 12, enter the difference [_____ . __] Check one: ☐ Apply to next return. ☐ Send a refund.

Part 2: Tell us about your deposit schedule and tax liability for this quarter.

If you're unsure about whether you're a monthly schedule depositor or a semiweekly schedule depositor, see section 11 of Pub. 15.

16 Check one: ☐ Line 12 on this return is less than $2,500 or line 12 on the return for the prior quarter was less than $2,500, and you didn't incur a $100,000 next-day deposit obligation during the current quarter. If line 12 for the prior quarter was less than $2,500 but line 12 on this return is $100,000 or more, you must provide a record of your federal tax liability. If you're a monthly schedule depositor, complete the deposit schedule below; if you're a semiweekly schedule depositor, attach Schedule B (Form 941). Go to Part 3.

☐ You were a monthly schedule depositor for the entire quarter. Enter your tax liability for each month and total liability for the quarter, then go to Part 3.

Tax liability: Month 1 [_____ . __]

Month 2 [_____ . __]

Month 3 [_____ . __]

Total liability for quarter [_____ . __] Total must equal line 12.

☐ You were a semiweekly schedule depositor for any part of this quarter. Complete Schedule B (Form 941), Report of Tax Liability for Semiweekly Schedule Depositors, and attach it to Form 941. Go to Part 3.

▶ You MUST complete all three pages of Form 941 and SIGN it. [Next ▶]

Form **941** (Rev. 3-2022)

4-12B (continued)

Name *(not your trade name)*	Employer identification number (EIN)
CLARKE'S ROOFING	00-0004701

Part 3: Tell us about your business. If a question does NOT apply to your business, leave it blank.

17 If your business has closed or you stopped paying wages . . . . ☐ Check here, and

enter the final date you paid wages [/ /] ; also attach a statement to your return. See instructions.

18 If you're a seasonal employer and you don't have to file a return for every quarter of the year . . . ☐ Check here.

19 Qualified health plan expenses allocable to qualified sick leave wages for leave taken before April 1, 2021   **19** [.]

20 Qualified health plan expenses allocable to qualified family leave wages for leave taken before April 1, 2021   **20** [.]

21 Reserved for future use . . . .   **21** [.]

22 Reserved for future use . . . .   **22** [.]

23 Qualified sick leave wages for leave taken after March 31, 2021, and before October 1, 2021   **23** [.]

24 Qualified health plan expenses allocable to qualified sick leave wages reported on line 23   **24** [.]

25 Amounts under certain collectively bargained agreements allocable to qualified sick leave wages reported on line 23 . . . .   **25** [.]

26 Qualified family leave wages for leave taken after March 31, 2021, and before October 1, 2021   **26** [.]

27 Qualified health plan expenses allocable to qualified family leave wages reported on line 26   **27** [.]

28 Amounts under certain collectively bargained agreements allocable to qualified family leave wages reported on line 26 . . . .   **28** [.]

Part 4: May we speak with your third-party designee?

Do you want to allow an employee, a paid tax preparer, or another person to discuss this return with the IRS? See the instructions for details.

☐ **Yes.** Designee's name and phone number [   ] [   ]

Select a 5-digit personal identification number (PIN) to use when talking to the IRS. ☐ ☐ ☐ ☐ ☐

☐ **No.**

Part 5: Sign here. You MUST complete all three pages of Form 941 and SIGN it.

Under penalties of perjury, I declare that I have examined this return, including accompanying schedules and statements, and to the best of my knowledge and belief, it is true, correct, and complete. Declaration of preparer (other than taxpayer) is based on all information of which preparer has any knowledge.

X Sign your name here [   ]

Print your name here [   ]
Print your title here [   ]

Date [/ /]

Best daytime phone [   ]

Paid Preparer Use Only

Check if you're self-employed . . . ☐

Preparer's name	[ ]	PTIN	[ ]
Preparer's signature	[ ]	Date	[/ /]
Firm's name (or yours if self-employed)	[ ]	EIN	[ ]
Address	[ ]	Phone	[ ]
City	[ ] State [ ]	ZIP code	[ ]

Page **3**   Form **941** (Rev. 3-2022)

4-13B • LO 3, 4   See Figure 4.8 on page 4-23, Figure 4.11 on page 4-28

During the first full week of 20--, the Payroll Department of Omni Corporation is preparing the Forms W-2 for distribution to its employees along with their payroll checks on January 10. In this problem, you will complete six of the forms in order to gain some experience in recording the different kinds of information required.

Assume each employee earned the same weekly salary for each of the 52 paydays in 20--, the previous year. Using the following information obtained from the personnel and payroll records of the firm, complete Copy A of the six Forms W-2 reproduced on the following pages. Also complete Form W-3. The form is to be signed by the president, Frank Kent, and is prepared by Vince Roper.

Company Information:

Address:	4800 River Road		
	Philadelphia, PA 19113-5548	Pennsylvania state identification number:	00-0-1066
Telephone number: (215) 555-0017		Federal identification number:	00-0000972
Fax number: (215) 555-0010		Philadelphia identification number:	0001895

Income Tax Information:

The wage-bracket method is used to determine federal income tax withholding. Calculate the annual federal income tax withheld by using the weekly wage-bracket table and multiply the answer by 52. The other taxes withheld are shown below.

Employee Data	Payroll Data	Annual Taxes Withheld	
See example of Randy A. Kellison's completed Form W-2 on next page.			
Randy A. Kellison	Single	Social security tax withheld	2,305.16
54 Gradison Place	$715 per week	Medicare tax withheld	539.24
Philadelphia, PA 19113-4054	SS#: 000-00-4310	State income tax withheld	1,141.40
	Deduction for 401(k) plan:	Local income tax withheld	1,427.40
	$50/week	State unemployment tax withheld**	22.36
Vince T. Roper	Married filing jointly	Social security tax withheld	3,175.64
56 Andrews Court, Apt. 7	$985 per week	Medicare tax withheld	742.56
Philadelphia, PA 19103-3356	SS#: 000-00-8804	State income tax withheld	1,572.48
	Dependent care payment: $950	Local income tax withheld	1,966.64
	$70/week—401(k)	State unemployment tax withheld**	30.68
Murray T. Rodson	Single	Social security tax withheld	2,466.36
770 Camac Street	$765 per week	Medicare tax withheld	576.68
Philadelphia, PA 19101-3770	SS#: 000-00-3316	State income tax withheld	1,221.48
	Union dues withheld: $102	Local income tax withheld	1,527.24
		State unemployment tax withheld**	23.92
Frank A. Kent	Married filing jointly	Social security tax withheld	6,061.29
338 North Side Avenue	$1,875 per week	Medicare tax withheld	1,417.69
Philadelphia, PA 19130-6638	SS#: 000-00-6839	State income tax withheld	2,993.12
	Cost of group-term life insurance	Local income tax withheld	3,744.00
	exceeding $50,000: $262.75* $100/week—401(k)	State unemployment tax withheld**	58.76
Carlie C. Christian	Married filing jointly	Social security tax withheld	2,514.72
4900 Gladwynne Terrace	$780 per week	Medicare tax withheld	588.12
Philadelphia, PA 19127-0049	SS#: 000-00-5771	State income tax withheld	1,245.40
	Union dues withheld: $102	Local income tax withheld	1,557.40
		State unemployment tax withheld**	24.44
Zana W. Amelia	Single	Social security tax withheld	2,546.96
480-A Hopkinson Tower	$790 per week	Medicare tax withheld	595.92
Philadelphia, PA 19101-3301	SS#: 000-00-8703	State income tax withheld	1,261.00
	Educational assistance payments	Local income tax withheld	1,577.16
	(job-required): $675	State unemployment tax withheld**	24.44
	$50/week—401(k)		

* The cost of excess group-term life insurance is added to gross wages for federal income tax, Social Security, and Medicare. Employers withhold OASDI and HI tax on these amounts but are not required to withhold federal income tax. The cost is not added to gross wages for state and local taxes; therefore, it is not subject to those taxes (see Figure 4.8 on page 4-23).

**State unemployment tax withheld for Pennsylvania labeled as PA SUI on Form W-2 Box 14.

4-13B (continued)

22222	Void ☐	**a** Employee's social security number 000-00-4310	For Official Use Only ▶ OMB No. 1545-0008	

b Employer identification number (EIN) 00-0000972		**1** Wages, tips, other compensation 34580.00*	**2** Federal income tax withheld 2444.00**

c Employer's name, address, and ZIP code Omni Corporation 4800 River Road Philadelphia, PA 19113-5548	**3** Social security wages 37180.00	**4** Social security tax withheld 2305.16
	5 Medicare wages and tips 37180.00	**6** Medicare tax withheld 539.24
	7 Social security tips	**8** Allocated tips

d Control number	**9**	**10** Dependent care benefits

e Employee's first name and initial Randy A.	Last name Kellison	Suff.	**11** Nonqualified plans	**12a** See instructions for box 12 D 2600.00
54 Gradison Place Philadelphia, PA 19113-4054			**13** Statutory employee ☐ Retirement plan ☒ Third-party sick pay ☐	**12b**
			14 Other PA SUI 22.36	**12c**
				12d

f Employee's address and ZIP code						
15 State Employer's state ID number PA 00-0-1066	**16** State wages, tips, etc. 37180.00	**17** State income tax 1141.40	**18** Local wages, tips, etc. 37180.00	**19** Local income tax 1427.40	**20** Locality name Phila.

Form **W-2** Wage and Tax Statement   **20 - -**

Department of the Treasury—Internal Revenue Service

Copy A For Social Security Administration — Send this entire page with Form W-3 to the Social Security Administration; photocopies are **not** acceptable.

For Privacy Act and Paperwork Reduction Act Notice, see the separate instructions.

Cat. No. 10134D

*[Weekly salary $715.00 − $50.00 Contribution for 401(k)] × 52 weeks
**Federal Income Tax Withheld $47.00 × 52 weeks

Do Not Cut, Fold, or Staple Forms on This Page

22222	Void ☐	**a** Employee's social security number	For Official Use Only ▶ OMB No. 1545-0008	

b Employer identification number (EIN)		**1** Wages, tips, other compensation	**2** Federal income tax withheld

c Employer's name, address, and ZIP code	**3** Social security wages	**4** Social security tax withheld
	5 Medicare wages and tips	**6** Medicare tax withheld
	7 Social security tips	**8** Allocated tips

d Control number	**9**	**10** Dependent care benefits

e Employee's first name and initial	Last name	Suff.	**11** Nonqualified plans	**12a** See instructions for box 12
			13 Statutory employee ☐ Retirement plan ☐ Third-party sick pay ☐	**12b**
			14 Other	**12c**
				12d

f Employee's address and ZIP code						
15 State Employer's state ID number	**16** State wages, tips, etc.	**17** State income tax	**18** Local wages, tips, etc.	**19** Local income tax	**20** Locality name

Form **W-2** Wage and Tax Statement   **20 - -**

Department of the Treasury—Internal Revenue Service

Copy A For Social Security Administration — Send this entire page with Form W-3 to the Social Security Administration; photocopies are **not** acceptable.

For Privacy Act and Paperwork Reduction Act Notice, see the separate instructions.

Cat. No. 10134D

Do Not Cut, Fold, or Staple Forms on This Page

Source: Internal Revenue Service.

4-13B (continued)

22222 Void ☐	**a** Employee's social security number	For Official Use Only ▶ OMB No. 1545-0008		

b Employer identification number (EIN)	**1** Wages, tips, other compensation	**2** Federal income tax withheld
c Employer's name, address, and ZIP code	**3** Social security wages	**4** Social security tax withheld
	5 Medicare wages and tips	**6** Medicare tax withheld
	7 Social security tips	**8** Allocated tips
d Control number	**9**	**10** Dependent care benefits
e Employee's first name and initial　　Last name　　Suff.	**11** Nonqualified plans	**12a** See instructions for box 12
	13 Statutory employee ☐　Retirement plan ☐　Third-party sick pay ☐	**12b**
	14 Other	**12c**
		12d
f Employee's address and ZIP code		

15 State　Employer's state ID number	**16** State wages, tips, etc.	**17** State income tax	**18** Local wages, tips, etc.	**19** Local income tax	**20** Locality name

Form **W-2** Wage and Tax Statement　　**20 - -**　　Department of the Treasury—Internal Revenue Service

Copy A For Social Security Administration — Send this entire page with Form W-3 to the Social Security Administration; photocopies are **not** acceptable.

For Privacy Act and Paperwork Reduction Act Notice, see the separate instructions.

Cat. No. 10134D

Do Not Cut, Fold, or Staple Forms on This Page

22222 Void ☐	**a** Employee's social security number	For Official Use Only ▶ OMB No. 1545-0008		

b Employer identification number (EIN)	**1** Wages, tips, other compensation	**2** Federal income tax withheld
c Employer's name, address, and ZIP code	**3** Social security wages	**4** Social security tax withheld
	5 Medicare wages and tips	**6** Medicare tax withheld
	7 Social security tips	**8** Allocated tips
d Control number	**9**	**10** Dependent care benefits
e Employee's first name and initial　　Last name　　Suff.	**11** Nonqualified plans	**12a** See instructions for box 12
	13 Statutory employee ☐　Retirement plan ☐　Third-party sick pay ☐	**12b**
	14 Other	**12c**
		12d
f Employee's address and ZIP code		

15 State　Employer's state ID number	**16** State wages, tips, etc.	**17** State income tax	**18** Local wages, tips, etc.	**19** Local income tax	**20** Locality name

Form **W-2** Wage and Tax Statement　　**20 - -**　　Department of the Treasury—Internal Revenue Service

Copy A For Social Security Administration — Send this entire page with Form W-3 to the Social Security Administration; photocopies are **not** acceptable.

For Privacy Act and Paperwork Reduction Act Notice, see the separate instructions.

Cat. No. 10134D

Do Not Cut, Fold, or Staple Forms on This Page

Source: Internal Revenue Service.

4-13B (continued)

22222	Void ☐	**a** Employee's social security number	For Official Use Only ▶ OMB No. 1545-0008		
b Employer identification number (EIN)			**1** Wages, tips, other compensation		**2** Federal income tax withheld
c Employer's name, address, and ZIP code			**3** Social security wages		**4** Social security tax withheld
			5 Medicare wages and tips		**6** Medicare tax withheld
			7 Social security tips		**8** Allocated tips
d Control number			**9**		**10** Dependent care benefits
e Employee's first name and initial — Last name — Suff.			**11** Nonqualified plans		**12a** See instructions for box 12
			13 Statutory employee ☐ Retirement plan ☐ Third-party sick pay ☐		**12b**
			14 Other		**12c**
					12d
f Employee's address and ZIP code					
15 State Employer's state ID number	**16** State wages, tips, etc.	**17** State income tax	**18** Local wages, tips, etc.	**19** Local income tax	**20** Locality name

Form **W-2** Wage and Tax Statement **20 - -** Department of the Treasury—Internal Revenue Service

Copy A For Social Security Administration — Send this entire page with Form W-3 to the Social Security Administration; photocopies are **not** acceptable.

For Privacy Act and Paperwork Reduction Act Notice, see the separate instructions.

Cat. No. 10134D

Do Not Cut, Fold, or Staple Forms on This Page

22222	Void ☐	**a** Employee's social security number	For Official Use Only ▶ OMB No. 1545-0008		
b Employer identification number (EIN)			**1** Wages, tips, other compensation		**2** Federal income tax withheld
c Employer's name, address, and ZIP code			**3** Social security wages		**4** Social security tax withheld
			5 Medicare wages and tips		**6** Medicare tax withheld
			7 Social security tips		**8** Allocated tips
d Control number			**9**		**10** Dependent care benefits
e Employee's first name and initial — Last name — Suff.			**11** Nonqualified plans		**12a** See instructions for box 12
			13 Statutory employee ☐ Retirement plan ☐ Third-party sick pay ☐		**12b**
			14 Other		**12c**
					12d
f Employee's address and ZIP code					
15 State Employer's state ID number	**16** State wages, tips, etc.	**17** State income tax	**18** Local wages, tips, etc.	**19** Local income tax	**20** Locality name

Form **W-2** Wage and Tax Statement **20 - -** Department of the Treasury—Internal Revenue Service

Copy A For Social Security Administration — Send this entire page with Form W-3 to the Social Security Administration; photocopies are **not** acceptable.

For Privacy Act and Paperwork Reduction Act Notice, see the separate instructions.

Cat. No. 10134D

Do Not Cut, Fold, or Staple Forms on This Page

Source: Internal Revenue Service.

DO NOT STAPLE

33333	a Control number	For Official Use Only ▶ OMB No. 1545-0008		

b Kind of Payer (Check one) ▶
941 ☐ Military ☐ 943 ☐ 944 ☐ CT-1 ☐ Hshld. emp. ☐ Medicare govt. emp. ☐

Kind of Employer (Check one) ▶
None apply ☐ 501c non-govt. ☐ State/local non-501c ☐ State/local 501c ☐ Federal govt. ☐

Third-party sick pay (Check if applicable) ☐

c Total number of Forms W-2	d Establishment number	1 Wages, tips, other compensation	2 Federal income tax withheld
e Employer identification number (EIN)		3 Social security wages	4 Social security tax withheld
f Employer's name		5 Medicare wages and tips	6 Medicare tax withheld
		7 Social security tips	8 Allocated tips
		9	10 Dependent care benefits
		11 Nonqualified plans	12a Deferred compensation
g Employer's address and ZIP code			
h Other EIN used this year		13 For third-party sick pay use only	12b
15 State Employer's state ID number		14 Income tax withheld by payer of third-party sick pay	
16 State wages, tips, etc.	17 State income tax	18 Local wages, tips, etc.	19 Local income tax
Employer's contact person		Employer's telephone number	For Official Use Only
Employer's fax number		Employer's email address	

Under penalties of perjury, I declare that I have examined this return and accompanying documents and, to the best of my knowledge and belief, they are true, correct, and complete.

Signature ▶   Title ▶   Date ▶

Form **W-3** **Transmittal of Wage and Tax Statements**   **20- -**   Department of the Treasury Internal Revenue Service

Source: Internal Revenue Service.

Supplement Problem Set • B

As we go to press, the federal income tax rates for 2023 are being determined by budget talks in Washington and not available for publication. For this edition, the 2022 federal income tax tables for Manual Payroll Systems with Forms W-4 from 2019 or earlier and 2022 FICA rates have been used.

*4-14B • LO 3   See Example 4-1 on page 4-5, Example 4-14 on page 4-40

Herman Swayne is a waiter at the Dixie Hotel. In his first weekly pay in March, he earned $360.00 for the 40 hours he worked. In addition, he reports his tips for February to his employer ($700.00), and the employer withholds the appropriate taxes for the tips from this first pay in March.

   Calculate his net take-home pay assuming the employer withheld federal income tax (**wage-bracket,** married, 2 allowances), social security taxes, and state income tax (2%) .... $_____

*4-15B • LO 3   See Example 4-13 on page 4-39

Use the *percentage method* to compute the federal income taxes to withhold from the wages or salaries of each employee.

Employee No.	Employee Name	Marital Status	No. of Withholding Allowances	Gross Wage or Salary	Amount to Be Withheld
1	Skymer, A.	M	4	$ 1,575 weekly	_____
2	Wolfe, T.	S	0	1,200 biweekly	_____
3	Klein, G.	S	5	12,600 quarterly	_____
4	Carey, P.	M	8	1,090 semimonthly	_____
5	Wu, M.	M	3	8,120 monthly	_____

*4-16B • LO 3   See Example 4-13 on page 4-39, Example 4-14 on page 4-40

Use (a) the percentage method and (b) the wage-bracket method to compute the federal income taxes to withhold from the wages or salaries of each employee.

Employee	Marital Status	No. of Withholding Allowances	Gross Wage or Salary	Amount to Be Withheld Percentage Method	Wage-Bracket Method
Ruiz, S.	S	2	$ 1,040 weekly	_____	_____
Flume, X.	S	1	1,800 weekly	_____	_____
Farley, H.	M	6	1,890 biweekly	_____	_____
Comey, P.	M	4	2,315 semimonthly	_____	_____
Hanks, R.	M	4	3,200 monthly	_____	_____

*4-17B • LO 3   See Example 4-14 on page 4-40

Ernesto Enterprises uses the *wage-bracket method* to determine federal income tax withholding on its employees. Find the amount to withhold from the wages paid each employee.

Employee	Marital Status	No. of Withholding Allowances	Payroll Period W = Weekly S = Semimonthly M = Monthly D = Daily	Wage	Amount to Be Withheld
Ed Boone	M	1	W	$ 1,250	_____
Ray Ortega	S	1	W	695	_____
Carl Lopez	S	3	W	915	_____
Terri Kim	M	6	M	3,070	_____
Kathy Horace	M	2	M	2,730	_____
John Gleam	M	8	S	1,200	_____
Rob Abreu	S	1	D	115	_____
Carmen Sanchez	S	4	S	2,040	_____
Howard Nee	M	4	M	3,500	_____

Date _____ Name _____

Refer to the partially completed payroll register which you worked on at the end of Chapter 3. You will now determine the amount of income tax to withhold for each employee, proceeding as follows:

1. In the appropriate columns of your payroll register, record the filing status for each employee using the information provided.
2. Record the payroll deductions for the SIMPLE plan that the employer has established for participating employees. All of the employees are participating, and their weekly contributions are listed below.

The tax deferral on these deductions applies only to the federal income tax.

3. Record the amount of federal income taxes using the wage-bracket method and standard withholding.
4. Record the state income taxes on the gross weekly earnings for each employee. The rate is 3.07% for the state of Pennsylvania.
5. Record the city income taxes on the gross weekly earnings of each employee. The rate is 3% for the city of Pittsburgh residents.

Time Card No.	Filing Status	No. of Withholding Allowances	SIMPLE Deductions
11	S	N/A	$20
12	S	N/A	50
13	MFJ	N/A	40
21	MFJ	N/A	50
22	S	N/A	20
31	MFJ	N/A	40
32	MFJ	N/A	50
33	S	N/A	60
51	MFJ	N/A	30
99	MFJ	N/A	80

Refer to the partially completed payroll register which you worked on at the end of Chapter 3. You will now determine the amount of income tax to withhold for each employee, proceeding as follows:

1. In the appropriate columns of your payroll register, record the filing status for each employee using the information provided.
2. Record the payroll deductions for the SIMPLE plan that the employer has established for participating employees. All of the employees are participating, and their weekly contributions are listed below.

The tax deferral on these deductions applies only to the federal income tax.

3. Record the amount of federal income taxes using the wage-bracket method and standard withholding.
4. Record the state income taxes on the gross weekly earnings for each employee. The rate is 3.07% for the state of Pennsylvania.
5. Record the local income taxes on the gross weekly earnings of each employee. The rate is 1.0% for the Chalfont Boro residents.

Time Card No.	Filing Status	No. of Withholding Allowances	SIMPLE Deductions
11	S	N/A	$20
12	S	N/A	50
13	MFJ	N/A	40
21	MFJ	N/A	60
22	S	N/A	20
31	MFJ	N/A	40
32	MFJ	N/A	50
33	S	N/A	50
51	MFJ	N/A	30
99	MFJ	N/A	80

Case Problems

C1. Answering Employees' Questions About Wage Reporting. LO 4.

During the past week, one of your newly employed pay-roll associates dropped into your office to ask several questions regarding wage reporting for federal income and social security tax purposes. If you were the payroll supervisor, how would you answer each of the following questions raised by your associate?

1. I just noticed that the social security number is wrong on three of the employees' W-2 forms.

C2. Classified as an Employee and Independent Contractor. LO 1.

Yeager Company pays John Kerr a salary as an employee and also fees for work he does as an independent contractor. Does this violate IRS rules?

How do I go about correcting the forms? Will the employees be penalized for filing incorrect forms?

2. Eileen Huang informed me today that we had withheld too much Medicare tax from her pay last year. She is right! What forms do I use to make the correction?

3. You asked me last week to locate one of our former employees, Warren Bucks. I can't seem to track him down. What should I do with his Form W-2?

4. Is it okay to use titles like "M.D." and "Esq." when I keyboard data in the W-2 forms?

Chapter 5

Unemployment Compensation Taxes

So we just lost our job? At least we can collect unemployment checks as we look for another job. How much do we get and how long can we collect? Who pays for these benefits? So, it's our former employer!

The program is a federal-state partnership based on the federal law. Each state designs its unemployment program in conformity with the guidelines of the federal requirements.

There are tax rates, tax limits, new deposit requirements, and tax forms to digest. Welcome to the world of unemployment taxes.

Learning Objectives

After studying this chapter, you should be able to:

1. Describe the basic requirements for an individual to be classified as an employer or an employee under the Federal Unemployment Tax Act.
2. Identify generally what is defined as taxable wages by the Federal Unemployment Tax Act.
3. Compute the federal unemployment tax, the credit against the tax, and any credit reductions that might apply.
4. Describe how an experience-rating system is used in determining employers' contributions to state unemployment compensation funds.
5. Complete the reports required by the Federal Unemployment Tax Act.
6. Describe the types of information reports under the various state unemployment compensation laws.

The Social Security Act of 1935 ordered every state to set up an unemployment compensation program in order to provide payments to workers during periods of temporary unemployment. Payroll taxes at both the federal and state levels fund this unemployment insurance program. The Federal Unemployment Tax Act (FUTA) imposes a tax on employers based on wages paid for covered employment. It is **not** collected or deducted from employees' wages. The funds collected by the federal government as a result of this tax pay the cost of administering both the federal and the state unemployment insurance programs. The FUTA tax is **not** used for the payment of weekly benefits to unemployed workers. Such benefits are paid by the states in accordance with each state's unemployment tax law (SUTA). These unemployment benefits are paid out of each state's trust fund, which is financed by state unemployment taxes. Because all states conform to standards specified in FUTA, considerable uniformity exists in the provisions of the state unemployment compensation laws. However, many variations in eligibility requirements, rates of contributions, benefits paid, and duration of benefits exist. All the states, Puerto Rico, the Virgin Islands, and the District of Columbia have enacted unemployment compensation laws that have been approved by the Social Security Administration.

In June 2022 the number of unemployed persons was 5.9 million out of a civilian labor force of about 164 million. At that time, the jobless rate was 3.6 percent. This rate shows a steady decrease as the country tries to recover from the pandemic (the rate was 20.8 percent in April 2020). **Unemployed persons**

Everett Historical/Shutterstock.com

News Alert

The average length of unemployment in June 2022 was 22.3 weeks.

include young people seeking positions for the first time, seasonal workers unemployed a part of each year, and workers who lost their jobs through various causes and cannot find other suitable employment.

LO 1

Describe the basic requirements for an individual to be classified as an employer or an employee under the Federal Unemployment Tax Act.

Coverage Under FUTA and SUTA

Other than a few significant exceptions as explained in this section, the coverage under FUTA is similar to that under FICA, as described in Chapter 3.

Employers—FUTA

The federal law levies a payroll tax on employers for the purpose of providing more uniform administration of the various state unemployment compensation laws. The federal law considers a person or a business an employer if *either* of the following two tests applies:

1. Pays wages of $1,500 or more during any calendar quarter in the current or preceding calendar year, or
2. Employs one or more persons, on at least some portion of one day, in each of 20 or more calendar weeks during the current or preceding taxable year.

A number of points serve to clarify the meaning of the two alternative tests: (a) a calendar week is defined as seven successive days beginning with Sunday; (b) the 20 weeks need not be consecutive; (c) the employees need not be the same employees; (d) regular, part-time, and temporary workers are considered employees; (e) in determining the employer's status, employees include individuals on vacation or sick leave; and (f) members of a partnership are not considered to be employees. As soon as an employer meets either test, the employer becomes liable for the FUTA tax for the entire calendar year.

For Vemor Company (a new employer), the 20th week of having one or more employees does not occur until November of 20--. The company becomes liable for FUTA tax on all taxable wages paid beginning with January 1 of that year.

% IRS Connection

Generally, religious, educational, scientific, and charitable organizations exempt from federal income tax are not subject to FUTA tax.

Other covered employers are:

1. *Agricultural employers* who in the present or previous year paid $20,000 or more to farm workers in any calendar quarter and/or employed 10 or more farm workers during some part of a day during any 20 different weeks. This includes wages paid to aliens who are in this country on a temporary basis to perform farmwork.
2. A *household employer* who during the present or previous year paid $1,000 or more during any quarter for household services in a private home, college club, or local fraternity or sorority club.

Once attained, the employer status continues until the employer fails to meet the test for coverage during a year. In this case, liability under FUTA would end as of January 1 of the next year.

Generally, the nature of the business organization has no relevance in determining employer status. Thus, the employer may be an individual, corporation, partnership, company, association, trust, or estate. There may be instances where it is difficult to determine which of two entities is the employer for purposes of FUTA. As under FICA, the question is answered by determining which entity has the ultimate right to direct and control the employees' activities. It is not necessary that the employer actually direct or control the manner in which the services are performed; it is sufficient if the employer has the right to do so. Other factors characteristic of an employer include the right to discharge and the furnishing of tools and a place to work.

Employers—SUTA

In general, employers specifically excluded under the federal law are also excluded under the state laws. However, as a result of variations found in state unemployment compensation laws, not all employers covered by the unemployment compensation laws of one or more states are covered by FUTA. For example, the services performed by some charitable organizations may be covered by a state's unemployment compensation act, but these same services may be exempt from FUTA coverage.

Employees—FUTA

Every individual is considered an employee if the relationship between the worker and the person for whom the services are performed is the legal common-law relationship of employer and employee. This individual would then be counted in determining whether the employer is subject to FUTA. Chapters 3 and 4 cover the nature of this common-law relationship.

For the purpose of the FUTA tax, the term "statutory employee" also means any of the following who perform service for remuneration:

1. An **agent-driver** or a **commission-driver** who distributes food or beverages (other than milk) or laundry or dry-cleaning services for the principal.

2. A **traveling** or a city **salesperson** engaged in full-time soliciting and transmitting to the principal orders for merchandise for resale or supplies for use in business operations.

Unlike FICA, under FUTA "statutory employees" do not include home workers (exempt unless they meet the definition of employee under the common-law test) and full-time life insurance agents. If a person in one of these categories has a substantial investment in facilities used to perform the services (not including transportation facilities), the individual is an independent contractor and not a covered employee.

The work performed by the employee for the employer includes any services of whatever nature performed within the United States, regardless of the citizenship or residence of either. FUTA coverage also includes service of any nature performed outside the United States by a citizen of the United States for an American employer. The major exception is that service performed in Canada or in any other adjoining country with which the United States has an agreement relating to unemployment does not constitute covered employment.

An employee may perform both included and excluded employment for the same employer during a pay period. In such a case, the services that predominate in the pay period determine the employee's status with that employer for the period. FUTA wholly exempts some services from coverage. Among those **excluded** from coverage are:

1. Casual laborers, unless cash remuneration paid for such service is $50 or more in a calendar quarter and the person to whom it is paid is regularly employed by the one for whom the services were performed during that period.

2. Directors of corporations, unless they perform services for the corporation other than those required by attending and participating in meetings of the board of directors.

3. Foreign students and exchange visitors who are carrying out the purposes for which they are admitted into the United States, such as studying, teaching, or conducting research. If employed for other purposes, they would not be excluded.

4. Government employees of international organizations, such as the United Nations.

On the Net

http://www.servicelocator
.org/OWSLinks.asp This
site provides a variety of
interactive maps concerning
individual states' status
on unemployment-related
issues.

5. Independent contractors, such as physicians, lawyers, dentists, veterinarians, contractors, subcontractors, public stenographers, auctioneers, and others who follow an independent trade, business, or profession in which they offer their services to the public.

6. Individuals under 18 years of age who deliver or distribute newspapers or shopping news (other than delivery or distribution to any point for subsequent delivery and distribution) and retail vendors of any age who sell and distribute newspapers and magazines to the ultimate consumer.

7. Insurance agents or solicitors paid solely on a commission basis.

8. Members of partnerships.

9. Service performed by an individual for a son, daughter, or spouse, or by a child under the age of 21 for a parent.

10. Services performed by a student who is enrolled and regularly attending classes at a school, college, or university, if service is performed for that school, college, or university.

11. Services performed by employees or employee representatives for employers covered by either the Railroad Retirement Tax Act or the Railroad Unemployment Insurance Act.

12. Services performed by individuals in fishing and related activities if the vessel is less than ten net tons.

13. Services performed in the employ of a religious, educational, or charitable organization that is exempt from federal income tax. This exemption includes service in church-sponsored elementary and secondary schools.

14. Services performed in the employ of foreign, federal, state, or local governments and certain of their instrumentalities. However, taxes imposed by FUTA apply to these federal instrumentalities: federal reserve banks, federal loan banks, and federal credit unions.

15. Students enrolled full time in a work-study or internship program, for work that is an integral part of the student's academic program.

16. Student nurses and hospital interns.

Employees—SUTA

The definition of "employee" as established by FUTA applies to a majority of the states, although minor variations exist in the state laws. Many states apply a simple "ABC" test to determine exclusion from coverage. All of the following requirements must be met for exclusion:

1. Free from control or direction.

2. Performed outside usual course of business.

3. Customarily engaged in an independent trade or business.

All states extend coverage to U.S. citizens working abroad for American employers (except in Canada).

Coverage of Interstate Employees

An **interstate employee** is an individual who works in more than one state. To prevent duplicate contributions on the services of interstate employees, all states have adopted a uniform four-part definition of employment to determine which state will cover such employees. This definition covers the entire services of an interstate worker in one state only—that state in which the worker will most likely look for a job if they become unemployed. Several factors that must be considered in determining coverage of interstate employees, in their order of application, include:

1. Place where the work is *localized.*
2. Location of *base of operations.*
3. Location of place from which operations are *directed or controlled.*
4. Location of *employee's residence.*

Over the Line

After nearly a year on the job in New York, an employee moved to Florida and telecommuted for another two years. She was laid off and received benefits from New York. The employer appealed, and a state appeals court ruled that she was ineligible because she had not worked in New York during the base period. Her out-of-state work must be incidental to the in-state work. That was not the case since the actual work was performed in Florida.

Place Where the Work Is Localized

Under this main criterion of coverage adopted by the states, if all the work is performed within one state, it is clearly "localized" in that state and constitutes "employment" under the law of that state. In some cases, however, part of the person's work may be performed outside the state. In such instances, the entire work may be treated as localized within the state if the services performed in other states are temporary or transitory in nature.

Carlin Parker is a sales representative whose regular sales territory lies within Arizona. Parker is covered by the laws of Arizona, with respect to their total employment, even though they make frequent trips to the firm's showrooms in Los Angeles to attend sales meetings and to look over new lines of goods.

Location of Base of Operations

Often, a worker may perform services continually in two or more states. In such situations, the employment in one state is not incidental to the employment in the other state. Thus, the test of localization does not apply, and the base of operations test must be considered. Under this test, the employee's services may be covered by the laws of a single state even though the services are not localized within that state. The base of operation is the place of a more or less permanent nature from which the employee starts work and to which the employee customarily returns. It could be a particular place where their (a) instructions are received, (b) business records are maintained, (c) supplies are sent, or (d) office is maintained (may be in the employee's home).

Mathew Hinges travels through four southern states for Irwin Company, which is headquartered in Georgia. His work is equally divided among the four states. When working in Georgia, he reports to the main office for instructions. The location of his base of operations is clearly Georgia, and his services are subject to the Georgia laws.

Location of Place from Which Operations Are Directed or Controlled

Often, an employee's services are not localized in any state. Or, it may be impossible to determine any base of operations. If the place of control can be fixed in a particular state in which some service is performed, that will be the state in which the individual is covered.

Afia Mendes is a sales representative whose sales territory is so widespread that she does not retain any fixed business address or office. She receives all orders or instructions by mail or wire wherever she may happen to be. Clearly, the work is not localized in any state, and no fixed base of operations exists. However, the services performed by Mendes may still come under the provisions of a single state law—the law of that state in which is located the place of direction or control, provided that some of Mendes's work is also performed in that state.

Location of Employee's Residence

If an employee's coverage cannot be determined by any of the three tests described, a final test, that of the employee's residence, is used. Thus, the worker's service is covered in its entirety in the state in which the employee lives, provided some of the service is performed in that state.

Randy Mueller is employed by Prang Company of Illinois. He lives in Iowa, and his work territory includes Iowa, Minnesota, and Wisconsin. Since neither the base of operations nor the place from which his work is directed is in a state in which he works, he is covered in his state of residence (Iowa).

Reciprocal Arrangements and Transfers of Employment

If coverage of interstate employees cannot be determined using these factors, states may enter into arrangements under which the employer may elect coverage of the employee in one state.

These agreements, known as **reciprocal arrangements**, provide unemployment insurance coverage and payment of benefits to interstate workers. The most widely accepted type of interstate coverage arrangement is the Interstate Reciprocal Coverage Arrangement. Under this arrangement, an employer can elect to cover all of the services of a worker in any one state in which (a) the employee performs any work, (b) the employee maintains a residence, or (c) the employer maintains the place of business.

Morris Davidson is a salesperson for Tannenbaum Company. His sales territory includes parts of Rhode Island and Massachusetts, and his services can be considered localized in both states. Under the Interstate Reciprocal Coverage Arrangement, the company elects to cover Davidson under the law of Massachusetts.

Instead of paying into two or more of the 50 states, an employer can elect a state based on such factors as low wage bases and contribution rates. Once the employer chooses the state in which all the services of the inter-state workers are to be covered and the employee consents to the coverage, this state approves the election of coverage. Then, the appropriate agencies of the other states in which services are performed are notified so that they can agree to the coverage in the state of election. Since they are usually done on a case-by-case basis, new arrangements must be agreed upon for each employee.

Another aspect of reciprocal arrangements concerns the transfer of an employee from one state to another during the same calendar year. An employer can include, for purposes of determining the taxable wage base in the second state, wages paid an employee with respect to employment covered by the unemployment compensation law of the previous state.

> **Example 5-1**
>
> Parlone Company has paid wages of $4,000 to an employee in State A. During the year, the employee is transferred to State B, which has a $7,000 taxable salary limitation for its state unemployment tax. The company has a credit of $4,000 against this $7,000 limit. Thus, the company has to pay State B's unemployment tax on only the next $3,000 of wages earned by that worker in State B during the remainder of the calendar year.

Coverage of Americans Working Overseas

As mentioned before, coverage extends to U.S. citizens working abroad for American employers. The state of the employer's principal place of business would provide the coverage. If the principal place of business cannot be determined, the state of incorporation or the state of residence of the individual owner would be the state of coverage.

Qualifying for Benefits

In order to qualify for benefits, claimants must have earned a minimum base-period wage and meet other requirements as established by the individual state.

For instance, in Colorado the claimant must:

- Have earned wages of at least 40 times the weekly benefit or $2,500, whichever is greater.
- Make a claim.
- Be able and available for work.
- Serve a one-week waiting period.
- Be actively looking for work.

Wages—FUTA

Generally, *wages* means all remuneration for employment, including the cash value of all remuneration paid in any medium other than cash, with certain exceptions.

Taxable wages include only the first $7,000 of remuneration paid by an employer to an employee with respect to employment during any calendar year. The basis upon which the remuneration is paid is immaterial. It may be paid on a piece-work basis or it may be a percentage of profits; it may be paid hourly, daily, weekly, biweekly, semimonthly, monthly, or annually. Some of the more common types of payments made to employees and the taxability status of these payments include the following:

> **LO 2**
> Identify generally what is defined as taxable wages by the Federal Unemployment Tax Act.

Taxable Wages for Unemployment Purposes

1. Advance payment for work to be done in the future.
2. Bonuses as remuneration for services.
3. Cash and noncash prizes and awards for doing outstanding work, for exceeding sales quotas, or for contributing suggestions that increase productivity or efficiency.
4. Christmas gifts, excluding noncash gifts of nominal value.
5. Commissions as compensation for covered employment.
6. Contributions by an employer to a supplemental unemployment individual-account plan to which the employee has a fully vested and nonforfeitable right.
7. Dismissal payments.
8. Employer contributions to cash or deferred arrangements to the extent that the contributions are not included in the employee's gross income.
9. Idle time and standby payments.
10. Payment by the employer of the employee's FICA tax or the employee's share of any state unemployment compensation tax without deduction from the employee's wages.
11. Payments representing compensation for services by an employee paid to the dependents after an employee's death. Payments in the nature of a gratuity rather than compensation for services are nontaxable. Any payments made by an employer to an employee's estate or to the employee's survivors after the calendar year in which the employee died are excluded from the definition of wages and thus may not be taxed.
12. Payments to employees or their dependents on account of sickness or accident disability. These payments are *not* taxable after the expiration of six months following the last calendar month in which the employee worked. Payments for work missed due to pregnancy are not classified as taxable wages during the first six months of absence.
13. Payments under a guaranteed annual wage plan.
14. Retroactive wage increases.
15. Tips, including charged tips, reported by the employee to the employer.
16. Transfer of stock by an employer to the employees as remuneration for services. (The fair market value of the stock at the time of payment is the taxable base.)
17. Vacation pay.

Nontaxable Wages for Unemployment Purposes

1. Advances or reimbursement of ordinary and necessary business expenses incurred in the business of the employer.
2. Allowances made to an individual by a prospective employer for expenses incurred in connection with interviews for possible employment.
3. Bonuses under a supplemental compensation plan paid upon retirement, death, or disability of an employee.
4. Caddy fees.
5. Commissions paid to insurance agents and solicitors who are paid solely by commission. Such persons are classified as independent contractors, not employees.

6. Courtesy discounts to employees and their families.

7. Educational assistance payments to workers.

8. Payments made by an employer under a plan established by the employer for health, accident, or life insurance, or retirement benefits on behalf of the employees or their dependents.

9. Reimbursement of an employee's moving expenses if, at the time of payment, it is reasonable to believe that the employee will be entitled to a deduction for those expenses at the time of filing their federal income tax return.

10. Retirement pay.

11. Strike benefits paid by a union to its members.

12. Value of meals and lodging furnished employees for the convenience of the employer.

13. Workers' compensation payments.

Perez Company paid wages of $515,000 for the year. Included in the payments was $250,000 paid to hourly employees over the $7,000 limit for each employee. The only employees who were not paid hourly were the president and vice president who were paid $125,000 and $90,000, respectively. Included in the wages was a payment of $2,000 to a director who only attended director meetings. Since the FUTA wage limit is $7,000 per employee, Perez Company would pay a FUTA tax on $62,000 [$515,000 − $250,000 − $201,000 (president and vice president over the limit by $118,000 and $83,000, respectively) − $2,000 (director's pay)].

Example 5-2

Wages—SUTA

The definition of taxable wages is fairly uniform under the various state unemployment compensation laws. However, some variations exist among the states as to the status of particular kinds of payments. For example, about one-sixth of the states have ruled that Christmas bonuses or gifts are "wages" when substantial, contractual, or based on a percentage of the employee's wages or length of service. New Hampshire, however, does not include gifts or gratuities of $25 or less as wages, unless paid under a contract related to past or future employment. A further variation in defining taxable wages among the states arises in the treatment of **dismissal payments**. Generally, such payments are considered wages whether or not the employer must legally make the payments. However, in some states (e.g., Kentucky), dismissal payments under a plan established for all employees or for a class of employees do not constitute wages. Puerto Rico does not consider any type of dismissal payment to be wages, nor are tips considered taxable wages.

Unemployment Compensation Taxes and Credits

The base of the unemployment compensation tax is **wages paid** rather than **wages payable**. Thus, an employer is liable for the unemployment compensation tax in the year in which wages are paid employees, not necessarily in the year in which the services are rendered. Thus, if an employee performs services in 2022 but is not paid for them until 2023, the employer is liable for the tax in 2023, and the 2023 tax rates apply. Wages are considered paid when actually paid or when **constructively paid**. Wages are considered constructively paid when credited to the account of, or set apart for, an employee so that they may be drawn upon at any time, even though they are not actually possessed by the employee.

Successor employers can include payments against the FUTA wage base that predecessor employers made to the employees who continue to work for the new employer. The predecessor employer must have been an employer for FUTA tax purposes.

Tax Rate—FUTA

Under FUTA, all employers, as defined earlier, are subject to a tax with respect to having individuals in their employ. The employer's tax rate is 6.0 percent of the first $7,000 wages paid each employee during the calendar year. Thus, an employer is liable for the FUTA tax on wages paid each employee until the employee's wages reach the $7,000 level. If an employee has more than one employer during the current year, the taxable wage base *applies separately* to each of those employers, unless one employer has transferred the business to the second.

Example 5-3

During this year, an employer had charged the wages account for $79,850. Of this amount, $720 will not be paid until the first payday in the next year. Further, the wages actually paid to employees in this year in excess of $7,000 each amounted to $29,840. The gross FUTA tax imposed on the employer is computed as follows:

Total amount charged to wages during this year		$79,850.00
Less:		
Wages not to be paid until the next year	$ 720	
Wages paid in excess of $7,000 limit	29,840	30,560.00
Total taxable wages		$49,290.00
Rate of tax		× 6.0%
Amount of gross FUTA tax		$ 2,957.40

LO 3

Compute the federal unemployment tax, the credit against the tax, and any credit reductions that might apply.

Credits Against FUTA Tax

The actual FUTA tax paid is usually only *0.6 percent,* since employers are entitled to a credit against their FUTA tax liability for contributions made under approved state unemployment compensation laws. The state unemployment taxes must have been paid in full, on time, and on all the same wages as are subject to the FUTA tax (as long as the state is not a **credit reduction state**, see page 5-12). The maximum credit permitted is 5.4 percent (90% of 6%). Thus, in the preceding example where the **gross** FUTA tax rate is 6.0 percent, the **net** FUTA rate would be 0.6 percent if the full 5.4 percent credit applied. Even if employers pay a SUTA rate of less than 5.4 percent, they still get the full credit against the FUTA tax.

Example 5-4

Total taxable earnings (above example)		$49,290.00
Net rate of tax (6.0% − 5.4%)		× 0.6%
Amount of net FUTA tax		$ 295.74

 On the Job

Eighty percent of the FUTA tax paid goes to pay federal (4 percent) and state (76 percent) administrative costs. The other 20 percent goes into an extended unemployment benefits account.

To obtain the maximum credit of 5.4 percent against the federal tax, the employer must make the state contributions on or before the due date for filing the annual return under FUTA (see page 5-28)—January 31 of the following year. If the employer is late in paying the state contributions, the credit is limited to 90 percent of the amount of the deposit that would have been allowed as a credit if the late contributions had been paid on time.

Example 5-5

Sutcliffe Company had taxable wages totaling $87,500. During the year, the company paid some of its state contributions after the January 31 cutoff of the following year. The penalty for tardiness is shown in the following calculation of the firm's net FUTA tax:

Amount of gross FUTA tax ($87,500 × 6.0%)..		$ 5,250.00
State taxable wages..	$87,500	
Sutcliffe's SUTA tax rate	× 5.4%	
Sutcliffe's SUTA tax..	$ 4,725	

Breakdown of Sutcliffe's SUTA tax payments:

Before 1/31 cutoff—$3,000 × 100% credit	(3,000.00)
After 1/31 cutoff—$1,725 × 90% credit..	(1,552.50)
Amount of net FUTA tax	$ 697.50

If the company had made timely payments of its state contributions, the amount of its net FUTA tax would have been reduced to $525, for a savings of $172.50, as follows:

Amount of gross FUTA tax ($87,500 × 6.0%)..		$ 5,250.00
Total taxable wages	$87,500	
Credit against tax..	× 5.4%	
Total credit..		4,725.00
Amount of net FUTA tax ($87,500 × 6.0%)...		$ 525.00

$697.50 − $525.00 = $172.50 savings

The credit against the FUTA tax for state contributions does not apply to any SUTA payments deducted from employees' pay and penalties and interest not included in the contribution rate assigned by the state.

Experience Rating

In some cases, employers may pay contributions into their state unemployment fund at a rate lower than 5.4 percent. The method by which the employer contributions may be adjusted because of a favorable employment record is referred to as **experience rating** or **merit rating**. Thus, an employer's favorable experience rate (employment record) qualifies the employer for a SUTA rate lower than 5.4 percent. As noted before, FUTA provides for a credit equal to the employer's SUTA rate plus an additional credit so that the **full 5.4 percent credit** still applies. In this way, employers who have steady employment histories, and therefore lower SUTA tax rates, are not penalized when the FUTA tax is paid.

Self-Study Quiz 5-1

Garo Company pays taxable wages (FUTA and SUTA) of $188,000. Garo Company has a state unemployment tax rate of 4.1 because of its past employment record. Compute Garo Company's FUTA and SUTA taxes.

    $_____ FUTA
    $_____ SUTA

Note: Answers to Self-Study Quizzes are on page 5-33.

If an employer receives an additional credit against the FUTA tax because the state experience rate is less than 5.4 percent, the additional credit is not subject to the 90 percent FUTA credit limitation for late SUTA payments. The credit reduction applies only to actual SUTA tax payments made after January 31 of the following year.

Example 5-6

Park Company has a $70,000 federal and state taxable payroll and has earned a reduced state tax rate of 4 percent. If none of its state tax payments are timely, the FUTA tax calculation is as follows:

Gross FUTA tax ($70,000 × 0.060)..		$4,200
Less 90% credit for state taxes paid late ($70,000 × 0.04 × 90%)............................	$2,520	
Less additional credit for state tax if rate were 5.4% [$70,000 × (0.054 − 0.04)]	980	
Total credit..		3,500
Net FUTA tax		$ 700

If Park Company had made its SUTA payments before the due date of Form 940, the credit for the payments (4%) and the additional credit (1.4%) would have provided a total credit of $3,780 and a FUTA tax savings of $280.

Where contributions are paid into more than one state unemployment compensation fund, the credit against the federal tax is still limited to 5.4 percent.

The contribution rate of Cruz Supply in Kansas is 5.5 percent and in Missouri, 2 percent. The credit against the gross FUTA tax on the wages paid is 5.4 percent in each state.

The unemployment compensation laws of certain states set the taxable wage base at a figure higher than the first $7,000 paid to each employee. For example, in Ohio, the wage base for 2022 was the first $9,000. In such states, the total contributions that the employer must pay into the state fund may exceed 5.4 percent of the taxable wages as established by FUTA (first $7,000 of each employee's earnings). However, the maximum credit that can be claimed against the gross FUTA tax for the state contributions is 5.4 percent of the first $7,000 of each individual employee's earnings.

Example 5-7

Shu Company located in Georgia had FUTA taxable wages of $130,000 and SUTA taxable wages (on first $9,500) were $210,000 with a 0.9 percent SUTA tax rate. The total unemployment taxes that Shu Company is liable for are:

$$\text{FUTA tax} - \$130,000 \times 0.6\% = \$ \ 780$$
$$\text{SUTA tax} - \$210,000 \times 0.9\% = 1,890$$
$$\text{Total unemployment taxes} = \underline{\$2,670}$$

Another reason that the net FUTA tax may be greater than 0.6 percent is the fact that some types of wages are not taxed by a particular state but are subject to the FUTA tax (e.g., group legal services in Arizona). In that case, the 5.4 percent credit can only be taken on the SUTA taxable wage amount.

Title XII Advances

States that experience financial difficulties and are unable to pay their unemployment compensation benefits may borrow funds from the federal government under Title XII of the Social Security Act. The states use these funds, called **Title XII advances**, to pay their regular unemployment benefits. Under the repayment provisions established by the federal government, if a state defaults in its payments, the credit against the gross FUTA tax is reduced by 0.3 percent beginning the **second taxable year after the advance**. This penalty increases by an additional 0.3 percent for each succeeding year in which there is a balance due the federal government. Thus, employers in those states have their gross FUTA tax rate increased by 0.3 percent the second year after the advance, then by 0.6 percent. The credit reduction is capped (0.6 percent) if certain solvency requirements are met by the state. The credit reduction can be avoided if the state repays the loan by November 10 of the year in which the reduction is scheduled to take effect. This additional FUTA tax is due with

the fourth-quarter deposit. In addition, a Benefit Cost Ratio (BCR) of 0.5 percent is added to the credit reduction beginning with the third or fourth consecutive year in which the federal loan has not been repaid and the credit reduction state's unemployment insurance rates do not meet the minimum federal levels.

At the beginning of 2022, only the Virgin Islands was affected by the credit reduction. The credit reduction was 4.1 percent.

Tax Rates—SUTA

Figure 5.1 presents a summary of each state's 2022 unemployment compensation laws, including the tax rates and the wage limitations.

The tax rate applied to each employer within a particular state yields the funds used by that state in paying benefits to its unemployed workers. Currently, all states have enacted **pooled-fund laws** as a basis for their unemployment insurance systems. By means of pooled funds, the cost of unemployment benefits is spread among all the employers in a particular state.

News Alert

At the start of 2022, there were 9 states that had outstanding FUTA loans. If not paid, the credit reductions of 0.3% will happen for 2022. Under the American Rescue Plan, states are now permitted to use Federal Recovery Funds not only to pay Title XII advances, but also to replenish their trust funds to pre-pandemic levels.

FIGURE 5.1

Summary of State Unemployment Compensation Laws (2022)
Warning: The provisions of the state laws are subject to change at any time.

State	Size of Firm (One employee in specified time and/or size of payroll[1])	Contributions (On first $7,000 unless otherwise indicated)		Benefits (Excluding dependency allowances)			
		Employer Min.–Max.	Employee	Waiting Period (weeks)	Max. per Week	Min. per Week	Max. Duration (weeks)
ALABAMA	20 weeks	0.65%–6.8% on first $8,000		none	$265	$ 45	26
ALASKA	any time	1.0%–5.4% on first $45,200	0.56% on first $45,200	1	370	56	26
ARIZONA	20 weeks	0.08%–20.93%**		1	240	60	26
ARKANSAS	10 days	0.3%–14.2% on first $10,000		1	451	81	26
CALIFORNIA	over $100 in any calendar quarter	1.5%–6.2%	1.1% on first $145,600	1	450	40	25

[1]This is $1,500 in any calendar quarter in current or preceding calendar year unless otherwise specified.
*2022 FUTA credit reduction state
**Allow voluntary contributions

FIGURE 5.1 (continued)

Summary of State Unemployment Compensation Laws (2022)

Warning: The provisions of the state laws are subject to change at any time.

State	Size of Firm (One employee in specified time and/or size of payroll[1])	Contributions (On first $7,000 unless otherwise indicated) Employer Min.–Max.	Employee	Waiting Period (weeks)	Max. per Week	Min. per Week	Max. Duration (weeks)
COLORADO	any time	0.75%–10.39% on first $17,000**		1	552	25	26
CONNECTICUT	20 weeks	1.9%–6.8% on first $15,000		none	631	15	26
DELAWARE	20 weeks	0.3%–8.2% on first $14,500		none	400	20	26
DISTRICT OF COLUMBIA	any time	1.9%–7.4% on first $9,000		1	444	50	26
FLORIDA	20 weeks	0.1%–5.4%		1	275	32	23
GEORGIA	20 weeks	0.04%–7.56% on first $9,500**		none	365	55	26
HAWAII	any time	0.2%–5.8% on first $51,600	0.5% of maximum weekly wages of $1,200.30 not to exceed $6.00 per week (disability ins)	1	648	5	26
IDAHO	20 weeks or $300 in any calendar quarter	0.252%–5.4% on first $46,500		1	410	72	26
ILLINOIS	20 weeks	0.725%–7.625% on first $12,960		1	449	51	25
INDIANA	20 weeks	0.5%–7.4% on first $9,500**		1	390	50	26
IOWA	20 weeks	0.0%–7.5% on first $34,800		none	531	79	26
KANSAS	20 weeks	0.2%–7.6% on first $14,000**		1	469	117	26
KENTUCKY	20 weeks	0.5%–9.5% on first $11,100**		none	569	39	26
LOUISIANA	20 weeks	0.09%–6.2% on first $7,700**		1	247	10	26
MAINE	20 weeks	0.49%–5.481% on first $12,000**		1	418	71	26
MARYLAND	any time	1.0%–10.5% on first $8,500		none	430	25	26
MASSACHUSETTS	13 weeks	0.94%–14.37% on first $15,000**		1	795	31	30
MICHIGAN	20 weeks or $1,000 in calendar year	0.06%–10.3% on first $9,500		none	362	81	20
MINNESOTA	20 weeks	0.5%–8.9% on first $38,000**		1	693	38	26
MISSISSIPPI	20 weeks	0.2%–5.6% on first $14,000		1	235	30	26
MISSOURI	20 weeks	0.0%–5.4% on first $11,000		1	320	48	26
MONTANA	Over $1,000 in current or preceding year	0.13%–6.3% on first $38,100		1	552	163	28
NEBRASKA	20 weeks	0.0%–5.4% on first $9,000**		1	414	30	26
NEVADA	$225 in any quarter	0.25%–5.4% on first $36,600		none	426	16	26
NEW HAMPSHIRE	20 weeks	0.1%–7.0% on first $14,000		none	427	32	20
NEW JERSEY	$1,000 in any year	0.5%–5.8% on first $39,800**	0.705% (0.14% for disability ins; 0.565% for unempl. Comp/family leave/workforce development funds) on first $39,800	1	731	73	26
NEW MEXICO	20 weeks or $450 in any quarter	0.33%–6.4% on first $28,700		1	442	82	26

[1]This is $1,500 in any calendar quarter in current or preceding calendar year unless otherwise specified.
*2022 FUTA credit reduction state
**Allow voluntary contributions

FIGURE 5.1 (concluded)
Summary of State Unemployment Compensation Laws (2022)
Warning: The provisions of the state laws are subject to change at any time.

State	Size of Firm (One employee in specified time and/or size of payroll[1])	Contributions (On first $7,000 unless otherwise indicated) Employer Min.–Max.	Employee	Waiting Period (weeks)	Max. per Week	Min. per Week	Max. Duration (weeks)
NEW YORK	$300 in any quarter	0.6%–7.9% on first $12,000**	0.5%-limit $0.60 weekly	1	420	100	26
NORTH CAROLINA	20 weeks	0.06%–5.76% on first $28,000**		1	350	46	26
NORTH DAKOTA	20 weeks	0.08%–9.69% on first $38,400**		1	640	43	26
OHIO	20 weeks	0.3%–9.7% on first $9,000**		1	443	111	26
OKLAHOMA	20 weeks	0.3%–7.5% on first $24,800		1	539	16	26
OREGON	20 weeks	0.9%–5.4% on first $47,700		1	590	138	26
PENNSYLVANIA	18 weeks or $225 in any quarter	1.2905%–9.9333% on first $10,000**	0.06% on total wages	1	573	35	26
PUERTO RICO	any time	1.2%–5.4%	0.3% on first $9,000 (disability ins)	1	133	7	26
RHODE ISLAND	any time	1.2%–9.59% on first $24,600**	1.3% on first $81,500 (disability ins)	1	599	58	26
SOUTH CAROLINA	any time	0.06%–5.46% on first $14,000		1	326	42	26
SOUTH DAKOTA	20 weeks	0.0%–9.3% on first $15,000**		1	402	28	26
TENNESSEE	20 weeks	0.01%–10.0%		1	275	30	26
TEXAS	20 weeks	0.36%–6.36% on first $9,000**		1	535	70	26
UTAH	$140 in calendar quarter in current or preceding calendar year	0.3%–7.3% on first $41,600		1	543	25	26
VERMONT	20 weeks	0.8%–6.5% on first $15,500		1	583	59	26
VIRGIN ISLANDS*	any time	2.5% on first $30,800		1	505	33	26
VIRGINIA	20 weeks	0.33%–6.43% on first $8,00		1	378	60	26
WASHINGTON	any time	0.033%–6.02% on first $62,500		1	929	295	26
WEST VIRGINIA	20 weeks	1.5%–8.5% on first $12,000**		1	424	24	26
WISCONSIN	20 weeks	0.0%–12.0% on first $14,000**		none	370	54	26
WYOMING	$500 in current or preceding calendar year	0.48%–9.78% on first $27,700		1	489	33	26

Source: *Payroll Guide*, published by Thomson Reuters.

[1]This is $1,500 in any calendar quarter in current or preceding calendar year unless otherwise specified.
*2022 FUTA credit reduction state
**Allow voluntary contributions

Employer Contributions

Every state has its own unemployment compensation law with varying tax rates and taxable wage bases.

Example 5-8

Tell Me More

1. Iqbal Company of Georgia had a FUTA taxable payroll of $215,600 and a SUTA taxable payroll of $255,700 with a 5.6 percent SUTA tax rate. The company would pay unemployment taxes of:

   FUTA $215,600 × 0.006 = $ 1,293.60
   SUTA $255,700 × 0.056 = 14,319.20
   Total taxes $15,612.80

2. Kresloff Company has only two employees and is located in a state that has set an unemployment tax for the company of 4.8 percent on the first $12,000 of each employee's earnings. Both employees are paid the same amount each week ($900) and have earned $11,500 up to this week's pay. The unemployment taxes that the company must pay for this week's pay would be $48.

   FUTA tax (both over $7,000) = $0.00
   SUTA tax ($1,000 × 0.048) = $48
   ($500 of each employee's pay is under the state taxable limit of $12,000)

As with FUTA tax, if an employee has more than one employer during the year, the taxable wage base (same state) or bases (different states) applies separately to each employer.

To minimize the impact of unemployment insurance taxes on newly covered employers, each state sets an initial contribution rate for new employers that will apply for a specific period of time. During this period of time, the new employer's employment record can be developed and an experience rating can later be established. A state may assign a contribution rate of not less than 1 percent to newly covered employers on some "reasonable basis" other than employment experience. Once the new employer has accumulated the experience required under the provisions of the state law, a new rate will be assigned. For example, Oklahoma applies 1.5 percent to new employers.

Employee Contributions

Some states, as shown in Figure 5.1, impose a contributions requirement on employees in addition to the contributions made by the employer.

Example 5-9

1. Fay Nannen earns $320 during the first week of February while working for Dango, Inc. Since the company is located in New Jersey, Nannen would have $2.26 deducted from her pay (0.705% of $320). This 0.705% percent tax would be deducted on the first $39,800 paid to her during the year. (In New Jersey, 0.14 percent of the employees' contributions is for the disability benefit plan and 0.565 percent for the unemployment insurance/family leave funds.)

2. Jose Salvador works in Puerto Rico and earns $450 each week. He would contribute $1.35 (0.3% of $450) of each pay to a disability fund. This 0.3 percent deduction would continue until his cumulative pay for the year reached $9,000.

Self-Study Quiz 5-2

Moss Company paid wages of $6,000 to John Castellano in Arizona. During the year, Castellano transferred to the company's office in Colorado, and he received $26,000 for the rest of the year. The company's unemployment tax rate for Colorado is 2.9%. What would Moss Company pay to Colorado for unemployment taxes on Castellano's wages? $_____

Experience Rating

As indicated earlier, the concept of experience rating is based upon the payment of state unemployment taxes according to the employer's stability of employment. As an employer experiences a lower employee turnover, generally the state unemployment tax rate will lower.

In all states, some type of experience-rating plan provides for a reduction in the employer's tax contributions based on the employer's experience with the risk of unemployment. There are four distinct systems: (1) reserve-ratio, (2) benefit-ratio, (3) benefit-wage-ratio, and (4) payroll variation formulas. Each measures every employer's experience with unemployment or benefit expenditures and compares this amount with a measure of exposure (usually payroll) to establish the relative experience of each employer. The most commonly used is the **reserve-ratio formula**:

$$\text{Reserve Ratio} = \frac{\text{Contributions} - \text{Benefits Paid}}{\text{Average Payroll}}$$

The amount of the unemployment compensation contributions (taxes paid), the benefits paid by the state, and the employer's payroll are entered by the state on each employer's record. The benefits paid are subtracted from the contributions, and the balance of the employer's account is divided by the average payroll for a stated period of time to determine the reserve ratio. Under this plan, the balance carried forward each year equals the difference between the employer's total contributions and the total benefits paid to former employees by the state. The contribution rates are then established according to a schedule under which the higher the reserve ratio, the lower the tax rate.

Employers who have built up a balance in their reserve account (contributions paid in less benefits charged) are sometimes referred to as **positive-balance employers**. The larger the positive balance in a company's reserve account, the lower its tax rate will be. Employers whose reserve accounts have been charged for more benefits paid out than contributions paid in are referred to as **negative-balance employers**, and their high tax rates reflect this fact.

Computing the Contribution Rate

In an experience-rating system, the rate of contributions for employers is based on the employment experience of the employer. The rate is determined by computing the total of the reserve built up by employer contributions over a certain period of time and by computing the ratio of the amount in the reserve account to the employer's average annual payroll as determined under the state's formula.

> **LO 4**
>
> Describe how an experience-rating system is used in determining employers' contributions to state unemployment compensation funds.

Example 5-10

Spencili Company is an employer located in a state with an unemployment compensation law containing merit-rating provisions for employers who meet certain requirements. Below is a summary of the total wages for the years 2019 to 2022, inclusive. For the purpose of the illustration, assume that the total wages and taxable wages are the same amount.

Quarter	2019	2020	2021	2022
1st	$11,000	$10,000	$ 8,500	$10,500
2nd	10,000	9,000	9,500	11,000
3rd	10,000	9,500	10,000	11,000
4th	10,500	9,750	9,500	9,500
Total	$41,500	$38,250	$37,500	$42,000

The State Unemployment Compensation Commission maintains a separate account for each employer. The account is credited with contributions paid into the unemployment compensation fund by the employer and is charged with unemployment benefits paid from the fund.

For 2023, the state law set up the following contribution rate schedule for employers:

Reserve Ratio	Rate
Negative reserve balance	6.7%
0% to less than 8%	5.9%
8% to less than 10%	5.0%
10% to less than 12%	4.1%
12% to less than 15%	3.2%
15% and over	2.5%

The state law under discussion defines: *average annual payroll*—average of last three years, *annual payroll*—wages paid from October 1 to September 30 each year.

The following computations show the state contributions made by Spencili Company for the calendar years 2019 to 2022 inclusive, the federal tax imposed under FUTA, and the method of arriving at the contribution rate for the calendar year 2023:

2019

Taxable wages..	$41,500	
Rate (SUTA)..	× 2.7%	
State contributions		$1,120.50
Federal tax: 0.6% of $41,500		249.00
Total unemployment tax..		$1,369.50

2020

Taxable wages..	$38,250	
Rate (SUTA)..	× 2.7%	
State contributions..		$1,032.75
Federal tax: 0.6% of $38,250		229.50
Total unemployment tax..		$1,262.25

2021

Taxable wages..	$37,500	
Rate (SUTA)	× 3.4%	
State contributions..		$1,275.00
Federal tax: 0.6% of $37,500		225.00
Total unemployment tax..		$1,500.00

2022

Taxable wages..	$42,000	
Rate (SUTA)..	× 3.7%	
State contributions..		$1,554.00
Federal tax: 0.6% of $42,000		252.00
Total unemployment tax..		$1,806.00

Remember that the average annual payroll is the average of the last three annual payrolls, with each annual payroll period running from October 1 to September 30.

Assume that Spencili Company paid state contributions of $960 in 2017 and $1,010 in 2018 and that $1,850 was charged to the employer's account for unemployment compensation benefits during 2021 and 2022. The contribution rate for 2023 is computed as follows:

Computation of rate for 2022:

Annual payroll period ending 9/30/20	$ 39,000
Annual payroll period ending 9/30/21	37,750
Annual payroll period ending 9/30/22	42,000
Total of last 3 annual payroll periods...	$118,750

Average annual payroll:

$$\$118,750 \div 3 = \$39,583$$

Contributions for 2017	$ 960.00
Contributions for 2018	1,010.00
Contributions for 2019	1,120.50
Contributions for 2020	1,032.75
Contributions for 2021	1,275.00
Contributions for 2022 (first nine months)..	1,202.50
Total contributions...	$6,600.75
Less amount of benefits paid..	1,850.00
Balance in reserve account 9/30/22	$4,750.75

$$\$4,750.75 \div \text{Average annual payroll, } \$39,583 = 12\%$$

Since the reserve is 12 percent of the average annual payroll, the tax rate for 2023 is 3.2 percent (the ratio is between 12% and 15%).

Voluntary Contributions

Tell Me More

In some states (see Figure 5.1, on pages 5-13 to 5-15), employers may obtain reduced unemployment compensation rates by making **voluntary contributions** to the state fund. Employers deliberately make these contributions in addition to their regularly required payments of state unemployment taxes. In reserve ratio states, voluntary contributions increase the balance in the employer's reserve account so that a lower contribution rate may be assigned for the following year. Thus, the new lower tax rate will save the employer more in future state unemployment tax payments than the amount of the voluntary contribution itself. New employers must have a minimum experience rating period before the employer can make a voluntary contribution.

An employer who desires to make a voluntary contribution usually must determine the amount of the contribution needed in order to obtain a lower contribution rate. In some states, the agencies provide worksheets that aid employers in determining the amount of voluntary contributions required. Ohio computes the voluntary contribution amount needed and includes it in the rate notices sent to all employers. As with the regular contributions, the state must receive the voluntary contributions by a certain date before they can be credited to the employer's account and be used in computing a new tax rate. In some states, the employer may have a certain number of days following the mailing of the tax rate notice to make the voluntary contributions. For instance, in Texas, the voluntary contributions must be paid within 60 days of the tax rate notice mailing in December.

News Alert

If there are unpaid taxes and penalties due, states may apply the voluntary contributions to these amounts first.

Example 5-11

To illustrate the tax saving that may be realized as a result of making voluntary contributions, consider the following case of Krane Company, which is subject to the unemployment compensation law of a state that uses the reserve-ratio formula to determine experience ratings. The following contribution rate schedule applies for 2024:

Reserve Ratio	Rate
0% to less than 1%	6.2%
1% to less than 1.4%	5.6%
1.4% to less than 1.8%	5.0%
1.8% to less than 2.2%	4.4%
2.2% to less than 2.6%	3.8%
2.6% to less than 3.0%	3.2%
3.0% and over	2.6%

For the three 12-month periods ending on June 30, 2023, the company had an average annual taxable payroll of $330,000. This is the base that the state uses as the average payroll. As of June 30, 2023, the credits to the employer's account exceeded the benefits paid by $6,800. Thus, the 2023 reserve ratio is 2.06 percent ($6,800 ÷ $330,000), which would result in the assignment of a 4.4 percent tax rate, as shown in the preceding table. If the employer's 2024 total taxable payroll were $390,000, the SUTA contribution would amount to $17,160.

If Krane Company makes a voluntary contribution into the state fund within the time period specified by the state law, the tax for 2024 will be less. For example, if the company contributes $460, the reserve ratio will be 2.2 percent ($7,260 ÷ $330,000). As a result, the tax rate will be reduced to 3.8 percent, with the following savings realized in 2024:

Tax payment with no voluntary contribution (4.4% × $390,000)		$17,160
Tax payment with voluntary contribution	$ 460	
Reserve ratio (3.8% 3 $390,000)	14,820	15,280
Tax savings		$ 1,880

Since these payments are not required payments, these voluntary contributions do not count as part of the credit against the FUTA tax.

Terminating Liability

Generally, an employer remains liable for two years—the year in which the employer first met the state's requirement and through the following year.

In order to terminate liability, an employer must file an application by the date set by the state's law. The employer's liability will end as of January 1 of any year if, during the preceding year, the employer did not employ the required number of employees for the required time, or did not have the dollar amount of payroll necessary to be covered. In most states, coverage cannot be terminated if the employer is subject to FUTA.

Nonprofits

A federal law allows nonprofits the option to reimburse the state for the actual amount of unemployment benefits paid to their former employees, instead of paying a set percentage for state unemployment taxes. The reimbursement takes place on a dollar-for-dollar basis when the state pays the benefits to the former employees.

Dumping

The **SUTA Dumping Prevention Act** requires states to enact laws that stop businesses from changing their business structure to avoid paying their proper amount of SUTA taxes. This law is designed to stop companies with poor experience ratings from forming new companies with lower new employer tax rates and then transferring the employees to the new company ("dumping" the original company's high tax rates).

Unemployment Compensation Reports Required of the Employer

Employers liable for both the FUTA and the SUTA tax must file periodic reports with both the federal and the state governments. For FUTA tax reporting, employers file an annual return (Form 940) and generally make quarterly tax payments. Also, employers covered by state unemployment compensation laws generally submit two major kinds of reports. One is a tax return, on which the employer reports the tax due the state. The other is a wage report, which reflects the amount of taxable wages paid to each of the employer's covered employees.

Annual FUTA Return—Form 940

Form 940, Employer's Annual Federal Unemployment (FUTA) Tax Return, is the prescribed form for making the return required of employers in reporting the tax imposed under FUTA. Figure 5.2, on pages 5-23 and 5-24, shows a filled-in copy of this form.

LO 5

Complete the reports required by the Federal Unemployment Tax Act.

On the Job

Business name changes must be sent to the IRS office where the returns are filed. If it is a change in the business address or responsible party, Form 8822-B must be completed and mailed.

FIGURE 5.2
Form 940, Employer's Annual Federal Unemployment (FUTA) Tax Return

Form **940 for 20--:** **Employer's Annual Federal Unemployment (FUTA) Tax Return**
Department of the Treasury — Internal Revenue Service

OMB No. 1545-0028

Employer identification number (EIN) 0 0 – 0 0 0 0 3 2 0

Name (not your trade name) SHANNON HEATING COMPANY

Trade name (if any)

Address P.O. BOX 1803
Number   Street   Suite or room number

LANSDOWNE   PA   19019-3636
City   State   ZIP code

Foreign country name   Foreign province/county   Foreign postal code

Type of Return
(Check all that apply.)
☐ **a.** Amended
☐ **b.** Successor employer
☐ **c.** No payments to employees in 20--
☐ **d.** Final: Business closed or stopped paying wages

Go to *www.irs.gov/Form940* for instructions and the latest information.

Read the separate instructions before you complete this form. Please type or print within the boxes.

Part 1: **Tell us about your return. If any line does NOT apply, leave it blank. See instructions before completing Part 1.**

1a If you had to pay state unemployment tax in one state only, enter the state abbreviation . **1a**

1b If you had to pay state unemployment tax in more than one state, you are a multi-state employer . **1b** ☒ Check here. Complete Schedule A (Form 940).

2 If you paid wages in a state that is subject to CREDIT REDUCTION . **2** ☐ Check here. Complete Schedule A (Form 940).

Part 2: **Determine your FUTA tax before adjustments. If any line does NOT apply, leave it blank.**

3 Total payments to all employees . **3** 122534 ▪ 29

4 Payments exempt from FUTA tax . **4** 4300 ▪ 00

Check all that apply: **4a** ☐ Fringe benefits **4c** ☒ Retirement/Pension **4e** ☐ Other
4b ☐ Group-term life insurance **4d** ☐ Dependent care

5 Total of payments made to each employee in excess of $7,000 . **5** 21017 ▪ 62

6 Subtotal (line 4 + line 5 = line 6) . **6** 25317 ▪ 62

7 Total taxable FUTA wages (line 3 – line 6 = line 7). See instructions . **7** 97216 ▪ 67

8 FUTA tax before adjustments (line 7 x 0.006 = line 8) . **8** 583 ▪ 30

Part 3: **Determine your adjustments. If any line does NOT apply, leave it blank.**

9 If ALL of the taxable FUTA wages you paid were excluded from state unemployment tax, multiply line 7 by 0.054 (line 7 × 0.054 = line 9). Go to line 12 . **9** ▪

10 If SOME of the taxable FUTA wages you paid were excluded from state unemployment tax, OR you paid ANY state unemployment tax late (after the due date for filing Form 940), complete the worksheet in the instructions. Enter the amount from line 7 of the worksheet . **10** ▪

11 If credit reduction applies, enter the total from Schedule A (Form 940) . **11** ▪

Part 4: **Determine your FUTA tax and balance due or overpayment. If any line does NOT apply, leave it blank.**

12 Total FUTA tax after adjustments (lines 8 + 9 + 10 + 11 = line 12) . **12** 583 ▪ 30

13 FUTA tax deposited for the year, including any overpayment applied from a prior year . **13** 562 ▪ 20

14 Balance due. If line 12 is more than line 13, enter the excess on line 14.
• If line 14 is more than $500, you must deposit your tax.
• If line 14 is $500 or less, you may pay with this return. See instructions . **14** 21 ▪ 10

15 Overpayment. If line 13 is more than line 12, enter the excess on line 15 and check a box below **15** ▪

▶ You **MUST** complete both pages of this form and **SIGN** it. Check one: ☐ Apply to next return. ☐ Send a refund.

Next ▶

For Privacy Act and Paperwork Reduction Act Notice, see the back of the Payment Voucher.   Cat. No. 11234O   Form **940** (2021)

FIGURE 5.2 (concluded)

Form 940, Employer's Annual Federal Unemployment (FUTA) Tax Return

---

Name *(not your trade name)*	**Employer identification number (EIN)**
SHANNON HEATING COMPANY	00-0000320

Part 5:   Report your FUTA tax liability by quarter only if line 12 is more than $500. If not, go to Part 6.

16   Report the amount of your FUTA tax liability for each quarter; do NOT enter the amount you deposited. If you had no liability for a quarter, leave the line blank.

     16a   **1st quarter** (January 1 – March 31) . . . .   **16a**   203 ∎ 42

     16b   **2nd quarter** (April 1 – June 30) . . . .   **16b**   259 ∎ 95

     16c   **3rd quarter** (July 1 – September 30) . . . .   **16c**   98 ∎ 83

     16d   **4th quarter** (October 1 – December 31) . . . .   **16d**   21 ∎ 10

17   **Total tax liability for the year** (lines 16a + 16b + 16c + 16d = line 17) **17**   583 ∎ 30   **Total must equal line 12.**

Part 6:   May we speak with your third-party designee?

Do you want to allow an employee, a paid tax preparer, or another person to discuss this return with the IRS? See the instructions for details.

☐ **Yes.**   Designee's name and phone number

            Select a 5-digit Personal Identification Number (PIN) to use when talking to IRS

☒ **No.**

Part 7:   Sign here. You MUST complete both pages of this form and SIGN it.

Under penalties of perjury, I declare that I have examined this return, including accompanying schedules and statements, and to the best of my knowledge and belief, it is true, correct, and complete, and that no part of any payment made to a state unemployment fund claimed as a credit was, or is to be, deducted from the payments made to employees. Declaration of preparer (other than taxpayer) is based on all information of which preparer has any knowledge.

✗ Sign your name here	*J.D. Shannon*	Print your name here	J.D.SHANNON
		Print your title here	PRESIDENT
Date	1/31/--	Best daytime phone	(215) 555 - 1234

Paid Preparer Use Only   Check if you are self-employed ☐

Preparer's name		PTIN	
Preparer's signature		Date	/ /
Firm's name (or yours if self-employed)		EIN	
Address		Phone	
City		State	ZIP code

Source: Internal Revenue Service.

FIGURE 5.3

Sources of Information for Completing Form 940

Line No.	Source of Information
Part 1—About Your Return	
1	State unemployment tax forms
Part 2—Determine Your FUTA Tax	
3	General ledger account(s) for wages and salaries
4	Employee information files
5	Employee earnings records
6	Follow directions for addition.
7	Follow directions for subtraction.
8	Follow directions for multiplication.
Part 3—Determine Your Adjustments	
9 and 10	From the appropriate states' unemployment tax returns
11	From the total on Schedule A
Part 4—Determine Your FUTA Tax	
12	Follow directions for addition.
13	From the debit postings to the FUTA taxes payable account in the general ledger
14, 15	Difference between lines 12 and 13
Part 5—FUTA Tax Liability for Each Quarter	
16	From the quarterly balances in the FUTA taxes payable account in the general ledger
17	Follow directions for addition.
Part 6—Third-Party Designee	
	Check the yes or no box.
Part 7—Sign Here	
	Sign, date, and list phone number.

Figure 5.3 provides sources of information for completing the form. If an employer who is not liable for FUTA tax receives a Form 940, check Box c in the top corner of the form and sign and return the form to the IRS.

Electronic Filing

Employers can also electronically file Form 940 through their payroll service provider (if they offer this service). In addition, the government provides a Web-based Internet system through which taxpayers enter data directly into IRS-approved software. The IRS e-file can be used to file Form 940 and e-pay (electronic funds withdrawal) the balance due in a single step.

Tell Me More

Completing the Return

In making entries on the form:

    a. Dollar signs and decimal points—not used (commas optional).

    b. Zero value line—leave blank.

    c. Negative amounts—use "minus" sign.

    d. Rounding—is optional and can be done to the nearest dollar for all entries.

Part 1

    1a. Employers who pay SUTA tax to only one state enter that state (use the two-letter, U.S. Postal Service abbreviation) in this box. If more than one state, check Box 1b.

    2. Employers who paid wages in a "credit reduction" state would check this box.

Part 2

Many of the entries are self-explanatory. The taxable wages adjustments relate to:

4. Some payments that are not included in the FUTA definition of "wages" or services that are not included in the definition of "employment" are entered here. Some of these payments would include the value of certain meals and lodging, contributions to accident or health plans for employees, employer contributions to employees' qualified retirement plans, and payments to children under the age of 21 for services provided to their parent(s). This also applies to the value of group-term life insurance in excess of $50,000—Box 4b (taxable for FICA, federal income tax, but not FUTA). Check the appropriate box(es).

5. Enter the total of the payments over $7,000 that were paid to each employee after subtracting exempt payments (line 4).

Part 3

Adjustments made to the FUTA tax:

9. If all the wages paid were excluded from state unemployment tax (e.g., wages were paid to employees in a specific excluded occupation), the employer must pay a 6.0 percent FUTA tax.

10. If this applies, the attached worksheet must be completed and the step-by-step process will determine the credit.

11. If the FUTA taxable wages were also subject to state unemployment taxes, enter the amount from Schedule A.

Part 4

Complete lines 12 through 15 to determine the balance due or the overpayment, whichever applies. If a balance is due, depending on the amount of the liability, the employer either deposits, electronically transfers, or remits the balance due directly to the IRS with Form 940. Employers may now use a major credit card to pay the balance due on the form. This does not apply to the payment of the quarterly deposits made during the year (page 5-28).

Part 5

Complete this part only if line 12 is more than $500. Enter the tax liability for each quarter. If a credit reduction applies (line 11), the amount owed for the reduction must be included with the fourth quarter liability.

Part 6

Check the appropriate box. If YES is checked, complete the designee's information.

Part 7

Form 940 must be signed by:

1. The individual, if a sole proprietorship.

2. The president, vice president, or other principal officer, if a corporation.

3. A responsible and duly authorized member, if a partnership or other unincorporated organization.

4. A fiduciary, if a trust or an estate.

Officers and authorized agents may sign the return by rubber stamp, mechanical device, or computer software. In the case of an electronically filed form, a ten-digit personal identification number (PIN) will be used by the authorized signer to electronically sign the Form 940. This PIN is sent to the business once the authorized signer(s) of the Form 94x series have been approved by the IRS.

Paid preparers, who are not employees of the filing entity, must manually sign Form 940 and provide the information requested in the PAID PREPARER USE ONLY section of Part 7. This section does not have to be completed by the reporting agents who have a Form 8655 (Reporting Agent Authorization) on file with the IRS.

Schedule A

This schedule (Figure 5.4) is only completed by employers who were required to pay state unemployment taxes in more than one state or paid wages in a state that is subject to the credit reduction.

Enter an "X" in the box for the appropriate states. If the states are subject to a FUTA credit reduction, calculate the credit reduction (FUTA taxable wages for that state, multiplied by the state's credit reduction rate). At the bottom of the schedule, total the amount of the credit reductions and enter this amount on line 11 of Form 940. This schedule will then be submitted along with Form 940.

Filing the Return

The employer must file the annual return no later than January 31 following the close of the calendar year. If, however, the employer has made timely deposits that pay the FUTA tax liability in full, as discussed later, the company may delay the filing of Form 940 until February 10. The return must be filed on a calendar-year basis even though the company operates on a fiscal-year basis different from the calendar year. If January 31 or February 10 falls on Saturday, Sunday, or a legal holiday, the return may be filed on the following business day. A mailed return bearing a postmark indicating it was mailed on or before the due date will be considered to have been timely filed even though received after the due date.

Upon application of the employer, the district director or the director of a service center may grant a reasonable extension of time in which to file the return, but not for payment of the tax. However, no extension will be granted for a period of more than 90 days. Generally, the application for an extension must be written on or before the filing due date. The return must be filed with the IRS center for the district in which the employer's principal place of business or office or agency is located. The instructions for Form 940 list the addresses of the IRS centers.

Once an employer has filed Form 940, the IRS will send the employer a pre-addressed Form 940 near the close of each subsequent calendar year.

Amending the Return

When filing a corrected return, the employer must complete a new Form 940 for the year being amended. The "Amended" box on Form 940 should be checked, and the correct figures should be completed on the form. The return must be signed, and an explanation of the reasons for filing an amended return should be attached.

Final Return

If a company has ceased doing business, a final Form 940 must be completed (check box on Form 940 to indicate a final return) and the balance of the tax paid. In addition, a statement giving the name and address of the person(s) in charge of the required payroll records must be included with Form 940. If the business was sold or transferred, the name and address of the acquiring company should be included in the statement.

% | IRS Connection

The IRS has estimated the average time spent in preparing, copying, assembling, and sending Form 940 to be 21 minutes and 15 minutes for Schedule A.

FIGURE 5.4
Required Form for Multi-State Employers

Schedule A (Form 940) for 20--:

Multi-State Employer and Credit Reduction Information
Department of the Treasury — Internal Revenue Service

OMB No. 1545-0028

Employer identification number (EIN) 0 0 — 0 0 0 0 3 2 0

Name *(not your trade name)* SHANNON HEATING COMPANY

See the instructions on page 2. File this schedule with Form 940.

Place an "X" in the box of EVERY state in which you had to pay state unemployment tax this year. For the U.S. Virgin Islands, enter the FUTA taxable wages and the reduction rate (see page 2). Multiply the FUTA taxable wages by the reduction rate and enter the credit reduction amount. Don't include in the *FUTA Taxable Wages* box wages that were excluded from state unemployment tax (see the instructions for Step 2). If any states don't apply to you, leave them blank.

	Postal Abbreviation	FUTA Taxable Wages	Reduction Rate	Credit Reduction		Postal Abbreviation	FUTA Taxable Wages	Reduction Rate	Credit Reduction
	AK	.		.		NC	.		.
	AL	.		.		ND	.		.
	AR	.		.		NE	.		.
	AZ	.		.		NH	.		.
X	CA	.		.		NJ	.		.
	CO	.		.		NM	.		.
	CT	.		.		NV	.		.
	DC	.		.		NY	.		.
	DE	.		.		OH	.		.
	FL	.		.		OK	.		.
	GA	.		.		OR	.		.
	HI	.		.	X	PA	.		.
	IA	.		.		RI	.		.
	ID	.		.		SC	.		.
	IL	.		.		SD	.		.
	IN	.		.		TN	.		.
	KS	.		.		TX	.		.
	KY	.		.		UT	.		.
	LA	.		.		VA	.		.
	MA	.		.		VT	.		.
	MD	.		.		WA	.		.
	ME	.		.		WI	.		.
	MI	.		.		WV	.		.
	MN	.		.		WY	.		.
	MO	.		.		PR	.		.
	MS	.		.		VI	.		.
	MT	.		.					

Total Credit Reduction. Add all amounts shown in the *Credit Reduction* boxes. Enter the total here and on Form 940, line 11 . . . .

For Privacy Act and Paperwork Reduction Act Notice, see the Instructions for Form 940.   Cat. No. 16997C   Schedule A (Form 940) 2021

Source: Internal Revenue Service.

Quarterly Deposit—FUTA

The employer computes the net FUTA tax on a quarterly basis during the month following the end of each calendar quarter by multiplying 0.6 percent by that part of the first $7,000 of each of the employee's annual wages that the employer paid during the quarter. If the employer's tax liability exceeds $500, the employer must pay before the last day of the month following the end of the quarter. Amounts owed due to a credit reduction (Title VII advances) should be included with the fourth-quarter deposit. The employer is required to deposit all federal depository tax liabilities (including FUTA) electronically. Chapter 3 enumerated the requirements for each employer. In order to make timely payments, the Electronic Federal Tax Payment System (EFTPS) payment transaction must be initiated at least one business day before the due date of the deposit. Electronic deposits can also be made on the employer's behalf by an arrangement with a tax professional, financial institution, payroll service, or other trusted third party. In addition, the employer can provide for its financial institution to initiate a same-day wire payment.

A similar computation and payment for each of the first three quarters of the year is made. If the tax liability for the first quarter is $500 or less, a payment is not required; however, the employer must add the amount of the liability to the amount subject to payment for the next quarter in order to compare the total tax due with the $500 threshold for that quarter. Amounts owed due to a credit reduction (Title XII advances) should be included with the fourth-quarter deposit.

As stated in Chapter 3, businesses are required to make their federal tax deposits electronically unless they have $2,500 or less in quarterly tax liabilities and pay their liability when they file their returns.

As shown in Figure 5.2, on pages 5-22 and 5-23, the accumulated tax liabilities of Shannon Heating Company for the 1st and 2nd quarters were less than $500; no payment was made for the first two quarters. Since the accumulated liability at the end of the 3rd quarter exceeded the $500 limit, a payment of $562.20 was made on October 31.

At the time of filing the annual return on Form 940, the employer pays the balance of tax owed for the prior year and not yet paid. If the amount of tax reportable on Form 940 exceeds by more than $500 the sum of amounts deposited each quarter, the employer must pay the total amount owed electronically on or before January 31 following the year for which Form 940 is filed. If the amount owed is $500 or less, the employer may remit it with the annual form. A payment voucher form, Form 940V, is completed and filed along with Form 940 and the check or money order. This form allows the government to process the payment more efficiently. As already stated, e-pay or a major credit card or debit card can be used to pay the balance due on the return but cannot be used for the required quarterly deposits.

If the full amount cannot be paid, the employer can apply for an installment agreement online. The amount owed can be paid back in monthly installments, provided the amount owed is less than $25,000 and is paid back in full in 24 months. The employer will be charged a fee and be subject to penalties and interest on the amount not paid by the due date of Form 940. In case of an overpayment of the tax, employers can either apply the overpayment to next year's return or get a refund.

Taxes—Household Employers

Household employers both report and pay their federal unemployment taxes for their household employees with their personal income tax return (Form 1040). Schedule H, **Household Employment Taxes**, is attached to their tax returns, and payment of the unemployment taxes for the previous year is due by April 15. If there are other employees involved in addition to household employees, the employers can choose to include the household employees on their Form 940.

Self-Study Quiz 5-3

The FUTA taxable wages of Kamar Company during 2023 follow. List the amount and the due date of each deposit of FUTA taxes for the year—not in a credit reduction state.

	Amount	Due Date
1st Quarter—$66,000	$ _____	_____
2nd Quarter—$64,000	$ _____	_____
3rd Quarter—$42,000	$ _____	_____
4th Quarter—$25,000	$ _____	_____

Penalties—FUTA

As indicated in Chapter 3, the Internal Revenue Code subjects employers to civil and criminal penalties for failing to file returns, pay the employment taxes when due, and make timely deposits. These penalties apply, generally, without regard to the type of tax or return involved. The employer is responsible even if the duties of depositing taxes and filing the return have been outsourced. If the third party fails to perform any required action, the employer is still accountable. The last section of Chapter 3 presents all of the penalties.

Information Reports—SUTA

A wide variation exists in the official forms that the states provide for filing the reports required under the unemployment compensation laws. Therefore, the employer must become familiar with the law and regulations of each state in which liability might be incurred. In an increasing number of states, electronic filing of the reports and electronic payment of tax liabilities are required. For instance, Maryland requires filing online using their BEACON 2.0 system.[1]

The reports required of the employers by the individual states determine (1) the employer's liability for the contributions, (2) the amount of the contribution due on a quarterly basis, and (3) the amount of benefits to which employees will be entitled if they become unemployed. The most important of the required reports follow:

1. Status reports
2. Contribution reports
3. Wage information reports
4. Separation reports
5. Partial unemployment notices

> **LO 6**
>
> Describe the types of information reports under the various state unemployment compensation laws.

---

[1] BEACON 2.0 is an IT system that integrates all benefits, appeals, tax, and reemployment functions of the Maryland unemployment insurance system.

Status Reports

Under the unemployment compensation laws of most states, new employers must register or file an initial statement or **status report**. This report determines the employer's liability for making contributions into the state unemployment compensation fund.

Contribution Reports

All employers liable for contributions under the unemployment compensation law of any state must submit a quarterly **contribution report** or tax return. This report provides a summary of the wages paid during the period and shows the computation of the tax or contribution. Usually, the report must be filed on or before the last day of the month following the close of the calendar quarter, and the tax or contribution must be paid at the same time. Figure 5.5 shows an illustration of a quarterly tax calculation report (Part I).

Wage Information Reports

In most states, employers must make **wage information reports** concerning individual employees. Usually, employers file these reports with the quarterly contribution reports. Figure 5.6 shows an example of a quarterly wage information report (Part II). On the report are listed all employee names, SSNs, taxable wages, taxable tips, and the employer's federal account number. In addition, the number of credit weeks earned by each employee during the quarter could be required. (A *credit week* is defined by the state's unemployment compensation law; for example, Pennsylvania defines a credit week as any calendar week in the quarter during which the person earned remuneration of not less than $50.)

FIGURE 5.5

Pennsylvania Form, UC-2. Employer's Report for Unemployment Compensation—Part I

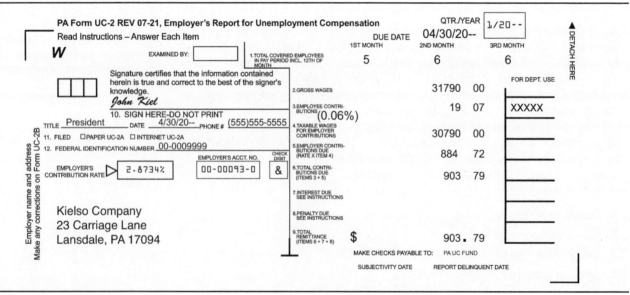

Source: PA Department of Labor & Industry.

FIGURE 5.6

Pennsylvania Form, UC-2A. Employers Report for Unemployment Compensation—Part II

pennsylvania
DEPARTMENT OF LABOR & INDUSTRY

**PA Form UC-2A, Employer's Quarterly
Report of Wages Paid to Each Employee**

See instructions on separate sheet. Information MUST be typewritten or printed in BLACK ink. Do NOT use commas (,) or dollar signs ($).
If typed, disregard vertical bars and type a consecutive string of characters. If hand printed, print in CAPS and within the boxes as below:

SAMPLE Typed: `1 2 3 4 5 6 . 0 0` SAMPLE Handwritten: `1 2 3 4 5 6 . 0 0` SAMPLE Filled-in: ●

Employer name (make corrections on Form UC-2B): **Kielso Company**

Employer PA UC account no.: `00 — 00093-0`

Check digit: `&`

Quarter and year Q / YYYY: `1/20--`

Quarter ending date MM / DD / YYYY: `03/31/20--`

1. Name and telephone number of preparer:
Nancy Heller
(555) 555-5555

2. Total number of pages in this report: `1`

3. Total number of employees listed in item 8 on all pages of Form UC-2A: `7`

4. Plant number (if approved):

5. Gross wages, MUST agree with item 2 on UC-2 and the sum of item 11 on all pages of Form UC-2A
`3 1 7 9 0 . 0 0`

6. Fill in this circle if you would like the Department to preprint your employee's names & SSNs on Form UC-2A next quarter ⊙

7. Employee's Social Security Number	8. Employee's name FI MI LAST	9. Gross wages paid this qtr Example: 123456.00	10. Credit Weeks
0 0 0 0 0 8 2 7 1	J L CORTEZ	6 3 0 0 . 0 0	1 3
0 0 0 0 0 1 9 1 8	C H LONG	1 9 0 0 . 0 0	5
0 0 0 0 0 3 7 9 0	H M DORSEY	2 9 9 0 . 0 0	1 3
0 0 0 0 0 6 5 1 0	M F ERNST	2 1 0 0 . 0 0	1 3
0 0 0 0 0 0 0 9 3	J B KIEL	1 0 5 0 0 . 0 0	1 3
0 0 0 0 0 9 0 0 8	A W PINKETT	4 1 0 0 . 0 0	1 3
0 0 0 0 0 1 7 9 2	L B SONG	3 9 0 0 . 0 0	1 3
		.	
		.	
		.	
		.	
		.	
		.	
		.	
		.	
		.	
		.	
		.	
		.	

List any additional employees on continuation sheets in the required format (see instructions).

11. Total gross wages for this page: `3 1 7 9 0 . 0 0`
12. Total number of employees for this page `7`

UC-2A REV 07-21

13. Page `1` **of** `1`

On the Job

In some industries, employers provide supplemental unemployment benefits (SUB plans) to their laid-off workers. A trust fund is financed (a cents-per-hour contribution) by the employer, and the employee draws weekly cash payments from the trust as well as state benefits.

Most states permit the use of the same magnetic tape for reporting state wage information that is used for federal social security reporting purposes. The pay-roll manager should contact the state agency to determine whether federal-state combined magnetic tape reporting is acceptable.

Separation Reports

Whenever a worker becomes separated from employment, a **separation report**, providing a wage and employment record of the separated employee and the reason for leaving, might be required. Usually, a copy of the report is given to the worker in order that the individual may be informed of any entitlement to unemployment insurance benefits.

Partial Unemployment Notices

Some states require employers to give **partial unemployment notices** to those workers who become "partially unemployed," so that they are informed of their potential eligibility for partial unemployment benefits. **Partial unemployment** refers to employment by the individual's regular employer but on a reduced scale because of lack of work. In most states, the notice must be given to the worker immediately after a week of partial employment has been completed. After that, the employer ordinarily furnishes the worker with some kind of low-earnings report during each week of partial employment so that the worker will be assured of the receipt of supplemental or partial benefits. In these states, benefit laws allow workers to receive benefits in proportion to the amount of reduction in their hours. The states require that the normal weekly hours of the affected employees be reduced by 10 to 60 percent (depending on the state) and that at least 10 percent of the employees in the affected unit are included in the plan.

Record Retention

Every state requires employers to maintain accurate records even if not covered by the state's unemployment compensation law. The records must show each worker's name, social security number, date of hire, separation, and rehire, dates of payment, and dates and hours worked. Each state sets a retention period for these recordings, ranging from three years in Idaho to as high as eight years in Minnesota.

Penalties—SUTA

All states have some form of penalty for failure to pay, for the late payment of contributions, and also for failure to file reports. Some states impose a 10 percent penalty if the failure to pay the tax is due to negligence, and in a few states, a 50 percent penalty is imposed if the failure to pay is due to fraud. Many states also deny experience rates to employers who are delinquent in filing reports or paying contributions. In some states, employers who have been delinquent in paying their contributions may be required to pay the contributions monthly rather than quarterly.

Key Terms

constructively paid (p. 5-9)

contribution report (p. 5-30)

credit reduction state (p. 5-10)

dismissal payments (p. 5-9)

experience rating (p. 5-11)

interstate employee (p. 5-4)

merit rating (p. 5-11)

negative-balance employers (p. 5-17)

partial unemployment (p. 5-32)

partial unemployment notices (p. 5-32)

pooled-fund laws (p. 5-13)

positive-balance employers (p. 5-17)

reciprocal arrangements (p. 5-6)

reserve-ratio formula (p. 5-17)

separation report (p. 5-32)

status report (p. 5-30)

Title XII advances (p. 5-12)

voluntary contributions (p. 5-19)

wage information reports (p. 5-30)

Answers to Self-Study Quizzes

Self-Study Quiz 5-1

4.1% of $188,000 = $7,708		SUTA tax
6.0% of $188,000 =	$11,280	Gross FUTA tax
4.1% of $188,000 = $7,708		Credit for SUTA tax paid
1.3% of $188,000 = <u> 2,444</u>	<u>10,152</u>	Additional credit to get to 5.4%
0.6% of $188,000 =	<u>$ 1,128</u>	Net FUTA tax

Self-Study Quiz 5-2

From the Summary of State Unemployment Compensation Laws (Figure 5.1 on page 5-14), the taxable wage in Colorado is $17,00. However, the company receives a credit of $6,000 against this limit because of unemployment taxes paid to Arizona on Castellano's wages in that state. Therefore, the calculation is:

Castellano's wages in Colorado	$26,000
Over taxable limit	<u> 9,000</u>
Colorado's SUTA wage limit	$17,000
Credit for wages taxed in Arizona	<u> 6,000</u>
Castellano's taxable wages in Colorado	$11,000
Moss's SUTA tax rate in Colorado	<u>× 2.9%</u>
Amount of the company's SUTA tax in Colorado	<u>$319.00</u>

Self-Study Quiz 5-3

1st Quarter—$66,000 × 0.006 = $396.00
           no deposit due

2nd Quarter—$64,000 × 0.006 = $384 + $396 = $780
           due on 7/31

3rd Quarter—$42,000 × 0.006 = $252.00
           no deposit due

4th Quarter—($25,000 × 0.006) + $252.00 = $402.00
           due on 1/31

Key Points Summary

	Learning Objectives	Key Points	Problem Sets A & B
LO1	Describe the basic requirements for an individual to be classified as an employer or an employee under the Federal Unemployment Tax Act.	• Employer—pays wages or $1,500 or more in a quarter or employs 1 or more persons in 20 or more weeks. • Employee—legal common-law relationship + agent/commission driver + travelling/city salesperson. • Interstate employees—where localized, base of operations, direction or control, or residence.	5-5, 5-6
LO2	Identify generally what is defined as taxable wages by the Federal Unemployment Tax Act.	• First $7,000 of each employee's earnings is taxed. • Fairly uniform under state laws.	5-14
LO3 ▶ Tell Me More	Compute the federal unemployment tax, the credit against the tax, and any credit reductions that might apply.	• 6.0 percent of first $7,000 of earnings – 5.4 percent credit (for SUTA taxes paid) = 0.6 percent net FUTA rate. • Experience ratings set SUTA rate for each employer based on past employment record.	5-1, 5-2, 5-3, 5-4, 5-7, 5-9, 5-10, 5-11
LO4 ▶ Tell Me More	Describe how an experience-rating system is used in determining employers' contributions to state unemployment compensation funds.	• Reserve-ratio formula determines tax rate for each employer (contributions – benefits paid/average payroll). • Some states allow voluntary contributions in order to lower SUTA tax rate.	5-8, 5-12, 5-13, 5-15
LO5 ▶ Tell Me More	Complete the reports required by the Federal Unemployment Tax Act.	• Annual Form 940 to be completed by January 31 of the following year. • Taxes paid quarterly (if liability each quarter is over $500). • Paid electronically.	5-16, 5-17
LO6	Describe the types of information reports under the various state unemployment compensation laws.	• Information reports, status reports, contribution reports, and wage information reports. • Quarterly contribution reports filed by end of the month following the quarter-end. • Taxes paid with reports.	N/A

Matching Quiz

_____ 1. Reciprocal arrangements
_____ 2. Title XII advances
_____ 3. Negative-balance employers
_____ 4. Dumping
_____ 5. Over $500
_____ 6. Merit rating
_____ 7. Form 940
_____ 8. Household employers
_____ 9. Wage information reports
_____ 10. Voluntary contributions

A. Extra state unemployment contributions made by the employers
B. Favorable employment records result in a lower SUTA tax
C. Annual Federal Unemployment Tax Return
D. Poor experience-rated companies form new companies with lower unemployment tax rates
E. Pay FUTA tax with Schedule H of Form 1040
F. Provide unemployment insurance coverage and payment of benefits to interstate workers
G. Borrowings from federal government to pay unemployment compensation benefits
H. Employers whose reserve account has been charged with more benefits paid out than contributions made
I. Quarterly threshold for mandatory depositing of FUTA taxes
J. Quarterly reports submitted to the state listing employees, SSNs, and taxable wages

Questions for Review

1. What two alternative tests are applied to a business in order to judge whether it is an "employer" and therefore subject to the FUTA tax?
2. What condition would make a household employer a covered employer under FUTA?
3. Charlie Kapoor is a full-time student at Wenonah College and works part time in the school's maintenance department. Must the college pay a FUTA tax on Kapoor's earnings?
4. Under the Interstate Reciprocal Coverage Arrangement, the services of a worker can be covered in the state of the election of the employer as long as one of three factors exists. What are those three conditions?
5. To what extent does FUTA coverage extend to services that a citizen of the United States performs for an American employer outside the United States?
6. Which of the following types of payments are taxable under FUTA?
   a. Commissions as compensation for covered employment.
   b. Christmas gifts of nominal value.
   c. Courtesy discounts to employees.
   d. Reimbursement of ordinary and necessary business expenses.
   e. Dismissal payments.
7. What is an employer required to do in order to obtain the maximum credit of 5.4 percent against the FUTA tax?
8. An employer, because of a favorable experience rating, is permitted to pay a state contribution at a reduced rate of 1.5 percent. What percentage of taxable wages must be paid in the aggregate to the federal and state governments?
9. What are three situations in which an employer could be liable for a net FUTA tax greater than 0.6 percent?
10. What is the purpose of Title XII advances?
11. In 2022:
    a. Which state had the widest range of SUTA tax rates for employers?
    b. Which state paid the highest weekly maximum benefit (excluding dependency allowances) to qualified unemployed workers?
    c. Which state had the highest taxable wage base for the SUTA tax?
12. How is the SUTA tax rate determined for a new employer?
13. a. For an employer who is subject to FUTA, what is the basic form that must be filed with the federal government?
    b. When must the form be filed?
    c. How are taxable wages computed on the annual return?
14. How are pretax contributions by employees into cafeteria plans presented on Form 940?
15. How does an employer file an amended Form 940?
16. What special steps must be taken when completing Form 940 for a company that has ceased operations during the year?
17. When and how does an employer pay the FUTA taxes?
18. What are the options for paying an amount due (under $500) with the filing of Form 940?
19. How often do employers file wage and contribution reports with their states?
20. What is a separation report?

Questions for Discussion

1. Can the owner of a small business receive unemployment compensation? Explain.
2. What arguments could be made for raising the upper limits of the SUTA tax rates?
3. Check the unemployment compensation law of your state and determine the answers to the following questions:
   a. How do nonprofit organizations, subject to coverage, make payments to the unemployment compensation fund?
   b. Can part-time teachers collect unemployment compensation between school terms?
   c. Can professional athletes receive unemployment compensation?
   d. Are aliens covered by the unemployment compensation law?
   e. How do employers protest or appeal benefit determinations and charges against their accounts?
   f. Briefly describe how a person's weekly benefit rate and maximum benefit amount are determined.
   g. Can an unemployed worker collect additional benefits if they have dependents? If so, how much is paid for each dependent?

h. Does the state provide payment of partial benefits?
i. Are benefits payable to a female during pregnancy?
j. Can employers make voluntary contributions to their state unemployment reserve accounts?
k. For what reasons may an unemployed worker be disqualified from receiving unemployment benefits?
l. What steps are taken by the state unemployment agency to prevent the improper payment of claims?

4. As a way of curbing the unemployment rate, California has a "shared-work compensation" program. Under this program, a company faced with a layoff of its workers may place its entire workforce on a four-day workweek during the period of hardship. During this period of reduced workweeks, the employees collect partial unemployment benefits. When business rebounds, the firm returns to its normal five-day workweek, and the unemployment compensation benefits cease. Participation in the program must be approved by both the employer and the unions. If, however, the firm is not unionized, management has the discretion of putting the plan into effect.

a. What are the benefits of such a shared-work compensation program to (1) the employer and (2) the employees?
b. What disadvantages do you see in the operation of a shared-work compensation program, especially from the viewpoint of organized labor?

Date _____ Name _____

Problem Set • A

Since the SUTA rates changes are made at the end of each year, the available 2022 rates were used for FUTA and SUTA.

5-1A • LO 3, 4   See Example 5-7 on page 5-12 [X]

During the year, Plum Company has a SUTA tax rate of 4.8%. The taxable payroll for the year for FUTA and SUTA is $123,400. Compute:

  a. Net FUTA tax .... $ _____
  b. Net SUTA tax .... $ _____
  c. Total unemployment taxes... $ _____

5-2A • LO 3, 4   See Example 5-8 on page 5-16 [X]

Qwan Company's payroll for the year is $737,910. Of this amount, $472,120 is for wages paid in excess of $7,000 to each individual employee. The SUTA rate in Qwan Company's state is 2.9% on the first $7,000 of each employee's earnings. Compute:

  a. Net FUTA tax .... $ _____
  b. Net SUTA tax .... $ _____
  c. Total unemployment taxes... $ _____

5-3A • LO 3, 4 See Example 5-8 on page 5-16

Garrison Shops had a SUTA tax rate of 3.7%. The state's taxable limit was $8,000 of each employee's earnings. For the year, Garrison Shops had FUTA taxable wages of $67,900 and SUTA taxable wages of $83,900. Compute:

  a. Net FUTA tax .... $ _____
  b. Net SUTA tax .... $ _____

5-4A • LO 3, 4 See Example 5-7 on page 5-12 [X]

Due to its experience rating, Ianelli, Inc., is required to pay unemployment taxes on its payroll as follows:
1. Under SUTA for Massachusetts on taxable payroll of $18,000, the contribution rate is 4%.
2. Under SUTA for New Hampshire on taxable payroll of $24,000, the contribution rate is 6.65%.
3. Under SUTA for Maine on taxable payroll of $79,000, the contribution rate is 2.9%.
4. Under FUTA, the taxable payroll is $103,500.

Compute:
  a. SUTA taxes paid to Massachusetts .... $ _____
  b. SUTA taxes paid to New Hampshire...................................... $ _____
  c. SUTA taxes paid to Maine .... $ _____
  d. FUTA taxes paid... $ _____

5-5A • LO 1, 3   See Example 5-4 on page 5-10

Banerjee Company began its operations in September of the current year. During September, the company paid wages of $23,400. For the last quarter of the year, the taxable wages paid amounted to $64,700. None of the employees was paid more than $7,000 this year.

5-5A (concluded)

a. Is Banerjee Company liable for FUTA tax this year? Explain.

_____

_____

b. What is the *net* FUTA tax?..................................... $ _____

5-6A • LO 1, 2, 3 See Example 5-8 on page 5-16

In September Manson Paint Corporation began operations in a state that requires new employers of one or more individuals to pay a state unemployment tax of 3.5% of the first $7,000 of wages paid each employee.

An analysis of the company's payroll for the year shows total wages paid of $177,610. The salaries of the president and the vice president of the company were $20,000 and $15,000, respectively, for the four-month period, but there were no other employees who received wages in excess of $7,000 for the four months. Included in the total wages were $900 paid to a director who only attended director meetings during the year, $6,300 paid to the factory superintendent, and $2,000 in employee contributions to a cafeteria plan made on a pretax basis—for both federal and state.

In addition to the total wages of $177,610, a payment of $2,430 was made to Andersen Accounting Company for an audit it performed on the company's books in December. Compute:

a. Net FUTA tax .... $ _____
b. SUTA tax... $ _____

5-7A • LO 3, 4 See Example 5-1 on page 5-7

In April of the current year, Freeman Steel Company transferred Herb Porter from its factory in Nebraska to its plant in Ohio. The company's SUTA tax rates based on its experience ratings are 3.2% in Nebraska and 3.8% in Ohio. Both states base the tax on the first $9,000 of each employee's earnings. This year, Freeman Steel Company paid Herb Porter wages of $20,900; $2,800 were paid in Nebraska and the remainder in Ohio. Compute:

a. Amount of SUTA tax the company must pay to Nebraska on Porter's wages................ $ _____
b. Amount of SUTA tax the company must pay to Ohio on Porter's wages .... $ _____
c. Amount of the net FUTA tax on Porter's wages... $ _____

5-8A • LO 4 See Figure 5.1 on page 5-13

Ron Valdez worked for two different employers. Until May, he worked for Rowland Construction Company in Ames, Iowa, and earned $22,000. The state unemployment rate for Rowland is 4.6%. He then changed jobs and worked for Ford Improvement Company in Topeka, Kansas, and earned $29,500 for the rest of the year. The state unemployment rate for Ford is 5.1%. Determine the unemployment taxes (FUTA and SUTA) that would be paid by:

a. Rowland Construction Company.. $ _____
b. Ford Improvement Company.. $ _____

5-9A • LO 3, 4 See Example 5-2 on page 5-9

The partnership of Keenan and Kludlow paid the following wages during this year:

M. Keenan (partner)..................................	$85,000
S. Kludlow (partner).................................	75,000
N. Perry (supervisor)	53,000
T. Lee (factory worker)	34,600
R. Rolf (factory worker).............................	29,800
D. Broch (factory worker)...........................	6,900
S. Ruiz (bookkeeper)................................	25,400
C. Rudolph (maintenance)...........................	5,100

5-9A (concluded)

In addition, the partnership owed $200 to Rudolph for work he performed during December. However, payment for this work will not be made until January of the following year. The state unemployment tax rate for the company is 2.95% on the first $9,000 of each employee's earnings. Compute:

a. Net FUTA tax for the partnership for this year.................................... $ _____

b. SUTA tax for this year.. $ _____

5-10A • LO 3, 4   See Example 5-6 on page 5-12

Peroni Company paid wages of $170,900 this year. Of this amount, $114,000 was taxable for net FUTA and SUTA purposes. The state's contribution tax rate is 3.1% for Peroni Company. Due to cash flow problems, the company did not make any SUTA payments until after the Form 940 filing date. Compute:

a. Amount of credit the company would receive against the FUTA tax for its
SUTA contributions .... $ _____

b. Amount that Peroni Company would pay to the federal government for
its FUTA tax.. $ _____

c. Amount that the company lost because of its late payments .... $ _____

5-11A • LO 3, 4   See Example 5-8 on page 5-16

Hinsky Company was subject to the Alaska state unemployment tax of 4.2%. The company's taxable wages for FUTA were $86,700 and for SUTA, $171,000. Compute:

a. SUTA tax that Hinsky Company would pay to the state of Alaska................................. $ _____

b. Net FUTA tax .... $ _____

c. Amount of employees' unemployment tax (use the employee's tax
rate shown in Figure 5.1 on page 5-13).. $ _____

5-12A • LO 4   See Example 5-10 on page 5-18

The following unemployment tax rate schedule is in effect for the calendar year 2023 in State A, which uses the reserve-ratio formula in determining employer contributions:

Reserve Ratio	Contribution Rate
0.0% or more, but less than 1.0%.............................	6.7%
1.0% or more, but less than 1.2%.............................	6.4%
1.2% or more, but less than 1.4%.............................	6.1%
1.4% or more, but less than 1.6%.............................	5.8%
1.6% or more, but less than 1.8%.............................	5.5%
1.8% or more, but less than 2.0%.............................	5.2%
2.0% or more, but less than 2.2%.............................	4.9%
2.2% or more, but less than 2.4%.............................	4.6%
2.4% or more, but less than 2.6%.............................	4.3%
2.6% or more, but less than 2.8%.............................	4.0%
2.8% or more, but less than 3.0%.............................	3.7%
3.0% or more, but less than 3.2%.............................	3.4%
3.2% or more...	3.1%

Hyram Company, which is located in State A, had an average annual payroll of $850,000 for the three 12-month periods ending on June 30, 2022 (the computation date for the tax year 2023). As of June 30, 2022, the total contributions that had been made to Hyram Company's reserve account, in excess of the benefits charged, amounted to $17,440. Compute:

a. Hyram Company's reserve ratio for 2022.. _____ %

b. 2023 contribution rate for the company.. _____ %

5-12A (concluded)

c. Smallest contribution that the company can make in order to reduce its tax rate if State A permits voluntary contributions .... $ _____

d. Tax savings realized by the company, taking into consideration the voluntary contribution made in (c) if the taxable payroll in 2023 is $980,000 .... $ _____

5-13A • LO 4   **See Example 5-11 on page 5-20**

As of June 30, 2022 (the computation date for the 2023 tax rate), Sanchez Company had a negative balance of $1,190 in its unemployment reserve account in State A. The company's average payroll over the last three 12-month periods amounted to $520,000. The unemployment compensation law of State A provides that the tax rate of an employer who has a negative balance on the computation date shall be 7.2% during the following calendar year.

Using the tax rate schedule presented in Problem 5-12A, compute:

a. The smallest voluntary contribution that Sanchez Company should make in order to effect a change in its tax rate .... $ _____

b. The amount of the tax savings as a result of the voluntary contribution if Sanchez Company's taxable payroll for 2023 is $660,000 .... $ _____

5-14A • LO 2, 3, 4   **See Example 5-8 on page 5-16**

Marlene Grady and Pauline Monroe are partners engaged in operating The G&M Doll Shop, which has employed the following persons since the beginning of the year:

V. Hoffman (general office worker)	$1,700 per month
A. Drugan (saleswoman)	$15,000 per year
G. Beiter (stock clerk)	$180 per week
S. Egan (deliveryman)	$220 per week
B. Lin (cleaning and maintenance, part-time)	$160 per week

Grady and Monroe are each paid a weekly salary allowance of $950.

The doll shop is located in a state that requires unemployment compensation contributions of employers of one or more individuals. The company is subject to state contributions at a rate of 3.1% for wages not in excess of $8,100. Compute each of the following amounts based upon the *41st weekly payroll period* for the week ending October 14, 20--:

a. Amount of FICA taxes (OASDI and HI) to be withheld from the earnings of each person. (Refer to Chapter 3.)

	OASDI	HI
M. Grady	$ _____	$ _____
P. Monroe	_____	_____
V. Hoffman	_____	_____
A. Drugan	_____	_____
G. Beiter	_____	_____
S. Egan	_____	_____
B. Lin..	_____	_____

b. Amount of the employer's FICA taxes for the weekly payroll .... _____ _____

c. Amount of state unemployment contributions for the weekly payroll .... $ _____

d. Amount of the net FUTA tax on the payroll .... $ _____

e. Total amount of the employer's payroll taxes for the weekly payroll .... $ _____

5-15A • LO 4   See Example 5-10 on page 5-18

Karlson Software Company is located in State H, which enables employers to reduce their contribution rates under the experience-rating system. From 2009 to 2018, inclusive, the company's total contributions to state unemployment compensation amounted to $14,695. For the calendar years 2019 to 2022, inclusive, the contribution rate for the Karlson Company was 2.7%.

The contributions of each employer are credited to an account maintained by the State Unemployment Compensation Commission. This account is credited with contributions paid into the account by the employer and is charged with unemployment benefits that are paid from the account. Starting January 1, 2023, the contributions rate for all employers in State H will be based on the following tax rate schedule:

Reserve Ratio	Contribution Rate
Contributions falling below benefits paid	7.0%
0.0% to 7.9%	5.5%
8.0% to 9.9%	4.5%
10.0% to 11.9%	3.5%
12.0% to 14.9%	2.5%
15.0% or more...	1.5%

The annual payroll for calculation purposes is the total wages payable during a 12-month period ending with the last day of the third quarter of any calendar year. The average annual payroll is the average of the last three annual payrolls. The SUTA tax rate for the year is computed using the information available (benefits received and taxes paid) as of September 30 of the preceding year.

The schedule below shows the total payroll and the taxable payroll for the calendar years 2019 to 2022.

Calendar Year

	2019		2020		2021		2022	
	Total Payroll	Taxable Payroll	Total Payroll	Taxable Payroll	Total Payroll	Taxable Payroll	Total Payroll	Taxable Payroll
First Quarter...........	$12,000	$12,000	$11,000	$11,000	$13,000	$13,000	$10,000	$10,000
Second Quarter.......	11,750	11,750	11,500	11,400	12,750	12,700	9,300	9,300
Third Quarter..........	12,500	12,250	12,750	12,400	12,200	12,000	9,350	9,350
Fourth Quarter........	13,000	12,500	12,500	12,200	14,000	13,750	—	—

Unemployment benefits became payable to the company's qualified unemployed workers on January 1, 2009. Between that time and September 30, 2022 total benefits amounting to $15,100.90 were charged against the employer's account. Compute:

a. Contribution rate for 2023.. _____ %

b. Rate for 2023 if $2,000 additional benefits had been charged by mistake to the account of Karlson Software Company by the State Unemployment Compensation .... _____ %

5-16A • LO 5 See Figure 5.2 on pages 5-22 and 5-23,

Show Me How

Figure 5.3 on page 5-24, Figure 5.4 on page 5-27

As the accountant for Runson Moving Company, you are preparing the company's annual return, Form 940 and Schedule A. Use the following information to complete Form 940 and Schedule A on pages 5-43 to 5-45.

The net FUTA tax liability for each quarter of 20-- was as follows: 1st, $220.10; 2nd, $107.60; 3rd, $101.00; and 4th, $56.10 plus the credit reduction.

5-16A (concluded)

Since the net FUTA tax liability did not exceed $500 until the 4th quarter, the company was required to make its first deposit of FUTA taxes on January 31 of the next year. Assume that the electronic payment was made on time.

a. One of the employees performs all of his duties in another state—Arizona.

b. Total payments made to employees during calendar year 20--:

California	$102,310
Arizona	18,490
Total	$120,800

c. Employer contributions in California into employees' 401(k) retirement plan: $3,500.

d. Payments made to employees in excess of $7,000: $36,500 ($11,490 from Arizona and $25,010 from California).

e. Form is to be signed by Mickey Vixon, Vice President, and dated 1/31/--.

f. Phone number—(219) 555-8310.

Form **940 for 20--:** **Employer's Annual Federal Unemployment (FUTA) Tax Return**

Department of the Treasury — Internal Revenue Service

OMB No. 1545-0028

Employer identification number (EIN) 0 0 – 0 0 0 3 7 9 3

Name (not your trade name) RUNSON MOVING COMPANY

Trade name (if any)

Address 423 BRISTOL PIKE

Number Street Suite or room number

SACRAMENTO CA 94203-4523

City State ZIP code

Foreign country name Foreign province/county Foreign postal code

Type of Return
(Check all that apply.)

☐ **a.** Amended

☐ **b.** Successor employer

☐ **c.** No payments to employees in 20--

☐ **d.** Final: Business closed or stopped paying wages

Go to *www.irs.gov/Form940* for instructions and the latest information.

Read the separate instructions before you complete this form. Please type or print within the boxes.

Part 1: **Tell us about your return. If any line does NOT apply, leave it blank. See instructions before completing Part 1.**

1a If you had to pay state unemployment tax in one state only, enter the state abbreviation . **1a** ☐ ☐

1b If you had to pay state unemployment tax in more than one state, you are a multi-state employer . . . . **1b** ☐ Check here. Complete Schedule A (Form 940).

2 If you paid wages in a state that is subject to **CREDIT REDUCTION** . . . . **2** ☐ Check here. Complete Schedule A (Form 940).

Part 2: **Determine your FUTA tax before adjustments. If any line does NOT apply, leave it blank.**

3 Total payments to all employees **3**

4 Payments exempt from FUTA tax **4**

Check all that apply: **4a** ☐ Fringe benefits **4c** ☐ Retirement/Pension **4e** ☐ Other
4b ☐ Group-term life insurance **4d** ☐ Dependent care

5 Total of payments made to each employee in excess of $7,000 . . . . **5**

6 **Subtotal** (line 4 + line 5 = line 6) **6**

7 **Total taxable FUTA wages** (line 3 – line 6 = line 7). See instructions **7**

8 FUTA tax before adjustments (line 7 x 0.006 = line 8) **8**

Part 3: **Determine your adjustments. If any line does NOT apply, leave it blank.**

9 If ALL of the taxable FUTA wages you paid were excluded from state unemployment tax, multiply line 7 by 0.054 (line 7 × 0.054 = line 9). Go to line 12 . . . . **9**

10 If SOME of the taxable FUTA wages you paid were excluded from state unemployment tax, OR you paid ANY state unemployment tax late (after the due date for filing Form 940), complete the worksheet in the instructions. Enter the amount from line 7 of the worksheet . . **10**

11 If credit reduction applies, enter the total from Schedule A (Form 940) **11**

Part 4: **Determine your FUTA tax and balance due or overpayment. If any line does NOT apply, leave it blank.**

12 Total FUTA tax after adjustments (lines 8 + 9 + 10 + 11 = line 12) **12**

13 FUTA tax deposited for the year, including any overpayment applied from a prior year . **13**

14 **Balance due.** If line 12 is more than line 13, enter the excess on line 14.
• If line 14 is more than $500, you must deposit your tax.
• If line 14 is $500 or less, you may pay with this return. See instructions **14**

15 **Overpayment.** If line 13 is more than line 12, enter the excess on line 15 and check a box below **15**

▶ You **MUST** complete both pages of this form and **SIGN** it. Check one: ☐ Apply to next return. ☐ Send a refund.

Next ▶

For Privacy Act and Paperwork Reduction Act Notice, see the back of the Payment Voucher. Cat. No. 11234O Form **940** (2021)

5-16A (continued)

Name *(not your trade name)*	Employer identification number (EIN)
RUNSON MOVING COMPANY	00-0003793

Part 5:   Report your FUTA tax liability by quarter only if line 12 is more than $500. If not, go to Part 6.

16   Report the amount of your FUTA tax liability for each quarter; do NOT enter the amount you deposited. If you had no liability for a quarter, leave the line blank.

16a   **1st quarter** (January 1 – March 31) . . . .   16a   [.   ]

16b   **2nd quarter** (April 1 – June 30) . . . .   16b   [.   ]

16c   **3rd quarter** (July 1 – September 30) . . . .   16c   [.   ]

16d   **4th quarter** (October 1 – December 31) . . . .   16d   [.   ]

17   Total tax liability for the year (lines 16a + 16b + 16c + 16d = line 17)   **17**   [.   ]   Total must equal line 12.

Part 6:   May we speak with your third-party designee?

Do you want to allow an employee, a paid tax preparer, or another person to discuss this return with the IRS? See the instructions for details.

☐ **Yes.**   Designee's name and phone number   [   ]   [   ]

       Select a 5-digit Personal Identification Number (PIN) to use when talking to IRS   [ ] [ ] [ ] [ ] [ ]

☐ **No.**

Part 7:   Sign here. You MUST complete both pages of this form and SIGN it.

Under penalties of perjury, I declare that I have examined this return, including accompanying schedules and statements, and to the best of my knowledge and belief, it is true, correct, and complete, and that no part of any payment made to a state unemployment fund claimed as a credit was, or is to be, deducted from the payments made to employees. Declaration of preparer (other than taxpayer) is based on all information of which preparer has any knowledge.

✗ **Sign your name here**   [   ]

    Print your name here   [   ]

    Print your title here   [   ]

Date   [/   /   ]

Best daytime phone   [   ]

Paid Preparer Use Only   Check if you are self-employed ☐

Preparer's name	[ ]	PTIN	[ ]
Preparer's signature	[ ]	Date	[/ /]
Firm's name (or yours if self-employed)	[ ]	EIN	[ ]
Address	[ ]	Phone	[ ]
City	[ ] State [ ]	ZIP code	[ ]

Page **2**   Form **940** (2021)

Source: Internal Revenue Service.

5-16A (concluded)

Schedule A (Form 940) for 20--:

Multi-State Employer and Credit Reduction Information

Department of the Treasury — Internal Revenue Service

OMB No. 1545-0028

Employer identification number (EIN) 0 0 — 0 0 0 3 7 9 3

Name (not your trade name) RUNSON MOVING COMPANY

See the instructions on page 2. File this schedule with Form 940.

Place an "X" in the box of EVERY state in which you had to pay state unemployment tax this year. For the U.S. Virgin Islands, enter the FUTA taxable wages and the reduction rate (see page 2). Multiply the FUTA taxable wages by the reduction rate and enter the credit reduction amount. Don't include in the *FUTA Taxable Wages* box wages that were excluded from state unemployment tax (see the instructions for Step 2). If any states don't apply to you, leave them blank.

Postal Abbreviation	FUTA Taxable Wages	Reduction Rate	Credit Reduction	Postal Abbreviation	FUTA Taxable Wages	Reduction Rate	Credit Reduction
☐ AK	.		.	☐ NC	.		.
☐ AL	.		.	☐ ND	.		.
☐ AR	.		.	☐ NE	.		.
☐ AZ	.		.	☐ NH	.		.
☐ CA	.		.	☐ NJ	.		.
☐ CO	.		.	☐ NM	.		.
☐ CT	.		.	☐ NV	.		.
☐ DC	.		.	☐ NY	.		.
☐ DE	.		.	☐ OH	.		.
☐ FL	.		.	☐ OK	.		.
☐ GA	.		.	☐ OR	.		.
☐ HI	.		.	☐ PA	.		.
☐ IA	.		.	☐ RI	.		.
☐ ID	.		.	☐ SC	.		.
☐ IL	.		.	☐ SD	.		.
☐ IN	.		.	☐ TN	.		.
☐ KS	.		.	☐ TX	.		.
☐ KY	.		.	☐ UT	.		.
☐ LA	.		.	☐ VA	.		.
☐ MA	.		.	☐ VT	.		.
☐ MD	.		.	☐ WA	.		.
☐ ME	.		.	☐ WI	.		.
☐ MI	.		.	☐ WV	.		.
☐ MN	.		.	☐ WY	.		.
☐ MO	.		.	☐ PR	.		.
☐ MS	.		.	☐ VI	.		.
☐ MT	.		.				

Total Credit Reduction. Add all amounts shown in the *Credit Reduction* boxes. Enter the total here and on Form 940, line 11   .   .   .   .   _____ .

For **Privacy Act and Paperwork Reduction Act Notice, see the Instructions for Form 940.**   Cat. No. 16997C   Schedule A (Form 940) 2021

Source: Internal Revenue Service.

5-17A • LO 5, 6 **See Figure 5.2 on pages 5-22 and 5-23, Figure 5.5 on page 5-30, Figure 5.6 on page 5-31**

The information listed below refers to the employees of Lemonica Company for the year ended December 31, 20--. The wages are separated into the quarters in which they were paid to the individual employees.

Name	Social Security #	1st Qtr.	2nd Qtr.	3rd Qtr.	4th Qtr.	Total
Robert G. Cramer	000-00-0001	$ 5,800	$ 5,000	$ 5,000	$ 5,200	$ 21,000
Daniel M. English (Foreman)	000-00-0003	13,000	13,400	13,400	13,400	53,200
Ruth A. Small	000-00-1998	2,000	2,300	2,300	2,400	9,000
Harry B. Klaus	000-00-7413	11,600	11,700	11,700	11,700	46,700
Kenneth N. George (Manager)	000-00-6523	13,600	14,000	14,500	15,000	57,100
Mavis R. Jones	000-00-6789	1,600	1,700	1,700	-0-	5,000
Marshall T. McCoy	000-00-3334	11,400	11,400	-0-	-0-	22,800
Bertram A. Gompers (President)	000-00-1014	24,500	25,000	25,500	26,300	101,300
Arthur S. Rooks	000-00-7277	-0-	700	1,700	1,700	4,100
Mary R. Bastian	000-00-8111	8,000	8,200	8,200	8,200	32,600
Klaus C. Werner	000-00-2623	2,300	2,500	2,500	2,500	9,800
Kathy T. Tyler	000-00-3534	-0-	-0-	11,300	11,700	23,000
Totals		$93,800	$95,900	$97,800	$98,100	$385,600

For 20--, State D's contribution rate for Lemonica Company, based on the experience-rating system of the state, was 2.8% of the first $7,000 of each employee's earnings. The state tax returns are due one month after the end of each calendar quarter. During 20--, the company paid $2,214.80 of contributions to State D's unemployment fund.

Employer's phone number: (613) 555-0029. Employer's State D reporting number: 00596.

Using the forms supplied on pages 5-47 to 5-49, complete the following for 20--:

a. Date and amount of the FUTA tax payment for the fourth quarter of 20-- (State D is not a credit reduction state).

Tax Payment:

Date _____   Amount $ _____

b. Employer's Report for Unemployment Compensation, State D—4th quarter only. Item 1 is the number of employees employed in the pay period that includes the 12th of each month in the quarter. For Lemonica Company, the number of employees is eight in October, seven in November, and eight in December. All employees earned 13 credit weeks during the last quarter except for Rooks (8) and Tyler (9).

c. Employer's Annual Federal Unemployment (FUTA) Tax Return—Form 940

Indicate on each form the date that the form should be submitted and the amount of money that must be paid. The president of the company prepares and signs all tax forms.

5-17A (continued)

b.

State D Form UC-2 REV 07-21, Employer's Report for Unemployment Compensation

QTR./YEAR 4/20--

Read Instructions – Answer Each Item

DUE DATE 01/31/20--

1ST MONTH 2ND MONTH 3RD MONTH

W

EXAMINED BY:

1. TOTAL COVERED EMPLOYEES IN PAY PERIOD INCL. 12TH OF MONTH

Signature certifies that the information contained herein is true and correct to the best of the signer's knowledge.

FOR DEPT. USE

2. GROSS WAGES

3. EMPLOYEE CONTRIBUTIONS

X X X X X X X X   X X   XXXXX

10. SIGN HERE-DO NOT PRINT

TITLE _____ DATE _____ PHONE # _____

4. TAXABLE WAGES FOR EMPLOYER CONTRIBUTIONS

11. FILED ☐ PAPER UC-2A ☐ INTERNET UC-2A

5. EMPLOYER CONTRIBUTIONS DUE (RATE X ITEM 4)

12. FEDERAL IDENTIFICATION NUMBER _____

EMPLOYER'S ACCT. NO. CHECK DIGIT

EMPLOYER'S CONTRIBUTION RATE ▷ 2.8%   00596   1

6. TOTAL CONTRIBUTIONS DUE (ITEMS 3 + 5)

7. INTEREST DUE SEE INSTRUCTIONS

Employer name and address
Make any corrections on Form UC-2B

8. PENALTY DUE SEE INSTRUCTIONS

Lemonica Company
123 Swamp Road
Pikesville, D State 10777-2017

9. TOTAL REMITTANCE (ITEMS 6 + 7 + 8) $.

MAKE CHECKS PAYABLE TO: State D UC FUND

SUBJECTIVITY DATE   REPORT DELINQUENT DATE

▲ DETACH HERE

State D Form UC-2A, Employer's Quarterly Report of Wages Paid to Each Employee

See instructions on separate sheet. Information MUST be typewritten or printed in BLACK ink. Do NOT use commas (,) or dollar signs ($).
If typed, disregard vertical bars and type a consecutive string of characters. If hand printed, print in CAPS and within the boxes as below:

SAMPLE Typed: `1 2 3 4 5 6 . 0 0`   SAMPLE Handwritten: `1 2 3 4 5 6 . 0 0`   SAMPLE Filled-in: → ●

Employer name (make corrections on Form UC-2B)   Employer State D UC account no.   Check digit   Quarter and year Q / YYYY   Quarter ending date MM / DD / YYYY

Lemonica Company   00596   1   4/20--   12/31/20--

1. Name and telephone number of preparer

2. Total number of pages in this report

3. Total number of employees listed in item 8 on all pages of Form UC-2A

4. Plant number (if approved)

5. Gross wages, MUST agree with item 2 on UC-2 and the sum of item 11 on all pages of Form UC-2A   ▲

6. Fill in this circle if you would like the Department to preprint your employee's names & SSNs on Form UC-2A next quarter   → ◉

7. Employee's Social Security Number	8. Employee's name FI MI LAST	9. Gross wages paid this qtr Example: 123456.00	10. Credit Weeks

List any additional employees on continuation sheets in the required format (see instructions).

▲   **11. Total gross wages for this page:** →
12. Total number of employees for this page _____   ▲

UC-2A REV 07-21   **13. Page ____ of ____**

5-17A (continued)

c.

Form **940** for 20--: **Employer's Annual Federal Unemployment (FUTA) Tax Return**

Department of the Treasury — Internal Revenue Service

OMB No. 1545-0028

Employer identification number (EIN) 0 0 – 0 0 0 6 4 2 1

Name (not your trade name) LEMONICA COMPANY

Trade name (if any)

Address 123 SWAMP ROAD
Number   Street   Suite or room number

PIKESVILLE   D   10777-2017
City   State   ZIP code

Foreign country name   Foreign province/county   Foreign postal code

Type of Return
(Check all that apply.)

☐ **a.** Amended
☐ **b.** Successor employer
☐ **c.** No payments to employees in 20--
☐ **d.** Final: Business closed or stopped paying wages

Go to *www.irs.gov/Form940* for instructions and the latest information.

Read the separate instructions before you complete this form. Please type or print within the boxes.

Part 1:   Tell us about your return. If any line does NOT apply, leave it blank. See instructions before completing Part 1.

1a If you had to pay state unemployment tax in one state only, enter the state abbreviation .   **1a** ☐ ☐

1b If you had to pay state unemployment tax in more than one state, you are a multi-state employer . . . .   **1b** ☐ Check here. Complete Schedule A (Form 940).

2   If you paid wages in a state that is subject to **CREDIT REDUCTION** . . . .   **2** ☐ Check here. Complete Schedule A (Form 940).

Part 2:   Determine your FUTA tax before adjustments. If any line does NOT apply, leave it blank.

3   Total payments to all employees . . . .   **3** [.]

4   Payments exempt from FUTA tax . . . .   **4** [.]

Check all that apply: **4a** ☐ Fringe benefits   **4c** ☐ Retirement/Pension   **4e** ☐ Other
                       4b ☐ Group-term life insurance **4d** ☐ Dependent care

5   Total of payments made to each employee in excess of $7,000 . . . .   **5** [.]

6   **Subtotal** (line 4 + line 5 = line 6) . . . .   **6** [.]

7   Total taxable FUTA wages (line 3 – line 6 = line 7). See instructions . . . .   **7** [.]

8   FUTA tax before adjustments (line 7 × 0.006 = line 8) . . . .   **8** [.]

Part 3:   Determine your adjustments. If any line does NOT apply, leave it blank.

9   If ALL of the taxable FUTA wages you paid were excluded from state unemployment tax, multiply line 7 by 0.054 (line 7 × 0.054 = line 9). Go to line 12 . . . .   **9** [.]

10 If SOME of the taxable FUTA wages you paid were excluded from state unemployment tax, OR you paid ANY state unemployment tax late (after the due date for filing Form 940), complete the worksheet in the instructions. Enter the amount from line 7 of the worksheet . .   **10** [.]

11 If credit reduction applies, enter the total from Schedule A (Form 940) . . . . . .   **11** [.]

Part 4:   Determine your FUTA tax and balance due or overpayment. If any line does NOT apply, leave it blank.

12 Total FUTA tax after adjustments (lines 8 + 9 + 10 + 11 = line 12) . . . .   **12** [.]

13 FUTA tax deposited for the year, including any overpayment applied from a prior year .   **13** [.]

14 **Balance due.** If line 12 is more than line 13, enter the excess on line 14.
    • If line 14 is more than $500, you must deposit your tax.
    • If line 14 is $500 or less, you may pay with this return. See instructions . . . .   **14** [.]

15 **Overpayment.** If line 13 is more than line 12, enter the excess on line 15 and check a box below **15** [.]

▶ You **MUST** complete both pages of this form and **SIGN** it.   Check one: ☐ Apply to next return. ☐ Send a refund.

Next ▶

For Privacy Act and Paperwork Reduction Act Notice, see the back of the Payment Voucher.   Cat. No. 11234O   Form **940** (2021)

5-17A (concluded)

d.

Name *(not your trade name)*	Employer identification number (EIN)
LEMONICA COMPANY	00-0006421

Part 5:   Report your FUTA tax liability by quarter only if line 12 is more than $500. If not, go to Part 6.

16   Report the amount of your FUTA tax liability for each quarter; do NOT enter the amount you deposited. If you had no liability for a quarter, leave the line blank.

     16a   **1st quarter** (January 1 – March 31) . . . . **16a**   [.   ]

     16b   **2nd quarter** (April 1 – June 30) . . . . **16b**   [.   ]

     16c   **3rd quarter** (July 1 – September 30) . . . . **16c**   [.   ]

     16d   **4th quarter** (October 1 – December 31) . . . . . . **16d**   [.   ]

17   **Total tax liability for the year** (lines 16a + 16b + 16c + 16d = line 17) **17**   [.   ]   **Total must equal line 12.**

Part 6:   May we speak with your third-party designee?

Do you want to allow an employee, a paid tax preparer, or another person to discuss this return with the IRS? See the instructions for details.

☐ **Yes.**   Designee's name and phone number

            Select a 5-digit Personal Identification Number (PIN) to use when talking to IRS   ☐ ☐ ☐ ☐ ☐

☐ **No.**

Part 7:   Sign here. You MUST complete both pages of this form and SIGN it.

Under penalties of perjury, I declare that I have examined this return, including accompanying schedules and statements, and to the best of my knowledge and belief, it is true, correct, and complete, and that no part of any payment made to a state unemployment fund claimed as a credit was, or is to be, deducted from the payments made to employees. Declaration of preparer (other than taxpayer) is based on all information of which preparer has any knowledge.

✗ Sign your name here

Print your name here

Print your title here

Date   /   /

Best daytime phone

Paid Preparer Use Only   Check if you are self-employed ☐

Preparer's name	PTIN
Preparer's signature	Date / /
Firm's name (or yours if self-employed)	EIN
Address	Phone
City State	ZIP code

Source: Internal Revenue Service.

Problem Set • B

Since the SUTA rates changes are made at the end of each year, the available 2022 rates were used for FUTA and SUTA.

5-1B • LO 3, 4 See Example 5-7 on page 5-12

During the year, Zeno Company has a SUTA tax rate of 6.3%. The taxable payroll for the year for FUTA and SUTA is $77,000. Compute:

a. Net FUTA tax .... $ _____

b. Net SUTA tax .... $ _____

c. Total unemployment taxes.. $ _____

5-2B • LO 3, 4 See Example 5-8 on page 5-16

Show Me How

Yengling Company's payroll for the year is $593,150. Of this amount, $211,630 is for wages paid in excess of $7,000 to each individual employee. The SUTA rate in Yengling Company's state is 2.9% on the first $7,000 of each employee's earnings. Compute:

a. Net FUTA tax .... $ _____

b. Net SUTA tax .... $ _____

c. Total unemployment taxes.. $ _____

5-3B • LO 3, 4 See Example 5-8 on page 5-16

Shibuno Shops had a SUTA tax rate of 2.7%. The state's taxable limit was $8,000 of each employee's earnings. For the year, Shibuno Shops had FUTA taxable wages of $77,900 and SUTA taxable wages of $93,900. Compute:

a. Net FUTA tax .... $ _____

b. Net SUTA tax .... $ _____

5-4B • LO 3, 4 See Example 5-7 on page 5-12

Show Me How

Due to its experience rating, Chang, Inc., is required to pay unemployment taxes on its payroll as follows:

1. Under SUTA for New Mexico on taxable payroll of $28,000, the contribution rate is 3.9%.

2. Under SUTA for Colorado on taxable payroll of $23,000, the contribution rate is 7.15%.

3. Under SUTA for Utah on taxable payroll of $65,000, the contribution rate is 4.1%.

4. Under FUTA, the taxable payroll is $94,500.

Compute:

a. SUTA taxes paid to New Mexico .... $ _____

b. SUTA taxes paid to Colorado .... $ _____

c. SUTA taxes paid to Utah.. $ _____

d. FUTA taxes paid... $ _____

5-5B • LO 1, 3 See Example 5-4 on page 5-10

Cowen Company began its operations in August of the current year. During August and September, the company paid wages of $2,450. For the last quarter of the year, the taxable wages paid amounted to $3,900. None of the employees were paid more than $7,000 this year.

5-5B (concluded)

a. Is Cowen Company liable for FUTA tax this year? Explain.

_____

_____

b. What is the *net* FUTA tax? .... $ _____

5-6B • LO 1, 2, 3   See Example 5-8 on page 5-16

In September, Painter Wax Corporation began operations in a state that requires new employers of one or more individuals to pay a state unemployment tax of 4.1% of the first $7,000 of wages paid each employee.

An analysis of the company's payroll for the year shows total wages paid of $212,640. The salaries of the president and the vice president of the company were $25,000 and $15,000, respectively, for the four-month period, but there were no other employees who received wages in excess of $7,000 for the four months. Included in the total wages were $900 paid to a director who only attended director meetings during the year, $6,300 paid to the factory superintendent, and $2,000 in employee contributions to a cafeteria plan made on a pretax basis—for both federal and state.

In addition to the total wages of $212,640, a payment of $2,000 was made to Andersen Accounting Company for an audit it performed on the company's books in December. Compute:

a. Net FUTA tax .... $ _____

b. SUTA tax .... $ _____

5-7B • LO 3, 4   See Example 5-1 on page 5-7

In April of the current year, Steelman Press Company transferred Ken Sherm from its factory in Louisiana to its plant in Florida. The company's SUTA tax rates based on its experience ratings are 3.2% in Louisiana and 3.8% in Florida. The taxable wage limits are $7,700 in Louisiana and $7,000 in Florida. This year, Steelman Press Company paid Ken Sherm wages of $14,190; $4,950 were paid in Louisiana and the remainder in Florida. Compute:

a. Amount of SUTA tax the company must pay to Louisiana on Sherm's wages........... $ _____

b. Amount of SUTA tax the company must pay to Florida on Sherm's wages.............. $ _____

c. Amount of the net FUTA tax on Sherm's wages .... $ _____

5-8B • LO 4 See Figure 5.1 on page 5-13

Sung Khang worked for two different employers. Until May, he worked for Wonderman Construction Company in Kansas City, Kansas, and earned $21,500. The state unemployment rate for Wonderman is 4.6%. He then changed jobs and worked for Buxmont Improvement Company in Mobile, Alabama, and earned $33,100 for the rest of the year. The state unemployment rate for Buxmont is 5.1%. Determine the unemployment taxes (FUTA and SUTA) that would be paid by:

a. Wonderman Construction Company .... $ _____

b. Buxmont Improvement Company .... $ _____

5-9B • LO 3, 4   See Example 5-2 on page 5-9

Show Me How

The partnership of Cox and Cohen paid the following wages during this year:

M. Cox (partner)	$45,000
S. Cohen (partner)	26,000
N. Rosario (supervisor)...	14,350
T. Gerenski (factory worker)	9,900
R. Sobowski (factory worker)...	9,450

D. Brunder (factory worker) 8,910
S. Carsoni (bookkeeper) 11,100
C. Chu (maintenance) 3,900

In addition, the partnership owed $200 to Chu for work he performed during December. However, payment for this work will not be made until January of the following year. The state unemployment tax rate for the company is 2.95% on the first $9,000 of each employee's earnings. Compute:

a. Net FUTA tax for the partnership for this year .... $ _____

b. SUTA tax for this year .... $ _____

5-10B • LO 3, 4 See Example 5-6 on page 5-12

Roofling Company paid wages of $319,600 this year. Of this amount, $193,900 was taxable for net FUTA and SUTA purposes. The state's contribution tax rate is 4.3% for Roofling Company. Due to cash flow problems, the company did not make any SUTA payments until after the Form 940 filing date. Compute:

a. Amount of credit the company would receive against the FUTA tax
for its SUTA contributions .... $ _____

b. Amount that Roofling Company would pay to the federal government
for its FUTA tax .... $ _____

c. Amount that the company lost because of its late payments .... $ _____

5-11B • LO 3, 4 See Example 5-8 on page 5-16

Pedro Company was subject to the New Jersey state unemployment tax of 5.1%. The company's taxable wages for FUTA were $93,400 and for SUTA, $194,300. Compute:

a. SUTA tax that Pedro Company would pay to the state of New Jersey .... $ _____

b. Net FUTA tax .... $ _____

c. Amount of employees' unemployment tax (use the employee's tax rate shown
in Figure 5.1 on page 5-14) .... $ _____

5-12B • LO 4 See Example 5-10 on page 5-18

The following unemployment tax rate schedule is in effect for the calendar year 2023 in State A, which uses the reserve-ratio formula in determining employer contributions:

Reserve Ratio	Contribution Rate
0.0% or more, but less than 1.0%...............................	6.7%
1.0% or more, but less than 1.2%...............................	6.4%
1.2% or more, but less than 1.4%...............................	6.1%
1.4% or more, but less than 1.6%...............................	5.8%
1.6% or more, but less than 1.8%...............................	5.5%
1.8% or more, but less than 2.0%...............................	5.2%
2.0% or more, but less than 2.2%...............................	4.9%
2.2% or more, but less than 2.4%...............................	4.6%
2.4% or more, but less than 2.6%...............................	4.3%
2.6% or more, but less than 2.8%...............................	4.0%
2.8% or more, but less than 3.0%...............................	3.7%
3.0% or more, but less than 3.2%...............................	3.4%
3.2% or more...	3.1%

Conrad Company, which is located in State A, had an average annual payroll of $1,150,000 for the three 12-month periods ending on June 30, 2022 (the computation date for the tax year 2023). As of June 30, 2022 the

5-12B (concluded)

total contributions that had been made to Conrad Company's reserve account, in excess of the benefits charged, amounted to $21,560. Compute:

a. Conrad Company's reserve ratio for 2022 .... _____ %

b. 2023 contribution rate for the company.. _____ %

c. Smallest contribution that the company can make in order to reduce its tax rate if State A permits voluntary contributions .... $ _____

d. Tax savings realized by the company, taking into consideration the voluntary contribution made in (c) if the taxable payroll in 2023 is $1,295,000.. $ _____

5-13B • LO 4   See Example 5-11 on page 5-20   Show Me How

As of June 30, 2022 (the computation date for the 2023 tax rate), Amanda Company had a negative balance of $1,015 in its unemployment reserve account in State A. The company's average payroll over the last three 12-month periods amounted to $525,000. The unemployment compensation law of State A provides that the tax rate of an employer who has a negative balance on the computation date shall be 7.2% during the following calendar year.

   Using the tax rate schedule presented in Problem 5-12B, compute:

a. The smallest voluntary contribution that Amanda Company should make in order to effect a change in its tax rate... $ _____

b. The amount of the tax savings as a result of the voluntary contribution if Amanda Company's taxable payroll for 2023 is $650,000...................................... $ _____

5-14B • LO 2, 3, 4   See Example 5-8 on page 5-16

Mary Givens and Peggy Moser are partners engaged in operating The G&M Doll Shop, which has employed the following persons since the beginning of the year:

T. Binn (general office worker)	$3,100 per month
W. Ashworth (saleswoman).......................................	$30,000 per year
K. Bitner (stock clerk)..	$280 per week
J. Vern (deliveryman)	$350 per week
A. Patel (cleaning and maintenance, part-time)	$240 per week

Givens and Moser are each paid a weekly salary allowance of $1,000.

   The doll shop is located in a state that requires unemployment compensation contributions of employers of one or more individuals. The company is subject to state contributions at a rate of 3.25% for wages not in excess of $10,000. Compute each of the following amounts based upon the *41st weekly payroll period* ending October 14, 20--:

a. Amount of FICA taxes (OASDI and HI) to be withheld from the earnings of each person. (Refer to Chapter 3.)

	OASDI	HI
M. Givens	$ _____	$ _____
P. Moser..	_____	_____
T. Binn..	_____	_____
W. Ashworth	_____	_____
K. Bitner...	_____	_____
J. Vern..	_____	_____
A. Patel	_____	_____

b. Amount of the employer's FICA taxes for the weekly payroll................... _____ _____

c. Amount of state unemployment contributions for the weekly payroll .... $ _____

d. Amount of the net FUTA tax on the payroll .... $ _____

e. Total amount of the employer's payroll taxes for the weekly payroll.................. $ _____

5-15B • LO 4 See Example 5-10 on page 5-18

Alfaro Security Company is located in State H, which enables employers to reduce their contribution rates under the experience-rating system. From 2009 to 2018, inclusive, the company's total contributions to state unemployment compensation amounted to $18,135. For the calendar years 2019 to 2022, inclusive, the contribution rate for the Alfaro Company was 3.7%.

The contributions of each employer are credited to an account maintained by the State Unemployment Compensation Commission. This account is credited with contributions paid into the account by the employer and is charged with unemployment benefits that are paid from the account. Starting January 1, 2023 the contributions rate for all employers in State H will be based on the following tax rate schedule:

Reserve Ratio	Contribution Rate
Contributions falling below benefits paid	7.0%
0.0% to 7.9%	5.5%
8.0% to 9.9%	4.5%
10.0% to 11.9%	3.5%
12.0% to 14.9%	2.5%
15.0% or more	1.5%

The annual payroll for calculation purposes is the total wages payable during a 12-month period ending with the last day of the third quarter of any calendar year. The average annual payroll is the average of the last three annual payrolls. The SUTA tax rate for the year is computed using the information available (benefits received and taxes paid) as of September 30 of the preceding year.

The schedule below shows the total payroll and the taxable payroll for the calendar years 2019 to 2022.

	Calendar Year							
	2019		2020		2021		2022	
	Total Payroll	Taxable Payroll	Total Payroll	Taxable Payroll	Total Payroll	Taxable Payroll	Total Payroll	Taxable Payroll
First Quarter............	$12,000	$12,000	$11,000	$11,000	$13,000	$13,000	$10,000	$10,000
Second Quarter	11,750	11,750	11,500	11,400	12,750	12,700	9,300	9,300
Third Quarter...........	12,500	12,250	12,750	12,400	12,200	12,000	9,350	9,350
Fourth Quarter.........	13,000	12,500	12,500	12,200	14,000	13,750	—	—

Unemployment benefits became payable to the company's qualified unemployed workers on January 1, 2009. Between that time and September 30, 2023, total benefits amounting to $23,194.15 were charged against the employer's account. Compute:

a. Contribution rate for 2023 .... _____ %

b. Rate for 2023 if $2,000 additional benefits had been charged by mistake to the account of Alfaro Security Company by the State Unemployment Compensation Commission .... _____ %

5-16B • LO 5   See Figure 5.2 on pages 5-22 and 5-23, Figure 5.3 on page 5-24, Figure 5.4 on page 5-27

Show Me How

As the accountant for Monroe Trucking Company, you are preparing the company's annual return, Form 940 and Schedule A. Use the following information to complete Form 940 and Schedule A on pages 5-57 to 5-59.

The net FUTA tax liability for each quarter of 20-- was as follows: 1st, $97.00; 2nd, $87.00; 3rd, $69.70; and 4th, $59.50.

5-16B (continued)

Since the net FUTA tax liability did not exceed $500, the company was not required to make its first deposit of FUTA taxes until January 31 of the next year. Assume that the electronic payment was made on time.

a. One of the employees performs all of his duties in another state—Louisiana.

b. Total payments made to employees during calendar year 20--:

Texas..	$53,450
Louisiana......................................	22,150
Total..	$75,600

c. Employer contributions into employees' 401(k) retirement plan: $1,250.

d. Payments made to employees in excess of $7,000: $22,150.

e. Form is to be signed by Vernon Scott, Vice President, and dated 1/31/--.

f. Phone number—(834) 555-5551.

5-16B (continued)

Form **940 for 20--:** **Employer's Annual Federal Unemployment (FUTA) Tax Return**

Department of the Treasury — Internal Revenue Service

OMB No. 1545-0028

Employer identification number (EIN) 0 0 – 0 0 0 3 7 9 3

Name (not your trade name) MONROE TRUCKING COMPANY

Trade name (if any)

Address 423 BRISTOL PIKE

Number   Street   Suite or room number

LAREDO   TX   78040-4523

City   State   ZIP code

Foreign country name   Foreign province/county   Foreign postal code

Type of Return
(Check all that apply.)

☐ **a.** Amended

☐ **b.** Successor employer

☐ **c.** No payments to employees in 20--

☐ **d.** Final: Business closed or stopped paying wages

Go to *www.irs.gov/Form940* for instructions and the latest information.

Read the separate instructions before you complete this form. Please type or print within the boxes.

Part 1: Tell us about your return. If any line does NOT apply, leave it blank. See instructions before completing Part 1.

1a If you had to pay state unemployment tax in one state only, enter the state abbreviation . **1a**

1b If you had to pay state unemployment tax in more than one state, you are a multi-state employer . . . . **1b** ☐ Check here. Complete Schedule A (Form 940).

2 If you paid wages in a state that is subject to CREDIT REDUCTION . . . . **2** ☐ Check here. Complete Schedule A (Form 940).

Part 2: Determine your FUTA tax before adjustments. If any line does NOT apply, leave it blank.

3 Total payments to all employees **3**

4 Payments exempt from FUTA tax **4**

Check all that apply: **4a** ☐ Fringe benefits   **4c** ☐ Retirement/Pension   **4e** ☐ Other
              4b ☐ Group-term life insurance   **4d** ☐ Dependent care

5 Total of payments made to each employee in excess of $7,000 . . . . . . **5**

6 Subtotal (line 4 + line 5 = line 6) **6**

7 Total taxable FUTA wages (line 3 – line 6 = line 7). See instructions **7**

8 FUTA tax before adjustments (line 7 x 0.006 = line 8) **8**

Part 3: Determine your adjustments. If any line does NOT apply, leave it blank.

9 If ALL of the taxable FUTA wages you paid were excluded from state unemployment tax, multiply line 7 by 0.054 (line 7 × 0.054 = line 9). Go to line 12 . . . . **9**

10 If SOME of the taxable FUTA wages you paid were excluded from state unemployment tax, OR you paid ANY state unemployment tax late (after the due date for filing Form 940), complete the worksheet in the instructions. Enter the amount from line 7 of the worksheet . . **10**

11 If credit reduction applies, enter the total from Schedule A (Form 940) **11**

Part 4: Determine your FUTA tax and balance due or overpayment. If any line does NOT apply, leave it blank.

12 Total FUTA tax after adjustments (lines 8 + 9 + 10 + 11 = line 12) **12**

13 FUTA tax deposited for the year, including any overpayment applied from a prior year . **13**

14 Balance due. If line 12 is more than line 13, enter the excess on line 14.
- If line 14 is more than $500, you must deposit your tax.
- If line 14 is $500 or less, you may pay with this return. See instructions **14**

15 Overpayment. If line 13 is more than line 12, enter the excess on line 15 and check a box below **15**

▶ You **MUST** complete both pages of this form and **SIGN** it.   Check one: ☐ Apply to next return. ☐ Send a refund.

Next ▶

For Privacy Act and Paperwork Reduction Act Notice, see the back of the Payment Voucher.   Cat. No. 11234O   Form **940** (2021)

5-16B (continued)

Name *(not your trade name)*	Employer identification number (EIN)
MONROE TRUCKING COMPANY	00-0003793

Part 5: Report your FUTA tax liability by quarter only if line 12 is more than $500. If not, go to Part 6.

16 Report the amount of your FUTA tax liability for each quarter; do NOT enter the amount you deposited. If you had no liability for a quarter, leave the line blank.

16a **1st quarter** (January 1 – March 31) . . . . 16a [.   ]

16b **2nd quarter** (April 1 – June 30) . . . . 16b [.   ]

16c **3rd quarter** (July 1 – September 30) . . . . 16c [.   ]

16d **4th quarter** (October 1 – December 31) . . . . 16d [.   ]

17 Total tax liability for the year (lines 16a + 16b + 16c + 16d = line 17) **17** [.   ] Total must equal line 12.

Part 6: May we speak with your third-party designee?

Do you want to allow an employee, a paid tax preparer, or another person to discuss this return with the IRS? See the instructions for details.

☐ **Yes.** Designee's name and phone number [   ] [   ]

Select a 5-digit Personal Identification Number (PIN) to use when talking to IRS [   ] [   ] [   ] [   ] [   ]

☐ **No.**

Part 7: Sign here. You MUST complete both pages of this form and SIGN it.

Under penalties of perjury, I declare that I have examined this return, including accompanying schedules and statements, and to the best of my knowledge and belief, it is true, correct, and complete, and that no part of any payment made to a state unemployment fund claimed as a credit was, or is to be, deducted from the payments made to employees. Declaration of preparer (other than taxpayer) is based on all information of which preparer has any knowledge.

✗ **Sign your name here** [   ]

Print your name here [   ]

Print your title here [   ]

Date [/   /   ]

Best daytime phone [   ]

Paid Preparer Use Only   Check if you are self-employed ☐

Preparer's name [ ]	PTIN [ ]
Preparer's signature [ ]	Date [/ /]
Firm's name (or yours if self-employed) [ ]	EIN [ ]
Address [ ]	Phone [ ]
City [ ] State [ ]	ZIP code [ ]

Source: Internal Revenue Service.

5-16B (concluded)

Schedule A (Form 940) for 20--:

Multi-State Employer and Credit Reduction Information
Department of the Treasury — Internal Revenue Service

OMB No. 1545-0028

Employer identification number (EIN) 0 0 – 0 0 0 3 7 9 3

Name *(not your trade name)* MONROE TRUCKING COMPANY

See the instructions on page 2. File this schedule with Form 940.

Place an "X" in the box of EVERY state in which you had to pay state unemployment tax this year. For the U.S. Virgin Islands, enter the FUTA taxable wages and the reduction rate (see page 2). Multiply the FUTA taxable wages by the reduction rate and enter the credit reduction amount. Don't include in the *FUTA Taxable Wages* box wages that were excluded from state unemployment tax (see the instructions for Step 2). If any states don't apply to you, leave them blank.

Postal Abbreviation	FUTA Taxable Wages	Reduction Rate	Credit Reduction	Postal Abbreviation	FUTA Taxable Wages	Reduction Rate	Credit Reduction
AK	.		.	NC	.		.
AL	.		.	ND	.		.
AR	.		.	NE	.		.
AZ	.		.	NH	.		.
CA	.		.	NJ	.		.
CO	.		.	NM	.		.
CT	.		.	NV	.		.
DC	.		.	NY	.		.
DE	.		.	OH	.		.
FL	.		.	OK	.		.
GA	.		.	OR	.		.
HI	.		.	PA	.		.
IA	.		.	RI	.		.
ID	.		.	SC	.		.
IL	.		.	SD	.		.
IN	.		.	TN	.		.
KS	.		.	TX	.		.
KY	.		.	UT	.		.
LA	.		.	VA	.		.
MA	.		.	VT	.		.
MD	.		.	WA	.		.
ME	.		.	WI	.		.
MI	.		.	WV	.		.
MN	.		.	WY	.		.
MO	.		.	PR	.		.
MS	.		.	VI	.		.
MT	.		.				

Total Credit Reduction. Add all amounts shown in the *Credit Reduction* boxes. Enter the total here and on Form 940, line 11 . . . .

For Privacy Act and Paperwork Reduction Act Notice, see the Instructions for Form 940.   Cat. No. 16997C   Schedule A (Form 940) 2021

Source: Internal Revenue Service.

5-17B • LO 5, 6   See Figure 5.2 on pages 5-22 and 5-23, Figure 5.5 on page 5-30, Figure 5.6 on page 5-31

The information listed below refers to the employees of Brennan Company for the year ended December 31, 20--. The wages are separated into the quarters in which they were paid to the individual employees.

Name	Social Security #	1st Qtr.	2nd Qtr.	3rd Qtr.	4th Qtr.	Total
May S. Sun	000-00-0001	$ -0-	$ 6,100	$ 6,300	$ 4,100	$ 16,500
David R. Maro (Foreman)	000-00-0003	4,000	3,800	4,200	4,700	16,700
Randy A. Wade	000-00-1998	2,900	2,700	2,900	3,200	11,700
Hilary B. Cahn	000-00-7413	3,800	4,100	4,900	5,500	18,300
Paul C. Morse (Manager)	000-00-6523	9,000	8,800	9,500	10,000	37,300
Morrie T. Black	000-00-6789	6,500	4,100	-0-	-0-	10,600
Kelly K. Woods	000-00-3334	2,500	2,300	1,900	1,800	8,500
Terry M. Brennan (President)	000-00-1014	15,000	14,700	15,500	16,900	62,100
Art A. Mintz	000-00-7277	-0-	-0-	7,000	9,800	16,800
Megan T. Rudolph	000-00-8111	8,800	8,400	8,900	-0-	26,100
Kurt A. Weiner	000-00-2623	-0-	7,500	7,700	8,400	23,600
Ryan C. Harrow	000-00-3534	5,300	5,700	6,100	2,400	19,500
Totals		$57,800	$68,200	$74,900	$66,800	$267,700

For 20--, State D's contribution rate for Brennan Company, based on the experience-rating system of the state, was 3.6% of the first $7,000 of each employee's earnings. The state tax returns are due one month after the end of each calendar quarter. During 20--, the company paid $3,024.00 of contributions to State D's unemployment fund.

Employer's phone number: (613) 555-0029. Employer's State D reporting number: 00596.

Using the forms supplied on pages 5-61 to 5-63, complete the following for 20--:

a. The last payment of the year is used to pay the FUTA tax for the fourth quarter of 20-- (the first three-quarter's liability was more than the $500 threshold). State D is not a credit reduction state.

   Tax Payment:

   Date _____   Amount $ _____

b. Employer's Report for Unemployment Compensation, State D—4th quarter only. Item 1 is the number of employees employed in the pay period that includes the 12th of each month in the quarter. For Brennan Company, the number of employees is ten in October, nine in November, and eight in December. All employees earned 13 credit weeks during the last quarter except for Sun (8) and Harrow (9).

c. Employer's Annual Federal Unemployment (FUTA) Tax Return—Form 940

Indicate on each form the date that the form should be submitted and the amount of money that must be paid. The president of the company prepares and signs all tax forms.

5-17B (continued)

b.

State D Form UC-2 REV 07-21, Employer's Report for Unemployment Compensation   QTR./YEAR 4/20--

Read Instructions – Answer Each Item   DUE DATE 01/31/20--

W   1ST MONTH   2ND MONTH   3RD MONTH   ▲ DETACH HERE

EXAMINED BY: [   ]   1. TOTAL COVERED EMPLOYEES IN PAY PERIOD INCL. 12TH OF MONTH

Signature certifies that the information contained herein is true and correct to the best of the signer's knowledge.   FOR DEPT. USE

[   ][   ][   ]   2. GROSS WAGES

10. SIGN HERE-DO NOT PRINT   3. EMPLOYEE CONTRI-BUTIONS   X X X X X X X X X   [XXXXX]

TITLE _____ DATE _____ PHONE # _____   4. TAXABLE WAGES FOR EMPLOYER CONTRIBUTIONS

11. FILED ☐ PAPER UC-2A ☐ INTERNET UC-2A   5. EMPLOYER CONTRI-BUTIONS DUE (RATE X ITEM 4)

12. FEDERAL IDENTIFICATION NUMBER _____

EMPLOYER'S CONTRIBUTION RATE ▷ 3.6%   EMPLOYER'S ACCT. NO. 00596   CHECK DIGIT 1   6. TOTAL CONTRI-BUTIONS DUE (ITEMS 3 + 5)

7. INTEREST DUE SEE INSTRUCTIONS

8. PENALTY DUE SEE INSTRUCTIONS

Brennan Company
123 Swamp Road
Pikesville, D State 10777-2017   9. TOTAL REMITTANCE (ITEMS 6 + 7 + 8) $ ▪

Employer name and address Make any corrections on Form UC-2B

MAKE CHECKS PAYABLE TO: State D UC FUND

SUBJECTIVITY DATE   REPORT DELINQUENT DATE

State D Form UC-2A, Employer's Quarterly Report of Wages Paid to Each Employee

See instructions on separate sheet. Information MUST be typewritten or printed in BLACK ink. Do NOT use commas (,) or dollar signs ($). If typed, disregard vertical bars and type a consecutive string of characters. If hand printed, print in CAPS and within the boxes as below:

SAMPLE Typed: [1][2][3][4][5][6][.][0][0]   SAMPLE Handwritten: [1][2][3][4][5][6][.][0][0]   SAMPLE Filled-in: ➡ ●

Employer name (make corrections on Form UC-2B)   Employer State D UC account no.   Check digit   Quarter and year Q / YYYY   Quarter ending date MM / DD / YYYY

Brennan Company   00596   1   4/20--   12/31/20--

1. Name and telephone number of preparer   2. Total number of pages in this report   3. Total number of employees listed in item 8 on all pages of Form UC-2A   4. Plant number (if approved)

5. Gross wages, MUST agree with item 2 on UC-2 and the sum of item 11 on all pages of Form UC-2A   ▲   6. Fill in this circle if you would like the Department to preprint your employee's names & SSNs on Form UC-2A next quarter   ➡ ◉

7. Employee's Social Security Number	8. Employee's name FI MI LAST	9. Gross wages paid this qtr Example: 123456.00	10. Credit Weeks

List any additional employees on continuation sheets in the required format (see instructions).

11. Total gross wages for this page:
12. Total number of employees for this page _____   ➡

UC-2A REV 07-21   **13. Page ____ of ____**

5-17B (continued)

c.

Form **940** for 20--: **Employer's Annual Federal Unemployment (FUTA) Tax Return**

Department of the Treasury — Internal Revenue Service

OMB No. 1545-0028

Employer identification number (EIN) 0 0 – 0 0 0 6 4 2 1

Name *(not your trade name)* BRENNAN COMPANY

Trade name *(if any)*

Address 123 SWAMP ROAD

Number   Street   Suite or room number

PIKESVILLE   D   10777-2017

City   State   ZIP code

Foreign country name   Foreign province/county   Foreign postal code

Type of Return
(Check all that apply.)

☐ **a.** Amended

☐ **b.** Successor employer

☐ **c.** No payments to employees in 20--

☐ **d.** Final: Business closed or stopped paying wages

Go to *www.irs.gov/Form940* for instructions and the latest information.

Read the separate instructions before you complete this form. Please type or print within the boxes.

Part 1: Tell us about your return. If any line does NOT apply, leave it blank. See instructions before completing Part 1.

1a If you had to pay state unemployment tax in one state only, enter the state abbreviation . **1a** ☐ ☐

1b If you had to pay state unemployment tax in more than one state, you are a multi-state employer . . . . **1b** ☐ Check here. Complete Schedule A (Form 940).

2 If you paid wages in a state that is subject to CREDIT REDUCTION . . . . . . **2** ☐ Check here. Complete Schedule A (Form 940).

Part 2: Determine your FUTA tax before adjustments. If any line does NOT apply, leave it blank.

3 Total payments to all employees . . . . **3** _____.

4 Payments exempt from FUTA tax . . . . . . **4** _____.

Check all that apply: **4a** ☐ Fringe benefits   **4c** ☐ Retirement/Pension   **4e** ☐ Other
4b ☐ Group-term life insurance   **4d** ☐ Dependent care

5 Total of payments made to each employee in excess of $7,000 . . . . **5** _____.

6 Subtotal (line 4 + line 5 = line 6) . . . . **6** _____.

7 Total taxable FUTA wages (line 3 – line 6 = line 7). See instructions . . . . **7** _____.

8 FUTA tax before adjustments (line 7 x 0.006 = line 8) . . . . **8** _____.

Part 3: Determine your adjustments. If any line does NOT apply, leave it blank.

9 If ALL of the taxable FUTA wages you paid were excluded from state unemployment tax, multiply line 7 by 0.054 (line 7 x 0.054 = line 9). Go to line 12 . . . . **9** _____.

10 If SOME of the taxable FUTA wages you paid were excluded from state unemployment tax, OR you paid ANY state unemployment tax late (after the due date for filing Form 940), complete the worksheet in the instructions. Enter the amount from line 7 of the worksheet . . **10** _____.

11 If credit reduction applies, enter the total from Schedule A (Form 940) . . . . . . **11** _____.

Part 4: Determine your FUTA tax and balance due or overpayment. If any line does NOT apply, leave it blank.

12 Total FUTA tax after adjustments (lines 8 + 9 + 10 + 11 = line 12) . . . . **12** _____.

13 FUTA tax deposited for the year, including any overpayment applied from a prior year . **13** _____.

14 Balance due. If line 12 is more than line 13, enter the excess on line 14.
• If line 14 is more than $500, you must deposit your tax.
• If line 14 is $500 or less, you may pay with this return. See instructions . . . . . . **14** _____.

15 Overpayment. If line 13 is more than line 12, enter the excess on line 15 and check a box below **15** _____.

▶ You **MUST** complete both pages of this form and **SIGN** it.   Check one: ☐ Apply to next return. ☐ Send a refund.

Next ▶

For Privacy Act and Paperwork Reduction Act Notice, see the back of the Payment Voucher.   Cat. No. 11234O   Form **940** (2021)

5-17B (concluded)

c.

Name *(not your trade name)*	Employer identification number (EIN)
BRENNAN COMPANY	00-0006421

Part 5:	Report your FUTA tax liability by quarter only if line 12 is more than $500. If not, go to Part 6.

16 Report the amount of your FUTA tax liability for each quarter; do NOT enter the amount you deposited. If you had no liability for a quarter, leave the line blank.

16a **1st quarter** (January 1 – March 31) . . . . **16a** [.]

16b **2nd quarter** (April 1 – June 30) . . . . **16b** [.]

16c **3rd quarter** (July 1 – September 30) . . . . **16c** [.]

16d **4th quarter** (October 1 – December 31) . . . . **16d** [.]

17 Total tax liability for the year (lines 16a + 16b + 16c + 16d = line 17) **17** [.] **Total must equal line 12.**

Part 6:	May we speak with your third-party designee?

Do you want to allow an employee, a paid tax preparer, or another person to discuss this return with the IRS? See the instructions for details.

☐ **Yes.** Designee's name and phone number [   ] [   ]

Select a 5-digit Personal Identification Number (PIN) to use when talking to IRS [ ] [ ] [ ] [ ] [ ]

☐ **No.**

Part 7:	Sign here. You MUST complete both pages of this form and SIGN it.

Under penalties of perjury, I declare that I have examined this return, including accompanying schedules and statements, and to the best of my knowledge and belief, it is true, correct, and complete, and that no part of any payment made to a state unemployment fund claimed as a credit was, or is to be, deducted from the payments made to employees. Declaration of preparer (other than taxpayer) is based on all information of which preparer has any knowledge.

✗ **Sign your name here** [   ]

Print your name here [   ]

Print your title here [   ]

Date [/ /]

Best daytime phone [   ]

Paid Preparer Use Only   Check if you are self-employed ☐

Preparer's name		PTIN	
Preparer's signature		Date	/ /
Firm's name (or yours if self-employed)		EIN	
Address		Phone	
City	State	ZIP code	

Form **940** (2021)

Source: Internal Revenue Service.

Continuing Payroll Problem • A

Refer to the partially completed payroll register that you worked on at the end of Chapter 4. Complete the SUTA deduction column—employees pay 0.06% on total gross pay. You will now compute the employer's liability for unemployment taxes (FUTA and SUTA) for the pay of January 14. These computations will be used at the end of Chapter 6 in recording the payroll tax entries.

To compute the employer's liability for unemployment taxes, proceed as follows:

1. Enter each employee's gross earnings in the Taxable Earnings—FUTA and SUTA columns.
2. Total the Taxable Earnings—FUTA and SUTA columns.

3. At the bottom of your payroll register, compute the following:
   a. Net FUTA tax. Since this is the first pay period of the year, none of the employees are near the $7,000 ceiling; therefore, each employee's gross earnings is subject to the FUTA tax.
   b. SUTA tax. Since Kipley Company is a new employer, Pennsylvania has assigned the company a contribution rate of 3.689% on the first $10,000 of each employee's earnings. Employees pay 0.06% on total gross pay.

Note: Retain your partially completed payroll register for use at the end of Chapter 6.

Continuing Payroll Problem • B

Refer to the partially completed payroll register that you worked on at the end of Chapter 4. Complete the SUTA deduction column—employees pay 0.06% on total gross pay. You will now compute the employer's liability for unemployment taxes (FUTA and SUTA) for the pay of January 14. These computations will be used at the end of Chapter 6 in recording the payroll tax entries.

To compute the employer's liability for unemployment taxes, proceed as follows:

1. Enter each employee's gross earnings in the Taxable Earnings—FUTA and SUTA columns.
2. Total the Taxable Earnings—FUTA and SUTA columns.

3. At the bottom of your payroll register, compute the following:
   a. Net FUTA tax. Since this is the first pay period of the year, none of the employees are near the $7,000 ceiling; therefore, each employee's gross earnings is subject to the FUTA tax.
   b. SUTA tax. Since Olney Company is a new employer, Pennsylvania has assigned the company a contribution rate of 3.689% on the first $10,000 of each employee's earnings. Employees pay 0.06% on total gross pay.

Note: Retain your partially completed payroll register for use at the end of Chapter 6.

Case Problem

C1. Reducing a High Unemployment Tax Rate.

Over the past two years, Kermit Stone, the controller of Hilton Company, has been concerned that the company has been paying a large amount of money for state unemployment taxes. On reviewing the "unemployment file" with the head accountant, Deborah Murtha, he learns that the company's tax rate is near the top of the range of the state's experience-rating system.

After calling the local unemployment office, Stone realizes that the turnover of employees at Hilton Company has had an adverse effect on the company's tax rates. In addition, after consulting with Murtha, he discovers that the eligibility reports that come from the state unemployment office are just signed and sent back to the state without any review

The eligibility reports are notices that an ex-employee has filed a claim for unemployment benefits. By signing these reports "blindly," the company, in effect, tells the state that the employee is eligible for the benefits. Any benefits paid are charged by the state against Hilton Company's account.

Stone is convinced that the rates the company is paying are too high, and he feels that part of the reason is the "blind" signing of the eligibility reports. Besides this, he wonders what other steps the company can take to lower its contributions rate and taxes.

Submit recommendations that might help Stone reduce the "unfair" burden that the unemployment compensation taxes are leveling on Hilton Company.

Chapter 6

Analyzing and Journalizing Payroll

As you know, the title of this book is **Payroll Accounting**. In the first five chapters, we focused on payroll discussions. Now is the time to look at the accounting part. You remember—the debits and the credits, the journal and the ledger, the payroll registers, and the employees' earnings records.

Payroll transactions must be journalized—recording the payroll, the employer's payroll taxes, the payment of the payroll-related liabilities, and the adjustment required at the end of the accounting period. These entries must then be posted to the appropriate general ledger accounts. Even if done through a computerized system, you need to understand the process and be able to explain how the dollar amounts are being generated.

Learning Objectives

After studying this chapter, you should be able to:

1. Record payrolls in payroll registers and post to employees' earnings records.
2. Identify the various deductions—both voluntary and involuntary (taxes and garnishments)—that are taken out of employees' gross pay.
3. Journalize the entries to record the payroll and payroll taxes.
4. Post to the various general ledger accounts that are used to accumulate information from the payroll entries.
5. Explain the recording of the payroll tax deposits.
6. Explain the need for end-of-period adjustments.

This chapter presents the procedures for recording the payroll in a payroll register, transferring information from the payroll register to the employees' earnings records, recording these transactions in the company's book of original entry, and posting them to the proper ledger accounts. Today, many of these functions are done by sophisticated computer programs. However, the payroll professional must understand the steps that the computer is performing.

We will also look at the various withholdings that can come out of an employee's pay and some issues that the employer must be aware of in making these deductions. In addition, the methods of paying employees are detailed in this chapter.

Puhhha/Shutterstock.com

The Payroll Register

As you have seen in Figure 1.9, on page 1-24, and in completing the Continuing Payroll Problem, the payroll register, which in most cases will be computer-generated, gives detailed information about the payroll for each pay period.

To summarize, the payroll register may provide the following types of information:

1. The title of the form.
2. The period covered by the payroll and the pay date.

LO 1
Record payrolls in payroll registers and post to employees' earnings records.

3. Department or branch. Some large businesses with many departments or branches prepare a separate sheet in the payroll register for each department or branch on each payday. Other firms provide "distribution" columns such as "Sales Salaries," "Office Salaries," and "Plant Wages" for classifying the gross wages and salaries according to the nature of the wage and salary expense. The total of each distribution column shows the total amount of that department's wage expense.

4. A column to record the name of each employee. Many businesses provide a column to record an identifying number such as the time clock number for each employee.

5. Filing status and number of withholding allowances. This information determines the income tax deductions. In some cases (for employees who already have Forms W-4 on file), this information is presented only in the employees' earnings records. For employees who completed Form W-4 from 2020 or later, the withholding allowances are not needed and are not listed on the form (e.g., in Figure 6.1, see employee number 23, LuAnn T. O'Brien).

6. A record of time worked. Many companies show detailed information in the payroll register as to hours worked each day by each employee. Separate columns can be used to show a total of regular hours worked and a total of overtime hours worked during the pay period. This information helps a business that schedules much overtime work.

7. The regular rate of pay and the amount earned at the regular rate.

8. A space to record the overtime rate and the total earnings at the overtime rate. Some companies prefer to show an Overtime Premium Earnings column in place of the Overtime Earnings column. With this approach, as discussed in Chapter 2, the regular earnings is equal to the regular hourly rate of pay multiplied by the total hours worked, and the overtime premium is equal to the extra one-half rate of pay multiplied by the overtime hours.

9. A column to record the total earnings.

10. Information about deductions from total earnings. A separate column may be provided for each type of deduction. The various deductions will be discussed later in this chapter.

11. A column to show the net amount paid (total earnings less deductions). When paying by check, a company usually provides a column for the number of each employee's paycheck.

12. Some firms provide special columns in the payroll register to indicate that portion of the employee's wages taxable under the Federal Insurance Contributions Act (OASDI and HI) and other laws that require payment of taxes only on wages up to the taxable limits.

Example 6-1

Chris Collins (the first employee in Figure 6.1) earns $15.20 per hour and worked 44 hours. His pay would be (using the overtime premium approach):

Regular pay	$15.20 × 44 hours =	$668.80
Overtime premium pay	$ 7.60 × 4 hours =	30.40
Total pay		$699.20

The only information needed to be entered will be the employee's number or name and the time worked. In some cases, this information would be automatically transferred from the time-keeping device. The program will then calculate and print the other information based on the data stored for each employee and the particular computer program. Only a small number of firms prepare the registers manually. The partial payroll register shown in Figure 6.1 contains most of the information outlined before. This register is used to compute the pay for hourly workers for a weekly pay period. The layout of the section devoted to time or hours worked will vary, depending on the payroll period and the work schedules of each individual business.

FIGURE 6.1
Payroll Register (left side)

FOR WEEK ENDING *January 17, 20--*   Payday January 17, 20--

	NO.	NAME	FILING STATUS	NO. W/H ALLOW.	TIME RECORD M	T	W	T	F	S	REGULAR EARNINGS HOURS	RATE PER HOUR	AMOUNT			OVERTIME EARNINGS HOURS	RATE PER HOUR	AMOUNT		
1	10	Collins, Chris R.	M	2	8	8	8	8	8	4	40	15 20	6 0 8	00		4	22 80	9 1	20	
2	12	Liu, Carolyn B.	M	4	8	8	8	8	10		40	17 10	6 8 4	00		2	25 65	5 1	30	
3	13	Carson, Henry S.	S	1	8	8	8	8	8		40	16 30	6 5 2	00						
4	23	O'Brien, LuAnn T.	MFJ	N/A	8	8	8	8	8	8	40	15 90	6 3 6	00		8	23 85	1 9 0	80	
5	24	Rudolph, Beth M.	S	1	8	8	8	0	8		32	16 10	5 1 5	20						
36		Totals											224 9 7	20				22 6 5	50	

FIGURE 6.1 (concluded)
Payroll Register (right side)

DEPT. ACCOUNTING— 10

TOTAL EARNINGS				DEDUCTIONS FICA OASDI	HI	FED. INCOME TAX	STATE INCOME TAX	GROUP INS.	NET PAID CHECK NO.	AMOUNT			TAXABLE EARNINGS FICA OASDI	HI	FUTA & SUTA	
6	9	9	20	4 3 35	10 14	29 00	4 78	9 00	898	6 0 2	93		6 9 9 20	6 9 9 20	6 9 9 20	1
7	3	5	30	4 5 59	10 66	15 00	6 11	9 00	899	6 4 8	94		7 3 5 30	7 3 5 30	7 3 5 30	2
6	5	2	00	4 0 42	9 45	54 00	5 04	3 90	900	5 3 9	19		6 5 2 00	6 5 2 00	6 5 2 00	3
8	2	6	80	5 1 26	11 99	33 00	6 14	9 00	901	7 1 5	41		8 2 6 80	8 2 6 80	8 2 6 80	4
5	1	5	20	3 1 94	7 47	38 00	3 90	3 90	902	4 2 9	99		5 1 5 20	5 1 5 20	5 1 5 20	5
247 6	2	70	15 35	29 3 59	06 37	14 00	5 5 25	5 4 70		190 4 4	40		247 6 2 70	247 6 2 70	247 6 2 70	36

Proving the Totals of the Payroll Register

As shown later in this chapter, the payroll register provides the information needed in preparing the journal entries to record (1) the wages earned, deductions from wages, and net amount paid each payday and (2) the employer's payroll taxes. Prior to making the journal entry to record the payroll, check the accuracy of the amounts entered in the payroll register by proving the totals of the money columns. Prove the partial payroll register shown in Figure 6.1 as follows:

Proof:

Regular earnings	$22,497.20	
Overtime earnings	2,265.50	
Total earnings		$24,762.70
FICA tax withheld—OASDI	$ 1,535.29	
FICA tax withheld—HI	359.06	
Federal income taxes withheld	3,714.00	
State income taxes withheld	55.25	
Group insurance withheld	54.70	
Total deductions		$ 5,718.30
Total net pay		19,044.40
Total earnings		$24,762.70

In preparing the journal entry to record a payroll, you make an entry each payday to record the aggregate amount of wages earned, deductions made, and net payments to all employees, as determined from the Totals line of the payroll register. After making the journal entry, you must transfer, or post, the information from the journal to the appropriate general ledger accounts.

In most companies having computer-driven payroll systems, the payroll programs are interfaced with the general ledger programs. In these systems, computers generate the payroll entries into a printed journal-entry format and post to the various general ledger accounts automatically from these entries.

Using the Information in the Payroll Register

In addition to serving as the source for preparing journal entries to record the payroll and the employer's payroll taxes, the payroll register provides information that meets some of the recordkeeping requirements of the various payroll acts. Also, the register provides data used in preparing periodic reports required by various laws (e.g., hours worked each day as required by the Fair Labor Standards Act).

Besides the information contained in the payroll register, businesses must provide information about the accumulated earnings of each employee. Therefore, companies keep a separate payroll record on each employee—the employee's earnings record. This record, introduced in Figure 1.10, on page 1-25, is discussed in the following section.

The Employee's Earnings Record

The employee's earnings record, a supplementary record, provides information for:

1. *Preparing the payroll register* from the earnings records, which contain the information needed to compute gross earnings and to determine the amount to withhold for income tax purposes.

2. ***Preparing reports*** required by state unemployment compensation or disability laws.

3. ***Determining when the accumulated wages of an employee reach the cutoff level*** for purposes of FICA (OASDI), FUTA, or SUTA. As shown in Figure 6.2, on page 6-6, a special "Cumulative Earnings" column is provided so that the total amount of accumulated wages can be recorded each pay period. Thus, when the FICA (OASDI), FUTA, or SUTA cutoff has been reached, the record shows that the employee or the employer no longer has a liability for that particular tax during the rest of the calendar year. [In Figure 6.1, the FUTA and SUTA taxable wage cutoffs are the same ($7,000). However, another separate column would be needed in the payroll register if there were a different cutoff for the SUTA tax.]

4. ***Preparing payroll analyses*** for governmental agencies and for internal management control. Information such as the department in which the employee works and the job title serves as the basis for such analyses.

5. ***Settling employee grievances*** regarding regular pay and overtime pay calculations and the withholding of amounts for income taxes and other purposes.

6. ***Completing Forms W-2,*** which show for each employee the annual gross earnings, income taxes withheld, wages subject to FICA taxes, and FICA taxes withheld.

A business keeps an employee's earnings record for each employee whose wages are recorded in the payroll register. Each payday, after the information has been recorded in the payroll register, the information for each employee is posted to the employee's earnings record. The columns are arranged so that the information can be transferred easily. The earnings record shown in Figure 6.2, on page 6-6, is arranged for weekly pay periods. You will note that totals are provided for each quarter so that you can enter information easily on the quarterly tax returns. The bottom of page 1 of the earnings record shows a line for semiannual totals. The bottom of page 2 of the form, which is not illustrated, shows a line for annual totals, which you will need in preparing Form 940, W-2s, and other annual reports.

With today's payroll programs, all of these functions are being done instantaneously. As soon as the information (just the hours worked) is entered in the system, the processing and transferring of the information is done immediately. In a lot of systems, the information does not even have to be entered since it comes right from the time-keeping device—to the payroll register, to the employee earnings record, to the paycheck, to the journal, to the ledger, and eventually, to the related tax returns.

Recording the Gross Payroll and Withholdings

After you have recorded the payroll in the payroll register and posted to the employees' earnings records, you must enter the information in the employer's accounting system. An entry for the totals of each payroll period should be made in the general journal and posted to the general ledger. You can obtain the amounts needed for this entry from the Totals line at the bottom of the last payroll register sheet. As stated at the beginning of this chapter, much of this transferring of information is now done automatically by computerized payroll programs.

FIGURE 6.2
Employee's Earnings Record (page 1)

WEEK	20— WEEK ENDING	TOTAL WORKED DAYS	TOTAL WORKED HRS.	REGULAR EARNINGS HRS.	REGULAR EARNINGS RATE	REGULAR EARNINGS AMOUNT	OVERTIME EARNINGS HRS.	OVERTIME EARNINGS RATE	OVERTIME EARNINGS AMOUNT	FICA OASDI	FICA HI	FEDERAL INCOME TAX	STATE INCOME TAX	GROUP INSURANCE	NET PAID CK. NO.	NET PAID AMOUNT	CUMULATIVE EARNINGS	TIME LOST
1	1/3	5	44	40	15 20	6 0 8 00	4	22 80	9 1 20	4 3 35	1 0 14	2 9 00	4 78	9 00	510	6 0 2 93	6 9 9 20	
2	1/10	5	42	40	15 20	6 0 8 00	2	22 80	4 5 60	4 0 52	9 48	2 4 00	4 47	9 00	706	5 6 6 13	13 5 2 80	
3	1/17	6	44	40	15 20	6 0 8 00	4	22 80	9 1 20	4 3 35	1 0 14	2 9 00	4 78	9 00	898	6 0 2 93	20 5 2 00	
4																		
5																		
6																		
7																		
8																		
9																		
10																		
11																		
12																		
13																		
QUARTER TOTAL																		
1																		
2																		
13																		
QUARTER TOTAL																		
SEMIANNUAL TOTAL																		

DEPARTMENT	OCCUPATION	WORKS IN (STATE)	S.S. ACCOUNT NO.	NAME-LAST	FIRST	MIDDLE	W/H ALLOW.	FILING STATUS
A-10	Adm. Ass't	XXX	000-00-1186	Collins	Chris	Ruth	N/A	M

The following journal entry to record the payroll includes a debit to the appropriate expense account(s) for the gross payroll and credits to the various liability accounts for the withholdings from the pay and for the net amount to be paid employees:

	Debit	Credit
Salaries Expense..	XXX	
Liabilities (Withholdings)...		XXX
Cash or Salaries Payable (Net Pay)..		XXX
To record the payment of salaries and the liabilities for the employees' taxes withheld.		

Gross Payroll

You should record the total gross payroll (regular earnings and overtime earnings) as the debit portion of the payroll entry. The account has a title such as **Wages Expense** or **Salaries Expense**. In the case of a company with many departments or cost centers, the accounts would have titles such as **Wages Expense—Department A**, **Wages Expense—Maintenance**, and **Wages Expense—Residential Services**. These accounts show the total gross earnings that the employer incurs as an **expense** each payday.

FICA Taxes—Employee

The employer must withhold FICA taxes for each employee. Since the employer has withheld these taxes from the pay of the employees and now owes this amount to the IRS, the taxes withheld represent a **liability** of the employer. When recording the payroll, you should credit accounts entitled **FICA Taxes Payable—OASDI** and **FICA Taxes Payable—HI** for the amounts withheld.

Federal Income Taxes

Employers must withhold a part of their employees' wages for income tax purposes. Chapter 4 presented the methods of determining the amounts to be withheld from wages for income tax purposes. As with FICA taxes withheld, the employer also owes to the IRS the federal income taxes withheld from the employees' pay. You should keep a separate account in the general ledger for recording the employer's **liability** for the amount of federal income taxes withheld.

A suitable title for this account, **Employees Federal Income Taxes Payable**, may be abbreviated to read **Employees FIT Payable**. The account is credited for the total amount of federal income taxes withheld each payday and is subsequently debited for the amounts paid to a depositary or to the IRS.

State and City Income Taxes

Employers may be required to withhold state and city income taxes in addition to the federal income taxes. You should keep a separate account in the general ledger for recording the employer's **liability** for the amount of each kind of income tax withheld. Account titles that may be used include **Employees State Income Taxes (SIT) Payable** and **Employees City Income Taxes (CIT) Payable.**

Employees' Contributions to State Funds

A few states require employees to contribute to state unemployment compensation or disability funds. In states requiring employee contributions, the employer deducts the amount of the contributions from the employees' wages

> **LO 2**
> Identify the various deductions—both voluntary and involuntary (taxes and garnishments)—that are taken out of employees' gross pay.

at the time the wages are paid. The *liability* for employees' contributions may be recorded in the same account as the employer's SUTA contributions; namely, *SUTA Taxes Payable*. If employees make contributions to a disability benefit fund, this amount is usually reported separately to the state and should be recorded in a separate liability account such as *Employees Disability Contributions Payable*.

Other Payroll Deductions

Besides FICA taxes, state unemployment contributions, and income taxes, most companies have other deductions that must be taken into consideration when preparing the payroll. Regardless of the number or the types of deductions made from employees' wages, we must provide a systematic means of keeping a record of the total wages for each employee, the deductions for each purpose, and the net amount paid.

Although you should have a separate column in the payroll register for each deduction, the payroll register may become too cumbersome if there are too many columns for deductions. Many businesses, therefore, use a payroll register with a separate column for each of the major deductions and lump all other deductions together in one column headed "Other Deductions." Some companies use only one column for deductions and place the entire total in that column. If this practice is followed, it is necessary to have a supplementary record of deductions showing a detailed breakdown of the total for each employee. This supplementary record serves as the basis for obtaining the figure for total deductions shown in the payroll register.

Many payroll deductions result from company policies, collective bargaining agreements, court orders, or employee authorizations. Some of the purposes for making deductions include:

1. Group insurance.
2. Health insurance.
3. Purchase of government savings bonds.
4. Union dues.
5. Garnishment of wages.
   a. Child support.
   b. Federal tax levy.
   c. Second garnishments.
6. Pension and retirement contributions.

Group Insurance

Many companies have a **group insurance** program for employees. Such programs usually permit employees to obtain life insurance at a much lower rate than would be possible if the employee purchased the insurance as an individual. Under some group insurance plans, the employer and the employee share the cost of the insurance premium. The employees' share may be deducted from their wages every payday, every month, or every quarter.

When recording a payroll that makes deductions from employees' wages for group insurance, the amount withheld from their wages is applied toward the payment of their share of the premium. The total amount withheld is credited to a *liability* account with a title such as *Group Insurance Premiums Collected* or *Group Insurance Payments Withheld*. This general ledger account serves the same purpose as the accounts used to record payroll taxes withheld from employees' wages. When the premiums are paid to the insurance company, the liability account will be debited.

Health Insurance

Many companies have developed their own health insurance plans for employees or are members of private insurance groups that provide coverage for employees of companies that are members of the group. If employees bear the cost or a portion of the cost of such insurance, the portion paid by the employees is usually deducted every payday from the wages of the employees. The amounts withheld from the employees' wages for health insurance are credited to a *liability* account such as **Health Insurance Premiums Collected**. If these withholdings are made by means of a salary reduction for a qualified benefit under an Internal Revenue Department approved cafeteria plan, the premiums are paid with pretax dollars (not included in taxable income for FIT withholding).

Employers often pay the premium for health insurance in advance to the insurance carrier. At the time of paying the premium, a prepaid expense account such as **Prepaid Health Insurance** is debited for the amount paid the carrier. This account is adjusted periodically through the health insurance or fringe benefit expense account and, if applicable, the employees' withholding account.

Health savings accounts and flexible-spending accounts (see page 4-8), which allow employees to save money to pay for out-of-pocket medical expenses, are deductions from the employee's pay and are done on a pretax basis. These deductions will also be set up as credits to appropriate liability accounts as part of the payroll entry.

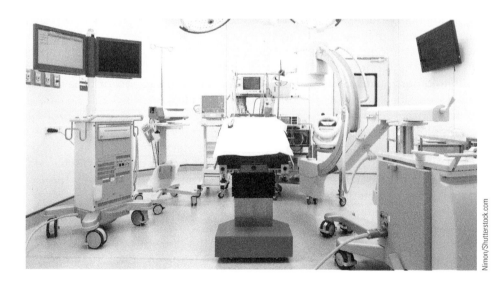

Nimon/Shutterstock.com

Purchase of Government Savings Bonds

Employees are encouraged to invest a certain amount of their wages in government savings bonds. Such plans or similar savings plans encourage employees to save a certain amount of each salary payment. The theory behind such deductions is that most employees will not miss a small amount that is set aside each payday, and over a period of time the deductions accumulate into a sizable amount.

Employees authorize their employer to make payroll deductions for the purchase of savings bonds by completing authorization forms that indicate the amount to be withheld and the frequency. The amounts withheld from the paychecks are sent to the employer's Treasury Direct accounts which are set up by the employees with the United States Treasury. In their Direct accounts, employees decide what type and dollar value of savings bond they want to purchase.

Union Dues

In companies in which employees are members of unions that require employees to pay dues to the union, many employees pay their dues, assessments, and initiation fees through deductions from wages, known as a **check-off system**. Amounts withheld from union members' wages are credited to a *liability* account such as ***Union Dues Payable***. Monthly, or as agreed upon by the union and the employer, the amounts withheld are turned over to the treasurer of the union. At this time, a journal entry is made in which the payment of union dues is recorded by debiting the liability account and crediting the cash account.

Garnishment of Wages

Tell Me More

Garnishment refers to the legal or equitable procedure by which a portion of the wages of any person must be withheld for payment of a debt. Through the garnishment process, a creditor, with the aid of the courts, may require the employer to hold back a portion of the debtor's wages and pay that amount to the court or to the creditor. In some companies, the amounts to be held back are deducted each payday from the employee's wages. Ignoring a garnishment order means the employee's debt becomes the company's debt by default judgment.

Generally, the following priority withholding order applies to these wage attachments: (1) federal tax levy or child support order, whichever is delivered first; (2) bankruptcy; and (3) creditor, student loan, or federal administrative wage garnishments. Bankruptcy orders under Chapter 13 of the Bankruptcy Act have the highest priority over all other claims. All other garnishment withholdings must stop with the exception of child support or repaying an employee's loan from their retirement plan account.

On the Job

There are eight types of wage attachments—child support, bankruptcy, federal administration levy, federal tax levy, student loans, state and local tax levies, and creditor repayments.

The provisions of the Consumer Credit Protection Act (CCPA) prohibit an employer from discharging an employee simply because the employee's wages are subject to garnishment for one indebtedness. If another garnishment for a second indebtedness should arise, the worker could be discharged, provided a considerable amount of time had not elapsed between the two occasions of indebtedness.

The CCPA defines "earnings" to include wages, salaries, commissions, bonuses, or other compensations. For garnishment purposes, lump-sum payments are treated as regular wages for the current pay period. In the case of tipped employees, this includes cash wages paid by the employer and the amount of tip credit claimed by the employer, but not tips received in excess of the tip credit amount. However, when tips are charged to a credit card, such tips are subject to withholding. CCPA restrictions on the amount of an employee's pay that can be garnished are based on an employee's disposable earnings. **Disposable earnings** are the earnings remaining after withholding for federal and state income taxes, FICA taxes, state unemployment and disability taxes, and deductions required for state employees' retirement systems.

Example 6-2

John Jenkins earns $1,290 per week. The deductions from his pay were:

FIT	$110.00
FICA—OASDI	79.98
FICA—HI	18.71
State income tax	31.00
State disability insurance	9.03
Credit union deduction	40.00
Health insurance premium	47.50
Charitable contribution	5.00

John's disposable earnings would be:

$$\$1,290.00 - \$110.00 \text{ (FIT)} - \$79.98 - \$18.71 \text{ (FICA deductions)}$$
$$- \$31.00 \text{ (SIT)} - \$9.03 \text{ (disability insurance)} = \$1,041.28$$

Service charges that are passed on to the employee by the employer are considered part of the disposable earnings equation. States may define disposable earnings differently and if the state law is more beneficial to the employee, the state law will apply.

The maximum amount of disposable earnings that can be garnished is the lesser of the disposable earnings minus:

25% of disposable earnings for the week; or the amount by which the disposable earnings for the week exceed 30 times the federal minimum wage rate (does not apply to garnishments for bankruptcy, child support, or federal or state tax levies).

Example 6-3

Sam Kuchenko's disposable earnings for this weekly pay period is $260. A creditor requires $70 be deducted from his pay each week to satisfy an outstanding debt. The maximum that can be deducted from his pay is:

$$\$260 \times 25\% = \$65$$
$$\$260 - \$217.50 \ (30 \times \$7.25) = \$42.50$$

Only $42.50 can be deducted from Kuchenko's pay this week in order to leave him with the statutory minimum of $217.50 a week of disposable pay.

Based on the type of garnishment, the Act limits the amount of wages subject to garnishment to:

- Child support: 50% of disposable earnings if supporting a child or spouse in addition to those named in the garnishment order
- 60% of disposable earnings if not supporting another spouse or child
- 5% additional in each case if there are past due accounts over 12 weeks
- Creditor garnishment: 25% of disposable earnings
- Administrative wage garnishment: 15% of disposable earnings
- Student loan garnishment: 15% of disposable earnings

These maximum deductions apply regardless of the number of garnishments received on an employee.

For federal tax levies, even though not subject to the limits of the CCPA, the IRS instructs employers to withhold the difference between the employee's take-home pay and the exempt amount. This allows the employee's voluntary deductions to continue. In the case of state tax levies, it is possible that an

On the Job

State garnishment laws either set a flat weekly exempt amount (e.g., Oregon) or use the state minimum wage to determine an exempt amount (e.g., Illinois).

employee's entire net pay can be used to satisfy a state tax levy (leaving the employee with no paycheck).

Part-time employees are granted full protection of the law for each job that they work, regardless of how much their total income may be. Employers only have to be concerned with the amount that they pay to their individual employees.

The Social Security Administration (SSA) has started to use the administrative wage garnishment to collect delinquent overpayments owed by former beneficiaries of the social security program. Unlike other credits, the SSA does not need a court order to initiate this garnishment process.

The payroll manager should also be aware that state garnishment laws that are more favorable to employees have priority over the federal law.

Child Support

The Family Support Act requires the immediate withholding for child support payments for all cases supported by a court order. The amount withheld is equal to the amount of the delinquency, subject to the limits prescribed in the federal garnishment law. Employers may withhold a fee, set by each state, for administrative costs. Tips are part of the disposable earnings for child support purposes—whether in the form of **cash**, debit or credit card receipts, or a set service charge.

Child support takes precedence over most voluntary and involuntary deductions. In the case of multiple support orders, the employer is to allocate monies to each order from the employee's available disposable income.

In the case of competing orders, the process begins with the deduction of the child support order. Then, the other garnishment is satisfied according to the rules stated above for repayment of a creditor debt.

On the Net

The Office of Child Support Enforcement has established an electronic income withholding order portal that is used by all of the states. States can electronically transmit income withholding orders to employers and employers can use the portal to notify states of the status of the withholding orders.

Example 6-4

Galvis Company has a child support order outstanding on one of its employees (Charles Suffert—$170 per week). Charles Suffert's disposable income is $950 per week. A new garnishment is received for a $5,000 debt to a credit card company. The company would take an additional $237.50 out of Suffert's pay.

Lesser of:

$25\% \times \$950$	=	$\underline{\$237.50}$	or
$\$950 - (30 \times \$7.25)$	=	$\underline{\$732.50}$	

On the Job

For child support withholding purposes, all new employees hired must be reported to the state. The reporting methods and time periods vary by state—no more than 20 days from the date of hire.

All states' child support agencies offer electronic payment options and close to 20 states require employers, who meet certain conditions, to remit the payments electronically. For example, employers in Florida with 10 or more employees or that pay $20,000 or more in annual state taxes must remit these support payments electronically. The Office of Child Support Enforcement requires these payments to be made within seven business days of paying wages to the employee—some states have shorter time limits. The payments for several employees can be combined if they are being sent to the same State Disbursement Unit. The case numbers and amounts withheld from each employee and the dates must be included in the filing.

If the employee is no longer employed, employers are required to report this as soon as possible to the agency that issued the withholding order. Depending on the state, the reporting may be done by phone, fax, mail, or electronic transmission.

Federal Tax Levy

Federal tax levies take second priority after wages withheld for child support (if received prior to the tax levy). If a tax levy is in place prior to the child support order, the employer must call the issuing agency so that an alternate payment plan can be worked out with the IRS. Each year, the IRS provides tables (see Figure 6.3) that show the amount of the individuals' take-home pay that is exempt from the levy based on the filing status, the standard deduction (see page 4-16), and an amount determined in part based on the number of dependents the employee is allowed for the year of the levy. As long as the employee does not change the number of dependents, the exempt table in the year the levy was issued will continue to be used. The IRS instructs employers to withhold the difference between the take-home pay and the exempt amount. The take-home pay is the gross pay less taxes and the deductions in effect before the levy was received (such as 401(k) plan contributions, credit union savings, and involuntary deductions for child support and creditor garnishments). These tax levies are suspended if a debtor declares bankruptcy.

FIGURE 6.3

2022 Table for Amount Exempt for Tax Levy (Single Person)

Filing Status: **Single**							
Pay Period	**Number of Dependents Claimed on Statement**						
	0	**1**	**2**	**3**	**4**	**5**	**More Than 5**
Daily	49.81	66.73	83.65	100.57	117.49	134.41	49.81 plus 16.92 for each dependent
Weekly	249.04	333.66	418.28	502.90	587.52	672.14	249.04 plus 84.62 for each dependent
Biweekly	498.08	667.13	836.54	1005.77	1175.00	1344.23	498.08 plus 169.23 for each dependent
Semimonthly	539.58	722.91	906.24	1089.57	1272.90	1456.23	539.58 plus 183.33 for each dependent
Monthly	1079.17	1445.84	1812.51	2179.18	2545.85	2912.52	1079.17 plus 366.67 for each dependent

Source: Internal Revenue Service.

The IRS uses Form 668-W—Notice of Levy on Wages, Salary and Other Income (not illustrated)—to notify an employer of a tax levy. Copies of the form must then be forwarded to the employee for completion of a statement of filing status and exemptions. This information will then allow the employer to compute the actual levy. If the employee fails to return the signed statement within three working days to the employer, the exempt amount is based on married-filing-separately status with one personal exemption. The employer must begin the withholding in accordance with the levy within 10 days.

The tax levy takes effect with the first wage payment made three days from the receipt of the tax levy notice. The employer then returns Part 3 of Form 668-W to the Internal Revenue Service along with the initial payment. Further payments are to be sent on the same day that the employee is paid.

The employer must continue to withhold until Form 668-D—Release of Levy/Release of Property from Levy (not illustrated)—is received. Failure to surrender any wages that are subject to a tax levy will incur a liability to pay the levy plus costs and interest. Unless there is a reasonable cause for failing to obey the law, an additional 50 percent penalty will be added.

Example 6-5

Borden Company received a federal tax levy on John Kline. Kline is single, claims 2 dependents, and had a take-home pay of $621.00 this week. The amount of the tax levy (in 2022) would be:

Take-home pay..	$621.00
Less: Exempt amount (from Figure 6.3, page 6-13).................	418.28
Federal tax levy..	$202.72

Second Garnishments

Deductions for back taxes, child support, or a bankruptcy do not qualify as deductions required by law. If the garnishment for these equals or exceeds 25% of an employee's disposable earnings, no deduction can be made to satisfy the second garnishment.

Example 6-6

Michael Mato pays child support of 30% of his disposable earnings. Then, his employer receives a court order to withhold 25% of Mato's disposable earnings for a second garnishment. Since the employer is already withholding in excess of the federal limit, Mato's income is exempt for the second garnishment.

Pension and Retirement Contributions

Since in many instances social security benefits are inadequate for retired employees and their dependents, many firms provide pension and retirement plans that will supplement the government benefits. Although the benefit formulas and eligibility rules vary, the coverage is about the same for production workers, office employees, and managers. Some pension plans are financed solely by employer contributions, but other plans involve employee contributions. With the passage of the Pension Protection Act of 2006, companies can automatically enroll employees in the company's retirement plan and start deducting contributions from their pays. Once these contributions are deducted from the employees' pay, they become a liability for the employer and are recorded as such in the payroll entry. This would also apply to employee contributions into 401(k) plans.

Some employers also provide their employees with the opportunity to set up their own Individual Retirement Accounts (IRA) through a payroll deduction plan (see page 4-9). These voluntary contributions are deducted from the paychecks of the employees who set up their own retirement accounts. These deductions are recorded as a liability in the payroll entry. This liability account will be cleared as the employer pays the contributions to the financial institution that is in charge of each employee's retirement account.

LO 3

Journalize the entries to record the payroll and payroll taxes.

Net Pay

The total of the net amount paid to the employees each payday is credited to either the **cash** account or the **salaries payable** account.

Example 6-7

The journal entry to record the payroll from Figure 6.1, on pages 6-3 and 6-4, would be:

	Debit	Credit
Wages Expense	24,762.70	
FICA Taxes Payable—OASDI		1,535.29
FICA Taxes Payable—HI		359.06
FIT Payable..		3,714.00
SIT Payable		55.25
Group Insurance Payments W/H.............................		54.70
Cash...		19,044.40

Self-Study Quiz 6-1

The totals from the payroll register of Olt Company for the week of January 25 show:

Gross earnings	$ 95,190.00
Withholdings:	
FICA taxes—OASDI	(5,901.78)
FICA taxes—HI	(1,380.26)
Federal income tax	(14,270.00)
State income tax	(1,427.85)
State unemployment tax—employee portion	(951.90)
Net pay	$ 71,258.21

Journalize the entry to record the payroll of January 25.

Note: Answers to Self-Study Quizzes are on page 6-37.

Methods of Paying Wages and Salaries

The four main methods used in paying wages and salaries include (1) cash, (2) check, (3) electronic transfer, and (4) pay cards.

Paying in Cash

When a company pays wages and salaries in cash, a common procedure is used, as follows:

1. Compute the total wages earned, the deductions, and the net amount to be paid and record this information in the payroll register, as shown in Figure 1.9, on page 1-24.

2. Prepare a supplementary payroll sheet showing the various denominations of bills and coins needed to pay the salary of each employee. The form in Figure 6.4, on page 6-16, provides columns to list the names of the employees, the net amount to be paid, the denominations needed to pay each employee, the total amount needed to pay all employees, and the total number of each denomination needed to pay all employees.

3. Prepare a payroll slip by using the total amount of each denomination needed for the payroll.

4. Write a check for the total amount of the payroll and present it to the bank with the payroll slip to obtain the proper denominations.

5. Place the amount due to each employee in an envelope with a receipt showing the total earnings, the deductions, and the net amount paid. Distribute the prepared envelopes to the employees.

Paying by Check

When paying wages and salaries by check, the employer prepares and signs the checks in the usual way. The check preparer should ensure the accuracy of the names of the payees and the net amounts of the checks. Employers must give employees a periodic statement showing the deductions that have been made from their wages for tax purposes. The employer may distribute these

On the Job

Biweekly pay is the most common payroll schedule with close to 40% of employers using this pay method.

On the Job

The National Automated Clearing House Association estimated that employees spend an average of 8 to 24 hours per year depositing or cashing paychecks. In many cases, these transactions are made on company time.

FIGURE 6.4
Supplementary Payroll Sheet

		Bills					Coins				
HENDRIX, INC. SUPPLEMENTARY PAYROLL SHEET — June 30, 20--											
Name of Employee	**Net Amount to Be Paid**	**$50**	**$20**	**$10**	**$5**	**$1**	**50¢**	**25¢**	**10¢**	**5¢**	**1¢**
Kapoor, Paul C.	$ 268.62	5		1	1	3	1		1		2
Connor, Rose T.	271.40	5	1			1		1	1	1	
Day, Joseph R.	297.28	5	2		1	2		1			3
Park, Margaret F.	704.92	14				4	1	1	1	1	2
Hawke, Sidney O.	271.64	5	1			1	1		1		4
Kirk, Evelyn A.	788.24	15	1	1	1	3			2		4
Lerro, Doris B.	268.12	5		1	1	3			1		2
Pesiri, Armand G.	878.80	17	1		1	3	1	1		1	
Topkis, Christine W.	284.65	5	1	1		4	1		1	1	
Vogel, John C.	724.10	14	1			4			1		
Total	$4,757.77	90	8	4	5	28	5	4	9	4	17

statements each payday or give them out monthly, quarterly, or annually. Also, employees receive a statement at the time they leave the employ of the company. Most employers who pay wages and salaries by check indicate on each check issued or on the check stub or earnings statement the various deductions made (see Figure 6.5).

Many businesses maintain a payroll account at their bank in addition to their regular checking account. In such a case, all checks to pay wages and salaries are issued against the payroll account rather than against the regular checking account. When the company maintains a separate payroll account, the usual procedure is as follows:

1. Sets up a payroll account with a certain balance to be maintained at all times. A transfer from the regular checking account is made to the payroll account. A small balance is desirable in the payroll account because it may be necessary to issue payroll checks before the regular payday. For example, if mistakes were made in an employee's paycheck, an additional check must be issued. These types of corrections will be shown in the next payday's payroll register.

2. Makes a transfer to payroll, drawn on the regular checking account, equal to the total net pay, and deposited in the special payroll account at the bank.

3. Prepares individual checks, drawn against the special payroll account, and records the numbers of the payroll checks in the payroll register. Many companies having a large number of employees may use automatic means of signing the checks.

By maintaining a separate payroll account at the bank, a listing of the canceled payroll checks, accompanied by a statement of the payroll account balance, are returned separately from the canceled checks lists drawn upon the regular checking account, making it easier to reconcile both accounts. The payroll account balance as shown on the bank statement should always be equal to the sum of the total of the outstanding payroll checks and any maintained balance, less any service charge.

FIGURE 6.5
Earnings Statement (Check Stub) Showing Payroll Deductions

EMPLOYEE'S NAME ARTHUR T. COCO											PENLAND EQUIPMENT COMPANY, SAN MATEO, FL 32088-2279
PAY PERIOD ENDING	HOURS		RATE	GROSS EARNINGS	OASDI TAX	HI TAX	FED. WITH. TAX	STATE WITH. TAX	UNION DUES		NET EARNINGS PAID
5/16/ --	REG. T. 40	O.T. 12	11.25 16.88	652.56	40.46	9.46	44.00		8.00		550.64
EMPLOYEE: THIS IS A STATEMENT OF YOUR EARNINGS AND DEDUCTIONS FOR PERIOD INDICATED. KEEP THIS FOR YOUR PERMANENT RECORD.											

Africa Studio/Shutterstock.com

Paying by Electronic Transfer

Under an **electronic funds transfer system (EFTS)**, employers do not have to issue a paycheck to each worker, although the worker is given a stub showing the amounts deducted. Instead, the employer creates a computerized record for each employee. This record indicates:

1. The employee's bank.
2. The account number at the bank.
3. The net amount to be paid.

A day or two before payday, the employer sends the information to the company's bank where the amounts due to any employees who also keep their accounts at that bank are removed and deposited to the appropriate accounts. That bank sends the remaining names to an automated clearinghouse which sorts out the other bank names and prepares a computer tape for each bank to receive funds electronically. For banks unable to receive entries in electronic form, the clearinghouse creates a printed statement showing the customers' names and the amounts for which their accounts are to be credited. The actual crediting of accounts and the settlement occur on payday.

Under a "paperless" deposit and bill-paying system, employers may deposit wages in bank accounts designated by the employees if the deposits are voluntarily authorized by the employees. Millions of written checks may be eliminated each month. After their net pay has been electronically transferred directly into their accounts, the employees can pay bills by authorizing the bank to automatically transfer funds from that account to the accounts of creditors such as the utility company and department stores.

The Electronic Fund Transfer Act (known as Regulation E) allows employers to make direct deposit mandatory as long as the employees can choose the bank in which their wages will be deposited.

On the state level, some rely on the federal mandate, while other states follow the mandate but require the employer to provide another payment method for the "unbanked" employee. A number of states require employers to have employees sign written requests for electronic wage payments.

Pay Cards

The major problem of direct deposit is to obtain up-to-date and timely banking information—employees changing accounts without notifying their employers, gathering information in time to make payroll for new employees, and paying into closed accounts.

Over 15 million American households do not have bank accounts; however, by using debit card-based accounts, the "unbanked" employees can opt for direct deposit of their paychecks. All transactions are completed electronically by using a pay card to make purchases at any point-of-sale terminal or to access cash at automated teller machines (ATMs) or through a bank teller.

National and regional banks issue these prepaid pay cards. Each pay period, funds are transferred from the employer's payroll account to the financial institution issuing the pay card. The card is then used like any debit or credit card and can also be used to access cash at certain automated teller machines (ATMs). Employees will then receive a monthly statement detailing their transactions and have access to card information at any time on the internet and by automated phone system.[1] These cards are reloadable, and each payday the cards will be "loaded up" with the pays without the employees needing to be anywhere near their employers.

A debit card can also be opened through a point-of-sale purchase at a retail store. The owner can then use the card like a bank account. ATM withdrawals and retail point-of-service transactions can be initiated using a personal identification number (PIN).

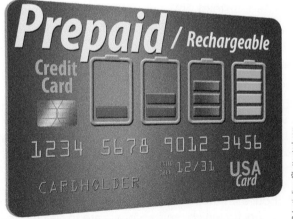

Robertindiana/Shutterstock.com

---

1 "Card-Based Payroll Solutions," *PAYTECH*, April 2002, p. 22.

Employers can eliminate paper paychecks by giving employees the choice between receiving their wages by direct deposit or on a pay card.[2] A few states allow employers to make these e-payment options a condition of employment. For instance, in Iowa it can be mandatory for new hires as long as the employees incur no bank charges. Some states require that the employee be allowed a certain number of free withdrawals from the ATMs. A recent bulletin from the Consumer Finance Protection Bureau (CFPB) cautioned employers to have available to the employees at least one other payment option in addition to payroll cards.

On the Job

Pay card benefits to the employees include:
- The unbanked can use.
- No need to wait to cash or deposit checks.
- No delays in getting the paycheck.
- Convenient access to ATM for withdrawals and to make purchases.
- Card information available on the internet.

Over the Line

The owners of 16 McDonald's franchises in Pennsylvania had to pay $1 million to settle charges that they broke the law by paying workers with fee-laden credit cards. It was argued in court that the pay cards did not meet the state's definition of "lawful money," since the cards charged fees for withdrawals, online payments, and other transactions.[3]

Earned Wage Access (EWA)

This method (also known as On-Demand pay) allows employees to be paid one day's wages or all the money they have earned during the current pay period. Thus, employees can receive their wages as they earn rather than wait for the next standard payday. Often, employees can only access a certain portion or maximum limit of their wages per pay period. Payroll processing companies that offer this option typically charge a fee that must be covered by the employee. These interim withdrawals are not taxed; however, the taxes on these payments must be deducted from the upcoming paycheck.

The advanced funds are then deducted from the employee's next paycheck and shown as a detailed line item on the check stub. The amount deducted is then remitted to the provider through Accounts Payable.

On the Job

Currently, it is estimated that 5% of employers offer an EWA program. It is expected to reach 20% by 2023.

Electronic Paystub

Cost savings can also be realized by offering employees **electronic paystubs**. In these cases, the company will make the information that is usually found on a paper paystub available through a secured Web site, kiosk, or interactive voice response system. As with electronic payments, one can eliminate paper, postage, and distribution costs.

Final Pay

Even though few states have no laws governing the timing of the disbursement of the final pay, most states set a time limit after notice of termination for the payment of an employee's final wage. The deadline depends on whether or not the worker is leaving voluntarily. Most states allow a lag time in which to process the final check—regulations in most states require payment by the next regular payday. However, if fired, California and Minnesota require immediate payment. If the employee quits, California requires payment within 72 hours (if 72 hours of notice were given, final wages are due at separation), while Minnesota, in either firing or quitting cases, requires payment on the next scheduled payday. In California, employees can sue for an equal amount in penalty wages for failure to timely pay final wages (up to 30 days' pay).[4]

---

2 "Pay Cards Are a Win-Win Solution," *PAYTECH,* June 2010, p. 24.

3 "In the News," *HR Employment Law,* December 2017, p. 1.

4 *Payroll Legal Alert,* March 2012, p. 1.

Even though there is no federal law that employers must pay workers for their stored-up vacation time when the employee departs, several states have such laws.[5]

Over the Line

Upon losing a government contract, employees of Catapult Technology, Ltd., accepted employment with a new contractor without giving notice to Catapult. Since the employees did not provide two weeks' notice (as specified in Catapult's employee handbook), Catapult refused to pay for the accrued unpaid universal leave time. The employees sued, and a Maryland appeals court ruled that universal leave is given "in remuneration" for employees' work and constitutes a wage. A company's personnel policy cannot contravene an employee's right to be compensated for their work.[6]

Unclaimed Wages

Occasionally, a worker may terminate employment or be terminated and not claim the final wage payment. The payroll manager is then faced with the question of what to do with the worker's unclaimed wages, which then become a form of abandoned property, subject to the state laws of escheat. This unclaimed property could also be in the form of unused payroll cards, expense reimbursements, and other employee benefits, such as flexible-spending accounts.

The first step in exercising due diligence would be to send a certified letter to the employee's last known address. If contact is not established during the period specified under state law, the paycheck can be voided and the funds transferred to an escrow account. Even though a uniform law (the Uniform Unclaimed Property Act) exists on the subject of unclaimed property, varying practices occur in those states that provide for the disposition of unclaimed property. The uniform law, followed by most states, provides that the holder of any unclaimed property must file a report after a specified statutory period (one year in most states) and then surrender the money to the state as abandoned property. In other states, the holder of unclaimed property files a report with the state, and the state then files suit for possession of the property. Generally, these reports must be filed annually and must state the employee's name, last known address, description of the abandoned wages, the amount, and the date of the last transaction with the employee.

The state would then hold the funds until the employee or heirs claim the funds. Each state has a Web site that allows people to search the database for unclaimed funds.[7] All of these issues surrounding uncashed payroll checks can be eliminated if employees are paid by direct deposit.

Audits conducted by a state agency are used to determine the adequacy of a firm's compliance program and, if found to be unsatisfactory, can result in interest, penalties, and even criminal prosecution. State statutory provisions for interest rates vary with the most common rate being 12 percent, and with the penalties for failure to report, ranging from $100 to $1,000 per day.

---

5 "Ask the Attorney," *The HR Law Weekly*, June 1, 2016, p. 4.
6 "Employers Cannot Put Strings on Final Wage Payments," *Payroll Manager's Letter*, Volume 24, No. 8, April 21, 2008, p. 3.
7 "How to Handle Uncashed Paychecks," *Payroll Manager's Letter*, Volume 31, No. 8, April 21, 2015, p. 5.

Because of the different practices among states, payroll managers must be well acquainted with the laws of their own states in the event they are faced with the difficult problem of disposing of unclaimed wages. They should periodically review their procedures to test the adequacy of their unclaimed property compliance program. Some of the procedures for the unclaimed paychecks should include an identification process, an aging record, a reporting and remitting plan, and a consistent recordkeeping system.[8]

Recording Payroll Taxes

In this section, we will analyze the journal entries that record the **employer's** payroll taxes, each of which has been discussed in preceding chapters:

1. **FICA:** Taxes imposed under the Federal Insurance Contributions Act for old-age, survivors, and disability insurance (OASDI) and hospital insurance (HI) benefits.
2. **FUTA:** Taxes imposed under the Federal Unemployment Tax Act.
3. **SUTA:** Contributions to the unemployment compensation funds of one or more states.

The following accounts will be needed in the general ledger if the employer is subject to FICA taxes, FUTA taxes, and SUTA taxes:

1. **Payroll Taxes:** An expense account for the FICA, FUTA, and SUTA taxes on the employer.
2. **FICA Taxes Payable—OASDI:** A liability account for the tax withheld from employees' wages plus the employer's portion of the tax.
3. **FICA Taxes Payable—HI:** A liability account for the tax withheld from employees' wages plus the employer's portion of the tax.
4. **FUTA Taxes Payable:** A liability account for the accumulation of the employer's federal unemployment taxes payable to the federal government.
5. **SUTA Taxes Payable:** A liability account for the amount payable to state unemployment compensation fund(s).

The following journal entry to record the payroll taxes includes a debit to the tax expense account for the total of the employer's payroll taxes and a credit to the various tax liability accounts:

	Debit	Credit
Payroll Taxes..	XXX	
Liabilities (various taxes)..		XXX
To record the payroll taxes and liabilities of the employer.		

FICA Taxes—Employer

The law states specifically that deductions made from the wages of employees under FICA should be recorded immediately as liabilities on the books of the company. The law does not require that employers record their part of the FICA taxes at the time the **wages are paid**. However, in order to place the tax expense in the proper accounting period, the common practice is to also record the employer's FICA tax liabilities each payday.

---

8 "Be Prepared for Unclaimed Property Audits," *PAYTECH*, April 2014, pp. 34–36.

The taxes on the employer represent both business expenses and liabilities of the employer. The employer may deduct the employer's FICA contributions as a **business expense** in the calculation of the company's net income for federal income tax purposes (and the costs of all other employer payroll taxes).

SUTA Taxes

Under the state unemployment compensation laws, employers must pay contributions into one or more state unemployment compensation funds. When an employer must make contributions to the state unemployment compensation funds of more than one state, it may be advisable to keep a separate liability account for the contributions payable to each state.

FUTA Tax

An employer subject to the gross FUTA tax of 6.0 percent may be able to claim credit in paying the federal tax because of contributions made to state unemployment compensation funds. As discussed in Chapter 5, the maximum credit is 5.4 percent, even though the amount of state contributions is more or less than 5.4 percent. Thus, the net FUTA tax (6.0% − 5.4%) is 0.6 percent. Although you do not actually claim the credit against the FUTA tax until Form 940 is filed with the Internal Revenue Service, you may record the FUTA tax at the net amount (0.6%) at the time you make the entry to record the employer's payroll taxes for each payroll period.

Example 6-8

The employees of Richardson Company earn wages during the year amounting to $26,400, all of which is subject to the gross FUTA tax of 6.0 percent. The company must make contributions to the unemployment compensation fund of the state in which the business is located at the rate of 2.8 percent of the wages paid each employee. Richardson computes the federal and state unemployment taxes as follows:

SUTA tax, 2.8% of $26,400		$739.20
Gross FUTA tax, 6.0% of $26,400	$1,584.00	
Less: Credit for SUTA tax, 5.4% of $26,400	1,425.60	158.40 (net FUTA tax)
Total unemployment taxes		$897.60

More simply, the net FUTA tax is computed by multiplying the taxable wages, $26,400, by the net FUTA tax rate, 0.6 percent, yielding $158.40.

The FUTA tax, like the FICA taxes and the contributions to the state for unemployment compensation purposes, is a social security tax. Thus, the FUTA tax can be charged to the same expense account as the other payroll taxes on the employer, the payroll taxes account. However, since employers may be required to pay the net FUTA tax quarterly and to pay the FICA taxes more frequently, an employer should keep separate liability accounts for recording these two taxes.

Example 6-9

The journal entry to record the payroll tax entry from Figure 6.1 on page 6-3 would be (assume a SUTA tax rate of 3.0%):

	Debit	Credit
Payroll Taxes	2,785.81	
FICA Taxes Payable—OASDI		1,535.29
FICA Taxes Payable—HI		359.06
FUTA Taxes Payable		148.58
SUTA Taxes Payable		742.88

Self-Study Quiz 6-2

Olt Company's gross payroll for the week of January 25 was $95,190.00. This total pay was taxable for federal (0.6%) and state (3.15%) unemployment taxes.

Journalize the entry to record Olt Company's payroll taxes for this pay.

Entries to Record Wages and Payroll Taxes

Tell Me More

In the following illustrations of recording (or journalizing) wages and the payroll taxes imposed under both the federal and state laws, the employer is responsible for the following taxes:

1. FICA tax—OASDI on employees: 6.2%.
2. FICA tax—HI on employees: 1.45% + 0.9% on an employee's wages in excess of $200,000.
3. FIT withheld from employees.
4. FICA tax—OASDI on employers: 6.2%.
5. FICA tax—HI on employers: 1.45%.
6. Net FUTA tax: 0.6%.
7. SUTA tax: 2.4%.

The weekly payroll amounts to $3,200, and the entire amount is subject to all social security and unemployment taxes. You record this information in two separate journal entries. In the first entry, you record the wages expense of the employer and the liabilities for the FICA taxes and FIT withheld in a two-column general journal as follows:

> **LO 4**
> Post to the various general ledger accounts that are used to accumulate information from the payroll entries.

	Debit	Credit
Wages Expense	3,200.00	
FICA Taxes Payable—OASDI		198.40[9]
FICA Taxes Payable—HI		46.40[10]
Employees FIT Payable..		230.00[11]
Cash...		2,725.20[12]
To record the payment of wages and the liability for the employees' FICA.		

---

9 The amount credited to FICA Taxes Payable—OASDI is computed as follows: 6.2% of $3,200 = $198.40, amount deducted from employees' wages.

10 The amount credited to FICA Taxes Payable—HI is computed as follows: 1.45% of $3,200 = $46.40, amount deducted from employees' wages.

11 The amount credited to Employees FIT Payable is obtained by using one of the withholding methods explained in Chapter 4.

12 The amount credited to Cash is computed as follows:

$3,200.00	gross wages earned
−474.80	employees' taxes withheld
$2,725.20	net amount paid employees

We can analyze this entry in T-accounts as follows:

WAGES EXPENSE		FICA TAXES PAYABLE—OASDI	
3,200.00			198.40
This debit represents the employees' gross earnings for the pay period. This results in an increase in the operating expenses of the employer.			This credit results in an increase in a liability of the employer.

FICA TAXES PAYABLE—HI		EMPLOYEES FIT PAYABLE	
	46.40		230.00
	This credit results in an increase in a liability of the employer.		This credit results in an increase in a liability of the employer.

CASH	
	2,725.20
	This credit results in a decrease in an asset.

In the second entry, you record the employer's payroll taxes as follows:

	Debit	Credit
Payroll Taxes	340.80[13]	
FICA Taxes Payable—OASDI		198.40
FICA Taxes Payable—HI		46.40
FUTA Taxes Payable		19.20
SUTA Taxes Payable		76.80

To record the payroll taxes and the employer's liability for the taxes.

Let's analyze this entry by means of T-accounts as shown below.

PAYROLL TAXES	
340.80	
This debit results in an increase in the operating expenses.	

FICA TAXES PAYABLE—OASDI		FICA TAXES PAYABLE—HI	
	198.40		46.40
	198.40		46.40
	The second credit amount, representing the employer's OASDI tax, also increases the employer's liability. The amount is determined as shown in the computation of the payroll taxes.		The second credit amount, representing the employer's HI tax, also increases the employer's liability. The amount is determined as shown in the computation of the payroll taxes.

13 The amount debited to Payroll Taxes is computed as follows:

6.2% of $3,200	=	$198.40	employer's OASDI tax
1.45% of $3,200	=	46.40	employer's HI tax
0.6% of $3,200	=	19.20	employer's net FUTA tax
2.4% of $3,200	=	76.80	employer's SUTA tax
Total payroll taxes		$340.80	

FUTA TAXES PAYABLE		SUTA TAXES PAYABLE	
	19.20		76.80
	This credit results in an increase in a liability of the employer. The amount is determined as shown in the computation of the payroll taxes.		This credit results in an increase in a liability of the employer. The amount is determined as shown in the computation of the payroll taxes.

In the preceding illustration, no contributions were required of employees for state unemployment compensation purposes. Assume that the employees had been required to make contributions of 1 percent to state unemployment compensation funds. The payroll entry would then appear as shown below.

	Debit	Credit
Wages Expense	3,200.00	
FICA Taxes Payable—OASDI		198.40
FICA Taxes Payable—HI		46.40
Employees FIT Payable		230.00
SUTA Taxes Payable		32.00
Cash		2,693.20
To record the payment of wages and the liability for the employees' FICA.		

In a small company with few employees, you can compute the hours worked, determine net pay, and prepare the paychecks or pay envelopes in a relatively short period of time. For such companies, a journal entry crediting the cash account for the total net pay is a logical, efficient procedure.

In larger companies, however, the calculation of hours worked, the determination of net pay, and the preparation of paychecks may extend over the greater part of a workday, or even longer. In such companies, because of the workload involved in meeting each payroll and especially when the paychecks must be mailed to far-flung branch offices, the paychecks may be prepared several days in advance of their actual distribution to the workers. Further, the preparation of the workers' paychecks may occur in one accounting period, although the actual payment is made in the following accounting period. Thus, to show an accurate picture of the firm's liability for the payroll, at the time of recording the payroll, the net pay is accrued and credited to a liability account such as Salaries Payable or Accrued Salaries Payable, instead of to the cash account. Later, when the paychecks are given to the workers, an entry is made to record the payment of the payroll.

	Debit	Credit
Salaries Payable	XXX	
Cash		XXX
To record the payment of wages for the pay period ended July 20, 20--.		

Recording Workers' Compensation Insurance Expense

As indicated in Chapter 1, most states have passed laws that require employers to provide workers' compensation insurance to protect their employees against losses due to injury or death incurred during employment. The expense account, **Workers' Compensation Insurance Expense,** can be used to record the premiums paid by the company to provide this

coverage. Usually, the employer estimates and pays the premium in advance. The insurance premium, often based upon the total gross payroll of the business, may be stated in terms of an amount for each $100 of weekly wages paid to employees. At the end of the year, all the payrolls are audited, and the company pays an additional premium or receives credit for an overpayment. Since the premium rate varies with the hazard involved in the work performed, your personnel and payroll records should provide for a careful classification of employees by kind or grade of work and a summary of labor costs according to the insurance premium classifications.

Example 6-10

Malindez Company has only two different grades of work—office clerical and machine shop. The premium rates for the year are $0.18 per $100 of payroll for the office clerical workers and $2.90 per $100 of payroll for the machine-shop workers. Based upon past experience and budgetary projections for the year, the company estimates its annual premium to be $8,900 and sends a check for that amount to the insurance carrier at the beginning of the year. The entry to record this transaction is as follows:

Workers' Compensation Insurance Expense	8,900.00	
Cash		8,900.00

The effect of this entry, when posted to the ledger accounts, increases the operating expenses of the company and decreases the assets.

At the end of the year, the payrolls for the year are audited and analyzed and the current rates are applied to determine the actual premium as follows:

Work Grade	Total Payroll	Rate per $100	Premium
Office clerical	$ 81,000	$0.18	$ 145.80
Machine shop	312,000	2.90	9,048.00
Total	$393,000		$9,193.80
Less: Estimated premium paid in January			8,900.00
Balance due			$ 293.80

A check is written for the balance due the insurance company, and the following entry is made in the journal:

Workers' Compensation Insurance Expense	293.80	
Cash		293.80

LO 5

Explain the recording of the payroll tax deposits.

Recording the Deposit or Payment of Payroll Taxes

The journal entries required to record the deposit or payment of FICA taxes and income taxes withheld and the payment of FUTA and SUTA taxes are explained below.

Depositing FICA Taxes and Federal Income Taxes Withheld

As explained in Chapter 3, the requirements for depositing FICA taxes and federal income taxes withheld from employees' wages and the employer's FICA match vary.

On April 15, 20--, the ledger accounts FICA Taxes Payable—OASDI, FICA Taxes Payable—HI, and Employees FIT Payable of Goosen Company appear as follows:

Example 6-11

FICA TAXES PAYABLE—OASDI

	4/15	697.07
	4/15	697.07
		1,394.14

FICA TAXES PAYABLE—HI

	4/15	163.02
	4/15	163.02
		326.04

EMPLOYEES FIT PAYABLE

	4/15	1,601.19

The company must electronically transfer the FICA and the federal income taxes. The following journal entry records this transaction:

FICA Taxes Payable—OASDI	1,394.14	
FICA Taxes Payable—HI	326.04	
Employees FIT Payable	1,601.19	
Cash		3,321.37

When posted, the debits of $1,394.14 and $326.04 to FICA Taxes Payable—OASDI and FICA Taxes Payable—HI remove the liabilities for the employer's share, as well as the employees' share, of the FICA taxes imposed. The debit to Employees FIT Payable removes the liability for the total amount of federal income taxes withheld from the employees' wages during the period. The credit to Cash reduces the assets of the company.

On the Job

More than 43 percent of companies outsource their payroll tax matters, and the majority of others handle it in-house using tax compliance software.

Paying State or City Income Taxes

When the employer turns over to the state or city the amount of income taxes withheld from employees' wages, the appropriate journal entry would be recorded as follows:

	Debit	Credit
Employees SIT Payable	XXX	
or		
Employees CIT Payable	XXX	
Cash		XXX

Paying FUTA and SUTA Taxes

At the time of depositing the FUTA taxes that have accumulated during the preceding calendar quarter, an entry is made as follows:

	Debit	Credit
FUTA Taxes Payable	XXX	
Cash		XXX

The quarterly payment of state unemployment contributions is recorded as follows:

	Debit	Credit
SUTA Taxes Payable	XXX	
Cash		XXX

Recording End-of-Period Adjustments

In most cases, the end of the fiscal (accounting) period does not coincide with the end of the payroll period. Therefore, adjustments are commonly made to record the end-of-period wages and accrued vacation pay.

Wages

To record the adjustment for end-of-period wages, the wages for this last payroll period must be split between the fiscal period just ending (accrued wages) and the fiscal period just beginning. For instance, if the fiscal period ends on Wednesday (e.g., December 31) and payday takes place every Friday, the wages earned by the employees on Monday, Tuesday, and Wednesday are an expense of the fiscal period just ended. However, the wages earned on Thursday and Friday (payday) apply to the new fiscal period.

In order to record the wage expense properly for the fiscal period ended, an adjusting entry must be made on the last day of the fiscal period. However, since there is no actual wage payment and, therefore, no withholding, there is no need to credit any withholding accounts. The debit part of the entry would be based on the gross pay for the workdays to be accrued. The credit part of the entry involves a single liability account for the total wage expense. In the case above, the wage expenses of Monday, Tuesday, and Wednesday would be recorded in the following **adjusting entry:**

	Debit	Credit
Wages Expense	XXX	
Wages Payable		XXX
To record wages incurred but unpaid as of the end of the fiscal period.		

With a sophisticated timekeeping system, hours worked and earnings for the accrued wages can be easily generated. In other cases, since the accumulation of payroll data (timesheets, registers, etc.) is such a time-consuming process, the amount of the adjustment could be based on a percentage of the previous period's payroll. For instance, if the accrual is for three workdays out of a five-workday week, 60 percent of the prior week's gross pay could be used as the amount of the adjustment.

In a situation where the employer holds back one week's pay (e.g., earnings for the current week are not paid until the following Friday), the adjusting entry for the example shown above would accrue eight days of expense (one full workweek plus Monday, Tuesday, and Wednesday).

Since the employer is not liable for the payroll taxes (FICA, FUTA, and SUTA) until the actual payday, payroll taxes are not accrued.

Vacation Pay

Another adjustment required at the end of the accounting period concerns vacation pay. If a company has a vacation policy, the employees earn the right for paid future absences during the current period. Therefore, an expense account should be created for the amount of the vacation time earned by the employees and a liability should be accrued at the end of the current period. Whether making the adjustment each payday, each month, or each year, the expense must be recorded when the liability is created, which is in the period when the employees earn it.

The employees of Parma Company are entitled to one day's vacation for each month worked. The average daily pay for each of the 50 employees is $130. The adjusting entry to record the vacation expense of $6,500 ($130 × 50) at the end of each month is:

Example 6-12

Vacation Benefits Expense	6,500.00	
Vacation Benefits Payable		6,500.00

When employees eventually use their vacation time, the payment entry debits Vacation Benefits Payable, not Wages Expense, since the expense was previously recorded in the adjusting entry, as shown above. Another method that is used by most companies ignores the split between regular pay and vacation pay in the payroll entry. Instead, an adjusting entry is made at the end of each month for the expense and the liability to bring the balance in the liability account (Vacation Benefits Payable) either up to or down to the current total of unused vacation for the company, with the offsetting debit or credit made to a vacation expense account.

Postretirement benefits such as health care and pensions also require adjusting entries of this type. These benefits must be reported as expenses during the employees' working years when they earn the entitlements.

On the Job

According to *24/7 Wall St.*, a financial news company, the average number of vacation days and paid holidays required by law to be provided to workers is 32 in Italy, 36 in France, 38 in Austria, 20 in Canada, and 0 in the United States.

Summary of Accounts Used in Recording Payroll Transactions

The following listing summarizes some of the general ledger accounts that may be used to record payroll transactions:

1. *Wages and Salaries:* An operating expense account in which the gross payroll is recorded.

2. *Payroll Taxes:* An operating expense account in which are recorded all payroll taxes on the employer under FICA, FUTA, and the various state unemployment compensation laws.

3. *Workers' Compensation Insurance Expense:* An operating expense account in which are recorded the premiums paid by the company to provide coverage for employees against employment-related injury or death.

4. *Vacation Benefits Expense:* An operating expense account in which are recorded the costs of the vacation time that has been earned by employees.

5. *FICA Taxes Payable—OASDI:* A current liability account in which are recorded deductions made from employees' wages and the employer's portion of the OASDI tax.

6. *FICA Taxes Payable—HI:* A current liability account in which are recorded deductions made from employees' wages and the employer's portion of the HI tax.

7. *FUTA Taxes Payable:* A current liability account in which are recorded the employer's federal unemployment taxes.

8. *SUTA Taxes Payable:* A current liability account in which are recorded the amounts due the states for the employer's unemployment compensation contributions. This account may also be credited for amounts deducted from employees' wages, if employees must contribute to state unemployment compensation funds.

9. *Employees FIT Payable:* A current liability account in which are recorded deductions made from employees' wages for federal income taxes.

10. *Employees SIT Payable:* A current liability account in which are recorded deductions made from employees' wages for state income taxes.

11. *Health Insurance Premiums Collected:* A current liability account in which are recorded deductions made from employees' wages for their share of the premiums paid for health insurance coverage.

12. *Union Dues Payable:* A current liability account in which are recorded the deductions made from union members' wages for their union dues, assessments, or initiation fees.

13. *Wages Payable:* A current liability account in which are recorded the net wages that have been earned by employees but not yet paid to them.

14. *Vacation Benefits Payable:* A current liability account in which are recorded the costs of the vacation time that has been earned by employees but not yet used.

Illustrative Case

The following illustrative case shows the accounting procedures used by Brookins Company in recording payroll transactions during the third quarter of its fiscal year. The fiscal year of the company ends on June 30, 20--. Brookins pays employees semimonthly on the 15th and the last day of the month. When the 15th or the last day of the month falls on Saturday or Sunday, employees are paid on the preceding Friday.

On January 1, 20--, the balances of the accounts used in recording payroll transactions follow. These account balances are shown in the general ledger on pages 6-35 and 6-36.

Acct. No.	Account Title	Account Balance
11	Cash	$85,000.00
20	FICA Taxes Payable—OASDI	961.00
21	FICA Taxes Payable—HI	224.75
22	FUTA Taxes Payable	91.50

23	SUTA Taxes Payable	350.75
25	Employees FIT Payable	1,472.00
26	Employees SIT Payable	474.42
28	Union Dues Payable	80.00
51	Wages and Salaries	46,500.00
55	Payroll Taxes	4,224.00

The first $147,000 in wages and salaries paid is subject to the OASDI tax on both the employer (6.2%) and the employees (6.2%). The total wages and salaries paid are subject to the HI tax on both the employer (1.45%) and the employees (1.45% + 0.9% on wages in excess of $200,000). The employer is also subject to a net FUTA tax of 0.6 percent, based on the first $7,000 in earnings paid each employee during a calendar year, and a SUTA tax of 2.3 percent, based on the first $7,000 in earnings paid during a calendar year. The state does not require contributions of employees for unemployment compensation or disability insurance.

The wage-bracket method tables are used to determine the amount of federal income taxes to be withheld from the employees' earnings. The state income tax law requires that a graduated percentage of the gross earnings of each employee be withheld each payday. Under the check-off system, union dues are withheld each payday from the union workers who are employed in the plant. On or before the fourth of each month, the dues collected during the preceding month are turned over to the treasurer of the union.

In the following narrative of transactions, the January 14 (Friday) payroll transaction is explained in detail. All other transactions are stated briefly. Adjacent to the narrative are the journal entries to record the transactions. The ledger accounts showing the transactions posted are on pages 6-35 and 6-36.

Narrative of Transactions	Journal	P.R.	Debit	Page 15 Credit
	20--			
Jan. 4. Paid the treasurer of the union $80, representing the union dues withheld from the workers' earnings during the month of December.	Jan. 4 Union Dues Payable	28	80.00	
	Cash	11		80.00
	To record payment of union dues withheld during December.			
Jan. 14. Paid total wages and salaries of all employees, $3,890. All the earnings are taxable under FICA. In addition to the social security taxes, the company withheld $455 from the employees' earnings for federal income taxes, $85.58 for state income taxes, and $45 for union dues. (See the explanation of the January 14 payroll transaction given below.)	14 Wages and Salaries	51	3,890.00	
	FICA Taxes Payable—OASDI	20		241.18
	FICA Taxes Payable—HI	21		56.41
	Employees FIT Payable	25		455.00
	Employees SIT Payable	26		85.58
	Union Dues Payable	28		45.00
	Cash	11		3,006.83
	To record the payment of wages and the liabilities for the employees' taxes withheld.			
Jan. 14. Recorded the employer's payroll taxes for the first pay in January. All the earnings are taxable under FICA, FUTA, and SUTA.	14 Payroll Taxes	55	410.40	
	FICA Taxes Payable—OASDI	20		241.18
	FICA Taxes Payable—HI	21		56.41
	FUTA Taxes Payable	22		23.34
	SUTA Taxes Payable	23		89.47
	To record the payroll taxes and liabilities of the employer.			
Jan. 18. Electronically transferred to the IRS the FICA taxes and employees' federal income taxes withheld on the two December payrolls. At the end of December, the total liability for FICA taxes and federal income taxes withheld was $2,657.75 (January 17—Monday—Martin Luther King, Jr.'s birthday is a bank holiday).	18 FICA Taxes Payable—OASDI	20	961.00	
	FICA Taxes Payable—HI	21	224.75	
	Employees FIT Payable	25	1,472.00	
	Cash	11		2,657.75
	To record deposit of FICA taxes and federal income taxes withheld for the 12/15 and 12/31 payrolls.			

Analysis of the January 14 payroll transaction follows:

1. Wages and Salaries is debited for $3,890, the total of the employees' gross earnings.

2. FICA Taxes Payable—OASDI is credited for $241.18, the amount withheld from the employees' earnings for OASDI taxes.

3. FICA Taxes Payable—HI is credited for $56.41, the amount withheld from the employees' earnings for HI taxes.

4. Employees FIT Payable is credited for $455, the amount withheld from employees' earnings for federal income tax purposes.

5. Employees SIT Payable is credited for $85.58, the amount withheld from employees' earnings for state income taxes.

6. Union Dues Payable is credited for $45, the amount withheld from union members' earnings.

7. Cash is credited for $3,006.83, the net amount paid the employees ($3,890 gross earnings − $241.18 OASDI − $56.41 HI − $455 FIT − $85.58 SIT − $45 union dues).

8. Payroll Taxes is debited for $410.40, the amount of taxes imposed on the employer under FICA, FUTA, and SUTA. The computation of the total payroll taxes is:

FICA—OASDI:	6.2% of $3,890 =	$241.18
FICA—HI:	1.45% of $3,890 =	56.41
FUTA:	0.6% of $3,890 =	23.34
SUTA:	2.3% of $3,890 =	89.47
Total payroll taxes		$410.40

9. FICA Taxes Payable—OASDI is credited for the amount of tax on the employer.

10. FICA Taxes Payable—HI is credited for the amount of tax on the employer.

11. FUTA Taxes Payable is credited for $23.34, the liability incurred because of the taxes imposed on the employer under FUTA.

12. SUTA Taxes Payable is credited for $89.47, the amount of the contributions payable to the state.

Narrative of Transactions		Journal	P.R.	Debit	Page 16 Credit
Jan. 18. Paid to the state the amount of state income taxes withheld from employees' pays for the quarter just ended.	Jan. 18	Employees SIT Payable	26	474.42	
		Cash	11		474.42
		To record payment of state income taxes withheld during 4th quarter.			
Jan. 31. Paid total wages and salaries, $4,100. All of this amount constitutes taxable earnings under FICA. Withheld $483 for federal income taxes, $90.20 for state income taxes, and $45 for union dues.	31	Wages and Salaries	51	4,100.00	
		FICA Taxes Payable—OASDI	20		254.20
		FICA Taxes Payable—HI	21		59.45
		Employees FIT Payable...	25		483.00
		Employees SIT Payable...	26		90.20
		Union Dues Payable	28		45.00
		Cash	11		3,168.15
		To record the payment of wages and the liabilities for the employees' taxes withheld.			
Jan. 31. Recorded the employer's payroll taxes for this payroll. All the earnings are taxable under FICA, FUTA, and SUTA.	31	Payroll Taxes...	55	432.55	
		FICA Taxes Payable—OASDI	20		254.20
		FICA Taxes Payable—HI	21		59.45
		FUTA Taxes Payable	22		24.60
		SUTA Taxes Payable...	23		94.30
		To record the payroll taxes and liabilities of the employer.			
Jan. 31. Filed the Employer's Annual Federal Unemployment (FUTA) Tax Return, Form 940, for the preceding calendar year. Electronically transferred $91.50 to remove the liability for FUTA taxes for the fourth quarter of the previous year.	31	FUTA Taxes Payable	22	91.50	
		Cash	11		91.50
		To record the deposit of FUTA taxes for the 4th quarter.			
Jan. 31. Filed the state unemployment contributions return for the quarter ending December 31, and paid $350.75 to the state unemployment compensation fund.	31	SUTA Taxes Payable	23	350.75	
		Cash	11		350.75
		To record payment of contributions to state unemployment compensation fund for the 4th quarter.			

Jan. 31. Filed the quarterly return (Form 941) with the IRS Center for the period ended December 31. No journal entry is required since the liability for FICA taxes and employees' federal income taxes withheld was removed by the timely transfer on January 18, 20--. No taxes were paid or deposited at the time of filing Form 941.

Feb. 4. Paid the treasurer of the union $90, representing the union dues withheld from the workers' earnings during the month of January.

	Feb. 4	Union Dues Payable	28	90.00	
		Cash	11		90.00
		To record the payment of the union dues withheld during January.			

Feb. 15. Paid total wages and salaries, $4,000. All of this amount is taxable under FICA. Withheld $470 for federal income taxes, $88 for state income taxes, and $45 for union dues.

	15	Wages and Salaries	51	4,000.00	
		FICA Taxes Payable—OASDI	20		248.00
		FICA Taxes Payable—HI	21		58.00
		Employees FIT Payable	25		470.00
		Employees SIT Payable	26		88.00
		Union Dues Payable	28		45.00
		Cash	11		3,091.00
		To record the payment of wages and the liabilities for the employees' taxes withheld.			

Narrative of Transactions		Journal	P.R.	Debit	Page 17 Credit
Feb. 15. Recorded the employer's payroll taxes. All the earnings are taxable under FICA, FUTA, and SUTA.	Feb. 15	Payroll Taxes	55	422.00	
		FICA Taxes Payable—OASDI	20		248.00
		FICA Taxes Payable—HI	21		58.00
		FUTA Taxes Payable	22		24.00
		SUTA Taxes Payable	23		92.00
		To record the payroll taxes and liabilities of the employer.			
Feb. 15. Electronically transferred $2,160.48 to remove the liability for the FICA taxes and the employees' federal income taxes withheld on the January 14 and January 31 payrolls.	15	FICA Taxes Payable—OASDI	20	990.76	
		FICA Taxes Payable—HI	21	231.72	
		Employees FIT Payable	25	938.00	
		Cash	11		2,160.48
		To record the deposit of FICA taxes and federal income taxes withheld for the January 14 and January 31 payrolls.			
Feb. 28. Paid total wages and salaries, $4,250. All of this amount is taxable under FICA. Withheld $502 for federal income taxes, $93.50 for state income taxes, and $50 for union dues.	28	Wages and Salaries	51	4,250.00	
		FICA Taxes Payable—OASDI	20		263.50
		FICA Taxes Payable—HI	21		61.63
		Employees FIT Payable	25		502.00
		Employees SIT Payable	26		93.50
		Union Dues Payable	28		50.00
		Cash	11		3,279.37
		To record the payment of wages and the liabilities for the employees' taxes withheld.			
Feb. 28. Recorded the employer's payroll taxes. All the earnings are taxable under FICA, FUTA, and SUTA.	28	Payroll Taxes	55	448.38	
		FICA Taxes Payable—OASDI	20		263.50
		FICA Taxes Payable—HI	21		61.63
		FUTA Taxes Payable	22		25.50
		SUTA Taxes Payable	23		97.75
		To record the payroll taxes and liabilities of the employer.			
Mar. 4. Paid the treasurer of the union $95, representing the union dues withheld from the workers' earnings during the month of February.	Mar. 4	Union Dues Payable	28	95.00	
		Cash	11		95.00
		To record the payment of the union dues withheld during February.			

Mar. 15. Paid total wages and salaries, $4,300. All of this amount is taxable under FICA. Withheld $554 for federal income taxes, $94.60 for state income taxes, and $50 for union dues.	15	Wages and Salaries	51	4,300.00	
		FICA Taxes Payable—OASDI	20		266.60
		FICA Taxes Payable—HI	21		62.35
		Employees FIT Payable...	25		554.00
		Employees SIT Payable...	26		94.60
		Union Dues Payable	28		50.00
		Cash	11		3,272.45
		To record the payment of wages and the liabilities for the employees' taxes withheld.			
Mar. 15. Recorded the employer's payroll taxes. All the earnings are taxable under FICA, FUTA, and SUTA.	15	Payroll Taxes...	55	453.65	
		FICA Taxes Payable—OASDI	20		266.60
		FICA Taxes Payable—HI	21		62.35
		FUTA Taxes Payable	22		25.80
		SUTA Taxes Payable	23		98.90
		To record the payroll taxes and liabilities of the employer.			

					Page 18
Narrative of Transactions		**Journal**	**P.R.**	**Debit**	**Credit**
Mar. 15. Electronically transferred $2,234.26 to remove the liability for FICA taxes and the employees' federal income taxes withheld on the February 15 and February 28 payrolls.	Mar. 15	FICA Taxes Payable—OASDI	20	1,023.00	
		FICA Taxes Payable—HI..	21	239.26	
		Employees FIT Payable	25	972.00	
		Cash	11		2,234.26
		To record the deposit of FICA taxes and federal income taxes withheld for the February 15 and February 28 payrolls.			
Mar. 31. Paid total wages and salaries, $4,320. All of this amount is taxable under FICA. Withheld $570 for federal income taxes, $95.04 for state income taxes, and $50 for union dues.	31	Wages and Salaries	51	4,320.00	
		FICA Taxes Payable—OASDI	20		267.84
		FICA Taxes Payable—HI	21		62.64
		Employees FIT Payable...	25		570.00
		Employees SIT Payable...	26		95.04
		Union Dues Payable	28		50.00
		Cash	11		3,274.48
		To record the payment of wages and the liabilities for the employees' taxes withheld.			
Mar. 31. Recorded the employer's payroll taxes. All of the earnings are taxable under FICA, FUTA, and SUTA.	31	Payroll Taxes...	55	455.76	
		FICA Taxes Payable—OASDI	20		267.84
		FICA Taxes Payable—HI	21		62.64
		FUTA Taxes Payable	22		25.92
		SUTA Taxes Payable	23		99.36
		To record the payroll taxes and liabilities of the employer.			

After journalizing and posting the transactions for January through March, the general ledger payroll accounts as shown on the next two pages carry the following balances:

1. **FICA Taxes Payable—OASDI:** $1,068.88, the amount of the liability for the taxes imposed on both the employer and the employees with respect to wages and salaries paid on March 15 and March 31. The FICA taxes, along with the employees' federal income taxes withheld, must be deposited by April 15.

2. **FICA Taxes Payable—HI:** $249.98, the amount of the liability for the taxes imposed on both the employer and the employees with respect to wages

and salaries paid on March 15 and March 31. The FICA taxes, along with the employees' federal income taxes withheld, must be paid by April 15.

3. **FUTA Taxes Payable:** $149.16, the accumulation of the amounts credited to this account each payday during the first three months of the calendar year. The balance of the account on March 31 need not be deposited since it is $500 or less. The $149.16 will be added to the second quarter's liability and deposited if the $500 threshold is passed.

4. **SUTA Taxes Payable:** $571.78, the amount due to the state unemployment compensation fund. This liability must be paid on or before May 2.

5. **Employees FIT Payable:** $1,124, the amount due for federal income taxes withheld from employees' earnings on March 15 and March 31. This amount, along with the balances of the FICA taxes payable accounts, represents a liability that must be paid by April 15.

6. **Employees SIT Payable:** $546.92, the amount due for state income taxes withheld from employees' earnings during the first three months of the calendar year. This amount must be paid to the treasurer of the state on the date specified in the state's income tax law.

7. **Union Dues Payable:** $100, amount due the treasurer of the union on or before April 4.

8. **Wages and Salaries:** $71,360, the total gross earnings for the three quarters of the company's fiscal year. The entire amount is an operating expense of the business.

9. **Payroll Taxes:** $6,846.74, the total payroll taxes for the three quarters imposed on the employer under FICA, FUTA, and SUTA. The entire amount is an operating expense of the business.

GENERAL LEDGER

		CASH				11				FICA TAXES PAYABLE—OASDI			20
					Balance							**Balance**	
Date	Item	P.R.	Dr.	Cr.	Dr.	Cr.	Date	Item	P.R.	Dr.	Cr.	Dr.	Cr.
20--							20--						
Jan. 1	Bal.	✓			85,000.00		Jan. 1	Bal.	✓				961.00
4		J15		80.00	84,920.00		14		J15		241.18		1,202.18
14		J15		3,006.83	81,913.17		14		J15		241.18		1,443.36
18		J15		2,657.75	79,255.42		18		J15	961.00			482.36
18		J16		474.42	78,781.00		31		J16		254.20		736.56
31		J16		3,168.15	75,612.85		31		J16		254.20		990.76
31		J16		91.50	75,521.35		Feb. 15		J16		248.00		1,238.76
31		J16		350.75	75,170.60		15		J17		248.00		1,486.76
Feb. 4		J16		90.00	75,080.60		15		J17	990.76			496.00
15		J16		3,091.00	71,989.60		28		J17		263.50		759.50
15		J17		2,160.48	69,829.12		28		J17		263.50		1,023.00
28		J17		3,279.37	66,549.75		Mar. 15		J17		266.60		1,289.60
Mar. 4		J17		95.00	66,454.75		15		J17		266.60		1,556.20
15		J17		3,272.45	63,182.30		15		J18	1,023.00			533.20
15		J18		2,234.26	60,948.04		31		J18		267.84		801.04
31		J18		3,274.48	57,673.56		31		J18		267.84		1,068.88

		FICA TAXES PAYABLE—HI				21				FUTA TAXES PAYABLE			22
					Balance							**Balance**	
Date	Item	P.R.	Dr.	Cr.	Dr.	Cr.	Date	Item	P.R.	Dr.	Cr.	Dr.	Cr.
20--							20--						
Jan. 1	Bal.	✓				224.75	Jan. 1	Bal.	✓				91.50
14		J15		56.41		281.16	14		J15		23.34		114.84
14		J15		56.41		337.57	31		J16		24.60		139.44
18		J15	224.75			112.82	31		J16	91.50			47.94
31		J16		59.45		172.27	Feb. 15		J17		24.00		71.94
31		J16		59.45		231.72	28		J17		25.50		97.44
Feb. 15		J16		58.00		289.72	Mar. 15		J17		25.80		123.24
15		J17		58.00		347.72	31		J18		25.92		149.16
15		J17	231.72			116.00							
28		J17		61.63		177.63							
28		J17		61.63		239.26							
Mar. 15		J17		62.35		301.61							
15		J17		62.35		363.96							
15		J18	239.26			124.70							
31		J18		62.64		187.34							
31		J18		62.64		249.98							

SUTA TAXES PAYABLE   23

Date		Item	P.R.	Dr.	Cr.	Balance Dr.	Balance Cr.
20--							
Jan.	1	Bal.	✓				350.75
	14		J15		89.47		440.22
	31		J16		94.30		534.52
	31		J16	350.75			183.77
Feb.	15		J17		92.00		275.77
	28		J17		97.75		373.52
Mar.	15		J17		98.90		472.42
	31		J18		99.36		571.78

EMPLOYEES FIT PAYABLE   25

Date		Item	P.R.	Dr.	Cr.	Balance Dr.	Balance Cr.
20--							
Jan.	1	Bal.	✓				1,472.00
	14		J15		455.00		1,927.00
	18		J15	1,472.00			455.00
	31		J16		483.00		938.00
Feb.	15		J16		470.00		1,408.00
	15		J17	938.00			470.00
	28		J17		502.00		972.00
Mar.	15		J17		554.00		1,526.00
	15		J18	972.00			554.00
	31		J18		570.00		1,124.00

EMPLOYEES SIT PAYABLE   26

Date		Item	P.R.	Dr.	Cr.	Balance Dr.	Balance Cr.
20--							
Jan.	1	Bal.	✓				474.42
	14		J15		85.58		560.00
	18		J16	474.42			85.58
	31		J16		90.20		175.78
Feb.	15		J16		88.00		263.78
	28		J17		93.50		357.28
Mar.	15		J17		94.60		451.88
	31		J18		95.04		546.92

UNION DUES PAYABLE   28

Date		Item	P.R.	Dr.	Cr.	Balance Dr.	Balance Cr.
20--							
Jan.	1	Bal.	✓				80.00
	4		J15	80.00		—	
	14		J15		45.00		45.00
	31		J16		45.00		90.00
Feb.	4		J16	90.00		—	
	15		J16		45.00		45.00
	28		J17		50.00		95.00
Mar.	4		J17	95.00		—	
	15		J17		50.00		50.00
	31		J18		50.00		100.00

WAGES AND SALARIES   51

Date		Item	P.R.	Dr.	Cr.	Balance Dr.	Balance Cr.
20--							
Jan.	1	Bal.	✓			46,500.00	
	14		J15	3,890.00		50,390.00	
	31		J16	4,100.00		54,490.00	
Feb.	15		J16	4,000.00		58,490.00	
	28		J17	4,250.00		62,740.00	
Mar.	15		J17	4,300.00		67,040.00	
	31		J18	4,320.00		71,360.00	

PAYROLL TAXES   55

Date		Item	P.R.	Dr.	Cr.	Balance Dr.	Balance Cr.
20--							
Jan.	1	Bal.	✓			4,224.00	
	14		J15	410.40		4,634.40	
	31		J16	432.55		5,066.95	
Feb.	15		J17	422.00		5,488.95	
	28		J17	448.38		5,937.33	
Mar.	15		J17	453.65		6,390.98	
	31		J18	455.76		6,846.74	

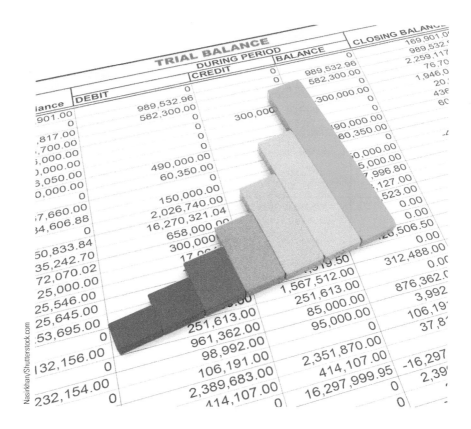

Key Terms

business expense (p. 6-22)

check-off system (p. 6-10)

disposable earnings (p. 6-10)

electronic funds transfer system (EFTS) (p. 6-17)

electronic paystubs (p. 6-19)

garnishment (p. 6-10)

group insurance (p. 6-8)

journal entries (p. 6-3)

Answers to Self-Study Quizzes

Self-Study Quiz 6-1

January 25	Salary Expense	95,190.00	
	FICA Taxes Payable—OASDI		5,901.78
	FICA Taxes Payable—HI		1,380.26
	Employees FIT Payable		14,270.00
	Employees SIT Payable		1,427.85
	SUTA Taxes Payable		951.90
	Salaries Payable (Cash)		71,258.21

Self-Study Quiz 6-2

January 25	Payroll Taxes	10,851.67	
	FICA Taxes Payable—OASDI		5,901.78
	FICA Taxes Payable—HI		1,380.26
	FUTA Taxes Payable		571.14
	SUTA Taxes Payable		2,998.49

Key Points Summary

	Learning Objectives	Key Points	Problem Sets A & B
LO1	Record payrolls in payroll registers and post to employees' earnings records.	• Separate P/R register for each payday.	6-16
		• Separate line for each employee.	
		• Totals of each column are used to record payroll journal entry.	
		• Information on each employee is transferred from the P/R register to the employee's earnings record.	
LO2	Identify the various deductions—both voluntary and involuntary (taxes and garnishments)—that are taken out of employees' gross pay. ▶ Tell Me More	• Amounts withheld for taxes (FICA, FIT, SIT, and CIT) are set up as liabilities in the P/R entry.	6-1, 6-2, 6-3, 6-4, 6-5, 6-6, 6-8, 6-14
		• All other deductions from employees' paychecks are set up as liabilities.	
		• Consumer Credit Protection Act limits the amount of wages subject to garnishment.	
		• With garnishments, child support is first, federal tax levies are second.	

LO3	Journalize the entries to record the payroll and payroll taxes. ▶ Tell Me More	• Wages Expense (gross payroll) XXX
		       Liabilities (all withholdings) XXX
		       Cash/Salary Payroll (net pay) XXX
			6-4 , 6-5, 6-6, 6-7, 6-9, 6-10, 6-17

		• Paying in cash, check, electronic transfer, pay cards.	

		• P/R Tax Expense (total) XXX
		     FICA Payable OASDI (employer's) XXX
		     FICA Payable HI (employer's) XXX
		     FUTA Payable XXX
		     SUTA Payable XXX	

LO4	Post to the various general ledger accounts that are used to accumulate information from the payroll entries.	• Copy the debits and credits from the journal entries into the individual ledger accounts in the general ledger.	6-17
LO5	Explain the recording of the payroll tax deposits.	• When tax payments are due: Specify Tax Liability Account XXX Cash XXX	6-11
LO6	Explain the need for end-of-period adjustments.	• End of accounting period and end of payroll period—different endings.	6-12, 6-13, 6-15

		• Adjusting entries needed for end-of-period wages and accrued vacation pay:
		Wages Expense XXX
		     Wages Payable XXX
		Vacation Benefits Expense XXX
		     Vacation Benefits Payable XXX	

Matching Quiz

_____ 1. Employee's earnings record
_____ 2. Pay cards
_____ 3. Disposable earnings
_____ 4. Regular earnings plus overtime earnings
_____ 5. Payroll Taxes
_____ 6. Overtime premium earnings
_____ 7. Wages Payable
_____ 8. Payroll register
_____ 9. Form 668-W
_____ 10. Garnishment

A. Expense account for FICA, FUTA, and SUTA taxes on the employer
B. Legal procedure by which a portion of the wages of any person is withheld for payment of a debt
C. Debit card-based accounts
D. Notifies employer of a tax levy
E. Used to complete Form W-2
F. Provides information needed in preparing the journal entries for payroll
G. Debit portion of payroll entry
H. Earnings remaining after withholding for income taxes and for other amounts required by law
I. One-half regular pay rate multiplied by overtime hours
J. Liability account for wages that have been earned by employees but not yet paid

Questions for Review

1. What are the main kinds of information contained in a payroll register?
2. For what reason are "distribution" columns sometimes provided in the payroll register?
3. Explain the use of the "Cumulative" column in the employee's earnings record.
4. In Philadelphia, Pennsylvania, most workers are subject to three income taxes upon their earnings—federal, state, and city. Should an employer in Philadelphia record the liability for the withholding of all three income taxes in one liability account such as Income Taxes Payable?
5. What is meant by the garnishment of wages?
6. What is general priority order concerning wage attachments?
7. Under the Consumer Credit Protection Act, what is the maximum percentage that can be deducted from an employee's pay to satisfy a student loan garnishment?
8. What portions of an employee's take-home pay are exempt from a federal tax levy?
9. How will payroll deductions from employees' wages for their portion of 401(k) plans be recorded?
10. How are employees who do not have bank accounts paid by an employer who uses an electronic funds transfer system for payroll?
11. How is the information that is usually on a paper paystub given to an employee if the employer is using electronic paystubs?

12. What must the employer do with unclaimed paychecks?
13. What special accounts must usually be opened in the general ledger to record payroll tax entries?
14. Is it necessary for an employer who is subject to FICA and FUTA taxes to keep a separate expense account for the taxes under each act?
15. What is the effect of each of the following postings upon the assets, liabilities, and owner's equity of a company?
    a. A debit to Wages.
    b. A credit to FICA Taxes Payable—HI.
    c. A debit to SUTA Taxes Payable.
    d. A credit to Cash.
16. Why is it necessary to classify employees by kind of work performed when computing the cost of workers' compensation insurance?
17. What accounts are debited and credited when an employer records the electronic transfer of FICA taxes and federal income taxes that have been withheld?
18. How is the amount of accrual entry for the portion of a weekly payroll that is accrued at the end of an accounting period determined?
19. When are expenses of benefits such as vacation pay and retirement pay recorded? Explain.
20. What payroll-related expenses does an employer incur because of its employees?

Questions for Discussion

1. Would it be a violation of the Consumer Credit Protection Act to suspend, demote, or transfer an employee who is subject to a garnishment?
2. Freisleven Corporation has undertaken a cost study of its operations. One area of concern to the company is the total cost of labor, particularly the cost of employee benefits. Prepare a list of the different kinds of costs that a company might incur as part of its "total package" salary cost.
3. If a salaried exempt employee was paid twice (direct deposit) for one pay period and the company was unable to recover the funds, what options are available to the company to correct this overpayment?

Problem Set • A

Omit the writing of explanations for the journal entries. For rounding rules, refer to page 2-37.

6-1A • LO 2   See Example 6-5 on page 6-14, Figure 6.3 on page 6-13

Carson Holiday has a federal tax levy of $4,119.90 against him. If Holiday is single with three dependents and had a take-home pay of $1,020.00 this week, how much would his employer take from his pay to satisfy part of the tax levy?

6-2A • LO 2   See Example 6-2 on page 6-11, Example 6-3 on page 6-11

Kalen O'Brien earned $730 this week. The deductions from her pay were as follows:

FIT	$54.00
FICA—OASDI	45.26
FICA—HI	10.59
State income tax	36.50
State disability insurance	8.61
Health insurance premium	19.50
Credit union contribution	35.00
United Fund contribution	5.00

O'Brien's employer just received a garnishment order (credit card debt of $3,500) against her pay. Compute the following:

a. O'Brien's disposable earnings .... $ _____

b. The amount of her pay subject to the garnishment .... $ _____

6-3A • LO 2 See Example 6-4 on page 6-12

Rico Samuel's employer receives a creditor garnishment order to withhold $80 from Samuel's paycheck each week. This week his disposable earnings were $300. How much will the employer withhold from this week's pay to satisfy the garnishment?

Garnishment .... $ _____

6-4A • LO 3   See Example 6-7 on page 6-14, Example 6-9 on page 6-22,
Example 6-11 on page 6-27

a. Cal Yanza, an employer, is subject to FICA taxes but exempt from FUTA and SUTA taxes. During the last quarter of the year, his employees earned monthly wages of $8,500, all of which is taxable. The amount of federal income taxes withheld each month is $1,040. Journalize the payment of wages, and record the payroll tax on November 29.

6-4A (concluded)

JOURNAL

	DATE	DESCRIPTION	POST. REF.	DEBIT	CREDIT	
1						1
2						2
3						3
4						4
5						5
6						6
7						7
8						8
9						9
10						10

b. Prior to posting the November 29 payroll transaction, FICA Taxes Payable—OASDI, FICA Taxes Payable—HI, and Employees FIT Payable had zero balances. Yanza must pay the FICA taxes and income taxes withheld on the November 29 payroll. Journalize the electronic transfer of the payroll taxes on December 16.

JOURNAL

	DATE	DESCRIPTION	POST. REF.	DEBIT	CREDIT	
1						1
2						2
3						3
4						4
5						5
6						6

6-5A • LO 3 See Example 6-7 on page 6-14, Example 6-9 on page 6-22

The employees of Donnelly Music Company earn total wages of $4,690 during January. The total amount is taxable under FICA, FUTA, and SUTA. The state contribution rate for the company is 3.6%. The amount withheld for federal income taxes is $685. Journalize the payment of the monthly wages, and record the payroll taxes.

6-5A (concluded)

JOURNAL

	DATE		DESCRIPTION	POST. REF.	DEBIT	CREDIT	
1							1
2							2
3							3
4							4
5							5
6							6
7							7
8							8
9							9
10							10
11							11
12							12
13							13
14							14

6-6A • LO 3 **See Example 6-7 on page 6-14, Example 6-9 on page 6-22** Show Me How

Vulcra, Inc., has a semimonthly payroll of $67,000 on September 15, 20--. The total payroll is taxable under FICA Taxes—HI; $63,850 is taxable under FICA Taxes—OASDI; and $10,300 is taxable under FUTA and SUTA. The state contribution rate for the company is 4.1%. The amount withheld for federal income taxes is $9,911. The amount withheld for state income taxes is $1,410.

a. Journalize the payment of the wages, and record the payroll taxes on September 15.

b. Assume that the employees of Vulcra, Inc., must also pay state contributions (disability insurance) of 1% on the taxable payroll of $62,100 and that the employees' contributions are to be deducted by the employer. Journalize the September 15 payment of wages, assuming that the state contributions of the employees are kept in a separate account.

6-6A (concluded)

JOURNAL

	DATE	DESCRIPTION	POST. REF.	DEBIT	CREDIT	
1						1
2						2
3						3
4						4
5						5
6						6
7						7
8						8
9						9
10						10
11						11
12						12
13						13
14						14
15						15
16						16
17						17
18						18
19						19
20						20
21						21
22						22
23						23
24						24
25						25
26						26
27						27

6-7A • LO 3 See Figure 6.4 on page 6-16

Gallardo, Inc., pays its employees' weekly wages in cash. A supplementary payroll sheet that lists the employees' names and their earnings for a certain week is shown below. Complete the payroll sheet by calculating the total amount of payroll and indicating the least possible number of denominations that can be used in paying each employee. However, no employees are to be given bills in denominations greater than $50.

GALLARDO, INC.

Supplementary Payroll Sheet

Name of Employee	Net Amount Paid	Bills						Coins				
		$50	$20	$10	$5	$1	50¢	25¢	10¢	5¢	1¢
Chad T. Biskis	$251.75											
Nicole A. Cibik	256.52											
Domingo M. Diaz	384.94											
Laura B. Elias	202.59											
Ari M. Fleischer	253.64											
Diane Y. Germano	296.50											
Arnold B. Herst	594.26											
Edward C. Kenner	399.89											
Kathleen J. Marfia	234.01											
Kimberly A. Picket	595.80											
Total												

6-8A • LO 2, 3  **See Example 6-7 on page 6-14, Example 6-9 on page 6-22**
Show
Me How

Kip Lee is owner and sole employee of KB Corporation. He pays himself a salary of $1,500 each week.

Additional tax information includes:

FICA tax—OASDI	6.2% on first $147,000
FICA tax—HI	1.45% on total pay
Federal income tax	$232.00 per pay
State income tax	22% of the federal income tax withholding
Federal unemployment tax	0.6% on first $7,000
State unemployment tax	0.05% on first $14,000

Additional payroll deductions include:

401(k) plan	3% per pay
Child support garnishment	$100 per pay
Health insurance premium	$95 per pay

Record the payroll entry and payroll tax entry for the pay of the week ended June 7 (his year-to-date pay is $31,500).

JOURNAL

	DATE	DESCRIPTION	POST. REF.	DEBIT	CREDIT	
1						1
2						2
3						3
4						4
5						5
6						6
7						7
8						8
9						9
10						10
11						11
12						12
13						13
14						14
15						15
16						16
17						17
18						18
19						19
20						20

6-9A • LO 3 See Example 6-7 on page 6-14, Example 6-9 on page 6-22

The employees of Pelter Company earn wages of $12,000 for the two weeks ending April 12. FIT taxes of $260 were withheld. The entire amount of wages is subject to the FICA taxes, but only $9,800 is taxable under the federal and state unemployment compensation laws. The state contribution rate of the employer is 2.9%. All employees are subject to state unemployment contributions of 0.5% on the April 12 taxable wages of $9,800, and the employees' contributions are to be deducted by the employer. Journalize the payment of the wages, and record the payroll taxes, assuming that the contributions of the employer and the employees are recorded in one account, SUTA Taxes Payable.

JOURNAL

	DATE	DESCRIPTION	POST. REF.	DEBIT	CREDIT	
1						1
2						2
3						3
4						4
5						5
6						6
7						7
8						8
9						9
10						10
11						11
12						12
13						13
14						14
15						15

6-10A • LO 3 See Example 6-7 on page 6-14, Example 6-9 on page 6-22

The following information pertains to a weekly payroll of Texera Tile Company:

a. The total wages earned by employees are $17,210.

b. The state unemployment insurance contribution rate is 3.5%.

c. The entire amount of wages is taxable under FICA, FUTA, and SUTA.

d. The amount withheld from the employees' wages for federal income taxes is $1,890; for state income taxes, $369.40; and for group insurance, $193.00.

Journalize the payment of wages, and record the payroll taxes for this payroll.

JOURNAL

	DATE	DESCRIPTION	POST. REF.	DEBIT	CREDIT	
1						1
2						2
3						3
4						4
5						5
6						6
7						7
8						8
9						9
10						10
11						11
12						12
13						13
14						14
15						15
16						16
17						17

6-11A • LO 5 See page 6-27

On December 31, Chang Company has a balance of $98.75 in the FUTA taxes payable account. This represents the employer's liability for the fourth quarter taxes. Journalize the entry Chang Company should make in January to record the last transfer (payment) of FUTA taxes.

JOURNAL

	DATE		DESCRIPTION	POST. REF.	DEBIT	CREDIT	
1							1
2							2
3							3
4							4
5							5
6							6

6-12A • LO 6 See page 6-28

On December 31, 20--, Karmansky Company needed to record its accrued wages for year-end. If December 31 is a Tuesday, then Karmansky Company must account for two days of wages.

The company operates on a five-day workweek, the prior week's gross pay was $32,650, and the net pay was $21,330.

Journalize the adjusting entry to be made on December 31 for the accrued wages.

JOURNAL

	DATE		DESCRIPTION	POST. REF.	DEBIT	CREDIT	
1							1
2							2
3							3
4							4
5							5
6							6

6-13A • LO 6   **See Example 6-1 on page 6-2 and page 6-28**   Show Me How

Kelsey Gunn is the only employee of Arsenault Company. His pay rate is $23.00 per hour with an overtime rate of 1½ times for hours over 40 in a workweek.

For the week ending March 31, 20--, he worked 48 hours. Calculate his gross pay for the week using the overtime premium approach to calculate the overtime pay.

Since the company holds back one week of pay, Gunn will not be paid until April 7, 20--. What adjusting entry would the company make in order to record Gunn's salary in the first quarter of this year?

a. Regular pay.. $ _____

b. Overtime premium pay.. $ _____

c. Gross pay .... $ _____

d. Adjusting entry

JOURNAL

	DATE	DESCRIPTION	POST. REF.	DEBIT	CREDIT	
1						1
2						2
3						3

6-14A • LO 2   **See Example 6-10 on page 6-26**

In Oregon, employers who are covered by the state workers' compensation law withhold employee contributions from the wages of covered employees for the workers' benefit fund at the rate of 1.1c / for each hour or part of an hour that the worker is employed. Every covered employer is also assessed 1.1c / per hour for each worker employed for each hour or part of an hour. The employer-employee contributions for workers' compensation are collected monthly, quarterly, or annually by the employer's insurance carrier, according to a schedule agreed upon by the employer and the carrier. The insurance carrier remits the contributions to the state's Workers' Compensation Department.

Cortez Company, a covered employer in Oregon, turns over the employer-employee workers' compensation contributions to its insurance carrier by the 15th of each month for the preceding month. During the month of July, the number of full-time employee-hours worked by the company's employees was 8,270; the number of part-time employee-hours was 1,950.

a. The amount the company should have withheld from its full- and part-time employees during the month of July for workers' compensation insurance is $ _____

b. The title you would give to the general ledger liability account to which the amount withheld from the employees' earnings would be credited is:

_____

c. Journalize the entry on July 31 to record the employer's liability for workers' compensation insurance for the month.

6-14A (concluded)

JOURNAL

	DATE		DESCRIPTION	POST. REF.	DEBIT	CREDIT	
1							1
2							2
3							3
4							4
5							5

d. Journalize the entry on August 15 to record payment to the insurance carrier of the amount withheld from the employees' earnings for workers' compensation insurance and the amount of the employer's liability.

JOURNAL

	DATE		DESCRIPTION	POST. REF.	DEBIT	CREDIT	
1							1
2							2
3							3
4							4
5							5

6-15A • LO 6   See Example 6-12 on page 6-29

At the end of April, Hernandez Company had a balance of $37,910 in the vacation benefits payable account. During May, employees earned an additional $2,790 in vacation benefits, but some employees used vacation days that amounted to $2,050 of the vacation benefits. The $2,050 was charged to Wages Expense when it was paid in May. What adjusting entry would Hernandez Company make at the end of May to bring the vacation benefits payable account up to date?

JOURNAL

	DATE		DESCRIPTION	POST. REF.	DEBIT	CREDIT	
1							1
2							2
3							3

6-16A • LO 1　See Figure 6.1 on pages 6-3 and 6-4

The form on page 6-53 shows the amounts that appear in the Earnings to Date column of the employees' earnings records for 10 full- and part-time workers in Unger Company. These amounts represent the cumulative earnings for each worker as of October 4, the company's last payday. The form also gives the gross amount of earnings to be paid each worker on the next payday, October 11.

In the state where Unger Company is located, the tax rates and bases are as follows:

Tax on Employees:

FICA—OASDI	6.2% on first $147,000
FICA—HI	1.45% on **total earnings**
SUTA	0.5% on first $8,000

Tax on Employer:

FICA—OASDI	6.2% on first $147,000
FICA—HI	1.45% on **total earnings**
FUTA	0.6% on first $7,000
SUTA...	1.8% on first $8,000

In the appropriate columns of the form on page 6-53, do the following:

1. Compute the amount to be withheld from each employee's earnings on October 11 for (a) FICA—OASDI, (b) FICA—HI, and (c) SUTA, and determine the total employee taxes.

2. Record the portion of each employee's earnings that is taxable under FICA, FUTA, and SUTA, and calculate the total employer's payroll taxes on the October 11 payroll.

Date _____ Name _____

UNGER COMPANY

Employee	Earnings to Date	Gross Earnings Oct. 11	Taxes to Be Withheld from Employees' Earnings Under			Employer Taxes: Portion of Employees' Earnings Taxable Under			
			FICA		SUTA	FICA		FUTA	SUTA
			OASDI	HI		OASDI	HI		
1. Weiser, Roberta A.	$158,500	$1,790	$	$	$	$	$	$	$
2. Stankard, Laurie C.	14,950	295							
3. Grow, Joan L.	4,060	240							
4. Rowe, Paul C.	8,190	235							
5. McNamara, Joyce M.	7,460	195							
6. O'Connor, Roger T.	146,710	1,810							
7. Carson, Ronald B.	8,905	280							
8. Chun, Ginni C.	4,325	175							
9. Lin, Virginia S.	57,010	590							
10. Wilson, Joe W.	3,615	205							
Total employee taxes...........			$	$	$	$	$	$	$
			1.(a)	1.(b)	1.(c)				

Total taxable earnings .... $ .... $ .... $ .... $

× Applicable tax rate ....

Totals........................ $ .... $ .... $ .... $

Total payroll taxes .... $ _____
                                        2.

6-17A • LO 3, 4, 5, 6 See Illustrative Case beginning on page 6-30

In the Illustrative Case in this chapter, payroll transactions for Brookins Company were analyzed, journalized, and posted for the third quarter of the fiscal year. In this problem, you are to record the payroll transactions for the last quarter of the firm's fiscal year. The last quarter begins on April 1, 20--.

Refer to the Illustrative Case on pages 6-30 to 6-36 and proceed as follows:

a. Analyze and journalize the transactions described in the following narrative. Use the two-column journal paper provided on pages 6-55 to 6-59. Omit the writing of explanations in the journal entries.

b. Post the journal entries to the general ledger accounts on pages 6-60 to 6-65.

Narrative of Transactions:

Apr. 1. Paid the treasurer of the union the amount of union dues withheld from workers' earnings during March.

15. Payroll: $6,105. All wages and salaries taxable. Withheld $565 for federal income taxes, $107.32 for state income taxes, and $50 for union dues.

15. Paid the treasurer of the state the amount of state income taxes withheld from workers' earnings during the first quarter.

15. Electronically transferred funds to remove the liability for FICA taxes and employees' federal income taxes withheld on the March payrolls.

29. Payroll: $5,850. All wages and salaries taxable. Withheld $509 for federal income taxes, $128.90 for state income taxes, and $55 for union dues.

29. Filed the Employer's Quarterly Federal Tax Return (Form 941) for the period ended March 31. No journal entry is required, since the FICA taxes and federal income taxes withheld have been timely paid.

29. Filed the state contribution return for the quarter ended March 31 and paid the amount to the state unemployment compensation fund.

May 2. Paid the treasurer of the union the amount of union dues withheld from workers' earnings during April.

13. Payroll: $5,810. All wages and salaries taxable. Withheld $507 for federal income taxes, $125.05 for state income taxes, and $55 for union dues.

16. Electronically transferred funds to remove the liability for FICA taxes and federal income taxes withheld on the April payrolls.

31. Payroll: $6,060. All wages and salaries taxable. Withheld $533 for federal income taxes, $119.00 for state income taxes, and $50 for union dues.

June 3. Paid the treasurer of the union the amount of union dues withheld from workers' earnings during May.

15. Payroll: $6,380. All wages and salaries taxable, except only $5,000 is taxable under FUTA and SUTA. Withheld $549 for federal income taxes, $128.70 for state income taxes, and $50 for union dues.

15. Electronically transferred funds to remove the liability for FICA taxes and federal income taxes withheld on the May payrolls.

30. Payroll: $6,250. All wages and salaries taxable, except only $4,770 is taxable under FUTA and SUTA. Withheld $538 for federal income taxes, $127.60 for state income taxes, and $50 for union dues.

6-17A (continued)

c. Answer the following questions:

1. The total amount of the liability for FICA taxes and federal income taxes withheld as of June 30 is .... $ _____

2. The total amount of the liability for state income taxes withheld as of June 30 is .... $ _____

3. The amount of FUTA taxes that must be paid to the federal government on or before August 1 (assume July 31 is a Sunday) is............................... $ _____

4. The amount of contributions that must be paid into the state unemployment compensation fund on or before August 1 is........................... $ _____

5. The total amount due the treasurer of the union is............................... $ _____

6. The total amount of wages and salaries expense since the beginning of the fiscal year is .... $ _____

7. The total amount of payroll taxes expense since the beginning of the fiscal year is .... $ _____

8. Using the partial journal below, journalize the entry to record the vacation accrual at the end of the company's fiscal year. The amount of Brookins Company's vacation accrual for the fiscal year is $15,000.

JOURNAL

	DATE	DESCRIPTION	POST. REF.	DEBIT	CREDIT	
1						1
2						2
3						3
4						4
5						5
6						6

6-17A (continued)

	DATE	DESCRIPTION	POST. REF.	DEBIT	CREDIT	
1						1
2						2
3						3
4						4
5						5
6						6
7						7
8						8
9						9
10						10
11						11
12						12
13						13
14						14
15						15
16						16
17						17
18						18
19						19
20						20
21						21
22						22
23						23
24						24
25						25
26						26
27						27
28						28
29						29
30						30
31						31
32						32
33						33
34						34

6-17A (continued)

JOURNAL

	DATE		DESCRIPTION	POST. REF.	DEBIT	CREDIT	
1							1
2							2
3							3
4							4
5							5
6							6
7							7
8							8
9							9
10							10
11							11
12							12
13							13
14							14
15							15
16							16
17							17
18							18
19							19
20							20
21							21
22							22
23							23
24							24
25							25
26							26
27							27
28							28
29							29
30							30
31							31
32							32
33							33
34							34

6-17A (continued)

	DATE	DESCRIPTION	POST. REF.	DEBIT	CREDIT	
1						1
2						2
3						3
4						4
5						5
6						6
7						7
8						8
9						9
10						10
11						11
12						12
13						13
14						14
15						15
16						16
17						17
18						18
19						19
20						20
21						21
22						22
23						23
24						24
25						25
26						26
27						27
28						28
29						29
30						30
31						31
32						32
33						33
34						34

6-17A (continued)

JOURNAL

	DATE		DESCRIPTION	POST. REF.	DEBIT	CREDIT	
1							1
2							2
3							3
4							4
5							5
6							6
7							7
8							8
9							9
10							10
11							11
12							12
13							13
14							14
15							15
16							16
17							17
18							18
19							19
20							20
21							21
22							22
23							23
24							24
25							25
26							26
27							27
28							28
29							29
30							30
31							31
32							32
33							33
34							34

6-17A (continued)

| ACCOUNT | CASH | | | | ACCOUNT NO. | 11 |

DATE		ITEM	POST. REF.	DEBIT	CREDIT	BALANCE	
						DEBIT	CREDIT
20-- Apr.	1	Balance	✓			5 7 6 7 3 56	

6-17A (continued)

ACCOUNT **FICA TAXES PAYABLE—OASDI**   ACCOUNT NO. 20

DATE	ITEM	POST. REF.	DEBIT	CREDIT	BALANCE	
					DEBIT	CREDIT
20-- Apr. 1	Balance	✓				1 0 6 8 88

6-17A (continued)

ACCOUNT **FICA TAXES PAYABLE—HI**   ACCOUNT NO. 21

DATE		ITEM	POST. REF.	DEBIT	CREDIT	BALANCE	
						DEBIT	CREDIT
20-- Apr.	1	Balance	✓				2 4 9 98

6-62

6-17A (continued)

ACCOUNT **FUTA TAXES PAYABLE**   ACCOUNT NO. 22

DATE		ITEM	POST. REF.	DEBIT	CREDIT	BALANCE	
						DEBIT	CREDIT
20-- Apr.	1	Balance	✓				1 4 9 16

ACCOUNT **SUTA TAXES PAYABLE**   ACCOUNT NO. 23

DATE		ITEM	POST. REF.	DEBIT	CREDIT	BALANCE	
						DEBIT	CREDIT
20-- Apr.	1	Balance	✓				5 7 1 78

6-17A (continued)

ACCOUNT **EMPLOYEES FIT PAYABLE** ACCOUNT NO. 25

DATE		ITEM	POST. REF.	DEBIT	CREDIT	BALANCE	
						DEBIT	CREDIT
20-- Apr.	1	Balance	✓				1 1 2 4 00

ACCOUNT **EMPLOYEES SIT PAYABLE** ACCOUNT NO. 26

DATE		ITEM	POST. REF.	DEBIT	CREDIT	BALANCE	
						DEBIT	CREDIT
20-- Apr.	1	Balance	✓				5 4 6 92

6-17A (concluded)

ACCOUNT **UNION DUES PAYABLE**   ACCOUNT NO. 28

DATE		ITEM	POST. REF.	DEBIT	CREDIT	BALANCE	
						DEBIT	CREDIT
20-- Apr.	1	Balance	✓				1 0 0 00

ACCOUNT **WAGES AND SALARIES**   ACCOUNT NO. 51

DATE		ITEM	POST. REF.	DEBIT	CREDIT	BALANCE	
						DEBIT	CREDIT
20-- Apr.	1	Balance	✓			7 1 3 6 0 00	

ACCOUNT **PAYROLL TAXES**   ACCOUNT NO. 55

DATE		ITEM	POST. REF.	DEBIT	CREDIT	BALANCE	
						DEBIT	CREDIT
20-- Apr.	1	Balance	✓			6 8 4 6 74	

Problem Set • B

Omit the writing of explanations for the journal entries. For rounding rules, refer to page 2-37.

6-1B • LO 2   See Example 6-5 on page 6-14, Figure 6.3 on page 6-13

Karen Salas has a federal tax levy of $2,100.50 against her. If Salas is single with two dependents and had a take-home pay of $499.00 this week, how much would her employer take from her pay to satisfy part of the tax levy?

6-2B • LO 2   See Example 6-2 on page 6-11, Example 6-3 on page 6-11

Garrett Hudson earned $895 this week. The deductions from his pay were as follows:

FIT	$74.00
FICA—OASDI	55.49
FICA—HI	12.98
State income tax	27.75
State disability insurance	6.71
Health insurance premium	31.00
Credit union contribution	50.00
United Fund contribution	10.00

Hudson's employer just received a garnishment order (credit card debt of $2,140) against his pay. Compute the following:

a. Hudson's disposable earnings .... $ _____

b. The amount of his pay subject to the garnishment .... $ _____

6-3B • LO 2   See Example 6-4 on page 6-12

Kirit Devi's employer receives a creditor garnishment order to withhold $100 from Devi's paycheck each week. This week his disposable earnings were $250. How much will the employer withhold from this week's pay to satisfy the garnishment?

Garnishment .... $ _____

6-4B • LO 3   See Example 6-7 on page 6-14, Example 6-9 on page 6-22, Example 6-11 on page 6-27

a. Harriet Pandel, an employer, is subject to FICA taxes but exempt from FUTA and SUTA taxes. During the last quarter of the year, her employees earned monthly wages of $16,900, all of which is taxable. The amount of federal income taxes withheld each month is $1,698. Journalize the payment of wages, and record the payroll tax on November 29.

6-4B (concluded)

JOURNAL

	DATE		DESCRIPTION	POST. REF.	DEBIT	CREDIT	
1							1
2							2
3							3
4							4
5							5
6							6
7							7
8							8
9							9
10							10

b. Prior to posting the November 29 payroll transaction, FICA Taxes Payable—OASDI, FICA Taxes Payable—HI, and Employees FIT Payable had zero balances. Pandel must pay the FICA taxes and income taxes withheld on the November 29 payroll. Journalize the electronic transfer of the payroll taxes on December 16.

JOURNAL

	DATE		DESCRIPTION	POST. REF.	DEBIT	CREDIT	
1							1
2							2
3							3
4							4
5							5
6							6

6-5B • LO 3 **See Example 6-7 on page 6-14, Example 6-9 on page 6-22**

The employees of Patel Bakery Company earn total wages of $7,780 during January. The total amount is taxable under FICA, FUTA, and SUTA. The state contribution rate for the company is 4.3%. The amount withheld for federal income taxes is $998. Journalize the payment of the monthly wages, and record the payroll taxes.

JOURNAL

	DATE	DESCRIPTION	POST. REF.	DEBIT	CREDIT	
1						1
2						2
3						3
4						4
5						5
6						6
7						7
8						8
9						9
10						10
11						11
12						12
13						13
14						14

6-6B • LO 3 **See Example 6-7 on page 6-14, Example 6-9 on page 6-22**

Yang, Inc., has a semimonthly payroll of $53,900 on September 15, 20--. The total payroll is taxable under FICA Taxes—HI; $50,400 is taxable under FICA Taxes—OASDI; and $7,300 is taxable under FUTA and SUTA. The state contribution rate for the company is 3.1%. The amount withheld for federal income taxes is $6,995. The amount withheld for state income taxes is $1,010.

a. Journalize the payment of the wages, and record the payroll taxes on September 15.

b. Assume that the employees of Yang, Inc., must also pay state contributions (disability insurance) of 1% on the taxable payroll of $24,100 and that the employees' contributions are to be deducted by the employer. Journalize the September 15 payment of wages, assuming that the state contributions of the employees are kept in a separate account.

JOURNAL

	DATE	DESCRIPTION	POST. REF.	DEBIT	CREDIT	
1						1
2						2
3						3
4						4
5						5
6						6
7						7
8						8
9						9
10						10
11						11
12						12
13						13
14						14
15						15
16						16
17						17
18						18
19						19
20						20
21						21
22						22
23						23
24						24
25						25
26						26
27						27

6-7B • LO 3 See Figure 6.4 on page 6-16

Adams, Inc., pays its employees' weekly wages in cash. A supplementary payroll sheet that lists the employees' names and their earnings for a certain week is shown below. Complete the payroll sheet by calculating the total amount of payroll and indicating the least possible number of denominations that can be used in paying each employee. However, no employees are to be given bills in denominations greater than $50.

ADAMS, INC.

Supplementary Payroll Sheet

Name of Employee	Net Amount Paid	Bills						Coins				
		$50	$20	$10	$5	$1	50¢	25¢	10¢	5¢	1¢
Ben Dowd	$639.57											
Erin Martin	248.95											
Dot Ruiz	491.95											
Randi Shin	832.14											
Rex Sundry	710.15											
Hal Roach	709.13											
Mandy Arnold	519.13											
Faye Montgomery	227.24											
Max Held	473.18											
Pedro Rodries	590.90											
Total												

Show
Me How

6-8B • LO 2, 3  **See Example 6-7 on page 6-14, Example 6-9 on page 6-22**

Carmen Santos is owner and sole employee of CS Corporation. He pays himself a salary of $2,400 this week.

Additional tax information includes:

FICA tax—OASDI..	6.2% on first $147,000
FICA tax—HI..	1.45% on total pay
Federal income tax	$532.00 per pay
State income tax	22% of the federal income tax withholding
Federal unemployment tax............................	0.6% on first $7,000
State unemployment tax	0.05% on first $14,000

Additional payroll deductions include:

401(k) plan	3% per pay
Child support garnishment	$125 per pay
Health insurance premium	$110 per pay

Record the payroll entry and payroll tax entry for the pay of the week ended June 7 (his year-to-date pay is $51,500).

JOURNAL

	DATE	DESCRIPTION	POST. REF.	DEBIT	CREDIT	
1						1
2						2
3						3
4						4
5						5
6						6
7						7
8						8
9						9
10						10
11						11
12						12
13						13
14						14
15						15
16						16
17						17
18						18
19						19
20						20

6-9B • LO 3 **See Example 6-7 on page 6-14, Example 6-9 on page 6-22**

The employees of Portonegra Company earn wages of $15,600 for the two weeks ending April 12. FIT taxes of $424 were withheld. The entire amount of wages is subject to the FICA taxes, but only $10,800 is taxable under the federal and state unemployment compensation laws. The state contribution rate of the employer is 3.9%. All employees are subject to state unemployment contributions of 0.5% on the April 12 taxable wages of $10,800, and the employees' contributions are to be deducted by the employer. Journalize the payment of the wages, and record the payroll taxes, assuming that the contributions of the employer and the employees are recorded in one account, SUTA Taxes Payable.

JOURNAL

	DATE	DESCRIPTION	POST. REF.	DEBIT	CREDIT	
1						1
2						2
3						3
4						4
5						5
6						6
7						7
8						8
9						9
10						10
11						11
12						12
13						13
14						14
15						15

6-10B • LO 3   **See Example 6-7 on page 6-14, Example 6-9 on page 6-22**

The following information pertains to a weekly payroll of Fanelli Fashion Company:

a. The total wages earned by employees are $2,910.

b. The state unemployment insurance contribution rate is 3.75%.

c. The entire amount of wages is taxable under FICA, FUTA, and SUTA.

d. The amount withheld from the employees' wages for federal income taxes is $491; for state income taxes, $49.10; and for group insurance, $87.10.

Journalize the payment of wages, and record the payroll taxes for this payroll.

JOURNAL

	DATE	DESCRIPTION	POST. REF.	DEBIT	CREDIT	
1						1
2						2
3						3
4						4
5						5
6						6
7						7
8						8
9						9
10						10
11						11
12						12
13						13
14						14
15						15
16						16
17						17

6-11B • LO 5 See page 6-27

On December 31, Kapoor Company has a balance of $619.24 in the FUTA taxes payable account. This represents the employer's liability for the fourth quarter taxes. Journalize the entry Kapoor Company should make in January to record the last transfer (payment) of FUTA taxes.

JOURNAL

	DATE		DESCRIPTION	POST. REF.	DEBIT	CREDIT	
1							1
2							2
3							3
4							4
5							5
6							6

6-12B • LO 6 See page 6-28   X Show Me How

On December 31, 20--, Sanchez Company needed to record its accrued wages for year-end. If December 31 is a Wednesday, then Sanchez Company must account for three days of wages.

The company operates on a five-day workweek, the prior week's gross pay was $29,870, and the net pay was $19,995.

Journalize the adjusting entry to be made on December 31 for the accrued wages.

JOURNAL

	DATE		DESCRIPTION	POST. REF.	DEBIT	CREDIT	
1							1
2							2
3							3
4							4
5							5
6							6

6-13B • LO 6   See Example 6-1 on page 6-2 and page 6-28

John Torre is the only employee of Bambert Company. His pay rate is $19.70 per hour with an overtime rate of 1½ times for hours over 40 in a workweek.

For the week ending March 31, 20--, he worked 44 hours. Calculate his gross pay for the week using the overtime premium approach to calculate the overtime pay.

Since the company holds back one week of pay, Torre will not be paid until April 7, 20--. What adjusting entry would the company make in order to record Torre's salary in the first quarter of this year?

a. Regular pay .... $ _____

b. Overtime premium pay .... $ _____

c. Gross pay .... $ _____

d. Adjusting entry

JOURNAL

	DATE	DESCRIPTION	POST. REF.	DEBIT	CREDIT	
1						1
2						2
3						3

6-14B • LO 2   See Example 6-10 on page 6-26

In Oregon, employers who are covered by the state workers' compensation law withhold employee contributions from the wages of covered employees for the workers' benefit fund at the rate of 1.1¢ for each hour or part of an hour that the worker is employed. Every covered employer is also assessed 1.1¢ per hour for each worker employed for each hour or part of an hour. The employer-employee contributions for workers' compensation are collected monthly, quarterly, or annually by the employer's insurance carrier, according to a schedule agreed upon by the employer and the carrier. The insurance carrier remits the contributions to the state's Workers' Compensation Department.

Umber Company, a covered employer in Oregon, turns over the employer-employee workers' compensation contributions to its insurance carrier by the 15th of each month for the preceding month. During the month of July, the number of full-time employee-hours worked by the company's employees was 26,110; the number of part-time employee-hours was 3,490.

a. The amount the company should have withheld from its full- and part-time employees during the month of July for workers' compensation insurance is $ _____

b. The title you would give to the general ledger account to which the amount withheld from the employees' earnings would be credited is:

_____

c. Journalize the entry on July 31 to record the employer's liability for workers' compensation insurance for the month.

6-14B (concluded)

JOURNAL

	DATE	DESCRIPTION	POST. REF.	DEBIT	CREDIT	
1						1
2						2
3						3
4						4
5						5

d. Journalize the entry on August 15 to record payment to the insurance carrier of the amount withheld from the employees' earnings for workers' compensation insurance and the amount of the employer's liability.

JOURNAL

	DATE	DESCRIPTION	POST. REF.	DEBIT	CREDIT	
1						1
2						2
3						3
4						4
5						5

6-15B • LO 6 See Example 6-12 on page 6-29

At the end of June, Morton Company had a balance of $49,900 in the vacation benefits payable account. During July, employees earned an additional $3,110 in vacation benefits, but some employees used vacation days that amounted to $2,490 of the vacation benefits. The $2,490 was charged to Wages Expense when it was paid in July. What adjusting entry would Morton Company make at the end of July to bring the vacation benefits payable account up to date?

JOURNAL

	DATE	DESCRIPTION	POST. REF.	DEBIT	CREDIT	
1						1
2						2
3						3

6-16B • LO 1 See Figure 6.1 on pages 6-3 and 6-4

The form on page 6-79 shows the amounts that appear in the Earnings to Date column of the employees' earnings records for 10 full- and part-time workers in Ranger Company. These amounts represent the cumulative earnings for each worker as of November 1, the company's last payday. The form also gives the gross amount of earnings to be paid each worker on the next payday, November 8.

In the state where Ranger Company is located, the tax rates and bases are as follows:

Tax on Employees:

FICA—OASDI .... 6.2% on first $147,000

FICA—HI .... 1.45% on **total earnings**

SUTA .... 0.5% on first $8,000

Tax on Employer:

FICA—OASDI .... 6.2% on first $147,000

FICA—HI .... 1.45% on **total earnings**

FUTA .... 0.6% on first $7,000

SUTA .... 2.8% on first $8,000

In the appropriate columns of the form on page 6-79, do the following:

1. Compute the amount to be withheld from each employee's earnings on November 8 for (a) FICA—OASDI, (b) FICA—HI, and (c) SUTA, and determine the total employee taxes.

2. Record the portion of each employee's earnings that is taxable under FICA, FUTA, and SUTA, and calculate the total employer's payroll taxes on the November 8 payroll.

6-16B (concluded)

RANGER COMPANY

Employee	Earnings to Date	Gross Earnings Nov. 8	Taxes to Be Withheld from Employees' Earnings Under			Employer Taxes: Portion of Employees' Earnings Taxable Under			
			FICA		SUTA	FICA		FUTA	SUTA
			OASDI	HI		OASDI	HI		
1. Watson, Ruth T.	$159,000	$1,890	$	$	$	$	$	$	$
2. Kinder, Ralph A.	14,950	410							
3. Sanchez, Robert T.	4,060	395							
4. Carey, Mary C.	8,190	295							
5. Cox, Mason M.	6,460	425							
6. Kenni, Jack T.	146,800	1,850							
7. Britmayer, Tim A.	8,905	490							
8. Candi, Mark B.	6,825	325							
9. Choi, Barbara C.	57,010	1,150							
10. McBride, James W.	3,615	195							
Total employee taxes			$	$	$	$	$	$	$
			1.(a)	1.(b)	1.(c)				

Total taxable earnings .... $ $ $

× Applicable tax rate ....

Totals .... $ $ $

Total payroll taxes .... $

2.

6-17B • LO 3, 4, 5, 6 See Illustrative Case beginning on page 6-30

In the Illustrative Case in this chapter, payroll transactions for Brookins Company were analyzed, journalized, and posted for the third quarter of the fiscal year. In this problem, you are to record the payroll transactions for the last quarter of the firm's fiscal year. The last quarter begins on April 1, 20--.

Refer to the Illustrative Case on pages 6-30 to 6-36 and proceed as follows:

a. Analyze and journalize the transactions described in the following narrative. Use the two-column journal paper provided on pages 6-81 to 6-85. Omit the writing of explanations in the journal entries.

b. Post the journal entries to the general ledger accounts on pages 6-86 to 6-91.

Narrative of Transactions:

Apr.	1.	Paid the treasurer of the union the amount of union dues withheld from workers' earnings during March.
	15.	Payroll: $8,310. All wages and salaries taxable. Withheld $890 for federal income taxes, $166.20 for state income taxes, and $140 for union dues.
	15.	Paid the treasurer of the state the amount of state income taxes withheld from workers' earnings during the first quarter.
	15.	Electronically transferred funds to remove the liability for FICA taxes and employees' federal income taxes withheld on the March payrolls.
	29.	Payroll: $7,975. All wages and salaries taxable. Withheld $815 for federal income taxes, $151.50 for state income taxes, and $135 for union dues.
	29.	Filed the Employer's Quarterly Federal Tax Return (Form 941) for the period ended March 31. No journal entry is required, since the FICA taxes and federal income taxes withheld have been timely paid.
	29.	Filed the state contribution return for the quarter ended March 31 and paid the amount to the state unemployment compensation fund.
May	2.	Paid the treasurer of the union the amount of union dues withheld from workers' earnings during April.
	13.	Payroll: $8,190. All wages and salaries taxable. Withheld $875 for federal income taxes, $160.05 for state income taxes, and $135 for union dues.
	16.	Electronically transferred funds to remove the liability for FICA taxes and federal income taxes withheld on the April payrolls.
	31.	Payroll: $8,755. All wages and salaries taxable. Withheld $971 for federal income taxes, $174.05 for state income taxes, and $140 for union dues.
June	3.	Paid the treasurer of the union the amount of union dues withheld from workers' earnings during May.
	15.	Payroll: $9,110. All wages and salaries taxable, except only $4,210 is taxable under FUTA and SUTA. Withheld $1,029 for federal income taxes, $187.15 for state income taxes, and $145 for union dues.
	15.	Electronically transferred funds to remove the liability for FICA taxes and federal income taxes withheld on the May payrolls.
	30.	Payroll: $8,960. All wages and salaries taxable, except only $2,280 is taxable under FUTA and SUTA. Withheld $988 for federal income taxes, $183.95 for state income taxes, and $145 for union dues.

6-17B (continued)

c. Answer the following questions:

1. The total amount of the liability for FICA taxes and federal income taxes withheld as of June 30 is .... $ _____

2. The total amount of the liability for state income taxes withheld as of June 30 is .... $ _____

3. The amount of FUTA taxes that must be paid to the federal government on or before August 1 (assume July 31 is a Sunday) is .... $ _____

4. The amount of contributions that must be paid into the state unemployment compensation fund on or before August 1 is .... $ _____

5. The total amount due the treasurer of the union is .... $ _____

6. The total amount of wages and salaries expense since the beginning of the fiscal year is .... $ _____

7. The total amount of payroll taxes expense since the beginning of the fiscal year is .... $ _____

8. Using the partial journal below, journalize the entry to record the vacation accrual at the end of the company's fiscal year. The amount of Brookins Company's vacation accrual for the fiscal year is $15,000.

JOURNAL

	DATE	DESCRIPTION	POST. REF.	DEBIT	CREDIT	
1						1
2						2
3						3
4						4
5						5
6						6

6-17B (continued)

JOURNAL

	DATE		DESCRIPTION	POST. REF.	DEBIT	CREDIT	
1							1
2							2
3							3
4							4
5							5
6							6
7							7
8							8
9							9
10							10
11							11
12							12
13							13
14							14
15							15
16							16
17							17
18							18
19							19
20							20
21							21
22							22
23							23
24							24
25							25
26							26
27							27
28							28
29							29
30							30
31							31
32							32
33							33
34							34

6-17B (continued)

JOURNAL

	DATE		DESCRIPTION	POST. REF.	DEBIT	CREDIT	
1							1
2							2
3							3
4							4
5							5
6							6
7							7
8							8
9							9
10							10
11							11
12							12
13							13
14							14
15							15
16							16
17							17
18							18
19							19
20							20
21							21
22							22
23							23
24							24
25							25
26							26
27							27
28							28
29							29
30							30
31							31
32							32
33							33
34							34

6-17B (continued)

JOURNAL

Page 21

	DATE		DESCRIPTION	POST. REF.	DEBIT	CREDIT	
1							1
2							2
3							3
4							4
5							5
6							6
7							7
8							8
9							9
10							10
11							11
12							12
13							13
14							14
15							15
16							16
17							17
18							18
19							19
20							20
21							21
22							22
23							23
24							24
25							25
26							26
27							27
28							28
29							29
30							30
31							31
32							32
33							33
34							34

6-17B (continued)

JOURNAL

	DATE		DESCRIPTION	POST. REF.	DEBIT	CREDIT	
1							1
2							2
3							3
4							4
5							5
6							6
7							7
8							8
9							9
10							10
11							11
12							12
13							13
14							14
15							15
16							16
17							17
18							18
19							19
20							20
21							21
22							22
23							23
24							24
25							25
26							26
27							27
28							28
29							29
30							30
31							31
32							32
33							33
34							34

6-17B (continued)

| ACCOUNT | CASH | | | | ACCOUNT NO. 11 |

DATE		ITEM	POST. REF.	DEBIT	CREDIT	BALANCE	
						DEBIT	CREDIT
20-- Apr.	1	Balance	✓			5 7 6 7 3 56	

6-17B (continued)

ACCOUNT **FICA TAXES PAYABLE—OASDI**   ACCOUNT NO. 20

DATE		ITEM	POST. REF.	DEBIT	CREDIT	BALANCE	
						DEBIT	CREDIT
20-- Apr.	1	Balance	✓				1 0 6 8 88

6-17B (continued)

ACCOUNT **FICA TAXES PAYABLE—HI**   ACCOUNT NO. 21

DATE		ITEM	POST. REF.	DEBIT	CREDIT	BALANCE	
						DEBIT	CREDIT
20-- Apr.	1	Balance	✓				2 4 9 98

6-17B (continued)

ACCOUNT **FUTA TAXES PAYABLE**   ACCOUNT NO. 22

DATE		ITEM	POST. REF.	DEBIT	CREDIT	BALANCE	
						DEBIT	CREDIT
20-- Apr.	1	Balance	✓				1 4 9 16

ACCOUNT **SUTA TAXES PAYABLE**   ACCOUNT NO. 23

DATE		ITEM	POST. REF.	DEBIT	CREDIT	BALANCE	
						DEBIT	CREDIT
20-- Apr.	1	Balance	✓				5 7 1 78

6-17B (continued)

ACCOUNT **EMPLOYEES FIT PAYABLE**   ACCOUNT NO. **25**

DATE		ITEM	POST. REF.	DEBIT	CREDIT	BALANCE	
						DEBIT	CREDIT
20-- Apr.	1	Balance	✓				1 1 2 4 00

ACCOUNT **EMPLOYEES SIT PAYABLE**   ACCOUNT NO. **26**

DATE		ITEM	POST. REF.	DEBIT	CREDIT	BALANCE	
						DEBIT	CREDIT
20-- Apr.	1	Balance	✓				5 4 6 92

6-17B (concluded)

ACCOUNT **UNION DUES PAYABLE**   ACCOUNT NO. 28

DATE		ITEM	POST. REF.	DEBIT	CREDIT	BALANCE	
						DEBIT	CREDIT
20-- Apr.	1	Balance	✓				1 0 0 00

ACCOUNT **WAGES AND SALARIES**   ACCOUNT NO. 51

DATE		ITEM	POST. REF.	DEBIT	CREDIT	BALANCE	
						DEBIT	CREDIT
20-- Apr.	1	Balance	✓			7 1 3 6 0 00	

ACCOUNT **PAYROLL TAXES**   ACCOUNT NO. 55

DATE		ITEM	POST. REF.	DEBIT	CREDIT	BALANCE	
						DEBIT	CREDIT
20-- Apr.	1	Balance	✓			6 8 4 6 74	

Continuing Payroll Problem • A

In this last phase of your work on the Continuing Payroll Problem A, you will record the amounts withheld for group and health insurance and calculate the net pay for each employee. Refer to the partially completed payroll registers upon which you were working at the end of Chapter 5, and proceed as follows:

1. In the appropriate column of the payroll register, record the amount to be withheld for group life insurance. Each employee contributes 85¢ each week toward the cost of group insurance coverage, with the exception of Smith and Schork (Kipley Company), who are not yet eligible for coverage under the company plan.
2. Record the amount to be withheld for health insurance. Each employee contributes $1.65 each week toward the cost of health insurance.
3. Record the net pay for each employee. The net pay for each employee is obtained by subtracting the total amount of all deductions from the total earnings.
4. Each worker is to be paid by check. Assign check numbers commencing with No. 313.
5. Foot all money columns of the payroll register, and prove the accuracy of the column totals.

6. On a separate sheet of paper:
    a. Prepare the journal entries as of January 12 to record the payroll and the payroll taxes for the week ending January 8. Credit Salaries Payable for the total net pay.
        Use the following tax rates and bases: employer's FICA—OASDI, 6.2% on the first $147,000; employer's FICA—HI, 1.45% on total earnings; FUTA, 0.6% on the first $7,000; and SUTA, 3.6890% on the first $10,000.
    b. Prepare the journal entry to record the payment of the payroll on January 14 when the paychecks are distributed to all workers.

Your work on the Continuing Payroll Problem A is now completed, and you may be asked to submit your payroll register to your instructor. The experience you have gained in working on each of the succeeding phases of the Continuing Payroll Problem will aid you in undertaking the payroll work involved in Chapter 7. In the Comprehensive Payroll Project, you will be responsible for all aspects of payroll operations for a company for an entire calendar quarter.

Continuing Payroll Problem • B

In this last phase of your work on the Continuing Payroll Problem B, you will record the amounts withheld for group and health insurance and calculate the net pay for each employee. Refer to the partially completed payroll registers upon which you were working at the end of Chapter 5, and proceed as follows:

1. In the appropriate column of the payroll register, record the amount to be withheld for group life insurance. Each employee contributes 85¢ each week toward the cost of group insurance coverage, with the exception of Palmetto and Wichman (Olney Company) who are not yet eligible for coverage under the company plan.
2. Record the amount to be withheld for health insurance. Each employee contributes $1.65 each week toward the cost of health insurance.
3. Record the net pay for each employee. The net pay for each employee is obtained by subtracting the total amount of all deductions from the total earnings.

4. Each worker is to be paid by check. Assign check numbers commencing with No. 313.
5. Foot all money columns of the payroll register, and prove the accuracy of the column totals.
6. On a separate sheet of paper:
    a. Prepare the journal entries as of January 12 to record the payroll and the payroll taxes for the week ending January 8. Credit Salaries Payable for the total net pay.
        Use the following tax rates and bases: employer's FICA—OASDI, 6.2% on the first $147,000; employer's FICA—HI, 1.45% on total earnings; FUTA, 0.6% on the first $7,000; and SUTA, 3.6890% on the first $10,000.
    b. Prepare the journal entry to record the payment of the payroll on January 14 when the paychecks are distributed to all workers.

Your work on the Continuing Payroll Problem B is now completed, and you may be asked to submit your payroll register to your instructor. The experience you have gained in working on each of the succeeding phases of the Continuing Payroll Problem will aid you in undertaking the payroll work involved in Chapter 7. In the Comprehensive Payroll Project, you will be responsible for all aspects of payroll operations for a company for an entire calendar quarter.

Case Problem

C1. Budgeting for Additional Payroll Costs.

Frank Flynn is the payroll manager for Powlus Supply Company. During the budgeting process, Sam Kinder, director of finance, asked Flynn to arrive at a set percentage that could be applied to each budgeted salary figure to cover the additional cost that will be incurred by Powlus Supply for each employee. After some discussion, it was determined that the best way to compute this percentage would be to base these additional costs of payroll on the average salary paid by the company.

Kinder wants this additional payroll cost percentage to cover payroll taxes (FICA, FUTA, and SUTA) and other payroll costs covered by the company (workers' compensation expense, health insurance costs, and vacation pay).

Flynn gathers the following information in order to complete the analysis:

Average annual salary	$24,000
FICA rates	6.2% and 1.45%
FUTA	0.6% on 1st $7,000
SUTA	3.3% on 1st $10,400
Workers' compensation costs	$0.97 per $100 of payroll
Health insurance costs	$75.15 per week
Vacation pay earned.......................................	2 weeks' pay earned each year to be used in following year

Compute the percentage that can be used in the budget.

Payroll Project

Comprehensive Payroll Project Overview

The following chapter and appendices represent three different methods of doing payroll. Each chapter or appendix is designed to stand alone. It is highly recommended that one manual payroll be completed if you are assigned either Appendix A or B.

Chapter 7—Payroll Project

In this chapter, you will manually complete the fourth quarter payroll transactions for Glo-Brite Paint Company. The first payroll on 10-09 is provided as a demonstration to get you started. Acting as the payroll clerk, you will apply the concepts learned in the previous chapters, which include:

- Completing the payroll register by calculating total earnings, withholdings and net pay
- Demonstrating the ability to use IRS Wage Bracket Tables to determine the amount of federal income tax to be withheld
- Posting the information from the payroll register to the employee earnings record
- Creating general journal entries to record payroll and payment of withholdings
- Posting entries from the general journal to the general ledger
- Creating the end-of-year tax reports for employees and federal, state and local governments either manually or in CNOWv2 and
- Creating adjust journal entries associated with payroll

All of this is done manually using the documents beginning on page 7-2. Since Chapter 7 and Appendix A use the same methods of calculating pay and taxes, the solutions for Chapter 7 and Appendix A are the same.

Appendix A—Excel Template Instructions for the Glo-Brite Payroll Project (Chapter 7: Short Version)

Appendix A is designed to acquaint you with Excel and to show you how a small company can maintain its payroll using Excel. The first section of the appendix includes an introduction to Excel and the templates you'll be using. As the payroll clerk, you will be completing the payroll transaction for the month of December and have been provided with a demonstration of the 11-20 payroll to get you started. The templates have been created to calculate tax withholdings with the exception of federal income tax. After completing the transactions for the month of December, you will complete the end-of-year reporting requirements using the forms provided in Chapter 7, beginning on page 7-53 or in CNOWv2. The solutions for Chapter 7 and Appendix A are the same.

Appendix B—Payroll Project Using Online Automated General Ledger Software

Appendix B is a computerized version of payroll utilizing *Automated General Ledger Software* similar to what is found in the industry. The project is only available through CNOWv2 either by completing all transactions for the quarter like Chapter 7 or the transactions for the month of December like Appendix A. Appendix B is completed entirely in CNOWv2. Since general ledger software uses the annualized method of calculating federal income tax withholding, the solutions for Appendix B will be different from those of Chapter 7 or Appendix A.

Payroll Project

What now? Can we process a payroll? How about the accounting entries and postings? Can we complete the deposit forms and the "dreaded" payroll tax returns? What have we learned in the previous six chapters? Did I waste this semester?

Let's find out. Here's your real-world test.

Learning Objectives

Chapter 7 consists of a simulation, or practice set, for payroll accounting. You will apply the knowledge acquired in this course to practical payroll situations. This simulation is a culmination of the information presented in the textbook.

After completing this chapter, you should be able to:

1. Prepare payroll registers.
2. Maintain employees' earnings records.
3. Journalize and post payroll and payroll tax entries.
4. Complete federal, state, and city tax deposit forms and journalize the transactions.
5. Prepare various quarter-end and year-end payroll tax forms.
6. Make the accrual entries for the payroll at the end of a year.

The Payroll Project will provide you with extended practice in keeping payroll records and accounting for payroll transactions. Your completion of this project involves an application of the information learned in the preceding chapters. The work provided resembles that prevailing in the office of every employer in the United States subject to the provisions of the Federal Wage and Hour Law, income tax withholding laws, social security laws, and unemployment compensation laws. Even though most payroll systems now employ computers, it is important that the practitioner understand the operations performed by the computer.

Zivica Kerkez/Shutterstock.com

If your assignment involves the use of Appendix A (computerized option using Excel for the short version project in Chapter 7) or Appendix B (computerized option using Automated General Ledger Software), it is suggested that you do at least one of the payrolls manually so that you gain a thorough understanding of the steps needed to be completed on a typical payday. Appendix B using Automated General Ledger Software can be used for both the short and long versions of the project.

In this project, you are employed by Glo-Brite Paint Company. As the payroll clerk in the Accounting Department, you have been in charge of the payroll records since the company first began operations on January 5 of the current year. The company employs about 800 individuals; but for the purpose of this project, payroll records will be kept for only a dozen or so employees. By understanding the principles of payroll accounting for a few employees, you should be able to keep similar records for several hundred employees.

For purposes of this project, you will assume that the payroll records, tax reports, and deposits have been completed and filed for the first three quarters of this year. Your work will involve the processing of the payrolls for the last quarter of the year and the completion of the last quarterly and annual tax reports and forms.

Books of Account and Payroll Records

The books of account and payroll records that you will use in this project are described in this section.

Journal

You will use a two-column general journal to record all transactions affecting the accounts in the general ledger. This book of original entry serves as a posting medium for transactions affecting the payroll accounts.

General Ledger

A general ledger, used in keeping the payroll accounts, is ruled with balance-column ruling, which makes it possible to keep a continuous record of each account balance. Some of the ledger accounts will have beginning balances carried over from the first three quarters of the year.

The chart of accounts in Figure 7.1 has been used in opening the general ledger accounts (pages 7-33 to 7-40). Glo-Brite Paint Company has other accounts in its general ledger, but those listed in the partial chart of accounts are the only accounts required in completing this project.

Payroll Register

The payroll register provides the information needed for journalizing each payroll and for posting to the employees' earnings records.

FIGURE 7.1
Partial Chart of Accounts

Account Title	Account No.
Cash	11
Payroll Cash	12
FICA Taxes Payable—OASDI	20.1
FICA Taxes Payable—HI	20.2
FUTA Taxes Payable	21
SUTA Taxes Payable—Employer	22
Employees FIT Payable	24
Employees SIT Payable	25
Employees SUTA Payable	25.1
Employees CIT Payable	26
Group Insurance Premiums Collected	27
Union Dues Payable	28
Simple Contributions Payable	29
Administrative Salaries	51
Office Salaries	52
Sales Salaries	53
Plant Wages	54
Payroll Taxes	56

Employee's Earnings Record

The employee's earnings record provides a summary of each employee's earnings, deductions, and taxable wages. The information recorded in this record is posted from the payroll register.

From the personnel data given in Figure 7.2, an employee's earnings record has been maintained for each employee (pages 7-42 to 7-48). The first line of each of these records shows the employee's cumulative figures for the first three quarters of the year. Note that only one-half page has been used for each employee's earnings record.

General Information

The home office and the manufacturing plant of Glo-Brite Paint Company are located at 2215 Salvador Street, Philadelphia, PA 19175-0682. The company's phone number is (215) 555-9559. The company's federal identification number is 00-0000660; the state account number, 000-0-3300; and the city identifying number, 000-0001855.

Regular Hours of Work

The workweek for all employees is 40 hours, except for the student's 36-hour schedule. The office is open from 8:00 A.M. to 5:00 P.M. each day, except weekends. Glo-Brite allows office employees one hour for lunch, 12:00 P.M. to 1:00 P.M. The plant operates on a five-day workweek of eight hours per day, with normal working hours from 7:00 A.M. to 11:00 A.M. and 12:00 P.M. to 4:00 P.M.

FIGURE 7.2
Glo-Brite Employees

Personnel Data—October 1, 20- -

BONNO, Anthony Victor, 694 Bristol Avenue, Philadelphia, PA 19135-0617. Married Filing Joint (MFJ). Telephone, 555-9827. Social Security No. 000-00-3481. Position, mixer operator in plant. Wages, $17.60 per hour. Group insurance, $55,000.

FERGUSON, Jamie Hadi, 808 Sixth Street, Philadelphia, PA 19106-0995. MFJ. Telephone, 555-8065. Social Security No. 000-00-8645. Position, sales manager. Salary, $58,500 per year. Group insurance, $88,000. Department: Sales.

FORD, Catherine Louise, 18 Dundee Avenue, Philadelphia, PA 19151-1919. Single. Telephone, 555-0235. Social Security No. 000-00-4567. Position, administrative assistant. Salary, $2,643.33 per month. Group insurance, $48,000. Department: Office.

MANN, Kari Casey, 3007 Bisque Drive, Philadelphia, PA 19199-0718. MFJ. Telephone, 555-0774. Social Security No. 000-00-9352. Position, sales representative. Salary, $2,925 per month. Group insurance, $53,000. Department: Sales.

O'NEILL, Joseph Tyler, 2100 Broad Street, Philadelphia, PA 19121-7189. MFJ. Telephone, 555-2332. Social Security No. 000-00-1534. Position, president. Salary, $60,000 per year, paid $2,307.69 biweekly. Group insurance, $90,000. Department: Administrative.

RUSSELL, Serdar Parker, 8004 Dowling Road, Philadelphia, PA 19135-9001. Single. Telephone, 555-3681. Social Security No. 000-00-6337. Position, time clerk. Salary, $2,600 per month. Group insurance, $47,000. Department: Office.

RYAN, Jeri Mischa, 7300 Harrison Street, Philadelphia, PA 19124-6699. MFJ. Telephone, 555-6660. Social Security No. 000-00-1223. Position, electrician in plant. Wages, $18.00 per hour. Group insurance, $56,000.

SOKOWSKI, Thomas James, 133 Cornwells Street, Philadelphia, PA 19171-5718. MFJ. Telephone, 555-5136. Social Security No. 000-00-8832. Position, supervisor in plant. Salary, $1,025 per week. Group insurance, $80,000.

STUDENT, 7018 Erdrick Street, Philadelphia, PA 19135-8517. Single. Position, accounting trainee. Wages, $15.00 per hour. Group insurance, $42,000. Department: Office.

WILLIAMS, Ruth Virginia, 9433 State Street, Philadelphia, PA 19149-0819. Single. Telephone, 555-5845. Social Security No. 000-00-6741. Position, programmer. Salary, $2,650 per month. Group insurance, $48,000. Department: Office.

Pay Points

For rounding rules refer to instructions on page 2-37.

Overtime

All employees except for the exempt administrative employees—the president (*O'Neill*), the sales manager (*Ferguson*), sales representative (*Mann*), and supervisor (*Sokowski*)—are paid *time and a half* for any overtime exceeding 40 hours a week. Workers in the plant (*Bonno and Ryan*) are paid *time and a half* for any hours worked over eight each workday and for work on Saturdays and *twice* the regular hourly rate of pay for work on Sundays or holidays.

Timekeeping

All office and plant employees, except the president, the sales manager, sales representatives, and supervisors, must ring in and out daily on a time clock. Also, those employees who ring in and out must notify the time clerk of the reason for lost time. (The unemployment compensation laws of some states require this information.) The time clerk prepares a weekly report of the hours worked by each employee.

The calendar for the last quarter of the year is presented below.

October

S	M	T	W	T	F	S
				1	2	3
4	5	6	7	8	9	10
11	12	13	14	15	16	17
18	19	20	21	22	23	24
25	26	27	28	29	30	31

November

S	M	T	W	T	F	S
1	2	3	4	5	6	7
8	9	10	11	12	13	14
15	16	17	18	19	20	21
22	23	24	25	26	27	28
29	30					

December

S	M	T	W	T	F	S
		1	2	3	4	5
6	7	8	9	10	11	12
13	14	15	16	17	18	19
20	21	22	23	24	25	26
27	28	29	30	31		

Payday

Employees are paid biweekly on Friday. The first payday in the fourth quarter is Friday, October 9. Since the weekly time clerk's report is not finished until the Monday following the end of each week, the first pay (October 9) will be for the two weeks September 20–26 and September 27–October 3. The company, in effect, holds back one week's pay. This policy applies to all employees. The next payday (October 23) will cover the days worked in the weeks ending October 10 and October 17.

Payroll Taxes—Contributions and Withholdings

Payroll taxes are levied upon Glo-Brite Paint Company and its employees as shown in Figure 7.3.

Depositing Taxes

The company must deposit federal, state, and city taxes during this quarter. The deposit rules that affect the company appear in Figure 7.4.

FIGURE 7.3
Glo-Brite Payroll Taxes

	Payroll Taxes Levied upon Glo-Brite Paint Company and Its Employees	
Federal Income Taxes (FIT)	Withheld from each employee's gross earnings in accordance with information given on Form W-4 (from 2020 or later) and employee's earnings record. Wage-bracket method tables on pages T-7 to T-8 (Manual Payroll Systems Biweekly Payroll Period with Standard Withholding) are used to determine FIT withholding.*	
Pennsylvania State Income Taxes (SIT)	3.07 percent withheld from each employee's gross earnings during the fourth quarter.*	
Philadelphia City Income Taxes (CIT)	3.8398 percent withheld from gross earnings of each resident employee.*	
Pennsylvania State Unemployment Taxes (SUTA)	*Employee:*	0.06 percent (0.0006) on total gross earnings (no limit for the employee's portion).*
	Employer:	3.6890 percent on first $10,000 gross earnings paid each employee during the calendar year (PA rate for new employers).
Federal Unemployment Taxes (FUTA)	*Employer:*	Net tax rate of 0.6 percent on first $7,000 gross earnings paid each worker in the calendar year.
Federal Insurance Contributions Act (FICA)	*OASDI—Employee and Employer:*	6.2 percent on first $147,000 of gross earnings paid each worker in the calendar year (maximum OASDI tax of $9,114.00).
	HI—Employee:	1.45 percent on total gross earnings paid each worker in the calendar year, plus an additional 0.9 percent on wages over $200,000.
	HI—Employer:	1.45 percent on total gross earnings paid each worker in the calendar year.

* Tax withholdings for FIT, FICA, SIT, CIT, and SUTA are based on rates used in 2022. Rates for 2023 were not available at the time of publishing.

FIGURE 7.4
Deposit Rules

	Deposit Rules for Glo-Brite Paint Company
Federal	The FICA taxes and FIT taxes must be deposited *on or before the 15th of the month following the month* in which the taxes were withheld. Since Glo-Brite is a new employer and has no tax liabilities during the lookback period, the company is subject to the monthly deposit rule.
Pennsylvania	Since the state income taxes withheld total $1,000 or more each quarter, the company must remit the withheld taxes semimonthly. The taxes must be remitted within three banking days after the semimonthly periods ending *on the 15th and the last day of the month.*
Philadelphia	Since the city income taxes withheld are more than $350 but less than $16,000 each month, the company is subject to the monthly rule. The city income taxes withheld during the month must be remitted *by the 15th day of the following month.*

Group Insurance

The company carries group-term life insurance on all its employees in an amount equal to one and one-half times the annual salary or wages paid each employee (rounded to the nearest thousand). The group insurance program covers full-time employees. A notation has been made on each employee's earnings record to show that each month *30¢ for each $1,000* of insurance coverage is deducted from the employee's earnings to pay a portion of the premium cost. *For example: Anthony Bonno has $55,000 of insurance coverage. Therefore, the calculation for his insurance deduction is ($55,000/$1,000) × .30 = $16.50.* The amount withheld is credited to a liability account entitled Group Insurance Premiums Collected. The taxable portion of group-term life insurance in excess of $50,000 is disregarded because the employees pay for group-term life insurance.

Pay Points

Deduct insurance premiums only on the last payday of each month.

Union Dues

Both workers in the plant (*Bonno and Ryan*) are union members. Under the check-off system, $8 is deducted *each payday* from the plant workers' earnings for union dues, assessments, and initiation fees. A notation to this effect has been made on each plant worker's earnings record. On or before the tenth of each month, the amounts withheld during the preceding month are turned over to the treasurer of the union.

Distribution of Labor Costs

Figure 7.5 shows how the salaries and wages are to be charged to the labor cost accounts.

Start of Payroll Project

October 9, 20--

No. 1 The first payroll in October covered the two workweeks that ended on September 26 and October 3. This payroll transaction has been entered for you in the payroll register, the employees' earnings records, the general journal, and the general ledger. By reviewing the calculations of the wages and deductions in the payroll register and the posting of the information to the employees' earnings records, you can see the procedure to be followed each payday.

Wages and salaries are paid by issuing special payroll checks. When the bank on which they are drawn receives such checks, they will be charged against the payroll cash account.

Observe the following rules in computing earnings each pay period:

1. Do not make any deduction from an employee's earnings if the employee loses less than 15 minutes of time in any day. Time lost that exceeds 15 minutes is rounded to the nearest quarter-hour and deducted. If the time lost by an employee is not to be deducted, the time clerk will make a notation to that effect on the Time Clerk's Report.

2. In completing the time record columns of the payroll register for all workers, you should place an 8 in the day column for each full day worked (refer to page PR-2 at the end of the book). If an employee works less than a full day, show the actual hours for which the employee will be paid.

FIGURE 7.5
Glo-Brite Labor Cost Accounts

Personnel	Accounts to Be Charged
President (O'Neill)	Administrative Salaries
Administrative Assistant (Ford) Programmer (Williams) Time Clerk (Russell) Accounting Trainee (Student)	Office Salaries
Sales Manager (Ferguson) Sales Representative (Mann)	Sales Salaries
Workers (Bonno and Ryan) Supervisor (Sokowski)	Plant Wages

3. In the case of an employee who begins work during a pay period, compute the earnings by paying the employees their weekly rate for *any full week* worked. For any *partial week*, compute the earnings for that week by multiplying the hours worked by the hourly rate of pay.

4. If time lost is to be deducted from a salaried employee's pay, the employee's pay must be determined by multiplying the actual hours worked for that week by the hourly rate. If hours are missed but no pay is deducted, include those hours in the Time Record columns on the payroll register. The following schedule shows the weekly and hourly wage rates of the salaried employees:

Employee	Weekly Rate	Hourly Rate
Ferguson, Jamie H.	$1,125.00	$28.13
Ford, Catherine L.	610.00	15.25
Mann, Kari C.	675.00	16.88
O'Neill, Joseph T.	2,307.69*	28.85
Russell, Serdar P.	600.00	15.00
Sokowski, Thomas J.	1,025.00	25.63
Williams, Ruth V.	611.54	15.29

*O'Neill is paid on a biweekly basis.

5. Plant workers (*Bonno and Ryan*), other than supervisors, are employed on an hourly basis. Compute the wages by multiplying the number of hours worked during the pay period by the employee's hourly rate.

6. The information needed and the sequence of steps that are completed for the payroll are presented in the following discussion.

Time Clerk's Report No. 38
For the Week Ending September 26, 20--

Employee	Time Record							Time Worked	Time Lost
	S	M	T	W	T	F	S		
Bonno, A. V.		8	8	8	8	8		40 hrs.	. . .
Ford, C. L.		8	8	8	8	8		40 hrs.	. . .
Russell, S. P.		8	8	8	8	8		40 hrs.	. . .
Ryan, J. M.		8	8	8	8	8		40 hrs.	. . .
Student		8	8	8	8	4		36 hrs.	. . .
Williams, R. V. . . .		8	8	D	8	8		32 hrs.	8 hrs.*

*Time lost because of personal business; charged to personal leave; no deduction for this time lost.
D = lost full day

Time Clerk's Report No. 39
For the Week Ending October 3, 20--

Employee	Time Record							Time Worked	Time Lost
	S	M	T	W	T	F	S		
Bonno, A. V.		8	8	8	8	8		40 hrs.	. . .
Ford, C. L.		8	8	8	8	8		40 hrs.	. . .
Russell, S. P.		8	8	8	8	8		40 hrs.	. . .
Ryan, J. M.		8	8	8	8	8		40 hrs.	. . .
Student		8	8	8	8	4		36 hrs.	. . .
Williams, R. V. . .		8	8	8	8	8		40 hrs.	. . .

The time clerk prepared Time Clerk's Report Nos. 38 and 39 from the time cards used by the employees for these workweeks. *In as much as the president, sales manager, sales representatives, and supervisors do not ring in and out on the time clock, their records are not included in the time clerks report, but their salaries must be included in the payroll.*

① The following schedule shows the hourly wage rates of the three hourly employees used in preparing the payroll register for the payday on October 9.

Employee	Hourly Rate
Bonno, Anthony V.	$17.60
Ryan, Jeri M.	18.00
Student	15.00

Pay Points

Tax calculations are to be taken to three decimal places and then rounded to two places.

② The entry required for each employee is recorded in the payroll register. The names of all employees are listed in alphabetical order, including yours as "Student." The fold-out payroll register forms needed to complete this project are bound at the back of the book (pages PR-2, PR-3, and PR-4).

No deduction has been made for the time lost by Williams. Thus, the total number of hours (80) for which payment was made is recorded in the Regular Earnings Hours column of the payroll register. However, a notation of the time lost (D) was made in the Time Record column. When posting to Williams' earnings record, 80 hours is recorded in the Regular Earnings Hours column (no deduction for the time lost).

In computing the federal income taxes to be withheld, the Wage Bracket Method Tables for Manual Payroll Systems With Forms W-4 From 2020 or Later (using standard withholding column) – Biweekly Payroll Period in Tax Table B at the back of the book were used (pages T-7 and T-8).

Pay Points

Use Wage Bracket Method Tables for Manual Payroll Systems With Forms W-4 From 2020 or Later (using standard withholding column) – Biweekly Payroll Period.

Each payday, $8 was deducted from the earnings of the two plant workers for union dues (*Bonno and Ryan*).

Payroll check numbers were assigned beginning with check no. 672.

In the Labor Cost Distribution columns at the extreme right of the payroll register, each employee's gross earnings were recorded in the column that identifies the department in which the employee regularly works. The totals of the Labor Cost Distribution columns provide the amounts to be charged to the appropriate salary and wage expense accounts and aid department managers and supervisors in comparing the actual labor costs with the budgeted amounts.

Once the net pay of each employee was computed, all the amount columns in the payroll register were footed, proved, and ruled.

③ An entry was made in the journal (page 7-24) transferring from the regular cash account to the payroll cash account the amount of the check issued to Payroll to cover the net amount of the payroll; next, the entry was posted.

④ Information from the payroll register was posted to the employees' earnings records (see pages 7-42 to 7-46).

Note that when posting the deductions for each employee, a column has been provided in the earnings record for recording each deduction for FICA (OASDI and HI), FIT, SIT, SUTA, and CIT. All other deductions for each employee are to be totaled and recorded as one amount in the Other Deductions column. Subsidiary ledgers are maintained for Group Insurance Premiums Collected and Union Dues Withheld. Thus, any question about the amounts withheld from an employee's earnings may be answered by referring to the appropriate subsidiary ledger. In this project, your work will not involve any recording in or reference to the subsidiary ledgers.

⑤ The proper journal entry recorded salaries, wages, taxes, and the net amount of cash paid from the totals of the payroll register. The journal entry to record the payroll for the first pay in the fourth quarter appears below and in the general journal (page 7-24).

Administrative Salaries	2,307.69	
Office Salaries	4,723.08	
Sales Salaries	3,600.00	
Plant Wages	4,898.00	
FICA Taxes Payable—OASDI		962.79
FICA Taxes Payable—HI		225.18
Employees FIT Payable		806.00
Employees SIT Payable		476.76
Employees SUTA Payable		9.30
Employees CIT Payable		596.28
Union Dues Payable		16.00
Payroll Cash		12,436.46

The amounts charged the salary and wage expense accounts were obtained from the totals of the Labor Cost Distribution columns in the payroll register. The salaries and wages were charged as follows:

Administrative Salaries

Joseph T. O'Neill (President)

Office Salaries

Catherine L. Ford (Administrative Assistant)
Serdar P. Russell (Time Clerk)
Student (Accounting Trainee)
Ruth V. Williams (Programmer)

Sales Salaries

Jamie H. Ferguson (Sales Manager)
Kari C. Mann (Sales Representative)

Plant Wages

Anthony V. Bonno (Mixer Operator)
Jeri M. Ryan (Electrician)
Thomas J. Sokowski (Supervisor)

FICA Taxes Payable—OASDI and FICA Taxes Payable—HI were credited for $962.79 and $225.18, respectively, the amounts deducted from employees' wages.

Employees FIT Payable, Employees SIT Payable, Employees SUTA Payable, Employees CIT Payable, and Union Dues Payable were credited for the total amount withheld for each kind of deduction from employees' wages. In subsequent payroll transactions, Group Insurance Premiums Collected will be credited for the amounts withheld from employees' wages for this type of deduction. Finally, Payroll Cash was credited for the sum of the net amounts paid all employees.

⑥ The payroll taxes for this pay were then recorded in the general journal (page 7-24) as follows:

Payroll Taxes	1,390.21	
FICA Taxes Payable—OASDI		962.78
FICA Taxes Payable—HI		225.17
FUTA Taxes Payable		23.34
SUTA Taxes Payable—Employer		178.92

Payroll Taxes was debited for the sum of the employer's FICA, FUTA, and SUTA taxes. The taxable earnings used in computing each of these payroll taxes were obtained from the appropriate column totals of the payroll register. Note that only part of *Ford's* wages are taxable ($700 out of $1,220 gross pay) for FUTA ($7,000 limit). The computation of the debit to Payroll Taxes was:

FICA—OASDI:	6.2% of $15,528.77 =	$ 962.78
FICA—HI:	1.45% of $15,528.77 =	225.17
FUTA:	0.6% of $3,890.00 =	23.34
SUTA:	3.6890% of $4,850.00 =	178.92
Total Payroll Taxes		$ 1,390.21

FICA Taxes Payable—OASDI was credited for $962.78, the amount of the liability for the employer's portion of the tax. FICA Taxes Payable—HI was credited for $225.17, the amount of the liability for the employer's share of this tax. FUTA Taxes Payable was credited for the amount of the tax on the employer for federal unemployment purposes ($23.34). SUTA Taxes Payable—Employer was credited for $178.92, which is the amount of the contribution required of *the employer* under the state unemployment compensation law.

⑦ The journal entries were posted to the proper ledger accounts (pages 7-33 to 7-40).

October 15

This is the day on which the deposits of FICA and FIT taxes and the city of Philadelphia income taxes for the September payrolls are due. However, in order to concentrate on the fourth-quarter payrolls, we will assume that the deposits for the third quarter and the appropriate entries were already completed.

October 20

No. 2   On this date, Glo-Brite Paint Company must deposit the Pennsylvania state income taxes withheld from the October 9 payroll.

The deposit rule states that if the employer expects the aggregate amount withheld each quarter to be $1,000 or more, the employer must pay the withheld tax semimonthly.

The tax must be remitted within three banking days after the close of the semimonthly periods ending on the 15th and the last day of the month.

① Prepare the journal entry to record the deposit of the taxes, and post to the appropriate ledger accounts.

② Pennsylvania has eliminated the filing of paper forms (replaced by telefile or online filing). The information needed to telefile is listed on page 7-50—complete the information worksheet needed for the first semimonthly period of October. The company's Pennsylvania employer account number is 000-0-3300, its EIN is 00-0000660, its filing password is GBPCOM, and its telephone number is (215) 555-9559.

October 23

No. 3   Prepare the payroll for the last pay period of October from Time Clerk's Report Nos. 40 and 41.

The proper procedure in recording the payroll follows:

① Complete the payroll register.

In as much as only a portion of the payroll register sheet was used in recording the October 9 payroll, the October 23 payroll should be recorded on the same sheet to save space. On the first blank ruled line after the October 9 payroll, insert "Payday October 23—For Period Ending October 17, 20--." On the following lines, record the payroll information for the last pay date of October. When recording succeeding payrolls, continue to conserve space by recording two payrolls on each separate payroll register sheet.

The workers in the plant (*Bonno and Ryan*) are paid **time and a half** for any hours worked over eight each workday and for work on Saturdays and are paid *twice* the regular hourly rate for work on Sundays or holidays.

With this pay period, the **cumulative earnings** of several employees exceed the taxable income base set up by FUTA and SUTA. This factor must be considered in preparing the payroll register and in computing the employer's payroll taxes. Refer to each employee's earnings record to see the amount of cumulative earnings.

LO 1
Prepare payroll registers.

Project Audit Test

✓ Net Paid $12,494.94

Pay Points

Even though they are not on the time clerk's report, remember to pay the president, sales manager, sales representatives, and supervisors.

Pay Points

The employees' Pennsylvania State Unemployment Tax (SUTA) is calculated (0.0006) on the total wages of each employee. There is no taxable wage limit on the employees' portion of the tax.

Pay Points

Be sure to deduct 30¢ premium for each $1,000 of group insurance carried by each employee (last payday of each month).

Time Clerk's Report No. 40
For the Week Ending October 10, 20--

Employee	Time Record							Time Worked	Time Lost
	S	M	T	W	T	F	S		
Bonno, A. V.		8	8	8	8	8	4	44 hrs.	. . .
Ford, C. L.		4	8	8	8	8		36 hrs.	4 hrs.*
Russell, S. P.		8	8	8	8	8		40 hrs.	. . .
Ryan, J. M.		8	8	8	8	8		40 hrs.	. . .
Student		8	8	8	8	4		36 hrs.	. . .
Williams, R. V. . . .		8	8	8	8	8		40 hrs.	. . .

*Time lost on account of death of relative; charged against annual personal leave; no deduction for time lost.

Time Clerk's Report No. 41
For the Week Ending October 17, 20--

Employee	Time Record							Time Worked	Time Lost
	S	M	T	W	T	F	S		
Bonno, A. V. . . .		8	8	8	8	8		40 hrs.	. . .
Ford, C. L.		8	8	8	8	8		40 hrs.	. . .
Russell, S. P.		8	8	8	8	8		40 hrs.	. . .
Ryan, J. M.		8	8	8	8	8	8	48 hrs.	. . .
Student		8	8	8	8	4		36 hrs.	. . .
Williams, R. V. . . .		8	8	8	8	8		40 hrs.	. . .

② Make the entry transferring from Cash to Payroll Cash the net amount of the total payroll, and post.

③ Post the required information from the payroll register to each employee's earnings record.

④ Record in the journal the salaries, wages, taxes withheld, group insurance premiums collected, union dues withheld, and net amount paid, and post to the proper ledger accounts.

The entry required to record the October 23 payroll is the same as that to record the October 9 payroll, except it is necessary to record the liability for the amount withheld from the employees' wages to pay their part of the group insurance premium. The amount withheld should be recorded as a credit to Group Insurance Premiums Collected.

⑤ Record in the journal the employer's payroll taxes and the liabilities created; post to the appropriate ledger accounts.

November 4

No. 4   Deposit with the state of Pennsylvania the amount of state income taxes withheld from the October 23 payroll and complete information worksheet.

No. 5   *Thomas J. Sokowski* completed a new Form W-4, showing that his filing status changed to single. Change Sokowski's earnings record accordingly.

November 6

No. 6   Pay the treasurer of the union the amount of union dues withheld during the month of October.

Time Clerk's Report No. 42 For the Week Ending October 24, 20--									
Employee	Time Record							Time Worked	Time Lost
	S	M	T	W	T	F	S		
Bonno, A. V. ...		8	8	8	8	8		40 hrs.	...
Ford, C. L.		8	8	8	8	8		40 hrs.	...
Russell, S. P.		8	8	8	8	6		38 hrs.	2 hrs.*
Ryan, J. M.		8	8	8	8	8		40 hrs.	...
Student		8	8	8	8	4		36 hrs.	...
Williams, R. V. ...		8	8	8	7	8		39 hrs.	1 hr.**

*Time lost on account of family function; deduct 2 hours' pay.
**Time lost because of tardiness; deduct 1 hour's pay.

Time Clerk's Report No. 43 For the Week Ending October 31, 20--									
Employee	Time Record							Time Worked	Time Lost
	S	M	T	W	T	F	S		
Bonno, A. V. ...		8	8	8	8	8		40 hrs.	...
Ford, C. L.		8	8	8	8	8		40 hrs.	...
Russell, S. P.		8	8	8	8	8		40 hrs.	...
Ryan, J. M.		8	8	8	8	8		40 hrs.	...
Student		8	8	8	8	4		36 hrs.	...
Williams, R. V. ...		8	8	8	8	8		40 hrs.	...

No. 7   Prepare the payroll for the first pay period in November from Time Clerk's Report Nos. 42 and 43 and record the paychecks issued to all employees. Record this payroll at the top of the second payroll register sheet.

Note: *Serdar Russell* worked only 38 hours in the week ending October 24. Therefore, compute Russell's pay for that week by multiplying 38 by $15.00 (hourly rate). *Ruth Williams* worked only 39 hours in the week ending October 24. Therefore, compute her pay for that week by multiplying 39 by $15.29 (hourly rate).

Also, record the employer's payroll taxes.

Pay Points

Make changes in November 6 pay. Refer to No. 5.

November 13

No. 8   Because of her excessive tardiness and absenteeism during the year, the company discharged *Ruth Williams* today. For the week ending November 7, she was late a total of six hours; and for this week, she missed two full days and was late two hours on another day. In lieu of two weeks' notice, Williams was given two full weeks' pay ($1,223.08). Along with dismissal pay ($1,223.08), she was paid for the week ending November 7 (34 hours, or $519.86) and the days worked this current week (22 hours, or $336.38). The total pay for the two partial weeks is $856.24.

Project Audit Test

✓ Net Paid $ 1,578.92

① Record a separate payroll register (on one line) to show Williams' total earnings, deductions, and net pay. The two weeks' dismissal pay is subject to all payroll taxes. Include dismissal pay with the total earnings but do not show the hours in the Time Record columns. Use the Wage Bracket Method Tables for Manual Payroll Systems With Forms W-4 From 2020 or Later (using standard withholding column) for the biweekly payroll period for the total gross pay ($2,079.32) of Williams.

The deduction for group insurance premiums is $14.40. In the Time Record column, make a note of Williams' discharge as of this date. Indicate the payroll check number used to prepare the final check for Williams. When posting to the earnings record, make a notation of Williams' discharge on this date.

② Prepare the journal entries to transfer the net cash and to record Williams' final pay and the employer's payroll taxes. Post to the ledger accounts.

③ See completed Form W-2 for Ruth Williams on page 7-60. Box "d" should be left blank, since Glo-Brite Paint Company does not use a control number to identify individual Forms W-2. (Please use this Form W-2 as an example to help in completing Forms W-2 at end of the year.)

November 16

No. 9   Electronically deposit the amount of FICA taxes and federal income taxes for the October payrolls and complete the Federal Deposit Information Worksheet (page 7-49). Since the company is subject to the monthly deposit rule, the deposit is due on the 15th of the following month. See the deposit requirements explained on page 3-18. November 15 is a Sunday; therefore, the deposit is to be made on the next business day.

Prepare the journal entry to record the deposit of the taxes, and post to the appropriate ledger accounts.

LO 4

Complete federal, state, and city tax deposit forms and journalize the transactions.

No. 10 Since Glo-Brite Paint Company withholds the city of Philadelphia income tax, you must deposit the taxes with the Department of Revenue. The deposit rule that affects Glo-Brite Paint Company states that if the withheld taxes are between $350 and $16,000 per month, the company must deposit the tax monthly by the 15th of the following month. The withheld taxes for the October payrolls were $1,214.76.

① Prepare the journal entry to record the deposit of the taxes, and post to the appropriate ledger accounts.

② Complete the Philadelphia Employer's Return of Tax Withheld coupon (Monthly Wage Tax), which appears on page 7-51.

Pay Points

On all tax and deposit forms requiring a signature, use Joseph O'Neill's name.

November 17

No. 11 Prepare an employee's earnings record for *Beth Anne Woods*, a new employee who began work today, Tuesday. Woods is single. She is employed as a programmer at a monthly salary of $2,600. Address, 8102 Franklin Court, Philadelphia, PA 19105-0915. Telephone, 555-1128. Social Security No. 000-00-1587. She is eligible for group insurance coverage of $47,000 immediately, although her first deduction for group insurance will not be made until December 18.

Department: Office
Weekly rate: $600.00
Hourly rate: $15.00

November 18

No. 12 Deposit with the state of Pennsylvania the amount of state income taxes withheld from the November 6 and 13 (*Ruth Williams*) payrolls and complete the information worksheet.

November 20

Project Audit Test

✓ Net Paid $9,538.43

No. 13 With this pay, the company has decided to offer employees a Savings Incentive Match Plan for Employees (SIMPLE Retirement Plan). Most of the employees opted to wait until the start of the following year to participate. However, the following employees have decided to take part in the plan for the remaining pay periods of the year.

Jamie Ferguson: $500 contribution per pay period
Kari Mann: $250 contribution per pay period
Joseph O'Neill: $700 contribution per pay period
Jeri Ryan: $200 contribution per pay period

The contributions are to be deducted from the participating employee's pay and are excluded from the employee's income for federal income tax purposes. The other payroll taxes still apply. On the payroll registers and the earnings record, use the blank column under "Deductions" for these contributions. Use the term "SIMPLE" as the new heading for this deduction column (on both the payroll register and employee's earnings record).

Use the account in the general ledger for SIMPLE Contributions Payable—account no. 29.

The company must match these contributions dollar for dollar, up to 3 percent of the employee's compensation. These payments will be processed through the Accounts Payable Department.

Prepare the payroll for the last pay period of November from Time Clerk's Report Nos. 44 and 45, and record the paychecks issued to all employees. Also, record the employer's payroll taxes.

Time Clerk's Report No. 44
For the Week Ending November 7, 20--

Employee	Time Record							Time Worked	Time Lost
	S	M	T	W	T	F	S		
Bonno, A. V. . . .		8	8	8	8	8		40 hrs.	. . .
Ford, C. L.		8	8	8	8	8		40 hrs.	. . .
Russell, S. P.		6	8	8	8	8		38 hrs.	2 hrs.*
Ryan, J. M.		8	8	8	8	8		40 hrs.	. . .
Student		8	8	8	8	4		36 hrs.	. . .
Williams, R. V. . . .		6	8	7	7	6		34 hrs.	6 hrs.**

*Time lost for personal business; deduct 2 hours' pay.
**Time lost because of tardiness; deduct 6 hours' pay.

Time Clerk's Report No. 45
For the Week Ending November 14, 20--

Employee	Time Record							Time Worked	Time Lost
	S	M	T	W	T	F	S		
Bonno, A. V. . . .		...	...	8	8	8		24 hrs.	. . .
Ford, C. L.		8	8	8	8	8		40 hrs.	. . .
Russell, S. P.		8	8	8	8	8		40 hrs.	. . .
Ryan, J. M.		8	8	8	8	8		40 hrs.	. . .
Student		8	8	8	8	4		36 hrs.	. . .
Williams, R. V. . . .		D	D	8	6	8		22 hrs.	18 hrs.*

*Time lost because of tardiness; deduct 2 hours' pay. Unexcused absences; deduct 16 hours' pay.

Remember to deduct the premiums on the group insurance for each employee.

No. 14 Salary increases of $30 per week, **effective for the two weeks covered in the December 4 payroll**, are given to *Catherine L. Ford* and *Serdar P. Russell*. The group insurance coverage for Ford will be increased to $50,000; for Russell, it will be increased to $49,000. Update the employees' earnings records accordingly. The new wage rates are listed below.

Pay Points
The new wage rates are effective for the December 4 payroll.

Employee	Weekly Rate	Hourly Rate
Ford, Catherine L.	$640.00	$16.00
Russell, Serdar P.	630.00	15.75

November 30

No. 15 Prepare an employee's earnings record for *Paul Winston Young*, the president's nephew, who began work today. Young is single. He is training as a field sales representative in the city where the home office is located. His beginning salary is $2,730 per month. Address, 7936 Holmes Drive, Philadelphia, PA 19107-0007. Telephone, 555-2096.

Social Security No. 000-00-6057. Young is eligible for group insurance coverage of $49,000.

Department: Sales
Weekly rate: $630.00
Hourly rate: $15.75

December 3

No. 16 Deposit with the state of Pennsylvania the amount of state income taxes withheld from the November 20 payroll using General Ledger balance for Account No. 25 and complete the information worksheet.

December 4

Project Audit Test

✓ Net Paid $11,109.84

No. 17 Prepare the payroll for the first biweekly pay period of December from Time Clerk's Report Nos. 46 and 47, and record the paychecks issued to all employees. Record this payroll at the top of the third payroll register sheet.

Note: Thursday, November 26, is a paid holiday for all workers.
Also, record the employer's payroll taxes.

Time Clerk's Report No. 46
For the Week Ending November 21, 20--

Employee	Time Record							Time Worked	Time Lost
	S	M	T	W	T	F	S		
Bonno, A. V. ...		8	8	8	8	8		40 hrs.	...
Ford, C. L.		8	8	8	8	8		40 hrs.	...
Russell, S. P.		8	8	8	8	8		40 hrs.	...
Ryan, J. M.		8	8	8	4	8		36 hrs.	4 hrs.*
Student		8	8	8	4	8		36 hrs.	...
Woods, B. A. ...		...	8	8	8	8		32 hrs.	...

*Time lost on account of personal business; deduct 4 hours' pay.

Time Clerk's Report No. 47
For the Week Ending November 28, 20--

Employee	Time Record							Time Worked	Time Lost
	S	M	T	W	T	F	S		
Bonno, A. V.	8*	8	8	8		8		48 hrs.	...
Ford, C. L.		8	8	8		8		40 hrs.	...
Russell, S. P.		8	8	8		8		40 hrs.	...
Ryan, J. M.		9	10	8	PAID HOLIDAY	8		43 hrs.	...
Student		8	8	8		4		36 hrs.	...
Woods, B. A.		8	8	8		8		40 hrs.	...

*Double time.

No. 18 Both *Anthony Bonno* and *Jeri Ryan* have been notified that their union dues will increase to $9 per pay, starting with the last pay period of the year. **Reflect these increases in the December 18 pay** and show the changes on their earnings records.

December 9

No. 19 Pay the treasurer of the union the amount of union dues withheld during the month of November.

December 11

No. 20 The Payroll Department was informed that *Serdar P. Russell* died in an automobile accident on the way home from work Thursday, December 10.

Pay Points

This final pay is not subject to withholding for FIT, SIT, or CIT purposes.

December 14

No. 21 ① Make a separate entry (on one line) in the payroll register to record the issuance of a check payable to the **Estate of Serdar P. Russell**. This check covers Russell's work for the weeks ending December 5 and 12 ($1,134.00) plus accrued vacation pay ($1,260.00). Do not show the vacation hours in the Time Record columns on the payroll register but include them in the Total Earnings column.

Russell's final biweekly pay for time worked and the vacation pay are subject to FICA, FUTA, and SUTA (employer and employee) taxes. Since Russell's cumulative earnings have surpassed the taxable earnings figures established by FUTA and SUTA, there will not be any unemployment tax on the **employer**. The deduction for group insurance premiums is $14.70.

② Make a notation of Russell's death in the payroll register and earnings record.

③ Prepare journal entries to transfer the net pay and to record Russell's final pay and the employer's payroll taxes. Post to the ledger accounts.

④ Include the final gross pay ($2,394.00) in Boxes 3 and 5 but not in Boxes 1, 16, and 18. Use the blank Form W-2 on page 7-60.

In addition, the last wage payment and vacation pay must be reported on Form 1099-MISC. A Form 1096 must also be completed. These forms will be completed in February before their due date. (See Transaction Nos. 38 and 39 on page 7-21.)

Project Audit Test

✓ Net Paid $2,194.72

Pay Points

Prepare a Wage and Tax Statement, Form W-2, which will be given to the executor of the estate along with the final paycheck.

December 15

No. 22 Electronically deposit the amount of FICA taxes and federal income taxes for the November payrolls and complete the Federal Deposit Information Worksheet.

No. 23 Deposit with the city of Philadelphia the amount of city income taxes withheld from the November payrolls.

December 18

No. 24 Deposit with the state of Pennsylvania the amount of state income taxes withheld from the December 4 payroll and complete the information worksheet.

No. 25 Glo-Brite has been notified by the insurance company that there will be no premium charge for the month of December on the policy for *Serdar Russell*. Prepare the entry for the check made payable to the estate of Serdar P. Russell for the amount that was withheld for insurance from the December 14 pay.

No. 26 Prepare an employee's earnings record for *Richard Lloyd Zimmerman*, who was employed today as time clerk to take the place left vacant by the death of Serdar P. Russell last week. His beginning salary is $2,600 per month. Address, 900 South Clark Street, Philadelphia, PA 19195-6247. Telephone, 555-2104. Social Security No. 000-00-1502. Zimmerman's filing status is married filing joint. Zimmerman is eligible for group insurance coverage of $47,000, although no deduction for group insurance premiums will be made until the last payday in January.

Department: Office
Weekly rate: $600.00
Hourly rate: $15.00

> **Project Audit Test**
>
> ✓ Net Paid $70,494.00

Pay Points

Calculate Federal Income tax on O'Neill's bonus using Method B—a flat 22 percent on the supplemental pay (see page 4-20).

Pay Points

Remember to deduct the premiums on the group insurance for each employee-note increase in Ford's pay.

No. 27 Prepare the payroll for the latter pay of December from Time Clerk's Report Nos. 48 and 49 and record the paychecks issued to all employees. Also, record the employer's payroll taxes.

In this pay, the president of the company, *Joseph O'Neill*, is paid his annual bonus. This does not affect O'Neill's insurance coverage, which is based on regular pay. This year, his bonus is *$95,000*. For withholding purposes, the bonus is considered a supplemental payment and is taxed at the supplemental rate of 22 percent. For this pay, O'Neill **has increased his SIMPLE deduction to $2,000**, which will reduce his salary for federal income tax purposes. To determine the federal income tax on the remaining taxable portion of his regular salary, use the Wage Bracket Method Tables for Manual Payroll Systems With Forms W-4 From 2020 or Later (using standard withholding column) – Biweekly Payroll Period in Table B (pages T-7 and T-8). In this pay, O'Neill has reached the OASDI ceiling. **To calculate O'Neill's OASDI tax, multiply the OASDI ceiling of $147,000 by 6.2 percent and then subtract the year-to-date OASDI taxes withheld up to this pay.** (Use O'Neill's Employee Earnings Record to view his year-to-date OASDI tax withheld.)

> *Note:* **After posting the information for this last pay to the employees' earnings records, calculate and enter the quarterly and yearly totals on each earnings record.**

	Time Clerk's Report No. 48 For the Week Ending December 5, 20--									
Employee	**Time Record**							**Time Worked**	**Time Lost**
	S	M	T	W	T	F	S		
Bonno, A. V. . . .	4	8	8	8	8	8		44 hrs.	. . .
Ford, C. L.		8	8	8	8	8		40 hrs.	. . .
Russell, S. P.		8	8	8	8	8		40 hrs.	. . .
Ryan, J. M.		8	9	9	9	9		44 hrs.	. . .
Student		8	8	7	8	4		35 hrs.	1 hr.*
Woods, B. A. . . .		8	8	8	8	8		40 hrs.	. . .
Young, P. W. . . .		8	8	8	8	8		40 hrs.	

*Time lost because of tardiness; deduct 1 hour's pay.

Time Clerk's Report No. 49
For the Week Ending December 12, 20--

Employee	Time Record							Time Worked	Time Lost
	S	M	T	W	T	F	S		
Bonno, A. V. . . .	8	8	8	8	8	8		48 hrs.	. . .
Ford, C. L.		4	8	8	8	8		36 hrs.	4 hrs.*
Russell, S. P.		8	8	8	8	D		32 hrs.	8 hrs.
Ryan, J. M.		10	8	8	9	8		43 hrs.	. . .
Student		4	8	8	8	4		32 hrs.	4 hrs.**
Woods, B. A. . . .		8	8	8	8	8		40 hrs.	. . .
Young, P. W. . . .		8	8	8	8	8		40 hrs.	

*Time spent in training session; no deduction in pay.
**Time lost in dentist appointment; no deduction in pay.

Note: This completes the project insofar as recording the payroll transactions for the last quarter is concerned. The following additional transactions are given to illustrate different types of transactions arising in connection with the accounting for payrolls and payroll taxes. Record these transactions in the journal, but do not post to the ledger.

End-of-Year Activities

January 6

No. 28 Deposit with the state of Pennsylvania the amount of state income taxes withheld from the December 18 payroll and complete the information worksheet.

January 8

No. 29 Pay the treasurer of the union the amount of union dues withheld during the month of December.

January 15

No. 30 Electronically deposit the amount of FICA taxes and federal income taxes for the December payrolls, and complete the Federal Deposit Information Worksheet.

No. 31 Deposit with the city of Philadelphia the amount of city income taxes withheld from the December payrolls.

February 1

No. 32 Prepare **Form 941, Employer's Quarterly Federal Tax Return,** with respect to wages paid during the last calendar quarter. Pages 7-54 to 7-56 contain a blank Form 941. The information needed in preparing the return should be obtained from the ledger accounts, payroll registers, employees' earnings records, and Federal Tax Deposit forms.

Form 941 and all forms that follow are to be signed by the president of the company, *Joseph T. O'Neill.*

Project Audit Test

January						
Su	Mo	Tu	We	Th	Fr	Sa
					1	2
3	4	5	6	7	8	9
10	11	12	13	14	15	16
17	18	19	20	21	22	23
24	25	26	27	28	29	30
31						

LO 5

Prepare various quarter-end and year-end payroll tax forms.

Washington Update

Since the Tax Cuts and Jobs Act (TCJA) eliminated personal withholding allowances, the Form W-4 employee's withholding certificate and tax withholding procedures were redesigned. Current employees will not have to complete a new Form W-4 unless they wish to make a change in the latest pre-2020 Form W-4 on file with their employer. Employers will now have to withhold income tax based on pre-2020 Forms W-4 and 2020 Forms W-4, which provide significantly different data. The IRS developed one set of withholding procedures and withholding tables to accommodate both versions of Form W-4. The new tables now include three filing statuses: married filing jointly, single or married filing separately, and head of household. The head of household tables should not be used if the Form W-4 is from before 2020. Publication 15-T was recently released and contains withholding procedures and tables. Please see Chapter 4 for recent legislation regarding the cares act. In this problem, Pennsylvania was not a credit reduction state. Also, see "As We Go to Press" on page iii and our "Online As We Go to Press" regarding current legislation.

No. 33 ① Complete *Form 940, Employer's Federal Unemployment (FUTA) Tax Return,* using the blank forms reproduced on pages 7-57 to 7-58. Also, complete the Federal Deposit Information Worksheet, using the blank form reproduced on page 7-49.

　　a. Total wages for the first three quarters was $142,224.57. FUTA taxable wages for the first three quarters was $65,490.00.

　　b. FUTA tax liability by quarter:

> 1st quarter—$204.53
> 2nd quarter—$105.25
> 3rd quarter—$83.16

　　The first FUTA deposit is now due.

　　c. Journalize the entry to record the electronic deposit for the FUTA tax liability.

No. 34 ① Prepare *Form UC-2, Employer's Report for Unemployment Compensation—Fourth Quarter,* using the blank form reproduced on page 7-59. In Pennsylvania, a credit week is any calendar week during the quarter in which the employee earned at least $50 (without regard to when paid). The maximum number of credit weeks in a quarter is 13. The telephone number of the company is (215) 555-9559. All other information needed in preparing the form can be obtained from the ledger accounts, the payroll registers, and the employees' earnings records.

② Journalize the entry to record the payment of the taxes for the fourth quarter.

No. 35 Complete *Form W-2, Wage and Tax Statement,* for each current employee, using the blank statements reproduced on pages 7-61 to 7-65. Use each employee's earnings record to obtain the information needed to complete the forms. The two plant workers (Bonno and Ryan) have had $121.00 in union dues withheld during the year. In addition to union dues withheld, include the Pennsylvania State Unemployment Tax (SUTA) withheld in Box 14.

No. 36   Complete **Form W-3, Transmittal of Wage and Tax Statements,** using the blank form reproduced on page 7-66. Use the information on all Forms W-2 to complete this form.

No. 37   Complete Pennsylvania **Form REV-1667, W-2 Transmittal,** using the blank form reproduced on page 7-66. Use the information on Forms W-2 to complete this report. The wages paid and the Pennsylvania tax withheld for the first three quarters are:

1st	$34,088.75	$1,046.52
2nd	$45,535.62	$1,397.94
3rd	$62,600.20	$1,921.83

No. 38   Complete **Form 1099-MISC, Miscellaneous Income,** for the payment to **the estate of Serdar P. Russell.** The full amount of the December 14 payment must be reported in Box 3. Page 7-67 contains a blank form.

     Note: These wages are to be reported as other income in Box 3 so that the IRS will not seek self-employment tax on such amounts.

No. 39   Complete **Form 1096, Annual Summary and Transmittal of U.S. Information Returns,** using the blank form on page 7-67. Use the information on Form 1099-MISC to complete this form.

No. 40   Pennsylvania's Quarterly Reconciliation of Income Tax Withheld is filed electronically. The information worksheet to be completed is on page 7-52. The telephone number of the company is (215) 555-9559.

No. 41   Prepare the Annual Reconciliation of Employer Wage Tax for Philadelphia, using the blank form on page 7-53. For lines 1, 3, and 4, use gross wages and salaries per general ledger less exempt wages paid to Russell ($2,394.00) on December 14. (This amount should agree with Form W-3 Box 18, local wages.) Tax paid during the first three quarters was $5,461.14. For reporting purposes, there were 10 Philadelphia residents for whom wage tax was remitted for the pay period ending March 12, 20--.

Recording End-of-Period Payroll Adjustments

LO 6

Make the accrual entries for the payroll at the end of a year.

1. On the financial statements prepared at the end of its first year of operations, the company must show an accurate picture of all expenses and all liabilities incurred. The last payday of the year was December 18. However, the payment to the employees on that day did not include the weeks ending December 19 and 26 and the four days (December 28–31) in the following week. These earnings will be reflected in the January payrolls. Two-column journal paper is provided for use in journalizing the following entry on the bottom of this page.

    Prepare the adjusting entry as of December 31 to record the salaries and wages that have accrued but remain unpaid as of the end of the year. When calculating the amount of the accrual for each hourly worker, assume each employee worked eight hours on each day during the period with no overtime (student works a 36-hour week—student worked 32 hours for the period December 28 through December 31). For each salaried worker, the accrual will amount to 14/10 of the worker's biweekly earnings, except for Zimmerman who worked only 10 days.

    Each of the labor cost accounts should be debited for the appropriate amount of the accrual, and Salaries and Wages Payable should be credited for the total amount of the accrual. There is no liability for payroll taxes on the accrued salaries and wages until the workers are actually paid. Therefore, the company follows the practice of not accruing payroll taxes.

2. Also, prepare the adjusting entry as of December 31 to record the accrued vacation pay as of the end of the year. Record the expense in a vacation benefits expense account, and credit the appropriate liability account. Use the journal paper provided below.

    As of December 31, the vacation time earned but not used by each employee is listed here.

Bonno	80 hours
Ferguson	three weeks
Ford	two weeks
Mann	one week
O'Neill	four weeks
Ryan	80 hours
Sokowski	two weeks
Student	72 hours
Woods	none
Young	none
Zimmerman	none

JOURNAL

Page ____

DATE	DESCRIPTION	POST. REF.	DEBIT	CREDIT

ACCOUNTING RECORDS AND REPORTS
Contents

Item	To Be Used with	Page
Journal..	Payroll Project.....................................	7-24
General Ledger	Payroll Project.....................................	7-33
Employees' Earnings Records	Payroll Project.....................................	7-42
Federal Deposit Information Worksheet	Payroll Project.....................................	7-49
State Filing Information Worksheet......................	Payroll Project.....................................	7-50
Employer's Coupons of Tax Withheld—City of Philadelphia..	Payroll Project.....................................	7-51
PA Employer's Quarterly Reconciliation Worksheet...	Payroll Project.....................................	7-52
Annual Reconciliation of Employer Wage Tax—Philadelphia..	Payroll Project.....................................	7-53
Employer's Quarterly Federal Tax Return (Form 941)...	Payroll Project.....................................	7-54
Employer's Annual Federal Unemployment (FUTA) Tax Return (Form 940)	Payroll Project.....................................	7-57
Employer's Report for Unemployment Compensation—Pennsylvania (Form UC-2)......	Payroll Project.....................................	7-59
Wage and Tax Statements (Form W-2)..................	Payroll Project.....................................	7-60
Transmittal of Wage and Tax Statements (Form W-3)	Payroll Project.....................................	7-66
W-2 Transmittal—Pennsylvania (Form REV-1667 AS)	Payroll Project.....................................	7-66
Miscellaneous Income (Form 1099-MISC).............	Payroll Project.....................................	7-67
Annual Summary and Transmittal of U.S. Information Returns (Form 1096)	Payroll Project.....................................	7-67
Project Audit Tests..	Payroll Project.....................................	7-69
Payroll Register—Kipley Company.......................	Continuing Payroll Problem A	PR-1
Payroll Register—Olney Company	Continuing Payroll Problem B	PR-1
Payroll Register—Glo-Brite Paint Company	Payroll Project.....................................	PR-2

JOURNAL

Page 41

	DATE		DESCRIPTION	POST. REF.	DEBIT	CREDIT	
1	20-- Oct.	9	Payroll Cash	12	1 2 4 3 6 46		1
2			Cash	11		1 2 4 3 6 46	2
3							3
4		9	Administrative Salaries	51	2 3 0 7 69		4
5			Office Salaries	52	4 7 2 3 08		5
6			Sales Salaries	53	3 6 0 0 00		6
7			Plant Wages	54	4 8 9 8 00		7
8			FICA Taxes Payable—OASDI	20.1		9 6 2 79	8
9			FICA Taxes Payable—HI	20.2		2 2 5 18	9
10			Employees FIT Payable	24		8 0 6 00	10
11			Employees SIT Payable	25		4 7 6 76	11
12			Employees SUTA Payable	25.1		9 30	12
13			Employees CIT Payable	26		5 9 6 28	13
14			Union Dues Payable	28		1 6 00	14
15			Payroll Cash	12		1 2 4 3 6 46	15
16							16
17		9	Payroll Taxes	56	1 3 9 0 21		17
18			FICA Taxes Payable—OASDI	20.1		9 6 2 78	18
19			FICA Taxes Payable—HI	20.2		2 2 5 17	19
20			FUTA Taxes Payable	21		2 3 34	20
21			SUTA Taxes Payable—Employer	22		1 7 8 92	21
22							22
23							23
24							24
25							25
26							26
27							27
28							28
29							29
30							30
31							31
32							32
33							33
34							34

JOURNAL

Page

	DATE		DESCRIPTION	POST. REF.	DEBIT	CREDIT	
1							1
2							2
3							3
4							4
5							5
6							6
7							7
8							8
9							9
10							10
11							11
12							12
13							13
14							14
15							15
16							16
17							17
18							18
19							19
20							20
21							21
22							22
23							23
24							24
25							25
26							26
27							27
28							28
29							29
30							30
31							31
32							32
33							33
34							34

JOURNAL

Page

	DATE		DESCRIPTION	POST. REF.	DEBIT	CREDIT	
1							1
2							2
3							3
4							4
5							5
6							6
7							7
8							8
9							9
10							10
11							11
12							12
13							13
14							14
15							15
16							16
17							17
18							18
19							19
20							20
21							21
22							22
23							23
24							24
25							25
26							26
27							27
28							28
29							29
30							30
31							31
32							32
33							33
34							34

JOURNAL

Page

	DATE		DESCRIPTION	POST. REF.	DEBIT	CREDIT	
1							1
2							2
3							3
4							4
5							5
6							6
7							7
8							8
9							9
10							10
11							11
12							12
13							13
14							14
15							15
16							16
17							17
18							18
19							19
20							20
21							21
22							22
23							23
24							24
25							25
26							26
27							27
28							28
29							29
30							30
31							31
32							32
33							33
34							34

JOURNAL

Page _____

	DATE	DESCRIPTION	POST. REF.	DEBIT	CREDIT	
1						1
2						2
3						3
4						4
5						5
6						6
7						7
8						8
9						9
10						10
11						11
12						12
13						13
14						14
15						15
16						16
17						17
18						18
19						19
20						20
21						21
22						22
23						23
24						24
25						25
26						26
27						27
28						28
29						29
30						30
31						31
32						32
33						33
34						34

JOURNAL

Page

	DATE	DESCRIPTION	POST. REF.	DEBIT	CREDIT	
1						1
2						2
3						3
4						4
5						5
6						6
7						7
8						8
9						9
10						10
11						11
12						12
13						13
14						14
15						15
16						16
17						17
18						18
19						19
20						20
21						21
22						22
23						23
24						24
25						25
26						26
27						27
28						28
29						29
30						30
31						31
32						32
33						33
34						34

JOURNAL

Page ____

	DATE		DESCRIPTION	POST. REF.	DEBIT	CREDIT	
1							1
2							2
3							3
4							4
5							5
6							6
7							7
8							8
9							9
10							10
11							11
12							12
13							13
14							14
15							15
16							16
17							17
18							18
19							19
20							20
21							21
22							22
23							23
24							24
25							25
26							26
27							27
28							28
29							29
30							30
31							31
32							32
33							33
34							34

JOURNAL

Page

	DATE	DESCRIPTION	POST. REF.	DEBIT	CREDIT	
1						1
2						2
3						3
4						4
5						5
6						6
7						7
8						8
9						9
10						10
11						11
12						12
13						13
14						14
15						15
16						16
17						17
18						18
19						19
20						20
21						21
22						22
23						23
24						24
25						25
26						26
27						27
28						28
29						29
30						30
31						31
32						32
33						33
34						34

JOURNAL

Page

	DATE		DESCRIPTION	POST. REF.	DEBIT	CREDIT	
1							1
2							2
3							3
4							4
5							5
6							6
7							7
8							8
9							9
10							10
11							11
12							12
13							13
14							14
15							15
16							16
17							17
18							18
19							19
20							20
21							21
22							22
23							23
24							24
25							25
26							26
27							27
28							28
29							29
30							30
31							31
32							32
33							33
34							34

GENERAL LEDGER

ACCOUNT **CASH**   ACCOUNT NO. **11**

DATE		ITEM	POST. REF.	DEBIT	CREDIT	BALANCE	
						DEBIT	CREDIT
20-- Oct.	1	*Balance*	✓			19 9 8 4 6 33	
	9		J41		1 2 4 3 6 46	18 7 4 0 9 87	

ACCOUNT **PAYROLL CASH**

ACCOUNT NO. **12**

DATE		ITEM	POST. REF.	DEBIT	CREDIT	BALANCE	
						DEBIT	CREDIT
20-- Oct.	9		J41	1 2 4 3 6 46		1 2 4 3 6 46	
	9		J41		1 2 4 3 6 46	– – – –	– – – –

ACCOUNT   **FICA TAXES PAYABLE—OASDI**

ACCOUNT NO. **20.1**

DATE		ITEM	POST. REF.	DEBIT	CREDIT	BALANCE	
						DEBIT	CREDIT
20-- Oct.	9		J41		9 6 2 79		9 6 2 79
	9		J41		9 6 2 78		1 9 2 5 57

ACCOUNT **FICA TAXES PAYABLE—HI**   ACCOUNT NO. **20.2**

DATE		ITEM	POST. REF.	DEBIT	CREDIT	BALANCE	
						DEBIT	CREDIT
20-- Oct.	9		J41		2 2 5 18		2 2 5 18
	9		J41		2 2 5 17		4 5 0 35

ACCOUNT **FUTA TAXES PAYABLE**   ACCOUNT NO. **21**

DATE		ITEM	POST. REF.	DEBIT	CREDIT	BALANCE	
						DEBIT	CREDIT
20-- Oct.	1	Balance	✓				3 9 2 94
	9		J41		2 3 34		4 1 6 28

ACCOUNT **SUTA TAXES PAYABLE—EMPLOYER**   ACCOUNT NO. **22**

DATE		ITEM	POST. REF.	DEBIT	CREDIT	BALANCE	
						DEBIT	CREDIT
20-- Oct.	9		J41		1 7 8 92		1 7 8 92

ACCOUNT **EMPLOYEES FIT PAYABLE**   ACCOUNT NO. **24**

DATE		ITEM	POST. REF.	DEBIT	CREDIT	BALANCE	
						DEBIT	CREDIT
20-- Oct.	9		J41		8 0 6 00		8 0 6 00

ACCOUNT **EMPLOYEES SIT PAYABLE**   ACCOUNT NO. **25**

DATE		ITEM	POST. REF.	DEBIT	CREDIT	BALANCE	
						DEBIT	CREDIT
20-- Oct.	9		J41		4 7 6 76		4 7 6 76

ACCOUNT **EMPLOYEES SUTA PAYABLE**　　　　　　　　ACCOUNT NO. **25.1**

DATE		ITEM	POST. REF.	DEBIT	CREDIT	BALANCE	
						DEBIT	CREDIT
20-- Oct.	9		J41		9 30		9 30

ACCOUNT **EMPLOYEES CIT PAYABLE**　　　　　　　　ACCOUNT NO. **26**

DATE		ITEM	POST. REF.	DEBIT	CREDIT	BALANCE	
						DEBIT	CREDIT
20-- Oct.	9		J41		5 9 6 28		5 9 6 28

ACCOUNT **GROUP INSURANCE PREMIUMS COLLECTED**　　　　　　　　ACCOUNT NO. **27**

DATE	ITEM	POST. REF.	DEBIT	CREDIT	BALANCE	
					DEBIT	CREDIT

ACCOUNT **UNION DUES PAYABLE**　　　　　　　　ACCOUNT NO. **28**

DATE		ITEM	POST. REF.	DEBIT	CREDIT	BALANCE	
						DEBIT	CREDIT
20-- Oct.	9		J41		1 6 00		1 6 00

ACCOUNT **SIMPLE CONTRIBUTIONS PAYABLE**   ACCOUNT NO. **29**

DATE	ITEM	POST. REF.	DEBIT	CREDIT	BALANCE DEBIT	BALANCE CREDIT

ACCOUNT **ADMINISTRATIVE SALARIES**   ACCOUNT NO. **51**

DATE		ITEM	POST. REF.	DEBIT	CREDIT	BALANCE DEBIT	BALANCE CREDIT
20-- Oct.	1	Balance	✓			42 692 27	
	9		J41	2 307 69		44 999 96	

ACCOUNT **OFFICE SALARIES**   ACCOUNT NO. **52**

DATE		ITEM	POST. REF.	DEBIT	CREDIT	BALANCE DEBIT	BALANCE CREDIT
20-- Oct.	1	Balance	✓			28 350 00	
	9		J41	4 723 08		33 073 08	

ACCOUNT **SALES SALARIES**

ACCOUNT NO. **53**

DATE		ITEM	POST. REF.	DEBIT	CREDIT	BALANCE	
						DEBIT	CREDIT
20-- Oct.	1	Balance	✓			2 8 5 2 5 00	
	9		J41	3 6 0 0 00		3 2 1 2 5 00	

ACCOUNT **PLANT WAGES**

ACCOUNT NO. **54**

DATE		ITEM	POST. REF.	DEBIT	CREDIT	BALANCE	
						DEBIT	CREDIT
20-- Oct.	1	Balance	✓			4 2 6 5 7 30	
	9		J41	4 8 9 8 00		4 7 5 5 5 30	

ACCOUNT **PAYROLL TAXES**

ACCOUNT NO. **56**

DATE		ITEM	POST. REF.	DEBIT	CREDIT	BALANCE	
						DEBIT	CREDIT
20-- Oct.	1	Balance	✓			1 4 3 5 3 07	
	9		J41	1 3 9 0 21		1 5 7 4 3 28	

EMPLOYEES' EARNINGS RECORD

Employee Earnings Record — BONNO, Anthony Victor

DEPARTMENT	Plant
OCCUPATION	Mixer Operator
WORKS IN (STATE)	PA
S.S. ACCOUNT NO.	000-00-3481
NAME—LAST	BONNO
FIRST	Anthony
MIDDLE	Victor
FILING STATUS	MFJ
W/H ALLOW.	N/A
SALARY	$
WEEKLY RATE	$
HOURLY RATE	$ 17.60
OVERTIME RATE	$ 26.40
GROUP INSURANCE	$55,000—30¢/M
OTHER DEDUCTIONS INFORMATION — UNION DUES	$8 each pay

20 PAYDAY	REGULAR EARNINGS HRS.	RATE	AMOUNT	OVERTIME EARNINGS HRS.	RATE	AMOUNT	CUMULATIVE EARNINGS	FICA OASDI	FICA HI	FIT	SIT	SUTA	CIT	OTHER DEDUCTIONS	CK. NO.	NET PAID AMOUNT
YEAR-TO-DATE TOTAL			10 2 9 3 40				113 2 2 00	7 0 1 96	1 6 4 17	8 1 0 00	3 4 7 59	6 79	4 3 4 74	2 1 6 80		86 3 9 95
1 10/9	80	17 60	14 0 8 00			10 2 8 60	127 3 0 00	8 7 30	2 0 42	4 0 00	4 3 23	0 84	54 06	8 00	672	11 5 4 15
2																
3																
4																
5																
6																
QUARTER TOTAL																
YEARLY TOTAL																

Employee Earnings Record — FERGUSON, Jamie Hadi

DEPARTMENT	Sales
OCCUPATION	Sales Manager
WORKS IN (STATE)	PA
S.S. ACCOUNT NO.	000-00-8645
NAME—LAST	FERGUSON
FIRST	Jamie
MIDDLE	Hadi
FILING STATUS	MFJ
W/H ALLOW.	N/A
SALARY	$ 58,500/yr.
WEEKLY RATE	$ 1,125.00
HOURLY RATE	$ 28.13
OVERTIME RATE	$
GROUP INSURANCE	$88,000—30¢/M

20 PAYDAY	REGULAR EARNINGS HRS.	RATE	AMOUNT	OVERTIME EARNINGS HRS.	RATE	AMOUNT	CUMULATIVE EARNINGS	FICA OASDI	FICA HI	FIT	SIT	SUTA	CIT	OTHER DEDUCTIONS	CK. NO.	NET PAID AMOUNT
YEAR-TO-DATE TOTAL			231 2 5 00				231 2 5 00	14 3 3 75	3 3 5 31	22 9 1 00	7 0 9 94	13 88	8 8 7 95	1 3 2 30		173 2 0 87
1 10/9	80		22 5 0 00				253 7 5 00	1 3 9 50	3 2 63	1 3 6 00	6 9 08	1 35	8 6 40		673	17 8 5 04
2																
3																
4																
5																
6																
QUARTER TOTAL																
YEARLY TOTAL																

Employee: FORD, Catherine Louise

DEPARTMENT	Office
OCCUPATION	Administrative Assistant
WORKS IN (STATE)	PA
S.S. ACCOUNT NO.	000-00-4567
NAME—LAST	FORD
FIRST	Catherine
MIDDLE	Louise
FILING STATUS	S
W/H ALLOW.	N/A
GROUP INSURANCE	$48,000—30¢/M
SALARY	$2,643.33/mo.
WEEKLY RATE	$610.00
HOURLY RATE	$15.25
OVERTIME RATE	22.88

20__ PAYDAY	REGULAR EARNINGS HRS.	RATE	AMOUNT	OVERTIME HRS.	RATE	AMOUNT	CUMULATIVE EARNINGS
YEAR-TO-DATE TOTAL			6300 00				63000 00
1 10/9	80		1220 00				75200 00

PAYDAY	OASDI	HI	FIT	SIT	SUTA	CIT	OTHER DEDUCTIONS	CK. NO.	NET PAID AMOUNT
YEAR-TO-DATE TOTAL	390 60	91 35	639 00	193 41	3 78	241 91			4702 15
1 10/9	75 64	17 69	79 00	37 45	0 73	46 85	37 80	674	962 64

Employee: MANN, Kari Casey

DEPARTMENT	Sales
OCCUPATION	Sales Representative
WORKS IN (STATE)	PA
S.S. ACCOUNT NO.	000-00-9352
NAME—LAST	MANN
FIRST	Kari
MIDDLE	Casey
FILING STATUS	MFJ
W/H ALLOW.	N/A
GROUP INSURANCE	$53,000—30¢/M
SALARY	$2,925.00/mo.
WEEKLY RATE	$675.00
HOURLY RATE	16.88

20__ PAYDAY	REGULAR EARNINGS HRS.	RATE	AMOUNT	OVERTIME HRS.	RATE	AMOUNT	CUMULATIVE EARNINGS
YEAR-TO-DATE TOTAL			5400 00				54000 00
1 10/9	80		1350 00				67500 00

PAYDAY	OASDI	HI	FIT	SIT	SUTA	CIT	OTHER DEDUCTIONS	CK. NO.	NET PAID AMOUNT
YEAR-TO-DATE TOTAL	334 80	78 30	332 00	165 78	3 24	207 35			4247 03
1 10/9	83 70	19 58	36 00	41 45	0 81	51 84	31 50	675	1116 62

Employee 1 — O'NEILL

DEPARTMENT	Admin.
OCCUPATION	President
WORKS IN (STATE)	PA
NAME–LAST	O'NEILL
FIRST	Joseph
MIDDLE	Tyler
S.S. ACCOUNT NO.	000-00-1534
FILING STATUS	MFJ
W/H ALLOW.	N/A
SALARY	$60,000/yr.
BIWEEKLY RATE	$2,307.69
HOURLY RATE	$
OVERTIME RATE	$
GROUP INSURANCE	$90,000—30¢/M

20— PAYDAY	REGULAR EARNINGS HRS.	RATE	AMOUNT	OVERTIME EARNINGS HRS.	RATE	AMOUNT	CUMULATIVE EARNINGS	FICA OASDI	FICA HI	FIT	SIT	SUTA	CIT	OTHER DEDUCTIONS	CK. NO.	NET PAID AMOUNT
YEAR-TO-DATE TOTAL			42692 27				426 9 2 27	2646 92	619 04	6116 00	1310 65	25 62	1639 30	202 50		3013 2 24
1 10/9	80		2307 69				449 9 9 96	143 08	33 46	142 00	70 85	1 38	88 61		676	1828 31
2																
3																
4																
5																
6																
QUARTER TOTAL																
YEARLY TOTAL																

Employee 2 — RUSSELL

DEPARTMENT	Office
OCCUPATION	Time Clerk
WORKS IN (STATE)	PA
NAME–LAST	RUSSELL
FIRST	Serdar
MIDDLE	Parker
S.S. ACCOUNT NO.	000-00-6337
FILING STATUS	S
W/H ALLOW.	N/A
SALARY	$2,600/mo.
WEEKLY RATE	$600.00
HOURLY RATE	$15.00
OVERTIME RATE	$22.50
GROUP INSURANCE	$47,000—30¢/M

20— PAYDAY	REGULAR EARNINGS HRS.	RATE	AMOUNT	OVERTIME EARNINGS HRS.	RATE	AMOUNT	CUMULATIVE EARNINGS	FICA OASDI	FICA HI	FIT	SIT	SUTA	CIT	OTHER DEDUCTIONS	CK. NO.	NET PAID AMOUNT
YEAR-TO-DATE TOTAL			6240 00				62 40 0 00	3868 88	904 8	642 00	191 56	3 74	239 60	31 50		4654 24
1 10/9	80		1200 00				74 40 0 00	74 40	17 40	76 00	36 84	0 72	46 08		677	948 56
2																
3																
4																
5																
6																
QUARTER TOTAL																
YEARLY TOTAL																

Employee Earnings Record — RYAN, Jeri Mischa

DEPARTMENT	Plant
OCCUPATION	Electrician
WORKS IN (STATE)	PA
S.S. ACCOUNT NO.	000-00-1223
NAME—LAST	RYAN
FIRST	Jeri
MIDDLE	Mischa
W/H ALLOW.	N/A
FILING STATUS	MFJ
SALARY	$
WEEKLY RATE	$
HOURLY RATE	$ 18.00
OVERTIME RATE	$ 27.00
GROUP INSURANCE	$56,000—30¢/M
OTHER DEDUCTIONS INFORMATION — UNION DUES	$8 each pay

PAYDAY 20—	REGULAR EARNINGS HRS	RATE	AMOUNT	OVERTIME EARNINGS HRS	RATE	AMOUNT	CUMULATIVE EARNINGS	FICA OASDI	HI	FIT	SIT	SUTA	CIT	OTHER DEDUCTIONS	NET PAID CK. NO.	AMOUNT
YEAR-TO-DATE TOTAL			13287 50			1397 80	14685 30	910 49	212 94	1070 00	450 84	8 81	563 89	235 70		11232 63
1 10/9	80	18 00	1440 00				16125 30	89 28	20 88	44 00	44 21	0 86	55 29	8 00	678	1177 48
2																
3																
4																
5																
6																
QUARTER TOTAL																
YEARLY TOTAL																

Employee Earnings Record — SOKOWSKI, Thomas James

DEPARTMENT	Plant
OCCUPATION	Supervisor
WORKS IN (STATE)	PA
S.S. ACCOUNT NO.	000-00-8832
NAME—LAST	SOKOWSKI
FIRST	Thomas
MIDDLE	James
W/H ALLOW.	N/A
FILING STATUS	MFJ
SALARY	$ 1,025.00
WEEKLY RATE	$
HOURLY RATE	$ 25.63
OVERTIME RATE	$
GROUP INSURANCE	$80,000—30¢/M
OTHER DEDUCTIONS INFORMATION — UNION DUES	

PAYDAY 20—	REGULAR EARNINGS HRS	RATE	AMOUNT	OVERTIME EARNINGS HRS	RATE	AMOUNT	CUMULATIVE EARNINGS	FICA OASDI	HI	FIT	SIT	SUTA	CIT	OTHER DEDUCTIONS	NET PAID CK. NO.	AMOUNT
YEAR-TO-DATE TOTAL			16650 00				16650 00	1032 30	241 43	2002 00	511 16	9 99	639 33	94 50		12119 29
1 10/9	80		2050 00				18700 00	127 10	29 73	112 00	62 94	1 23	78 72		679	1638 28
2																
3																
4																
5																
6																
QUARTER TOTAL																
YEARLY TOTAL																

Employee 1

DEPARTMENT	Office
OCCUPATION	Accounting Trainee
WORKS IN (STATE)	PA
NAME—LAST / FIRST / MIDDLE	
S.S. ACCOUNT NO.	
W/H ALLOW.	N/A
FILING STATUS	S
GROUP INSURANCE	$42,000—30¢/M
SALARY	$
WEEKLY RATE	$
HOURLY RATE	$ 15.00
OVERTIME RATE	$ 22.50

20-- PAYDAY	Reg. HRS	RATE	Reg. AMOUNT	CUMULATIVE EARNINGS	OASDI	HI	FIT	SIT	SUTA	CIT	OTHER DEDUCTIONS	CK. NO.	NET PAID AMOUNT
YEAR-TO-DATE TOTAL			5550 00	5550 00	344 10	80 48	409 00	170 38	3 33	213 11			4297 20
1 10/9	72	15 00	1080 00	6630 00	66 96	15 66	62 00	33 16	0 65	41 47	32 40	680	860 10

Employee 2

DEPARTMENT	Office
OCCUPATION	Programmer
WORKS IN (STATE)	PA
NAME—LAST	WILLIAMS
FIRST	Ruth
MIDDLE	Virginia
S.S. ACCOUNT NO.	000-00-6741
W/H ALLOW.	N/A
FILING STATUS	S
GROUP INSURANCE	$48,000—30¢/M
SALARY	$ 2,650/mo.
WEEKLY RATE	$ 611.54
HOURLY RATE	$ 15.29
OVERTIME RATE	$ 22.94

20-- PAYDAY	Reg. HRS	RATE	Reg. AMOUNT	CUMULATIVE EARNINGS	OASDI	HI	FIT	SIT	SUTA	CIT	OTHER DEDUCTIONS	CK. NO.	NET PAID AMOUNT
YEAR-TO-DATE TOTAL			10260 00	10260 00	636 12	148 77	1606 00	314 98	6 16	393 96			7094 61
1 10/9	80		1223 08	11483 08	75 83	17 73	79 00	37 55	0 73	46 96	59 40	681	965 28

Employee Earnings Record (Left)

DEPARTMENT | OCCUPATION | WORKS IN (STATE) | S.S. ACCOUNT NO. | NAME—LAST | FIRST | MIDDLE

GROUP INSURANCE | OTHER DEDUCTIONS INFORMATION — UNION DUES — OTHER | SALARY $ | WEEKLY RATE $ | HOURLY RATE $ | OVERTIME RATE $ | W/H ALLOW. | FILING STATUS

20 ___ PAYDAY	REGULAR EARNINGS		OVERTIME EARNINGS			CUMULATIVE EARNINGS	DEDUCTIONS							NET PAID	
	HRS.	RATE	AMOUNT	HRS.	RATE	AMOUNT		FICA OASDI	FICA HI	FIT	SIT	SUTA	CIT	OTHER DEDUCTIONS	CK. NO.	AMOUNT
YEAR-TO-DATE TOTAL																
1																
2																
3																
4																
5																
6																
QUARTER TOTAL																
YEARLY TOTAL																

Employee Earnings Record (Right)

DEPARTMENT | OCCUPATION | WORKS IN (STATE) | S.S. ACCOUNT NO. | NAME—LAST | FIRST | MIDDLE

GROUP INSURANCE | OTHER DEDUCTIONS INFORMATION — UNION DUES — OTHER | SALARY $ | WEEKLY RATE $ | HOURLY RATE $ | OVERTIME RATE $ | W/H ALLOW. | FILING STATUS

20 ___ PAYDAY	REGULAR EARNINGS		OVERTIME EARNINGS			CUMULATIVE EARNINGS	DEDUCTIONS							NET PAID	
	HRS.	RATE	AMOUNT	HRS.	RATE	AMOUNT		FICA OASDI	FICA HI	FIT	SIT	SUTA	CIT	OTHER DEDUCTIONS	CK. NO.	AMOUNT
YEAR-TO-DATE TOTAL																
1																
2																
3																
4																
5																
6																
QUARTER TOTAL																
YEARLY TOTAL																

Employee Earnings Record (Form 1)

DEPARTMENT	OCCUPATION	WORKS IN (STATE)	S.S. ACCOUNT NO.	NAME—LAST	FIRST	MIDDLE

OTHER DEDUCTIONS INFORMATION

GROUP INSURANCE				SALARY	$	FILING STATUS
OTHER		UNION DUES		WEEKLY RATE	$	W/H ALLOW.
				HOURLY RATE	$	
				OVERTIME RATE	$	

20 __ PAYDAY	REGULAR EARNINGS			OVERTIME EARNINGS			CUMULATIVE EARNINGS	DEDUCTIONS								NET PAID	
	HRS.	RATE	AMOUNT	HRS.	RATE	AMOUNT		OASDI	HI	FIT	SIT	SUTA	CIT	OTHER DEDUCTIONS	CK. NO.	AMOUNT
								FICA									

YEAR-TO-DATE TOTAL

1
2
3
4
5
6

QUARTER TOTAL

YEARLY TOTAL

Employee Earnings Record (Form 2)

DEPARTMENT	OCCUPATION	WORKS IN (STATE)	S.S. ACCOUNT NO.	NAME—LAST	FIRST	MIDDLE

OTHER DEDUCTIONS INFORMATION

GROUP INSURANCE				SALARY	$	FILING STATUS
OTHER		UNION DUES		WEEKLY RATE	$	W/H ALLOW.
				HOURLY RATE	$	
				OVERTIME RATE	$	

20 __ PAYDAY	REGULAR EARNINGS			OVERTIME EARNINGS			CUMULATIVE EARNINGS	DEDUCTIONS								NET PAID	
	HRS.	RATE	AMOUNT	HRS.	RATE	AMOUNT		OASDI	HI	FIT	SIT	SUTA	CIT	OTHER DEDUCTIONS	CK. NO.	AMOUNT
								FICA									

YEAR-TO-DATE TOTAL

1
2
3
4
5
6

QUARTER TOTAL

YEARLY TOTAL

Transaction No. 9

FEDERAL DEPOSIT INFORMATION WORKSHEET

Employer
Identification Number   _____   Name   _____

Month Tax Year Ends   _____   Amount of Deposit   _____

Type of Tax (Form)   _____   Tax Period   _____

Address   _____   Phone Number   _____

City, State, Zip   _____

Transaction No. 22

FEDERAL DEPOSIT INFORMATION WORKSHEET

Employer
Identification Number   _____   Name   _____

Month Tax Year Ends   _____   Amount of Deposit   _____

Type of Tax (Form)   _____   Tax Period   _____

Address   _____   Phone Number   _____

City, State, Zip   _____

Transaction No. 30

FEDERAL DEPOSIT INFORMATION WORKSHEET

Employer
Identification Number   _____   Name   _____

Month Tax Year Ends   _____   Amount of Deposit   _____

Type of Tax (Form)   _____   Tax Period   _____

Address   _____   Phone Number   _____

City, State, Zip   _____

Transaction No. 33

FEDERAL DEPOSIT INFORMATION WORKSHEET

Employer
Identification Number   _____   Name   _____

Month Tax Year Ends   _____   Amount of Deposit   _____

Type of Tax (Form)   _____   Tax Period   _____

Address   _____   Phone Number   _____

City, State, Zip   _____

Transaction No. 2

STATE FILING INFORMATION WORKSHEET

Company Name _____   Payment Frequency _____

Employer Account # _____   Gross Compensation _____

Employer ID # _____   PA Withholding Tax _____

Employer Password _____   Credits _____

Quarter Ending Date _____   Interest _____

Telephone Number _____   Payment _____

Transaction No. 4

STATE FILING INFORMATION WORKSHEET

Company Name _____   Payment Frequency _____

Employer Account # _____   Gross Compensation _____

Employer ID # _____   PA Withholding Tax _____

Employer Password _____   Credits _____

Quarter Ending Date _____   Interest _____

Telephone Number _____   Payment _____

Transaction No. 12

STATE FILING INFORMATION WORKSHEET

Company Name _____   Payment Frequency _____

Employer Account # _____   Gross Compensation _____

Employer ID # _____   PA Withholding Tax _____

Employer Password _____   Credits _____

Quarter Ending Date _____   Interest _____

Telephone Number _____   Payment _____

Transaction No. 16

STATE FILING INFORMATION WORKSHEET

Company Name _____	Payment Frequency _____
Employer Account # _____	Gross Compensation _____
Employer ID # _____	PA Withholding Tax _____
Employer Password _____	Credits _____
Quarter Ending Date _____	Interest _____
Telephone Number _____	Payment _____

Transaction No. 24

STATE FILING INFORMATION WORKSHEET

Company Name _____	Payment Frequency _____
Employer Account # _____	Gross Compensation _____
Employer ID # _____	PA Withholding Tax _____
Employer Password _____	Credits _____
Quarter Ending Date _____	Interest _____
Telephone Number _____	Payment _____

Transaction No. 28

STATE FILING INFORMATION WORKSHEET

Company Name _____	Payment Frequency _____
Employer Account # _____	Gross Compensation _____
Employer ID # _____	PA Withholding Tax _____
Employer Password _____	Credits _____
Quarter Ending Date _____	Interest _____
Telephone Number _____	Payment _____

Transaction No. 10

Monthly Wage Tax

GLO-BRITE PAINT COMPANY
2215 SALVADOR STREET
PHILADELPHIA, PA 19175-0682

Signature:_____
I hereby certify that I have examined this return
and that it is correct to the best of my knowledge.

Phone #:_____

Account #: **0001855**   From: **10/01**

Tax Type: **01**   To: **10/31**

Period/Yr: **10/—**   Due Date: **11/15**

Philadelphia Department of Revenue
P.O. Box 8040
Philadelphia, PA 19101-8040

1. TAX DUE PER WORKSHEET, *Line 8*

2. INTEREST AND PENALTY

3. TOTAL DUE (LINE 1 & 2)

Make checks payable to:
CITY OF PHILADELPHIA

Source: Philadelphia Department of Revenue.

Transaction No. 23

Monthly Wage Tax

GLO-BRITE PAINT COMPANY
2215 SALVADOR STREET
PHILADELPHIA, PA 19175-0682

Account #: **0001855**   From: **11/01**

Tax Type: **01**   To: **11/30**

Period/Yr: **11/—**   Due Date: **12/15**

Signature: _____
I hereby certify that I have examined this return
and that it is correct to the best of my knowledge.

Phone #: _____

Philadelphia Department of Revenue
P.O. Box 8040
Philadelphia, PA 19101-8040

1. TAX DUE PER WORKSHEET, *Line 8*

2. INTEREST AND PENALTY

3. TOTAL DUE (LINE 1 & 2)

Make checks payable to:
CITY OF PHILADELPHIA

Source: Philadelphia Department of Revenue.

Transaction No. 31

Monthly Wage Tax

GLO-BRITE PAINT COMPANY
2215 SALVADOR STREET
PHILADELPHIA, PA 19175-0682

Account #: **0001855**   From: **12/01**

Tax Type: **01**   To: **12/31**

Period/Yr: **12/—**   Due Date: **1/15**

Signature: _____
I hereby certify that I have examined this return
and that it is correct to the best of my knowledge.

Phone #: _____

Philadelphia Department of Revenue
P.O. Box 8040
Philadelphia, PA 19101-8040

1. TAX DUE PER WORKSHEET, *Line 8*

2. INTEREST AND PENALTY

3. TOTAL DUE (LINE 1 & 2)

Make checks payable to:
CITY OF PHILADELPHIA

Source: Philadelphia Department of Revenue.

Transaction No. 40

PA Employer's Quarterly Reconciliation Worksheet

Company Name _____

Account Number _____

ID # _____

Telephone # _____

Quarter Ending Date _____

Record of PA Withholding Tax:

1st half of month _____

2nd half of month _____

1st half of month _____

2nd half of month _____

1st half of month _____

2nd half of month _____

TOTAL _____

1. Total Compensation _____

2. Total PA W/H Tax _____

3. Total Deposits/Quarter _____

4. Tax Due _____

Transaction No. 41

CITY OF PHILADELPHIA
ANNUAL RECONCILIATION OF
20-- EMPLOYER WAGE TAX

5 0 1 3

DUE DATE: FEBRUARY 28, 20--

City Account Number

0	0	0	1	8	5	5

┌─ Taxpayer Name and Address ─────────────┐

GLO-BRITE PAINT COMPANY

2215 Salvador Street
Philadelphia, PA 19175-0682

└──┘

Federal Identification Number

0	0	–	0	0	0	0	6	6	0

If your business terminated in 20--, enter the
termination date **AND** file a CHANGE FORM.

m	m	–	d	d	–	y	y	y	y

YOU MUST USE THE CHANGE FORM TO REPORT A
CHANGE OF ADDRESS OR TO CANCEL THIS ACCOUNT.

If this is an amended return place an "X" here:

A. Enter the number of Philadelphia Residents for whom wage tax was remitted for the pay period including
March 12, 20--..A.

B. Enter the number of **nonresidents** (employees living outside Philadelphia city limits) for whom wage tax
was remitted for the pay period including March 12, 20--..B.

C. Total number of employees **for all company locations** reported on the Employer's Federal Quarterly
Tax Return for the first quarter of 20-- (for the pay period including March 12, 20--).........................C.

D. Number of employees working **at company locations within Philadelphia city limits**, for the pay period
including March 12, 20--...D.

1. Gross Compensation per W-2 forms for all employees...1.   .00

2. Non-Taxable Gross Compensation included in Line 1.
(Paid to nonresidents working outside of Philadelphia)..2.   .00

3. Gross Compensation per W-2 forms on which Philadelphia Wage Tax was
withheld or due (Line 1 minus Line 2)..3.   .00

4. **Taxable Gross Compensation paid to residents of Philadelphia**
in 20- -..4.   .00

5. Tax Due (Line 4 times .038398)..5.   .00

6. **Taxable Gross Compensation paid to nonresidents of Philadelphia**
in 20- -..6.   .00

7. Tax Due (Line 6 times .034481)..7.   .00

8. **Total Tax Due** (Add Lines 5 and 7)..8.   .00

9. **Tax previously paid for 20--**...9.   .00

10. **ADDITIONAL TAX DUE** If Line 8 is greater than Line 9, enter the amount here....................10.   .00

11. **TAX OVERPAID** If Line 9 is greater than Line 8, enter the amount here.
See instructions for filing a Refund Petition...11.   .00

Under penalties of perjury, as set forth in 18 PA C.S. §§ 4902-4903 as amended, I swear that I have reviewed this return
and accompanying statements and schedules, and to the best of my knowledge and belief, they are true and complete.

Taxpayer Signature_____ Date_____ Phone #_____

Preparer Signature_____ Date_____ Phone #_____

5013 Internet 11-7-2013

Transaction No. 32

Form **941 for 20--:** **Employer's QUARTERLY Federal Tax Return**
(Rev. March 2022)
Department of the Treasury — Internal Revenue Service

OMB No. 1545-0029

Employer identification number (EIN) `0 0 – 0 0 0 0 6 6 0`

Name *(not your trade name)* GLO-BRITE PAINT COMPANY

Trade name *(if any)*

Address 2215 SALVADOR STREET
Number   Street   Suite or room number

PHILADELPHIA   PA   19175-0682
City   State ZIP code

Foreign country name   Foreign province/county   Foreign postal code

Report for this Quarter of 20--
(Check one.)

☐ **1:** January, February, March

☐ **2:** April, May, June

☐ **3:** July, August, September

☐ **4:** October, November, December

Go to *www.irs.gov/Form941* for
instructions and the latest information.

Read the separate instructions before you complete Form 941. Type or print within the boxes.

Part 1: Answer these questions for this quarter.

1 Number of employees who received wages, tips, or other compensation for the pay period
   including: *Mar. 12 (Quarter 1)* . . . . **1** _____

2 Wages, tips, and other compensation . . . . **2** _____

3 Federal income tax withheld from wages, tips, and other compensation . . . . . . **3** _____

4 If no wages, tips, and other compensation are subject to social security or Medicare tax   ☐ Check and go to line 6.

	Column 1		Column 2	
5a Taxable social security wages* . .	_____	× 0.124 =	_____	*Include taxable qualified sick and family leave wages paid in 2022 for leave taken after March 31, 2021, and before October 1, 2021, on line 5a. Use lines 5a(i) and 5a(ii) only for taxable qualified sick and family leave wages paid in 2022 for leave taken after March 31, 2020, and before April 1, 2021.*
5a (i) Qualified sick leave wages* .	_____	× 0.062 =	_____	
5a (ii) Qualified family leave wages* .	_____	× 0.062 =	_____	
5b Taxable social security tips . . .	_____	× 0.124 =	_____	
5c Taxable Medicare wages & tips . .	_____	× 0.029 =	_____	
5d Taxable wages & tips subject to Additional Medicare Tax withholding	_____	× 0.009 =	_____	

5e Total social security and Medicare taxes. Add Column 2 from lines 5a, 5a(i), 5a(ii), 5b, 5c, and 5d   **5e** _____

5f Section 3121(q) Notice and Demand—Tax due on unreported tips *(see instructions)* . . **5f** _____

6 Total taxes before adjustments. Add lines 3, 5e, and 5f . . . . **6** _____

7 Current quarter's adjustment for fractions of cents . . . . **7** _____

8 Current quarter's adjustment for sick pay . . . . **8** _____

9 Current quarter's adjustments for tips and group-term life insurance . . . . . . **9** _____

10 Total taxes after adjustments. Combine lines 6 through 9 . . . . **10** _____

11a Qualified small business payroll tax credit for increasing research activities. Attach Form 8974   **11a** _____

11b Nonrefundable portion of credit for qualified sick and family leave wages for leave taken
    before April 1, 2021 . . . . **11b** _____

11c Reserved for future use . . . . **11c** _____

▶ You MUST complete all three pages of Form 941 and SIGN it.   Next ▶

For Privacy Act and Paperwork Reduction Act Notice, see the back of the Payment Voucher.   Cat. No. 17001Z   Form **941** (Rev. 3-2022)

Transaction No. 32 (continued)

Name *(not your trade name)*	Employer identification number (EIN)
GLO-BRITE PAINT COMPANY	00-0000660

Part 1:   Answer these questions for this quarter. *(continued)*

11d   Nonrefundable portion of credit for qualified sick and family leave wages for leave taken after March 31, 2021, and before October 1, 2021   . . . .   **11d** [.   ]

11e   Nonrefundable portion of COBRA premium assistance credit (see instructions for applicable quarter) . . . .   **11e** [.   ]

11f   Number of individuals provided COBRA premium assistance   [   ]

11g   **Total nonrefundable credits.** Add lines 11a, 11b, 11d, and 11e   . . . .   **11g** [.   ]

12   **Total taxes after adjustments and nonrefundable credits.** Subtract line 11g from line 10   .   **12** [.   ]

13a   Total deposits for this quarter, including overpayment applied from a prior quarter and overpayments applied from Form 941-X, 941-X (PR), 944-X, or 944-X (SP) filed in the current quarter   **13a** [.   ]

13b   Reserved for future use   . . . .   **13b** [.   ]

13c   Refundable portion of credit for qualified sick and family leave wages for leave taken before April 1, 2021   . . . .   **13c** [.   ]

13d   Reserved for future use   . . . .   **13d** [.   ]

13e   Refundable portion of credit for qualified sick and family leave wages for leave taken after March 31, 2021, and before October 1, 2021 . . . .   **13e** [.   ]

13f   Refundable portion of COBRA premium assistance credit (see instructions for applicable quarter)   . . . .   **13f** [.   ]

13g   **Total deposits and refundable credits.** Add lines 13a, 13c, 13e, and 13f   . . . .   **13g** [.   ]

13h   Reserved for future use   . . . .   **13h** [.   ]

13i   Reserved for future use   . . . .   **13i** [.   ]

14   **Balance due.** If line 12 is more than line 13g, enter the difference and see instructions   . . .   **14** [.   ]

15   **Overpayment.** If line 13g is more than line 12, enter the difference   [.   ]   Check one: ☐ Apply to next return.   ☐ Send a refund.

Part 2:   Tell us about your deposit schedule and tax liability for this quarter.

If you're unsure about whether you're a monthly schedule depositor or a semiweekly schedule depositor, see section 11 of Pub. 15.

16   Check one: ☐   Line 12 on this return is less than $2,500 or line 12 on the return for the prior quarter was less than $2,500, and you didn't incur a $100,000 next-day deposit obligation during the current quarter. If line 12 for the prior quarter was less than $2,500 but line 12 on this return is $100,000 or more, you must provide a record of your federal tax liability. If you're a monthly schedule depositor, complete the deposit schedule below; if you're a semiweekly schedule depositor, attach Schedule B (Form 941). Go to Part 3.

☐   **You were a monthly schedule depositor for the entire quarter.** Enter your tax liability for each month and total liability for the quarter, then go to Part 3.

Tax liability: Month 1   [.   ]

Month 2   [.   ]

Month 3   [.   ]

Total liability for quarter   [.   ]   Total must equal line 12.

☐   **You were a semiweekly schedule depositor for any part of this quarter.** Complete Schedule B (Form 941), Report of Tax Liability for Semiweekly Schedule Depositors, and attach it to Form 941. Go to Part 3.

▶ **You MUST complete all three pages of Form 941 and SIGN it.**   Next ▶

Form **941** (Rev. 3-2022)

Transaction No. 32 (continued)

Name *(not your trade name)*	Employer identification number (EIN)
GLO-BRITE PAINT COMPANY	00-0000660

Part 3: Tell us about your business. If a question does NOT apply to your business, leave it blank.

17 If your business has closed or you stopped paying wages . . . . ☐ Check here, and

enter the final date you paid wages [/ /] ; also attach a statement to your return. See instructions.

18 If you're a seasonal employer and you don't have to file a return for every quarter of the year . . . ☐ Check here.

19 Qualified health plan expenses allocable to qualified sick leave wages for leave taken before April 1, 2021   19 [.]

20 Qualified health plan expenses allocable to qualified family leave wages for leave taken before April 1, 2021   20 [.]

21 Reserved for future use . . . .   21 [.]

22 Reserved for future use . . . .   22 [.]

23 Qualified sick leave wages for leave taken after March 31, 2021, and before October 1, 2021   23 [.]

24 Qualified health plan expenses allocable to qualified sick leave wages reported on line 23   24 [.]

25 Amounts under certain collectively bargained agreements allocable to qualified sick leave wages reported on line 23 . . . .   25 [.]

26 Qualified family leave wages for leave taken after March 31, 2021, and before October 1, 2021   26 [.]

27 Qualified health plan expenses allocable to qualified family leave wages reported on line 26   27 [.]

28 Amounts under certain collectively bargained agreements allocable to qualified family leave wages reported on line 26 . . . .   28 [.]

Part 4: May we speak with your third-party designee?

Do you want to allow an employee, a paid tax preparer, or another person to discuss this return with the IRS? See the instructions for details.

☐ Yes. Designee's name and phone number [   ] [   ]

Select a 5-digit personal identification number (PIN) to use when talking to the IRS. ☐ ☐ ☐ ☐ ☐

☐ No.

Part 5: Sign here. You MUST complete all three pages of Form 941 and SIGN it.

Under penalties of perjury, I declare that I have examined this return, including accompanying schedules and statements, and to the best of my knowledge and belief, it is true, correct, and complete. Declaration of preparer (other than taxpayer) is based on all information of which preparer has any knowledge.

X   **Sign your name here** [   ]   Print your name here [   ]
Print your title here [   ]

Date [/ /]   Best daytime phone [   ]

Paid Preparer Use Only   Check if you're self-employed . . . ☐

Preparer's name	[ ]	PTIN	[ ]
Preparer's signature	[ ]	Date	[/ /]
Firm's name (or yours if self-employed)	[ ]	EIN	[ ]
Address	[ ]	Phone	[ ]
City	[ ] State [ ]	ZIP code	[ ]

Transaction No. 33

Form **940 for 20--:** **Employer's Annual Federal Unemployment (FUTA) Tax Return**
Department of the Treasury — Internal Revenue Service

OMB No. 1545-0028

Employer identification number (EIN)

`0 0 — 0 0 0 0 6 6 0`

Name *(not your trade name)* GLO-BRITE PAINT COMPANY

Trade name *(if any)*

Address 2215 SALVADOR STREET
Number   Street   Suite or room number

PHILADELPHIA   PA   19175-0682
City   State   ZIP code

Foreign country name   Foreign province/county   Foreign postal code

Type of Return
(Check all that apply.)

☐ **a.** Amended

☐ **b.** Successor employer

☐ **c.** No payments to employees in 20--

☐ **d.** Final: Business closed or stopped paying wages

Go to *www.irs.gov/Form940* for instructions and the latest information.

Read the separate instructions before you complete this form. Please type or print within the boxes.

Part 1: Tell us about your return. If any line does NOT apply, leave it blank. See instructions before completing Part 1.

1a If you had to pay state unemployment tax in one state only, enter the state abbreviation . **1a**

1b If you had to pay state unemployment tax in more than one state, you are a multi-state employer . . . . **1b** ☐ Check here. Complete Schedule A (Form 940).

2 If you paid wages in a state that is subject to CREDIT REDUCTION . . . . **2** ☐ Check here. Complete Schedule A (Form 940).

Part 2: Determine your FUTA tax before adjustments. If any line does NOT apply, leave it blank.

3 Total payments to all employees **3**

4 Payments exempt from FUTA tax **4**

Check all that apply: **4a** ☐ Fringe benefits   **4c** ☐ Retirement/Pension   **4e** ☐ Other
4b ☐ Group-term life insurance   **4d** ☐ Dependent care

5 Total of payments made to each employee in excess of $7,000 . . . . **5**

6 **Subtotal** (line 4 + line 5 = line 6) **6**

7 **Total taxable FUTA wages** (line 3 – line 6 = line 7). See instructions . **7**

8 **FUTA tax before adjustments** (line 7 x 0.006 = line 8) **8**

Part 3: Determine your adjustments. If any line does NOT apply, leave it blank.

9 If ALL of the taxable FUTA wages you paid were excluded from state unemployment tax, multiply line 7 by 0.054 (line 7 × 0.054 = line 9). Go to line 12 . . . . **9**

10 If SOME of the taxable FUTA wages you paid were excluded from state unemployment tax, OR you paid ANY state unemployment tax late (after the due date for filing Form 940), complete the worksheet in the instructions. Enter the amount from line 7 of the worksheet . . **10**

11 If credit reduction applies, enter the total from Schedule A (Form 940) **11**

Part 4: Determine your FUTA tax and balance due or overpayment. If any line does NOT apply, leave it blank.

12 **Total FUTA tax after adjustments** (lines 8 + 9 + 10 + 11 = line 12) **12**

13 FUTA tax deposited for the year, including any overpayment applied from a prior year . **13**

14 **Balance due.** If line 12 is more than line 13, enter the excess on line 14.
• If line 14 is more than $500, you must deposit your tax.
• If line 14 is $500 or less, you may pay with this return. See instructions **14**

15 **Overpayment.** If line 13 is more than line 12, enter the excess on line 15 and check a box below **15**

▶ You **MUST** complete both pages of this form and **SIGN** it.   Check one: ☐ Apply to next return.   ☐ Send a refund.

Next ▶

For Privacy Act and Paperwork Reduction Act Notice, see the back of the Payment Voucher.   Cat. No. 11234O   Form **940** (2021)

Transaction No. 33 (concluded)

Name *(not your trade name)*	Employer identification number (EIN)
GLO-BRITE PAINT COMPANY	00-0000660

Part 5: Report your FUTA tax liability by quarter only if line 12 is more than $500. If not, go to Part 6.

16 Report the amount of your FUTA tax liability for each quarter; do NOT enter the amount you deposited. If you had no liability for a quarter, leave the line blank.

16a **1st quarter** (January 1 – March 31) **16a**

16b **2nd quarter** (April 1 – June 30) **16b**

16c **3rd quarter** (July 1 – September 30) **16c**

16d **4th quarter** (October 1 – December 31) **16d**

17 **Total tax liability for the year** (lines 16a + 16b + 16c + 16d = line 17) **17**   Total must equal line 12.

Part 6: May we speak with your third-party designee?

Do you want to allow an employee, a paid tax preparer, or another person to discuss this return with the IRS? See the instructions for details.

☐ **Yes.** Designee's name and phone number

Select a 5-digit personal identification number (PIN) to use when talking to the IRS.

☐ **No.**

Part 7: Sign here. You MUST complete both pages of this form and SIGN it.

Under penalties of perjury, I declare that I have examined this return, including accompanying schedules and statements, and to the best of my knowledge and belief, it is true, correct, and complete, and that no part of any payment made to a state unemployment fund claimed as a credit was, or is to be, deducted from the payments made to employees. Declaration of preparer (other than taxpayer) is based on all information of which preparer has any knowledge.

✗ **Sign your name here**

Print your name here

Print your title here

Date   /   /

Best daytime phone

Paid Preparer Use Only

Check if you are self-employed ☐

Preparer's name		PTIN
Preparer's signature		Date / /
Firm's name (or yours if self-employed)		EIN
Address		Phone
City	State	ZIP code

Source: Internal Revenue Service.

Transaction No. 34

PA Form UC-2 REV 07-21, Employer's Report for Unemployment Compensation

Read Instructions – Answer Each Item

W

EXAMINED BY: _____

QTR./YEAR

DUE DATE 01/31/20--

1ST MONTH   2ND MONTH   3RD MONTH

4/20 - -

◄ DETACH HERE

1.TOTAL COVERED EMPLOYEES IN PAY PERIOD INCL. 12TH OF MONTH

Signature certifies that the information contained herein is true and correct to the best of the signer's knowledge.

10. SIGN HERE-DO NOT PRINT

FOR DEPT. USE

2.GROSS WAGES

TITLE _____ DATE _____ PHONE # _____

11. FILED ☐PAPER UC-2A ☐INTERNET UC-2A

12. FEDERAL IDENTIFICATION NUMBER _____

3.EMPLOYEE CONTRI-BUTIONS (0.06%)

4.TAXABLE WAGES FOR EMPLOYER CONTRIBUTIONS

EMPLOYER'S CONTRIBUTION RATE	EMPLOYER'S ACCT. NO.	CHECK DIGIT
EMPLOYER'S CONTRIBUTION RATE ▷ 3.6890%	000-0-3300 -	1

5.EMPLOYER CONTRI-BUTIONS DUE (RATE X ITEM 4)

6.TOTAL CONTRI-BUTIONS DUE (ITEMS 3 + 5)

7.INTEREST DUE SEE INSTRUCTIONS

8.PENALTY DUE SEE INSTRUCTIONS

GLO-BRITE PAINT COMPANY
2215 SALVADOR STREET
PHILADELPHIA, PA 19175-0682

9.TOTAL REMITTANCE (ITEMS 6 + 7 + 8)

$

MAKE CHECKS PAYABLE TO: PA UC FUND

SUBJECTIVITY DATE   REPORT DELINQUENT DATE

Employer name and address
Make any corrections on Form UC-2B

---

pennsylvania
DEPARTMENT OF LABOR & INDUSTRY

PA Form UC-2A, Employer's Quarterly
Report of Wages Paid to Each Employee

See instructions on separate sheet. Information MUST be typewritten or printed in BLACK ink. Do NOT use commas (,) or dollar signs ($).
If typed, disregard vertical bars and type a consecutive string of characters. If hand printed, print in CAPS and within the boxes as below:

| SAMPLE Typed: | 1 2 3 4 5 6 . 0 0 | SAMPLE Handwritten: | 1 2 3 4 5 6 . 0 0 | SAMPLE Filled-in: | ➜ ● |

Employer name (make corrections on Form UC-2B)	Employer PA UC account no.	Check digit	Quarter and year Q/ YYYY	Quarter ending date MM / DD / YYYY
Glo-Brite Paint Company	000-0-3300		4/20--	12/31/20--

1. Name and telephone number of preparer

2. Total number of pages in this report

3. Total number of employees listed in item 8 on all pages of Form UC-2A

4. Plant number (if approved)

5. Gross wages, MUST agree with item 2 on UC-2 and the sum of item 11 on all pages of Form UC-2A

6. Fill in this circle if you would like the Department to preprint your employee's names & SSNs on Form UC-2A next quarter ➜ ◉

7. Employee's Social Security Number	8. Employee's name FI MI LAST	9. Gross wages paid this qtr Example: 123456.00	10. Credit Weeks

List any additional employees on continuation sheets in the required format (see instructions).

11. Total gross wages for this page: ➜
12. Total number of employees for this page _____

UC-2A REV 07-21

13. Page 1 of 1

Source: PA Department of Labor & Industry.

Transaction No. 8

22222	Void ☐	**a** Employee's social security number 000-00-6741	**For Official Use Only ▶** OMB No. 1545-0008	
b Employer identification number (EIN) 00-0000660			**1** Wages, tips, other compensation 15993.33	**2** Federal income tax withheld 2022.00
c Employer's name, address, and ZIP code Glo-Brite Paint Company 2215 Salvador Street Philadelphia, PA 19175-0682			**3** Social security wages 15993.33	**4** Social security tax withheld 991.59
			5 Medicare wages and tips 15993.33	**6** Medicare tax withheld 231.89
			7 Social security tips	**8** Allocated tips
d Control number			**9**	**10** Dependent care benefits
e Employee's first name and initial Ruth V.	Last name Williams	Suff.	**11** Nonqualified plans	**12a** See instructions for box 12
			13 Statutory employee ☐ Retirement plan ☐ Third-party sick pay ☐	**12b**
9433 STATE STREET PHILADELPHIA, PA 19149-0819			**14** Other PA SUI 9.59	**12c**
				12d
f Employee's address and ZIP code				

15 State	Employer's state ID number	**16** State wages, tips, etc.	**17** State income tax	**18** Local wages, tips, etc.	**19** Local income tax	**20** Locality name
PA	000-0-3300	15993.33	491.00	15993.33	614.10	PHILA.

Form **W-2** **Wage and Tax Statement**　20- -　Department of the Treasury—Internal Revenue Service

Copy A For Social Security Administration — Send this entire page with Form W-3 to the Social Security Administration; photocopies are **not** acceptable.

For Privacy Act and Paperwork Reduction Act Notice, see the separate instructions.

Cat. No. 10134D

Do Not Cut, Fold, or Staple Forms on This Page

Transaction No. 21

22222	Void ☐	**a** Employee's social security number	**For Official Use Only ▶** OMB No. 1545-0008	
b Employer identification number (EIN)			**1** Wages, tips, other compensation	**2** Federal income tax withheld
c Employer's name, address, and ZIP code			**3** Social security wages	**4** Social security tax withheld
			5 Medicare wages and tips	**6** Medicare tax withheld
			7 Social security tips	**8** Allocated tips
d Control number			**9**	**10** Dependent care benefits
e Employee's first name and initial	Last name	Suff.	**11** Nonqualified plans	**12a** See instructions for box 12
			13 Statutory employee ☐ Retirement plan ☐ Third-party sick pay ☐	**12b**
			14 Other	**12c**
				12d
f Employee's address and ZIP code				

15 State	Employer's state ID number	**16** State wages, tips, etc.	**17** State income tax	**18** Local wages, tips, etc.	**19** Local income tax	**20** Locality name

Form **W-2** **Wage and Tax Statement**　20- -　Department of the Treasury—Internal Revenue Service

Copy A For Social Security Administration — Send this entire page with Form W-3 to the Social Security Administration; photocopies are **not** acceptable.

For Privacy Act and Paperwork Reduction Act Notice, see the separate instructions.

Cat. No. 10134D

Do Not Cut, Fold, or Staple Forms on This Page

Transaction No. 35

22222	Void ☐	**a** Employee's social security number	**For Official Use Only ▶** OMB No. 1545-0008	
b Employer identification number (EIN)			**1** Wages, tips, other compensation	**2** Federal income tax withheld
c Employer's name, address, and ZIP code			**3** Social security wages	**4** Social security tax withheld
			5 Medicare wages and tips	**6** Medicare tax withheld
			7 Social security tips	**8** Allocated tips
d Control number			**9**	**10** Dependent care benefits
e Employee's first name and initial	Last name	Suff.	**11** Nonqualified plans	**12a** See instructions for box 12
			13 Statutory employee ☐ Retirement plan ☐ Third-party sick pay ☐	**12b**
			14 Other	**12c**
				12d
f Employee's address and ZIP code				

15 State Employer's state ID number	**16** State wages, tips, etc.	**17** State income tax	**18** Local wages, tips, etc.	**19** Local income tax	**20** Locality name

Form **W-2** **Wage and Tax Statement**   20 - -   Department of the Treasury—Internal Revenue Service

Copy A For Social Security Administration — Send this entire page with Form W-3 to the Social Security Administration; photocopies are **not** acceptable.

For Privacy Act and Paperwork Reduction Act Notice, see the separate instructions.

Cat. No. 10134D

Do Not Cut, Fold, or Staple Forms on This Page

22222	Void ☐	**a** Employee's social security number	**For Official Use Only ▶** OMB No. 1545-0008	
b Employer identification number (EIN)			**1** Wages, tips, other compensation	**2** Federal income tax withheld
c Employer's name, address, and ZIP code			**3** Social security wages	**4** Social security tax withheld
			5 Medicare wages and tips	**6** Medicare tax withheld
			7 Social security tips	**8** Allocated tips
d Control number			**9**	**10** Dependent care benefits
e Employee's first name and initial	Last name	Suff.	**11** Nonqualified plans	**12a** See instructions for box 12
			13 Statutory employee ☐ Retirement plan ☐ Third-party sick pay ☐	**12b**
			14 Other	**12c**
				12d
f Employee's address and ZIP code				

15 State Employer's state ID number	**16** State wages, tips, etc.	**17** State income tax	**18** Local wages, tips, etc.	**19** Local income tax	**20** Locality name

Form **W-2** **Wage and Tax Statement**   20 - -   Department of the Treasury—Internal Revenue Service

Copy A For Social Security Administration — Send this entire page with Form W-3 to the Social Security Administration; photocopies are **not** acceptable.

For Privacy Act and Paperwork Reduction Act Notice, see the separate instructions.

Cat. No. 10134D

Do Not Cut, Fold, or Staple Forms on This Page

Transaction No. 35 (continued)

22222 Void ☐	**a** Employee's social security number	**For Official Use Only ▶** OMB No. 1545-0008

b Employer identification number (EIN)	**1** Wages, tips, other compensation	**2** Federal income tax withheld

c Employer's name, address, and ZIP code	**3** Social security wages	**4** Social security tax withheld
	5 Medicare wages and tips	**6** Medicare tax withheld
	7 Social security tips	**8** Allocated tips

d Control number	**9**	**10** Dependent care benefits

e Employee's first name and initial · Last name · Suff.	**11** Nonqualified plans	**12a** See instructions for box 12
	13 Statutory employee ☐ Retirement plan ☐ Third-party sick pay ☐	**12b**
	14 Other	**12c**
		12d

f Employee's address and ZIP code

15 State · Employer's state ID number	**16** State wages, tips, etc.	**17** State income tax	**18** Local wages, tips, etc.	**19** Local income tax	**20** Locality name

Form **W-2** Wage and Tax Statement   20 - -

Department of the Treasury—Internal Revenue Service

Copy A For Social Security Administration — Send this entire page with Form W-3 to the Social Security Administration; photocopies are **not** acceptable.

For Privacy Act and Paperwork Reduction Act Notice, see the separate instructions.

Cat. No. 10134D

Do Not Cut, Fold, or Staple Forms on This Page

22222 Void ☐	**a** Employee's social security number	**For Official Use Only ▶** OMB No. 1545-0008

b Employer identification number (EIN)	**1** Wages, tips, other compensation	**2** Federal income tax withheld

c Employer's name, address, and ZIP code	**3** Social security wages	**4** Social security tax withheld
	5 Medicare wages and tips	**6** Medicare tax withheld
	7 Social security tips	**8** Allocated tips

d Control number	**9**	**10** Dependent care benefits

e Employee's first name and initial · Last name · Suff.	**11** Nonqualified plans	**12a** See instructions for box 12
	13 Statutory employee ☐ Retirement plan ☐ Third-party sick pay ☐	**12b**
	14 Other	**12c**
		12d

f Employee's address and ZIP code

15 State · Employer's state ID number	**16** State wages, tips, etc.	**17** State income tax	**18** Local wages, tips, etc.	**19** Local income tax	**20** Locality name

Form **W-2** Wage and Tax Statement   20 - -

Department of the Treasury—Internal Revenue Service

Copy A For Social Security Administration — Send this entire page with Form W-3 to the Social Security Administration; photocopies are **not** acceptable.

For Privacy Act and Paperwork Reduction Act Notice, see the separate instructions.

Cat. No. 10134D

Do Not Cut, Fold, or Staple Forms on This Page

Transaction No. 35 (continued)

22222	Void ☐	**a** Employee's social security number	For Official Use Only ▶ OMB No. 1545-0008	

b Employer identification number (EIN)	**1** Wages, tips, other compensation	**2** Federal income tax withheld
c Employer's name, address, and ZIP code	**3** Social security wages	**4** Social security tax withheld
	5 Medicare wages and tips	**6** Medicare tax withheld
	7 Social security tips	**8** Allocated tips
d Control number	**9**	**10** Dependent care benefits

e Employee's first name and initial	Last name	Suff.	**11** Nonqualified plans	**12a** See instructions for box 12
			13 Statutory employee ☐ Retirement plan ☐ Third-party sick pay ☐	**12b**
			14 Other	**12c**
				12d
f Employee's address and ZIP code				

15 State	Employer's state ID number	**16** State wages, tips, etc.	**17** State income tax	**18** Local wages, tips, etc.	**19** Local income tax	**20** Locality name

Form **W-2** **Wage and Tax Statement**   **20 - -**   Department of the Treasury—Internal Revenue Service

Copy A For Social Security Administration — Send this entire page with Form W-3 to the Social Security Administration; photocopies are **not** acceptable.

For Privacy Act and Paperwork Reduction Act Notice, see the separate instructions.

Cat. No. 10134D

Do Not Cut, Fold, or Staple Forms on This Page

22222	Void ☐	**a** Employee's social security number	For Official Use Only ▶ OMB No. 1545-0008	

b Employer identification number (EIN)	**1** Wages, tips, other compensation	**2** Federal income tax withheld
c Employer's name, address, and ZIP code	**3** Social security wages	**4** Social security tax withheld
	5 Medicare wages and tips	**6** Medicare tax withheld
	7 Social security tips	**8** Allocated tips
d Control number	**9**	**10** Dependent care benefits

e Employee's first name and initial	Last name	Suff.	**11** Nonqualified plans	**12a** See instructions for box 12
			13 Statutory employee ☐ Retirement plan ☐ Third-party sick pay ☐	**12b**
			14 Other	**12c**
				12d
f Employee's address and ZIP code				

15 State	Employer's state ID number	**16** State wages, tips, etc.	**17** State income tax	**18** Local wages, tips, etc.	**19** Local income tax	**20** Locality name

Form **W-2** **Wage and Tax Statement**   **20 - -**   Department of the Treasury—Internal Revenue Service

Copy A For Social Security Administration — Send this entire page with Form W-3 to the Social Security Administration; photocopies are **not** acceptable.

For Privacy Act and Paperwork Reduction Act Notice, see the separate instructions.

Cat. No. 10134D

Do Not Cut, Fold, or Staple Forms on This Page

Source: Internal Revenue Service.

Transaction No. 35 (continued)

22222	Void ☐	**a** Employee's social security number	**For Official Use Only ▶** OMB No. 1545-0008		
b Employer identification number (EIN)			**1** Wages, tips, other compensation		**2** Federal income tax withheld
c Employer's name, address, and ZIP code			**3** Social security wages		**4** Social security tax withheld
			5 Medicare wages and tips		**6** Medicare tax withheld
			7 Social security tips		**8** Allocated tips
d Control number			**9**		**10** Dependent care benefits
e Employee's first name and initial	Last name	Suff.	**11** Nonqualified plans		**12a** See instructions for box 12
			13 Statutory employee ☐ Retirement plan ☐ Third-party sick pay ☐		**12b**
			14 Other		**12c**
					12d
f Employee's address and ZIP code					

15 State Employer's state ID number	**16** State wages, tips, etc.	**17** State income tax	**18** Local wages, tips, etc.	**19** Local income tax	**20** Locality name

Form **W-2** **Wage and Tax Statement**   **20 - -**

Copy A For Social Security Administration — Send this entire page with
Form W-3 to the Social Security Administration; photocopies are **not** acceptable.

Department of the Treasury—Internal Revenue Service
**For Privacy Act and Paperwork Reduction
Act Notice, see the separate instructions.**
Cat. No. 10134D

Do Not Cut, Fold, or Staple Forms on This Page

22222	Void ☐	**a** Employee's social security number	**For Official Use Only ▶** OMB No. 1545-0008		
b Employer identification number (EIN)			**1** Wages, tips, other compensation		**2** Federal income tax withheld
c Employer's name, address, and ZIP code			**3** Social security wages		**4** Social security tax withheld
			5 Medicare wages and tips		**6** Medicare tax withheld
			7 Social security tips		**8** Allocated tips
d Control number			**9**		**10** Dependent care benefits
e Employee's first name and initial	Last name	Suff.	**11** Nonqualified plans		**12a** See instructions for box 12
			13 Statutory employee ☐ Retirement plan ☐ Third-party sick pay ☐		**12b**
			14 Other		**12c**
					12d
f Employee's address and ZIP code					

15 State Employer's state ID number	**16** State wages, tips, etc.	**17** State income tax	**18** Local wages, tips, etc.	**19** Local income tax	**20** Locality name

Form **W-2** **Wage and Tax Statement**   **20 - -**

Copy A For Social Security Administration — Send this entire page with
Form W-3 to the Social Security Administration; photocopies are **not** acceptable.

Department of the Treasury—Internal Revenue Service
**For Privacy Act and Paperwork Reduction
Act Notice, see the separate instructions.**
Cat. No. 10134D

Do Not Cut, Fold, or Staple Forms on This Page

Source: Internal Revenue Service.

Transaction No. 35 (concluded)

22222	Void ☐	**a** Employee's social security number	For Official Use Only ▶ OMB No. 1545-0008		
b Employer identification number (EIN)				**1** Wages, tips, other compensation	**2** Federal income tax withheld
c Employer's name, address, and ZIP code				**3** Social security wages	**4** Social security tax withheld
				5 Medicare wages and tips	**6** Medicare tax withheld
				7 Social security tips	**8** Allocated tips
d Control number				**9**	**10** Dependent care benefits
e Employee's first name and initial Last name Suff.				**11** Nonqualified plans	**12a** See instructions for box 12
				13 Statutory employee Retirement plan Third-party sick pay	**12b**
				14 Other	**12c**
					12d
f Employee's address and ZIP code					
15 State Employer's state ID number	**16** State wages, tips, etc.	**17** State income tax	**18** Local wages, tips, etc.	**19** Local income tax	**20** Locality name

Form **W-2** **Wage and Tax Statement**   **20 - -**   Department of the Treasury—Internal Revenue Service

Copy A For Social Security Administration — Send this entire page with Form W-3 to the Social Security Administration; photocopies are **not** acceptable.

For Privacy Act and Paperwork Reduction Act Notice, see the separate instructions.

Cat. No. 10134D

Do Not Cut, Fold, or Staple Forms on This Page

22222	Void ☐	**a** Employee's social security number	For Official Use Only ▶ OMB No. 1545-0008		
b Employer identification number (EIN)				**1** Wages, tips, other compensation	**2** Federal income tax withheld
c Employer's name, address, and ZIP code				**3** Social security wages	**4** Social security tax withheld
				5 Medicare wages and tips	**6** Medicare tax withheld
				7 Social security tips	**8** Allocated tips
d Control number				**9**	**10** Dependent care benefits
e Employee's first name and initial Last name Suff.				**11** Nonqualified plans	**12a** See instructions for box 12
				13 Statutory employee Retirement plan Third-party sick pay	**12b**
				14 Other	**12c**
					12d
f Employee's address and ZIP code					
15 State Employer's state ID number	**16** State wages, tips, etc.	**17** State income tax	**18** Local wages, tips, etc.	**19** Local income tax	**20** Locality name

Form **W-2** **Wage and Tax Statement**   **20 - -**   Department of the Treasury—Internal Revenue Service

Copy A For Social Security Administration — Send this entire page with Form W-3 to the Social Security Administration; photocopies are **not** acceptable.

For Privacy Act and Paperwork Reduction Act Notice, see the separate instructions.

Cat. No. 10134D

Do Not Cut, Fold, or Staple Forms on This Page

Source: Internal Revenue Service.

Transaction No. 36

DO NOT STAPLE

a Control number: 33333	For Official Use Only ▶ OMB No. 1545-0008		

| b **Kind of Payer** (Check one) ▶ | 941 ☐ Military ☐ 943 ☐ 944 ☐ CT-1 ☐ Hshld. emp. ☐ Medicare govt. emp. ☐ | **Kind of Employer** (Check one) ▶ | None apply ☐ 501c non-govt. ☐ State/local non-501c ☐ State/local 501c ☐ Federal govt. ☐ | Third-party sick pay ☐ (Check if applicable) |

c Total number of Forms W-2	d Establishment number	1 Wages, tips, other compensation	2 Federal income tax withheld
e Employer identification number (EIN)		3 Social security wages	4 Social security tax withheld
f Employer's name		5 Medicare wages and tips	6 Medicare tax withheld
		7 Social security tips	8 Allocated tips
		9	10 Dependent care benefits
		11 Nonqualified plans	12a Deferred compensation
g Employer's address and ZIP code			
h Other EIN used this year		13 For third-party sick pay use only	12b
15 State Employer's state ID number		14 Income tax withheld by payer of third-party sick pay	
16 State wages, tips, etc.	17 State income tax	18 Local wages, tips, etc.	19 Local income tax
Employer's contact person		Employer's telephone number	For Official Use Only
Employer's fax number		Employer's email address	

Under penalties of perjury, I declare that I have examined this return and accompanying documents and, to the best of my knowledge and belief, they are true, correct, and complete.

Signature ▶ _____   Title ▶ _____   Date ▶ _____

Form **W-3** **Transmittal of Wage and Tax Statements**   **20 - -**   Department of the Treasury Internal Revenue Service

Source: Internal Revenue Service.

Transaction No. 37

pennsylvania DEPARTMENT OF REVENUE REV-1667 (AS) 12-17

START	YEAR	EMPLOYER ACCOUNT ID	ENTITY ID (EIN)
	2 0 - -	0 0 0 0 3 3 0 0	0 0 0 0 0 0 6 6 0

Part I   RECONCILIATION

1a	Number of W-2 forms attached	
1b	Number of 1099 forms with PA withholding	
2	Total compensation/distribution subject to PA withholding	$ •
3	PA personal income tax withheld	$ •

DUE DATE JANUARY 31

ANNUAL WITHHOLDING RECONCILIATION STATEMENT

BUSINESS NAME AND ADDRESS

Part II   ANNUAL RECONCILIATION

	Wages/distribution paid subject to PA withholding	PA tax withheld
1st Quarter		
2nd Quarter		
3rd Quarter		
4th Quarter		
TOTAL		

LEGAL NAME
GLO-BRITE PAINT COMPANY
TRADE NAME

ADDRESS
2215 SALVADOR STREET
CITY, STATE, ZIP
PHILADELPHIA, PA 19175-0682

DO NOT SEND PAYMENT WITH THIS FORM.

[RESET FORM] [PRINT]

MM/DD/YYYY
DATE   DAYTIME TELEPHONE #   EXT.   TITLE   SIGNATURE

Source: PA Department of Revenue.

Transaction No. 38

9595   ☐ VOID   ☐ CORRECTED

PAYER'S name, street address, city or town, state or province, country, ZIP or foreign postal code, and telephone no.	1 Rents $	OMB No. 1545-0115	Miscellaneous Information
	2 Royalties $	Form **1099-MISC** (Rev. January 2022) For calendar year 20 ___	
	3 Other income $	4 Federal income tax withheld $	Copy A For Internal Revenue Service Center
PAYER'S TIN RECIPIENT'S TIN	5 Fishing boat proceeds $	6 Medical and health care payments $	File with Form 1096.
RECIPIENT'S name	7 Payer made direct sales totaling $5,000 or more of consumer products to recipient for resale ☐	8 Substitute payments in lieu of dividends or interest $	For Privacy Act and Paperwork Reduction Act Notice, see the **current General Instructions for Certain Information Returns.**
Street address (including apt. no.)	9 Crop insurance proceeds $	10 Gross proceeds paid to an attorney $	
City or town, state or province, country, and ZIP or foreign postal code	11 Fish purchased for resale $	12 Section 409A deferrals $	
	13 FATCA filing requirement ☐	14 Excess golden parachute payments $	15 Nonqualified deferred compensation $
Account number (see instructions)	2nd TIN not. ☐	16 State tax withheld $ $	17 State/Payer's state no.	18 State income $ $

Form **1099-MISC** (Rev. 1-2022)   Cat. No. 14425J   www.irs.gov/Form1099MISC   Department of the Treasury - Internal Revenue Service

Do Not Cut or Separate Forms on This Page — Do Not Cut or Separate Forms on This Page

Source: Internal Revenue Service.

Transaction No. 39

Do Not Staple   6969

Form **1096** Department of the Treasury Internal Revenue Service	**Annual Summary and Transmittal of U.S. Information Returns**	OMB No. 1545-0108 20--

FILER'S name

Street address (including room or suite number)

City or town, state or province, country, and ZIP or foreign postal code

Name of person to contact	Telephone number	**For Official Use Only**
Email address	Fax number	

1 Employer identification number	2 Social security number	3 Total number of forms	4 Federal income tax withheld $	5 Total amount reported with this Form 1096 $

6 Enter an "X" in only one box below to indicate the type of form being filed.

W-2G 32	1097-BTC 50	1098 81	1098-C 78	1098-E 84	1098-F 03	1098-Q 74	1098-T 83	1099-A 80	1099-B 79	1099-C 85	1099-CAP 73	1099-DIV 91	1099-G 86	1099-INT 92	1099-K 10	1099-LS 16
☐	☐	☐	☐	☐	☐	☐	☐	☐	☐	☐	☐	☐	☐	☐	☐	☐

1099-LTC 93	1099-MISC 95	1099-NEC 71	1099-OID 96	1099-PATR 97	1099-Q 31	1099-QA 1A	1099-R 98	1099-S 75	1099-SA 94	1099-SB 43	3921 25	3922 26	5498 28	5498-ESA 72	5498-QA 2A	5498-SA 27
☐	☐	☐	☐	☐	☐	☐	☐	☐	☐	☐	☐	☐	☐	☐	☐	☐

Return this entire page to the Internal Revenue Service. Photocopies are not acceptable.

Under penalties of perjury, I declare that I have examined this return and accompanying documents and, to the best of my knowledge and belief, they are true, correct, and complete.

Source: Internal Revenue Service.

Name_____

Project Audit Test

OCTOBER 9 PAYROLL: (Answers are provided below for the illustrative pay period.)

Payroll Register

1. What is Jamie H. Ferguson's filing status? .... Married Filing Joint
2. What is the gross pay for Jeri M. Ryan? .... $ 1,440.00
3. What is the amount of HI withheld for the current pay period for Ruth V. Williams? .... $ 17.73
4. What is the total net pay for all employees? .... $ 12,436.46
5. What is the total SIT withheld for all employees? .... $ 476.76

Journal

6. What is the amount of the debit to Office Salaries? .... $ 4,723.08
7. What is the amount of the debit to Payroll Taxes? .... $ 1,390.21
8. What is the amount of the credit to Cash? .... $ 12,436.46

General Ledger

9. What is the Cash (account number 11) account balance? .... $ 187,409.87
10. What is the total Administrative Salaries paid to date? .... $ 44,999.96

- -

Name_____

Project Audit Test

OCTOBER 23 PAYROLL: (As you complete your work, answer the following questions.)

Payroll Register

1. What is the gross pay for Anthony V. Bonno? .... _____
2. What is the amount of OASDI withheld for Catherine L. Ford? .... _____
3. What is the total net pay for all employees? .... _____
4. What is the total amount of group insurance withheld for all employees? .... _____

Journal

5. What is the amount of the credit to Employees FIT Payable? .... _____
6. What is the amount of the debit to Payroll Taxes? .... _____
7. What is the amount of the credit to SUTA Taxes Payable—Employer? .... _____
8. What is the amount of the debit to Employees SIT Payable on October 20? .... _____

General Ledger

9. What is the balance of FICA Taxes Payable—OASDI? .... _____
10. What is the balance of Union Dues withheld for the employees? .... _____

Name_____

Project Audit Test

NOVEMBER 6 PAYROLL: (As you complete your work, answer the following questions.)

Payroll Register

1. What is the amount of FIT withheld for Joseph T. O'Neill? .... _____
2. What is the total gross pay for all employees? .... _____
3. What is the total amount of CIT withheld for all employees? .... _____
4. What is the total net pay for all employees? .... _____

Journal

5. What is the amount of the credit to FICA Taxes Payable—OASDI for employees? .... _____
6. What is the amount of the credit to FICA Taxes Payable—HI for employees? .... _____
7. What is the amount of the debit to Payroll Taxes? .... _____
8. What is the amount of the debit to Employees SIT Payable on November 4? .... _____

General Ledger

9. What is the balance in the Cash (account number 11) account? .... _____
10. What is the amount of Sales Salaries paid to date? .... _____

Name_____

Project Audit Test

NOVEMBER 13 PAYROLL: (As you complete your work, answer the following questions.)

Payroll Register

1. What is the amount of FIT withheld for Ruth V. Williams? .... _____
2. What is Ruth V. Williams' current net pay .... _____
3. What is the amount of CIT withheld for Ruth V. Williams? .... _____
4. What is Ruth V. Williams' filing status? .... _____

Journal

5. What is the amount of Ruth V. Williams' Group Insurance withheld? .... _____
6. What is the amount of the debit to Payroll Taxes? .... _____

General Ledger

7. What is the total amount of Payroll Taxes (account number 56) to date? .... _____
8. What is the balance in the FICA Taxes Payable—HI account? .... _____
9. What is the balance in the Cash Account? .... _____
10. What is the balance in the Employees FIT Payable account? .... _____

Name_____

Project Audit Test

NOVEMBER 20 PAYROLL: (As you complete your work, answer the following questions.)

Payroll Register

1. What is the amount of FIT withheld for Kari C. Mann? .... _____

2. What is the total amount of SUTA withheld this period for all employees? .... _____

3. What is the total gross pay for all employees? .... _____

Journal

4. What is the November 16 credit to Cash for the deposit of FICA & FIT taxes? .... _____

5. What is the amount of the debit to Payroll Taxes? .... _____

6. What is the November 16 debit to Employees CIT Payable? .... _____

General Ledger

7. What is the balance of Employees SIT Payable? .... _____

8. What is the amount of Office Salaries paid to date? .... _____

9. What is the balance of Simple Contributions Payable? .... _____

10. What is the Cash account balance? .... _____

- -

Name_____

Project Audit Test

DECEMBER 4 PAYROLL: (As you complete your work, answer the following questions.)

Payroll Register

1. What is the net pay for Joseph T. O'Neill? .... _____

2. What is the amount of OASDI withheld for Jeri M. Ryan? .... _____

3. What is the total net pay for all employees? .... _____

4. What is the total CIT withheld for all employees? .... _____

Journal

5. What is the amount of the debit to Employees SIT Payable on December 3? .... _____

6. What is the amount of the credit to Employees FIT Payable? .... _____

7. What is the amount of the debit to Payroll Taxes? .... _____

General Ledger

8. What is the balance of SUTA Taxes Payable—Employer? .... _____

9. What is the balance of Employees CIT Payable? .... _____

10. What is the Cash account balance? .... _____

Name_____

Project Audit Test

DECEMBER 14 PAYROLL: (As you complete your work, answer the following questions.)

Payroll Register

1. What is the amount of FIT withheld for Serdar P. Russell? .... _____
2. What is the amount of net pay received by Serdar P. Russell's estate? .... _____
3. What was Serdar P. Russell's filing status? .... _____

Journal

4. What is the amount of the debit to Union Dues Payable on December 9? .... _____
5. What is the amount of the debit to Payroll Cash? .... _____
6. What is the amount of the credit to Employees SUTA Payable? .... _____

General Ledger

7. What is the amount that was credited to Group Insurance Premiums Collected
   (account number 27) during this period? .... _____
8. What is the amount paid for office salaries to date? .... _____
9. What is the balance of FICA Taxes Payable—OASDI? .... _____
10. What is the balance of Payroll Taxes? .... _____

- -

Name_____

Project Audit Test

DECEMBER 18 PAYROLL: (As you complete your work, answer the following questions.)

Payroll Register

1. What is the amount of FIT withheld for Joseph T. O'Neill? .... _____
2. What is the total current net pay for all employees? .... _____
3. What is the total gross pay for all employees? .... _____
4. What is the taxable amount of Joseph T. O'Neill's gross pay for OASDI? .... _____

Journal

5. What is the amount of the credit to cash for FICA and FIT taxes on December 15? .... _____
6. What is the amount of the debit to Payroll Taxes? .... _____
7. What is the amount of the debit to Employees CIT Payable on December 15? .... _____

General Ledger

8. What is the balance in the Cash account? .... _____
9. What is the total amount of Plant Wages to date? .... _____
10. What is the total amount of Payroll Taxes to date? .... _____

Name_____

Project Audit Test

END-OF-YEAR ACTIVITIES

Journal

1. What is the amount of the deposit for Pennsylvania state income taxes withheld from the December 18 payroll? .... _____

2. What is the amount of FICA Taxes Payable—OASDI deposited from the December payrolls? .... _____

3. What is the amount of the city of Philadelphia employees income tax deposited from the December payrolls? .... _____

4. What is the amount of FUTA Taxes Payable deposited for the quarter? .... _____

5. What is the amount of the credit to cash for SUTA Taxes Payable on February 1? .... _____

Payroll Adjusting Entries

6. What is the amount of the credit to Salaries and Wages Payable for the December 31 adjusting entry? .... _____

7. What is the amount of the debit to Vacation Benefits Expense for the December 31 adjusting entry? .... _____

Calculations

8. What is the total Payroll Tax Expense incurred by the employer on salaries and wages paid during the quarter ended December 31? .... _____

9. What is the total Payroll Tax Expense incurred by the employer on the total earnings of Joseph T. O'Neill during the fourth quarter? .... _____

10. O'Neill has decided to give all current employees (excluding himself) a bonus payment during January equal to 5% of their gross pay for last year. What is the total of this bonus payment? .... _____

Excel Template Instructions for the Glo-Brite Payroll Project (Chapter 7: Short Version)

The Excel template for the Payroll Project is an electronic version of the books of account and payroll records. This is not an automated payroll system, but an example of how you might use a spreadsheet program to keep payroll records and account for payroll transactions. Appendix B (Computerized option using Automated General Ledger Software) is available for both the long version in Chapter 7 and the short version in Appendix A. You will follow the instructions in this appendix to complete the Short Version project. The instructions provided below will enable you to use the Excel template in place of the manual journal, general ledger, payroll register, and employee's earnings records. Other forms, such as tax forms, are required for the Payroll Project. You will use those provided at the end of Chapter 7 (pages 7-49 to 7-67).

Appendix A is divided into five sections: Getting to Know Excel, Excel Templates for Payroll Project's Short Version, Illustrative Case, Short Payroll Project, and End-of-Year Activities. Getting to Know Excel provides basic information about Excel including creating formulas, rounding in Excel, and saving files. If you are familiar with Excel, this will be a refresher for you. Excel Templates for Payroll Project's Short Version provides specific information about the workbook used for the project including how the workbook is set up, the use of checkpoints, and error messages when amounts are incorrect and when trying to enter data into protected cells. Illustrative Case takes you through the November 20 payroll and November 30 employee changes. Short Payroll Project includes information needed to complete activities by Glo-Brite Company for the month of December. End-of-Year Activities includes all the year-end reporting requirements and transactions for January and February.

 I. Getting to know Excel .... pages A-2 to A-6

 II. Excel Templates for Payroll Project's Short Version... pages A-6 to A-12

 III. Illustrative Case (November 20 Payroll) .... pages A-12 to A-19

 IV. Short Payroll Project .... pages A-19 to A-22

 V. End-of-Year Activities .... pages A-22 to A-26

 VI. Project Audit Tests .... pages A-28 to A-32

I. Getting to Know Excel

Excel files are called **workbooks**. A single workbook can store many worksheets, which are stored like pages in a notebook. The workbook for this project has five worksheets: a worksheet including basic Excel instructions, the journal, the general ledger, the payroll register, and employee's earnings records.

Each worksheet is made up of rows and columns. Rows are numbered from 1 to 65,536, and columns are labeled with letters. Column 1 is A, Column 26 is Z, Column 27 is AA, and so on. The intersection of a row and column is called a cell. Cells have addresses based on the row and column in which they appear. Each **cell** can hold a number, text, a mathematical formula, or nothing at all. If you need to correct the data in a cell, simply enter the data as if the cell were empty.

The Excel Screen

This workbook has the look of a typical Excel screen. The first blue bar should say Microsoft Excel. The bar below that is the menu bar and is a typical Microsoft Windows menu bar. The next bar is the standard toolbar (now called ribbons), which is very similar to that of Microsoft Word. (You can move the arrow to a particular icon, and the command to be issued will appear.) Below that is the formatting toolbar, which won't be used much in this project. The next bar has the name-box on the left, displaying the address of the active cell.

One of the cells in a worksheet is always the active cell. (The active cell is the one with a thicker border.) Its contents appear in the formula bar, which is to the right of the name-box, in the area next to the **fx** (or the equals sign in older versions of Excel). Some of the cells in this workbook are locked or protected so that you cannot enter data. Others have their contents hidden. This was done intentionally when this template was created.

Navigation

You can navigate through a worksheet by using the arrow keys or Page Up and Page Down keys. This will change the active cell. Or you can use the scroll bars to the right and bottom of the screen and then click on the cell you want to activate.

You can also move to another cell by typing its address in the name-box. In this template, some cells have been named to make navigation easier. There is a drop-down list with cell names from which to choose.

You can switch from one worksheet to another within the same workbook by clicking on the appropriate tab at the bottom of the screen. For this project, there will be tabs labeled for the Journal, General Ledger, Payroll Register, and Employee's Earnings Records.

Excel Help and How-to

Excel Help and How-to is an interactive help tool, which can respond to natural language questions. To make the office assistant visible, click on the question mark icon in the standard toolbar.

Copy and Paste

Much of the work you do in this Payroll Project involves posting information from one place to another. You can accomplish this in Excel by using the Copy and Paste commands. (For this project, it is important that you use the Paste Special command, or else the format of the cell to hold the data will be changed.) Three ways to issue the Copy and Paste commands are:

1. Click on the cell you want to copy from, making it the active cell. Select Edit, Copy from the menu bar. This will highlight the active cell. Click on the cell you want to hold the copy. Select Edit, Paste Special, click on Values, and press OK. Press Esc to remove the highlighting.

2. Click on the cell you want to copy from, making it the highlighted active cell. Select the Copy icon from the standard toolbar. (This is the icon that looks like two pieces of paper.) This will highlight the active cell. Click on the cell you want to hold the copy. Select the Paste Special icon from the standard toolbar, click on Values, and press OK. Press Esc key to remove the highlighting.

3. Right-click on the cell you want to copy from, making it the highlighted active cell and bringing up a shortcut menu. Select Copy. Right-click on the cell you want to hold the copy. Select Paste Special, click on Values, and press OK. Press Esc key to remove the highlighting.

Copying and pasting can be done from one worksheet to another. For example, you will need to post from the journal to the ledger. After you have highlighted the cell you want to copy from, click on the tab of the worksheet you want to copy to, and then click on that particular cell.

Copy and paste can be done from one cell to another cell or from a range of cells to another range of cells. To copy a range of cells, highlight the cells by clicking on one cell, and while holding the mouse button down, drag the pointer over the desired cells. These cells will be highlighted. Paste using the desired method described above. The range of cells that will be holding the copy must have the same number of cells as the range being copied.

Remember, for this worksheet, you should always use Paste Special, not just Paste.

Entering Formulas

A formula is a special type of cell entry that returns a result. When you enter a formula into a cell, the cell displays the result of the formula. The formula itself can be seen in the formula bar when the cell is activated.

A formula begins with an equals sign (=) and can consist of any of the following elements:

- Operators such as + (for addition), − (for subtraction), * (for multiplication), / (for division)
- Cell references, including cell addresses such as B52, as well as named cells and ranges
- Values and text
- Worksheet functions (such as SUM)

You can enter a formula into a cell manually (typing it in) or by pointing to the cells.

To enter a formula manually, follow these steps.

1. Move the cell pointer to the cell that you want to hold the formula.

2. Type an equals sign (=) to signal the fact that the cell contains a formula.

3. Type the formula and press Enter.

As you type, the characters appear in the cell as well as in the formula bar. When you press Enter, the value resulting from the formula will show on the worksheet, but the formula itself will appear in the formula bar.

The following chart shows an example of four formulas. Values have been entered in the cells in Columns A and B. The formulas are entered in the cells in the C column. Notice, for example, that 9 appears in cell C1, but the formula that was entered in that cell is = A1 + B1.

Excel Chart

	A	B	C
1	6	3	9
2	6	3	3
3	6	3	18
4	6	3	2
5	24	12	32
6	1.5	17.65	26.48

Formulas as they appear in the formula bar cells in Column C

$=A1+B1$

$=A2-B2$

$=A3*B3$

$=A4/B4$

$=SUM(C1:C4)$

$=ROUND(A5*B5,2)$

The best way to explain the pointing method is by giving an example. Suppose you want to subtract the value in cell B2 from the value in cell A2 and you want the result to appear in cell C2. To enter the formula =A2−B2 in cell C2 by using the pointing method, follow these steps.

1. Make C2 the active cell by clicking on it.
2. Type an equals sign (=) to begin the formula.
3. Click on cell A2. This will highlight the cell.
4. Type a minus sign (−).
5. Click on cell B2.
6. Press Enter to end the formula.

The value of the result will appear in cell C2 whether it is the active cell or not, but when C2 is active, you will see = A2 − B2 in the formula bar.

This workbook has not been formatted to round numbers to either the nearest whole number or the nearest cent. For example, $17.65 \times 1.5 = 26.475$. When that formula is entered into a cell in this workbook, the cell will display 26.48 and hold the value 26.475. Excel's rounding function must be used to have the cell display and hold the value 26.48, which can then be used in other formulae. Referring back to the Excel Chart on the previous page, the formula for cell C6 is written as =ROUND (A5*B5,2). This tells Excel to take the value in A6 (1.5) times B6 (17.65) to get 26.475 and round to 26.48. Failure to use the Round function will cause penny errors in the project.

Saving Your Work

When you save a workbook, Excel overwrites the previous copy of your file. You can save your work at any time. You can save the file to the current name, or you may want to keep multiple versions of your work by saving each successive version under a different name. To save to the current name, you can select File, Save from the menu bar or click on the disk icon in the standard toolbar. It is recommended, however, that you save the file to a new name that identifies the file as yours, such as Excel_Templates_Payroll_Project_John_Doe.xlsx. To save under a different name, follow these steps.

1. Select File, Save As to display the Save As type drop-box and choose Excel Workbook (*.xlsx).
2. Select the folder in which to store the workbook.
3. Enter a new filename in the File name box.
4. Click Save.

This Excel Template

The four worksheets in this workbook have been created to look as much like their paper counterparts as possible. Some formulas have been created for you; others will have to be created by you.

Checkpoints have also been created for you so that you can periodically check the accuracy of your work. These are light blue cells on the worksheets that have been set up to verify the data entered. A message is returned if the data entered are not correct for that checkpoint. For the checkpoints to work properly, DO NOT USE COPY AND PASTE. Validation DOES NOT occur if the user *pastes* invalid data. Validation can occur only when data are entered manually in the checkpoint cell.

Journal

Record your journal in this Excel template just as you would on paper. To change pages, scroll down the worksheet. At the bottom of the journal pages is an equality check for total debits and credits. This area is highlighted in yellow. If your total debits in the journal do not equal your total credits, a warning message will appear in red.

Directly below that are the journal checkpoints. For easier navigation to the journal checkpoints, click on the drop-down list of the name-box and click on Journal_Check_points. Checkpoints are provided for the end of each month. After all journal entries have been made for the month, enter the amount of the total debits in the appropriate blue cell. Remember, DO NOT USE COPY AND PASTE. No indication is needed for debit or credit. A message will be returned only if the amount is not correct.

General Ledger

Use the Copy and Paste Special commands described above when posting amounts from the journal to the ledger. The new balance for each account is calculated after posting an amount to the account. Excel does the calculation for you because of the formula set up in the Balance column. The formula is set with an "IF" statement so that the balance only appears in a row when an amount has been posted to that row.

Checkpoints for each month are to the right of each account in the general ledger worksheet. Again, these cells are blue and are provided to verify the balance in each account at the end of each month. Since the balance for an account can be a debit or a credit, you must enter the data in the appropriate checkpoint cell. Remember, DO NOT USE COPY AND PASTE. A message will be returned only if the amount is not correct.

Payroll Register

This worksheet is wider than an Excel screen and also has many column headings. When you scroll through a worksheet this size, it's easy to get lost when the row or column headings scroll out of view. The payroll register in this template is set up so that row and column headings are "frozen." This enables headings to remain visible as you scroll through the worksheet. The dark lines indicate the frozen rows and columns. There is not a separate sheet for each payday, but rather a section for each payday on one worksheet.

The formulas for total earnings, taxes with a fixed percentage, net pay amounts, and column totals are already entered in the template. Checkpoints are created for total earnings and net paid for each payday. These blue cells are to the right of the payroll register. The cell for the first set of checkpoints is listed as Payroll_Check_points in the drop-down list of the name-box. Remember, DO NOT USE COPY AND PASTE. A message will be returned only if the amount is not correct.

Employee's Earnings Record

As with the other three worksheets, this one has been set up to look as much like the paper counterpart as possible. Earnings records are provided for all employees who worked for Glo-Brite during the quarter covered by the Payroll Project. For employees hired late in the quarter, enter data in the appropriate row for the pay period.

To post amounts from the Payroll Register worksheet to the Employee's Earnings Records worksheet, you may use Copy and Paste Special as described above. The formulas for cumulative earnings, taxes with a fixed percentage, net pay amounts, and column totals are already entered in the template.

Checkpoints are provided for quarter and yearly totals of cumulative earnings and net paid for each employee. The blue cells are at the bottom of each employee's record. Remember, DO NOT USE COPY AND PASTE. A message will be returned only if the amount you enter is incorrect.

Printing

As a final note, all pages and print areas have been defined but can be changed by the student. If you are unfamiliar with page setup and defining print areas, don't worry! It's been done for you. Simply click on the printer icon on the standard toolbar (or click on the File Ribbon and select print) and you're done!

II. Excel Templates for Payroll Project's Short Version

The payroll project that follows is the Excel version of the Chapter 7 project beginning on page 7-14 of your text. For this project, you will use the **Appendix A: Payroll Project Short Version** file. You are employed by Glo-Brite Paint Company as the person in the Accounting Department responsible for the company's payroll processing using Excel.

This is the short version of the payroll project presented in Chapter 7. You will complete the payrolls for the month of December and the optional last quarter and year-end activities. The opening balance file you will use already contains all the processing through the first two months of the fourth quarter. In order for you to complete all the transactions for the month of December, a review of the transactions starting with the November 20 payroll are explained. In subsequent pay period processing, whenever a new operational procedure is used for the first time, additional instruction will be provided.

The Excel workbook has been set up like the project in Chapter 7. As explained earlier, there are five worksheets: a worksheet including basic Excel instructions, the journal, the general ledger, the payroll register, and employees' earnings records. Figure A.1, below, shows the five worksheets. To navigate between worksheets, click the appropriate tab.

Figure A.1
Worksheet Tabs

21	
22	5. **Rounding**: These templates have not been formatted to round numbers to either the nearest whole number or the nearest cent. For example,
23	17.65 x 1.5=26.475. The template will display 26.48 but hold 26.475. If you want to use 26.48 you will need to use Excel's rounding function.
24	In order to tell Excel to round to the nearest whole penny you must enter the formula as: =round(17.65*1.5,2). This tells Excel to multiply 17.65 x 1.5,
25	then round to 2 decimals. Excel will now display and hold the amount as 26.48. You must use the ROUND function when entering the payroll tax entry in the Journal.
26	There are two methods to use to enter a formula. This first is shown above in 3. This method is easy when you want to type the formula yourself or if you are using cells in the same spreadsheet.

Excel Instructions | Journal | General Ledger | Payroll Register | Employees' Earnings Records | ⊕

Ready

Source: Microsoft Corporation

1. Excel Instructions worksheet has a shortened explanation of Excel. The first part of this appendix should be reviewed whenever you have a question about Excel.

   In addition, each Excel worksheet has been protected. This means certain cells have been protected so changes can't be made to the information in those cells. Cells have been protected because of formatting and when common equations are used. Looking at the partial payroll register worksheet in Figure A.2, if you try to enter an amount in cell Z55 you will receive an error message that looks like the screen below. The cell contains a formula used to automatically calculate total earnings for you and is protected so you aren't able to change it.

Figure A.2
Protected Cell Error Message

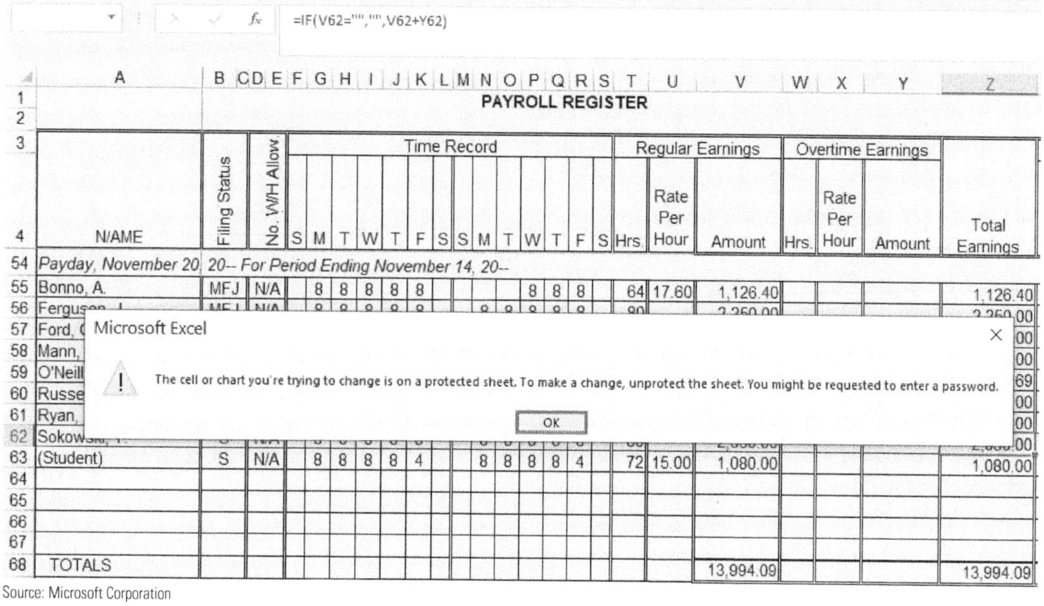

Source: Microsoft Corporation

2. Journal is called the book of original entry. Transactions are recorded and then posted to the general ledger accounts. Information for each payroll is taken from the Payroll Register to record the payroll entry.

3. General Ledger is used to keep a continuous record of each account balance. The chart of accounts in Figure A.3, on page A-8, is a partial list of Glo-Brite's accounts and only includes the accounts necessary to complete this payroll project.

Figure A.3
Partial Chart of Accounts

Account Title	Account No.
Cash	11
Payroll Cash	12
FICA Taxes Payable—OASDI	20.1
FICA Taxes Payable—HI	20.2
FUTA Taxes Payable	21
SUTA Taxes Payable—Employer	22
Employees FIT Payable	24
Employees SIT Payable	25
Employees SUTA Payable	25.1
Employees CIT Payable	26
Group Insurance Premiums Collected	27
Union Dues Payable	28
Simple Contributions Payable	29
Administrative Salaries	51
Office Salaries	52
Sales Salaries	53
Plant Wages	54
Payroll Taxes	56

4. Payroll Register provides the information needed for journalizing each payroll and for posting to the employees' earnings records.

5. Employees' Earnings Records provides a summary of each employee's earnings, deductions, and taxable wages. The information recorded in this worksheet is posted from the Payroll Register. In addition, information in these records is used to prepare a **Form W-2 Wage and Tax Statement** for each employee.

   From the personnel data given in Figure A.4, an employee's earnings record has been maintained for each employee. These records have been maintained through the November 20 payroll and represent all earnings, wage changes, etc., through November 30.

Figure A.4
Glo-Brite Employees

Personnel Data—November 30, 20- -

BONNO, Anthony Victor, 694 Bristol Avenue, Philadelphia, PA 19135-0617. Married Filing Joint (MFJ). Telephone, 555-9827.
Social Security No. 000-00-3481. Position, mixer operator in plant. Wages, $17.60 per hour. Group insurance, $55,000.

FERGUSON, Jamie Hadi, 808 Sixth Street, Philadelphia, PA 19106-0995. MFJ. Telephone, 555-8065.
Social Security No. 000-00-8645. Position, sales manager. Salary, $58,500 per year. Group insurance, $88,000. Department: Sales.

FORD, Catherine Louise, 18 Dundee Avenue, Philadelphia, PA 19151-1919. Single. Telephone, 555-0235.
Social Security No. 000-00-4567. Position, administrative assistant. Salary, $2,773.33 per month. Group insurance, $50,000. Department: Office.

MANN, Kari Casey, 3007 Bisque Drive, Philadelphia, PA 19199-0718. MFJ. Telephone, 555-0774.
Social Security No. 000-00-9352. Position, sales representative. Salary, $2,925 per month. Group insurance, $53,000. Department: Sales.

O'NEILL, Joseph Tyler, 2100 Broad Street, Philadelphia, PA 19121-7189. MFJ. Telephone, 555-2332.
Social Security No. 000-00-1534. Position, president. Salary, $60,000 per year, paid $2,307.69 biweekly. Group insurance, $90,000. Department: Administrative.

RUSSELL, Serdar Parker, 8004 Dowling Road, Philadelphia, PA 19135-9001. Single. Telephone, 555-3681.
Social Security No. 000-00-6337. Position, time clerk. Salary, $2,730 per month. Group insurance, $49,000. Department: Office.

RYAN, Jeri Mischa, 7300 Harrison Street, Philadelphia, PA 19124-6699. MFJ. Telephone, 555-6660.
Social Security No. 000-00-1223. Position, electrician in plant. Wages, $18.00 per hour. Group insurance, $56,000.

SOKOWSKI, Thomas James, 133 Cornwells Street, Philadelphia, PA 19171-5718. Single. Telephone, 555-5136.
Social Security No. 000-00-8832. Position, supervisor in plant. Salary, $1,025 per week. Group insurance, $80,000.

STUDENT, 7018 Erdrick Street, Philadelphia, PA 19135-8517. Single. Position, accounting trainee. Wages, $15.00 per hour.
Group insurance, $42,000. Department: Office.

WILLIAMS, Ruth Virginia, 9433 State Street, Philadelphia, PA 19149-0819. Single. Telephone, 555-5845.
Social Security No. 000-00-6741. Position, programmer. Salary, $2,650 per month. Group insurance, $48,000. Department: Office.

WOODS, Beth Anne, 8102 Franklin Court, Philadelphia, PA 19105-0915. Single. Telephone, 555-1128.
Social Security No. 000-00-1587. Position, programmer. Salary, $2,600 per month. Group insurance, $47,000. Department: Office.

Additional information from Chapter 7 you will need while completing the short version:

1. General company information for Glo-Brite Paint Company: located at 2215 Salvador Street, Philadelphia, PA 19175-0682, phone number is 215-555-9559, federal identification number is 00-0000660, state account number is 000-0-3300, and city identifying number is 000-0001855.

2. In completing the time record columns of the payroll register for all workers, you should place an 8 in the day column for each full day worked. If an employee works less than a full day, show the actual hours for which the employee will be paid.

3. In the case of an employee who begins work during a pay period, compute the earnings by paying the employees their weekly rate for ***any full week*** worked. For any ***partial week***, compute the earnings for that week by multiplying the hours worked by the hourly rate of pay.

4. If time lost is to be deducted from a salaried employee's pay, the employee's pay must be determined by multiplying the actual hours worked for that week by the hourly rate. If hours are missed but no pay is deducted, include those hours in the Time Record columns on the payroll register.

The following schedule shows the weekly and hourly wage rates of the salaried employees:

Employee	Weekly Rate	Hourly Rate
Ferguson, Jamie H.	$1,125.00	$28.13
Ford, Catherine L.	610.00	15.25
Mann, Kari C.	675.00	16.88
O'Neill, Joseph T.	2,307.69*	28.85
Russell, Serdar P.	600.00	15.00
Sokowski, Thomas J.	1,025.00	25.63
Williams, Ruth V.	611.54	15.29

*O'Neill is paid on a biweekly basis.

5. The workweek for all employees is 40 hours, except for the student's 36-hour workweek.

6. Overtime is paid to all employees except exempt administrative employees—the president (O'Neill), the sales manager (Ferguson), the sales representative (Mann), and the supervisor (Sokowski). Overtime is paid at time and a half for any overtime exceeding 40 hours a week. Bonno and Ryan are paid time and a half for any hours worked over eight each workday and for work on Saturdays and twice the regular hourly rate of pay for work on Sundays or holidays.

7. Employees are paid biweekly on Friday. Information for each pay period is provided in the time clerk's report.

8. Federal income tax withholding is determined using the Wage Bracket Method Tables for Manual Payroll Systems With Forms W-4 From 2020 or Later – Biweekly Payroll Period – Standard columns located on pages T-7 and T-8 in the back of the textbook. The filing status for each employee can be located on the Employees' Earnings Records.

9. Group-term life insurance is carried on all employees in an amount equal to one and one-half times the annual salary or wages paid each employee (rounded to the nearest thousand). A notation has been made on each employee's earnings record to show that each month, on the last payday of the month, **30¢ for each $1,000** of insurance coverage is deducted from the employee's earnings to pay a portion of the premium cost. The amount deducted is credited to the liability account titled Group Insurance Premiums Collected. The taxable portion of group-term life insurance in excess of $50,000 is ignored since the employees pay for the insurance.

Example: Anthony Bonno's earnings record indicates group insurance coverage in the amount of $55,000. The deduction for Group Insurance Premiums Collected would be $16.50 [($55,000/$1,000) × $.30]. The $5,000 in coverage in excess of $50,000 is not taxable since Bonno is paying for the insurance coverage.

10. Union dues of $8 are deducted **each pay** period from the wages of Bonno and Ryan. The amount deducted is credited to the liability account titled Union Dues Payable. The amount withheld during the preceding month is remitted to the union treasurer on or before the tenth of the month.

11. Figure A.5 shows how salaries and wages are to be debited to the labor cost accounts. This information is first entered in the Payroll Register in the columns titled Labor Cost Distribution. Remember the Payroll Register is completed first and is used to update Employees' Earnings Records and to make the Journal entry.

12. Payroll taxes are levied upon Glo-Brite Company and its employees as shown in Figure A.6.
13. Payroll taxes are deposited according the rules shown in Figure A.7, on page A-12.

Figure A.5
Glo-Brite Labor Cost Accounts

Personnel	Accounts to Be Charged
President (O'Neill)	Administrative Salaries
Administrative Assistant (Ford) Programmer (Williams) Time Clerk (Russell) Accounting Trainee (Student)	Office Salaries
Sales Manager (Ferguson) Sales Representative (Mann)	Sales Salaries
Workers (Bonno and Ryan) Supervisor (Sokowski)	Plant Wages

FIGURE A.6
Glo-Brite Payroll Taxes

	Payroll Taxes Levied upon Glo-Brite Paint Company and Its Employees
Federal Income Taxes (FIT)	Withheld from each employee's gross earnings in accordance with information given on Form W-4 (from 2020 or later) and employee's earnings record. Wage-bracket method tables on pages T-7 and T-8 (Manual Payroll Systems Biweekly Payroll Period with Standard Withholding) are used to determine FIT withholding.*
Pennsylvania State Income Taxes (SIT)	3.07 percent withheld from each employee's gross earnings during the fourth quarter.*
Philadelphia City Income Taxes (CIT)	3.8398 percent withheld from gross earnings of each resident employee.*
Pennsylvania State Unemployment Taxes (SUTA)	*Employee:* 0.06 percent (0.0006) on total gross earnings (no limit for the employee's portion).*
	Employer: 3.6890 percent on first $10,000 gross earnings paid each employee during the calendar year (PA rate for new employers).
Federal Unemployment Taxes (FUTA)	*Employer:* Net tax rate of 0.6 percent on first $7,000 gross earnings paid each worker in the calendar year.
Federal Insurance Contributions Act (FICA)	*OASDI—Employee and Employer:* 6.2 percent on first $147,000 of gross earnings paid each worker in the calendar year (maximum OASDI tax of $9,114.00).
	HI—Employee: 1.45 percent on total gross earnings paid each worker in the calendar year, plus an additional 0.9 percent on wages over $200,000.
	HI—Employer: 1.45 percent on total gross earnings paid each worker in the calendar year.

* Tax withholdings for FIT, FICA, SIT, CIT, and SUTA are based on rates used in 2022. Rates for 2023 were not available at the time of publishing.

Figure A.7
Deposit Rules

Deposit Rules for Glo-Brite Paint Company	
Federal	The FICA taxes and FIT taxes must be deposited *on or before the 15th of the month following the month* in which the taxes were withheld. Since Glo-Brite is a new employer and has no tax liabilities during the lookback period, the company is subject to the monthly deposit rule.
Pennsylvania	Since the state income taxes withheld total $1,000 or more each quarter, the company must remit the withheld taxes semimonthly. The taxes must be remitted within three banking days after the semimonthly periods ending *on the 15th and the last day of the month.*
Philadelphia	Since the city income taxes withheld are more than $350 but less than $16,000 each month, the company is subject to the monthly rule. The city income taxes withheld during the month must be remitted *by the 15th day of the following month.*

III. Illustrative Case

November 20

Project Audit Test

✓ Net Paid $9,538.43

a. The company has decided to offer a Savings Incentive Match Plan (SIMPLE) to its employees. **Note:** The SIMPLE deduction reduces income subject to federal income tax (FIT) but does not reduce income for FICA–OASDI, FICA–HI, state, and local taxes. The company must match these employee contributions dollar for dollar up to 3 percent of the employee's compensation. You will not be responsible for recording the employer's portion since this is handled by the Accounts Payable Department. The following employees have decided to participate this year:

Jamie Ferguson	$500 contribution per pay period
Kari Mann	$250 contribution per pay period
Joseph O'Neill	$700 contribution per pay period
Jeri Ryan	$200 contribution per pay period

b. Payroll Register—Use the Time Clerk's Report Nos. 44 and 45 to complete the Payroll Register. The time clerk prepared the Time Clerk's Report Nos. 44 and 45 from the time cards used by the employees for these workweeks. **In as much as the president, sales manager, sales representatives, and supervisors do not ring in and out on the time clock, their records are not included in the time clerk's report, but their salaries must be included in the payroll.**

Bonno, Ryan, and "Student" are paid an hourly rate. All the other employees are paid a weekly rate. Since Russell had "time lost" weeks in this pay period, for these weeks, calculate pay using hourly rate for the partial week plus a full week's salary. All pay rates are found on the Employees' Earnings Records.

Time Clerk's Report No. 44
For the Week Ending November 7, 20--

Employee	Time Record							Time Worked	Time Lost
	S	M	T	W	T	F	S		
Bonno, A. V. ...		8	8	8	8	8		40 hrs.	. . .
Ford, C. L.		8	8	8	8	8		40 hrs.	. . .
Russell, S. P.		6	8	8	8	8		38 hrs.	2 hrs.*
Ryan, J. M.		8	8	8	8	8		40 hrs.	. . .
Student........		8	8	8	8	4		36 hrs.	. . .
Williams, R. V. ...		6	8	7	7	6		34 hrs.	6 hrs.**

*Time lost for personal business; deduct 2 hours' pay.
**Time lost because of tardiness; deduct 6 hours' pay.

Time Clerk's Report No. 45
For the Week Ending November 14, 20--

Employee	Time Record							Time Worked	Time Lost
	S	M	T	W	T	F	S		
Bonno, A. V. ...		...	...	8	8	8		24 hrs.	. . .
Ford, C. L.		8	8	8	8	8		40 hrs.	. . .
Russell, S. P.		8	8	8	8	8		40 hrs.	. . .
Ryan, J. M.		8	8	8	8	8		40 hrs.	. . .
Student........		8	8	8	8	4		36 hrs.	. . .
Williams, R. V. ...		D	D	8	6	8		22 hrs.	18 hrs.*

*Time lost because of tardiness; deduct 2 hours' pay. Unexcused absences; deduct 16 hours' pay.

The Payroll Register shown in Figure A.8, on page A-14, is the starting point for recording payroll. The column titled Filing Status is used to determine the FIT deduction for this pay period. Each pay period the Employees' Earnings Records should be checked to be sure the filing status, pay rate, and other deductions such as group insurance and union dues are correct. Glo-Brite is a new company and all Forms W-4 on file are from 2020; therefore, the entry in the Number of Withholding Allowances column is not applicable (N/A).

Figure A.8
Payroll Register—Earnings Section

PAYROLL REGISTER

NAME	Filing Status	No. W/H Allow.	Time Record S	M	T	W	T	F	S	S	M	T	W	T	F	S	Reg Hrs.	Rate per Hour	Regular Amount	OT Hrs.	Rate per Hour	Overtime Amount	Total Earnings
Payday, November 20, 20-- For Period Ending November 14, 20--																						
Bonno, A.	MFJ	N/A		8	8	8	8	8					8	8	8		64	17.60	1,126.40				1,126.40
Ferguson, J.	MFJ	N/A		8	8	8	8	8			8	8	8	8	8		80		2,250.00				2,250.00
Ford, C.	S	N/A		8	8	8	8	8			8	8	8	8	8		80		1,220.00				1,220.00
Mann, K.	MFJ	N/A		8	8	8	8	8			8	8	8	8	8		80		1,350.00				1,350.00
O'Neill, J.	MFJ	N/A		8	8	8	8	8			8	8	8	8	8		80		2,307.69				2,307.69
Russell, S.	S	N/A		6	8	8	8	8			8	8	8	8	8		78		1,170.00				1,170.00
Ryan, J.	MFJ	N/A		8	8	8	8	8			8	8	8	8	8		80	18.00	1,440.00				1,440.00
Sokowski, T.	S	N/A		8	8	8	8	8			8	8	8	8	8		80		2,050.00				2,050.00
(Student)	S	N/A		8	8	8	8	4			8	8	8	8	4		72	15.00	1,080.00				1,080.00
TOTALS																			13,994.09				13,994.09

Once the total earnings have been calculated, you will complete the deductions section of the Payroll Register shown in Figure A.9. The advantage of using Excel is the use of formulas to calculate the deductions for OASDI, HI, SIT, SUTA, and CIT. Since these are routine calculations, the worksheet already contains the necessary formulas to do these calculations. You will be entering the amounts for FIT, Union Dues, Group Insurance (when necessary), and SIMPLE contributions. Once these amounts have been entered, the Net Pay will automatically calculate.

Figure A.9
Payroll Register—Deductions Section

GLO-BRITE PAINT COMPANY

NAME	Total Earnings	OASDI	HI	FIT	SIT	SUTA	CIT	Group Ins.	Union Dues	SIMPLE	Ck. No.	Amount
Payday, November 20, 20-- For Period Ending November 14, 20--												
Bonno, A.	1,126.40	69.84	16.33	12.00	34.58	0.68	43.625	16.50	8.00		703	925.22
Ferguson, J.	2,250.00	139.50	32.63	76.00	69.08	1.35	86.40	26.40		500.00	704	1,318.64
Ford, C.	1,220.00	75.64	17.69	79.00	37.45	0.73	46.85	14.40			705	948.24
Mann, K.	1,350.00	83.70	19.58	10.00	41.45	0.81	51.84	15.90		250.00	706	876.72
O'Neill, J.	2,307.69	143.08	33.46	60.00	70.85	1.38	88.61	27.00		700.00	707	1,183.31
Russell, S.	1,170.00	72.54	16.97	74.00	35.92	0.70	44.93	14.10			708	910.84
Ryan, J.	1,440.00	89.28	20.88	24.00	44.21	0.86	55.29	16.80	8.00	200.00	709	980.68
Sokowski, T.	2,050.00	127.10	29.73	179.00	62.94	1.23	78.72	24.00			710	1,547.28
(Student)	1,080.00	66.96	15.66	62.00	33.16	0.65	41.47	12.60			711	847.50
TOTALS	13,994.09	867.64	202.93	576.00	429.64	8.39	537.36	167.70	16.00	1,650.00		9,538.43

The wage-bracket tables will be used to determine the deduction for FIT. **Note:** The amount to look up in the table will be total earnings minus the SIMPLE contribution, so for Ferguson the taxable earnings for FIT will be $2,250 − $500 = $1,750. The SIMPLE only reduces taxable earnings for FIT!

The last section of the Payroll Register as shown in Figure A.10 helps the employer calculate payroll taxes and the entry to total earnings by category. The Taxable Earnings section is completed based on the earnings this period that would still be subject to the employer taxes. The taxable base for OASDI is $147,000. Since the cumulative earnings for each employee are under that amount, all earnings are subject to OASDI tax. HI has no limit so each employee's total earnings will be entered here. FUTA tax is based on the first $7,000 earned. Since all employees have exceeded this base, none of the earnings are taxable. Let's now look at the employer's SUTA tax. As shown in Figure A.6, the employer pays 3.6890 percent on the first $10,000. Once again, you will need to refer to the Employees' Earnings Records to see if the cumulative earning is less than $10,000. As you can see from the completed payroll record, four employees have not exceeded the taxable SUTA earnings. In the case of Kari Mann, cumulative earnings were $9,450. To calculate taxable earnings, you take $10,000 − $9,450 = $550.

Note: Checkpoints—once you've completed the Payroll Register, use the Checkpoint to check your work. Enter the amount of total earnings; you can get this amount from the Taxable Earnings column for HI. If the amount is correct, the box will appear as shown in Figure A.10. If the amount is incorrect, you will see a message like the one in Figure A.11, on page A-16, where the incorrect amount for "Net paid" was entered. (Remember—do not use Copy and Paste to enter the amount.)

Figure A.10
Payroll Register—Taxable Earnings and Labor Cost Distribution

N/AME	OASDI	HI	FUTA	SUTA	Admin.	Office	Sales	Plant
TOTALS	2,079.32	2,079.32	0.00	0.00	0.00	2,079.32	0.00	0.00
Payday, November 20								
Bonno, A.	1,126.40	1,126.40						1,126.40
Ferguson, J.	2,250.00	2,250.00					2,250.00	
Ford, C.	1,220.00	1,220.00		40.00		1,220.00		
Mann, K	1,350.00	1,350.00		550.00			1,350.00	
O'Neill, J.	2,307.69	2,307.69			2,307.69			
Russell, S.	1,170.00	1,170.00		190.00		1,170.00		
Ryan, J.	1,440.00	1,440.00						1,440.00
Sokowski, T.	2,050.00	2,050.00						2,050.00
(Student)	1,080.00	1,080.00		1,080.00		1,080.00		
TOTALS	13,994.09	13,994.09	0.00	1,860.00	2,307.69	3,470.00	3,600.00	4,616.40

Checkpoints

Total earnings	13,994.09
Net paid	9,538.43

Figure A.11
Payroll Register—Checkpoint Error Message

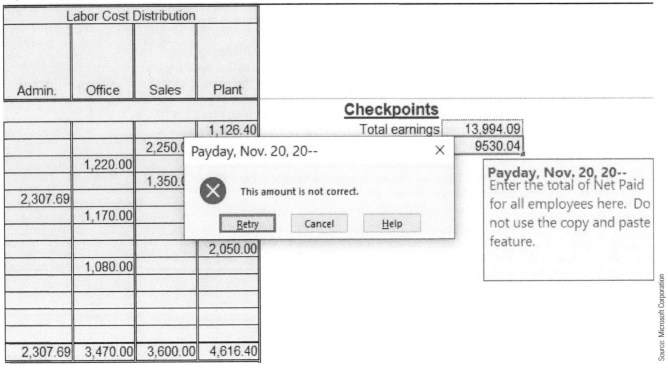

c. Journal—after completing the Payroll Register, you are ready to journalize
the payroll. Three entries will be made each period: transfer of cash
from the Cash account to the Payroll Cash account entry, payroll entry,
and payroll tax entry. The first two entries are shown in Figure A.12. All of
the amounts for these two entries are taken directly from the completed
Payroll Register.

Figure A.12
Journalized Payroll Entries

	20	Payroll Cash	12	9,538.43	
		Cash	11		9,538.43
	20	Administrative Salaries	51	2,307.69	
		Office Salaries	52	3,470.00	
		Sales Salaries	53	3,600.00	
		Plant Wages	54	4,616.40	
		FICA Taxes Payable - OASDI	20.1		867.64
		FICA Taxes Payable - HI	20.2		202.93
		Employees FIT Payable	24		576.00
		Employees SIT Payable	25		429.64
		Employees SUTA Payable	25.1		8.39
		Employees CIT Payable	26		537.36
		Group Insurance Premiums Collected	27		167.70
		Union Dues Payable	28		16.00
		SIMPLE Contributions Payable	29		1,650.00
		Payroll Cash	12		9,538.43

The last journal entry in the payroll process shown in Figure A.13 is to record the employer's payroll taxes. The tax is calculated on the total taxable amount for each category using the payroll register's Taxable Earnings columns.

OASDI tax	$13,994.09 × 0.062	=	$ 867.63
HI tax	$13,994.09 × 0.0145	=	202.91
SUTA tax	$ 1,860.00 × 0.03689	=	68.62
Total Payroll Taxes...		=	$1,139.16

Figure A.13

Journal Entry for Payroll Taxes

	JOURNAL				Page **45**

DATE		DESCRIPTION	POST. REF.	DEBIT	CREDIT
20--					
Nov.	20	Payroll Taxes	56	1,139.16	
		FICA Taxes Payable - OASDI	20.1		867.63
		FICA Taxes Payable - HI	20.2		202.91
		SUTA Taxes Payable - Employer	22		68.62

Total debits and credits (calculated automatically):   125,953.15 125,953.15

Your debits and credits should be equal after each journal entry is complete

Cumulative Journal Checkpoint Through Month Ending

59,572.70	October 31, 20--	December 31, 20--	
125,953.15	November 30, 20--	January 31, 20--	

Note: When calculating the employer's payroll taxes, you must use the ROUND function in Excel. See Entering Formulas on page A-3, or the Excel Instructions in the Excel workbook.

Notice: The Journal has a running total of debits and credits; if at any point these do not equal, you have recorded an entry incorrectly. Be sure to use the Checkpoint to check for accuracy.

d. General Ledger—after journalizing the entries in the Journal, you will post the amounts to the appropriate accounts. Figure A.14, on page A-18, shows the postings to the Cash account. Notice the account has a Debit column, Credit column, and Balance column which provides a running total of the amount in the account. Each general ledger account also contains a checkpoint used at the end of each month. (Remember— do not use Copy and Paste to enter numbers in the Checkpoints.)

Figure A.14
General Ledger—Cash Account

GENERAL LEDGER

ACCOUNT: **CASH**   ACCOUNT NO. **11**

DATE		ITEM	POST. REF.	DEBIT	CREDIT	BALANCE DEBIT	BALANCE CREDIT
20--							
Oct.	1	Balance	✔			199,846.33	
	9		J41		12,436.46	187,409.87	
	20		J41		476.76	186,933.11	
	23		J41		12,494.94	174,438.17	
Nov.	4		J42		486.63	173,951.54	
	6		J42		32.00	173,919.54	
	6		J43		12,335.83	161,583.71	
	13		J43		1,578.92	160,004.79	
	16		J44		6,447.03	153,557.76	
	16		J44		1,204.92	152,352.84	
	16		J44		539.21	151,813.63	
	20		J44		9,538.43	142,275.20	

Checkpoints

	Debit Balance	Credit Balance
Oct. 31, 20--	174,438.17	
Nov. 30, 20--	142,275.20	
Dec. 31, 20--		

e. Employees' Earnings Records—now it is time to transfer the information from the Payroll Register to the Employees' Earnings Records. Figure A.15 shows the completed earnings record for Jeri Ryan. The workbook is set up to automatically fill many of the fields for you once you've entered the earnings information. You will need to enter the amounts from the Payroll Register for: FIT, SIMPLE, Other Deductions, and Check No. The Other Deductions column contains union dues and group insurance.

Figure A.15
Employee's Earnings Record

DEPARTMENT	OCCUPATION	WORKS IN (STATE)	S.S. ACCOUNT NO.	NAME - LAST	FIRST		MIDDLE
Plant	Electrician	PA	000-00-1223	RYAN	Jeri		Mischa

OTHER DEDUCTIONS INFORMATION			SALARY	$		W/H ALLOW.	FILING STATUS
GROUP INSURANCE	UNION DUES	OTHER	WEEKLY RATE	$			
			HOURLY RATE	$ 18.00			
$56,000 -- $.30/M	$8 each pay		OVERTIME RATE	$ 27.00		N/A	MFJ

20__ PAYDAY		REGULAR EARNINGS HRS.	RATE	AMOUNT	OVERTIME EARNINGS HRS.	RATE	AMOUNT	CUMULATIVE EARNINGS	DEDUCTIONS FICA OASDI	HI	FIT	SIT	SUTA	CIT	SIMPLE	OTHER DEDUCTIONS	CK. NO.	NET PAID AMOUNT
YEAR-TO-DATE				13,287.50			1,397.80	14,685.30	910.49	212.94	1,070.00	450.84	8.81	563.89		235.70		11,232.63
1	10/9	80	18.00	1,440.00			0.00	16,125.30	89.28	20.88	44.00	44.21	0.86	55.29		8.00	678	1,177.48
2	10/23	80	18.00	1,440.00	8	27.00	216.00	17,781.30	102.67	24.01	66.00	50.84	0.99	63.59		24.80	688	1,323.10
3	11/6	80	18.00	1,440.00			0.00	19,221.30	89.28	20.88	44.00	44.21	0.86	55.29		8.00	698	1,177.48
4	11/20	80	18.00	1,440.00			0.00	20,661.30	89.28	20.88	24.00	44.21	0.86	55.29	200.00	24.80	709	980.68
5	12/4						0.00											
6	12/18						0.00											
QTR. TOT.																		
YR. TOT.																		
		Checkpoint									Checkpoint							

f. The salaries for Ford and Russell will increase with the next pay period. The employee's earnings record for each of these employees has been updated with the following information:

Employee	Weekly Rate	Hourly Rate	Group Insurance
Ford, Catherine L.	$640.00	$16.00	$50,000 – $.30/M
Russell, Serdar P.	$630.00	$15.75	$49,000 – $.30/M

November 30

a. A new employee by the name of Paul Winston Young was hired and began work on November 30. Young is single. He is training as a field sales representative in the city where the home office is located. His beginning salary is $2,730 per month. Address, 7936 Holmes Drive, Philadelphia, PA 19107-6107. Telephone, 555-2096. Social Security No. 000-00-6057. Young is eligible for group insurance coverage of $49,000. Department: Sales, weekly rate: $630.00, and hourly rate: $15.75. Young's completed earnings record is shown in Figure A.16.

Figure A.16
New Employee's Earnings Record

IV. Short Payroll Project

Audit Tests are presented on pages A-28 to A-32. If assigned, answer questions for the Audit Tests as you complete processing of each pay period.

Page references to forms and information worksheets in Chapter 7 have been provided in these instructions. Please verify with your instructor if you will be required to complete these items.

> ### Project Audit Test
>
> At the start of each pay period, remove the Project Audit Test beginning on page A-28. Answer the questions as you complete each pay period.

December 3

a. Deposit with the state of Pennsylvania the amount of state income taxes withheld from the November payroll. (Transaction No. 16 on page 7-51)

December 4

a. Prepare the payroll using the Time Clerk's Report Nos. 46 and 47. Note: Thursday, November 26, is a paid holiday for all workers. Complete the Payroll Register; journalize transfer of cash to the Payroll Cash account, the payroll entry, and payroll tax entry; post the amounts to the General Ledger accounts; and update the Employees' Earnings Records.

Project Audit Test
✓ Net Paid $11,109.84

Time Clerk's Report No. 46
For the Week Ending November 21, 20--

Employee	Time Record							Time Worked	Time Lost
	S	M	T	W	T	F	S		
Bonno, A. V. . . .		8	8	8	8	8		40 hrs.	. . .
Ford, C. L.		8	8	8	8	8		40 hrs.	. . .
Russell, S. P.		8	8	8	8	8		40 hrs.	. . .
Ryan, J. M.		8	8	8	4	8		36 hrs.	4 hrs.*
Student.		8	8	8	4	8		36 hrs.	. . .
Woods, B. A. . . .		. . .	8	8	8	8		32 hrs.	. . .

*Time lost on account of personal business; deduct 4 hours' pay.

Time Clerk's Report No. 47
For the Week Ending November 28, 20--

Employee	Time Record							Time Worked	Time Lost
	S	M	T	W	T	F	S		
Bonno, A. V.	8*	8	8	8	PAID HOLIDAY	8		48 hrs.	. . .
Ford, C. L.		8	8	8		8		40 hrs.	. . .
Russell, S. P.		8	8	8		8		40 hrs.	. . .
Ryan, J. M.		9	10	8		8		43 hrs.	. . .
Student.		8	8	8		4		36 hrs.	. . .
Woods, B. A.		8	8	8		8		40 hrs.	. . .

*Double time.

b. Increase the union dues to $9 each pay on Bonno's and Ryan's earnings records. This change is **effective on the last pay of the year (December 18).**

December 9

a. Pay the union treasurer the amount of union dues withheld during the month of November.

December 11

a. The Payroll Department was informed Serdar Russell died in an automobile accident on the way home from work on Thursday, December 10.

December 14

a. A special payroll needs to be completed to process Russell's final paycheck made payable to the **Estate of Serdar P. Russell**.
  - This check covers Russell's work for the weeks ending December 5 and 12 ($1,134.00) plus accrued vacation pay ($1,260.00). Do not show the vacation hours in the Time Record columns on the payroll register, but include them in the Regular Earnings column.

Project Audit Test

✓ Net Paid $2,194.72

- Russell's final biweekly pay is subject to FICA, FUTA, and SUTA. **This final pay is not subject to FIT, SIT, or CIT.** Since Russell's cumulative earnings have surpassed the taxable earnings figures for FUTA and SUTA, there will not be any unemployment tax on the employer.
- The deduction for group insurance is $14.70 [($49,000/$1,000) × $.30].
- Make a notation of Russell's death on the Payroll Register and Employee's Earnings Record.
- Prepare all the entries for the special pay; post to the General Ledger accounts and Employees' Earnings Records.
- If required by your instructor complete:
  - Form W-2 (Transaction No. 21 on page 7-60): Include the final gross pay in Boxes 3 and 5, but not in Boxes 1, 16, and 18. This Form W-2 will be given to the executor of the estate along with the final paycheck. Russell's address is 8004 Dowling Road, Philadelphia, PA 19135-9001.
  - Form 1099-MISC and Form 1096 (Transaction No. 38 and No. 39 on page 7-67) will be completed in February before their due date to report the last wage payment and vacation pay ($2,394.00).

December 15

a. Electronically deposit the amount of FICA taxes and federal income taxes for the November payrolls. (Transaction No. 22 on page 7-49)

b. Deposit with the city of Philadelphia the amount of city income taxes withheld for the November payrolls. (Transaction No. 23 on page 7-52)

December 18

a. Deposit with the state of Pennsylvania the amount of state income taxes withheld from the December 4 payroll. (Transaction No. 24 on page 7-51)

b. Glo-Brite received notification there will be no premium charge for the month of December on the policy for Serdar Russell. Prepare an entry for a check payable to the estate of Serdar P. Russell for the amount withheld for insurance from her December pay.

c. Prepare an employee's earnings record for Richard Lloyd Zimmerman who was employed starting today to take Serdar Russell's place.

Richard Lloyd Zimmerman	Married filing jointly (MFJ)
900 South Clark Street	$2,600 per month
Philadelphia, PA 19195-6247	$600.00 per week
Phone: 555-2104	$15.00 per hour
Soc. Sec. No.: 000-00-1502	Group ins.: $47,000 beginning next year
Department: Office	Position: Time Clerk

d. Using the information from the Time Clerk's Report Nos. 48 and 49, prepare the last pay for December and record the paychecks issued all employees. Also, record the employer's payroll taxes.

> **Project Audit Test**
> ✓ Net Paid $70,494.00

- In this pay, O'Neill is paid his annual bonus of **$95,000**. This does not affect his group insurance coverage. For withholding purposes, the bonus is considered a supplemental payment and taxed at the supplemental rate of 22 percent.
- O'Neill changed his SIMPLE contribution this pay to **$2,000**, which will reduce his salary for federal income tax purposes.

- To determine federal income tax on the remaining taxable portion of his regular salary, use the Wage Bracket Method Tables for Manual Payroll Systems With Forms W-4 From 2020 or Later – Biweekly Payroll Period – Standard columns (pages T-7 and T-8). In calculating the tax, do not round the aggregate to the nearest earnings dollar.
- In this pay, O'Neill has reached the OASDI ceiling. **To calculate O'Neill's OASDI tax, multiply the OASDI ceiling of $147,000 by 6.2 percent and then subtract the OASDI taxes withheld up to this pay.**

Note: After posting the information for this last pay to the Employees' Earnings Records, the quarterly and yearly totals on each earnings record will automatically be calculated using the protected formulas.

Time Clerk's Report No. 48
For the Week Ending December 5, 20--

Employee	Time Record							Time Worked	Time Lost
	S	M	T	W	T	F	S		
Bonno, A. V. . . .	4	8	8	8	8	8		44 hrs.	. . .
Ford, C. L.		8	8	8	8	8		40 hrs.	. . .
Russell, S. P.		8	8	8	8	8		40 hrs.	. . .
Ryan, J. M.		8	9	9	9	9		44 hrs.	. . .
Student		8	8	7	8	4		35 hrs.	1 hr.*
Woods, B. A. . . .		8	8	8	8	8		40 hrs.	. . .
Young, P. W. . . .		8	8	8	8	8		40 hrs.	

*Time lost because of tardiness; deduct 1 hour's pay.

Time Clerk's Report No. 49
For the Week Ending December 12, 20--

Employee	Time Record							Time Worked	Time Lost
	S	M	T	W	T	F	S		
Bonno, A. V. . . .	8	8	8	8	8	8		48 hrs.	. . .
Ford, C. L.		4	8	8	8	8		36 hrs.	4 hrs.*
Russell, S. P.		8	8	8	8	D		32 hrs.	8 hrs.
Ryan, J. M.		10	8	8	9	8		43 hrs.	. . .
Student		4	8	8	8	4		32 hrs.	4 hrs.**
Woods, B. A. . . .		8	8	8	8	8		40 hrs.	. . .
Young, P. W. . . .		8	8	8	8	8		40 hrs.	

*Time spent in training session; no deduction in pay.
**Time lost in dentist appointment; no deduction in pay.

Project Audit Test

January						
Su	Mo	Tu	We	Th	Fr	Sa
					1	2
3	4	5	6	7	8	9
10	11	12	13	14	15	16
17	18	19	20	21	22	23
24	25	26	27	28	29	30
31						

V. End-of-Year Activities

This completes the project insofar as recording the payroll transactions for the last quarter. The following additional transactions are given to illustrate different types of transactions arising in connection with the accounting for payroll taxes.

Record these transactions in the Journal, but do not post to the General Ledger.

January 6

a. Deposit with the state of Pennsylvania the amount of state income taxes withheld from the December 18 payroll. Use the current balance of account 25, Employees SIT Payable. (Transaction No. 28 on page 7-51)

January 8

a. Pay the treasurer of the union the amount withheld during the month of December. Use the current balance of account 28, Union Dues Payable.

January 15

a. Electronically deposit the amount of FICA taxes and federal income taxes for the December payrolls. (Transaction No. 30 on page 7-49)

b. Deposit with the city of Philadelphia the amount of city income taxes withheld from the December payrolls. (Transaction No. 31 on page 7-52)

February 1

a. Prepare **Form 941, Employer's Quarterly Federal Tax Return**, for the fourth quarter. The information needed to prepare Form 941 can be obtained from the ledger accounts, payroll registers, employees' earnings records, and Federal Deposit forms. The wages paid to Serdar Russell ($2,394.00) and the SIMPLE plan deductions need to be deducted from Line 2 total quarterly wages. Line 5a wages are total quarterly wages paid less the amount paid to O'Neill in excess of the $147,000 cap on Social Security wages, while line 5c is total quarterly wages. (Transaction No. 32 on pages 7-54 to 7-56)

　　Form 941 and all forms that follow are to be signed by the president of the company, Joseph T. O'Neill.

b. Prepare **Form 940, Employer's Annual Federal Unemployment (FUTA) Tax Return**. Line 3 is the annual gross pay. Line 7 is the total amount of earnings for the year that are subject to FUTA tax. Since the wage base for FUTA is $7,000, you will check the earnings records to see who has earnings in excess of the wage base. Add $7,000 for each employee over the wage base plus the total earnings of any employee earning less than the wage base. Lines 5 and 6 are the difference between these two amounts and represent the earnings in excess of the FUTA wage base of $7,000. (Remember any amount in excess of $7,000 is not taxed for FUTA.) Line 8 total tax paid should equal the February 1 payment. (Transaction No. 33 on pages 7-57 and 7-58)

　　Journalize the entry to record the electronic deposit for the FUTA tax liability. (Transaction No. 33 on pages 7-49)

c. Prepare **Form UC-2, Employer's Report for Unemployment Compensation-Fourth Quarter**. In Pennsylvania, a credit week is any calendar week during the quarter in which the employee earned at least $50 (without regard to when paid). The maximum number of credit weeks in a quarter is 13. (Transaction No. 34 on page 7-59)

　　Journalize the entry to record the payment of the SUTA taxes (employer and employee) for the fourth quarter.

d. Complete a **Form W-2, Wage and Tax Statement**, for each current employee using the employees' earnings records and address information from Figure A.4 on page A-9. **Note:** You will need to adjust total earnings in Box 1 if the employee made SIMPLE contributions. Use each employee's earnings record to obtain the information needed to complete the forms. The two plant workers (Bonno and Ryan) have had $121.00 in union dues withheld during the year. In addition to union dues withheld, include Pennsylvania State Unemployment Tax (SUTA) withheld in Box 14. (Transaction No. 35 on pages 7-61 through 7-65)

e. Complete **Form W-3, Transmittal of Wage and Tax Statements**. Use the information from all Forms W-2 to complete this form. (Transaction No. 36 on page 7-66)

f. Complete Pennsylvania **Form REV-1667, W-2 Transmittal**. Use the information on Forms W-2 to complete this report. **Remember:** Russell's final check was not subject to SIT. (Transaction No. 37 on page 7-66) The wages paid and the Pennsylvania tax withheld for the first three quarters are provided in Figure A.17.

Figure A.17
Pennsylvania State Income Tax

Quarter	Wages Paid	Tax Withheld
1st	$34,088.75	$1,046.52
2nd	$45,535.62	$1,397.94
3rd	$62,600.20	$1,921.83

g. Complete **Form 1099-MISC, Miscellaneous Income**, for the payment to the Estate of Serdar P. Russell. This is the gross amount of Russell's last pay. Because the check was written to the estate, this amount is reported as "Other income" in Box 3 so that the IRS will not seek self-employment tax on the amount and it should not appear on the W-2, as noted in (d) above. (Transaction No. 38 on page 7-67)

h. Complete **Form 1096, Annual Summary and Transmittal of U.S. Information Returns**. Use the information on Form 1099-MISC to complete this form. (Transaction No. 39 on page 7-67)

i. **Pennsylvania Quarterly Reconciliation of Income Tax Withheld** is filed electronically. (Transaction No. 40 on page 7-52)

j. Prepare the **Annual Reconciliation of Employer Wage Tax for Philadelphia**. For Lines 1, 3, and 4, use gross wages and salaries per General Ledger less the exempt wages paid to the Estate of Serdar P. Russell. (This amount should agree with Form W-3, Box 18, local wages.) Tax paid during the first three quarters was $5,461.14. For reporting purposes, there were 10 Philadelphia residents for whom wage tax was remitted for the pay period ending March 12, 20--. (Transaction No. 41 on page 7-53)

Recording End-of-Year Payroll Adjustments

a. On the financial statements prepared at the end of its first year of operations, the company must show an accurate picture of all expenses and all liabilities incurred. The last payday of the year was December 18. However, the payment to the employees on that day did not include the weeks ending December 19 and 26 and the four days (December 28–31) in the following week. These earnings will be reflected in the January payrolls. Two-column journal paper is provided for use in journalizing the following entry on the next page.

Prepare the adjusting entry as of December 31 to record the salaries and wages that have accrued but remain unpaid as of the end of the year. When calculating the amount of the accrual for each hourly worker, assume each employee worked eight hours on each day during the period with no overtime (student works a 36-hour week—student worked 32 hours for the period December 28 through December 31). For each salaried worker, the accrual will amount to 14/10 of the worker's biweekly earnings, except for Zimmerman who worked only 10 days.

Each of the labor cost accounts should be debited for the appropriate amount of the accrual, and Salaries and Wages Payable should be credited for the total amount of the accrual. There is no liability for payroll taxes on the accrued salaries and wages until the workers are actually paid. Therefore, the company follows the practice of not accruing payroll taxes.

b. Also, prepare the adjusting entry as of December 31 to record the accrued vacation pay as of the end of the year. Record the expense in a vacation benefits expense account, and credit the appropriate liability account. Use the journal paper provided on the following page.

As of December 31, the vacation time earned but not used by each employee is listed here.

Bonno	80 hours
Ferguson	three weeks
Ford	two weeks
Mann	one week
O'Neill	four weeks
Ryan	80 hours
Sokowski	two weeks
Student	72 hours
Woods	none
Young	none
Zimmerman	none

JOURNAL

Page ____

DATE	DESCRIPTION	POST. REF.	DEBIT	CREDIT

Name _____

VI. Project Audit Tests

NOVEMBER 20 PAYROLL: (Answers are provided below for the Illustrative Case.)

Payroll Register

1. What is the amount of FIT withheld for Kari C. Mann?......................................	$ 14.00
2. What is the total amount of SUTA withheld this period for all employees?......................	$ 8.39
3. What is the total gross pay for all employees?	$ 13,994.09

Journal

4. What is the November 16 credit to Cash for the deposit of FICA & FIT taxes?	$ 6,447.03
5. What is the amount of the debit to Payroll Taxes?	$ 1,139.16
6. What is the November 16 debit to Employees CIT Payable?...	$ 1,204.92

General Ledger

7. What is the balance of Employees SIT Payable?..	$ 429.64
8. What is the amount of Office Salaries paid to date?	$ 48,023.33
9. What is the balance of Simple Contributions Payable?	$ 1,650.00
10. What is the Cash account balance?	$ 142,275.20

- -

Name _____

Project Audit Test

DECEMBER 4 PAYROLL: (As you complete your work, answer the following questions.)

Payroll Register

1. What is the net pay for Joseph T. O'Neill?	_____
2. What is the amount of OASDI withheld for Jeri M. Ryan?..	_____
3. What is the total net pay for all employees?	_____
4. What is the total CIT withheld for all employees?...	_____

Journal

5. What is the amount of the debit to Employees SIT Payable on December 3?................	_____
6. What is the amount of the credit to Employees FIT Payable?..	_____
7. What is the amount of the debit to Payroll Taxes?..	_____

General Ledger

8. What is the balance of SUTA Taxes Payable—Employer?	_____
9. What is the balance of Employees CIT Payable?	_____
10. What is the Cash account balance?	_____

Name _____

Project Audit Test

DECEMBER 14 PAYROLL: (As you complete your work, answer the following questions.)

Payroll Register

1. What is the amount of FIT withheld for Serdar P. Russell?.. _____

2. What is the amount of net pay received by Serdar P. Russell's estate? .... _____

3. What was Serdar P. Russell's filing status?.. _____

Journal

4. What is the amount of the debit to Union Dues Payable on December 9?..................... _____

5. What is the amount of the debit to Payroll Cash? .... _____

6. What is the amount of the credit to Employees SUTA Payable? .... _____

General Ledger

7. What is the amount that was credited to Group Insurance Premiums Collected
(account number 27) during this period?.. _____

8. What is the amount paid for office salaries to date? .... _____

9. What is the balance of FICA Taxes Payable—OASDI? .... _____

10. What is the balance of Payroll Taxes? .... _____

- -

Name _____

Project Audit Test

DECEMBER 18 PAYROLL: (As you complete your work, answer the following questions.)

Payroll Register

1. What is the amount of FIT withheld for Joseph T. O'Neill?... _____

2. What is the total current net pay for all employees? .... _____

3. What is the total gross pay for all employees?.. _____

4. What is the taxable amount of Joseph T. O'Neill's gross pay for OASDI?...................... _____

Journal

5. What is the amount of the credit to Cash for the deposit of FICA and FIT taxes
on December 15? .... _____

6. What is the amount of the debit to Payroll Taxes? .... _____

7. What is the amount of the debit to Employees CIT Payable on December 15?............. _____

General Ledger

8. What is the Cash account balance? .... _____

9. What is the total amount of Plant Wages to date?... _____

10. What is the total amount of Payroll Taxes to date? .... _____

Name _____

Project Audit Test

END-OF-YEAR ACTIVITIES

Journal

1. What is the amount of the deposit for Pennsylvania state income taxes withheld from the December 18 payroll? .... _____

2. What is the amount of FICA Taxes Payable—OASDI deposited from the December payrolls? .... _____

3. What is the amount of the city of Philadelphia employees income tax deposited from the December payrolls? .... _____

4. What is the amount of FUTA Taxes Payable deposited for the quarter? .... _____

5. What is the amount of the credit to Cash for SUTA Taxes Payable for the fourth quarter? .... _____

Payroll Adjusting Entries

6. What is the amount of the credit to Salaries and Wages Payable for the December 31 adjusting entry? .... _____

7. What is the amount of the debit to Vacation Benefits Expense for the December 31 adjusting entry? .... _____

Calculations

8. What is the total payroll tax expense incurred by the employer on salaries and wages paid during the quarter ended December 31? .... _____

9. What is the total payroll tax expense incurred by the employer on the total earnings of Joseph T. O'Neill during the fourth quarter? .... _____

10. O'Neill has decided to give all current employees (excluding himself) a bonus payment during January equal to 5% of their total gross pay for last year. What is the total of this bonus payment? .... _____

Payroll Project Using Online Automated General Ledger Software

This edition of *Payroll Accounting* contains two different options for student solution: the complete, full version of the payroll project (which follows), and a short version. Both versions are identical except the short version requires only the completion of the December payrolls (as well as the last quarter and annual tax reports and forms). The short version's step-by-step instructions begin on page B-23 of this appendix. Be sure to ask your instructor which of the two versions you are to complete.

I.	Payroll Project	B-1
II.	Illustrative Case—Full Project	B-3
III.	Payroll Project (Short Version)	B-23
IV.	Illustrative Case—Short Project	B-25
V.	End-of-Year Activities	B-39
VI.	Project Audit Tests	B-43

I. Payroll Project

The payroll project that follows is the computerized version of the same project you completed manually in Chapter 7 beginning on page 7-6 of the text book.

Appendix B is divided into six sections, which include Illustrative Cases, instructions for the payroll project and short payroll projects, End-of-Year Activities, and Project Audit Tests.

In this project, you are employed by Glo-Brite Paint Company as the person in the accounting department responsible for the company's payroll processing using the computerized payroll system described in the preceding material. Like the manual project in Chapter 7, you will assume that the payroll records, tax reports, and deposits have been completed and filed for the first three quarters of this year. Your work will involve the computer processing of the payrolls for the last quarter of the year and the completion of the last quarter and annual tax reports and forms. You may complete the required deposit, quarterly, yearly, etc., forms described in Chapter 7 in CengageNOWv2. If you have already completed these forms for the manual student project, check them as you progress through this project and note any differences.

To help you get started, the first pay period is provided as a tutorial problem that illustrates the principles and procedures required to process payroll transactions using the *Automated General Ledger Software*. In subsequent pay period processing, whenever a new operational procedure is used for the first time, additional instruction will be provided. Each of the following step-by-step instructions lists a task to be completed at the computer.

Cengage
CNOWv2

This project has been broken down into several assignments comprising all or part of the project in your text. The assignments are delivered online using the CengageNOWv2 learning management system, with each assignment being graded automatically and submitted to your instructor. Your instructor may choose to have you complete only part of this project, so watch the dates and follow the instructions carefully.

Note: Throughout this project, some of the computer-calculated withholding amounts (e.g., federal income tax) will differ slightly from the amounts (from the tax tables) in the manual payroll project in Chapter 7. This occurs because the software uses the annualized percentage method from *IRS Publication 15-T* rather than the table look-up to compute withholding taxes (see Figure B-1). The differences here should be less than two dollars per pay period, and usually are much less. Also, the accounts differ slightly from those in Chapter 7, but there is a "Partial Chart of Accounts" available in the software to help you quickly find the accounts you need, or refer to Figure B.2.

Figure B.1

2022 Percentage Method Tables for Automated Payroll Systems

STANDARD Withholding Rate Schedules (Use these if the Form W-4 is from 2019 or earlier, or if the Form W-4 is from 2020 or later and the box in Step 2 of Form W-4 is **NOT** checked. Also use these for Form W-4P from any year.)				
If the Adjusted Annual Wage Amount on Worksheet 1A or the Adjusted Annual Payment Amount on Worksheet 1B is:		**The tentative amount to withhold is:**	**Plus this percentage—**	**of the amount that the Adjusted Annual Wage or Payment exceeds—**
At least—	**But less than—**			
A	**B**	**C**	**D**	**E**
Married Filing Jointly				
$0	$13,000	$0.00	0%	$0
$13,000	$33,550	$0.00	10%	$13,000
$33,550	$96,550	$2,055.00	12%	$33,550
$96,550	$191,150	$9,615.00	22%	$96,550
$191,150	$353,100	$30,427.00	24%	$191,150
$353,100	$444,900	$69,295.00	32%	$353,100
$444,900	$660,850	$98,671.00	35%	$444,900
$660,850		$174,253.50	37%	$660,850
Single or Married Filing Separately				
$0	$4,350	$0.00	0%	$0
$4,350	$14,625	$0.00	10%	$4,350
$14,625	$46,125	$1,027.50	12%	$14,625
$46,125	$93,425	$4,807.50	22%	$46,125
$93,425	$174,400	$15,213.50	24%	$93,425
$174,400	$220,300	$34,647.50	32%	$174,400
$220,300	$544,250	$49,335.50	35%	$220,300
$544,250		$162,718.00	37%	$544,250

Source: Internal Revenue Service

Figure B.2
Partial Chart of Accounts comparison

Classification	Account Number	Text Account Number	Account Title
Assets	11	11	Cash
	12	12	Payroll Cash
Liabilities	20.1	20.1	FICA Taxes Payable—OASDI
	20.2	20.2	FICA Taxes Payable—HI
	21	21	FUTA Taxes Payable
	22	22	SUTA Taxes Payable—Employer
	24	24	Employees FIT Payable
	25	25	Employees SIT Payable
	25.1	25.1	Employees SUTA Payable
	26	26	Employees CIT Payable
	27	27	Group Insurance Premium Collected
	28	28	Union Dues Payable
	29	29	SIMPLE Contributions Payable
Capital	30	N/A	Capital
Expenses	51	51	Administrative Salaries
	52	52	Office Salaries
	53	53	Sales Salaries
	54	54	Plant Wages
	56	56	Payroll Taxes

II. Illustrative Case—Full Project

October 9 Payroll

The *Automated General Ledger Software* is set up to guide you through completing the fourth quarter's payroll project from Chapter 7. The software provides two very important directions you'll need to go through before starting the instructions. **Get Started** walks you through the features of the software, such as identifying the modules you'll be using, how and where to access reports, how to resize screens, and introduces Source Documents and Instructions. **General Instructions** provide an overview of what you will be doing and explain why some amounts will differ from those in Chapter 7. It is very important that you complete the Get Started and General Instructions before you begin the October 9 Payroll.

The *Automated General Ledger Software* menu bar on the left side of the screen is where you will find the modules you'll be using to complete the assignments in this project. There are three primary modules: Company, General Ledger, and Payroll. When you click on a module, the icon will be highlighted.

On the right side of the screen is the assignment panel. This panel contains instruction to get you started on the assignment and in some cases you will be referred to a Source Document. The Source Documents represent real-world documents that you will refer to in order to complete the assignment. Included in the Source Documents are instructions to guide you through the Source Document. Source Document references have been included in the demonstration assignments for the long version demonstration assignment. All other Source Documents are shown in the Assignment Instruction panel and accessed on the bottom of the panel by clicking on the Source Document button.

Follow the steps below to complete the **October 9** payroll transactions using the *Automated General Ledger Software*. To access additional Help for any function, click on the **Help** (?) button that appears at the top right of the screen. There is a **Help** screen with additional information and sample screens for every menu option in the program. Click on the **Save** button at the lower right of your screen at any point to save your work if you need to stop working to continue later. Your work will automatically be restored when you return.

1. Ensure the **System Date** at the top of the screen is **October 9, 2023**. Note that the year needs to be **2023** in order for the problem to grade correctly.

2. Click on the **General Ledger** module and select the **Chart of Accounts** from the **Account Lists** menu. Review this list to understand how the software designates the Payroll accounts.

3. Enter the employee maintenance data. Click on the **Payroll** module and **Maintain Employees** task from the **Tasks** menu bar. Scroll down to select employee number **180** (Student), enter your own name in the **Employee Name** field (enter your last name in all capital letters similar to the other employees), then **Tab** out of the field. Click on the **Close** button, and answer "Yes" to accept your changes. **Note:** Do not change any of the other fields. If you do, your solutions will not be correct.

4. Display the Employee List report. Click on the **Employee List** from the **Reports** menu on the top menu bar of the **Payroll** module. The report is shown in Figure B.3 (Source Document 1 of 11). Verify the accuracy of the maintenance input from step 3 above and make any corrections via the **Maintain Employees** option.

Figure B.3
Employee List

Emp. No.	Employee Name/Address	Social Security /Filing Status	# Pay Periods	G.L. Accounts	Salary /Rate
100	BONNO, Anthony Victor 694 Bristol Avenue Philadelphia, PA 19135-0617	000-00-3481 Married Filing Joint W/H NA	26	54	0.00 17.60
110	FERGUSON, Jamie Hadi 808 Sixth Street Philadelphia, PA 19106-0995	000-00-8645 Married Filing Joint W/H NA	26	52	2,250.00 0.00
120	FORD, Catherine Louise 18 Dundee Avenue Philadelphia, PA 19151-1919	000-00-4567 Single W/H N/A	26	52	1,220.00 0.00
130	MANN, Kari Casey 3007 Bisque Drive Philadelphia, PA 19199-0718	000-00-9352 Married Filing Joint W/H N/A	26	53	1,350.00 0.00
140	O'NEILL, Joseph Tyler 2100 Broad Street Philadelphia, PA 19121-7189	000-00-1534 Married Filing Joint W/H N/A	26	51	2,307.69 0.00
150	RUSSELL, Serdar Parker 8004 Dowling Road Philadelphia, PA 19135-9001	000-00-6337 Single W/H N/A	26	52	1,200.00 0.00
160	RYAN, Jeri Mischa 7300 Harrison Street Philadelphia, PA 19124-6699	000-00-1233 Married Filing Joint W/H N/A	26	54	0.00 18.00
170	SOKOWSKI, Thomas James 133 Cornwells Street Philadelphia, PA 19171-5718	000-00-8832 Married Filing Joint W/H N/A	26	54	2,050.00 0.00
180	STUDENT 7018 Erdrick Street Philadelphia, PA 19135-8517	000-00-5555 Single W/H N/A	26	52	0.00 15.00
190	WILLIAMS, Ruth Virginia 9433 State Street Philadelphia, PA 19149-0819	000-00-6741 Single W/H N/A	26	52	1,223.08 0.00

5. Enter the Payroll transactions for the period using the detailed instructions in steps (a) through (j). Refer to the Figure B.4 for this period (Source Document 2 of 11):

To enter the payroll records, click on **Pay Employees** from the **Tasks** menu of the **Payroll** module. If you need more space, you can collapse the Assignment panel on the right side of your screen by clicking on the arrow. In addition, you can move the form by grabbing the top of the Payroll form with your mouse to reposition it to better fit on your screen. You should also scroll over to grab the lower-right corner of the form to drag it down to fill the screen. Source Documents can be moved and resized by doing the same thing.

a. The prior quarters payroll information is already entered, and will show up in the Yearly column of the reports, but NOT in the payroll entry screens.

b. For each pay period, you will need to add a new record to this payroll register for each employee to be paid. Click on the **Add** button to add a new pay record for each of the above employees, and then enter the corresponding fields. You may need to scroll down to the bottom of the payroll form to see the newly added line.

c. **Date:** Make sure the date is set to **10/09/23** for each new record, or use the pop-up calendar to change it. Payroll recording is <u>very</u> dependent on having the correct dates, so **verify this date**, especially for the first employee in any payroll set.

d. **Employee Name:** Select the name from the drop-down list or key the first letter of the employee's last name until the correct name appears.

e. **Check No.:** Start with check number **672** to continue from where the previous quarter left off. This number will automatically increase by 1 for each subsequent employee. It is critical to get this check number correct for each employee, along with the date, as this is how the software matches up your entries for grading.

Figure B.4
Employees To Be Paid This Pay Period

Check Number	Employee Number	Employee Name	Salary / Reg. Hrs.	Bonus	Overtime @ Time 1 1/2	Overtime @ Double	Group Ins.	Union Dues	SIMPLE Contribution
672	100	Bonno, Anthony Victor	80					$ 8.00	
673	110	Ferguson, Jamie Hadi	reg. salary						
674	120	Ford, Catherine Louise	reg. salary						
675	130	Mann, Kari Casey	reg. salary						
676	140	O'Neill, Joseph Tyler	reg. salary						
677	150	Russell, Serdar Parker	reg. salary						
678	160	Ryan, Jeri Mischa	80					$ 8.00	
679	170	Sokowski, Thomas James	reg. salary						
680	180	Student (your name)	72						
681	190	Williams, Ruth Virginia	reg. salary						

f. **Salary or Hours worked:** For salaried employees, the salary should display automatically. For hourly employees, click on the **Reg. Hours** field and enter the number of regular work hours shown above.

g. For the two union employees noted above, enter $8.00 into the **Union Dues** field.

h. Click on the **Calculate Taxes** button for each employee to fill the remaining fields. **Net Pay** will calculate automatically, and **Gross Pay** will display at the bottom of the form.

i. Review the amounts calculated for reasonableness.

j. Click **Add** to start a new employee or **Save** when done. It is extremely important that you **Save** the employee information you have entered and see a message like the one below. Failure to **Save** the payroll will cause errors on the **Payroll Report**. You may need to confirm the data you entered or the changes you made. If you make a mistake, just go to the appropriate line and field, and change the value. Click on the **Calculate Taxes** button to recalculate these amounts. **Net Pay** will re-compute automatically.

6. Display the Payroll Report. Click on the **Payroll Report** from the **Reports** menu at the top of the **Payroll** module. The payroll report for Employee 100; Bonno, Anthony Victor, followed by the payroll summary, is shown in Figure B.5 (Source Document 4 of 11). Due to its length, only the first employee and the summary are shown. If the summary is incorrect, review the list of employees to be paid from step 5 above. Check your numbers, and make any changes using the **Pay Employees** task.

7. Generate and post the journal entry for the current payroll. Click on the **Current Payroll Journal Entry** in the **Tasks** menu of the **Payroll** module. Click **Yes** when asked if you want to generate the journal entry. If your journal entries do not match those shown in Figure B.6 (Source Document 5 of 11), check your employee list and payroll report for keying errors, and go back to make the necessary corrections. If they are correct, click on **Post**. The journal entry will reappear, posted, in the General Journal.

Figure B.5
Payroll Report 10/09

		Current	Quarterly	Yearly
100 - BONNO, Anthony Victor	Gross Pay	1,408.00	1,408.00	12,730.00
54 - Plant Wages	FIT	41.18	41.18	851.18
Married Acct. 54	SIT	43.23	43.23	390.82
W/H 000-00-3481	Soc. Sec. (OASDI)	87.30	87.30	789.26
Pay Periods 26	Medicare (HI)	20.42	20.42	184.59
Salary 0.00	CIT	54.06	54.06	488.80
Hourly Rate 17.60	Group Ins.	-	-	144.80
Reg. Hours 80.00	Union Dues	8.00	8.00	80.00
O.T. Hours	Simple Plan	-	-	-
Check Number 672	Employee SUTA	0.84	0.84	7.63
Check Date 10/09/23	Net Pay	1,152.97	1,152.97	9,792.92
Payroll Summary	Gross Pay	15,528.77	15,528.77	157,753.34
	FIT	803.91	803.91	16,720.91
	SIT	476.76	476.76	4,843.05
	Soc. Sec. (OASDI)	962.79	962.79	9,780.71
	Medicare (HI)	225.18	225.18	2,287.45
	CIT	596.28	596.28	6,057.42
	Group Ins.	-	-	930.40
	Union Dues	16.00	16.00	160.00
	Simple Plan	-	-	-
	Employee SUTA	9.30	9.30	94.64
	Net Pay	12,438.55	12,438.55	116,878.76

Figure B.6
Current Payroll Journal Entries

Acct.	Title	Debit	Credit
51	Administrative Salaries	2,307.69	
52	Office Salaries	4,723.08	
53	Sales Salaries	3,600.00	
54	Plant Wages	4,898.00	
12	Payroll Cash		12,438.55
20.1	FICA Taxes Payable - OASDI		962.79
20.2	FICA Taxes Payable - HI		225.18
24	Employees FIT Payable		803.91
25	Employees SIT Payable		476.76
25.1	Employees SUTA Payable		9.30
26	Employees CIT Payable		596.28
28	Union Dues Payable		16.00

8. Generate and post the employer's payroll taxes journal entry. Click on the **Employer's Payroll Taxes Journal Entry** in the **Tasks** menu of the **Payroll** module. Compare your entries as they appear in the **Payroll Taxes Journal Entries** dialog box to Figure B.7 (Source Document 6 of 11). Click **Yes** when asked if you want to generate the journal entry. If they are correct, click on **Post**, otherwise go back and re-check your inputs. After you accept the entries, they will reappear, posted, in the General Journal.

9. Enter and post the October 9 General Journal entry to record the deposit of cash for the total net amount owed to employees in the payroll cash account. This is also found as the current period **Net Pay** value on the Payroll Report. From the **General Ledger** module, select **Tasks** and the **General Journal**. Enter the journal transaction shown in Figure B.8 (Source Documents 7 and 8 of 11), by first clicking on the **Add New Entry** button. Verify the date and enter **General** as the reference. Next, click on the **Insert Debit/Credit** button, enter the first account number (**12**) or click on the pop-up **Chart of Accounts** icon to display a list for selection. Enter the debit amount to clear the existing credit to **Payroll Cash** from the first journal entry above. Then click on **Insert Debit/Credit** again to enter the credit to the **Cash** account (**11**). Finally, click on the **Post** button to post this entry to the General Ledger.

Figure B.7
Payroll Taxes Journal Entries

Acct.	Title	Debit	Credit
56	Payroll Taxes	1,390.21	
20.1	FICA Taxes Payable - OASDI		962.78
20.2	FICA Taxes Payable - HI		225.17
21	FUTA Taxes Payable		23.34
22	SUTA Taxes Payable - Employer		178.92

Figure B.8
General Journal Payroll Cash Entries

Acct.	Title	Debit	Credit
12	Payroll Cash	12,438.55	
11	Cash		12,438.55

10. Display the General Journal report. With the **General Ledger** module still displayed, select **General Journal** from the **Journal Reports** menu on the top menu bar. The General Journal report is shown in Figure B.9 (Source Document 9 of 11). Note that you can change the dates of the report to match the dates of the assignment, which you will need to do for subsequent assignments. Simply select the range of dates and click **Apply**. You can also customize the report to display only certain **Reference** values or account numbers.

11. Display the General Ledger report. With the **General Ledger** module selected, click on **General Ledger** from the **Ledger Reports** menu on the top menu bar. The General Ledger report is shown in Figure B.10 (Source Document 10 of 11), on page B-10. You can customize this report to list only a selected range of accounts.

Figure B.9
General Journal Report

Date	Refer.	Acct.	Title	Debit	Credit
10/09/23	Payroll	51	Administrative Salaries	2,307.69	
10/09/23	Payroll	52	Office Salaries	4,723.08	
10/09/23	Payroll	53	Sales Salaries	3,600.00	
10/09/23	Payroll	54	Plant Wages	4,898.00	
10/09/23	Payroll	12	Payroll Cash		12,438.55
10/09/23	Payroll	20.1	FICA Taxes Payable - OASDI		962.79
10/09/23	Payroll	20.2	FICA Taxes Payable - HI		225.18
10/09/23	Payroll	24	Employees FIT Payable		803.91
10/09/23	Payroll	25	Employees SIT Payable		476.76
10/09/23	Payroll	25.1	Employees SUTA Payable		9.30
10/09/23	Payroll	26	Employees CIT Payable		596.28
10/09/23	Payroll	28	Union Dues Payable		16.00
10/09/23	Payroll	56	Payroll Taxes	1,390.21	
10/09/23	Payroll	20.1	FICA Taxes Payable - OASDI		962.78
10/09/23	Payroll	20.2	FICA Taxes Payable - HI		225.17
10/09/23	Payroll	21	FUTA Taxes Payable		23.34
10/09/23	Payroll	22	SUTA Taxes Payable - Employer		178.92
10/09/23	General	12	Payroll Cash	12,438.55	
10/09/23	General	11	Cash		12,438.55
			Totals	29,357.53	29,357.53

Figure B.10

General Ledger Report

Account	Journal	Date	Reference	Debit	Credit	Balance
11-Cash						
11-Cash	Balance Forward					199,846.33 Dr
11-Cash	General	10/9/2023	General	0	12,438.55	187407.78 Dr
12-Payroll Cash						
12-Payroll Cash	General	10/9/2023	Payroll	0	12,438.55	12,438.55 Cr
12-Payroll Cash	General	10/9/2023	General	12,438.55	0	0
20.1-FICA Taxes Payable-OASDI						
20.1-FICA Taxes Payable-OASDI	General	10/9/2023	Payroll	0	962.79	962.79 Cr
20.1-FICA Taxes Payable-OASDI	General	10/9/2023	Payroll	0	962.78	1,925.57 Cr
20.2-FICA Taxes Payable-HI						
20.2-FICA Taxes Payable-HI	General	10/9/2023	Payroll	0	225.18	225.18 Cr
20.2-FICA Taxes Payable-HI	General	10/9/2023	Payroll	0	225.17	450.35 Cr
21-FUTA Taxes Payable						
21-FUTA Taxes Payable	Balance Forward					392.94 Cr
21-FUTA Taxes Payable	General	10/9/2023	Payroll	0	23.34	416.28 Cr
22-SUTA Taxes Payable-Employer						
22-SUTA Taxes Payable-Employer	General	10/9/2023	Payroll	0	178.92	178.92 Cr
24-Employees FIT Payable						
24-Employees FIT Payable	General	10/9/2023	Payroll	0	803.91	803.91 Cr
25-Employees SIT Payable						
25-Employees SIT Payable	General	10/9/2023	Payroll	0	476.76	476.76 Cr
25.1-Employees SUTA Payable						
25.1-Employees SUTA Payable	General	10/9/2023	Payroll	0	9.30	9.30 Cr
26-Employees CIT Payable						
26-Employees CIT Payable	General	10/9/2023	Payroll	0	596.28	596.28 Cr
27-Group Insurance Premium Collected						
27-Group Insurance Premium Collected	No Activity					
28-Union Dues Payable						
28-Union Dues Payable	General	10/9/2023	Payroll	0	16.00	16.00 Cr
29-SIMPLE Contributions Payable						
29-SIMPLE Contributions Payable	No Activity					
30-Capital						
30-Capital	Balance Forward					356,031.03 Cr
51-Administrative Salaries						
51-Administrative Salaries	Balance Forward					42,692.27 Dr
51-Administrative Salaries	General	10/9/2023	Payroll	2,307.69	0	44,999.96 Dr
52-Office Salaries						
52-Office Salaries	Balance Forward					28,350.00 Dr
52-Office Salaries	General	10/9/2023	Payroll	4,723.08	0	33,073.08 Dr
53-Sales Salaries						
53-Sales Salaries	Balance Forward					28,525.00 Dr
53-Sales Salaries	General	10/9/2023	Payroll	3,600.00	0	32,125.00 Dr
54-Plant Wages						
54-Plant Wages	Balance Forward					42,657.30 Dr
54-Plant Wages	General	10/9/2023	Payroll	4,898.00	0	47,555.30 Dr
56-Payroll Taxes						
56-Payroll Taxes	Balance Forward					14,353.07 Dr
56-Payroll Taxes	General	10/9/2023	Payroll	1,390.21	0	15,743.28 Dr

12. Generate a labor distribution graph. Click on the **Company** module and select **Labor Distribution** from the Graphs menu bar to generate the graph shown in Figure B.11. Note that the *Automated General Ledger Software* creates the graph from the year-to-date values.

13. If there is a **Check** link on the lower right of your screen, click on that link to review your work. A Check My Work report will be generated and a percentage complete will be shown next to the **Check** button. If you have errors, go back and check the Payroll Report. After fixing individual employees using the **Pay Employees** task, you can delete any of the journal entries, using the **General Journal** task from the **General Ledger** module, and retry any or all of the steps above. If you can't find the errors, you can **Reset** the assignment to the beginning by selecting **Company Setup** in the **Company Information** menu of the **Company** module.

14. When you are comfortable that you have completed all steps of the problem correctly, click on the **Submit Assignment for Grading** button on the lower right of your screen. You will be graded primarily on three criteria for the payroll problems:

- Are the pay settings for each employee correct (rate, deductions, etc.)?
- Are all period's payroll entries correct for each employee?
- Are the ending balances in each General Ledger account correct?

Note that the journal entries themselves are not graded. If the journal entries are correct, the final General Ledger balances will then also be correct. This allows you to create, edit, delete, and re-enter journal entries in any order.

Figure B.11
Labor Distribution

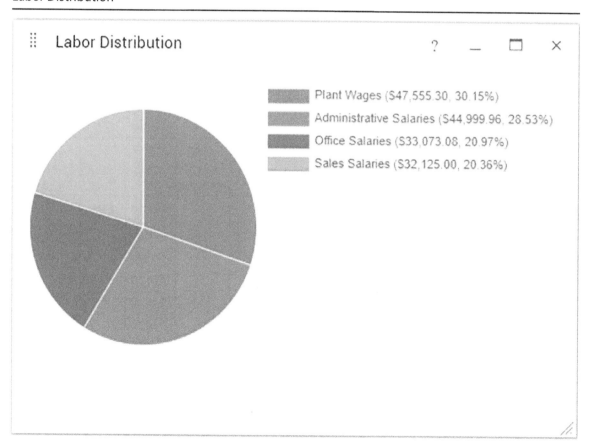

Labor Distribution

- Plant Wages ($47,555.30, 30.15%)
- Administrative Salaries ($44,999.96, 28.53%)
- Office Salaries ($33,073.08, 20.97%)
- Sales Salaries ($32,125.00, 20.36%)

Project Audit Test

✓ Net Paid $12,498.87

October 23 Payroll

When you load this section of the project from your **CengageNOWv2** assignment list, note that all transactions from the prior section are now correctly entered, allowing you to start this section of the project cleanly. You can review the journal and payroll reports through the menu reporting items you used in the last session, and these entries will appear. They will not appear in the journal entry or payroll task screens, however, and cannot be altered.

Click on the **Save** button at the lower right of your screen at any point to save your work if you need to stop working to continue later. Your work will automatically be restored when you return.

1. Ensure the **System Date** at the top right of the screen is set to **October 20, 2023**. Note that the year needs to be **2023** in order for the problem to grade correctly.

2. Enter and post the October 20 transaction required to record the deposit of the Pennsylvania state income taxes withheld from the October 9 payroll. Go to the **General Ledger** module and **General Journal** in the **Tasks** menu bar. Pay the current balance in the Employees SIT Payable account.

3. Change the **System Date** to October 23, 2023, and enter the employee maintenance data. Click on the **Payroll** module and **Maintain Employees** from the **Tasks** menu bar. Scroll down to select employee number **180** (Student), key your own name in the **Employee Name** field (enter your last name in all capital letters similar to the other employees), then **Tab** out of the field. Click on the **Close** button, and answer "Yes" to accept your changes. **Note:** Do not change any of the other fields. If you do, your solutions will not be correct.

4. Enter the Payroll transactions referring to Figure B.12 and detailed instructions that follow. <u>Do</u> deduct Group Insurance. <u>Do</u> deduct Union Dues for the appropriate employees. <u>Do not</u> deduct SIMPLE Contributions. Begin the sequence with **Check No. 682**. Note that the group insurance amounts are monthly. In addition, note that two employees have earned overtime pay, with the hours to be recorded in the **Overtime @ Time 1 1/2** column of the payroll record.

Figure B.12
Employees to Be Paid This Pay Period

Check Number	Employee Number	Employee Name	Salary / Reg. Hrs.	Bonus	Overtime @ Time 1 1/2	Overtime @ Double	Group Ins.	Union Dues	SIMPLE Contribution
682	100	Bonno, Anthony Victor	80		4		$16.50	$8.00	
683	110	Ferguson, Jamie Hadi	reg. salary				$26.40		
684	120	Ford, Catherine Louise	reg. salary				$14.40		
685	130	Mann, Kari Casey	reg. salary				$15.90		
686	140	O'Neill, Joseph Tyler	reg. salary				$27.00		
687	150	Russell, Serdar Parker	reg. salary				$14.10		
688	160	Ryan, Jeri Mischa	80		8		$16.80	$8.00	
689	170	Sokowski,Thomas James	reg. salary				$24.00		
690	180	Student (your name)	72				$12.60		
691	190	Williams, Ruth Virginia	reg. salary				$14.40		

To enter the payroll records, click on **Tasks** and **Pay Employees** from the top menu bar. Enter the information for each employee as you did for the previous payroll period, and click on the **Calculate Taxes** button after entering all deductions for each employee to fill the remaining fields. Be sure to **Save**.

5. Display the **Payroll Report**. Click on **Payroll Report** from the **Reports** menu bar and verify the results compared with input data.

6. Generate and post the journal entry for the current payroll by selecting **Current Payroll Journal Entry** from the **Tasks** menu bar. Click **Yes** when asked if you want to generate the journal entry. When the entry appears in the Current Payroll Journal Entries dialog box, click on **Post**. The journal entry will reappear, posted, in the General Journal.

7. Generate and post the employer's payroll taxes journal entry. With the **Payroll** module still selected, click on **Employer's Payroll Taxes Journal Entry** from the **Tasks** menu bar. Click **Yes** when asked if you want to generate the journal entry. Verify the result and click **Post** to post the entry to the General Journal. After you accept the entries, they will reappear, posted, in the General Journal.

8. Enter and post the October 23 General Journal entry to record the deposit of cash for the total net amount owed to employees in the payroll cash account. Click on the **General Ledger** module and **General Journal** in the **Tasks** menu bar. Based on the current period Net Pay summary information in the payroll report, enter the journal transaction.

9. Display the General Journal report. With the **General Ledger** module still displayed, click on the **General Journal** report from the **Journal Reports** section of menu bar. Note that you can change the dates of the report to match the dates of the assignment (10/20/23 through 10/23/23) to view only the entries for this part of the assignment.

10. Display the General Ledger report. With the **General Ledger** module selected, click on **General Ledger** from **Ledger Reports** of the menu bar. Review the entries for the period.

11. If there is a **Check** link on the lower right of your screen, click on that link to review a summary report of your work and a percentage complete next to the **Check** button. Try to locate the source of the errors and correct them. A good place to start is the Payroll Report and the General Ledger. You are graded on ending general ledger balances and payroll entries. Make sure the check number and employee name are the same as on the Employees to Be Paid This Pay Period form. Remember you can start over from the **Company** module and select **Company Setup** and **Company Information**. The **Reset** command is on the bottom.

12. When you are comfortable that you have completed all steps of the problem correctly, click on the **Submit Assignment for Grading** button on the lower right of your screen.

November 6 Payroll

Follow the steps below to complete the **November 6** payroll transactions, for the period ending October 31.

> **Project Audit Test**
> ✓ Net Paid $12,337.67

1. Ensure the **System Date** at the top of the screen is set to **November 4, 2023**. Note that the year needs to be **2023** in order for the problem to grade correctly.

2. Enter and post the following transactions, using the **General Journal** task under the **General Ledger** module. You can determine current account balances from the **General Ledger** Report in the **Ledger Reports** menu bar.

   - November 4: Deposited the Pennsylvania state income taxes withheld from the October 23 payroll. Pay the balance in the Employees SIT Payable account (25).

- Change the **System Date** to November 6: Paid the treasurer of the union the amount of union dues withheld during the month of October. Pay the balance in the Union Dues Payable account (28).

3. Enter the following information, using **Maintain Employees** in the **Tasks** menu of the **Payroll** module.

   - Change employee 180 from "Student" to your name.
   - Change Thomas J. Sokowski's filing status to Single.

4. Display an **Employee List** report and verify the changes you made in step 3.

Figure B.13
Employees to Be Paid Pay Period

Check Number	Employee Number	Employee Name	Salary / Reg. Hrs.	Bonus	Overtime @ Time 1 1/2	Overtime @ Double	Group Ins.	Union Dues	SIMPLE Contribution
692	100	Bonno, Anthony Victor	80					$8.00	
693	110	Ferguson, Jamie Hadi	reg. salary						
694	120	Ford, Catherine Louise	reg. salary						
695	130	Mann, Kari Casey	reg. salary						
696	140	O'Neill, Joseph Tyler	reg. salary						
697	150	Russell, Serdar Parker	$1,170.00 (loss of 2 hours)						
698	160	Ryan, Jeri Mischa	80					$8.00	
699	170	Sokowski,Thomas James	reg. salary						
700	180	Student (your name)	72						
701	190	Williams, Ruth Virginia	$1,207.85 (loss of 1 hours)						

5. Enter the Payroll transactions referring to Figure B.13 and detailed instructions that follow. <u>Do not</u> deduct Group Insurance. <u>Do</u> deduct Union Dues for the appropriate employees. <u>Do not</u> deduct SIMPLE Contributions. Begin the sequence with **Check No. 692**. Note that you need to enter the salary amounts shown for Virginia Russell and Ruth Williams to override their regular salary amounts. Once you've entered all the employees to be paid, be sure to **Save**.

6. Display and review the **Payroll Report**.

7. Generate and post the journal entry for the current payroll by selecting **Current Payroll Journal Entry** from the **Tasks** menu bar. Click **Yes** when asked if you want to generate the journal entry. When the entry appears in the Current Payroll Journal Entries dialog box, click on **Post**. The journal entry will reappear, posted, in the General Journal.

8. Generate and post the employer's payroll taxes journal entry. With the **Payroll** module still selected, click on **Employer's Payroll Taxes Journal Entry** from the **Tasks** menu bar. Click **Yes** on when asked if you want to generate the journal entry. Verify the result and click **Post** to post the entry to the General Journal. After you accept the entries, they will reappear, posted, in the General Journal.

9. Enter and post the November 6 General Journal entry to record the deposit of cash for the total net amount owed to employees in the payroll cash account. Click on the **General Ledger** module and **General Journal** from the **Tasks** menu. Based on the current period Net Pay summary information in the payroll report, enter the journal transaction.

10. Display and review the General Journal report. With the **General Ledger** module still displayed, click on the **General Journal** report from the **Journal Reports** section of the top menu bar. Note that you should change the dates of the report to match the dates of the assignment (11/4/23 through 11/6/23) to view only the entries for this part of the assignment.

11. Display the General Ledger report. With the **General Ledger** module selected, click on **General Ledger** from the **Ledger Reports** section of the top menu bar.

12. If there is a **Check** link on the lower right of your screen, click on that link to review your work. A Check My Work summary report will be displayed and a percentage correct will show next to the **Check** link. Try to locate the source of the errors and correct them. A good place to start is the Payroll Report and the General Ledger. You are graded on ending general ledger balances and payroll entries. Make sure the check number and employee name are the same as on the Employees to Be Paid This Pay Period form. Remember you can start over from the **Company** module and select **Company Setup** and **Company Information**. The **Reset** command is on the bottom.

13. When you are comfortable that you have completed all steps of the problem correctly, click on the **Submit Assignment for Grading** button on the lower right of your screen.

November 13 Payroll

A special payroll needs to be run to process a discharged employee (Ruth Williams has been discharged because of her excessive tardiness and absenteeism). The step-by-step instructions for completing the November 13 special payroll are listed below.

> **Project Audit Test**
> ✓ Net Paid $1,579.07

1. Ensure the **System Date** at the top of the screen is **November 13, 2023**.

2. Enter Ruth V. Williams' payroll transaction (<u>do</u> deduct Group Ins of $14.40). Enter **Check No. 702** with $2,079.32 in her salary—two partial weeks of work ($856.24), plus two full weeks' pay ($1,223.08) in lieu of two weeks' notice for her final pay. To enter the payroll record, click on the **Pay Employees** task from the top menu bar in the **Payroll** module. Click on the **Calculate Taxes** button after entering all information to fill the remaining fields.

3. Display and review the **Payroll Report**. Click on the **Payroll Report** from the **Reports** menu bar.

4. Generate and post the journal entry for the current payroll by selecting **Current Payroll Journal Entry** from the **Tasks** menu bar. Click **Yes** when asked if you want to generate the journal entry. When the entry appears in the Current Payroll Journal Entries dialog box, click on **Post**. The journal entry will reappear, posted, in the General Journal.

5. Generate and post the employer's payroll taxes journal entry. With the **Payroll** module still selected, click on **Employer's Payroll Taxes Journal Entry** from the **Tasks** menu bar. Click **Yes** when asked if you want to generate the journal entry. Verify the result and click **Post** to post the entry to the General Journal. After you accept the entries, they will reappear, posted, in the General Journal.

6. Enter and post the November 13 general journal entry to record the deposit of cash for the total net amount of Ruth Williams' pay in the payroll cash account. Click on the **General Ledger** module and the **General Journal** task. Based on the current period Net Pay summary information in the Payroll Report, enter the journal transaction.

7. Display and review the **General Journal** report for 11/7/2023 through 11/13/2023.

8. Display and review the **General Ledger** report.

9. If there is a **Check** link on the lower right of your screen, click on that link to review your work. A Check My Work summary report will be displayed and a percentage correct will show next to the **Check** link. Try to locate the source of the errors and correct them. A good place to start is the Payroll Report and the General Ledger. You are graded on ending general ledger balances and payroll entries. Make sure the check number and employee name are the same as on the Employees to Be Paid This Pay Period form. Remember you can start over from the **Company** module and select **Company Setup** and **Company Information**. The **Reset** command is on the bottom.

10. When you are comfortable that you have completed all steps of the problem correctly, click on the **Submit Assignment for Grading** button on the lower right of your screen.

> **Project Audit Test**

✓ Net Paid $9,538.40

November 20 Payroll

Follow the steps below to complete the **November 20** payroll transactions, for the period ending November 14.

1. Ensure the **System Date** at the top of the screen is set to **November 16, 2023**.

2. Enter and post the following transactions, using the **General Journal** task under the **General Ledger** tab. You can determine current account balances from the **General Ledger** Report in the Ledger Reports menu.

   - November 16: Deposited with City Bank the amount of FICA taxes and federal income taxes for the October payrolls. Pay the balance in the two FICA Taxes Payable accounts (20.1 and 20.2) and Employees FIT Payable (24) <u>as of the end of October</u>.

   - November 16: Deposited the city of Philadelphia employees withheld income tax ($1,204.92) with the Department of Revenue for the October payrolls (see the Employees CIT Payable account balance in the general ledger report <u>as of the end of October</u>).

   - Change the **System Date** to November 18: Deposited the Pennsylvania state income taxes withheld from the November 6 regular payroll and November 13 special payroll (pay the balance in the Employees SIT Payable account).

3. Enter the following information, using the **Maintain Employees** task in the **Payroll** module.

   - Change employee 180 from "Student" to your name.

   - Add new employee: Employee number 200; WOODS, Beth Anne; 8102 Franklin Court, Philadelphia, PA 19105-0915; social security number, 000-00-1587; single, salaried, $1,200.00; number of pay periods per year, 26; Account No. 52 (Office Salaries).

4. Make sure the **System Date** at the top of the screen is set to 11/20/23, and enter the Payroll transactions, using the **Pay Employees** task and referring Figure B.14 and detailed instructions that follow. <u>Do</u> deduct Group Insurance. <u>Do</u> deduct Union Dues for the appropriate employees. <u>Do</u> deduct

SIMPLE Contributions as shown. Begin the sequence with **Check No. 703**. In addition, note that you need to enter the salary amount shown for Virginia Russell to override her regular salary amount.

Note: This is the first pay in which the company offers a savings incentive match plan. The computer software has been designed to use the key terms "SIMPLE Contributions" to instruct it to exclude this deduction from the employee's income for FIT purposes. The general ledger account **SIMPLE Contributions Payable** is associated with this deduction for updating during payroll transaction processing.

Note: You need to press the **Calculate Taxes** button AFTER you enter the SIMPLE Contributions amount for each employee in order for taxes to calculate correctly, as this value affects the FIT calculation.

Figure B.14
Employee to Be Paid This Pay Period

Check Number	Employee Number	Employee Name	Salary / Reg. Hrs.	Bonus	Overtime @ Time 1 1/2	Overtime @ Double	Group Ins.	Union Dues	SIMPLE Contribution
703	100	Bonno, Anthony Victor	64				$16.50	$8.00	
704	110	Ferguson, Jamie Hadi	reg. salary				$26.40		$500.00
705	120	Ford, Catherine Louise	reg. salary				$14.40		
706	130	Mann, Kari Casey	reg. salary				$15.90		$250.00
707	140	O'Neill, Joseph Tyler	reg. salary				$27.00		$700.00
708	150	Russell, Serdar Parker	$1,170.00 (Loss of 2 hours)				$14.10		
709	160	Ryan, Jeri Mischa	80				$16.80	$8.00	$200.00
710	170	Sokowski, Thomas James	reg. salary				$24.00		
711	180	Student (your name)	72				$12.60		

5. Display an **Employee List** report and verify information on the new employee.

6. Display and review the **Payroll Report**.

7. Generate and post the journal entry for the current payroll by selecting **Current Payroll Journal Entry** from the **Tasks** menu bar. Click **Yes** when asked if you want to generate the journal entry. When the entry appears in the Current Payroll Journal Entries dialog box, click on **Post**. The journal entry will reappear, posted, in the General Journal.

8. Generate and post the employer's payroll taxes journal entry. With the **Payroll** top tab still selected, click on **Employer's Payroll Taxes Journal Entry** from the **Tasks** menu bar. Click **Yes** when asked if you want to generate the journal entry. Verify the result and click **Post** to post the entry to the General Journal. After you accept the entries, they will reappear, posted, in the General Journal.

9. Enter and post the November 20 General Journal entry to record the deposit of cash for the total net amount owed to employees in the payroll cash account. Click on the **General Ledger** module and select **Tasks** and **General Journal**. Based on the current period Net Pay summary information in the Payroll Report, enter the journal transaction.

10. Display and review the **General Journal** report for 11/14/2023 through 11/20/2023.

11. Display and review the **General Ledger** report.

12. If there is a **Check** link on the lower right of your screen, click on that link to review your work. A Check My Work summary report will be displayed and a percentage correct will show next to the **Check** link. Try to locate the source of the errors and correct them. A good place to start is the **Payroll Report** and the **General Ledger**. You are graded on ending general ledger balances and payroll entries. Make sure the check number and employee name are the same as on the Employees to Be Paid This Pay Period form. Remember you can start over from the **Company** module and select **Company Setup** and **Company Information**. The **Reset** command is on the bottom.

13. When you are comfortable that you have completed all steps of the problem correctly, click on the **Submit Assignment for Grading** button on the lower right of your screen.

Project Audit Test

✓ Net Paid $11,107.66

December 4 Payroll

Follow the steps below to complete the **December 4** payroll transactions, for the period ending November 30.

1. Set the **System Date** at the top of the screen to **December 3, 2023**.

2. Enter and post the following transaction, using the **General Journal** task under the **General Ledger** tab. You can determine current account balances from the **General Ledger** Report in the **Ledger Reports** menu.

   - December 3: Deposited the Pennsylvania state income taxes withheld from the November 20 payroll (Employees SIT Payable).

3. Enter the following information, using the **Maintain Employees** task under the **Payroll** tab.

   - Change employee 180 from "Student" to your name.
   - Change Catherine L. Ford's salary amount to $1,280.00 because of a salary increase.
   - Change Serdar Russell's salary amount to $1,260.00 because of a salary increase.
   - Add new employee: Employee number 210; YOUNG, Paul Winston; 7936 Holmes Drive, Philadelphia, PA 19107-6107; social security number, 000-00-6057; single, salaried, $1,260.00; number of pay periods per year, 26; Account No. 53 (Sales Salaries).

4. Display an **Employee List** report under **Tasks** in the **Payroll** module, and verify information you changed and added.

5. Make sure the **System Date** at the top of the screen is set to 12/04/23, and enter the Payroll transactions, using the **Pay Employees** task and referring to Figure B.15 and detailed instructions that follow. <u>Do not</u> deduct Group Insurance. <u>Do</u> deduct Union Dues for the appropriate employees. <u>Do</u> deduct SIMPLE Contributions for the appropriate employees. Begin the sequence with **Check No. 712**. Finally, note that one employee has earned hours of double time pay, so put those hours in the **Overtime @ Double** column. Enter the information for each employee as you did for the previous payroll period, and click on the **Calculate Taxes** button after entering all deductions for each employee to fill the remaining fields.

6. Display and review the **Payroll Report**.

7. Generate and post the journal entry for the current payroll by selecting **Current Payroll Journal Entry** from the **Tasks** menu bar. Click **Yes** when asked if you want to generate the journal entry. When the entry appears in the Current Payroll Journal Entries dialog box, click on **Post**. The journal entry will reappear, posted, in the General Journal.

Figure B.15

Employee to Be Paid This Pay Period

Check Number	Employee Number	Employee Name	Salary / Reg. Hrs.	Bonus	Overtime @ Time 1 1/2	Overtime @ Double	Group Ins.	Union Dues	SIMPLE Contribution
712	100	Bonno, Anthony Victor	80			8		$8.00	
713	110	Ferguson, Jamie Hadi	reg. salary						$500.00
714	120	Ford, Catherine Louise	reg. salary						
715	130	Mann, Kari Casey	reg. salary						$250.00
716	140	O'Neill, Joseph Tyler	reg. salary						$700.00
717	150	Russell, Serdar Parker	reg. salary						
718	160	Ryan, Jeri Mischa	80		3			$8.00	$200.00
716	170	Sokowski, Thomas James	reg. salary						
720	180	Student (your name)	72						
721	200	Woods, Beth Ann	$1,080.00 (First Payroll)						

8. Generate and post the employer's payroll taxes journal entry. With the **Payroll** module still selected, click on **Employer's Payroll Taxes Journal Entry** from the **Tasks** menu bar. Click **Yes** when asked if you want to generate the journal entry. Verify the result and click **Post** to post the entry to the General Journal. After you accept the entries, they will reappear, posted, in the General Journal.

9. Enter and post the December 4 General Journal entry to record the deposit of cash for the total net amount owed to employees in the payroll cash account. Click on the **General Ledger** module and select **Tasks** and **General Journal**. Based on the current period Net Pay summary information in the Payroll Report, enter the journal transaction.

10. Display and review the **General Journal** report for 11/21/2023 through 12/04/2023.

11. Display and review the **General Ledger** report.

12. If there is a **Check** link on the lower right of your screen, click on that link to review your work. A Check My Work summary report will be displayed and a percentage correct will show next to the **Check** link. Try to locate the source of the errors and correct them. A good place to start is the Payroll Report and the General Ledger. You are graded on ending general ledger balances and payroll entries. Make sure the check number and employee name are the same as on the Employees to Be Paid This Pay Period form. Remember you can start over from the **Company** module and select **Company Setup** and **Company Information**. The **Reset** command is on the bottom.

13. When you are comfortable that you have completed all steps of the problem correctly, click on the **Submit Assignment for Grading** button on the lower right of your screen.

Project Audit Test

✓ Net Paid $2,194.72

December 14 Payroll

A special payroll needs to be run to process the death of an employee (Serdar P. Russell). The step-by-step instructions for completing the December 14 special payroll follow.

1. Set the **System Date** at the top of the screen to **December 9, 2023**.

2. Enter and post the following transaction, using the **General Journal** task under the **General Ledger** module. You can determine current account balances from the **General Ledger** Report in the **Ledger Reports** menu bar.

   - December 9: Paid the treasurer of the union the amount of union dues withheld during the month of November (the balance in Union Dues Payable as of Nov. 30).

3. Change the **System Date** to **December 14, 2023**. Pay Serdar P. Russell (pay will go to the estate). Enter $2,394.00 in salary amount, using **Check No. 722**, which is two partial weeks of work ($1,134.00) plus accrued vacation pay ($1,260.00) for the final check. **Note:** After clicking on the **Calculate Taxes** button, remove the calculated withholding amounts for FIT, SIT, and CIT by keying zeros in these grid cells (final pay is not subject to these withholdings). <u>Do</u> deduct $14.70 for Group Insurance.

4. Display and review the **Payroll Report**.

5. Generate and post the journal entry for the current payroll by selecting **Current Payroll Journal Entry**. Click **Yes** when asked if you want to generate the journal entry. When the entry appears in the Current Payroll Journal Entries dialog box, click on **Post**. The journal entry will reappear, posted, in the General Journal.

6. Generate and post the employer's payroll taxes journal entry. With the **Payroll** module still selected, click on **Tasks** and **Employer's Payroll Taxes Journal Entry**. Click **Yes** when asked if you want to generate the journal entry. Verify the result and click **Post** to post the entry to the General Journal. After you accept the entries, they will reappear, posted, in the General Journal.

7. Enter and post the December 14 general journal entry to record the deposit of cash for Serdar P. Russell's net amount in the payroll cash account. Click on the **General Ledger** module and select **Tasks** and **General Journal**. Based on the current period Net Pay summary information in the Payroll Report, enter the journal transaction.

8. Display and review the **General Journal** report for 12/5/2023 through 12/14/2023.

9. Display and review the **General Ledger** report.

10. If there is a **Check** link on the lower right of your screen, click on that link to review your work. A Check My Work summary report will be displayed and a percentage correct will show next to the **Check** link. Try to locate the source of the errors and correct them. A good place to start is the Payroll Report and the General Ledger. You are graded on ending general ledger balances and payroll entries. Make sure the check number and employee name are the same as on the Employees

to Be Paid This Pay Period form. Remember you can start over from the **Company** module and select **Company Setup** and **Company Information**. The **Reset** command is on the bottom.

11. When you are comfortable that you have completed all steps of the problem correctly, click on the **Submit Assignment for Grading** button on the lower right of your screen.

December 18 Payroll

Follow the steps below to complete the **December 18** payroll transactions, for the period ending December 15.

1. Set the **System Date** at the top of the screen to **December 15, 2023**.
2. Enter and post the following transactions, using the **General Journal** in **Tasks** from the **General Ledger** module. You can determine current account balances from the **General Ledger** Report item in the **Ledger Reports** menu bar.

   - December 15: Deposited with City Bank the amount of FICA taxes and federal income taxes for the November payrolls. Pay the balance in the two FICA Taxes Payable accounts (20.1 and 20.2) and Employees FIT Payable (24) as of the end of November.
   - December 15: Deposited the city of Philadelphia employees withheld income tax with the Department of Revenue for the November payrolls (see the Employees CIT Payable account balance in the general ledger report as of the end of November).
   - Change **System Date** to December 18: Deposited the Pennsylvania state income taxes withheld from the December 4 payroll (Employees SIT Payable).
   - December 18: Wrote check to Serdar Russell's estate from the regular cash account to reimburse the amount withheld from the December 14 pay for insurance (review the December 14 credit to Group Insurance Premiums Payable to determine this amount).

3. Enter the following information, using **Maintain Employees** in the **Tasks** menu of the **Payroll** module.

   - Change employee 180 from "Student" to your name.
   - Add new employee: Employee number 220; ZIMMERMAN, Richard Lewis; 900 South Clark Street, Philadelphia, PA 19195-6247; social security number, 000-00-1502; married filing joint, salaried, $1,200.00; number of pay periods per year, 26; Account No. 52 (Office Salaries).

4. Display an **Employee List** report and verify information you changed and added.

5. Enter the Payroll transactions, using **Pay Employees** in the **Tasks** menu and referring Figure B.16, on page B-22, and detailed instructions that follow. <u>Do</u> deduct Group Insurance. <u>Do</u> deduct Union Dues for the appropriate employees. <u>Do</u> deduct SIMPLE Contributions for the appropriate employees. Begin the sequence with **Check No. 723**. Note: Be sure to enter the changes and amounts of Group Insurance deductions for the new employees and the $9.00 Union Dues, as noted below.

Project Audit Test

✓ Net Paid $70,494.41

Figure B.16
Employee to Be Paid This Pay Period

Check Number	Employee Number	Employee Name	Salary / Reg. Hrs.	Bonus	Overtime @ Time 1 1/2	Overtime @ Double	Group Ins.	Union Dues	SIMPLE Contribution
723	100	Bonno, Anthony Victor	80			12	$16.50	$9.00	
724	110	Ferguson, Jamie Hadi	reg. salary				$26.40		$500.00
725	120	Ford, Catherine Louise	reg. salary				$15.00		
726	130	Mann, Kari Casey	reg. salary				$15.90		$250.00
727	140	O'Neill, Joseph Tyler	reg. salary	$95,000.00			$27.00		$2,000.00
728	160	Ryan, Jeri Mischa	80		7		$16.80	$9.00	$200.00
729	170	Sokowski, Thomas James	reg. salary				$24.00		
730	180	Student (your name)	71				$12.60		
731	200	Woods, Beth Ann	reg.salary				$14.10		
732	210	Young, Paul Winston	reg. salary				$14.70		

In this pay, the president of the company, *Joseph O'Neill*, is paid his annual bonus. This does not affect O'Neill's insurance coverage, which is based on regular pay. This year, his bonus is **$95,000**. For withholding purposes, the bonus is considered a supplemental payment and is taxed at the supplemental rate of 22 percent. For this pay, O'Neill **has increased his SIMPLE Contributions to $2,000**, which will reduce his salary for federal income tax purposes. The software calculates the tax on the annualized net earnings (gross salary – Simple) and then adds 22 percent times the bonus to arrive at the amount of FIT for this pay period. In addition, the software takes into consideration the OASDI limit of $147,000 to calculate the OASDI tax. Click on the **Calculate Taxes** button after entering all deductions for each employee to fill the remaining fields.

6. Display and review the **Payroll Report**.

7. Generate and post the journal entry for the current payroll by selecting **Current Payroll Journal Entry** from the **Tasks** menu bar. Click **Yes** when asked if you want to generate the journal entry. When the entry appears in the Current Payroll Journal Entries dialog box, click on **Post**. The journal entry will reappear, posted, in the General Journal.

8. Generate and post the employer's payroll taxes journal entry. With the **Payroll** module still selected, click on the **Employer's Payroll Taxes Journal Entry** from the **Tasks** menu bar. Click **Yes** when asked if you want to generate the journal entry. Verify the result and click **Post** to post the entry to the General Journal. After you accept the entries, they will reappear, posted, in the General Journal.

9. Enter and post the December 18 General Journal entry to record the deposit of cash for the total net amount owed to employees in the payroll cash account using the **General Journal** in the **Tasks** menu of the **General Ledger** module. Based on the current period Net Pay summary information in the Payroll Report, enter the journal transaction.

10. Display and review the **General Journal** report for 12/15/2023 through 12/18/2023.

11. Display and review the **General Ledger** report.

12. If there is a **Check** link on the lower right of your screen, click on that link to review your work. A Check My Work Summary report will be displayed and a percentage correct will show next to the **Check** link. Try to locate the source of the errors and correct them. A good place to start is the Payroll Report and the General Ledger. You are graded on ending general ledger balances and payroll entries. Make sure the check number and employee name are the same as on the Employees to Be Paid This Pay Period form. Remember you can start over from the **Company** module and select **Company Setup** and **Company Information**. The **Reset** command is on the bottom.

13. If your instructor has assigned the completion of the forms beginning in step 5 on page B-40, do not submit you assignment for grading until you have completed the forms as you will need to review some of the reports in the software to extract key numbers.

14. When you are comfortable that you have completed all steps of the problem correctly, click on the **Submit Assignment for Grading** button on the lower right of your screen.

If assigned by your instructor, continue to the "End-of-Year Activities" section on page B-39.

III. Payroll Project (Short Version)

The payroll project that follows is the online version of the same project you completed manually in Chapter 7 of your text. For this project, you will use the *Automated General Ledger Software* to simulate how a real company would use general ledger software to maintain payroll records and payroll journal transactions. In this project, you are employed by Glo-Brite Paint Company as the person in the accounting department responsible for the company's payroll processing using the computerized payroll system.

However, unlike the payroll project in Chapter 7, you will only complete the last payroll in November and the payrolls for the month of December and, if assigned, the end-of-year activities. The opening balance file you will use will already contain all the processing for the quarter up to the November payroll.

Your work will involve the computer processing of the payrolls for the last month of the year and the completion of the last quarter and annual tax reports and forms. You may complete the required deposit, quarterly, yearly, etc., forms in CengageNOWv2. If you have already completed these forms for the manual student project, you can use these as a reference as you progress through this project.

To help you get started, the last pay period of November is provided as a tutorial problem that illustrates the principles and procedures required to process payroll transactions using the *Automated General Ledger Software*. In subsequent pay period processing, whenever a new operational procedure is used for the first time, additional instruction will be provided.

This project has been broken down into several assignments comprising all or part of the project in your text. The assignments are delivered online using the **CengageNOWv2** learning management system, with each assignment being graded automatically and submitted to your instructor. Your instructor may choose to have you complete only part of this project, so watch the dates and follow the instructions carefully.

Note: Throughout this project, some of the computer-calculated withholding amounts (e.g., federal income tax) will differ slightly from the amounts (from the tax tables) in the manual payroll project in Chapter 7. This occurs because the software uses the annualized percentage method from *IRS Publication 15-T* rather than the table look-up to compute withholding taxes (see IRS 2022 Percentage Method Tables for Automated Payroll Systems in Figure B.17). The differences here should be less than two dollars per pay period, and usually are much less. Also, the accounts differ slightly from those in Chapter 7, but there is a "Partial Chart of Accounts" available in the software to help you quickly find the accounts you need, or refer to Figure B.18.

Figure B.17
2022 Percentage Method Tables for Automated Payroll Systems

STANDARD Withholding Rate Schedules
(Use these if the Form W-4 is from 2019 or earlier, or if the Form W-4 is from 2020 or later and the box in Step 2 of Form W-4 is **NOT** checked. Also use these for Form W-4P from any year.)

If the Adjusted Annual Wage Amount on Worksheet 1A or the Adjusted Annual Payment Amount on Worksheet 1B is:		The tentative amount to withhold is:	Plus this percentage—	of the amount that the Adjusted Annual Wage or Payment exceeds—
At least—	But less than—			
A	B	C	D	E
Married Filing Jointly				
$0	$13,000	$0.00	0%	$0
$13,000	$33,550	$0.00	10%	$13,000
$33,550	$96,550	$2,055.00	12%	$33,550
$96,550	$191,150	$9,615.00	22%	$96,550
$191,150	$353,100	$30,427.00	24%	$191,150
$353,100	$444,900	$69,295.00	32%	$353,100
$444,900	$660,850	$98,671.00	35%	$444,900
$660,850		$174,253.50	37%	$660,850
Single or Married Filing Separately				
$0	$4,350	$0.00	0%	$0
$4,350	$14,625	$0.00	10%	$4,350
$14,625	$46,125	$1,027.50	12%	$14,625
$46,125	$93,425	$4,807.50	22%	$46,125
$93,425	$174,400	$15,213.50	24%	$93,425
$174,400	$220,300	$34,647.50	32%	$174,400
$220,300	$544,250	$49,335.50	35%	$220,300
$544,250		$162,718.00	37%	$544,250

Source: Internal Revenue Service

Figure B.18
Partial Chart of Accounts Comparison

Classification	Account Number	Text Account Number	Account Title
Assets	11	11	Cash
	12	12	Payroll Cash
Liabilities	20.1	20.1	FICA Taxes Payable—OASDI
	20.2	20.2	FICA Taxes Payable—HI
	21	21	FUTA Taxes Payable
	22	22	SUTA Taxes Payable—Employer
	24	24	Employees FIT Payable
	25	25	Employees SIT Payable
	25.1	25.1	Employees SUTA Payable
	26	26	Employees CIT Payable
	27	27	Group Insurance Premium Collected
	28	28	Union Dues Payable
	29	29	SIMPLE Contributions Payable
Capital	30	N/A	Capital
Expenses	51	51	Administrative Salaries
	52	52	Office Salaries
	53	53	Sales Salaries
	54	54	Plant Wages
	56	56	Payroll Taxes

IV. Illustrative Case—Short Project

November 20 Payroll

The *Automated General Ledger Software* is set up to guide you through completing the fourth quarter's payroll project from Chapter 7. The software provides two very important directions you'll need to go through before starting the instructions. **Get Started** walks you through the features of the software such as identifying the modules you'll be using, how and where to access reports, and resizing screens and introduces Source Documents and Instructions. **General Instructions** provide an overview of what you will be doing and explain why some amounts will differ from those in Chapter 7. It is very important that you complete the Get Started and General Instructions before you begin the November 20 payroll.

The *Automated General Ledger Software* menu bar on the left side of the screen is where you will find the modules you'll be using to complete the assignments in this project. There are three primary modules; Company, General Ledger and Payroll. When you click on a module the icon will be highlighted.

On the right side of the screen is the assignment panel. This panel contains instruction to get you started on the assignment and in some cases you will be referred to a Source Document. The Source Documents represent real world documents that you will refer to in order to complete the assignment. Included in the Source Documents are instructions to guide you through the Source Document. Source Document references have been included in the demonstration assignments for the short version demonstration assignment. All other Source

Project Audit Test

✓ Net Paid $9,538.40

Project Audit Test

At the start of each assignment, remove the Project Audit Test beginning on page B-43. Answer the questions for each audit test as you complete processing for each pay period.

Documents are shown in the Assignment Instruction panel and accessed on the bottom of the panel by clicking on the Source Document button.

Follow the steps below to complete the **November 20** payroll transactions, for the period ending November 14, using *Automated General Ledger Software*.

To access additional **Help** for any function, click on the **Help** button that appears at the top of the screen. There is a **Help** screen with additional information and sample screens for every menu option in the program. Click on the Save button at the lower right of your screen at any point to save your work if you need to stop working and continue your work later. Your work will automatically be restored when you return.

The first three quarters and all transactions for the month of November have been completed up to this payroll.

1. Set the **System Date** at the top of the screen to **November 20, 2023**. Note that the year needs to be 2023 in order for the problem to grade correctly.

2. Click on the **General Ledger** module and select **Account Lists** from the top menu bar and **Chart of Accounts**. Review this list to understand how the software designates the Payroll Accounts.

3. Enter the employee maintenance data. Click on the **Payroll** module and select **Tasks** menu from the top bar and **Maintain Employees**. Scroll down to select employee number **180** (Student), enter your own name in the **Employee Name** field (enter your last name in all capital letters similar to the other employees), and then **Tab** out of the field. Click on the **Close** button, and answer "Yes" to accept your changes. Note: Do not change any of the other fields. If you do, your solutions will not be correct.

4. Display an **Employee List** report. From the **Payroll** module, select <u>Reports</u> menu on the top bar and **Employee List**. The report is shown in Figure B.19 (Source Document 1 of 11). Verify the accuracy of the maintenance input from step 3 above and make any corrections via the **Maintain Employees** option.

5. Enter the Payroll transactions for the period using the detailed instructions in steps (a) through (j) below. References to **Source Documents** from the *Automated General Ledger Software* are included to familiarize you with the **Source Documents**. Each **Source Document** includes Instructions to help with completing the step. Refer to the Figure B.20 for this period (Source Document 2 of 11):

Note: This is the first pay in which the company offers a savings incentive match plan. The computer software has been designed to use the key terms "SIMPLE Contributions" to instruct it to exclude this deduction from the employee's income for FIT purposes. The general ledger account **SIMPLE Contributions Payable** is associated with this deduction for updating during the payroll transaction processing.

To enter the payroll records, click on **Payroll** module and select **Tasks** from the top menu bar and **Pay Employees**. Make sure the **System Date** is set to November 20, 2023.

a. The prior payroll information is already entered, and will show up in the reports, but NOT in the payroll entry system.

Figure B.19
Employee List

Emp. No.	Employee Name/Address	Social Security /Filing Status	# Pay Periods	G.L. Accounts	Salary /Rate
100	BONNO, Anthony Victor 694 Bristol Avenue Philadelphia, PA 19135-0617	000-00-3481 Married Filing Joint W/H NA	26	54	0.00 17.60
110	FERGUSON, Jamie Hadi 808 Sixth Street Philadelphia, PA 19106-0995	000-00-8645 Married Filing Joint W/H NA	26	52	2,250.00 0.00
120	FORD, Catherine Louise 18 Dundee Avenue Philadelphia, PA 19151-1919	000-00-4567 Single W/H N/A	26	52	1,220.00 0.00
130	MANN, Kari Casey 3007 Bisque Drive Philadelphia, PA 19199-0718	000-00-9352 Married Filing Joint W/H N/A	26	53	1,350.00 0.00
140	O'NEILL, Joseph Tyler 2100 Broad Street Philadelphia, PA 19121-7189	000-00-1534 Married Filing Joint W/H N/A	26	51	2,307.69 0.00
150	RUSSELL, Serdar Parker 8004 Dowling Road Philadelphia, PA 19135-9001	000-00-6337 Single W/H N/A	26	52	1,200.00 0.00
160	RYAN, Jeri Mischa 7300 Harrison Street Philadelphia, PA 19124-6699	000-00-1233 Married Filing Joint W/H N/A	26	54	0.00 18.00
170	SOKOWSKI, Thomas James 133 Cornwells Street Philadelphia, PA 19171-5718	000-00-8832 Married Filing Joint W/H N/A	26	54	2,050.00 0.00
180	STUDENT 7018 Erdrick Street Philadelphia, PA 19135-8517	000-00-5555 Single W/H N/A	26	52	0.00 15.00
190	WILLIAMS, Ruth Virginia 9433 State Street Philadelphia, PA 19149-0819	000-00-6741 Single W/H N/A	26	52	1,223.08 0.00
200	WOODS, Beth Ann 8102 Franklin Court Philadelphia, PA 19105-0915	000-00-1587 Single	26	52	1,200.00 0.00

Figure B.15
Employee to Be Paid This Pay Period

Check Number	Employee Number	Employee Name	Salary / Reg. Hrs.	Bonus	Overtime @ Time 1 1/2	Overtime @ Double	Group Ins.	Union Dues	SIMPLE Contribution
703	100	Bonno, Anthony Victor	64				$16.50	$8.00	
704	110	Ferguson, Jamie Hadi	reg. salary				$26.40		$500.00
705	120	Ford, Catherine Louise	reg. salary				$14.40		
706	130	Mann, Kari Casey	reg. salary				$15.90		$250.00
707	140	O'Neill, Joseph Tyler	reg. salary				$27.00		$700.00
708	150	Russell, Serdar Parker	$1,170.00 (Loss of 2 hours)				$14.10		
709	160	Ryan, Jeri Mischa	80				$16.80	$8.00	$200.00
710	170	Sokowski, Thomas James	reg. salary				$24.00		
711	180	Student (your name)	72				$12.60		

b. For each pay period, you will need to add a new record to this payroll register for each employee to be paid. Click on the **Add** button to add a new pay record for each of the above employees and then enter the corresponding fields.

c. Date: Make sure the date is set to 11/20/2023 for each new record or use the pop-up calendar to change it. Payroll recording is very dependent on having the correct dates, so verify this date, especially for the first employee in any payroll assignment.

d. Employee Name: Select the name from the drop-down list or key the first letter of the employee's name until the correct name appears.

e. Check No.: Start with check number **703** to continue from where the current quarter left off. This number will automatically increase by 1 for each subsequent employee. It is critical to get this check number correct for each employee, along with the date, as this is how the software matches up your entries for grading.

f. Salary or Hours worked: For salaried employees, the salary should display automatically. For hourly employees, click on the **Reg. Hours** field and enter the number of regular work hours shown above. You can override a salaried employee by clicking on the salary and entering the correct amount.

g. Deductions: Do deduct union dues, Group Ins. and SIMPLE Contributions. Group Ins. is deducted once a month while union dues and SIMPLE Contributions are deducted each pay period.

h. Click on the **Calculate Taxes** button for each employee to fill the remaining fields. **Net pay** will calculate automatically, and **Gross Pay** will display at the bottom of the form. Note: You need to press the **Calculate Taxes** button AFTER you enter the Simple Plan amount for each employee in order for taxes to calculate correctly, as the value affects the FIT calculation.

i. Review the amounts calculated for reasonableness.

j. Click **Add** to start a new employee or **Save** when done. If you make a mistake, just go back and fix it; click on the **Calculate Taxes** button to recalculate these amounts. If you forget an employee, be sure the check number and name are the same as shown on the Employees to Be Paid This Pay Period form; otherwise, you will have errors. Before you leave the **Pay Employees** screen, be sure to **Save**. You will see the screen below.

6. Display and review the **Payroll Report**. From the **Payroll** module, select **Reports** menu from the top bar and **Payroll Report**. The payroll report for Employee 100: Bonno, Anthony Victor, followed by the payroll summary, is shown in Figure B.21 (Source Document 4 of 11). If the summary is incorrect, review the list of employees to be paid from step 3 above. Check your numbers against name and make any changes using the **Pay Employees** task.

Figure B.21
Payroll Report

		Current	Quarterly	Yearly
100 - BONNO, Anthony Victor	Gross Pay	1,126.40	5,456.00	16,778.00
54 - Plant Wages	FIT	13.02	147.12	957.12
Married Acct. 54	SIT	34.58	167.51	515.10
W/H 000-00-3481	Soc. Sec. (OASDI)	69.84	338.28	1,040.24
Pay Periods 26	Medicare (HI)	16.33	79.12	243.29
Salary 0.00	CIT	43.25	209.49	644.23
Hourly Rate 17.60	Group Ins.	16.50	33.00	177.80
Reg. Hours 80.00	Union Dues	8.00	32.00	104.00
O.T. Hours	Simple Plan	-	-	-
Check Number 703	Employee SUTA	0.68	3.27	10.06
Check Date 11/20/23	Net Pay	924.20	4,446.21	13,086.16
Payroll Summary	Gross Pay	13,994.09	62,936.09	205,160.66
	FIT	576.03	3,264.02	19,181.02
	SIT	429.64	1,932.24	6,298.53
	Soc. Sec. (OASDI)	867.64	3,902.06	12,719.98
	Medicare (HI)	202.93	912.63	2,974.90
	CIT	537.36	2,416.67	7,877.81
	Group Ins.	167.70	364.20	1,294.60
	Union Dues	16.00	64.00	208.00
	Simple Plan	1,650.00	1,650.00	1,650.00
	Employee SUTA	8.39	37.71	123.05
	Net Pay	9,538.40	48,392.56	152,832.77

7. Generate and post the journal entry for the current payroll by selecting **Current Payroll Journal Entry** from the **Tasks** menu bar. Click Yes when asked if you want to generate the journal entry. If your journal entries do not match those shown in Figure B.22 (Source Document 5 of 11) on page B-30, check your employee list and payroll report for errors, and go back to make the corrections. When the entry appears in the Current Payroll Journal Entries dialog box, click on **Post**. The journal entry will reappear, posted, in the General Journal.

Figure B.22

Current Payroll Journal Entries

Account #	Account Title	Debit	Credit
51	Administrative Salaries	2,307.69	
52	Office Salaries	3,470.00	
53	Sales Salaries	3,600.00	
54	Plant Wages	4,616.40	
12	Payroll Cash		9,538.40
20.1	FICA Taxes Payable - OASDI		867.64
20.2	FICA Taxes Payable - HI		202.93
24	Employees FIT Payable		576.03
25	Employees SIT Payable		429.64
25.1	Employees SUTA Payable		8.39
26	Employees CIT Payable		537.36
27	Group Insurance Premiums Collected		167.70
28	Union Dues Payable		16.00
29	SIMPLE Contributions Payable		1,650.00

8. Generate and post the employer's payroll taxes journal entry. With the **Payroll** module still selected, click on **Employer's Payroll Taxes Journal Entry** from the **Tasks** menu bar. Enter the journal transaction shown in Figure B.23 (Source Document 6 of 11). Click **Yes** when asked if you want to generate the journal entry. Verify the result and click **Post** to post the entry to the General Journal. After you accept the entries, they will reappear, posted, in the General Journal.

Figure B.23

Payroll Taxes Journal Entries

Account #	Account Title	Debit	Credit
56	Payroll Taxes	1,139.16	
20.1	FICA Taxes Payable - OASDI		867.63
20.2	FICA Taxes Payable - HI		202.91
22	SUTA Taxes Payable - Employer		68.62

9. Enter and post the November 20 General Journal entry to record the deposit of cash for the total net amount owed to employees in the payroll cash account. Click on the **General Ledger** module, and select **Tasks** and **General Journal**. Enter the journal transaction shown in Figure B.24 (Source Documents 7 and 8 of 11) by first clicking on the **Add New Entry** button. Verify the date and enter **General** as the reference. Next click on the **Insert Debit/Credit** button, enter the first account number (12), or click on the pop-up **Chart of Accounts** icon to display a list for selection. Enter the debit amount. Click on **insert Debit/Credit** again to enter the credit to **Cash** (account 11).

Figure B.24

General Journal Payroll Cash Entries

Date	Refer.	Account #	Account Title	Debit	Credit
11/20/2023	General	12	Payroll Cash	9,538.40	
		11	Cash		9,538.40

10. Display and review the **General Journal** report for 11/20/2023. From the **General Ledger** module, select **Journal Reports** from the top menu bar and **General Journal**. Modify the report by selecting the start and end dates and click on **Apply**. The General Journal report is shown in Figure B.25 (Source Document 9 of 11).

Figure B.25
General Journal Report

Date	Refer.	Acct.	Title	Debit	Credit
11/20/2023	Payroll	51	Administrative Salaries	2,307.69	
11/20/2023	Payroll	52	Office Salaries	3,470.00	
11/20/2023	Payroll	53	Sales Salaries	3,600.00	
11/20/2023	Payroll	54	Plant Wages	4,616.40	
11/20/2023	Payroll	12	Payroll Cash		9,538.40
11/20/2023	Payroll	20.1	FICA Taxes Payable--OASDI		867.64
11/20/2023	Payroll	20.2	FICA Taxes Payable--HI		202.93
11/20/2023	Payroll	24	Employees FIT Payable		576.03
11/20/2023	Payroll	25	Employees SIT Payable		429.64
11/20/2023	Payroll	25.1	Employees SUTA Payable		8.39
11/20/2023	Payroll	26	Employees CIT Payable		537.36
11/20/2023	Payroll	27	Group Ins. Prem. Collected		167.70
11/20/2023	Payroll	28	Union Dues Payable		16.00
11/20/2023	Payroll	29	SIMPLE Contributions Payable		1,650.00
11/20/2023	Payroll	56	Payroll Taxes	1,139.16	
11/20/2023	Payroll	20.1	FICA Taxes Payable--OASDI		867.63
11/20/2023	Payroll	20.2	FICA Taxes Payable--HI		202.91
11/20/2023	Payroll	22	SUTA Taxes Payable-Employer		68.62
11/20/2023	General	12	Payroll Cash	9,538.40	
11/20/2023	General	11	Cash		9,538.40
			Totals	24,671.65	24,671.65

11. Display and review the **General Ledger** report. From the **General Ledger** module, select **Ledger Reports** on the menu bar and **General Ledger**. The General Ledger report is shown in Figure B.26 (Source Document 10 of 11).

Figure B.26
General Ledger Partial Report

Account	Journal	Date	Reference	Debit	Credit	Balance
11-Cash						
11-Cash	Balance Forward					199,846.33 Dr
11-Cash	General	10/09/2023	General	0.00	12,438.55	187,407.78 Dr
11-Cash	General	10/20/2023	Pay Tax	0.00	476.76	186,931.02 Dr
11-Cash	General	10/23/2023	General	0.00	12,498.87	174,432.15 Dr
11-Cash	General	11/04/2023	Pay Tax	0.00	486.63	173,945.52 Dr
11-Cash	General	11/06/2023	General	0.00	32.00	173,913.52 Dr
11-Cash	General	11/06/2023	General	0.00	12,337.67	161,575.85 Dr
11-Cash	General	11/13/2023	General	0.00	1,579.07	159,996.78 Dr
11-Cash	General	11/16/2023	Pay Tax	0.00	6,441.01	153,555.77 Dr
11-Cash	General	11/16/2023	Pay Tax	0.00	1,204.92	152,350.85 Dr
11-Cash	General	11/18/2023	Pay Tax	0.00	539.21	151,811.64 Dr
11-Cash	General	11/20/2023	General	0.00	9,538.40	142,273.24 Dr
56-Payroll Taxes						
56-Payroll Taxes	Balance Forward					14,353.07 Dr
56-Payroll Taxes	General	10/09/2023	Payroll	1,390.21	0.00	15,743.28 Dr
56-Payroll Taxes	General	10/23/2023	Payroll	1,395.19	0.00	17,138.47 Dr
56-Payroll Taxes	General	11/06/2023	Payroll	1,362.30	0.00	18,500.77 Dr
56-Payroll Taxes	General	11/13/2023	Payroll	159.07	0.00	18,659.84 Dr
56-Payroll Taxes	General	11/20/2023	Payroll	1,139.16	0.00	19,799.00 Dr

12. Generate a labor distribution graph. From the **Company** module, select **Graphs** from the top bar and **Labor Distribution** to generate the graph shown in Figure B.27 (Source Document 11 of 11). Note: The *Automated General Ledger Software* generates a graph from the year-to-date values.

Figure B.27
Labor Distribution

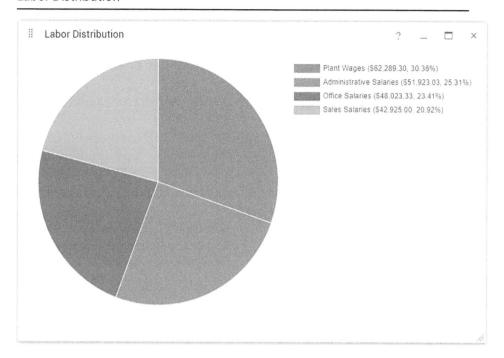

13. If there is a **Check** link on the lower right of your screen, click on that link to review your work. A Check My Work summary report will be displayed and a percentage correct will show next to the **Check** link. Try to locate the source of the errors and correct them. A good place to start is the Payroll Report and the General Ledger. You are graded on ending general ledger balances and payroll entries. Make sure the check number and employee name are the same as on the Employees to Be Paid This Pay Period form. Remember you can start over from the **Company** module and select **Company Setup** and **Company Information**. The **Reset** command is on the bottom.

14. When you are comfortable that you have completed all steps of the problem correctly, click on the **Submit Assignment for Grading** button on the lower right of your screen. You will be graded primarily on three criteria for the payroll problems.

    Are the pay settings for each employee correct (rate, deductions, etc.)?
    Are all periods' payroll entries correct for each employee?
    Are the ending balances in General Ledger account correct?

    Note that the journal entries themselves are not graded. If the journal entries are correct, the final General Ledger balances will then also be correct. This allows you to create, edit, delete, and re-enter journal entries in any order.

December 4 Payroll

Follow the steps below to complete the December 4 payroll transactions. To access additional Help for any function, click on the **Help** button that appears at the top right of the screen. There is a Help screen with additional information and sample screens for every menu option in the program. Click on the **Save** button at the lower right of your screen at any point to save your work if you need to stop working to continue later. Your work will automatically be restored when you return.

Project Audit Test

✓ Net Paid $11,107.66

1. Set the **System Date** at the top of the screen to **December 4, 2023**. Note that the year needs to be **2023** in order for the problem to grade correctly.

2. Enter the employee maintenance data. Click on the **Payroll** module, and select **Tasks** from the top menu bar and **Maintain Employees**.

   - Change Catherine L. Ford's salary amount to $1,280.00 because of a salary increase.
   - Change Serdar Russell's salary amount to $1,260.00 because of a salary increase.
   - Scroll down to select employee number **180** (Student), key your own name in the **Employee Name** field (enter your last name in all capital letters similar to the other employees), then **Tab** out of the field. Note: Do not change any of the other fields. If you do, your solutions will not be correct.
   - Add new employee: Employee number 210; YOUNG, Paul Winston; 7936 Holmes Drive, Philadelphia, PA 19107-6107; social security number, 000-00-6057; single, salaried, $1,260.00; number of pay periods per year, 26; Account No. 53 (Sales Salaries).
   - Click on the **Close** button, and click "Yes" to accept your changes.

3. Display the **Employee List** report. From the **Payroll** module, select **Reports** from the top menu bar and **Employee List**. Verify the information you changed and added.

4. Change the **System Date** to December 3, 2023. Enter and post the following transaction, using the **General Ledger** module, and select **Tasks** on the top menu bar and **General Journal**.

   - December 3: Deposited the Pennsylvania state income taxes withheld from the November 20 payroll (Employees SIT Payable). First determine current account balances using the **General Ledger Report** in the **Ledger Reports** menu bar in the **General Ledger** module. Look for the outstanding balance in account #25. Next, select the **General Journal** task and click on the **Add New Entry button**. Enter the first account number (**25**) or click on the pop-up **Chart of Accounts** icon to display a list for selection. Enter the debit amount to clear the existing credit to **Employees SIT Payable**. Then click on **Insert Debit/Credit** again to enter the credit (the same amount) to the **Cash** account (**11**). Finally, click on the **Post** button to post this entry to the General Ledger.

5. Change the **System Date** to December 4, 2023, and enter the Payroll transactions for the period using the **Payroll** module; select **Tasks** and **Pay Employees**. <u>Do</u> deduct Union Dues and SIMPLE Contributions this period. Note the overtime hours on the hourly employee. Beth Woods hasn't worked a full pay period so you will need to adjust her salary. Begin with **Check No. 712**. Enter the information for each employee as you did for the previous payroll period, and click on the **Calculate Taxes** button after entering all the deductions for each employee. **Save**. Refer to the Figure B.28 for this period.

Figure B.28
Employee to Be Paid This Pay Period

Check Number	Employee Number	Employee Name	Salary / Reg. Hrs.	Bonus	Overtime @ Time 1 1/2	Overtime @ Double	Group Ins.	Union Dues	SIMPLE Contribution
712	100	Bonno, Anthony Victor	80			8		$8.00	
713	110	Ferguson, Jamie Hadi	reg. salary						$500.00
714	120	Ford, Catherine Louise	reg. salary						
715	130	Mann, Kari Casey	reg. salary						$250.00
716	140	O'Neill, Joseph Tyler	reg. salary						$700.00
717	150	Russell, Serdar Parker	reg. salary						
718	160	Ryan, Jeri Mischa	80		3			$8.00	$200.00
716	170	Sokowski, Thomas James	reg. salary						
720	180	Student (your name)	72						
721	200	Woods, Beth Ann	$1,080.00 (First Payroll)						

6. Display and review the **Payroll Report**. Click on the **Payroll Report** in the **Reports** menu on the top menu bar.

7. Generate and post the journal entry for the current payroll. Click on **Current Payroll Journal Entry** in the **Task** menu on the top menu bar. Click **Yes** when asked if you want to generate the journal entry. When the entry appears in the Current Payroll Journal Entries dialog box, click on **Post**. The journal entry will reappear, posted, in the General Journal.

8. Generate and post the employer's payroll taxes journal entry. Click on the **Employer's Payroll Taxes Journal Entry** in **Tasks** on the top menu bar. Click **Yes** when asked if you want to generate the journal entry. Verify the results and click on **Post**. After you accept the entries, they will reappear, posted, in the General Journal.

9. Enter and post the December 4 General Journal entry to record the deposit of cash for the total net amount owed to employees in the payroll cash account. This is also found as the current period **Net Pay** value on the Payroll Report. Click on the **General Ledger** module and **General Journal** from the **Tasks** menu on the menu bar. Enter the transaction by first clicking on the **Add New Entry** button. Verify the date and enter **General** as the reference. Next, click on the **Insert Debit/Credit** button, enter the first account number (**12**) or click on the pop-up **Chart of Accounts** icon to display a list for selection. Then click on **Insert Debit/Credit** again to enter the credit to the **Cash** account. Finally, click on the **Post** button to post this entry to the General Ledger.

10. Display the General Journal report. With the General Ledger module still displayed, click on the **General Journal** report from the **Journal Reports** section of the top menu bar.

11. Display the General Ledger report. With the **General Ledger** module selected, click on **General Ledger** from the **Ledger Reports** menu of the top menu bar. You can also customize this report to list only a selected range of accounts.

12. If there is a **Check** link on the lower right of your screen, click on that link to review your work. A Check My Work Summary report will be generated and a percentage complete will be shown next to the **Check** button. If you have errors, go back and check the Payroll Report. After fixing individual employees using the **Pay Employees** task, you can delete any of the journal entries, using the **General Journal** task in the **General Ledger** module, and retry any or all of the steps above. If you can't find the errors, you can **Reset** the assignment to the beginning by selecting **Company Setup** in the **Company Information** menu of the **Company** module.

13. When you are comfortable that you have completed all steps of the problem correctly, click on the **Submit Assignment for Grading** button on the lower right of your screen.

    Note that the journal entries themselves are not graded. If the journal entries are correct, the final General Ledger balances will then also be correct.

> **Project Audit Test**
>
> ✓ Net Paid $2,194.72

December 14 Payroll

A special payroll needs to be run to process the death of an employee (Serdar P. Russell). The step-by-step instructions for completing the December 14 special payroll follow.

1. Set the **System Date** at the top of the screen to **December 9, 2022**.

2. Enter and post the following transaction, using the **General Journal** in the **Tasks** menu of the **General Ledger** module. You can determine current account balances from the **General Ledger** Report in the **Ledger Reports** menu bar.

   - December 9: Paid the treasurer of the union the amount of union dues withheld during the month of November (the balance in Union Dues Payable as of Nov. 30).

3. Change the **System Date** to **December 14, 2022**. Pay Serdar P. Russell (pay will go to the estate). Enter $2,394.00 in salary amount, using **Check No. 722**, which is two partial weeks of work ($1,134.00) plus accrued vacation pay ($1,260.00) for the final check. **Note:** After clicking on the **Calculate Taxes** button, remove the calculated withholding amounts for FIT, SIT, and CIT by keying zeros in these grid cells (final pay is not subject to these withholdings). Do deduct $14.70 for Group Insurance.

4. Display and review the **Payroll Report**. From the **Payroll** module, select **Reports** menu from the top bar and **Payroll Report**.

5. Generate and post the journal entry for the current payroll by selecting **Current Payroll Journal Entry** in **Tasks** on the top menu bar. Click **Yes** when asked if you want to generate the journal entry. When the entry appears in the Current Payroll Journal Entries dialog box, click on **Post**. The journal entry will reappear, posted, in the General Journal.

6. Generate and post the employer's payroll taxes journal entry. With the **Payroll** module still selected, click on the **Tasks** menu on the top bar and **Employer's Payroll Taxes Journal**. Click **Yes** when asked if you want to generate the journal entry. Verify the result and click **Post** to post the entry to the General Journal. After you accept the entries, they will reappear, posted, in the General Journal.

7. Enter and post the December 14 general journal entry to record the deposit of cash for Serdar P. Russell's net amount in the payroll cash account. Click on the **General Ledger** module and select **Tasks** and **General Journal**. Based on the current period Net Pay summary information in the Payroll Report, enter the journal transaction.

8. Display and review the **General Journal** report for 12/5/2023 through 12/14/2023.

9. Display and review the **General Ledger** report. While still in the **General Ledger** module, select the **Ledger Reports** menu on the top menu bar and **General Ledger**.

10. If there is a **Check** link on the lower right of your screen, click on that link to review your work. A Check My Work Summary report will be displayed and a percentage correct will show next to the **Check** link. Try to locate the source of the errors and correct them. A good place to start is the Payroll Report and the General Ledger. You are graded on ending general ledger balances and payroll entries. Make sure the check number and employee name are the same as on the Employees to Be Paid This Pay Period form. Remember you can start over from the **Company** module and select **Company Setup** and **Company Information**. The **Reset** command is on the bottom.

11. When you are comfortable that you have completed all steps of the problem correctly, click on the **Submit Assignment for Grading** button on the lower right of your screen.

December 18 Payroll

Follow the steps below to complete the **December 18** payroll transactions, for the period ending December 15.

Project Audit Test

✓ Net Paid $70,494.41

1. Set the **System Date** at the bottom of the screen to **December 15, 2023**.

2. Enter and post the following transactions, using the **General Journal** task under the **General Ledger** tab. You can determine current account balances from the **General Ledger** Report item in the left menu bar.

   • December 15: Deposited with City Bank the amount of FICA taxes and federal income taxes for the November payrolls. Pay the balance in the two FICA Taxes Payable accounts (20.1 and 20.2) and Employees FIT Payable (24) as of the end of November.

   • December 15: Deposited the city of Philadelphia employees withheld income tax with the Department of Revenue for the November payrolls (see the Employees CIT Payable account balance in the general ledger report as of the end of November).

   • Change the **System Date** to December 18: Deposited the Pennsylvania state income taxes withheld from the December 4 payroll (Employees SIT Payable).

   • December 18: Wrote check to Serdar Russell's estate from the regular cash account to reimburse the amount withheld from the December 14 pay for insurance (review the December 14 credit to Group Insurance Premiums Payable to determine this amount).

3. Enter the following information, using the **Maintain Employees** task under the **Payroll** tab.

   • Change employee 180 from "Student" to your name.

   • Add new employee: Employee number 220; ZIMMERMAN, Richard Lewis; 900 South Clark Street, Philadelphia, PA 19195-6247; social security number, 000-00-1502; married filing joint, salaried, $1,200.00; number of pay periods per year, 26; Account No. 52 (Office Salaries).

4. Display an **Employee List** report and verify information you changed and added.

5. Enter the Payroll transactions, using the **Pay Employees** task and referring to Figure B.29 and detailed instructions that follow. <u>Do</u> deduct Group Insurance. <u>Do</u> deduct Union Dues for the appropriate employees. <u>Do</u> deduct SIMPLE Contributions for the appropriate employees. Begin the sequence with **Check No. 723**. **Note:** Be sure to enter the changes and amounts of Group Insurance deductions for the new employees, O'Neill's increase in SIMPLE Contributions, and the $9.00 Union Dues, as noted below.

Figure B.29
Current Payroll Journal Entries

Check Number	Employee Number	Employee Name	Salary / Reg. Hrs.	Bonus	Overtime @ Time 1 1/2	Overtime @ Double	Group Ins.	Union Dues	SIMPLE Contribution
723	100	Bonno, Anthony Victor	80			12	$16.50	$9.00	
724	110	Ferguson, Jamie Hadi	reg. salary				$26.40		$500.00
725	120	Ford, Catherine Louise	reg. salary				$15.00		
726	130	Mann, Kari Casey	reg. salary				$15.90		$250.00
727	140	O'Neill, Joseph Tyler	reg. salary	$95,000.00			$27.00		$2,000.00
728	160	Ryan, Jeri Mischa	80		7		$16.80	$9.00	$200.00
729	170	Sokowski, Thomas James	reg. salary				$24.00		
730	180	Student (your name)	71				$12.60		
731	200	Woods, Beth Ann	reg. salary				$14.10		
732	210	Young, Paul Winston	reg. salary				$14.70		

In this pay, the president of the company, *Joseph O'Neill*, is paid his annual bonus. This does not affect O'Neill's insurance coverage, which is based on regular pay. This year, his bonus is **$95,000**. For withholding purposes, the bonus is considered a supplemental payment and is taxed at the supplemental rate of 22 percent. For this pay, O'Neill **has increased his SIMPLE deduction to $2,000**, which will reduce his salary for federal income tax purposes. The software calculates the tax on the annualized net earnings (gross salary – Simple) and then adds 22 percent times the bonus to arrive at the amount of FIT for this pay period. In addition, the software takes into consideration the OASDI limit of $147,000 to calculate the OASDI tax. Click on the **Calculate Taxes** button after entering all deductions for each employee to fill the remaining fields.

6. Display and review the **Payroll Report**. Select the **Reports** menu on the top menu bar and **Payroll Report**.

7. Generate and post the journal entry for the current payroll by selecting **Current Payroll Journal Entry** from the **Tasks** menu on the top menu bar. Click **Yes** when asked if you want to generate the journal entry. When the entry appears in the Current Payroll Journal Entries dialog box, click on **Post**. The journal entry will reappear, posted, in the General Journal.

8. Generate and post the employer's payroll taxes journal entry. With the **Payroll** module still selected, click on the **Employer's Payroll Taxes Journal Entry** in the **Tasks** menu from the top menu bar. Click **Yes** when asked if you want to generate the journal entry. Verify the result and click **Post** to post the entry to the General Journal. After you accept the entries, they will reappear, posted, in the General Journal.

9. Enter and post the December 18 General Journal entry to record the deposit of cash for the total net amount owed to employees in the payroll cash account using the **General Journal** in the **Tasks** menu in the **General Ledger** module. Based on the current period Net Pay summary information in the **Payroll Report**, enter the journal transaction.

10. Display and review the **General Journal** report for 12/15/2023 through 12/18/2023. From the **General Ledger** module, select the **Tasks** menu from the top menu bar and **General Journal**.

11. Display and review the **General Ledger** report. While still in the **General Ledger** module, select **Ledger Reports** and **General Ledger**.

12. If there is a **Check** link on the lower right of your screen, click on that link to review your work. A Check My Work Summary report will be displayed and a percentage correct will show next to the Check link. Try to locate the source of the errors and correct them. A good place to start is the Payroll Report and the General Ledger. You are graded on ending general ledger balances and payroll entries. Make sure the check number and employee name are the same as on the Employees to Be Paid This Pay Period form. Remember you can start over from the Company module and select Company Setup and Company Information. The Reset command is on the bottom.

13. If your instructor has assigned the completion of the forms beginning in step 5 below, do not submit you assignment for grading until you have completed the forms as you will need to review some of the reports in the software to extract key numbers.

14. When you are comfortable that you have completed all steps of the problem correctly, click on the **Submit Assignment for Grading** button on the lower right of your screen.

V. End-of-Year Activities

The following optional additional transactions are given to illustrate different types of transactions arising in the subsequent year in connection with the accounting for payrolls and payroll taxes. These correspond with the activities beginning in the Chapter 7 Payroll Project beginning with the date of January 6.

Note: before you begin this activity, you should have a printed copy of the December 18 **Payroll Report**. if you do not have this report, you need to print one BEFORE you change the date in step 1 below. It is found in the **Payroll** module in the **Reports** menu.

1. Set the System Date to **January 6, 2024**, Make sure the year has advanced to 2024.

2. Enter and post the following transactions, using the **General Journal** task under the **General Ledger** module. You can determine current account balances from the **General Ledger** Report in the **Ledger Reports** menu bar.

    -   January 6: Deposited the Pennsylvania state income taxes withheld from the December 18 payroll. Use the current balance of account 25, Employees SIT Payable.

    -   January 8: Paid the treasurer of the union the amount of union dues withheld during the month of December. Use the current balance of account 28, Union Dues Payable.

> **Project Audit Test**
>
> At the start of each assignment, remove the Project Audit Test beginning on page B-43. Answer the questions for each pay period as you complete processing for each pay period.

- January 15: Deposited with City Bank the amount of FICA taxes and federal income taxes for the December payrolls. Pay the balance in the two FICA Taxes Payable accounts (20.1 and 20.2) and Employees FIT Payable (24) as of the end of December.
- January 15: Deposited the city of Philadelphia employees' income tax withheld with the Department of Revenue from the December payrolls. Use the current balance of account 26, Employees CIT Payable.
- February 1: Deposited FUTA Taxes Payable for the quarter. Use the current balance of account 21.
- February 1: Paid the SUTA Taxes Payable—Employer (22) and Employees SUTA Payable (25.1) for the fourth quarter.

3. Display and review the **General Journal** report for 1/1/2024 through 2/1/2024.

4. If there is a **Check** link in the lower right of your screen, click on that link to review your work. Do not submit for grading until you have completed the forms requested by your instructor in step 5 below, as you will need to review some of the reports in the software to extract key numbers.

5. Use the information contained in the payroll accounting reports to complete the following forms, if not completed in the student project in Chapter 7. If completed in Chapter 7, check the forms and note any differences. Because of calculation rounding and the use of the percentage method for Federal Income Tax calculation, some amounts may differ. Refer to the February 1 narrative regarding the forms to be completed (on pages 7-53 through 7-67) in the manual student project in Chapter 7, if necessary. Complete those forms assigned by your instructor.

    a. Form 941, Employer's Quarterly Federal Tax Return. Use the total Quarterly numbers in the December 18 **Payroll Report**. The final wages paid to Serdar Russell ($2,394.00) and the SIMPLE Contributions quarterly need to be deducted from the Line 2 total quarterly wages. Line 3 is the total quarterly FIT amount withheld. Line 5a wages are total quarterly wages paid less the amount paid to Joseph O'Neill in excess of the $147,000 cap on Social Security wages, while Line 5c is total quarterly wages. To calculate the Line 11 amount, review the **General Journal** report for the total amount paid to the federal government in the transactions of 11/17/2023, 12/15/2023, and 1/15/2024 (also shown in the General Ledger report for accounts 20.1, 20.2, and 24).

    b. Form 940, Employer's Annual Federal Unemployment (FUTA) Tax Return. Line 3 is the annual gross pay from the December 18 Payroll Report. For Line 7, subtract $7,000 each for ten employees ($70,000) and the under $7,000 total wages for Beth Anne Woods and Paul Winston Young. Lines 5 and 6 are the difference between these two amounts. The Line 8 total tax paid should equal the February 1 payment.

    c. Form UC-2, Employer's Report for Unemployment Compensation—Fourth Quarter. Total fourth quarter wages come from the December 18 Payroll Report quarterly column. Employee SUTA contributions were $115.37 for the quarter. Taxable SUTA wages were $ 20,050.00.

    d. Form W-2. Review the Wage and Tax Statement for each employee if you printed them in preparation for this activity. Note that you will need to manually calculate the taxable federal wages for employees with Simple deductions. You will also need to issue a manually corrected W-2 for Serdar Russell to show that Line 1 Wages do not include her last pay of $2,394.00.

e. Form W-3, Transmittal of Wage and Tax Statements. The final wages paid to Virginia Russell and the Simple Plan total need to be deducted from the total annual wages on the December 18 Payroll Report for computing Box 1. Box 3 wages are total annual wages paid less the amount paid to Joseph O'Neill in excess of the $147,000 cap on Social Security wages. Box 16 and 18 wages are total annual wages less the final wages paid to Serdar Russell. The other values can be derived from the December 18 Payroll Report.

f. Pennsylvania Form REV-1667, W-2 Transmittal. Use the amounts below for the wages paid and the Pennsylvania tax withheld for the first three quarters. The Line 2 annual and Part II fourth quarter gross pay amounts are the total gross pay minus Serdar Russell's final wages. Find SIT taxes withheld for the quarter from the last Payroll Report.

Quarter	Wages Paid	Tax Withheld
1st	$34,088.75	$1,046.52
2nd	$45,535.62	$1,397.94
3rd	$62,600.20	$1,921.83

g. Form 1099-MISC, Miscellaneous Income (for Serdar P. Russell). This is the gross amount of her last (December 14) pay. Because that check was written to the estate, this amount is reported as "Other income" and should not appear on the W-2, as noted in step (d) above.

h. Form 1096, Annual Summary and Transmittal of U.S. Information Returns (same amount as 1099-MISC). This form must also be completed for Serdar P. Russell's last pay.

i. City of Philadelphia Annual Reconciliation of Employer Wage Tax. For Line 1, deduct Serdar Russell's final wages from the annual gross wages paid (rounded to the nearest dollar). Tax paid during the first three quarters was $5,461.14. Note that ten employees were residents of Philadelphia in March.

Recording End-of-Period Payroll Adjustments

1. On the financial statements prepared at the end of its first year of operations, the company must show an accurate picture of all expenses and all liabilities incurred. The last payday of the year was December 18. However, the payment to the employees on that day did not include the weeks ending December 19 and 26 and the four days (December 28–31) in the following week. These earnings will be reflected in the January payrolls. Two-column journal paper is provided for use in journalizing the following entry on the bottom of this page.

   Prepare the adjusting entry as of December 31 to record the salaries and wages that have accrued but remain unpaid as of the end of the year. When calculating the amount of the accrual for each hourly worker, assume each employee worked eight hours on each day during the period with no overtime (student works a 36-hour week—student worked

32 hours for the period December 28 through December 31). For each salaried worker, the accrual will amount to 14/10 of the worker's biweekly earnings, except for Zimmerman who worked only 10 days.

Each of the labor cost accounts should be debited for the appropriate amount of the accrual, and Salaries and Wages Payable should be credited for the total amount of the accrual. There is no liability for payroll taxes on the accrued salaries and wages until the workers are actually paid. Therefore, the company follows the practice of not accruing payroll taxes.

2. Also, prepare the adjusting entry as of December 31 to record the accrued vacation pay as of the end of the year. Record the expense in a vacation benefits expense account, and credit the appropriate liability account. Use the journal paper provided below.

As of December 31, the vacation time earned but not used by each employee is listed here.

Bonno	80 hours
Ferguson	three weeks
Ford	two weeks
Mann	one week
O'Neill	four weeks
Ryan	80 hours
Sokowski	72 hours
Student	none
Woods	none
Young	none
Zimmerman	none

JOURNAL   Page ____

DATE	DESCRIPTION	POST. REF.	DEBIT	CREDIT

Name_____

VI. Project Audit Test

OCTOBER 9 PAYROLL: (As you complete your work, answer the following questions.)

Payroll Report

1. What is Jamie H. Ferguson's filing status? .... _____

2. What is the current gross pay for Jeri M. Ryan? .... _____

3. What is the current amount of HI withheld for the current pay period
for Ruth V. Williams? .... _____

4. What is the current net pay for all employees? .... _____

5. What is the current SIT withheld for all employees? .... _____

Journal Entries Report

6. What is the amount of the debit to Office Salaries?.. _____

7. What is the amount of the debit to Payroll Taxes? .... _____

8. What is the amount of the credit to Cash? .... _____

General Ledger Report

9. What is the Cash (account number 11) account balance? .... _____

10. What is the total Administrative Salaries paid to date?... _____

Name_____

Project Audit Test

OCTOBER 23 PAYROLL: (As you complete your work, answer the following questions.)

Payroll Report

1. What is the gross pay for Anthony V. Bonno?... _____

2. What is the current amount of OASDI withheld for Catherine L. Ford?...................... _____

3. What is the current net pay for all employees?... _____

4. What is the current amount of group insurance withheld for all employees?.............. _____

Journal Entries Report

5. What is the amount of the credit to Employees FIT Payable? .... _____

6. What is the amount of the debit to Payroll Taxes?... _____

7. What is the amount of the credit to SUTA Taxes Payable—Employer? .... _____

8. What is the amount of the debit to Employees SIT Payable on October 20? .... _____

General Ledger Report

9. What is the balance of FICA Taxes Payable—OASDI? .... _____

10. What is the balance of Union Dues withheld for the employees?................................ _____

Name_____

Project Audit Test

NOVEMBER 6 PAYROLL: (As you complete your work, answer the following questions.)

Payroll Report

1. What is the current amount of FIT withheld for Joseph T. O'Neill?.............................. _____

2. What is the current gross pay for all employees?.. _____

3. What is the current amount of CIT withheld for all employees?.................................. _____

4. What is the current net pay for all employees?.. _____

Journal Entries Report

5. What is the amount of the credit to FICA Taxes Payable—OASDI for employees?....... _____

6. What is the amount of the credit to FICA Taxes Payable—HI for employees?.............. _____

7. What is the amount of the debit to Payroll Taxes?... _____

8. What is the amount of the debit to Employees SIT Payable on November 4?.............. _____

General Ledger Report

9. What is the balance in the Cash (account number 11) account? .... _____

10. What is the amount of Sales Salaries paid to date?... _____

Name_____

Project Audit Test

NOVEMBER 13 PAYROLL: (As you complete your work, answer the following questions.)

Payroll Report

1. What is the amount of FIT withheld for the year for Ruth V. Williams?......................... _____

2. What is Ruth V. Williams' current net pay?... _____

3. What is the current amount of CIT withheld for Ruth V. Williams?.............................. _____

4. What is Ruth V. Williams' filing status? .... _____

Journal Entries Report

5. What is the amount of Ruth V. Williams' Group Insurance withheld?.......................... _____

6. What is the amount of the debit to Payroll Taxes?... _____

General Ledger Report

7. What is the total amount of Payroll Taxes (account number 56) to date?..................... _____

8. What is the balance in the FICA Taxes Payable—HI account?.................................. _____

9. What is the balance in the Cash account?... _____

10. What is the balance in the Employees FIT Payable account?................................... _____

Name_____

Project Audit Test

NOVEMBER 20 PAYROLL: (As you complete your work, answer the following questions.)

Payroll Report

1. What is the current amount of FIT withheld for Kari C. Mann?................................... _____
2. What is the current amount of SUTA withheld this period for all employees?............. _____
3. What is the current gross pay for all employees? .... _____

Journal Entries Report

4. What is the November 16 credit to Cash for the deposit of FICA & FIT taxes?............ _____
5. What is the amount of the debit to Payroll Taxes?.. _____
6. What is the November 16 debit to Employees CIT Payable?...................................... _____

General Ledger Report

7. What is the balance of Employees SIT Payable?.. _____
8. What is the amount of Office Salaries paid to date?.. _____
9. What is the balance of SIMPLE Contributions Payable?.. _____
10. What is the Cash account balance? .... _____

Name_____

Project Audit Test

DECEMBER 4 PAYROLL: (As you complete your work, answer the following questions.)

Payroll Report

1. What is the current net pay for Joseph T. O'Neill? .... _____
2. What is the current amount of OASDI withheld for Jeri M. Ryan? .... _____
3. What is the current net pay for all employees?... _____
4. What is the current CIT withheld for all employees?... _____

Journal Entries Report

5. What is the amount of the debit to Employees SIT Payable on December 3?............. _____
6. What is the amount of the credit to Employees FIT Payable? .... _____
7. What is the amount of the debit to Payroll Taxes?.. _____

General Ledger Report

8. What is the balance of SUTA Taxes Payable —Employer?.. _____
9. What is the balance of Employees CIT Payable? .... _____
10. What is the Cash account balance? .... _____

Name_____

Project Audit Test

DECEMBER 14 PAYROLL: (As you complete your work, answer the following questions.)

Payroll Report

1. What is the current amount of FIT withheld for Serdar P. Russell? .... _____

2. What is the amount of net pay received by Serdar P. Russell's estate? .... _____

3. What was Serdar P. Russell's filing status? .... _____

Journal Entries Report

4. What is the amount of the debit to Union Dues Payable on December 9? .... _____

5. What is the amount of the debit to Payroll Cash? .... _____

6. What is the amount of the credit to Employees SUTA Payable? .... _____

General Ledger Report

7. What is the amount that was credited to Group Insurance Premiums
Collected (account number 27) during this period? .... _____

8. What is the amount paid for office salaries to date? .... _____

9. What is the balance of FICA Taxes Payable—OASDI? .... _____

10. What is the balance of Payroll Taxes? .... _____

- -

Name_____

Project Audit Test

DECEMBER 18 PAYROLL: (As you complete your work, answer the following questions.)

Payroll Report

1. What is the amount of FIT withheld for Joseph T. O'Neill? .... _____

2. What is the total current net pay for all employees? .... _____

3. What is the total yearly gross pay for all employees? .... _____

4. What is the yearly amount of OASDI withheld from Joseph T. O'Neill? .... _____

Journal Entries Report

5. What is the amount of the credit to Cash for FICA and FIT taxes on December 15? ... _____

6. What is the amount of the debit to Payroll Taxes? .... _____

7. What is the amount of the debit to Employees CIT Payable on December 15? .... _____

General Ledger Report

8. What is the balance in the Cash account? .... _____

9. What is the total amount of Plant Wages to date? .... _____

10. What is the total amount of Payroll Taxes to date? .... _____

Name_____

Project Audit Test

END-OF-YEAR ACTIVITIES

Journal

1. What is the amount of the deposit for Pennsylvania state income taxes withheld from the December 18 payroll? .... _____

2. What is the amount of FICA Taxes Payable—OASDI deposited from the December payrolls? .... _____

3. What is the amount of the city of Philadelphia employees income tax deposited from the December payrolls? .... _____

4. What is the amount of FUTA Taxes Payable deposited for the quarter? .... _____

5. What is the amount of the credit to cash for SUTA Taxes Payable on February 1? .... _____

Payroll Adjusting Entries

6. What is the amount of the credit to Salaries and Wages Payable for the December 31 adjusting entry? .... _____

7. What is the amount of the debit to Vacation Benefits Expense for the December 31 adjusting entry? .... _____

Calculations

8. What is the total Payroll Tax Expense incurred by the employer on salaries and wages paid during the quarter ended December 31? .... _____

9. What is the total Payroll Tax Expense incurred by the employer on the total earnings of Joseph T. O'Neill during the fourth quarter? .... _____

10. O'Neill has decided to give all current employees (excluding himself) a bonus payment during January equal to 5% of their gross pay for last year. What is the total of this bonus payment? .... _____

Tax Tables

The following tables were in effect during 2022:

TAX TABLE A: 2022 PERCENTAGE METHOD TABLES FOR MANUAL
PAYROLL SYSTEMS WITH FORMS W-4 FROM 2020 OR LATER .... T - 2 - T - 4

TAX TABLE B: 2022 WAGE BRACKET METHOD TABLES FOR MANUAL
PAYROLL SYSTEMS WITH FORMS W-4 FROM 2020 OR LATER .... T - 5 - T - 13

TABLE OF ALLOWANCES .... T - 14

TAX TABLE *C: 2022 PERCENTAGE METHOD TABLES FOR MANUAL
PAYROLL SYSTEMS WITH FORMS W-4 FROM 2019 OR EARLIER .... T - 15 - T - 16

TAX TABLE *D: 2022 WAGE BRACKET METHOD TABLES FOR MANUAL
PAYROLL SYSTEMS WITH FORMS W-4 FROM 2019 OR EARLIER .... T - 17 - T - 34

Tax Tables with an asterisk (*) refer to the Chapter 4 Supplement.

TAX TABLE A

2022 Percentage Method Tables for Manual Payroll Systems With Forms W-4 From 2020 or Later
WEEKLY Payroll Period

STANDARD Withholding Rate Schedules (Use these if the box in Step 2 of Form W-4 is **NOT** checked)					Form W-4, Step 2, Checkbox, Withholding Rate Schedules (Use these if the box in Step 2 of Form W-4 **IS** checked)				
If the Adjusted Wage Amount (line 1h) is:		The tentative amount to withhold is:	Plus this percentage—	of the amount that the Adjusted Wage exceeds—	If the Adjusted Wage Amount (line 1h) is:		The tentative amount to withhold is:	Plus this percentage—	of the amount that the Adjusted Wage exceeds—
At least—	But less than—				At least—	But less than—			
A	B	C	D	E	A	B	C	D	E
Married Filing Jointly					**Married Filing Jointly**				
$0	$498	$0.00	0%	$0	$0	$249	$0.00	0%	$0
$498	$893	$0.00	10%	$498	$249	$447	$0.00	10%	$249
$893	$2,105	$39.50	12%	$893	$447	$1,052	$19.80	12%	$447
$2,105	$3,924	$184.94	22%	$2,105	$1,052	$1,962	$92.40	22%	$1,052
$3,924	$7,038	$585.12	24%	$3,924	$1,962	$3,519	$292.60	24%	$1,962
$7,038	$8,804	$1,332.48	32%	$7,038	$3,519	$4,402	$666.28	32%	$3,519
$8,804	$12,957	$1,897.60	35%	$8,804	$4,402	$6,478	$948.84	35%	$4,402
$12,957		$3,351.15	37%	$12,957	$6,478		$1,675.44	37%	$6,478
Single or Married Filing Separately					**Single or Married Filing Separately**				
$0	$249	$0.00	0%	$0	$0	$125	$0.00	0%	$0
$249	$447	$0.00	10%	$249	$125	$223	$0.00	10%	$125
$447	$1,052	$19.80	12%	$447	$223	$526	$9.80	12%	$223
$1,052	$1,962	$92.40	22%	$1,052	$526	$981	$46.16	22%	$526
$1,962	$3,519	$292.60	24%	$1,962	$981	$1,760	$146.26	24%	$981
$3,519	$4,402	$666.28	32%	$3,519	$1,760	$2,201	$333.22	32%	$1,760
$4,402	$10,632	$948.84	35%	$4,402	$2,201	$5,316	$474.34	35%	$2,201
$10,632		$3,129.34	37%	$10,632	$5,316		$1,564.59	37%	$5,316
Head of Household					**Head of Household**				
$0	$373	$0.00	0%	$0	$0	$187	$0.00	0%	$0
$373	$655	$0.00	10%	$373	$187	$327	$0.00	10%	$187
$655	$1,448	$28.20	12%	$655	$327	$724	$14.00	12%	$327
$1,448	$2,086	$123.36	22%	$1,448	$724	$1,043	$61.64	22%	$724
$2,086	$3,643	$263.72	24%	$2,086	$1,043	$1,822	$131.82	24%	$1,043
$3,643	$4,526	$637.40	32%	$3,643	$1,822	$2,263	$318.78	32%	$1,822
$4,526	$10,756	$919.96	35%	$4,526	$2,263	$5,378	$459.90	35%	$2,263
$10,756		$3,100.46	37%	$10,756	$5,378		$1,550.15	37%	$5,378

2022 Percentage Method Tables for Manual Payroll Systems With Forms W-4 From 2020 or Later
BIWEEKLY Payroll Period

STANDARD Withholding Rate Schedules (Use these if the box in Step 2 of Form W-4 is **NOT** checked)					Form W-4, Step 2, Checkbox, Withholding Rate Schedules (Use these if the box in Step 2 of Form W-4 **IS** checked)				
If the Adjusted Wage Amount (line 1h) is:		The tentative amount to withhold is:	Plus this percentage—	of the amount that the Adjusted Wage exceeds—	If the Adjusted Wage Amount (line 1h) is:		The tentative amount to withhold is:	Plus this percentage—	of the amount that the Adjusted Wage exceeds—
At least—	But less than—				At least—	But less than—			
A	B	C	D	E	A	B	C	D	E
Married Filing Jointly					**Married Filing Jointly**				
$0	$996	$0.00	0%	$0	$0	$498	$0.00	0%	$0
$996	$1,787	$0.00	10%	$996	$498	$893	$0.00	10%	$498
$1,787	$4,210	$79.10	12%	$1,787	$893	$2,105	$39.50	12%	$893
$4,210	$7,848	$369.86	22%	$4,210	$2,105	$3,924	$184.94	22%	$2,105
$7,848	$14,077	$1,170.22	24%	$7,848	$3,924	$7,038	$585.12	24%	$3,924
$14,077	$17,608	$2,665.18	32%	$14,077	$7,038	$8,804	$1,332.48	32%	$7,038
$17,608	$25,913	$3,795.10	35%	$17,608	$8,804	$12,957	$1,897.60	35%	$8,804
$25,913		$6,701.85	37%	$25,913	$12,957		$3,351.15	37%	$12,957
Single or Married Filing Separately					**Single or Married Filing Separately**				
$0	$498	$0.00	0%	$0	$0	$249	$0.00	0%	$0
$498	$893	$0.00	10%	$498	$249	$447	$0.00	10%	$249
$893	$2,105	$39.50	12%	$893	$447	$1,052	$19.80	12%	$447
$2,105	$3,924	$184.94	22%	$2,105	$1,052	$1,962	$92.40	22%	$1,052
$3,924	$7,038	$585.12	24%	$3,924	$1,962	$3,519	$292.60	24%	$1,962
$7,038	$8,804	$1,332.48	32%	$7,038	$3,519	$4,402	$666.28	32%	$3,519
$8,804	$21,263	$1,897.60	35%	$8,804	$4,402	$10,632	$948.84	35%	$4,402
$21,263		$6,258.25	37%	$21,263	$10,632		$3,129.34	37%	$10,632
Head of Household					**Head of Household**				
$0	$746	$0.00	0%	$0	$0	$373	$0.00	0%	$0
$746	$1,310	$0.00	10%	$746	$373	$655	$0.00	10%	$373
$1,310	$2,896	$56.40	12%	$1,310	$655	$1,448	$28.20	12%	$655
$2,896	$4,171	$246.72	22%	$2,896	$1,448	$2,086	$123.36	22%	$1,448
$4,171	$7,287	$527.22	24%	$4,171	$2,086	$3,643	$263.72	24%	$2,086
$7,287	$9,052	$1,275.06	32%	$7,287	$3,643	$4,526	$637.40	32%	$3,643
$9,052	$21,512	$1,839.86	35%	$9,052	$4,526	$10,756	$919.96	35%	$4,526
$21,512		$6,200.86	37%	$21,512	$10,756		$3,100.46	37%	$10,756

Source: Internal Revenue Service.

TAX TABLE A (Continued)

2022 Percentage Method Tables for Manual Payroll Systems With Forms W-4 From 2020 or Later

SEMIMONTHLY Payroll Period

STANDARD Withholding Rate Schedules (Use these if the box in Step 2 of Form W-4 is **NOT** checked)					Form W-4, Step 2, Checkbox, Withholding Rate Schedules (Use these if the box in Step 2 of Form W-4 **IS** checked)				
If the Adjusted Wage Amount (line 1h) is:		The tentative amount to withhold is:	Plus this percentage—	of the amount that the Adjusted Wage exceeds—	If the Adjusted Wage Amount (line 1h) is:		The tentative amount to withhold is:	Plus this percentage—	of the amount that the Adjusted Wage exceeds—
At least—	But less than—				At least—	But less than—			
A	B	C	D	E	A	B	C	D	E
Married Filing Jointly					**Married Filing Jointly**				
$0	$1,079	$0.00	0%	$0	$0	$540	$0.00	0%	$0
$1,079	$1,935	$0.00	10%	$1,079	$540	$968	$0.00	10%	$540
$1,935	$4,560	$85.60	12%	$1,935	$968	$2,280	$42.80	12%	$968
$4,560	$8,502	$400.60	22%	$4,560	$2,280	$4,251	$200.24	22%	$2,280
$8,502	$15,250	$1,267.84	24%	$8,502	$4,251	$7,625	$633.86	24%	$4,251
$15,250	$19,075	$2,887.36	32%	$15,250	$7,625	$9,538	$1,443.62	32%	$7,625
$19,075	$28,073	$4,111.36	35%	$19,075	$9,538	$14,036	$2,055.78	35%	$9,538
$28,073		$7,260.66	37%	$28,073	$14,036		$3,630.08	37%	$14,036
Single or Married Filing Separately					**Single or Married Filing Separately**				
$0	$540	$0.00	0%	$0	$0	$270	$0.00	0%	$0
$540	$968	$0.00	10%	$540	$270	$484	$0.00	10%	$270
$968	$2,280	$42.80	12%	$968	$484	$1,140	$21.40	12%	$484
$2,280	$4,251	$200.24	22%	$2,280	$1,140	$2,126	$100.12	22%	$1,140
$4,251	$7,625	$633.86	24%	$4,251	$2,126	$3,813	$317.04	24%	$2,126
$7,625	$9,538	$1,443.62	32%	$7,625	$3,813	$4,769	$721.92	32%	$3,813
$9,538	$23,035	$2,055.78	35%	$9,538	$4,769	$11,518	$1,027.84	35%	$4,769
$23,035		$6,779.73	37%	$23,035	$11,518		$3,389.99	37%	$11,518
Head of Household					**Head of Household**				
$0	$808	$0.00	0%	$0	$0	$404	$0.00	0%	$0
$808	$1,419	$0.00	10%	$808	$404	$709	$0.00	10%	$404
$1,419	$3,138	$61.10	12%	$1,419	$709	$1,569	$30.50	12%	$709
$3,138	$4,519	$267.38	22%	$3,138	$1,569	$2,259	$133.70	22%	$1,569
$4,519	$7,894	$571.20	24%	$4,519	$2,259	$3,947	$285.50	24%	$2,259
$7,894	$9,806	$1,381.20	32%	$7,894	$3,947	$4,903	$690.62	32%	$3,947
$9,806	$23,304	$1,993.04	35%	$9,806	$4,903	$11,652	$996.54	35%	$4,903
$23,304		$6,717.34	37%	$23,304	$11,652		$3,358.69	37%	$11,652

2022 Percentage Method Tables for Manual Payroll Systems With Forms W-4 From 2020 or Later

MONTHLY Payroll Period

STANDARD Withholding Rate Schedules (Use these if the box in Step 2 of Form W-4 is **NOT** checked)					Form W-4, Step 2, Checkbox, Withholding Rate Schedules (Use these if the box in Step 2 of Form W-4 **IS** checked)				
If the Adjusted Wage Amount (line 1h) is:		The tentative amount to withhold is:	Plus this percentage—	of the amount that the Adjusted Wage exceeds—	If the Adjusted Wage Amount (line 1h) is:		The tentative amount to withhold is:	Plus this percentage—	of the amount that the Adjusted Wage exceeds—
At least—	But less than—				At least—	But less than—			
A	B	C	D	E	A	B	C	D	E
Married Filing Jointly					**Married Filing Jointly**				
$0	$2,158	$0.00	0%	$0	$0	$1,079	$0.00	0%	$0
$2,158	$3,871	$0.00	10%	$2,158	$1,079	$1,935	$0.00	10%	$1,079
$3,871	$9,121	$171.30	12%	$3,871	$1,935	$4,560	$85.60	12%	$1,935
$9,121	$17,004	$801.30	22%	$9,121	$4,560	$8,502	$400.60	22%	$4,560
$17,004	$30,500	$2,535.56	24%	$17,004	$8,502	$15,250	$1,267.84	24%	$8,502
$30,500	$38,150	$5,774.60	32%	$30,500	$15,250	$19,075	$2,887.36	32%	$15,250
$38,150	$56,146	$8,222.60	35%	$38,150	$19,075	$28,073	$4,111.36	35%	$19,075
$56,146		$14,521.20	37%	$56,146	$28,073		$7,260.66	37%	$28,073
Single or Married Filing Separately					**Single or Married Filing Separately**				
$0	$1,079	$0.00	0%	$0	$0	$540	$0.00	0%	$0
$1,079	$1,935	$0.00	10%	$1,079	$540	$968	$0.00	10%	$540
$1,935	$4,560	$85.60	12%	$1,935	$968	$2,280	$42.80	12%	$968
$4,560	$8,502	$400.60	22%	$4,560	$2,280	$4,251	$200.24	22%	$2,280
$8,502	$15,250	$1,267.84	24%	$8,502	$4,251	$7,625	$633.86	24%	$4,251
$15,250	$19,075	$2,887.36	32%	$15,250	$7,625	$9,538	$1,443.62	32%	$7,625
$19,075	$46,071	$4,111.36	35%	$19,075	$9,538	$23,035	$2,055.78	35%	$9,538
$46,071		$13,559.96	37%	$46,071	$23,035		$6,779.73	37%	$23,035
Head of Household					**Head of Household**				
$0	$1,617	$0.00	0%	$0	$0	$808	$0.00	0%	$0
$1,617	$2,838	$0.00	10%	$1,617	$808	$1,419	$0.00	10%	$808
$2,838	$6,275	$122.10	12%	$2,838	$1,419	$3,138	$61.10	12%	$1,419
$6,275	$9,038	$534.54	22%	$6,275	$3,138	$4,519	$267.38	22%	$3,138
$9,038	$15,788	$1,142.40	24%	$9,038	$4,519	$7,894	$571.20	24%	$4,519
$15,788	$19,613	$2,762.40	32%	$15,788	$7,894	$9,806	$1,381.20	32%	$7,894
$19,613	$46,608	$3,986.40	35%	$19,613	$9,806	$23,304	$1,993.04	35%	$9,806
$46,608		$13,434.65	37%	$46,608	$23,304		$6,717.34	37%	$23,304

TAX TABLE A (*Concluded*)

2022 Percentage Method Tables for Manual Payroll Systems With Forms W-4 From 2020 or Later

DAILY Payroll Period

STANDARD Withholding Rate Schedules (Use these if the box in Step 2 of Form W-4 is **NOT** checked)					Form W-4, Step 2, Checkbox, Withholding Rate Schedules (Use these if the box in Step 2 of Form W-4 **IS** checked)				
If the Adjusted Wage Amount (line 1h) is:		The tentative amount to withhold is:	Plus this percentage—	of the amount that the Adjusted Wage exceeds—	If the Adjusted Wage Amount (line 1h) is:		The tentative amount to withhold is:	Plus this percentage—	of the amount that the Adjusted Wage exceeds—
At least—	But less than—				At least—	But less than—			
A	B	C	D	E	A	B	C	D	E
Married Filing Jointly					**Married Filing Jointly**				
$0.00	$99.60	$0.00	0%	$0.00	$49.80	$89.30	$0.00	0%	$0.00
$99.60	$178.70	$0.00	10%	$99.60	$89.30	$210.50	$3.95	12%	$89.30
$178.70	$421.00	$7.91	12%	$178.70	$89.30	$210.50	$3.95	12%	$89.30
$421.00	$784.80	$36.99	22%	$421.00	$210.50	$392.40	$18.49	22%	$210.50
$784.80	$1,407.70	$117.02	24%	$784.80	$392.40	$703.80	$58.51	24%	$392.40
$1,407.70	$1,760.80	$266.52	32%	$1,407.70	$703.80	$880.40	$133.25	32%	$703.80
$1,760.80	$2,591.30	$379.51	35%	$1,760.80	$880.40	$1,295.70	$189.76	35%	$880.40
$2,591.30		$670.19	37%	$2,591.30	$1,295.70		$335.12	37%	$1,295.70
Single or Married Filing Separately					**Single or Married Filing Separately**				
$0.00	$49.80	$0.00	0%	$0.00	$0.00	$24.90	$0.00	0%	$0.00
$49.80	$89.30	$0.00	10%	$49.80	$24.90	$44.70	$0.00	10%	$24.90
$89.30	$210.50	$3.95	12%	$89.30	$44.70	$105.20	$1.98	12%	$44.70
$210.50	$392.40	$18.49	22%	$210.50	$105.20	$196.20	$9.24	22%	$105.20
$392.40	$703.80	$58.51	24%	$392.40	$196.20	$351.90	$29.26	24%	$196.20
$703.80	$880.40	$133.25	32%	$703.80	$351.90	$440.20	$66.63	32%	$351.90
$880.40	$2,126.30	$189.76	35%	$880.40	$440.20	$1,063.20	$94.88	35%	$440.20
$2,126.30		$625.83	37%	$2,126.30	$1,063.20		$312.93	37%	$1,063.20
Head of Household					**Head of Household**				
$0.00	$74.60	$0.00	0%	$0.00	$0.00	$37.30	$0.00	0%	$0.00
$74.60	$131.00	$0.00	10%	$74.60	$37.30	$65.50	$0.00	10%	$37.30
$131.00	$289.60	$5.64	12%	$131.00	$65.50	$144.80	$2.82	12%	$65.50
$289.60	$417.10	$24.67	22%	$289.60	$144.80	$208.60	$12.34	22%	$144.80
$417.10	$728.70	$52.72	24%	$417.10	$208.60	$364.30	$26.37	24%	$208.60
$728.70	$905.20	$127.51	32%	$728.70	$364.30	$452.60	$63.74	32%	$364.30
$905.20	$2,151.20	$183.99	35%	$905.20	$452.60	$1,075.60	$92.00	35%	$452.60
$2,151.20		$620.09	37%	$2,151.20	$1,075.60		$310.05	37%	$1,075.60

TAX TABLE B

WEEKLY PAYROLL PERIOD

2022 Wage Bracket Method Tables for Manual Payroll Systems with Forms W-4 From 2020 or Later
WEEKLY Payroll Period

The Tentative Withholding Amount is:

If the Adjusted Wage Amount (line 1h) is		Married Filing Jointly		Head of Household		Single or Married Filing Separately	
At least	But less than	Standard withholding	Form W-4, Step 2, Checkbox withholding	Standard withholding	Form W-4, Step 2, Checkbox withholding	Standard withholding	Form W-4, Step 2, Checkbox withholding
$0	$125	$0	$0	$0	$0	$0	$0
$125	$135	$0	$0	$0	$0	$0	$1
$135	$145	$0	$0	$0	$0	$0	$2
$145	$155	$0	$0	$0	$0	$0	$3
$155	$165	$0	$0	$0	$0	$0	$4
$165	$175	$0	$0	$0	$0	$0	$5
$175	$185	$0	$0	$0	$0	$0	$6
$185	$195	$0	$0	$0	$0	$0	$7
$195	$205	$0	$0	$0	$1	$0	$8
$205	$215	$0	$0	$0	$2	$0	$9
$215	$225	$0	$0	$0	$3	$0	$10
$225	$235	$0	$0	$0	$4	$0	$11
$235	$245	$0	$0	$0	$5	$0	$12
$245	$255	$0	$0	$0	$6	$0	$13
$255	$265	$0	$1	$0	$7	$1	$14
$265	$275	$0	$2	$0	$8	$2	$15
$275	$285	$0	$3	$0	$9	$3	$17
$285	$295	$0	$4	$0	$10	$4	$18
$295	$305	$0	$5	$0	$11	$5	$19
$305	$315	$0	$6	$0	$12	$6	$20
$315	$325	$0	$7	$0	$13	$7	$21
$325	$335	$0	$8	$0	$14	$8	$23
$335	$345	$0	$9	$0	$16	$9	$24
$345	$355	$0	$10	$0	$17	$10	$25
$355	$365	$0	$11	$0	$18	$11	$26
$365	$375	$0	$12	$1	$19	$12	$27
$375	$385	$0	$13	$2	$20	$13	$29
$385	$395	$0	$14	$3	$22	$14	$30
$395	$405	$0	$15	$4	$23	$15	$31
$405	$415	$0	$16	$5	$24	$16	$32
$415	$425	$0	$17	$6	$25	$17	$33
$425	$435	$0	$18	$7	$26	$18	$35
$435	$445	$0	$19	$8	$28	$19	$36
$445	$455	$0	$20	$9	$29	$20	$37
$455	$465	$0	$21	$10	$30	$21	$38
$465	$475	$0	$23	$11	$31	$23	$39
$475	$485	$0	$24	$12	$32	$24	$41
$485	$495	$0	$25	$13	$34	$25	$42
$495	$505	$0	$26	$14	$35	$26	$43
$505	$515	$1	$27	$15	$36	$27	$44
$515	$525	$2	$29	$16	$37	$29	$45
$525	$535	$3	$30	$17	$38	$30	$47
$535	$545	$4	$31	$18	$40	$31	$49
$545	$555	$5	$32	$19	$41	$32	$51
$555	$565	$6	$33	$20	$42	$33	$54
$565	$575	$7	$35	$21	$43	$35	$56
$575	$585	$8	$36	$22	$44	$36	$58
$585	$595	$9	$37	$23	$46	$37	$60
$595	$605	$10	$38	$24	$47	$38	$62
$605	$615	$11	$39	$25	$48	$39	$65
$615	$625	$12	$41	$26	$49	$41	$67
$625	$635	$13	$42	$27	$50	$42	$69
$635	$645	$14	$43	$28	$52	$43	$71
$645	$655	$15	$44	$29	$53	$44	$73
$655	$665	$16	$45	$30	$54	$45	$76
$665	$675	$17	$47	$31	$55	$47	$78
$675	$685	$18	$48	$32	$56	$48	$80
$685	$695	$19	$49	$33	$58	$49	$82
$695	$705	$20	$50	$34	$59	$50	$84
$705	$715	$21	$51	$35	$60	$51	$87
$715	$725	$22	$53	$36	$61	$53	$89
$725	$735	$23	$54	$37	$63	$54	$91
$735	$745	$24	$55	$38	$65	$55	$93
$745	$755	$25	$56	$40	$67	$56	$95
$755	$765	$26	$57	$41	$70	$57	$98

2022 Wage Bracket Method Tables for Manual Payroll Systems with Forms W-4 From 2020 or Later
WEEKLY Payroll Period

The Tentative Withholding Amount is:

If the Adjusted Wage Amount (line 1h) is		Married Filing Jointly		Head of Household		Single or Married Filing Separately	
At least	But less than	Standard withholding	Form W-4, Step 2, Checkbox withholding	Standard withholding	Form W-4, Step 2, Checkbox withholding	Standard withholding	Form W-4, Step 2, Checkbox withholding
$765	$775	$27	$59	$42	$72	$59	$100
$775	$785	$28	$60	$43	$74	$60	$102
$785	$795	$29	$61	$44	$76	$61	$104
$795	$805	$30	$62	$46	$78	$62	$106
$805	$815	$31	$63	$47	$81	$63	$109
$815	$825	$32	$65	$48	$83	$65	$111
$825	$835	$33	$66	$49	$85	$66	$113
$835	$845	$34	$67	$50	$87	$67	$115
$845	$855	$35	$68	$52	$89	$68	$117
$855	$865	$36	$69	$53	$92	$69	$120
$865	$875	$37	$71	$54	$94	$71	$122
$875	$885	$38	$72	$55	$96	$72	$124
$885	$895	$39	$73	$56	$98	$73	$126
$895	$905	$40	$74	$58	$100	$74	$128
$905	$915	$42	$75	$59	$103	$75	$131
$915	$925	$43	$77	$60	$105	$77	$133
$925	$935	$44	$78	$61	$107	$78	$135
$935	$945	$45	$79	$62	$109	$79	$137
$945	$955	$46	$80	$64	$111	$80	$139
$955	$965	$48	$81	$65	$114	$81	$142
$965	$975	$49	$83	$66	$116	$83	$144
$975	$985	$50	$84	$67	$118	$84	$146
$985	$995	$51	$85	$68	$120	$85	$148
$995	$1,005	$52	$86	$70	$122	$86	$151
$1,005	$1,015	$54	$87	$71	$125	$87	$153
$1,015	$1,025	$55	$89	$72	$127	$89	$156
$1,025	$1,035	$56	$90	$73	$129	$90	$158
$1,035	$1,045	$57	$91	$74	$131	$91	$160
$1,045	$1,055	$58	$92	$76	$134	$92	$163
$1,055	$1,065	$60	$94	$77	$136	$94	$165
$1,065	$1,075	$61	$96	$78	$138	$96	$168
$1,075	$1,085	$62	$99	$79	$141	$99	$170
$1,085	$1,095	$63	$101	$80	$143	$101	$172
$1,095	$1,105	$64	$103	$82	$146	$103	$175
$1,105	$1,115	$66	$105	$83	$148	$105	$177
$1,115	$1,125	$67	$107	$84	$150	$107	$180
$1,125	$1,135	$68	$110	$85	$153	$110	$182
$1,135	$1,145	$69	$112	$86	$155	$112	$184
$1,145	$1,155	$70	$114	$88	$158	$114	$187
$1,155	$1,165	$72	$116	$89	$160	$116	$189
$1,165	$1,175	$73	$118	$90	$162	$118	$192
$1,175	$1,185	$74	$121	$91	$165	$121	$194
$1,185	$1,195	$75	$123	$92	$167	$123	$196
$1,195	$1,205	$76	$125	$94	$170	$125	$199
$1,205	$1,215	$78	$127	$95	$172	$127	$201
$1,215	$1,225	$79	$129	$96	$174	$129	$204
$1,225	$1,235	$80	$132	$97	$177	$132	$206
$1,235	$1,245	$81	$134	$98	$179	$134	$208
$1,245	$1,255	$82	$136	$100	$182	$136	$211
$1,255	$1,265	$84	$138	$101	$184	$138	$213
$1,265	$1,275	$85	$140	$102	$186	$140	$216
$1,275	$1,285	$86	$143	$103	$189	$143	$218
$1,285	$1,295	$87	$145	$104	$191	$145	$220
$1,295	$1,305	$88	$147	$106	$194	$147	$223
$1,305	$1,315	$90	$149	$107	$196	$149	$225
$1,315	$1,325	$91	$151	$108	$198	$151	$228
$1,325	$1,335	$92	$154	$109	$201	$154	$230
$1,335	$1,345	$93	$156	$110	$203	$156	$232
$1,345	$1,355	$94	$158	$112	$206	$158	$235
$1,355	$1,365	$96	$160	$113	$208	$160	$237
$1,365	$1,375	$97	$162	$114	$210	$162	$240
$1,375	$1,385	$98	$165	$115	$213	$165	$242
$1,385	$1,395	$99	$167	$116	$215	$167	$244
$1,395	$1,405	$100	$169	$118	$218	$169	$247
$1,405	$1,415	$102	$171	$119	$220	$171	$249

Source: Internal Revenue Service.

TAX TABLE B (Continued)

2022 Wage Bracket Method Tables for Manual Payroll Systems with Forms W-4 From 2020 or Later

WEEKLY PAYROLL PERIOD

WEEKLY Payroll Period

If the Adjusted Wage Amount (line 1h) is		Married Filing Jointly		Head of Household		Single or Married Filing Separately	
At least	But less than	Standard withholding	Form W-4, Step 2, Checkbox withholding	Standard withholding	Form W-4, Step 2, Checkbox withholding	Standard withholding	Form W-4, Step 2, Checkbox withholding
		The Tentative Withholding Amount is:					
$1,415	$1,425	$103	$173	$120	$222	$173	$252
$1,425	$1,435	$104	$176	$121	$225	$176	$254
$1,435	$1,445	$105	$178	$122	$227	$178	$256
$1,445	$1,455	$106	$180	$124	$230	$180	$259
$1,455	$1,465	$108	$182	$126	$232	$182	$261
$1,465	$1,475	$109	$184	$128	$234	$184	$264
$1,475	$1,485	$110	$187	$130	$237	$187	$266
$1,485	$1,495	$111	$189	$133	$239	$189	$268
$1,495	$1,505	$112	$191	$135	$242	$191	$271
$1,505	$1,515	$114	$193	$137	$244	$193	$273
$1,515	$1,525	$115	$195	$139	$246	$195	$276
$1,525	$1,535	$116	$198	$141	$249	$198	$278
$1,535	$1,545	$117	$200	$144	$251	$200	$280
$1,545	$1,555	$118	$202	$146	$254	$202	$283
$1,555	$1,565	$120	$204	$148	$256	$204	$285
$1,565	$1,575	$121	$206	$150	$258	$206	$288
$1,575	$1,585	$122	$209	$152	$261	$209	$290
$1,585	$1,595	$123	$211	$155	$263	$211	$292
$1,595	$1,605	$124	$213	$157	$266	$213	$295
$1,605	$1,615	$126	$215	$159	$268	$215	$297
$1,615	$1,625	$127	$217	$161	$270	$217	$300
$1,625	$1,635	$128	$220	$163	$273	$220	$302
$1,635	$1,645	$129	$222	$166	$275	$222	$304
$1,645	$1,655	$130	$224	$168	$278	$224	$307
$1,655	$1,665	$132	$226	$170	$280	$226	$309
$1,665	$1,675	$133	$228	$172	$282	$228	$312
$1,675	$1,685	$134	$231	$174	$285	$231	$314
$1,685	$1,695	$135	$233	$177	$287	$233	$316
$1,695	$1,705	$136	$235	$179	$290	$235	$319
$1,705	$1,715	$138	$237	$181	$292	$237	$321
$1,715	$1,725	$139	$239	$183	$294	$239	$324
$1,725	$1,735	$140	$242	$185	$297	$242	$326
$1,735	$1,745	$141	$244	$188	$299	$244	$328
$1,745	$1,755	$142	$246	$190	$302	$246	$331
$1,755	$1,765	$144	$248	$192	$304	$248	$333
$1,765	$1,775	$145	$250	$194	$306	$250	$336
$1,775	$1,785	$146	$253	$196	$309	$253	$340
$1,785	$1,795	$147	$255	$199	$311	$255	$343
$1,795	$1,805	$148	$257	$201	$314	$257	$346
$1,805	$1,815	$150	$259	$203	$316	$259	$349
$1,815	$1,825	$151	$261	$205	$318	$261	$352
$1,825	$1,835	$152	$264	$207	$321	$264	$356
$1,835	$1,845	$153	$266	$210	$325	$266	$359
$1,845	$1,855	$154	$268	$212	$328	$268	$362
$1,855	$1,865	$156	$270	$214	$331	$270	$365
$1,865	$1,875	$157	$272	$216	$334	$272	$368
$1,875	$1,885	$158	$275	$218	$337	$275	$372
$1,885	$1,895	$159	$277	$221	$341	$277	$375
$1,895	$1,905	$160	$279	$223	$344	$279	$378
$1,905	$1,915	$162	$281	$225	$347	$281	$381
$1,915	$1,925	$163	$283	$227	$350	$283	$384

TAX TABLE B (Continued)

BIWEEKLY PAYROLL PERIOD

2022 Wage Bracket Method Tables for Manual Payroll Systems with Forms W-4 From 2020 or Later — BIWEEKLY Payroll Period

The Tentative Withholding Amount is:

If the Adjusted Wage Amount (line 1h) is: At least	But less than	Married Filing Jointly — Standard withholding	Married Filing Jointly — Form W-4, Step 2, Checkbox withholding	Head of Household — Standard withholding	Head of Household — Form W-4, Step 2, Checkbox withholding	Single or Married Filing Separately — Standard withholding	Single or Married Filing Separately — Form W-4, Step 2, Checkbox withholding
$0	$250	$0	$0	$0	$0	$0	$0
$250	$260	$0	$0	$0	$0	$0	$1
$260	$270	$0	$0	$0	$0	$0	$2
$270	$280	$0	$0	$0	$0	$0	$3
$280	$290	$0	$0	$0	$0	$0	$4
$290	$300	$0	$0	$0	$0	$0	$5
$300	$310	$0	$0	$0	$0	$0	$6
$310	$320	$0	$0	$0	$0	$0	$7
$320	$330	$0	$0	$0	$0	$0	$8
$330	$340	$0	$0	$0	$0	$0	$9
$340	$350	$0	$0	$0	$0	$0	$10
$350	$360	$0	$0	$0	$0	$0	$11
$360	$370	$0	$0	$0	$0	$0	$12
$370	$380	$0	$0	$0	$0	$0	$13
$380	$390	$0	$0	$0	$0	$0	$14
$390	$400	$0	$0	$0	$0	$0	$15
$400	$410	$0	$0	$0	$2	$0	$16
$410	$420	$0	$0	$0	$3	$0	$17
$420	$430	$0	$0	$0	$5	$0	$18
$430	$440	$0	$0	$0	$6	$0	$19
$440	$450	$0	$0	$0	$8	$0	$20
$450	$465	$0	$0	$0	$9	$0	$21
$465	$480	$0	$0	$0	$11	$0	$23
$480	$495	$0	$0	$0	$12	$0	$25
$495	$510	$0	$0	$0	$14	$0	$26
$510	$525	$0	$1	$0	$15	$1	$28
$525	$540	$0	$3	$0	$17	$3	$30
$540	$555	$0	$4	$0	$18	$4	$32
$555	$570	$0	$6	$0	$20	$6	$34
$570	$585	$0	$7	$0	$21	$7	$35
$585	$600	$0	$9	$0	$23	$9	$37
$600	$615	$0	$10	$0	$24	$10	$39
$615	$630	$0	$12	$0	$25	$12	$41
$630	$645	$0	$13	$0	$27	$13	$43
$645	$660	$0	$15	$0	$28	$15	$44
$660	$675	$0	$17	$0	$30	$17	$46
$675	$690	$0	$18	$0	$31	$18	$48
$690	$705	$0	$20	$0	$33	$20	$50
$705	$720	$0	$21	$0	$35	$21	$51
$720	$735	$0	$23	$0	$37	$23	$53
$735	$750	$0	$24	$0	$39	$24	$55
$750	$765	$0	$25	$1	$40	$25	$57
$765	$780	$0	$27	$3	$42	$27	$59
$780	$795	$0	$28	$4	$44	$28	$61
$795	$810	$0	$30	$6	$46	$30	$62
$810	$825	$0	$31	$7	$48	$31	$64
$825	$840	$0	$33	$9	$49	$33	$66
$840	$855	$0	$35	$10	$51	$35	$68
$855	$870	$0	$36	$12	$53	$36	$70
$870	$885	$0	$38	$13	$55	$38	$71
$885	$900	$0	$39	$15	$57	$39	$73
$900	$915	$0	$41	$16	$58	$41	$75
$915	$930	$0	$43	$18	$60	$43	$77
$930	$945	$0	$45	$19	$62	$45	$79
$945	$960	$0	$47	$21	$64	$47	$80
$960	$975	$0	$48	$22	$66	$48	$82
$975	$990	$0	$50	$24	$67	$50	$84
$990	$1,005	$0	$52	$25	$69	$52	$86
$1,005	$1,020	$2	$54	$27	$71	$54	$88
$1,020	$1,035	$3	$56	$28	$73	$56	$89
$1,035	$1,050	$5	$57	$30	$75	$57	$91
$1,050	$1,070	$6	$60	$31	$77	$60	$94
$1,070	$1,090	$8	$62	$33	$79	$62	$99
$1,090	$1,110	$10	$64	$35	$82	$64	$103
$1,110	$1,130	$12	$67	$37	$84	$67	$107

2022 Wage Bracket Method Tables for Manual Payroll Systems with Forms W-4 From 2020 or Later — BIWEEKLY Payroll Period

The Tentative Withholding Amount is:

If the Adjusted Wage Amount (line 1h) is: At least	But less than	Married Filing Jointly — Standard withholding	Married Filing Jointly — Form W-4, Step 2, Checkbox withholding	Head of Household — Standard withholding	Head of Household — Form W-4, Step 2, Checkbox withholding	Single or Married Filing Separately — Standard withholding	Single or Married Filing Separately — Form W-4, Step 2, Checkbox withholding
$1,130	$1,150	$14	$69	$39	$86	$69	$112
$1,150	$1,170	$16	$72	$41	$89	$72	$116
$1,170	$1,190	$18	$74	$43	$91	$74	$121
$1,190	$1,210	$20	$76	$45	$94	$76	$125
$1,210	$1,230	$22	$79	$47	$96	$79	$129
$1,230	$1,250	$24	$81	$49	$98	$81	$134
$1,250	$1,270	$26	$84	$51	$101	$84	$138
$1,270	$1,290	$28	$86	$53	$103	$86	$143
$1,290	$1,310	$30	$88	$55	$106	$88	$147
$1,310	$1,330	$32	$91	$58	$108	$91	$151
$1,330	$1,350	$34	$93	$60	$110	$93	$156
$1,350	$1,370	$36	$96	$62	$113	$96	$160
$1,370	$1,390	$38	$98	$65	$115	$98	$165
$1,390	$1,410	$40	$100	$67	$118	$100	$169
$1,410	$1,430	$42	$103	$70	$120	$103	$173
$1,430	$1,450	$44	$105	$72	$122	$105	$178
$1,450	$1,470	$46	$108	$74	$126	$108	$182
$1,470	$1,490	$48	$110	$77	$130	$110	$187
$1,490	$1,510	$50	$112	$79	$135	$112	$191
$1,510	$1,530	$52	$115	$82	$139	$115	$195
$1,530	$1,550	$54	$117	$84	$144	$117	$200
$1,550	$1,570	$56	$120	$86	$148	$120	$204
$1,570	$1,590	$58	$122	$89	$152	$122	$209
$1,590	$1,610	$60	$124	$91	$157	$124	$213
$1,610	$1,630	$62	$127	$94	$161	$127	$217
$1,630	$1,650	$64	$129	$96	$166	$129	$222
$1,650	$1,670	$66	$132	$98	$170	$132	$226
$1,670	$1,690	$68	$134	$101	$174	$134	$231
$1,690	$1,710	$70	$136	$103	$179	$136	$235
$1,710	$1,730	$72	$139	$106	$183	$139	$239
$1,730	$1,750	$74	$141	$108	$188	$141	$244
$1,750	$1,770	$76	$144	$110	$192	$144	$248
$1,770	$1,790	$78	$146	$113	$196	$146	$253
$1,790	$1,810	$81	$148	$115	$201	$148	$257
$1,810	$1,830	$83	$151	$118	$205	$151	$261
$1,830	$1,850	$85	$153	$120	$210	$153	$266
$1,850	$1,870	$88	$156	$122	$214	$156	$270
$1,870	$1,890	$90	$158	$125	$218	$158	$275
$1,890	$1,910	$93	$160	$127	$223	$160	$279
$1,910	$1,930	$95	$163	$130	$227	$163	$283
$1,930	$1,950	$97	$165	$132	$232	$165	$288
$1,950	$1,970	$100	$168	$134	$236	$168	$292
$1,970	$1,995	$103	$170	$137	$241	$170	$297
$1,995	$2,020	$106	$173	$140	$246	$173	$303
$2,020	$2,045	$109	$176	$143	$252	$176	$309
$2,045	$2,070	$112	$179	$146	$257	$179	$315
$2,070	$2,095	$115	$182	$149	$263	$182	$321
$2,095	$2,120	$118	$185	$152	$269	$185	$327
$2,120	$2,145	$121	$191	$155	$275	$191	$333
$2,145	$2,170	$124	$196	$158	$281	$196	$339
$2,170	$2,195	$127	$202	$161	$287	$202	$345
$2,195	$2,220	$130	$207	$164	$293	$207	$351
$2,220	$2,245	$133	$213	$167	$299	$213	$357
$2,245	$2,270	$136	$218	$170	$305	$218	$363
$2,270	$2,295	$139	$224	$173	$311	$224	$369
$2,295	$2,320	$142	$229	$176	$317	$229	$375
$2,320	$2,345	$145	$235	$179	$323	$235	$381
$2,345	$2,370	$148	$240	$182	$329	$240	$387
$2,370	$2,395	$151	$246	$185	$335	$246	$393
$2,395	$2,420	$154	$251	$188	$341	$251	$399
$2,420	$2,445	$157	$257	$191	$347	$257	$405
$2,445	$2,470	$160	$262	$194	$353	$262	$411
$2,470	$2,495	$163	$268	$197	$359	$268	$417
$2,495	$2,520	$166	$273	$200	$365	$273	$423
$2,520	$2,545	$169	$279	$203	$371	$279	$429

TAX TABLE B (Continued)

BIWEEKLY PAYROLL PERIOD

2022 Wage Bracket Method Tables for Manual Payroll Systems with Forms W-4 From 2020 or Later

BIWEEKLY Payroll Period

If the Adjusted Wage Amount (line 1h) is		Married Filing Jointly		Head of Household		Single or Married Filing Separately	
At least	But less than	Standard withholding	Form W-4, Step 2, Checkbox withholding	Standard withholding	Form W-4, Step 2, Checkbox withholding	Standard withholding	Form W-4, Step 2, Checkbox withholding
		The Tentative Withholding Amount is:					
$2,545	$2,570	$172	$284	$206	$377	$284	$435
$2,570	$2,595	$175	$290	$209	$383	$290	$441
$2,595	$2,620	$178	$295	$212	$389	$295	$447
$2,620	$2,645	$181	$301	$215	$395	$301	$453
$2,645	$2,670	$184	$306	$218	$401	$306	$459
$2,670	$2,695	$187	$312	$221	$407	$312	$465
$2,695	$2,720	$190	$317	$224	$413	$317	$471
$2,720	$2,745	$193	$323	$227	$419	$323	$477
$2,745	$2,770	$196	$328	$230	$425	$328	$483
$2,770	$2,795	$199	$334	$233	$431	$334	$489
$2,795	$2,820	$202	$339	$236	$437	$339	$495
$2,820	$2,845	$205	$345	$239	$443	$345	$501
$2,845	$2,870	$208	$350	$242	$449	$350	$507
$2,870	$2,895	$211	$356	$245	$455	$356	$513
$2,895	$2,920	$214	$361	$249	$461	$361	$519
$2,920	$2,945	$217	$367	$255	$467	$367	$525
$2,945	$2,970	$220	$372	$260	$473	$372	$531
$2,970	$2,995	$223	$378	$266	$479	$378	$537
$2,995	$3,020	$226	$383	$271	$485	$383	$543
$3,020	$3,045	$229	$389	$277	$491	$389	$549
$3,045	$3,070	$232	$394	$282	$497	$394	$555
$3,070	$3,095	$235	$400	$288	$503	$400	$561
$3,095	$3,120	$238	$405	$293	$509	$405	$567
$3,120	$3,145	$241	$411	$299	$515	$411	$573
$3,145	$3,170	$244	$416	$304	$521	$416	$579
$3,170	$3,195	$247	$422	$310	$527	$422	$585
$3,195	$3,220	$250	$427	$315	$533	$427	$591
$3,220	$3,245	$253	$433	$321	$539	$433	$597
$3,245	$3,270	$256	$438	$326	$545	$438	$603
$3,270	$3,295	$259	$444	$332	$551	$444	$609
$3,295	$3,320	$262	$449	$337	$557	$449	$615
$3,320	$3,345	$265	$455	$343	$563	$455	$621
$3,345	$3,370	$268	$460	$348	$569	$460	$627
$3,370	$3,395	$271	$466	$354	$575	$466	$633
$3,395	$3,420	$274	$471	$359	$581	$471	$639
$3,420	$3,445	$277	$477	$365	$587	$477	$645
$3,445	$3,470	$280	$482	$370	$593	$482	$651
$3,470	$3,495	$283	$488	$376	$599	$488	$657
$3,495	$3,520	$286	$493	$381	$605	$493	$663
$3,520	$3,545	$289	$499	$387	$611	$499	$671
$3,545	$3,570	$292	$504	$392	$617	$504	$679
$3,570	$3,595	$295	$510	$398	$623	$510	$687
$3,595	$3,620	$298	$515	$403	$629	$515	$695
$3,620	$3,645	$301	$521	$409	$635	$521	$703
$3,645	$3,670	$304	$526	$414	$642	$526	$711
$3,670	$3,695	$307	$532	$420	$650	$532	$719
$3,695	$3,720	$310	$537	$425	$658	$537	$727
$3,720	$3,745	$313	$543	$431	$666	$543	$735
$3,745	$3,770	$316	$548	$436	$674	$548	$743
$3,770	$3,795	$319	$554	$442	$682	$554	$751
$3,795	$3,820	$322	$559	$447	$690	$559	$759

TAX TABLE B (Continued)

SEMIMONTHLY PAYROLL PERIOD

2022 Wage Bracket Method Tables for Manual Payroll Systems with Forms W-4 From 2020 or Later

SEMIMONTHLY Payroll Period

The Tentative Withholding Amount is:

If the Adjusted Wage Amount (line 1h) is		Married Filing Jointly		Head of Household		Single or Married Filing Separately	
At least	But less than	Standard withholding	Form W-4, Step 2, Checkbox withholding	Standard withholding	Form W-4, Step 2, Checkbox withholding	Standard withholding	Form W-4, Step 2, Checkbox withholding
$0	$270	$0	$0	$0	$0	$0	$0
$270	$280	$0	$0	$0	$0	$0	$1
$280	$290	$0	$0	$0	$0	$0	$2
$290	$300	$0	$0	$0	$0	$0	$3
$300	$310	$0	$0	$0	$0	$0	$4
$310	$320	$0	$0	$0	$0	$0	$5
$320	$330	$0	$0	$0	$0	$0	$6
$330	$340	$0	$0	$0	$0	$0	$7
$340	$350	$0	$0	$0	$0	$0	$8
$350	$360	$0	$0	$0	$0	$0	$9
$360	$370	$0	$0	$0	$0	$0	$10
$370	$380	$0	$0	$0	$0	$0	$11
$380	$390	$0	$0	$0	$0	$0	$12
$390	$400	$0	$0	$0	$0	$0	$13
$400	$410	$0	$0	$0	$0	$0	$14
$410	$420	$0	$0	$0	$1	$0	$15
$420	$430	$0	$0	$0	$2	$0	$16
$430	$440	$0	$0	$0	$3	$0	$17
$440	$450	$0	$0	$0	$4	$0	$18
$450	$460	$0	$0	$0	$5	$0	$19
$460	$470	$0	$0	$0	$6	$0	$20
$470	$480	$0	$0	$0	$7	$0	$21
$480	$495	$0	$0	$0	$8	$0	$22
$495	$510	$0	$0	$0	$10	$0	$24
$510	$525	$0	$0	$0	$11	$0	$25
$525	$540	$0	$0	$0	$13	$0	$27
$540	$555	$0	$1	$0	$14	$1	$29
$555	$570	$0	$2	$0	$16	$2	$31
$570	$585	$0	$4	$0	$17	$4	$33
$585	$600	$0	$5	$0	$19	$5	$34
$600	$615	$0	$7	$0	$20	$7	$36
$615	$630	$0	$8	$0	$22	$8	$38
$630	$645	$0	$10	$0	$23	$10	$40
$645	$660	$0	$11	$0	$25	$11	$42
$660	$675	$0	$13	$0	$26	$13	$43
$675	$690	$0	$14	$0	$28	$14	$45
$690	$705	$0	$16	$0	$29	$16	$47
$705	$720	$0	$17	$0	$31	$17	$49
$720	$735	$0	$19	$0	$33	$19	$51
$735	$750	$0	$20	$0	$34	$20	$52
$750	$765	$0	$22	$0	$36	$22	$54
$765	$780	$0	$23	$0	$38	$23	$56
$780	$795	$0	$25	$0	$40	$25	$58
$795	$810	$0	$26	$0	$42	$26	$60
$810	$825	$0	$28	$1	$43	$28	$61
$825	$840	$0	$29	$2	$45	$29	$63
$840	$855	$0	$31	$4	$47	$31	$65
$855	$870	$0	$32	$5	$49	$32	$67
$870	$885	$0	$34	$7	$51	$34	$69
$885	$900	$0	$35	$8	$52	$35	$70
$900	$915	$0	$37	$10	$54	$37	$72
$915	$930	$0	$38	$11	$56	$38	$74
$930	$945	$0	$40	$13	$58	$40	$76
$945	$960	$0	$41	$14	$60	$41	$78
$960	$975	$0	$43	$16	$61	$43	$79
$975	$990	$0	$45	$17	$63	$45	$81
$990	$1,005	$0	$46	$19	$65	$46	$83
$1,005	$1,020	$0	$48	$20	$67	$48	$85
$1,020	$1,035	$0	$50	$22	$69	$50	$87
$1,035	$1,050	$0	$52	$23	$70	$52	$88
$1,050	$1,065	$0	$54	$25	$72	$54	$90
$1,065	$1,080	$0	$55	$26	$74	$55	$92
$1,080	$1,095	$1	$57	$28	$76	$57	$94
$1,095	$1,110	$2	$59	$29	$78	$59	$96
$1,110	$1,125	$4	$61	$31	$79	$61	$97

2022 Wage Bracket Method Tables for Manual Payroll Systems with Forms W-4 From 2020 or Later

SEMIMONTHLY Payroll Period

The Tentative Withholding Amount is:

If the Adjusted Wage Amount (line 1h) is		Married Filing Jointly		Head of Household		Single or Married Filing Separately	
At least	But less than	Standard withholding	Form W-4, Step 2, Checkbox withholding	Standard withholding	Form W-4, Step 2, Checkbox withholding	Standard withholding	Form W-4, Step 2, Checkbox withholding
$1,125	$1,140	$5	$63	$32	$81	$63	$99
$1,140	$1,160	$7	$65	$34	$83	$65	$102
$1,160	$1,180	$9	$67	$36	$86	$67	$107
$1,180	$1,200	$11	$69	$38	$88	$69	$111
$1,200	$1,220	$13	$72	$40	$91	$72	$116
$1,220	$1,240	$15	$74	$42	$93	$74	$120
$1,240	$1,260	$17	$77	$44	$95	$77	$124
$1,260	$1,280	$19	$79	$46	$98	$79	$129
$1,280	$1,300	$21	$81	$48	$100	$81	$133
$1,300	$1,320	$23	$84	$50	$103	$84	$138
$1,320	$1,340	$25	$86	$52	$105	$86	$142
$1,340	$1,360	$27	$89	$54	$107	$89	$146
$1,360	$1,380	$29	$91	$56	$110	$91	$151
$1,380	$1,400	$31	$93	$58	$112	$93	$155
$1,400	$1,420	$33	$96	$60	$115	$96	$160
$1,420	$1,440	$35	$98	$62	$117	$98	$164
$1,440	$1,460	$37	$101	$65	$119	$101	$168
$1,460	$1,480	$39	$103	$67	$122	$103	$173
$1,480	$1,500	$41	$105	$70	$124	$105	$177
$1,500	$1,520	$43	$108	$72	$127	$108	$182
$1,520	$1,540	$45	$110	$74	$129	$110	$186
$1,540	$1,560	$47	$113	$77	$131	$113	$190
$1,560	$1,580	$49	$115	$79	$134	$115	$195
$1,580	$1,600	$51	$117	$82	$138	$117	$199
$1,600	$1,620	$53	$120	$84	$143	$120	$204
$1,620	$1,640	$55	$122	$86	$147	$122	$208
$1,640	$1,660	$57	$125	$89	$152	$125	$212
$1,660	$1,680	$59	$127	$91	$156	$127	$217
$1,680	$1,700	$61	$129	$94	$160	$129	$221
$1,700	$1,720	$63	$132	$96	$165	$132	$226
$1,720	$1,740	$65	$134	$98	$169	$134	$230
$1,740	$1,760	$67	$137	$101	$174	$137	$234
$1,760	$1,780	$69	$139	$103	$178	$139	$239
$1,780	$1,800	$71	$141	$106	$182	$141	$243
$1,800	$1,820	$73	$144	$108	$187	$144	$248
$1,820	$1,840	$75	$146	$110	$191	$146	$252
$1,840	$1,860	$77	$149	$113	$196	$149	$256
$1,860	$1,880	$79	$151	$115	$200	$151	$261
$1,880	$1,900	$81	$153	$118	$204	$153	$265
$1,900	$1,920	$83	$156	$120	$209	$156	$270
$1,920	$1,940	$85	$158	$122	$213	$158	$274
$1,940	$1,960	$87	$161	$125	$218	$161	$278
$1,960	$1,980	$90	$163	$127	$222	$163	$283
$1,980	$2,000	$92	$165	$130	$226	$165	$287
$2,000	$2,020	$95	$168	$132	$231	$168	$292
$2,020	$2,040	$97	$170	$134	$235	$170	$296
$2,040	$2,060	$99	$173	$137	$240	$173	$300
$2,060	$2,080	$102	$175	$139	$244	$175	$305
$2,080	$2,100	$104	$177	$142	$248	$177	$309
$2,100	$2,120	$107	$180	$144	$253	$180	$314
$2,120	$2,140	$109	$182	$146	$257	$182	$318
$2,140	$2,170	$112	$185	$149	$263	$185	$324
$2,170	$2,200	$116	$189	$153	$269	$189	$331
$2,200	$2,230	$119	$192	$157	$276	$192	$338
$2,230	$2,260	$123	$196	$160	$282	$196	$346
$2,260	$2,290	$126	$200	$164	$289	$200	$353
$2,290	$2,320	$130	$206	$167	$297	$206	$360
$2,320	$2,350	$134	$212	$171	$304	$212	$367
$2,350	$2,380	$137	$219	$175	$311	$219	$374
$2,380	$2,410	$141	$226	$178	$318	$226	$382
$2,410	$2,440	$144	$232	$182	$325	$232	$389
$2,440	$2,470	$148	$239	$185	$333	$239	$396
$2,470	$2,500	$152	$245	$189	$340	$245	$403
$2,500	$2,530	$155	$252	$193	$347	$252	$410
$2,530	$2,560	$159	$259	$196	$354	$259	$418

TAX TABLE B (Continued)

2022 Wage Bracket Method Tables for Manual Payroll Systems with Forms W-4 From 2020 or Later

SEMIMONTHLY Payroll Period

SEMIMONTHLY PAYROLL PERIOD

If the Adjusted Wage Amount (line 1h) is		Married Filing Jointly		Head of Household		Single or Married Filing Separately	
At least	But less than	Standard withholding	Form W-4, Step 2, Checkbox withholding	Standard withholding	Form W-4, Step 2, Checkbox withholding	Standard withholding	Form W-4, Step 2, Checkbox withholding
		The Tentative Withholding Amount is:					
$2,560	$2,590	$162	$265	$200	$361	$265	$425
$2,590	$2,620	$166	$272	$203	$369	$272	$432
$2,620	$2,650	$170	$278	$207	$376	$278	$439
$2,650	$2,680	$173	$285	$211	$383	$285	$446
$2,680	$2,710	$177	$292	$214	$390	$292	$454
$2,710	$2,740	$180	$298	$218	$397	$298	$461
$2,740	$2,770	$184	$305	$221	$405	$305	$468
$2,770	$2,800	$188	$311	$225	$412	$311	$475
$2,800	$2,830	$191	$318	$229	$419	$318	$482
$2,830	$2,860	$195	$325	$232	$426	$325	$490
$2,860	$2,890	$198	$331	$236	$433	$331	$497
$2,890	$2,920	$202	$338	$239	$441	$338	$504
$2,920	$2,950	$206	$344	$243	$448	$344	$511
$2,950	$2,980	$209	$351	$247	$455	$351	$518
$2,980	$3,010	$213	$358	$250	$462	$358	$526
$3,010	$3,040	$216	$364	$254	$469	$364	$533
$3,040	$3,070	$220	$371	$257	$477	$371	$540
$3,070	$3,100	$224	$377	$261	$484	$377	$547
$3,100	$3,130	$227	$384	$265	$491	$384	$554
$3,130	$3,160	$231	$391	$269	$498	$391	$562
$3,160	$3,190	$234	$397	$276	$505	$397	$569
$3,190	$3,220	$238	$404	$282	$513	$404	$576
$3,220	$3,250	$242	$410	$289	$520	$410	$583
$3,250	$3,280	$245	$417	$295	$527	$417	$590
$3,280	$3,310	$249	$424	$302	$534	$424	$598
$3,310	$3,340	$252	$430	$309	$541	$430	$605
$3,340	$3,370	$256	$437	$315	$549	$437	$612
$3,370	$3,400	$260	$443	$322	$556	$443	$619
$3,400	$3,430	$263	$450	$328	$563	$450	$626
$3,430	$3,460	$267	$457	$335	$570	$457	$634
$3,460	$3,490	$270	$463	$342	$577	$463	$641
$3,490	$3,520	$274	$470	$348	$585	$470	$648
$3,520	$3,550	$278	$476	$355	$592	$476	$655
$3,550	$3,580	$281	$483	$361	$599	$483	$662
$3,580	$3,610	$285	$490	$368	$606	$490	$670
$3,610	$3,640	$288	$496	$375	$613	$496	$677
$3,640	$3,670	$292	$503	$381	$621	$503	$684
$3,670	$3,700	$296	$509	$388	$628	$509	$691
$3,700	$3,730	$299	$516	$394	$635	$516	$698
$3,730	$3,760	$303	$523	$401	$642	$523	$706
$3,760	$3,790	$306	$529	$408	$649	$529	$713
$3,790	$3,820	$310	$536	$414	$657	$536	$720
$3,820	$3,850	$314	$542	$421	$664	$542	$729
$3,850	$3,880	$317	$549	$427	$671	$549	$739
$3,880	$3,910	$321	$556	$434	$678	$556	$748
$3,910	$3,940	$324	$562	$441	$685	$562	$758
$3,940	$3,970	$328	$569	$447	$693	$569	$767
$3,970	$4,000	$332	$575	$454	$703	$575	$777
$4,000	$4,030	$335	$582	$460	$712	$582	$787
$4,030	$4,060	$339	$589	$467	$722	$589	$796
$4,060	$4,090	$342	$595	$474	$732	$595	$806
$4,090	$4,120	$346	$602	$480	$741	$602	$815

TAX TABLE B (Continued)

MONTHLY PAYROLL PERIOD

2022 Wage Bracket Method Tables for Manual Payroll Systems with Forms W-4 From 2020 or Later — MONTHLY Payroll Period

The Tentative Withholding Amount is:

If the Adjusted Wage Amount (line 1h) is		Married Filing Jointly		Head of Household		Single or Married Filing Separately	
At least	But less than	Standard withholding	Form W-4, Step 2, Checkbox withholding	Standard withholding	Form W-4, Step 2, Checkbox withholding	Standard withholding	Form W-4, Step 2, Checkbox withholding
$0	$540	$0	$0	$0	$0	$0	$0
$540	$560	$0	$0	$0	$0	$0	$1
$560	$580	$0	$0	$0	$0	$0	$3
$580	$600	$0	$0	$0	$0	$0	$5
$600	$620	$0	$0	$0	$0	$0	$7
$620	$640	$0	$0	$0	$0	$0	$9
$640	$660	$0	$0	$0	$0	$0	$11
$660	$680	$0	$0	$0	$0	$0	$13
$680	$700	$0	$0	$0	$0	$0	$15
$700	$720	$0	$0	$0	$0	$0	$17
$720	$740	$0	$0	$0	$0	$0	$19
$740	$760	$0	$0	$0	$0	$0	$21
$760	$780	$0	$0	$0	$0	$0	$23
$780	$800	$0	$0	$0	$0	$0	$25
$800	$820	$0	$0	$0	$0	$0	$27
$820	$840	$0	$0	$0	$0	$0	$29
$840	$860	$0	$0	$0	$0	$2	$31
$860	$880	$0	$0	$0	$0	$4	$33
$880	$900	$0	$0	$0	$0	$6	$35
$900	$920	$0	$0	$0	$0	$8	$37
$920	$940	$0	$0	$0	$0	$10	$39
$940	$960	$0	$0	$0	$0	$12	$41
$960	$980	$0	$0	$0	$0	$14	$43
$980	$1,010	$0	$0	$0	$0	$16	$46
$1,010	$1,040	$0	$0	$0	$0	$19	$50
$1,040	$1,070	$0	$0	$0	$0	$25	$53
$1,070	$1,100	$0	$0	$0	$1	$28	$57
$1,100	$1,130	$0	$0	$0	$4	$31	$60
$1,130	$1,160	$0	$0	$0	$7	$34	$64
$1,160	$1,190	$0	$0	$0	$10	$37	$68
$1,190	$1,220	$0	$0	$0	$13	$40	$71
$1,220	$1,250	$0	$0	$0	$16	$43	$75
$1,250	$1,280	$0	$0	$0	$19	$46	$78
$1,280	$1,310	$0	$0	$0	$22	$49	$82
$1,310	$1,340	$0	$0	$0	$25	$52	$86
$1,340	$1,370	$0	$0	$0	$28	$55	$89
$1,370	$1,400	$0	$0	$0	$31	$58	$93
$1,400	$1,430	$0	$0	$0	$34	$61	$96
$1,430	$1,460	$0	$0	$0	$37	$64	$100
$1,460	$1,490	$0	$0	$0	$40	$68	$104
$1,490	$1,520	$0	$0	$0	$43	$71	$107
$1,520	$1,550	$0	$0	$0	$46	$75	$111
$1,550	$1,580	$0	$0	$0	$49	$79	$114
$1,580	$1,610	$0	$0	$0	$52	$82	$118
$1,610	$1,640	$0	$0	$1	$55	$86	$122
$1,640	$1,670	$0	$0	$4	$58	$89	$125
$1,670	$1,700	$0	$0	$7	$61	$93	$129
$1,700	$1,730	$0	$0	$10	$64	$97	$132
$1,730	$1,760	$0	$0	$13	$67	$100	$136
$1,760	$1,790	$0	$0	$16	$70	$104	$140
$1,790	$1,820	$0	$0	$19	$73	$107	$143
$1,820	$1,850	$0	$0	$22	$76	$111	$147
$1,850	$1,880	$0	$0	$25	$79	$115	$150
$1,880	$1,910	$0	$0	$28	$82	$118	$154
$1,910	$1,940	$0	$0	$31	$85	$122	$158
$1,940	$1,970	$0	$0	$34	$88	$125	$161
$1,970	$2,000	$0	$0	$37	$92	$129	$165
$2,000	$2,030	$0	$0	$40	$95	$132	$168
$2,030	$2,060	$0	$0	$43	$99	$136	$172
$2,060	$2,090	$0	$0	$46	$102	$140	$176
$2,090	$2,120	$0	$0	$49	$106	$143	$179
$2,120	$2,150	$0	$0	$52	$110	$147	$183
$2,150	$2,180	$0	$0	$55	$113	$151	$186
$2,180	$2,210	$0	$0	$58	$117	$154	$190
$2,210	$2,240	$0	$0	$61	$120	$158	$194

2022 Wage Bracket Method Tables for Manual Payroll Systems with Forms W-4 From 2020 or Later — MONTHLY Payroll Period (continued)

The Tentative Withholding Amount is:

If the Adjusted Wage Amount (line 1h) is		Married Filing Jointly		Head of Household		Single or Married Filing Separately	
At least	But less than	Standard withholding	Form W-4, Step 2, Checkbox withholding	Standard withholding	Form W-4, Step 2, Checkbox withholding	Standard withholding	Form W-4, Step 2, Checkbox withholding
$2,240	$2,270	$10	$124	$64	$161	$124	$197
$2,270	$2,300	$13	$128	$67	$165	$128	$201
$2,300	$2,340	$16	$132	$70	$169	$132	$209
$2,340	$2,380	$20	$137	$74	$174	$137	$218
$2,380	$2,420	$24	$141	$78	$179	$141	$227
$2,420	$2,460	$28	$146	$82	$184	$146	$235
$2,460	$2,500	$32	$151	$86	$188	$151	$244
$2,500	$2,540	$36	$156	$90	$193	$156	$253
$2,540	$2,580	$40	$161	$94	$198	$161	$262
$2,580	$2,620	$44	$165	$98	$203	$165	$271
$2,620	$2,660	$48	$170	$102	$208	$170	$279
$2,660	$2,700	$52	$175	$106	$212	$175	$288
$2,700	$2,740	$56	$180	$110	$217	$180	$297
$2,740	$2,780	$60	$185	$114	$222	$185	$306
$2,780	$2,820	$64	$189	$118	$227	$189	$315
$2,820	$2,860	$68	$194	$122	$232	$194	$323
$2,860	$2,900	$72	$199	$127	$236	$199	$332
$2,900	$2,940	$76	$204	$132	$241	$204	$341
$2,940	$2,980	$80	$209	$137	$246	$209	$350
$2,980	$3,020	$84	$213	$142	$251	$213	$359
$3,020	$3,060	$88	$218	$146	$256	$218	$367
$3,060	$3,100	$92	$223	$151	$260	$223	$376
$3,100	$3,140	$96	$228	$156	$265	$228	$385
$3,140	$3,180	$100	$233	$161	$272	$233	$394
$3,180	$3,220	$104	$237	$166	$281	$237	$403
$3,220	$3,260	$108	$242	$170	$290	$242	$411
$3,260	$3,300	$112	$247	$175	$299	$247	$420
$3,300	$3,340	$116	$252	$180	$307	$252	$429
$3,340	$3,380	$120	$257	$185	$316	$257	$438
$3,380	$3,420	$124	$261	$190	$325	$261	$447
$3,420	$3,460	$128	$266	$194	$334	$266	$455
$3,460	$3,500	$132	$271	$199	$343	$271	$464
$3,500	$3,540	$136	$276	$204	$351	$276	$473
$3,540	$3,580	$140	$281	$209	$360	$281	$482
$3,580	$3,620	$144	$285	$214	$369	$285	$491
$3,620	$3,660	$148	$290	$218	$378	$290	$499
$3,660	$3,700	$152	$295	$223	$387	$295	$508
$3,700	$3,740	$156	$300	$228	$395	$300	$517
$3,740	$3,780	$160	$305	$233	$404	$305	$526
$3,780	$3,820	$164	$309	$238	$413	$309	$535
$3,820	$3,860	$168	$314	$242	$422	$314	$543
$3,860	$3,900	$172	$319	$247	$431	$319	$552
$3,900	$3,940	$177	$324	$252	$439	$324	$561
$3,940	$3,980	$182	$329	$257	$448	$329	$570
$3,980	$4,020	$187	$333	$262	$457	$333	$579
$4,020	$4,060	$192	$338	$266	$466	$338	$587
$4,060	$4,100	$196	$343	$271	$475	$343	$596
$4,100	$4,140	$201	$348	$276	$483	$348	$605
$4,140	$4,180	$206	$353	$281	$492	$353	$614
$4,180	$4,220	$211	$357	$286	$501	$357	$623
$4,220	$4,260	$216	$362	$290	$510	$362	$631
$4,260	$4,320	$222	$368	$296	$521	$368	$643
$4,320	$4,380	$229	$375	$304	$534	$375	$658
$4,380	$4,440	$236	$383	$311	$547	$383	$672
$4,440	$4,500	$243	$390	$318	$560	$390	$686
$4,500	$4,560	$250	$397	$325	$574	$397	$701
$4,560	$4,620	$258	$407	$332	$588	$407	$715
$4,620	$4,680	$265	$420	$340	$603	$420	$730
$4,680	$4,740	$272	$434	$347	$617	$434	$744
$4,740	$4,800	$279	$447	$354	$631	$447	$758
$4,800	$4,860	$286	$460	$361	$646	$460	$773
$4,860	$4,920	$294	$473	$368	$660	$473	$787
$4,920	$4,980	$301	$486	$376	$675	$486	$802
$4,980	$5,040	$308	$500	$383	$689	$500	$816
$5,040	$5,100	$315	$513	$390	$703	$513	$830

TAX TABLE B (Continued)

2022 Wage Bracket Method Tables for Manual Payroll Systems with Forms W-4 From 2020 or Later

MONTHLY Payroll Period

MONTHLY PAYROLL PERIOD

If the Adjusted Wage Amount (line 1h) is		Married Filing Jointly		Head of Household		Single or Married Filing Separately	
At least	But less than	Standard withholding	Form W-4, Step 2, Checkbox withholding	Standard withholding	Form W-4, Step 2, Checkbox withholding	Standard withholding	Form W-4, Step 2, Checkbox withholding
		The Tentative Withholding Amount is:					
$5,100	$5,160	$322	$526	$397	$718	$526	$845
$5,160	$5,220	$330	$539	$404	$732	$539	$859
$5,220	$5,280	$337	$552	$412	$747	$552	$874
$5,280	$5,340	$344	$566	$419	$761	$566	$888
$5,340	$5,400	$351	$579	$426	$775	$579	$902
$5,400	$5,460	$358	$592	$433	$790	$592	$917
$5,460	$5,520	$366	$605	$440	$804	$605	$931
$5,520	$5,580	$373	$618	$448	$819	$618	$946
$5,580	$5,640	$380	$632	$455	$833	$632	$960
$5,640	$5,700	$387	$645	$462	$847	$645	$974
$5,700	$5,760	$394	$658	$469	$862	$658	$989
$5,760	$5,820	$402	$671	$476	$876	$671	$1,003
$5,820	$5,880	$409	$684	$484	$891	$684	$1,018
$5,880	$5,940	$416	$698	$491	$905	$698	$1,032
$5,940	$6,000	$423	$711	$498	$919	$711	$1,046
$6,000	$6,060	$430	$724	$505	$934	$724	$1,061
$6,060	$6,120	$438	$737	$512	$948	$737	$1,075
$6,120	$6,180	$445	$750	$520	$963	$750	$1,090
$6,180	$6,240	$452	$764	$527	$977	$764	$1,104
$6,240	$6,300	$459	$777	$534	$991	$777	$1,118
$6,300	$6,360	$466	$790	$547	$1,006	$790	$1,133
$6,360	$6,420	$474	$803	$560	$1,020	$803	$1,147
$6,420	$6,480	$481	$816	$573	$1,035	$816	$1,162
$6,480	$6,540	$488	$830	$586	$1,049	$830	$1,176
$6,540	$6,600	$495	$843	$599	$1,063	$843	$1,190
$6,600	$6,660	$502	$856	$613	$1,078	$856	$1,205
$6,660	$6,720	$510	$869	$626	$1,092	$869	$1,219
$6,720	$6,780	$517	$882	$639	$1,107	$882	$1,234
$6,780	$6,840	$524	$896	$652	$1,121	$896	$1,248
$6,840	$6,900	$531	$909	$665	$1,135	$909	$1,262
$6,900	$6,960	$538	$922	$679	$1,150	$922	$1,277
$6,960	$7,020	$546	$935	$692	$1,164	$935	$1,291
$7,020	$7,080	$553	$948	$705	$1,179	$948	$1,306
$7,080	$7,140	$560	$962	$718	$1,193	$962	$1,320
$7,140	$7,200	$567	$975	$731	$1,207	$975	$1,334
$7,200	$7,260	$574	$988	$745	$1,222	$988	$1,349
$7,260	$7,320	$582	$1,001	$758	$1,236	$1,001	$1,363
$7,320	$7,380	$589	$1,014	$771	$1,251	$1,014	$1,378
$7,380	$7,440	$596	$1,028	$784	$1,265	$1,028	$1,392
$7,440	$7,500	$603	$1,041	$797	$1,279	$1,041	$1,406
$7,500	$7,560	$610	$1,054	$811	$1,294	$1,054	$1,421
$7,560	$7,620	$618	$1,067	$824	$1,308	$1,067	$1,435
$7,620	$7,680	$625	$1,080	$837	$1,323	$1,080	$1,452
$7,680	$7,740	$632	$1,094	$850	$1,337	$1,094	$1,471
$7,740	$7,800	$639	$1,107	$863	$1,351	$1,107	$1,490
$7,800	$7,860	$646	$1,120	$877	$1,366	$1,120	$1,509
$7,860	$7,920	$654	$1,133	$890	$1,380	$1,133	$1,528
$7,920	$7,980	$661	$1,146	$903	$1,399	$1,146	$1,548
$7,980	$8,040	$668	$1,160	$916	$1,418	$1,160	$1,567
$8,040	$8,100	$675	$1,173	$929	$1,438	$1,173	$1,586
$8,100	$8,160	$682	$1,186	$943	$1,457	$1,186	$1,605
$8,160	$8,220	$690	$1,199	$956	$1,476	$1,199	$1,624
$8,220	$8,280	$697	$1,212	$969	$1,495	$1,212	$1,644

TAX TABLE B (Concluded)

DAILY PAYROLL PERIOD

2022 Wage Bracket Method Tables for Manual Payroll Systems with Forms W-4 From 2020 or Later — DAILY Payroll Period

The Tentative Withholding Amount is:

If the Adjusted Wage Amount (line 1h) is		Married Filing Jointly		Head of Household		Single or Married Filing Separately	
At least	But less than	Standard withholding	Form W-4, Step 2, Checkbox withholding	Standard withholding	Form W-4, Step 2, Checkbox withholding	Standard withholding	Form W-4, Step 2, Checkbox withholding
$0	$25	$0.00	$0.00	$0.00	$0.00	$0.00	$0.00
$25	$30	$0.00	$0.00	$0.00	$0.00	$0.00	$0.30
$30	$35	$0.00	$0.00	$0.00	$0.00	$0.00	$0.80
$35	$40	$0.00	$0.00	$0.00	$0.00	$0.00	$1.30
$40	$45	$0.00	$0.00	$0.00	$0.00	$0.00	$1.80
$45	$50	$0.00	$0.00	$0.00	$0.00	$0.00	$2.30
$50	$55	$0.00	$0.30	$0.00	$0.30	$0.30	$2.90
$55	$60	$0.00	$0.80	$0.00	$1.00	$0.80	$3.50
$60	$65	$0.00	$1.30	$0.00	$1.70	$1.30	$4.10
$65	$70	$0.00	$1.80	$0.00	$2.40	$1.80	$4.70
$70	$75	$0.00	$2.30	$0.00	$3.10	$2.30	$5.30
$75	$80	$0.00	$2.80	$0.30	$3.80	$2.80	$5.90
$80	$85	$0.00	$3.30	$0.80	$4.50	$3.30	$6.50
$85	$90	$0.00	$3.80	$1.30	$5.20	$3.80	$7.10
$90	$95	$0.00	$4.30	$1.80	$5.90	$4.30	$7.70
$95	$100	$0.00	$4.90	$2.30	$6.60	$4.90	$8.30
$100	$105	$0.30	$5.50	$2.80	$7.30	$5.50	$8.90
$105	$110	$0.80	$6.10	$3.30	$8.00	$6.10	$9.70
$110	$115	$1.30	$6.70	$3.80	$8.70	$6.70	$10.80
$115	$120	$1.80	$7.30	$4.30	$9.40	$7.30	$11.90
$120	$125	$2.30	$7.90	$4.80	$10.10	$7.90	$13.00
$125	$130	$2.80	$8.50	$5.30	$10.80	$8.50	$14.10
$130	$135	$3.30	$9.10	$5.80	$11.50	$9.10	$15.20
$135	$140	$3.80	$9.70	$6.40	$12.20	$9.70	$16.30
$140	$145	$4.30	$10.30	$7.00	$12.90	$10.30	$17.40
$145	$150	$4.80	$10.90	$7.60	$13.60	$10.90	$18.50
$150	$155	$5.30	$11.50	$8.20	$14.00	$11.50	$19.60
$155	$160	$5.80	$12.10	$8.80	$15.10	$12.10	$20.70
$160	$165	$6.30	$12.70	$9.40	$16.20	$12.70	$21.80
$165	$170	$6.80	$13.30	$10.00	$17.30	$13.30	$22.90
$170	$175	$7.30	$13.90	$10.60	$18.40	$13.90	$24.00
$175	$180	$7.80	$14.50	$11.20	$19.50	$14.50	$25.10
$180	$185	$8.40	$15.10	$11.80	$20.60	$15.10	$26.20
$185	$190	$9.00	$15.70	$12.40	$21.70	$15.70	$27.30
$190	$195	$9.60	$16.30	$13.00	$22.80	$16.30	$28.40
$195	$200	$10.20	$16.90	$13.60	$23.90	$16.90	$29.60
$200	$205	$10.80	$17.50	$14.20	$25.00	$17.50	$30.80
$205	$210	$11.40	$18.10	$14.80	$26.10	$18.10	$32.00
$210	$215	$12.00	$18.90	$15.40	$27.30	$18.90	$33.20
$215	$220	$12.60	$20.00	$16.00	$28.50	$20.00	$34.40
$220	$225	$13.20	$21.10	$16.60	$29.70	$21.10	$35.60
$225	$230	$13.80	$22.20	$17.20	$30.90	$22.20	$36.80
$230	$235	$14.40	$23.30	$17.80	$32.10	$23.30	$38.00
$235	$240	$15.00	$24.40	$18.40	$33.30	$24.40	$39.20
$240	$245	$15.60	$25.50	$19.00	$34.50	$25.50	$40.40
$245	$250	$16.20	$26.60	$19.60	$35.70	$26.60	$41.60
$250	$255	$16.80	$27.70	$20.20	$36.90	$27.70	$42.80
$255	$260	$17.40	$28.80	$20.80	$38.10	$28.80	$44.00
$260	$265	$18.00	$29.90	$21.40	$39.30	$29.90	$45.20
$265	$270	$18.60	$31.00	$22.00	$40.50	$31.00	$46.40
$270	$275	$19.20	$32.10	$22.60	$41.70	$32.10	$47.60
$275	$280	$19.80	$33.20	$23.20	$42.90	$33.20	$48.80
$280	$285	$20.40	$34.30	$23.80	$44.10	$34.30	$50.00
$285	$290	$21.00	$35.40	$24.40	$45.30	$35.40	$51.20
$290	$295	$21.60	$36.50	$25.30	$46.50	$36.50	$52.40
$295	$300	$22.20	$37.60	$26.40	$47.70	$37.60	$53.60
$300	$305	$22.80	$38.70	$27.50	$48.90	$38.70	$54.80
$305	$310	$23.40	$39.80	$28.60	$50.10	$39.80	$56.00
$310	$315	$24.00	$40.90	$29.70	$51.30	$40.90	$57.20
$315	$320	$24.60	$42.00	$30.80	$52.50	$42.00	$58.40
$320	$325	$25.20	$43.10	$31.90	$53.70	$43.10	$59.60
$325	$330	$25.80	$44.20	$33.00	$54.90	$44.20	$60.80
$330	$335	$26.40	$45.30	$34.10	$56.10	$45.30	$62.00
$335	$340	$27.00	$46.40	$35.20	$57.30	$46.40	$63.20
$340	$345	$27.60	$47.50	$36.30	$58.50	$47.50	$64.40

2022 Wage Bracket Method Tables for Manual Payroll Systems with Forms W-4 From 2020 or Later — DAILY Payroll Period

The Tentative Withholding Amount is:

If the Adjusted Wage Amount (line 1h) is		Married Filing Jointly		Head of Household		Single or Married Filing Separately	
At least	But less than	Standard withholding	Form W-4, Step 2, Checkbox withholding	Standard withholding	Form W-4, Step 2, Checkbox withholding	Standard withholding	Form W-4, Step 2, Checkbox withholding
$345	$350	$28.20	$48.60	$37.40	$59.70	$48.60	$65.60
$350	$355	$28.80	$49.70	$38.50	$60.90	$49.70	$66.80
$355	$360	$29.40	$50.80	$39.60	$62.10	$50.80	$68.40
$360	$365	$30.00	$51.90	$40.70	$63.30	$51.90	$70.00
$365	$370	$30.60	$53.00	$41.80	$64.80	$53.00	$71.60
$370	$375	$31.20	$54.10	$42.90	$66.40	$54.10	$73.20
$375	$380	$31.80	$55.20	$44.00	$68.00	$55.20	$74.80
$380	$385	$32.40	$56.30	$45.10	$69.60	$56.30	$76.40
$385	$390	$33.00	$57.40	$46.20	$71.20	$57.40	$78.00

TABLE OF ALLOWANCE VALUES FOR PERCENTAGE METHOD TABLES FOR MANUAL PAYROLL SYSTEMS WITH FORMS W-4 FROM 2019 OR EARLIER

Payroll Period	One Withholding Allowance
Weekly	$ 83.00
Biweekly	165.00
Semimonthly	179.00
Monthly	358.00
Quarterly	1,075.00
Semiannually	2,150.00
Annually	4,300.00
Daily or miscellaneous (each day of the payroll period)	17.00

TAX TABLE *C

2022 Percentage Method Tables for Manual Payroll Systems With Forms W-4 From 2019 or Earlier

WEEKLY Payroll Period

MARRIED Persons					SINGLE Persons				
If the Adjusted Wage Amount (line 1d) is		The tentative amount to withhold is...	Plus this percentage ...	of the amount that the wage exceeds...	If the Adjusted Wage Amount (line 1d) is		The tentative amount to withhold is...	Plus this percentage ...	of the amount that the wage exceeds...
at least...	But less than...				at least...	But less than...			
A	B	C	D	E	A	B	C	D	E
$0	$250	$0.00	0%	$0	$0	$84	$0.00	0%	$0
$250	$645	$0.00	10%	$250	$84	$281	$0.00	10%	$84
$645	$1,857	$39.50	12%	$645	$281	$887	$19.70	12%	$281
$1,857	$3,676	$184.94	22%	$1,857	$887	$1,797	$92.42	22%	$887
$3,676	$6,790	$585.12	24%	$3,676	$1,797	$3,354	$292.62	24%	$1,797
$6,790	$8,556	$1,332.48	32%	$6,790	$3,354	$4,237	$666.30	32%	$3,354
$8,556	$12,709	$1,897.60	35%	$8,556	$4,237	$10,466	$948.86	35%	$4,237
$12,709		$3,351.15	37%	$12,709	$10,466		$3,129.01	37%	$10,466

BIWEEKLY Payroll Period

MARRIED Persons					SINGLE Persons				
If the Adjusted Wage Amount (line 1d) is		The tentative amount to withhold is...	Plus this percentage ...	of the amount that the wage exceeds...	If the Adjusted Wage Amount (line 1d) is		The tentative amount to withhold is...	Plus this percentage ...	of the amount that the wage exceeds...
at least...	But less than...				at least...	But less than...			
A	B	C	D	E	A	B	C	D	E
$0	$500	$0.00	0%	$0	$0	$167	$0.00	0%	$0
$500	$1,290	$0.00	10%	$500	$167	$563	$0.00	10%	$167
$1,290	$3,713	$79.00	12%	$1,290	$563	$1,774	$39.60	12%	$563
$3,713	$7,352	$369.76	22%	$3,713	$1,774	$3,593	$184.92	22%	$1,774
$7,352	$13,581	$1,170.34	24%	$7,352	$3,593	$6,708	$585.10	24%	$3,593
$13,581	$17,112	$2,665.30	32%	$13,581	$6,708	$8,473	$1,332.70	32%	$6,708
$17,112	$25,417	$3,795.22	35%	$17,112	$8,473	$20,933	$1,897.50	35%	$8,473
$25,417		$6,701.97	37%	$25,417	$20,933		$6,258.50	37%	$20,933

SEMIMONTHLY Payroll Period

MARRIED Persons					SINGLE Persons				
If the Adjusted Wage Amount (line 1d) is		The tentative amount to withhold is...	Plus this percentage ...	of the amount that the wage exceeds...	If the Adjusted Wage Amount (line 1d) is		The tentative amount to withhold is...	Plus this percentage ...	of the amount that the wage exceeds...
at least...	But less than...				at least...	But less than...			
A	B	C	D	E	A	B	C	D	E
$0	$542	$0.00	0%	$0	$0	$181	$0.00	0%	$0
$542	$1,398	$0.00	10%	$542	$181	$609	$0.00	10%	$181
$1,398	$4,023	$85.60	12%	$1,398	$609	$1,922	$42.80	12%	$609
$4,023	$7,965	$400.60	22%	$4,023	$1,922	$3,893	$200.36	22%	$1,922
$7,965	$14,713	$1,267.84	24%	$7,965	$3,893	$7,267	$633.98	24%	$3,893
$14,713	$18,538	$2,887.36	32%	$14,713	$7,267	$9,179	$1,443.74	32%	$7,267
$18,538	$27,535	$4,111.36	35%	$18,538	$9,179	$22,677	$2,055.58	35%	$9,179
$27,535		$7,260.31	37%	$27,535	$22,677		$6,779.88	37%	$22,677

MONTHLY Payroll Period

MARRIED Persons					SINGLE Persons				
If the Adjusted Wage Amount (line 1d) is		The tentative amount to withhold is...	Plus this percentage ...	of the amount that the wage exceeds...	If the Adjusted Wage Amount (line 1d) is		The tentative amount to withhold is...	Plus this percentage ...	of the amount that the wage exceeds...
at least...	But less than...				at least...	But less than...			
A	B	C	D	E	A	B	C	D	E
$0	$1,083	$0.00	0%	$0	$0	$363	$0.00	0%	$0
$1,083	$2,796	$0.00	10%	$1,083	$363	$1,219	$0.00	10%	$363
$2,796	$8,046	$171.30	12%	$2,796	$1,219	$3,844	$85.60	12%	$1,219
$8,046	$15,929	$801.30	22%	$8,046	$3,844	$7,785	$400.60	22%	$3,844
$15,929	$29,425	$2,535.56	24%	$15,929	$7,785	$14,533	$1,267.62	24%	$7,785
$29,425	$37,075	$5,774.60	32%	$29,425	$14,533	$18,358	$2,887.14	32%	$14,533
$37,075	$55,071	$8,222.60	35%	$37,075	$18,358	$45,354	$4,111.14	35%	$18,358
$55,071		$14,521.20	37%	$55,071	$45,354		$13,559.74	37%	$45,354

Source: Internal Revenue Service.

TAX TABLE *C (*Concluded*)

2022 Percentage Method Tables for Manual Payroll Systems With Forms W-4 From 2019 or Earlier

QUARTERLY Payroll Period

MARRIED Persons					SINGLE Persons				
If the Adjusted Wage Amount (line 1d) is		The tentative amount to withhold is...	Plus this percentage ...	of the amount that the wage exceeds...	If the Adjusted Wage Amount (line 1d) is		The tentative amount to withhold is...	Plus this percentage ...	of the amount that the wage exceeds...
at least...	But less than...				at least...	But less than...			
A	B	C	D	E	A	B	C	D	E
$0	$3,250	$0.00	0%	$0	$0	$1,088	$0.00	0%	$0
$3,250	$8,388	$0.00	10%	$3,250	$1,088	$3,656	$0.00	10%	$1,088
$8,388	$24,138	$513.80	12%	$8,388	$3,656	$11,531	$256.80	12%	$3,656
$24,138	$47,788	$2,403.80	22%	$24,138	$11,531	$23,356	$1,201.80	22%	$11,531
$47,788	$88,275	$7,606.80	24%	$47,788	$23,356	$43,600	$3,803.30	24%	$23,356
$88,275	$111,225	$17,323.68	32%	$88,275	$43,600	$55,075	$8,661.86	32%	$43,600
$111,225	$165,213	$24,667.68	35%	$111,225	$55,075	$136,063	$12,333.86	35%	$55,075
$165,213		$43,563.48	37%	$165,213	$136,063		$40,679.66	37%	$136,063

SEMIANNUAL Payroll Period

MARRIED Persons					SINGLE Persons				
If the Adjusted Wage Amount (line 1d) is		The tentative amount to withhold is...	Plus this percentage ...	of the amount that the wage exceeds...	If the Adjusted Wage Amount (line 1d) is		The tentative amount to withhold is...	Plus this percentage ...	of the amount that the wage exceeds...
at least...	But less than...				at least...	But less than...			
A	B	C	D	E	A	B	C	D	E
$0	$6,500	$0.00	0%	$0	$0	$2,175	$0.00	0%	$0
$6,500	$16,775	$0.00	10%	$6,500	$2,175	$7,313	$0.00	10%	$2,175
$16,775	$48,275	$1,027.50	12%	$16,775	$7,313	$23,063	$513.80	12%	$7,313
$48,275	$95,575	$4,807.50	22%	$48,275	$23,063	$46,713	$2,403.80	22%	$23,063
$95,575	$176,550	$15,213.50	24%	$95,575	$46,713	$87,200	$7,606.80	24%	$46,713
$176,550	$222,450	$34,647.50	32%	$176,550	$87,200	$110,150	$17,323.68	32%	$87,200
$222,450	$330,425	$49,335.50	35%	$222,450	$110,150	$272,125	$24,667.68	35%	$110,150
$330,425		$87,126.75	37%	$330,425	$272,125		$81,358.93	37%	$272,125

ANNUAL Payroll Period

MARRIED Persons					SINGLE Persons				
If the Adjusted Wage Amount (line 1d) is		The tentative amount to withhold is...	Plus this percentage ...	of the amount that the wage exceeds...	If the Adjusted Wage Amount (line 1d) is		The tentative amount to withhold is...	Plus this percentage ...	of the amount that the wage exceeds...
at least...	But less than...				at least...	But less than...			
A	B	C	D	E	A	B	C	D	E
$0	$13,000	$0.00	0%	$0	$0	$4,350	$0.00	0%	$0
$13,000	$33,550	$0.00	10%	$13,000	$4,350	$14,625	$0.00	10%	$4,350
$33,550	$96,550	$2,055.00	12%	$33,550	$14,625	$46,125	$1,027.50	12%	$14,625
$96,550	$191,150	$9,615.00	22%	$96,550	$46,125	$93,425	$4,807.50	22%	$46,125
$191,150	$353,100	$30,427.00	24%	$191,150	$93,425	$174,400	$15,213.50	24%	$93,425
$353,100	$444,900	$69,295.00	32%	$353,100	$174,400	$220,300	$34,647.50	32%	$174,400
$444,900	$660,850	$98,671.00	35%	$444,900	$220,300	$544,250	$49,335.50	35%	$220,300
$660,850		$174,253.50	37%	$660,850	$544,250		$162,718.00	37%	$544,250

DAILY Payroll Period

MARRIED Persons					SINGLE Persons				
If the Adjusted Wage Amount (line 1d) is		The tentative amount to withhold is...	Plus this percentage ...	of the amount that the wage exceeds...	If the Adjusted Wage Amount (line 1d) is		The tentative amount to withhold is...	Plus this percentage ...	of the amount that the wage exceeds...
at least...	But less than...				at least...	But less than...			
A	B	C	D	E	A	B	C	D	E
$0.00	$50.00	$0.00	0%	$0.00	$0.00	$16.70	$0.00	0%	$0.00
$50.00	$129.00	$0.00	10%	$50.00	$16.70	$56.30	$0.00	10%	$16.70
$129.00	$371.30	$7.90	12%	$129.00	$56.30	$177.40	$3.96	12%	$56.30
$371.30	$735.20	$36.98	22%	$371.30	$177.40	$359.30	$18.49	22%	$177.40
$735.20	$1,358.10	$117.03	24%	$735.20	$359.30	$670.80	$58.51	24%	$359.30
$1,358.10	$1,711.20	$266.53	32%	$1,358.10	$670.80	$847.30	$133.27	32%	$670.80
$1,711.20	$2,541.70	$379.52	35%	$1,711.20	$847.30	$2,093.30	$189.75	35%	$847.30
$2,541.70		$670.20	37%	$2,541.70	$2,093.30		$625.85	37%	$2,093.30

TAX TABLE *D

WEEKLY — MARRIED PERSONS

2022 Wage Bracket Method Tables for Manual Payroll Systems With Forms W-4 From 2019 or Earlier

WEEKLY Payroll Period — MARRIED Persons

If the Wage Amount (line 1a) is — And the number of allowances is: — The Tentative Withholding Amount is:

At least	But less than	0	1	2	3	4	5	6	7	8	9	10
$0	$250	$0	$0	$0	$0	$0	$0	$0	$0	$0	$0	$0
$250	$260	$1	$0	$0	$0	$0	$0	$0	$0	$0	$0	$0
$260	$270	$2	$0	$0	$0	$0	$0	$0	$0	$0	$0	$0
$270	$280	$3	$0	$0	$0	$0	$0	$0	$0	$0	$0	$0
$280	$290	$4	$0	$0	$0	$0	$0	$0	$0	$0	$0	$0
$290	$300	$5	$0	$0	$0	$0	$0	$0	$0	$0	$0	$0
$300	$310	$6	$0	$0	$0	$0	$0	$0	$0	$0	$0	$0
$310	$320	$7	$0	$0	$0	$0	$0	$0	$0	$0	$0	$0
$320	$330	$8	$0	$0	$0	$0	$0	$0	$0	$0	$0	$0
$330	$340	$9	$0	$0	$0	$0	$0	$0	$0	$0	$0	$0
$340	$350	$10	$1	$0	$0	$0	$0	$0	$0	$0	$0	$0
$350	$360	$11	$2	$0	$0	$0	$0	$0	$0	$0	$0	$0
$360	$370	$12	$3	$0	$0	$0	$0	$0	$0	$0	$0	$0
$370	$380	$13	$4	$0	$0	$0	$0	$0	$0	$0	$0	$0
$380	$390	$14	$5	$0	$0	$0	$0	$0	$0	$0	$0	$0
$390	$400	$15	$6	$0	$0	$0	$0	$0	$0	$0	$0	$0
$400	$410	$16	$7	$0	$0	$0	$0	$0	$0	$0	$0	$0
$410	$420	$17	$8	$0	$0	$0	$0	$0	$0	$0	$0	$0
$420	$430	$18	$9	$0	$0	$0	$0	$0	$0	$0	$0	$0
$430	$440	$19	$10	$1	$0	$0	$0	$0	$0	$0	$0	$0
$440	$450	$20	$11	$2	$0	$0	$0	$0	$0	$0	$0	$0
$450	$460	$21	$12	$3	$0	$0	$0	$0	$0	$0	$0	$0
$460	$470	$22	$13	$4	$0	$0	$0	$0	$0	$0	$0	$0
$470	$480	$23	$14	$5	$0	$0	$0	$0	$0	$0	$0	$0
$480	$490	$24	$15	$6	$0	$0	$0	$0	$0	$0	$0	$0
$490	$500	$25	$16	$7	$0	$0	$0	$0	$0	$0	$0	$0
$500	$510	$26	$17	$8	$1	$0	$0	$0	$0	$0	$0	$0
$510	$520	$27	$18	$9	$2	$0	$0	$0	$0	$0	$0	$0
$520	$530	$28	$19	$10	$3	$0	$0	$0	$0	$0	$0	$0
$530	$540	$29	$20	$11	$4	$0	$0	$0	$0	$0	$0	$0
$540	$550	$30	$21	$12	$5	$0	$0	$0	$0	$0	$0	$0
$550	$560	$31	$22	$13	$6	$0	$0	$0	$0	$0	$0	$0
$560	$570	$32	$23	$14	$7	$0	$0	$0	$0	$0	$0	$0
$570	$580	$33	$24	$15	$8	$0	$0	$0	$0	$0	$0	$0
$580	$590	$34	$25	$16	$9	$0	$0	$0	$0	$0	$0	$0
$590	$600	$35	$26	$17	$10	$1	$0	$0	$0	$0	$0	$0
$600	$610	$36	$27	$18	$11	$2	$0	$0	$0	$0	$0	$0
$610	$620	$37	$28	$19	$12	$3	$0	$0	$0	$0	$0	$0
$620	$630	$38	$29	$20	$13	$4	$0	$0	$0	$0	$0	$0
$630	$640	$39	$30	$21	$14	$5	$0	$0	$0	$0	$0	$0
$640	$650	$40	$31	$22	$15	$6	$0	$0	$0	$0	$0	$0
$650	$665	$41	$32	$24	$16	$8	$0	$0	$0	$0	$0	$0
$665	$680	$43	$34	$26	$17	$9	$1	$0	$0	$0	$0	$0
$680	$695	$45	$35	$27	$19	$11	$2	$0	$0	$0	$0	$0
$695	$710	$46	$37	$29	$20	$12	$4	$0	$0	$0	$0	$0
$710	$725	$48	$38	$30	$22	$14	$5	$0	$0	$0	$0	$0
$725	$740	$50	$40	$32	$23	$15	$7	$0	$0	$0	$0	$0
$740	$755	$52	$42	$33	$25	$17	$8	$0	$0	$0	$0	$0
$755	$770	$54	$44	$35	$26	$18	$10	$1	$0	$0	$0	$0
$770	$785	$55	$45	$36	$28	$20	$11	$2	$0	$0	$0	$0
$785	$800	$57	$47	$38	$29	$21	$13	$4	$0	$0	$0	$0
$800	$815	$59	$49	$39	$31	$23	$14	$6	$0	$0	$0	$0
$815	$830	$61	$51	$41	$32	$24	$16	$8	$0	$0	$0	$0
$830	$845	$63	$53	$43	$34	$26	$17	$9	$1	$0	$0	$0
$845	$860	$64	$54	$45	$35	$27	$19	$11	$2	$0	$0	$0
$860	$875	$66	$56	$46	$37	$29	$20	$12	$4	$0	$0	$0
$875	$890	$68	$58	$48	$40	$30	$22	$14	$5	$0	$0	$0
$890	$905	$70	$60	$50	$42	$32	$23	$15	$7	$0	$0	$0
$905	$920	$72	$62	$52	$44	$33	$25	$17	$8	$0	$0	$0
$920	$935	$73	$63	$54	$45	$35	$26	$18	$10	$2	$0	$0
$935	$950	$75	$65	$55	$47	$36	$28	$20	$11	$3	$0	$0
$950	$965	$77	$67	$57	$49	$38	$29	$21	$13	$5	$0	$0
$965	$980	$79	$69	$59	$51	$39	$31	$23	$14	$6	$0	$0
$980	$995	$81	$71	$61	$53	$41	$32	$24	$16	$8	$0	$0
$995	$1,010	$82	$72	$63	$54	$43	$34	$26	$17	$9	$1	$0
$1,010	$1,025	$84	$74	$64	$56	$45	$35	$27	$19	$11	$2	$0
$1,025	$1,040	$86	$76	$66	$58	$46	$37	$29	$20	$12	$4	$0
$1,040	$1,055	$88	$78	$68	$60	$48	$38	$30	$22	$14	$5	$0
$1,055	$1,070	$90	$80	$70	$62	$50	$40	$32	$23	$15	$7	$0
$1,070	$1,085	$91	$81	$72	$63	$52	$42	$33	$25	$17	$8	$0
$1,085	$1,100	$93	$83	$73	$65	$54	$44	$35	$26	$18	$10	$2
$1,100	$1,115	$95	$85	$75	$67	$55	$45	$36	$28	$20	$11	$3
$1,115	$1,130	$97	$87	$77	$69	$57	$47	$38	$29	$21	$13	$5
$1,130	$1,145	$99	$89	$79	$71	$59	$49	$39	$31	$23	$14	$6
$1,145	$1,160	$100	$90	$81	$72	$61	$51	$41	$32	$24	$16	$8
$1,160	$1,175	$102	$92	$82	$74	$63	$53	$43	$34	$26	$17	$9
$1,175	$1,190	$104	$94	$84	$76	$64	$54	$44	$35	$27	$19	$11
$1,190	$1,205	$106	$96	$86	$78	$66	$56	$46	$37	$29	$20	$12
$1,205	$1,220	$108	$98	$88	$80	$68	$58	$48	$38	$30	$22	$14
$1,220	$1,235	$109	$99	$90	$81	$70	$60	$50	$40	$32	$23	$15
$1,235	$1,250	$111	$101	$91	$83	$72	$62	$52	$42	$33	$25	$17
$1,250	$1,265	$113	$103	$93	$85	$73	$63	$53	$44	$35	$26	$18
$1,265	$1,280	$115	$105	$95	$87	$75	$65	$55	$45	$36	$28	$20
$1,280	$1,295	$117	$107	$97	$89	$77	$67	$57	$47	$38	$29	$21
$1,295	$1,310	$118	$108	$99	$90	$79	$69	$59	$49	$39	$31	$23
$1,310	$1,325	$120	$110	$100	$92	$81	$71	$61	$51	$41	$32	$24
$1,325	$1,340	$122	$112	$102	$94	$82	$72	$62	$53	$43	$34	$26
$1,340	$1,355	$124	$114	$104	$96	$84	$74	$64	$54	$44	$35	$27
$1,355	$1,370	$126	$116	$106	$98	$86	$76	$66	$56	$46	$37	$29
$1,370	$1,385	$127	$117	$108	$99	$88	$78	$68	$58	$48	$38	$30
$1,385	$1,400	$129	$119	$109	$101	$90	$80	$70	$60	$50	$40	$32
$1,400	$1,415	$131	$121	$111	$103	$91	$81	$71	$62	$52	$42	$33
$1,415	$1,430	$133	$123	$113	$105	$93	$83	$73	$63	$53	$43	$35
$1,430	$1,445	$135	$125	$115	$107	$95	$85	$75	$65	$55	$45	$36
$1,445	$1,460	$136	$126	$117	$108	$97	$87	$77	$67	$57	$47	$38
$1,460	$1,475	$138	$128	$118	$110	$99	$89	$79	$69	$59	$49	$39
$1,475	$1,490	$140	$130	$120	$112	$100	$90	$80	$71	$61	$51	$41
$1,490	$1,505	$142	$132	$122	$114	$102	$92	$82	$72	$62	$52	$43
$1,505	$1,520	$144	$134	$124	$115	$104	$94	$84	$74	$64	$54	$44
$1,520	$1,535	$145	$135	$126	$117	$106	$96	$86	$76	$66	$56	$46
$1,535	$1,550	$147	$137	$127	$118	$108	$98	$88	$78	$68	$58	$48
$1,550	$1,565	$149	$139	$129	$119	$109	$99	$89	$80	$70	$60	$50

Source: Internal Revenue Service.

TAX TABLE *D (Continued)

2022 Wage Bracket Method Tables for Manual Payroll Systems With Forms W-4 From 2019 or Earlier

WEEKLY Payroll Period

WEEKLY MARRIED PERSONS

If the Wage Amount (line 1a) is		MARRIED Persons — And the number of allowances is:										
At least	But less than	0	1	2	3	4	5	6	7	8	9	10
		The Tentative Withholding Amount is:										
$1,565	$1,580	$151	$141	$131	$121	$111	$101	$91	$81	$71	$61	$52
$1,580	$1,595	$153	$143	$133	$123	$113	$103	$93	$83	$73	$63	$53
$1,595	$1,610	$154	$144	$135	$125	$115	$105	$95	$85	$75	$65	$55
$1,610	$1,625	$156	$146	$136	$126	$117	$107	$97	$87	$77	$67	$57
$1,625	$1,640	$158	$148	$138	$128	$118	$108	$98	$89	$79	$69	$59
$1,640	$1,655	$160	$150	$140	$130	$120	$110	$100	$90	$80	$70	$61
$1,655	$1,670	$162	$152	$142	$132	$122	$112	$102	$92	$82	$72	$62
$1,670	$1,685	$163	$153	$144	$134	$124	$114	$104	$94	$84	$74	$64
$1,685	$1,700	$165	$155	$145	$135	$126	$116	$106	$96	$86	$76	$66
$1,700	$1,715	$167	$157	$147	$137	$127	$117	$107	$98	$88	$78	$68
$1,715	$1,730	$169	$159	$149	$139	$129	$119	$109	$99	$89	$79	$70
$1,730	$1,745	$171	$161	$151	$141	$131	$121	$111	$101	$91	$81	$71
$1,745	$1,760	$172	$162	$153	$143	$133	$123	$113	$103	$93	$83	$73
$1,760	$1,775	$174	$164	$154	$144	$135	$125	$115	$105	$95	$85	$75
$1,775	$1,790	$176	$166	$156	$146	$136	$126	$116	$107	$97	$87	$77
$1,790	$1,805	$178	$168	$158	$148	$138	$128	$118	$108	$98	$88	$79
$1,805	$1,820	$180	$170	$160	$150	$140	$130	$120	$110	$100	$90	$80
$1,820	$1,835	$181	$171	$162	$152	$142	$132	$122	$112	$102	$92	$82
$1,835	$1,850	$183	$173	$163	$153	$144	$134	$124	$114	$104	$94	$84
$1,850	$1,865	$185	$175	$165	$155	$145	$135	$125	$116	$106	$96	$86
$1,865	$1,880	$188	$177	$167	$157	$147	$137	$127	$117	$107	$97	$88
$1,880	$1,895	$192	$179	$169	$159	$149	$139	$129	$119	$109	$99	$89
$1,895	$1,910	$195	$180	$171	$161	$151	$141	$131	$121	$111	$101	$91
$1,910	$1,925	$198	$182	$172	$162	$153	$143	$133	$123	$113	$103	$93

TAX TABLE *D (Continued)

WEEKLY SINGLE PERSONS

2022 Wage Bracket Method Tables for Manual Payroll Systems With Forms W-4 From 2019 or Earlier — WEEKLY Payroll Period — SINGLE Persons

If the Wage Amount (line 1a) is — At least	But less than	0	1	2	3	4	5	6	7	8	9	10
		The Tentative Withholding Amount is:										
$0	$85	$0	$0	$0	$0	$0	$0	$0	$0	$0	$0	$0
$85	$95	$1	$0	$0	$0	$0	$0	$0	$0	$0	$0	$0
$95	$105	$2	$0	$0	$0	$0	$0	$0	$0	$0	$0	$0
$105	$115	$3	$0	$0	$0	$0	$0	$0	$0	$0	$0	$0
$115	$125	$4	$0	$0	$0	$0	$0	$0	$0	$0	$0	$0
$125	$135	$5	$0	$0	$0	$0	$0	$0	$0	$0	$0	$0
$135	$145	$6	$0	$0	$0	$0	$0	$0	$0	$0	$0	$0
$145	$155	$7	$0	$0	$0	$0	$0	$0	$0	$0	$0	$0
$155	$165	$8	$0	$0	$0	$0	$0	$0	$0	$0	$0	$0
$165	$175	$9	$0	$0	$0	$0	$0	$0	$0	$0	$0	$0
$175	$185	$10	$1	$0	$0	$0	$0	$0	$0	$0	$0	$0
$185	$195	$11	$2	$0	$0	$0	$0	$0	$0	$0	$0	$0
$195	$205	$12	$3	$0	$0	$0	$0	$0	$0	$0	$0	$0
$205	$215	$13	$4	$0	$0	$0	$0	$0	$0	$0	$0	$0
$215	$225	$14	$5	$0	$0	$0	$0	$0	$0	$0	$0	$0
$225	$235	$15	$6	$0	$0	$0	$0	$0	$0	$0	$0	$0
$235	$245	$16	$7	$0	$0	$0	$0	$0	$0	$0	$0	$0
$245	$255	$17	$8	$0	$0	$0	$0	$0	$0	$0	$0	$0
$255	$265	$18	$9	$0	$0	$0	$0	$0	$0	$0	$0	$0
$265	$275	$19	$10	$0	$0	$0	$0	$0	$0	$0	$0	$0
$275	$285	$20	$11	$1	$0	$0	$0	$0	$0	$0	$0	$0
$285	$300	$21	$12	$3	$0	$0	$0	$0	$0	$0	$0	$0
$300	$315	$23	$14	$4	$0	$0	$0	$0	$0	$0	$0	$0
$315	$330	$25	$16	$6	$0	$0	$0	$0	$0	$0	$0	$0
$330	$345	$27	$17	$7	$0	$0	$0	$0	$0	$0	$0	$0
$345	$360	$28	$19	$9	$0	$0	$0	$0	$0	$0	$0	$0
$360	$375	$30	$20	$10	$1	$0	$0	$0	$0	$0	$0	$0
$375	$390	$32	$22	$12	$3	$0	$0	$0	$0	$0	$0	$0
$390	$405	$34	$24	$14	$5	$0	$0	$0	$0	$0	$0	$0
$405	$420	$36	$26	$16	$7	$0	$0	$0	$0	$0	$0	$0
$420	$435	$37	$27	$17	$8	$0	$0	$0	$0	$0	$0	$0
$435	$450	$39	$29	$19	$10	$0	$0	$0	$0	$0	$0	$0
$450	$465	$41	$31	$21	$12	$2	$0	$0	$0	$0	$0	$0
$465	$480	$43	$33	$23	$14	$4	$0	$0	$0	$0	$0	$0
$480	$495	$45	$35	$25	$16	$6	$0	$0	$0	$0	$0	$0
$495	$510	$46	$36	$26	$17	$7	$0	$0	$0	$0	$0	$0
$510	$525	$48	$38	$28	$19	$9	$0	$0	$0	$0	$0	$0
$525	$540	$50	$40	$30	$21	$11	$1	$0	$0	$0	$0	$0
$540	$555	$52	$42	$32	$23	$13	$3	$0	$0	$0	$0	$0
$555	$570	$54	$44	$34	$25	$15	$5	$0	$0	$0	$0	$0
$570	$585	$55	$45	$35	$26	$16	$6	$0	$0	$0	$0	$0
$585	$600	$57	$47	$37	$28	$18	$8	$0	$0	$0	$0	$0
$600	$615	$59	$49	$39	$30	$20	$10	$1	$0	$0	$0	$0
$615	$630	$61	$51	$41	$32	$22	$12	$3	$0	$0	$0	$0
$630	$645	$63	$53	$43	$34	$24	$14	$5	$0	$0	$0	$0
$645	$660	$64	$54	$44	$35	$25	$15	$6	$0	$0	$0	$0
$660	$675	$66	$56	$46	$37	$27	$17	$8	$1	$0	$0	$0
$675	$690	$68	$58	$48	$39	$29	$19	$10	$3	$0	$0	$0
$690	$705	$70	$60	$50	$41	$31	$21	$12	$5	$0	$0	$0
$705	$720	$72	$62	$52	$43	$33	$23	$14	$7	$0	$0	$0
$720	$735	$73	$63	$53	$44	$34	$24	$15	$8	$0	$0	$0

2022 Wage Bracket Method Tables for Manual Payroll Systems With Forms W-4 From 2019 or Earlier — WEEKLY Payroll Period — SINGLE Persons

If the Wage Amount (line 1a) is — At least	But less than	0	1	2	3	4	5	6	7	8	9	10
		The Tentative Withholding Amount is:										
$735	$750	$75	$65	$55	$45	$35	$25	$16	$8	$0	$0	$0
$750	$765	$77	$67	$57	$47	$37	$27	$18	$9	$1	$0	$0
$765	$780	$79	$69	$59	$49	$39	$29	$19	$11	$3	$0	$0
$780	$795	$81	$71	$61	$51	$41	$31	$21	$12	$4	$0	$0
$795	$810	$82	$72	$62	$53	$43	$33	$23	$14	$6	$0	$0
$810	$825	$84	$74	$64	$54	$44	$34	$25	$15	$7	$0	$0
$825	$840	$86	$76	$66	$56	$46	$36	$26	$17	$9	$0	$0
$840	$855	$88	$78	$68	$58	$48	$38	$28	$18	$10	$0	$0
$855	$870	$90	$80	$70	$60	$50	$40	$30	$20	$12	$2	$0
$870	$885	$91	$81	$71	$62	$52	$42	$32	$21	$13	$3	$0
$885	$900	$94	$83	$73	$63	$53	$43	$34	$23	$15	$5	$0
$900	$915	$97	$85	$75	$65	$55	$45	$35	$24	$16	$6	$0
$915	$930	$100	$87	$77	$67	$57	$47	$37	$26	$18	$8	$0
$930	$945	$104	$89	$79	$69	$59	$49	$39	$27	$19	$9	$0
$945	$960	$107	$90	$80	$71	$61	$51	$41	$29	$21	$11	$1
$960	$975	$110	$92	$82	$72	$62	$52	$43	$31	$23	$13	$3
$975	$990	$113	$95	$84	$74	$64	$54	$44	$33	$25	$15	$5
$990	$1,005	$117	$99	$86	$76	$66	$56	$46	$34	$26	$16	$6
$1,005	$1,020	$120	$102	$88	$78	$68	$58	$48	$36	$28	$18	$8
$1,020	$1,035	$123	$105	$89	$80	$70	$60	$50	$38	$30	$20	$10
$1,035	$1,050	$127	$108	$91	$81	$71	$61	$52	$40	$32	$22	$12
$1,050	$1,065	$130	$112	$94	$83	$73	$63	$53	$42	$34	$24	$14
$1,065	$1,080	$133	$115	$97	$85	$75	$65	$55	$43	$35	$25	$15
$1,080	$1,095	$137	$118	$100	$87	$77	$67	$57	$45	$37	$27	$17
$1,095	$1,110	$140	$122	$103	$89	$79	$69	$59	$47	$39	$29	$19
$1,110	$1,125	$143	$125	$107	$90	$80	$70	$61	$49	$41	$31	$21
$1,125	$1,140	$146	$128	$110	$92	$82	$72	$62	$51	$43	$33	$23
$1,140	$1,155	$150	$132	$113	$95	$84	$74	$64	$52	$44	$34	$24
$1,155	$1,170	$153	$135	$117	$98	$86	$76	$66	$54	$46	$36	$26
$1,170	$1,185	$156	$138	$120	$102	$89	$78	$68	$56	$48	$38	$28
$1,185	$1,200	$160	$141	$123	$105	$91	$80	$70	$58	$50	$40	$30
$1,200	$1,215	$163	$145	$127	$108	$93	$82	$71	$60	$52	$42	$32
$1,215	$1,230	$166	$148	$130	$112	$95	$84	$73	$61	$53	$43	$33
$1,230	$1,245	$170	$151	$133	$115	$97	$86	$75	$63	$55	$45	$35
$1,245	$1,260	$173	$155	$136	$118	$100	$88	$77	$65	$57	$47	$37
$1,260	$1,275	$176	$158	$140	$122	$103	$91	$79	$67	$59	$49	$39
$1,275	$1,290	$179	$161	$143	$125	$107	$93	$80	$69	$61	$51	$41
$1,290	$1,305	$183	$165	$146	$128	$110	$95	$82	$71	$62	$52	$42
$1,305	$1,320	$186	$168	$150	$131	$113	$97	$84	$72	$64	$54	$44
$1,320	$1,335	$189	$171	$153	$135	$117	$100	$86	$74	$66	$56	$46
$1,335	$1,350	$193	$174	$156	$138	$120	$103	$88	$76	$68	$58	$48
$1,350	$1,365	$196	$178	$160	$141	$123	$107	$91	$78	$70	$60	$50
$1,365	$1,380	$199	$181	$163	$145	$126	$110	$93	$80	$71	$61	$51
$1,380	$1,395	$203	$184	$166	$148	$130	$113	$95	$81	$73	$63	$53
$1,395	$1,410	$206	$188	$169	$151	$133	$115	$97	$83	$75	$65	$55
$1,410	$1,425	$209	$191	$173	$155	$136	$118	$100	$85	$77	$67	$57
$1,425	$1,440	$212	$194	$176	$158	$140	$121	$103	$88	$79	$69	$59
$1,440	$1,455	$216	$198	$179	$161	$143	$125	$107	$90	$80	$70	$60
$1,455	$1,470	$219	$201	$183	$164	$146	$128	$110	$91	$82	$72	$61
$1,470	$1,485	$222	$204	$186	$168	$150	$131	$113	$95	$84	$74	$64
$1,485	$1,500	$226	$207	$189	$171	$153	$135	$117	$98	$86	$76	$66

TAX TABLE *D (Continued)

2022 Wage Bracket Method Tables for Manual Payroll Systems With Forms W-4 From 2019 or Earlier

WEEKLY Payroll Period

WEEKLY SINGLE PERSONS

SINGLE Persons

If the Wage Amount (line 1a) is		And the number of allowances is:										
At least	But less than	0	1	2	3	4	5	6	7	8	9	10
		The Tentative Withholding Amount is:										
$1,500	$1,515	$229	$211	$193	$174	$156	$138	$120	$102	$88	$78	$68
$1,515	$1,530	$232	$214	$196	$178	$159	$141	$123	$105	$89	$79	$69
$1,530	$1,545	$236	$217	$199	$181	$163	$145	$126	$108	$91	$81	$71
$1,545	$1,560	$239	$221	$202	$184	$166	$148	$130	$112	$93	$83	$73
$1,560	$1,575	$242	$224	$206	$188	$169	$151	$133	$115	$97	$85	$75
$1,575	$1,590	$245	$227	$209	$191	$173	$154	$136	$118	$100	$87	$77
$1,590	$1,605	$249	$231	$212	$194	$176	$158	$140	$121	$103	$88	$78
$1,605	$1,620	$252	$234	$216	$197	$179	$161	$143	$125	$107	$90	$80
$1,620	$1,635	$255	$237	$219	$201	$183	$164	$146	$128	$110	$92	$82
$1,635	$1,650	$259	$240	$222	$204	$186	$168	$150	$131	$113	$95	$84
$1,650	$1,665	$262	$244	$226	$207	$189	$171	$153	$135	$116	$98	$86
$1,665	$1,680	$265	$247	$229	$211	$192	$174	$156	$138	$120	$102	$87
$1,680	$1,695	$269	$250	$232	$214	$196	$178	$159	$141	$123	$105	$89
$1,695	$1,710	$272	$254	$235	$217	$199	$181	$163	$145	$126	$108	$91
$1,710	$1,725	$275	$257	$239	$221	$202	$184	$166	$148	$130	$111	$93
$1,725	$1,740	$278	$260	$242	$224	$206	$187	$169	$151	$133	$115	$97
$1,740	$1,755	$282	$264	$245	$227	$209	$191	$173	$154	$136	$118	$100
$1,755	$1,770	$285	$267	$249	$230	$212	$194	$176	$158	$140	$121	$103
$1,770	$1,785	$288	$270	$252	$234	$216	$197	$179	$161	$143	$125	$106
$1,785	$1,800	$292	$273	$255	$237	$219	$201	$183	$164	$146	$128	$110
$1,800	$1,815	$295	$277	$259	$240	$222	$204	$186	$168	$149	$131	$113

TAX TABLE *D (Continued)

BIWEEKLY — MARRIED PERSONS

2022 Wage Bracket Method Tables for Manual Payroll Systems With Forms W-4 From 2019 or Earlier — BIWEEKLY Payroll Period — MARRIED Persons

The Tentative Withholding Amount is (And the number of allowances is):

At least	But less than	0	1	2	3	4	5	6	7	8	9	10
$0	$500	$0	$0	$0	$0	$0	$0	$0	$0	$0	$0	$0
$500	$510	$1	$0	$0	$0	$0	$0	$0	$0	$0	$0	$0
$510	$520	$2	$0	$0	$0	$0	$0	$0	$0	$0	$0	$0
$520	$530	$3	$0	$0	$0	$0	$0	$0	$0	$0	$0	$0
$530	$540	$4	$0	$0	$0	$0	$0	$0	$0	$0	$0	$0
$540	$550	$5	$0	$0	$0	$0	$0	$0	$0	$0	$0	$0
$550	$560	$6	$0	$0	$0	$0	$0	$0	$0	$0	$0	$0
$560	$570	$7	$0	$0	$0	$0	$0	$0	$0	$0	$0	$0
$570	$580	$8	$0	$0	$0	$0	$0	$0	$0	$0	$0	$0
$580	$590	$9	$0	$0	$0	$0	$0	$0	$0	$0	$0	$0
$590	$600	$10	$0	$0	$0	$0	$0	$0	$0	$0	$0	$0
$600	$610	$11	$0	$0	$0	$0	$0	$0	$0	$0	$0	$0
$610	$620	$12	$0	$0	$0	$0	$0	$0	$0	$0	$0	$0
$620	$630	$13	$0	$0	$0	$0	$0	$0	$0	$0	$0	$0
$630	$640	$14	$0	$0	$0	$0	$0	$0	$0	$0	$0	$0
$640	$650	$15	$0	$0	$0	$0	$0	$0	$0	$0	$0	$0
$650	$660	$16	$0	$0	$0	$0	$0	$0	$0	$0	$0	$0
$660	$670	$17	$0	$0	$0	$0	$0	$0	$0	$0	$0	$0
$670	$680	$18	$1	$0	$0	$0	$0	$0	$0	$0	$0	$0
$680	$690	$19	$2	$0	$0	$0	$0	$0	$0	$0	$0	$0
$690	$700	$20	$3	$0	$0	$0	$0	$0	$0	$0	$0	$0
$700	$710	$21	$4	$0	$0	$0	$0	$0	$0	$0	$0	$0
$710	$720	$22	$5	$0	$0	$0	$0	$0	$0	$0	$0	$0
$720	$730	$23	$6	$0	$0	$0	$0	$0	$0	$0	$0	$0
$730	$740	$24	$7	$0	$0	$0	$0	$0	$0	$0	$0	$0
$740	$750	$25	$8	$0	$0	$0	$0	$0	$0	$0	$0	$0
$750	$760	$26	$9	$0	$0	$0	$0	$0	$0	$0	$0	$0
$760	$770	$27	$10	$0	$0	$0	$0	$0	$0	$0	$0	$0
$770	$780	$28	$11	$0	$0	$0	$0	$0	$0	$0	$0	$0
$780	$790	$29	$12	$0	$0	$0	$0	$0	$0	$0	$0	$0
$790	$800	$30	$13	$0	$0	$0	$0	$0	$0	$0	$0	$0
$800	$810	$31	$14	$0	$0	$0	$0	$0	$0	$0	$0	$0
$810	$820	$32	$15	$0	$0	$0	$0	$0	$0	$0	$0	$0
$820	$830	$33	$16	$0	$0	$0	$0	$0	$0	$0	$0	$0
$830	$840	$34	$17	$0	$0	$0	$0	$0	$0	$0	$0	$0
$840	$850	$35	$18	$1	$0	$0	$0	$0	$0	$0	$0	$0
$850	$860	$36	$19	$2	$0	$0	$0	$0	$0	$0	$0	$0
$860	$870	$37	$20	$3	$0	$0	$0	$0	$0	$0	$0	$0
$870	$880	$38	$21	$4	$0	$0	$0	$0	$0	$0	$0	$0
$880	$890	$39	$22	$5	$0	$0	$0	$0	$0	$0	$0	$0
$890	$900	$40	$23	$6	$0	$0	$0	$0	$0	$0	$0	$0
$900	$910	$41	$24	$7	$0	$0	$0	$0	$0	$0	$0	$0
$910	$920	$42	$25	$8	$0	$0	$0	$0	$0	$0	$0	$0
$920	$930	$43	$26	$9	$0	$0	$0	$0	$0	$0	$0	$0
$930	$940	$44	$27	$10	$0	$0	$0	$0	$0	$0	$0	$0
$940	$950	$45	$28	$11	$0	$0	$0	$0	$0	$0	$0	$0
$950	$960	$46	$29	$12	$0	$0	$0	$0	$0	$0	$0	$0
$960	$970	$47	$30	$13	$0	$0	$0	$0	$0	$0	$0	$0
$970	$980	$48	$31	$14	$0	$0	$0	$0	$0	$0	$0	$0
$980	$990	$49	$32	$15	$0	$0	$0	$0	$0	$0	$0	$0
$990	$1,000	$50	$33	$16	$0	$0	$0	$0	$0	$0	$0	$0

2022 Wage Bracket Method Tables for Manual Payroll Systems With Forms W-4 From 2019 or Earlier — BIWEEKLY Payroll Period — MARRIED Persons

The Tentative Withholding Amount is (And the number of allowances is):

At least	But less than	0	1	2	3	4	5	6	7	8	9	10
$1,000	$1,010	$51	$34	$17	$1	$0	$0	$0	$0	$0	$0	$0
$1,010	$1,020	$52	$35	$18	$2	$0	$0	$0	$0	$0	$0	$0
$1,020	$1,030	$53	$36	$19	$3	$0	$0	$0	$0	$0	$0	$0
$1,030	$1,040	$54	$37	$20	$4	$0	$0	$0	$0	$0	$0	$0
$1,040	$1,050	$55	$38	$21	$5	$0	$0	$0	$0	$0	$0	$0
$1,050	$1,060	$56	$39	$22	$6	$0	$0	$0	$0	$0	$0	$0
$1,060	$1,070	$57	$40	$23	$7	$0	$0	$0	$0	$0	$0	$0
$1,070	$1,080	$58	$41	$24	$8	$0	$0	$0	$0	$0	$0	$0
$1,080	$1,090	$59	$42	$25	$9	$0	$0	$0	$0	$0	$0	$0
$1,090	$1,100	$60	$43	$26	$10	$0	$0	$0	$0	$0	$0	$0
$1,100	$1,110	$61	$44	$27	$11	$0	$0	$0	$0	$0	$0	$0
$1,110	$1,120	$62	$45	$28	$12	$0	$0	$0	$0	$0	$0	$0
$1,120	$1,130	$63	$46	$29	$13	$0	$0	$0	$0	$0	$0	$0
$1,130	$1,140	$64	$47	$30	$14	$0	$0	$0	$0	$0	$0	$0
$1,140	$1,150	$65	$48	$31	$15	$0	$0	$0	$0	$0	$0	$0
$1,150	$1,160	$66	$49	$32	$16	$0	$0	$0	$0	$0	$0	$0
$1,160	$1,170	$67	$50	$33	$17	$0	$0	$0	$0	$0	$0	$0
$1,170	$1,180	$68	$51	$34	$18	$1	$0	$0	$0	$0	$0	$0
$1,180	$1,190	$69	$52	$35	$19	$2	$0	$0	$0	$0	$0	$0
$1,190	$1,200	$70	$53	$36	$20	$3	$0	$0	$0	$0	$0	$0
$1,200	$1,210	$71	$54	$37	$21	$4	$0	$0	$0	$0	$0	$0
$1,210	$1,220	$72	$55	$38	$22	$5	$0	$0	$0	$0	$0	$0
$1,220	$1,230	$73	$56	$39	$23	$6	$0	$0	$0	$0	$0	$0
$1,230	$1,240	$74	$57	$40	$24	$7	$0	$0	$0	$0	$0	$0
$1,240	$1,250	$75	$58	$41	$25	$8	$0	$0	$0	$0	$0	$0
$1,250	$1,260	$76	$59	$42	$26	$9	$0	$0	$0	$0	$0	$0
$1,260	$1,270	$77	$60	$43	$27	$10	$0	$0	$0	$0	$0	$0
$1,270	$1,280	$78	$61	$44	$28	$11	$0	$0	$0	$0	$0	$0
$1,280	$1,290	$79	$62	$45	$29	$12	$0	$0	$0	$0	$0	$0
$1,290	$1,330	$81	$64	$48	$31	$15	$2	$0	$0	$0	$0	$0
$1,330	$1,370	$86	$68	$52	$35	$19	$6	$0	$0	$0	$0	$0
$1,370	$1,410	$91	$72	$56	$39	$23	$10	$0	$0	$0	$0	$0
$1,410	$1,450	$96	$76	$60	$43	$27	$14	$0	$0	$0	$0	$0
$1,450	$1,490	$101	$81	$64	$47	$31	$18	$0	$0	$0	$0	$0
$1,490	$1,530	$105	$86	$68	$51	$35	$18	$2	$0	$0	$0	$0
$1,530	$1,570	$110	$90	$72	$55	$39	$22	$6	$0	$0	$0	$0
$1,570	$1,610	$115	$95	$76	$59	$43	$26	$10	$0	$0	$0	$0
$1,610	$1,650	$120	$100	$80	$63	$47	$30	$14	$0	$0	$0	$0
$1,650	$1,690	$125	$105	$85	$67	$51	$34	$18	$1	$0	$0	$0
$1,690	$1,730	$129	$110	$90	$71	$55	$38	$22	$5	$0	$0	$0
$1,730	$1,770	$134	$114	$95	$75	$59	$42	$26	$9	$0	$0	$0
$1,770	$1,810	$139	$119	$99	$79	$63	$46	$30	$13	$0	$0	$0
$1,810	$1,850	$144	$124	$104	$84	$67	$50	$34	$17	$1	$0	$0
$1,850	$1,890	$149	$129	$109	$89	$71	$54	$38	$21	$5	$0	$0
$1,890	$1,930	$153	$134	$114	$94	$75	$58	$42	$25	$9	$0	$0
$1,930	$1,970	$158	$138	$119	$99	$79	$62	$46	$29	$13	$0	$0
$1,970	$2,010	$163	$143	$123	$103	$84	$66	$50	$33	$17	$0	$0
$2,010	$2,050	$168	$148	$128	$108	$88	$70	$54	$37	$21	$4	$0
$2,050	$2,090	$173	$153	$133	$113	$93	$75	$58	$41	$25	$8	$0
$2,090	$2,130	$177	$158	$138	$118	$98	$79	$62	$45	$29	$12	$0
$2,130	$2,170	$182	$162	$143	$123	$103	$83	$66	$49	$33	$16	$0

TAX TABLE *D (Continued)

BIWEEKLY MARRIED PERSONS

2022 Wage Bracket Method Tables for Manual Payroll Systems With Forms W-4 From 2019 or Earlier

BIWEEKLY Payroll Period

MARRIED Persons

If the Wage Amount (line 1a) is		And the number of allowances is:										
At least	But less than	0	1	2	3	4	5	6	7	8	9	10
		The Tentative Withholding Amount is:										
$2,170	$2,210	$187	$167	$147	$127	$108	$88	$70	$53	$37	$20	$4
$2,210	$2,250	$192	$172	$152	$132	$112	$93	$74	$57	$41	$24	$8
$2,250	$2,290	$197	$177	$157	$137	$117	$97	$78	$61	$45	$28	$12
$2,290	$2,330	$201	$182	$162	$142	$122	$102	$82	$65	$49	$32	$16
$2,330	$2,370	$206	$186	$167	$147	$127	$107	$87	$69	$53	$36	$20
$2,370	$2,410	$211	$191	$171	$151	$132	$112	$92	$73	$57	$40	$24
$2,410	$2,450	$216	$196	$176	$156	$136	$117	$97	$77	$61	$44	$28
$2,450	$2,490	$221	$201	$181	$161	$141	$121	$102	$82	$65	$48	$32
$2,490	$2,530	$225	$206	$186	$166	$146	$126	$106	$86	$69	$52	$36
$2,530	$2,570	$230	$210	$191	$171	$151	$131	$111	$91	$73	$56	$40
$2,570	$2,610	$235	$215	$195	$175	$156	$136	$116	$96	$77	$60	$44
$2,610	$2,650	$240	$220	$200	$180	$160	$141	$121	$101	$81	$64	$48
$2,650	$2,690	$245	$225	$205	$185	$165	$145	$126	$106	$86	$68	$52
$2,690	$2,730	$249	$230	$210	$190	$170	$150	$130	$110	$91	$72	$56
$2,730	$2,770	$254	$234	$215	$195	$175	$155	$135	$115	$95	$76	$60
$2,770	$2,810	$259	$239	$219	$199	$180	$160	$140	$120	$100	$80	$64
$2,810	$2,850	$264	$244	$224	$204	$184	$165	$145	$125	$105	$85	$68
$2,850	$2,890	$269	$249	$229	$209	$189	$169	$150	$130	$110	$90	$72
$2,890	$2,930	$273	$254	$234	$214	$194	$174	$154	$134	$115	$95	$76
$2,930	$2,970	$278	$258	$239	$219	$199	$179	$159	$139	$119	$100	$80
$2,970	$3,010	$283	$263	$243	$223	$204	$184	$164	$144	$124	$104	$85
$3,010	$3,050	$288	$268	$248	$228	$208	$189	$169	$149	$129	$109	$89
$3,050	$3,090	$293	$273	$253	$233	$213	$193	$174	$154	$134	$114	$94
$3,090	$3,130	$297	$278	$258	$238	$218	$198	$178	$158	$139	$119	$99
$3,130	$3,170	$302	$282	$263	$243	$223	$203	$183	$163	$143	$124	$104
$3,170	$3,210	$307	$287	$267	$247	$228	$208	$188	$168	$148	$128	$109
$3,210	$3,250	$312	$292	$272	$252	$232	$213	$193	$173	$153	$133	$113
$3,250	$3,290	$317	$297	$277	$257	$237	$217	$198	$178	$158	$138	$118
$3,290	$3,330	$321	$302	$282	$262	$242	$222	$202	$182	$163	$143	$123
$3,330	$3,370	$326	$306	$287	$267	$247	$227	$207	$187	$167	$148	$128
$3,370	$3,410	$331	$311	$291	$271	$252	$232	$212	$192	$172	$152	$133
$3,410	$3,450	$336	$316	$296	$276	$256	$237	$217	$197	$177	$157	$137

TAX TABLE *D (Continued)

BIWEEKLY SINGLE PERSONS

2022 Wage Bracket Method Tables for Manual Payroll Systems
With Forms W-4 From 2019 or Earlier
BIWEEKLY Payroll Period — SINGLE Persons

If the Wage Amount (line 1a) is: At least	But less than	And the number of allowances is: 0	1	2	3	4	5	6	7	8	9	10
		The Tentative Withholding Amount is:										
$0	$170	$0	$0	$0	$0	$0	$0	$0	$0	$0	$0	$0
$170	$180	$1	$0	$0	$0	$0	$0	$0	$0	$0	$0	$0
$180	$190	$2	$0	$0	$0	$0	$0	$0	$0	$0	$0	$0
$190	$200	$3	$0	$0	$0	$0	$0	$0	$0	$0	$0	$0
$200	$210	$4	$0	$0	$0	$0	$0	$0	$0	$0	$0	$0
$210	$220	$5	$0	$0	$0	$0	$0	$0	$0	$0	$0	$0
$220	$230	$6	$0	$0	$0	$0	$0	$0	$0	$0	$0	$0
$230	$240	$7	$0	$0	$0	$0	$0	$0	$0	$0	$0	$0
$240	$250	$8	$0	$0	$0	$0	$0	$0	$0	$0	$0	$0
$250	$260	$9	$0	$0	$0	$0	$0	$0	$0	$0	$0	$0
$260	$270	$10	$0	$0	$0	$0	$0	$0	$0	$0	$0	$0
$270	$280	$11	$0	$0	$0	$0	$0	$0	$0	$0	$0	$0
$280	$290	$12	$0	$0	$0	$0	$0	$0	$0	$0	$0	$0
$290	$300	$13	$0	$0	$0	$0	$0	$0	$0	$0	$0	$0
$300	$310	$14	$0	$0	$0	$0	$0	$0	$0	$0	$0	$0
$310	$320	$15	$0	$0	$0	$0	$0	$0	$0	$0	$0	$0
$320	$330	$16	$0	$0	$0	$0	$0	$0	$0	$0	$0	$0
$330	$340	$17	$0	$0	$0	$0	$0	$0	$0	$0	$0	$0
$340	$350	$18	$1	$0	$0	$0	$0	$0	$0	$0	$0	$0
$350	$360	$19	$2	$0	$0	$0	$0	$0	$0	$0	$0	$0
$360	$370	$20	$3	$0	$0	$0	$0	$0	$0	$0	$0	$0
$370	$380	$21	$4	$0	$0	$0	$0	$0	$0	$0	$0	$0
$380	$390	$22	$5	$0	$0	$0	$0	$0	$0	$0	$0	$0
$390	$400	$23	$6	$0	$0	$0	$0	$0	$0	$0	$0	$0
$400	$410	$24	$7	$0	$0	$0	$0	$0	$0	$0	$0	$0
$410	$420	$25	$8	$0	$0	$0	$0	$0	$0	$0	$0	$0
$420	$430	$26	$9	$0	$0	$0	$0	$0	$0	$0	$0	$0
$430	$440	$27	$10	$0	$0	$0	$0	$0	$0	$0	$0	$0
$440	$450	$28	$11	$0	$0	$0	$0	$0	$0	$0	$0	$0
$450	$460	$29	$12	$0	$0	$0	$0	$0	$0	$0	$0	$0
$460	$470	$30	$13	$0	$0	$0	$0	$0	$0	$0	$0	$0
$470	$480	$31	$14	$0	$0	$0	$0	$0	$0	$0	$0	$0
$480	$490	$32	$15	$0	$0	$0	$0	$0	$0	$0	$0	$0
$490	$500	$33	$16	$0	$0	$0	$0	$0	$0	$0	$0	$0
$500	$510	$34	$17	$1	$0	$0	$0	$0	$0	$0	$0	$0
$510	$520	$35	$18	$2	$0	$0	$0	$0	$0	$0	$0	$0
$520	$530	$36	$19	$3	$0	$0	$0	$0	$0	$0	$0	$0
$530	$540	$37	$20	$4	$0	$0	$0	$0	$0	$0	$0	$0
$540	$550	$38	$21	$5	$0	$0	$0	$0	$0	$0	$0	$0
$550	$560	$39	$22	$6	$0	$0	$0	$0	$0	$0	$0	$0
$560	$590	$41	$24	$8	$0	$0	$0	$0	$0	$0	$0	$0
$590	$620	$45	$27	$11	$0	$0	$0	$0	$0	$0	$0	$0
$620	$650	$48	$30	$14	$0	$0	$0	$0	$0	$0	$0	$0
$650	$680	$52	$33	$17	$1	$0	$0	$0	$0	$0	$0	$0
$680	$710	$55	$36	$20	$3	$0	$0	$0	$0	$0	$0	$0
$710	$740	$59	$39	$23	$6	$0	$0	$0	$0	$0	$0	$0
$740	$770	$63	$43	$26	$9	$0	$0	$0	$0	$0	$0	$0
$770	$800	$66	$46	$29	$12	$0	$0	$0	$0	$0	$0	$0
$800	$830	$70	$50	$32	$15	$0	$0	$0	$0	$0	$0	$0
$830	$860	$73	$54	$35	$18	$2	$0	$0	$0	$0	$0	$0
$860	$890	$77	$57	$38	$21	$5	$0	$0	$0	$0	$0	$0

2022 Wage Bracket Method Tables for Manual Payroll Systems
With Forms W-4 From 2019 or Earlier
BIWEEKLY Payroll Period — SINGLE Persons

If the Wage Amount (line 1a) is: At least	But less than	And the number of allowances is: 0	1	2	3	4	5	6	7	8	9	10
		The Tentative Withholding Amount is:										
$890	$920	$81	$61	$41	$24	$8	$0	$0	$0	$0	$0	$0
$920	$950	$84	$64	$45	$27	$11	$0	$0	$0	$0	$0	$0
$950	$980	$88	$68	$48	$30	$14	$0	$0	$0	$0	$0	$0
$980	$1,010	$91	$72	$52	$33	$17	$0	$0	$0	$0	$0	$0
$1,010	$1,040	$95	$75	$55	$36	$20	$3	$0	$0	$0	$0	$0
$1,040	$1,070	$99	$79	$59	$39	$23	$6	$0	$0	$0	$0	$0
$1,070	$1,100	$102	$82	$63	$43	$26	$9	$0	$0	$0	$0	$0
$1,100	$1,130	$106	$86	$66	$46	$29	$12	$0	$0	$0	$0	$0
$1,130	$1,160	$109	$90	$70	$50	$32	$15	$0	$0	$0	$0	$0
$1,160	$1,190	$113	$93	$73	$53	$35	$18	$2	$0	$0	$0	$0
$1,190	$1,220	$117	$97	$77	$57	$38	$21	$5	$0	$0	$0	$0
$1,220	$1,250	$120	$100	$81	$61	$41	$24	$8	$0	$0	$0	$0
$1,250	$1,280	$124	$104	$84	$64	$44	$27	$11	$0	$0	$0	$0
$1,280	$1,310	$127	$108	$88	$68	$48	$30	$14	$0	$0	$0	$0
$1,310	$1,340	$131	$111	$91	$71	$52	$33	$17	$0	$0	$0	$0
$1,340	$1,370	$135	$115	$95	$75	$55	$36	$20	$3	$0	$0	$0
$1,370	$1,400	$138	$118	$99	$79	$59	$39	$23	$6	$0	$0	$0
$1,400	$1,430	$142	$122	$102	$82	$62	$43	$26	$9	$0	$0	$0
$1,430	$1,460	$145	$126	$106	$86	$66	$46	$29	$12	$0	$0	$0
$1,460	$1,490	$149	$129	$109	$89	$70	$50	$32	$15	$0	$0	$0
$1,490	$1,520	$153	$133	$113	$93	$73	$53	$35	$18	$1	$0	$0
$1,520	$1,550	$156	$136	$117	$97	$77	$57	$38	$21	$4	$0	$0
$1,550	$1,580	$160	$140	$120	$100	$80	$61	$41	$24	$7	$0	$0
$1,580	$1,610	$163	$144	$124	$104	$84	$64	$44	$27	$10	$0	$0
$1,610	$1,640	$167	$147	$127	$107	$88	$68	$48	$30	$13	$0	$0
$1,640	$1,670	$171	$151	$131	$111	$91	$71	$52	$33	$16	$1	$0
$1,670	$1,700	$174	$154	$135	$115	$95	$75	$55	$36	$19	$4	$0
$1,700	$1,730	$178	$158	$138	$118	$98	$79	$59	$39	$22	$7	$0
$1,730	$1,760	$181	$162	$142	$122	$102	$82	$62	$42	$25	$10	$0
$1,760	$1,790	$185	$165	$145	$125	$106	$86	$66	$46	$28	$13	$0
$1,790	$1,830	$193	$169	$150	$130	$110	$90	$70	$50	$32	$16	$3
$1,830	$1,870	$202	$174	$154	$134	$115	$95	$75	$55	$36	$19	$7
$1,870	$1,910	$210	$179	$159	$139	$119	$100	$80	$60	$40	$23	$11
$1,910	$1,950	$219	$184	$164	$144	$124	$104	$85	$65	$45	$27	$15
$1,950	$1,990	$228	$192	$169	$149	$129	$109	$89	$69	$50	$31	$19
$1,990	$2,030	$237	$200	$174	$154	$134	$114	$94	$74	$54	$35	$23
$2,030	$2,070	$246	$209	$178	$158	$139	$119	$99	$79	$59	$39	$27
$2,070	$2,110	$254	$218	$183	$163	$143	$124	$104	$84	$64	$44	$31
$2,110	$2,150	$263	$227	$190	$168	$148	$128	$109	$89	$69	$49	$35
$2,150	$2,190	$272	$236	$199	$173	$153	$133	$113	$93	$74	$54	$39
$2,190	$2,230	$281	$244	$208	$182	$158	$138	$118	$98	$78	$59	$44
$2,230	$2,270	$290	$253	$217	$189	$163	$143	$123	$103	$83	$63	$48
$2,270	$2,310	$298	$262	$226	$198	$167	$148	$128	$108	$88	$68	$53
$2,310	$2,350	$307	$271	$234	$207	$172	$152	$133	$113	$93	$73	$58
$2,350	$2,390	$316	$280	$243	$216	$177	$157	$137	$117	$98	$78	$63
$2,390	$2,430	$325	$288	$252	$224	$182	$162	$142	$122	$102	$83	$68
$2,430	$2,470	$334	$297	$261	$233	$188	$167	$147	$127	$107	$87	$72
$2,470	$2,510	$342	$306	$270	$242	$197	$172	$152	$132	$112	$92	$77
$2,510	$2,550	$351	$315	$278	$251	$206	$176	$157	$137	$117	$97	$82
$2,550	$2,590	$360	$324	$287	$260	$214	$181	$161	$141	$122	$102	$82
$2,590	$2,630	$369	$332	$296	$260	$223	$187	$166	$146	$126	$107	$87

TAX TABLE *D (Continued)

2022 Wage Bracket Method Tables for Manual Payroll Systems With Forms W-4 From 2019 or Earlier

BIWEEKLY Payroll Period

SINGLE Persons

BIWEEKLY SINGLE PERSONS

If the Wage Amount (line 1a) is		And the number of allowances is:										
At least	But less than	0	1	2	3	4	5	6	7	8	9	10
		The Tentative Withholding Amount is:										
$2,630	$2,670	$378	$341	$305	$268	$232	$196	$171	$151	$131	$111	$92
$2,670	$2,710	$386	$350	$314	$277	$241	$204	$176	$156	$136	$116	$96
$2,710	$2,750	$395	$359	$322	$286	$250	$213	$181	$161	$141	$121	$101
$2,750	$2,790	$404	$368	$331	$295	$258	$222	$186	$165	$146	$126	$106
$2,790	$2,830	$413	$376	$340	$304	$267	$231	$195	$170	$150	$131	$111
$2,830	$2,870	$422	$385	$349	$312	$276	$240	$203	$175	$155	$135	$116
$2,870	$2,910	$430	$394	$358	$321	$285	$248	$212	$180	$160	$140	$120
$2,910	$2,950	$439	$403	$366	$330	$294	$257	$221	$185	$165	$145	$125
$2,950	$2,990	$448	$412	$375	$339	$302	$266	$230	$193	$170	$150	$130
$2,990	$3,030	$457	$420	$384	$348	$311	$275	$239	$202	$174	$155	$135
$3,030	$3,070	$466	$429	$393	$356	$320	$284	$247	$211	$179	$159	$140
$3,070	$3,110	$474	$438	$402	$365	$329	$292	$256	$220	$184	$164	$144
$3,110	$3,150	$483	$447	$410	$374	$338	$301	$265	$229	$192	$169	$149
$3,150	$3,190	$492	$456	$419	$383	$346	$310	$274	$237	$201	$174	$154
$3,190	$3,230	$501	$464	$428	$392	$355	$319	$283	$246	$210	$179	$159
$3,230	$3,270	$510	$473	$437	$400	$364	$328	$291	$255	$219	$183	$164
$3,270	$3,310	$518	$482	$446	$409	$373	$336	$300	$264	$227	$191	$168
$3,310	$3,350	$527	$491	$454	$418	$382	$345	$309	$273	$236	$200	$173
$3,350	$3,390	$536	$500	$463	$427	$390	$354	$318	$281	$245	$209	$178
$3,390	$3,430	$545	$508	$472	$436	$399	$363	$327	$290	$254	$217	$183
$3,430	$3,470	$554	$517	$481	$444	$408	$372	$335	$299	$263	$226	$190

TAX TABLE *D (Continued)

SEMIMONTHLY — MARRIED PERSONS

2022 Wage Bracket Method Tables for Manual Payroll Systems With Forms W-4 From 2019 or Earlier
SEMIMONTHLY Payroll Period — MARRIED Persons

And the number of allowances is: — The Tentative Withholding Amount is:

If the Wage Amount (line 1a) is — At least	But less than	0	1	2	3	4	5	6	7	8	9	10
$0	$545	$0	$0	$0	$0	$0	$0	$0	$0	$0	$0	$0
$545	$555	$1	$0	$0	$0	$0	$0	$0	$0	$0	$0	$0
$555	$565	$2	$0	$0	$0	$0	$0	$0	$0	$0	$0	$0
$565	$575	$3	$0	$0	$0	$0	$0	$0	$0	$0	$0	$0
$575	$585	$4	$0	$0	$0	$0	$0	$0	$0	$0	$0	$0
$585	$595	$5	$0	$0	$0	$0	$0	$0	$0	$0	$0	$0
$595	$605	$6	$0	$0	$0	$0	$0	$0	$0	$0	$0	$0
$605	$615	$7	$0	$0	$0	$0	$0	$0	$0	$0	$0	$0
$615	$625	$8	$0	$0	$0	$0	$0	$0	$0	$0	$0	$0
$625	$635	$9	$0	$0	$0	$0	$0	$0	$0	$0	$0	$0
$635	$645	$10	$0	$0	$0	$0	$0	$0	$0	$0	$0	$0
$645	$655	$11	$0	$0	$0	$0	$0	$0	$0	$0	$0	$0
$655	$665	$12	$0	$0	$0	$0	$0	$0	$0	$0	$0	$0
$665	$675	$13	$0	$0	$0	$0	$0	$0	$0	$0	$0	$0
$675	$685	$14	$0	$0	$0	$0	$0	$0	$0	$0	$0	$0
$685	$695	$15	$0	$0	$0	$0	$0	$0	$0	$0	$0	$0
$695	$705	$16	$0	$0	$0	$0	$0	$0	$0	$0	$0	$0
$705	$715	$17	$0	$0	$0	$0	$0	$0	$0	$0	$0	$0
$715	$725	$18	$0	$0	$0	$0	$0	$0	$0	$0	$0	$0
$725	$735	$19	$1	$0	$0	$0	$0	$0	$0	$0	$0	$0
$735	$745	$20	$2	$0	$0	$0	$0	$0	$0	$0	$0	$0
$745	$755	$21	$3	$0	$0	$0	$0	$0	$0	$0	$0	$0
$755	$765	$22	$4	$0	$0	$0	$0	$0	$0	$0	$0	$0
$765	$775	$23	$5	$0	$0	$0	$0	$0	$0	$0	$0	$0
$775	$785	$24	$6	$0	$0	$0	$0	$0	$0	$0	$0	$0
$785	$795	$25	$7	$0	$0	$0	$0	$0	$0	$0	$0	$0
$795	$805	$26	$8	$0	$0	$0	$0	$0	$0	$0	$0	$0
$805	$815	$27	$9	$0	$0	$0	$0	$0	$0	$0	$0	$0
$815	$825	$28	$10	$0	$0	$0	$0	$0	$0	$0	$0	$0
$825	$835	$29	$11	$0	$0	$0	$0	$0	$0	$0	$0	$0
$835	$845	$30	$12	$0	$0	$0	$0	$0	$0	$0	$0	$0
$845	$855	$31	$13	$0	$0	$0	$0	$0	$0	$0	$0	$0
$855	$865	$32	$14	$0	$0	$0	$0	$0	$0	$0	$0	$0
$865	$875	$33	$15	$0	$0	$0	$0	$0	$0	$0	$0	$0
$875	$885	$34	$16	$0	$0	$0	$0	$0	$0	$0	$0	$0
$885	$895	$35	$17	$0	$0	$0	$0	$0	$0	$0	$0	$0
$895	$905	$36	$18	$0	$0	$0	$0	$0	$0	$0	$0	$0
$905	$915	$37	$19	$1	$0	$0	$0	$0	$0	$0	$0	$0
$915	$925	$38	$20	$2	$0	$0	$0	$0	$0	$0	$0	$0
$925	$935	$39	$21	$3	$0	$0	$0	$0	$0	$0	$0	$0
$935	$945	$40	$22	$4	$0	$0	$0	$0	$0	$0	$0	$0
$945	$955	$41	$23	$5	$0	$0	$0	$0	$0	$0	$0	$0
$955	$965	$42	$24	$6	$0	$0	$0	$0	$0	$0	$0	$0
$965	$975	$43	$25	$7	$0	$0	$0	$0	$0	$0	$0	$0
$975	$985	$44	$26	$8	$0	$0	$0	$0	$0	$0	$0	$0
$985	$995	$45	$27	$9	$0	$0	$0	$0	$0	$0	$0	$0
$995	$1,005	$46	$28	$10	$0	$0	$0	$0	$0	$0	$0	$0
$1,005	$1,015	$47	$29	$11	$0	$0	$0	$0	$0	$0	$0	$0
$1,015	$1,025	$48	$30	$12	$0	$0	$0	$0	$0	$0	$0	$0
$1,025	$1,035	$49	$31	$13	$0	$0	$0	$0	$0	$0	$0	$0
$1,035	$1,045	$50	$32	$14	$0	$0	$0	$0	$0	$0	$0	$0

2022 Wage Bracket Method Tables for Manual Payroll Systems With Forms W-4 From 2019 or Earlier
SEMIMONTHLY Payroll Period — MARRIED Persons

And the number of allowances is: — The Tentative Withholding Amount is:

If the Wage Amount (line 1a) is — At least	But less than	0	1	2	3	4	5	6	7	8	9	10
$1,045	$1,055	$51	$33	$15	$0	$0	$0	$0	$0	$0	$0	$0
$1,055	$1,065	$52	$34	$16	$0	$0	$0	$0	$0	$0	$0	$0
$1,065	$1,075	$53	$35	$17	$0	$0	$0	$0	$0	$0	$0	$0
$1,075	$1,085	$54	$36	$18	$0	$0	$0	$0	$0	$0	$0	$0
$1,085	$1,095	$55	$37	$19	$1	$0	$0	$0	$0	$0	$0	$0
$1,095	$1,105	$56	$38	$20	$2	$0	$0	$0	$0	$0	$0	$0
$1,105	$1,115	$57	$39	$21	$3	$0	$0	$0	$0	$0	$0	$0
$1,115	$1,125	$58	$40	$22	$4	$0	$0	$0	$0	$0	$0	$0
$1,125	$1,135	$59	$41	$23	$5	$0	$0	$0	$0	$0	$0	$0
$1,135	$1,145	$60	$42	$24	$6	$0	$0	$0	$0	$0	$0	$0
$1,145	$1,155	$61	$43	$25	$7	$0	$0	$0	$0	$0	$0	$0
$1,155	$1,165	$62	$44	$26	$8	$0	$0	$0	$0	$0	$0	$0
$1,165	$1,175	$63	$45	$27	$9	$0	$0	$0	$0	$0	$0	$0
$1,175	$1,185	$64	$46	$28	$10	$0	$0	$0	$0	$0	$0	$0
$1,185	$1,195	$65	$47	$29	$11	$0	$0	$0	$0	$0	$0	$0
$1,195	$1,205	$66	$48	$30	$12	$0	$0	$0	$0	$0	$0	$0
$1,205	$1,215	$67	$49	$31	$13	$0	$0	$0	$0	$0	$0	$0
$1,215	$1,225	$68	$50	$32	$14	$0	$0	$0	$0	$0	$0	$0
$1,225	$1,235	$69	$51	$33	$15	$0	$0	$0	$0	$0	$0	$0
$1,235	$1,245	$70	$52	$34	$16	$0	$0	$0	$0	$0	$0	$0
$1,245	$1,255	$71	$53	$35	$17	$0	$0	$0	$0	$0	$0	$0
$1,255	$1,265	$72	$54	$36	$18	$0	$0	$0	$0	$0	$0	$0
$1,265	$1,275	$73	$55	$37	$19	$1	$0	$0	$0	$0	$0	$0
$1,275	$1,285	$74	$56	$38	$20	$2	$0	$0	$0	$0	$0	$0
$1,285	$1,295	$75	$57	$39	$21	$3	$0	$0	$0	$0	$0	$0
$1,295	$1,305	$76	$58	$40	$22	$4	$0	$0	$0	$0	$0	$0
$1,305	$1,315	$77	$59	$41	$23	$5	$0	$0	$0	$0	$0	$0
$1,315	$1,325	$78	$60	$42	$24	$6	$0	$0	$0	$0	$0	$0
$1,325	$1,335	$79	$61	$43	$25	$7	$0	$0	$0	$0	$0	$0
$1,335	$1,345	$80	$62	$44	$26	$8	$0	$0	$0	$0	$0	$0
$1,345	$1,355	$81	$63	$45	$27	$9	$0	$0	$0	$0	$0	$0
$1,355	$1,365	$82	$64	$46	$28	$10	$0	$0	$0	$0	$0	$0
$1,365	$1,375	$83	$65	$47	$29	$11	$0	$0	$0	$0	$0	$0
$1,375	$1,385	$84	$66	$48	$30	$12	$0	$0	$0	$0	$0	$0
$1,385	$1,395	$85	$67	$49	$31	$13	$0	$0	$0	$0	$0	$0
$1,395	$1,405	$86	$68	$50	$32	$14	$0	$0	$0	$0	$0	$0
$1,405	$1,445	$89	$70	$51	$35	$17	$0	$0	$0	$0	$0	$0
$1,445	$1,485	$94	$74	$55	$39	$21	$3	$0	$0	$0	$0	$0
$1,485	$1,525	$98	$78	$59	$43	$25	$7	$0	$0	$0	$0	$0
$1,525	$1,565	$103	$82	$63	$47	$29	$11	$0	$0	$0	$0	$0
$1,565	$1,605	$108	$87	$67	$51	$33	$15	$0	$0	$0	$0	$0
$1,605	$1,645	$113	$91	$72	$55	$37	$19	$1	$0	$0	$0	$0
$1,645	$1,685	$118	$96	$76	$59	$41	$23	$5	$0	$0	$0	$0
$1,685	$1,725	$122	$101	$81	$63	$45	$27	$9	$0	$0	$0	$0
$1,725	$1,765	$127	$106	$85	$67	$49	$31	$13	$0	$0	$0	$0
$1,765	$1,805	$132	$111	$89	$71	$53	$35	$17	$0	$0	$0	$0
$1,805	$1,845	$137	$115	$94	$75	$57	$39	$21	$3	$0	$0	$0
$1,845	$1,885	$142	$120	$99	$79	$61	$43	$25	$7	$0	$0	$0
$1,885	$1,925	$146	$125	$103	$83	$65	$47	$29	$11	$0	$0	$0
$1,925	$1,965	$151	$130	$108	$87	$69	$51	$33	$15	$0	$0	$0
$1,965	$2,005	$156	$135	$113	$92	$73	$55	$37	$19	$1	$0	$0

TAX TABLE *D (Continued)

2022 Wage Bracket Method Tables for Manual Payroll Systems With Forms W-4 From 2019 or Earlier

SEMIMONTHLY Payroll Period

SEMIMONTHLY MARRIED PERSONS

MARRIED Persons

If the Wage Amount (line 1a) At least	But less than	And the number of allowances is:										
		0	1	2	3	4	5	6	7	8	9	10
		The Tentative Withholding Amount is:										
$2,005	$2,045	$161	$139	$118	$96	$77	$59	$41	$23	$5	$0	$0
$2,045	$2,085	$166	$144	$123	$101	$81	$63	$45	$27	$9	$0	$0
$2,085	$2,125	$170	$149	$127	$106	$85	$67	$49	$31	$13	$0	$0
$2,125	$2,165	$175	$154	$132	$111	$89	$71	$53	$35	$17	$0	$0
$2,165	$2,205	$180	$159	$137	$116	$94	$75	$57	$39	$21	$3	$0
$2,205	$2,245	$185	$163	$142	$120	$99	$79	$61	$43	$25	$7	$0
$2,245	$2,285	$190	$168	$147	$125	$104	$83	$65	$47	$29	$11	$0
$2,285	$2,325	$194	$173	$151	$130	$108	$87	$69	$51	$33	$15	$0
$2,325	$2,365	$199	$178	$156	$135	$113	$92	$73	$55	$37	$19	$1
$2,365	$2,405	$204	$183	$161	$140	$118	$97	$77	$59	$41	$23	$5
$2,405	$2,445	$209	$187	$166	$144	$123	$101	$81	$63	$45	$27	$9
$2,445	$2,485	$214	$192	$171	$149	$128	$106	$85	$67	$49	$31	$13
$2,485	$2,525	$218	$197	$175	$154	$132	$111	$89	$71	$53	$35	$17
$2,525	$2,565	$223	$202	$180	$159	$137	$116	$94	$75	$57	$39	$21
$2,565	$2,605	$228	$207	$185	$164	$142	$121	$99	$79	$61	$43	$25
$2,605	$2,645	$233	$211	$190	$168	$147	$125	$104	$83	$65	$47	$29
$2,645	$2,685	$238	$216	$195	$173	$152	$130	$109	$87	$69	$51	$33
$2,685	$2,725	$242	$221	$199	$178	$156	$135	$113	$92	$73	$55	$37
$2,725	$2,765	$247	$226	$204	$183	$161	$140	$118	$97	$77	$59	$41
$2,765	$2,805	$252	$231	$209	$188	$166	$145	$123	$102	$81	$63	$45
$2,805	$2,845	$257	$235	$214	$192	$171	$149	$128	$106	$85	$67	$49
$2,845	$2,885	$262	$240	$219	$197	$176	$154	$133	$111	$90	$71	$53
$2,885	$2,925	$266	$245	$223	$202	$180	$159	$137	$116	$94	$75	$57
$2,925	$2,965	$271	$250	$228	$207	$185	$164	$142	$121	$99	$79	$61
$2,965	$3,005	$276	$255	$233	$212	$190	$169	$147	$126	$104	$83	$65
$3,005	$3,045	$281	$259	$238	$216	$195	$173	$152	$130	$109	$87	$69
$3,045	$3,085	$286	$264	$243	$221	$200	$178	$157	$135	$114	$92	$73
$3,085	$3,125	$290	$269	$247	$226	$204	$183	$161	$140	$118	$97	$77
$3,125	$3,165	$295	$274	$252	$231	$209	$188	$166	$145	$123	$102	$81
$3,165	$3,205	$300	$279	$257	$236	$214	$193	$171	$150	$128	$107	$85
$3,205	$3,245	$305	$283	$262	$240	$219	$197	$176	$154	$133	$111	$90
$3,245	$3,285	$310	$288	$267	$245	$224	$202	$181	$159	$138	$116	$95

TAX TABLE *D (Continued)

SEMIMONTHLY SINGLE PERSONS

2022 Wage Bracket Method Tables for Manual Payroll Systems With Forms W-4 From 2019 or Earlier — SEMIMONTHLY Payroll Period — SINGLE Persons

If the Wage Amount (line 1a) is — And the number of allowances is: — The Tentative Withholding Amount is:

At least	But less than	0	1	2	3	4	5	6	7	8	9	10
$0	$185	$0	$0	$0	$0	$0	$0	$0	$0	$0	$0	$0
$185	$195	$1	$0	$0	$0	$0	$0	$0	$0	$0	$0	$0
$195	$205	$2	$0	$0	$0	$0	$0	$0	$0	$0	$0	$0
$205	$215	$3	$0	$0	$0	$0	$0	$0	$0	$0	$0	$0
$215	$225	$4	$0	$0	$0	$0	$0	$0	$0	$0	$0	$0
$225	$235	$5	$0	$0	$0	$0	$0	$0	$0	$0	$0	$0
$235	$245	$6	$0	$0	$0	$0	$0	$0	$0	$0	$0	$0
$245	$255	$7	$0	$0	$0	$0	$0	$0	$0	$0	$0	$0
$255	$265	$8	$0	$0	$0	$0	$0	$0	$0	$0	$0	$0
$265	$275	$9	$0	$0	$0	$0	$0	$0	$0	$0	$0	$0
$275	$285	$10	$0	$0	$0	$0	$0	$0	$0	$0	$0	$0
$285	$295	$11	$0	$0	$0	$0	$0	$0	$0	$0	$0	$0
$295	$305	$12	$0	$0	$0	$0	$0	$0	$0	$0	$0	$0
$305	$315	$13	$0	$0	$0	$0	$0	$0	$0	$0	$0	$0
$315	$325	$14	$0	$0	$0	$0	$0	$0	$0	$0	$0	$0
$325	$335	$15	$0	$0	$0	$0	$0	$0	$0	$0	$0	$0
$335	$345	$16	$0	$0	$0	$0	$0	$0	$0	$0	$0	$0
$345	$355	$17	$0	$0	$0	$0	$0	$0	$0	$0	$0	$0
$355	$365	$18	$0	$0	$0	$0	$0	$0	$0	$0	$0	$0
$365	$375	$19	$0	$0	$0	$0	$0	$0	$0	$0	$0	$0
$375	$385	$20	$0	$0	$0	$0	$0	$0	$0	$0	$0	$0
$385	$395	$21	$1	$0	$0	$0	$0	$0	$0	$0	$0	$0
$395	$405	$22	$2	$0	$0	$0	$0	$0	$0	$0	$0	$0
$405	$415	$23	$3	$0	$0	$0	$0	$0	$0	$0	$0	$0
$415	$425	$24	$4	$0	$0	$0	$0	$0	$0	$0	$0	$0
$425	$435	$25	$5	$0	$0	$0	$0	$0	$0	$0	$0	$0
$435	$445	$26	$6	$0	$0	$0	$0	$0	$0	$0	$0	$0
$445	$455	$27	$7	$0	$0	$0	$0	$0	$0	$0	$0	$0
$455	$465	$28	$8	$0	$0	$0	$0	$0	$0	$0	$0	$0
$465	$475	$29	$9	$0	$0	$0	$0	$0	$0	$0	$0	$0
$475	$485	$30	$10	$0	$0	$0	$0	$0	$0	$0	$0	$0
$485	$495	$31	$11	$0	$0	$0	$0	$0	$0	$0	$0	$0
$495	$505	$32	$12	$0	$0	$0	$0	$0	$0	$0	$0	$0
$505	$515	$33	$13	$0	$0	$0	$0	$0	$0	$0	$0	$0
$515	$525	$34	$14	$0	$0	$0	$0	$0	$0	$0	$0	$0
$525	$535	$35	$15	$0	$0	$0	$0	$0	$0	$0	$0	$0
$535	$545	$36	$16	$0	$0	$0	$0	$0	$0	$0	$0	$0
$545	$555	$37	$17	$0	$0	$0	$0	$0	$0	$0	$0	$0
$555	$565	$38	$18	$1	$0	$0	$0	$0	$0	$0	$0	$0
$565	$575	$39	$19	$2	$0	$0	$0	$0	$0	$0	$0	$0
$575	$585	$40	$20	$3	$0	$0	$0	$0	$0	$0	$0	$0
$585	$595	$41	$21	$4	$0	$0	$0	$0	$0	$0	$0	$0
$595	$605	$42	$22	$5	$0	$0	$0	$0	$0	$0	$0	$0
$605	$615	$43	$23	$6	$0	$0	$0	$0	$0	$0	$0	$0
$615	$655	$46	$27	$10	$0	$0	$0	$0	$0	$0	$0	$0
$655	$695	$51	$31	$14	$0	$0	$0	$0	$0	$0	$0	$0
$695	$735	$55	$35	$18	$0	$0	$0	$0	$0	$0	$0	$0
$735	$775	$60	$39	$22	$4	$0	$0	$0	$0	$0	$0	$0
$775	$815	$65	$44	$26	$8	$0	$0	$0	$0	$0	$0	$0
$815	$855	$70	$48	$30	$12	$0	$0	$0	$0	$0	$0	$0
$855	$895	$75	$53	$34	$16	$0	$0	$0	$0	$0	$0	$0

2022 Wage Bracket Method Tables for Manual Payroll Systems With Forms W-4 From 2019 or Earlier — SEMIMONTHLY Payroll Period — SINGLE Persons

If the Wage Amount (line 1a) is — And the number of allowances is: — The Tentative Withholding Amount is:

At least	But less than	0	1	2	3	4	5	6	7	8	9	10
$895	$935	$79	$58	$38	$20	$2	$0	$0	$0	$0	$0	$0
$935	$975	$84	$63	$42	$24	$6	$0	$0	$0	$0	$0	$0
$975	$1,015	$89	$68	$46	$28	$10	$0	$0	$0	$0	$0	$0
$1,015	$1,055	$94	$72	$51	$32	$14	$0	$0	$0	$0	$0	$0
$1,055	$1,095	$99	$77	$56	$36	$18	$0	$0	$0	$0	$0	$0
$1,095	$1,135	$103	$82	$60	$40	$22	$4	$0	$0	$0	$0	$0
$1,135	$1,175	$108	$87	$65	$44	$26	$8	$0	$0	$0	$0	$0
$1,175	$1,215	$113	$92	$70	$49	$30	$12	$0	$0	$0	$0	$0
$1,215	$1,255	$118	$96	$75	$53	$34	$16	$0	$0	$0	$0	$0
$1,255	$1,295	$123	$101	$80	$58	$38	$20	$2	$0	$0	$0	$0
$1,295	$1,335	$127	$106	$84	$63	$42	$24	$6	$0	$0	$0	$0
$1,335	$1,375	$132	$111	$89	$68	$46	$28	$10	$0	$0	$0	$0
$1,375	$1,415	$137	$116	$94	$73	$51	$32	$14	$0	$0	$0	$0
$1,415	$1,455	$142	$120	$99	$77	$56	$36	$18	$1	$0	$0	$0
$1,455	$1,495	$147	$125	$104	$82	$61	$40	$22	$4	$0	$0	$0
$1,495	$1,535	$151	$130	$108	$87	$65	$44	$26	$8	$0	$0	$0
$1,535	$1,575	$156	$135	$113	$92	$70	$49	$30	$12	$0	$0	$0
$1,575	$1,615	$161	$140	$118	$97	$75	$54	$34	$16	$0	$0	$0
$1,615	$1,655	$166	$144	$123	$101	$80	$58	$38	$20	$2	$0	$0
$1,655	$1,695	$171	$149	$128	$106	$85	$63	$42	$24	$6	$0	$0
$1,695	$1,735	$175	$154	$132	$111	$89	$68	$46	$28	$10	$0	$0
$1,735	$1,775	$180	$159	$137	$116	$94	$73	$51	$32	$14	$0	$0
$1,775	$1,815	$185	$164	$142	$121	$99	$78	$56	$36	$18	$1	$0
$1,815	$1,855	$190	$168	$147	$125	$104	$82	$61	$40	$22	$4	$0
$1,855	$1,895	$195	$173	$152	$130	$109	$87	$65	$44	$26	$8	$0
$1,895	$1,935	$199	$178	$156	$135	$113	$92	$70	$49	$30	$12	$0
$1,935	$1,975	$208	$183	$161	$140	$118	$97	$75	$54	$34	$16	$0
$1,975	$2,015	$216	$188	$166	$145	$123	$102	$80	$58	$38	$20	$2
$2,015	$2,055	$225	$192	$171	$149	$128	$106	$85	$63	$42	$24	$6
$2,055	$2,095	$234	$197	$176	$154	$133	$111	$89	$68	$47	$28	$10
$2,095	$2,135	$243	$203	$180	$159	$137	$116	$94	$73	$51	$32	$14
$2,135	$2,175	$252	$212	$185	$164	$142	$121	$99	$78	$56	$36	$18
$2,175	$2,215	$260	$221	$190	$169	$147	$126	$104	$82	$61	$40	$22
$2,215	$2,255	$269	$230	$195	$173	$152	$130	$108	$87	$66	$44	$26
$2,255	$2,295	$278	$239	$200	$178	$157	$135	$113	$92	$71	$49	$30
$2,295	$2,335	$287	$247	$208	$183	$161	$140	$118	$97	$75	$54	$34
$2,335	$2,375	$296	$256	$217	$188	$166	$145	$123	$102	$80	$59	$38
$2,375	$2,415	$304	$265	$226	$193	$171	$150	$128	$106	$85	$64	$42
$2,415	$2,455	$313	$274	$234	$197	$176	$154	$132	$111	$90	$68	$47
$2,455	$2,495	$322	$283	$243	$204	$181	$159	$137	$116	$95	$73	$52
$2,495	$2,535	$331	$291	$252	$213	$185	$164	$142	$121	$99	$78	$56
$2,535	$2,575	$340	$300	$261	$221	$190	$169	$147	$126	$104	$83	$61
$2,575	$2,615	$348	$309	$270	$230	$195	$174	$152	$130	$109	$88	$66
$2,615	$2,655	$357	$318	$278	$239	$200	$178	$156	$135	$114	$92	$71
$2,655	$2,695	$366	$327	$287	$248	$208	$183	$161	$140	$119	$97	$76
$2,695	$2,735	$375	$335	$296	$257	$217	$188	$166	$145	$123	$102	$80
$2,735	$2,775	$384	$344	$305	$265	$226	$193	$171	$150	$128	$107	$85
$2,775	$2,815	$392	$353	$314	$274	$235	$198	$176	$154	$133	$112	$90
$2,815	$2,855	$401	$362	$322	$283	$244	$204	$181	$159	$138	$116	$95
$2,855	$2,895	$410	$371	$331	$292	$252	$213	$186	$164	$143	$121	$100
$2,895	$2,935	$419	$379	$340	$301	$261	$222	$190	$169	$147	$126	$104

TAX TABLE *D (Continued)

2022 Wage Bracket Method Tables for Manual Payroll Systems With Forms W-4 From 2019 or Earlier

SEMIMONTHLY SINGLE PERSONS

SEMIMONTHLY Payroll Period — SINGLE Persons

| If the Wage Amount (line 1a) is | | And the number of allowances is: | | | | | | | | | | |
At least	But less than	0	1	2	3	4	5	6	7	8	9	10
		The Tentative Withholding Amount is:										
$2,935	$2,975	$428	$388	$349	$309	$270	$231	$195	$174	$152	$131	$109
$2,975	$3,015	$436	$397	$358	$318	$279	$239	$200	$179	$157	$136	$114
$3,015	$3,055	$445	$406	$366	$327	$288	$248	$209	$183	$162	$140	$119
$3,055	$3,095	$454	$415	$375	$336	$296	$257	$218	$188	$167	$145	$124
$3,095	$3,135	$463	$423	$384	$345	$305	$266	$226	$193	$171	$150	$128
$3,135	$3,175	$472	$432	$393	$353	$314	$275	$235	$198	$176	$155	$133
$3,175	$3,215	$480	$441	$402	$362	$323	$283	$244	$204	$181	$160	$138
$3,215	$3,255	$489	$450	$410	$371	$332	$292	$253	$213	$186	$164	$143
$3,255	$3,295	$498	$459	$419	$380	$340	$301	$262	$222	$191	$169	$148
$3,295	$3,335	$507	$467	$428	$389	$349	$310	$270	$231	$195	$174	$152
$3,335	$3,375	$516	$476	$437	$397	$358	$319	$279	$240	$200	$179	$157
$3,375	$3,415	$524	$485	$446	$406	$367	$327	$288	$248	$209	$184	$162
$3,415	$3,455	$533	$494	$454	$415	$376	$336	$297	$257	$218	$188	$167
$3,455	$3,495	$542	$503	$463	$424	$384	$345	$306	$266	$227	$193	$172
$3,495	$3,535	$551	$511	$472	$433	$393	$354	$314	$275	$235	$198	$176
$3,535	$3,575	$560	$520	$481	$441	$402	$363	$323	$284	$244	$205	$181
$3,575	$3,615	$568	$529	$490	$450	$411	$371	$332	$292	$253	$214	$186
$3,615	$3,655	$577	$538	$498	$459	$420	$380	$341	$301	$262	$222	$191
$3,655	$3,695	$586	$547	$507	$468	$428	$389	$350	$310	$271	$231	$196
$3,695	$3,735	$595	$555	$516	$477	$437	$398	$358	$319	$279	$240	$201
$3,735	$3,775	$604	$564	$525	$485	$446	$407	$367	$328	$288	$249	$209
$3,775	$3,815	$612	$573	$534	$494	$455	$415	$376	$336	$297	$258	$218
$3,815	$3,855	$621	$582	$542	$503	$464	$424	$385	$345	$306	$266	$227
$3,855	$3,895	$630	$591	$551	$512	$472	$433	$394	$354	$315	$275	$236
$3,895	$3,935	$639	$599	$560	$521	$481	$442	$402	$363	$323	$284	$245
$3,935	$3,975	$649	$608	$569	$529	$490	$451	$411	$372	$332	$293	$253
$3,975	$4,015	$658	$617	$578	$538	$499	$459	$420	$380	$341	$302	$262
$4,015	$4,055	$668	$626	$586	$547	$508	$468	$429	$389	$350	$310	$271

TAX TABLE *D (Continued)

MONTHLY MARRIED PERSONS

2022 Wage Bracket Method Tables for Manual Payroll Systems With Forms W-4 From 2019 or Earlier — MONTHLY Payroll Period — MARRIED Persons

And the number of allowances is: — The Tentative Withholding Amount is:

If the Wage Amount (line 1a) is												
At least	But less than	0	1	2	3	4	5	6	7	8	9	10
$0	$1,085	$0	$0	$0	$0	$0	$0	$0	$0	$0	$0	$0
$1,085	$1,125	$2	$0	$0	$0	$0	$0	$0	$0	$0	$0	$0
$1,125	$1,165	$6	$0	$0	$0	$0	$0	$0	$0	$0	$0	$0
$1,165	$1,205	$10	$0	$0	$0	$0	$0	$0	$0	$0	$0	$0
$1,205	$1,245	$14	$0	$0	$0	$0	$0	$0	$0	$0	$0	$0
$1,245	$1,285	$18	$0	$0	$0	$0	$0	$0	$0	$0	$0	$0
$1,285	$1,325	$22	$0	$0	$0	$0	$0	$0	$0	$0	$0	$0
$1,325	$1,365	$26	$0	$0	$0	$0	$0	$0	$0	$0	$0	$0
$1,365	$1,405	$30	$0	$0	$0	$0	$0	$0	$0	$0	$0	$0
$1,405	$1,445	$34	$0	$0	$0	$0	$0	$0	$0	$0	$0	$0
$1,445	$1,485	$38	$2	$0	$0	$0	$0	$0	$0	$0	$0	$0
$1,485	$1,525	$42	$6	$0	$0	$0	$0	$0	$0	$0	$0	$0
$1,525	$1,565	$46	$10	$0	$0	$0	$0	$0	$0	$0	$0	$0
$1,565	$1,605	$50	$14	$0	$0	$0	$0	$0	$0	$0	$0	$0
$1,605	$1,645	$54	$18	$0	$0	$0	$0	$0	$0	$0	$0	$0
$1,645	$1,685	$58	$22	$0	$0	$0	$0	$0	$0	$0	$0	$0
$1,685	$1,725	$62	$26	$0	$0	$0	$0	$0	$0	$0	$0	$0
$1,725	$1,765	$66	$30	$0	$0	$0	$0	$0	$0	$0	$0	$0
$1,765	$1,805	$70	$34	$0	$0	$0	$0	$0	$0	$0	$0	$0
$1,805	$1,845	$74	$38	$2	$0	$0	$0	$0	$0	$0	$0	$0
$1,845	$1,885	$78	$42	$6	$0	$0	$0	$0	$0	$0	$0	$0
$1,885	$1,925	$82	$46	$10	$0	$0	$0	$0	$0	$0	$0	$0
$1,925	$1,965	$86	$50	$14	$0	$0	$0	$0	$0	$0	$0	$0
$1,965	$2,005	$90	$54	$18	$0	$0	$0	$0	$0	$0	$0	$0
$2,005	$2,045	$94	$58	$22	$0	$0	$0	$0	$0	$0	$0	$0
$2,045	$2,085	$98	$62	$26	$0	$0	$0	$0	$0	$0	$0	$0
$2,085	$2,125	$102	$66	$30	$0	$0	$0	$0	$0	$0	$0	$0
$2,125	$2,165	$106	$70	$34	$0	$0	$0	$0	$0	$0	$0	$0
$2,165	$2,205	$110	$74	$38	$2	$0	$0	$0	$0	$0	$0	$0
$2,205	$2,245	$114	$78	$42	$6	$0	$0	$0	$0	$0	$0	$0
$2,245	$2,285	$118	$82	$46	$10	$0	$0	$0	$0	$0	$0	$0
$2,285	$2,325	$122	$86	$50	$14	$0	$0	$0	$0	$0	$0	$0
$2,325	$2,365	$126	$90	$54	$18	$0	$0	$0	$0	$0	$0	$0
$2,365	$2,405	$130	$94	$58	$22	$0	$0	$0	$0	$0	$0	$0
$2,405	$2,445	$134	$98	$62	$26	$0	$0	$0	$0	$0	$0	$0
$2,445	$2,485	$138	$102	$66	$30	$0	$0	$0	$0	$0	$0	$0
$2,485	$2,525	$142	$106	$70	$34	$0	$0	$0	$0	$0	$0	$0
$2,525	$2,565	$146	$110	$74	$38	$2	$0	$0	$0	$0	$0	$0
$2,565	$2,605	$150	$114	$78	$42	$6	$0	$0	$0	$0	$0	$0
$2,605	$2,645	$154	$118	$82	$46	$10	$0	$0	$0	$0	$0	$0
$2,645	$2,685	$158	$122	$86	$50	$14	$0	$0	$0	$0	$0	$0
$2,685	$2,725	$162	$126	$90	$54	$18	$0	$0	$0	$0	$0	$0
$2,725	$2,765	$166	$130	$94	$58	$22	$0	$0	$0	$0	$0	$0
$2,765	$2,805	$170	$134	$98	$62	$26	$0	$0	$0	$0	$0	$0
$2,805	$2,865	$176	$139	$104	$68	$32	$0	$0	$0	$0	$0	$0
$2,865	$2,925	$183	$145	$110	$74	$38	$2	$0	$0	$0	$0	$0
$2,925	$2,985	$190	$151	$116	$80	$44	$8	$0	$0	$0	$0	$0
$2,985	$3,045	$198	$157	$122	$86	$50	$14	$0	$0	$0	$0	$0
$3,045	$3,105	$205	$163	$128	$92	$56	$20	$0	$0	$0	$0	$0
$3,105	$3,165	$212	$169	$134	$98	$62	$26	$0	$0	$0	$0	$0
$3,165	$3,225	$219	$176	$140	$104	$68	$32	$0	$0	$0	$0	$0

2022 Wage Bracket Method Tables for Manual Payroll Systems With Forms W-4 From 2019 or Earlier — MONTHLY Payroll Period — MARRIED Persons

And the number of allowances is: — The Tentative Withholding Amount is:

If the Wage Amount (line 1a) is												
At least	But less than	0	1	2	3	4	5	6	7	8	9	10
$3,225	$3,285	$226	$183	$146	$110	$74	$38	$2	$0	$0	$0	$0
$3,285	$3,345	$234	$191	$152	$116	$80	$44	$8	$0	$0	$0	$0
$3,345	$3,405	$241	$198	$158	$122	$86	$50	$14	$0	$0	$0	$0
$3,405	$3,465	$248	$205	$164	$128	$92	$56	$20	$0	$0	$0	$0
$3,465	$3,525	$255	$212	$170	$134	$98	$62	$26	$0	$0	$0	$0
$3,525	$3,585	$262	$219	$176	$140	$104	$68	$32	$0	$0	$0	$0
$3,585	$3,645	$270	$227	$184	$146	$110	$74	$38	$2	$0	$0	$0
$3,645	$3,705	$277	$234	$191	$152	$116	$80	$44	$8	$0	$0	$0
$3,705	$3,765	$284	$241	$198	$158	$122	$86	$50	$14	$0	$0	$0
$3,765	$3,825	$291	$248	$205	$164	$128	$92	$56	$20	$0	$0	$0
$3,825	$3,885	$298	$255	$212	$170	$134	$98	$62	$26	$0	$0	$0
$3,885	$3,945	$306	$263	$220	$177	$140	$104	$68	$32	$0	$0	$0
$3,945	$4,005	$313	$270	$227	$184	$146	$110	$74	$38	$3	$0	$0
$4,005	$4,065	$320	$277	$234	$191	$152	$116	$80	$44	$9	$0	$0
$4,065	$4,125	$327	$284	$241	$198	$158	$122	$86	$50	$15	$0	$0
$4,125	$4,185	$334	$291	$248	$205	$164	$128	$92	$56	$21	$0	$0
$4,185	$4,245	$342	$299	$256	$213	$170	$134	$98	$62	$27	$0	$0
$4,245	$4,305	$349	$306	$263	$220	$177	$140	$104	$68	$33	$0	$0
$4,305	$4,365	$356	$313	$270	$227	$184	$146	$110	$74	$39	$3	$0
$4,365	$4,425	$363	$320	$277	$234	$191	$152	$116	$80	$45	$9	$0
$4,425	$4,485	$370	$327	$284	$241	$198	$158	$122	$86	$51	$15	$0
$4,485	$4,545	$378	$335	$292	$249	$205	$164	$128	$92	$57	$21	$0
$4,545	$4,605	$385	$342	$299	$256	$213	$170	$134	$98	$63	$27	$0
$4,605	$4,665	$392	$349	$306	$263	$220	$177	$140	$104	$69	$33	$0
$4,665	$4,725	$399	$356	$313	$270	$227	$184	$146	$110	$75	$39	$3
$4,725	$4,785	$406	$363	$320	$277	$234	$191	$152	$116	$81	$45	$9
$4,785	$4,845	$414	$371	$328	$285	$242	$199	$158	$122	$87	$51	$15
$4,845	$4,905	$421	$378	$335	$292	$249	$206	$164	$128	$93	$57	$21
$4,905	$4,965	$428	$385	$342	$299	$256	$213	$170	$134	$99	$63	$27
$4,965	$5,025	$435	$392	$349	$306	$263	$220	$177	$140	$105	$69	$33
$5,025	$5,085	$442	$399	$356	$313	$270	$227	$184	$146	$111	$75	$39
$5,085	$5,145	$450	$407	$364	$321	$278	$235	$192	$152	$117	$81	$45
$5,145	$5,205	$457	$414	$371	$328	$285	$242	$199	$158	$123	$87	$51
$5,205	$5,265	$464	$421	$378	$335	$292	$249	$206	$164	$129	$93	$57
$5,265	$5,325	$471	$428	$385	$342	$299	$256	$213	$170	$135	$99	$63
$5,325	$5,385	$478	$435	$392	$349	$306	$263	$220	$177	$141	$105	$69
$5,385	$5,445	$486	$443	$400	$357	$314	$271	$228	$185	$147	$111	$75
$5,445	$5,505	$493	$450	$407	$364	$321	$278	$235	$192	$153	$117	$81
$5,505	$5,565	$500	$457	$414	$371	$328	$285	$242	$199	$159	$123	$87
$5,565	$5,625	$507	$464	$421	$378	$335	$292	$249	$206	$165	$129	$93
$5,625	$5,685	$514	$471	$428	$385	$342	$299	$256	$213	$171	$135	$99
$5,685	$5,745	$522	$479	$436	$393	$350	$307	$264	$221	$178	$141	$105
$5,745	$5,805	$529	$486	$443	$400	$357	$314	$271	$228	$185	$147	$111
$5,805	$5,865	$536	$493	$450	$407	$364	$321	$278	$235	$192	$153	$117
$5,865	$5,925	$543	$500	$457	$414	$371	$328	$285	$242	$199	$159	$123
$5,925	$5,985	$550	$507	$464	$421	$378	$335	$292	$249	$206	$165	$129
$5,985	$6,045	$558	$515	$472	$429	$386	$343	$300	$257	$214	$171	$135
$6,045	$6,105	$565	$522	$479	$436	$393	$350	$307	$264	$221	$178	$141
$6,105	$6,165	$572	$529	$486	$443	$400	$357	$314	$271	$228	$185	$147
$6,165	$6,225	$579	$536	$493	$450	$407	$364	$321	$278	$235	$192	$153
$6,225	$6,285	$586	$543	$500	$457	$414	$371	$328	$285	$242	$199	$159

TAX TABLE *D (Continued)

2022 Wage Bracket Method Tables for Manual Payroll Systems With Forms W-4 From 2019 or Earlier

MONTHLY Payroll Period

MARRIED Persons

MONTHLY MARRIED PERSONS

If the Wage Amount (line 1a) is		And the number of allowances is:										
At least	But less than	0	1	2	3	4	5	6	7	8	9	10
		The Tentative Withholding Amount is:										
$6,285	$6,345	$594	$551	$508	$465	$422	$379	$336	$293	$250	$207	$165
$6,345	$6,405	$601	$558	$515	$472	$429	$386	$343	$300	$257	$214	$171
$6,405	$6,465	$608	$565	$522	$479	$436	$393	$350	$307	$264	$221	$178
$6,465	$6,525	$615	$572	$529	$486	$443	$400	$357	$314	$271	$228	$185
$6,525	$6,585	$622	$579	$536	$493	$450	$407	$364	$321	$278	$235	$192
$6,585	$6,645	$630	$587	$544	$501	$458	$415	$372	$329	$286	$243	$200
$6,645	$6,705	$637	$594	$551	$508	$465	$422	$379	$336	$293	$250	$207
$6,705	$6,765	$644	$601	$558	$515	$472	$429	$386	$343	$300	$257	$214
$6,765	$6,825	$651	$608	$565	$522	$479	$436	$393	$350	$307	$264	$221
$6,825	$6,885	$658	$615	$572	$529	$486	$443	$400	$357	$314	$271	$228
$6,885	$6,945	$666	$623	$580	$537	$494	$451	$408	$365	$322	$279	$236
$6,945	$7,005	$673	$630	$587	$544	$501	$458	$415	$372	$329	$286	$243
$7,005	$7,065	$680	$637	$594	$551	$508	$465	$422	$379	$336	$293	$250
$7,065	$7,125	$687	$644	$601	$558	$515	$472	$429	$386	$343	$300	$257
$7,125	$7,185	$694	$651	$608	$565	$522	$479	$436	$393	$350	$307	$264
$7,185	$7,245	$702	$659	$616	$573	$530	$487	$444	$401	$358	$315	$272
$7,245	$7,305	$709	$666	$623	$580	$537	$494	$451	$408	$365	$322	$279
$7,305	$7,365	$716	$673	$630	$587	$544	$501	$458	$415	$372	$329	$286
$7,365	$7,425	$723	$680	$637	$594	$551	$508	$465	$422	$379	$336	$293
$7,425	$7,485	$730	$687	$644	$601	$558	$515	$472	$429	$386	$343	$300
$7,485	$7,545	$738	$695	$652	$609	$566	$523	$480	$437	$394	$351	$308
$7,545	$7,605	$745	$702	$659	$616	$573	$530	$487	$444	$401	$358	$315
$7,605	$7,665	$752	$709	$666	$623	$580	$537	$494	$451	$408	$365	$322
$7,665	$7,725	$759	$716	$673	$630	$587	$544	$501	$458	$415	$372	$329
$7,725	$7,785	$766	$723	$680	$637	$594	$551	$508	$465	$422	$379	$336
$7,785	$7,845	$774	$731	$688	$645	$602	$559	$516	$473	$430	$387	$344
$7,845	$7,905	$781	$738	$695	$652	$609	$566	$523	$480	$437	$394	$351
$7,905	$7,965	$788	$745	$702	$659	$616	$573	$530	$487	$444	$401	$358
$7,965	$8,025	$795	$752	$709	$666	$623	$580	$537	$494	$451	$408	$365
$8,025	$8,085	$803	$759	$716	$673	$630	$587	$544	$501	$458	$415	$372
$8,085	$8,155	$818	$767	$724	$681	$638	$595	$552	$509	$466	$423	$380
$8,155	$8,225	$833	$776	$733	$690	$647	$604	$561	$518	$475	$432	$389

TAX TABLE *D (Continued)

MONTHLY SINGLE PERSONS

2022 Wage Bracket Method Tables for Manual Payroll Systems With Forms W-4 From 2019 or Earlier

MONTHLY Payroll Period — SINGLE Persons

And the number of allowances is: — The Tentative Withholding Amount is:

If the Wage Amount (line 1a) is — At least	But less than	0	1	2	3	4	5	6	7	8	9	10
$0	$365	$0	$0	$0	$0	$0	$0	$0	$0	$0	$0	$0
$365	$395	$2	$0	$0	$0	$0	$0	$0	$0	$0	$0	$0
$395	$425	$5	$0	$0	$0	$0	$0	$0	$0	$0	$0	$0
$425	$455	$8	$0	$0	$0	$0	$0	$0	$0	$0	$0	$0
$455	$485	$11	$0	$0	$0	$0	$0	$0	$0	$0	$0	$0
$485	$515	$14	$0	$0	$0	$0	$0	$0	$0	$0	$0	$0
$515	$545	$17	$0	$0	$0	$0	$0	$0	$0	$0	$0	$0
$545	$575	$20	$0	$0	$0	$0	$0	$0	$0	$0	$0	$0
$575	$605	$23	$0	$0	$0	$0	$0	$0	$0	$0	$0	$0
$605	$635	$26	$0	$0	$0	$0	$0	$0	$0	$0	$0	$0
$635	$665	$29	$0	$0	$0	$0	$0	$0	$0	$0	$0	$0
$665	$695	$32	$0	$0	$0	$0	$0	$0	$0	$0	$0	$0
$695	$725	$35	$0	$0	$0	$0	$0	$0	$0	$0	$0	$0
$725	$755	$38	$0	$0	$0	$0	$0	$0	$0	$0	$0	$0
$755	$785	$41	$0	$0	$0	$0	$0	$0	$0	$0	$0	$0
$785	$815	$44	$8	$0	$0	$0	$0	$0	$0	$0	$0	$0
$815	$845	$47	$11	$0	$0	$0	$0	$0	$0	$0	$0	$0
$845	$875	$50	$14	$0	$0	$0	$0	$0	$0	$0	$0	$0
$875	$905	$53	$17	$0	$0	$0	$0	$0	$0	$0	$0	$0
$905	$935	$56	$20	$0	$0	$0	$0	$0	$0	$0	$0	$0
$935	$965	$59	$23	$0	$0	$0	$0	$0	$0	$0	$0	$0
$965	$995	$62	$26	$0	$0	$0	$0	$0	$0	$0	$0	$0
$995	$1,025	$65	$29	$0	$0	$0	$0	$0	$0	$0	$0	$0
$1,025	$1,055	$68	$32	$0	$0	$0	$0	$0	$0	$0	$0	$0
$1,055	$1,085	$71	$35	$0	$0	$0	$0	$0	$0	$0	$0	$0
$1,085	$1,115	$74	$38	$2	$0	$0	$0	$0	$0	$0	$0	$0
$1,115	$1,145	$77	$41	$5	$0	$0	$0	$0	$0	$0	$0	$0
$1,145	$1,175	$80	$44	$8	$0	$0	$0	$0	$0	$0	$0	$0
$1,175	$1,205	$83	$47	$11	$0	$0	$0	$0	$0	$0	$0	$0
$1,205	$1,235	$86	$50	$14	$0	$0	$0	$0	$0	$0	$0	$0
$1,235	$1,295	$91	$54	$19	$0	$0	$0	$0	$0	$0	$0	$0
$1,295	$1,355	$98	$60	$25	$0	$0	$0	$0	$0	$0	$0	$0
$1,355	$1,415	$106	$66	$31	$0	$0	$0	$0	$0	$0	$0	$0
$1,415	$1,475	$113	$72	$37	$1	$0	$0	$0	$0	$0	$0	$0
$1,475	$1,535	$120	$78	$43	$7	$0	$0	$0	$0	$0	$0	$0
$1,535	$1,595	$127	$84	$49	$13	$0	$0	$0	$0	$0	$0	$0
$1,595	$1,655	$134	$91	$55	$19	$0	$0	$0	$0	$0	$0	$0
$1,655	$1,715	$142	$99	$61	$25	$0	$0	$0	$0	$0	$0	$0
$1,715	$1,775	$149	$106	$67	$31	$0	$0	$0	$0	$0	$0	$0
$1,775	$1,835	$156	$113	$73	$37	$1	$0	$0	$0	$0	$0	$0
$1,835	$1,895	$163	$120	$79	$43	$7	$0	$0	$0	$0	$0	$0
$1,895	$1,955	$170	$127	$85	$49	$13	$0	$0	$0	$0	$0	$0
$1,955	$2,015	$178	$135	$92	$55	$19	$0	$0	$0	$0	$0	$0
$2,015	$2,075	$185	$142	$99	$61	$25	$0	$0	$0	$0	$0	$0
$2,075	$2,135	$192	$149	$106	$67	$31	$0	$0	$0	$0	$0	$0
$2,135	$2,195	$199	$156	$113	$73	$37	$1	$0	$0	$0	$0	$0
$2,195	$2,255	$206	$163	$120	$79	$43	$7	$0	$0	$0	$0	$0
$2,255	$2,315	$214	$171	$128	$85	$49	$13	$0	$0	$0	$0	$0
$2,315	$2,375	$221	$178	$135	$92	$55	$19	$0	$0	$0	$0	$0
$2,375	$2,435	$228	$185	$142	$99	$61	$25	$0	$0	$0	$0	$0
$2,435	$2,495	$235	$192	$149	$106	$67	$31	$0	$0	$0	$0	$0

2022 Wage Bracket Method Tables for Manual Payroll Systems With Forms W-4 From 2019 or Earlier

MONTHLY Payroll Period — SINGLE Persons

And the number of allowances is: — The Tentative Withholding Amount is:

If the Wage Amount (line 1a) is — At least	But less than	0	1	2	3	4	5	6	7	8	9	10
$2,495	$2,555	$242	$199	$156	$113	$73	$37	$1	$0	$0	$0	$0
$2,555	$2,615	$250	$207	$164	$121	$79	$43	$7	$0	$0	$0	$0
$2,615	$2,675	$257	$214	$171	$128	$85	$49	$13	$0	$0	$0	$0
$2,675	$2,735	$264	$221	$178	$135	$92	$55	$19	$0	$0	$0	$0
$2,735	$2,795	$271	$228	$185	$142	$99	$61	$25	$0	$0	$0	$0
$2,795	$2,855	$278	$235	$192	$149	$106	$67	$31	$0	$0	$0	$0
$2,855	$2,915	$286	$243	$200	$157	$114	$73	$37	$0	$0	$0	$0
$2,915	$2,975	$293	$250	$207	$164	$121	$79	$43	$0	$0	$0	$0
$2,975	$3,035	$300	$257	$214	$171	$128	$85	$49	$13	$0	$0	$0
$3,035	$3,095	$307	$264	$221	$178	$135	$92	$55	$19	$0	$0	$0
$3,095	$3,155	$314	$271	$228	$185	$142	$99	$61	$25	$0	$0	$0
$3,155	$3,215	$322	$279	$236	$193	$150	$107	$67	$31	$0	$0	$0
$3,215	$3,275	$329	$286	$243	$200	$157	$114	$73	$37	$2	$0	$0
$3,275	$3,335	$336	$293	$250	$207	$164	$121	$79	$43	$8	$0	$0
$3,335	$3,395	$343	$300	$257	$214	$171	$128	$85	$49	$14	$0	$0
$3,395	$3,455	$350	$307	$264	$221	$178	$135	$92	$55	$20	$0	$0
$3,455	$3,515	$358	$315	$272	$229	$186	$143	$100	$61	$26	$0	$0
$3,515	$3,575	$365	$322	$279	$236	$193	$150	$107	$67	$32	$0	$0
$3,575	$3,635	$372	$329	$286	$243	$200	$157	$114	$73	$38	$2	$0
$3,635	$3,695	$379	$336	$293	$250	$207	$164	$121	$79	$44	$8	$0
$3,695	$3,755	$386	$343	$300	$257	$214	$171	$128	$85	$50	$14	$0
$3,755	$3,815	$394	$351	$308	$265	$222	$179	$136	$93	$56	$20	$0
$3,815	$3,875	$401	$358	$315	$272	$229	$186	$143	$100	$62	$26	$0
$3,875	$3,945	$415	$366	$323	$280	$237	$194	$151	$108	$68	$32	$0
$3,945	$4,015	$431	$374	$331	$288	$245	$202	$159	$116	$75	$39	$3
$4,015	$4,085	$446	$382	$339	$296	$253	$210	$167	$124	$82	$46	$10
$4,085	$4,155	$461	$391	$348	$305	$262	$219	$176	$133	$90	$53	$17
$4,155	$4,225	$477	$399	$356	$313	$270	$227	$184	$141	$98	$60	$24
$4,225	$4,295	$492	$413	$365	$322	$279	$236	$193	$150	$107	$67	$31
$4,295	$4,365	$508	$429	$373	$330	$287	$244	$201	$158	$115	$74	$38
$4,365	$4,435	$523	$444	$381	$338	$295	$252	$209	$166	$123	$81	$45
$4,435	$4,505	$538	$460	$390	$347	$304	$261	$218	$175	$132	$89	$52
$4,505	$4,575	$554	$475	$398	$355	$312	$269	$226	$183	$140	$97	$59
$4,575	$4,645	$569	$490	$412	$364	$321	$278	$235	$192	$149	$106	$66
$4,645	$4,715	$585	$506	$427	$372	$329	$286	$243	$200	$157	$114	$73
$4,715	$4,785	$600	$521	$442	$380	$337	$294	$251	$208	$165	$122	$80
$4,785	$4,855	$615	$537	$458	$389	$346	$303	$260	$217	$174	$131	$88
$4,855	$4,925	$631	$552	$473	$397	$354	$311	$268	$225	$182	$139	$96
$4,925	$4,995	$646	$567	$489	$410	$363	$320	$277	$234	$191	$148	$105
$4,995	$5,065	$662	$583	$504	$425	$371	$328	$285	$242	$199	$156	$113
$5,065	$5,135	$677	$598	$519	$441	$379	$336	$293	$250	$207	$164	$121
$5,135	$5,205	$692	$614	$535	$456	$388	$345	$302	$259	$216	$173	$130
$5,205	$5,275	$708	$629	$550	$471	$396	$353	$310	$267	$224	$181	$138
$5,275	$5,345	$723	$644	$566	$487	$408	$362	$319	$276	$233	$190	$147
$5,345	$5,415	$739	$660	$581	$502	$423	$370	$327	$284	$241	$198	$155
$5,415	$5,485	$754	$675	$596	$518	$439	$378	$335	$292	$249	$206	$163
$5,485	$5,555	$769	$691	$612	$533	$454	$387	$344	$301	$258	$215	$172
$5,555	$5,625	$785	$706	$627	$548	$469	$395	$352	$309	$266	$223	$180
$5,625	$5,695	$800	$721	$643	$564	$485	$406	$361	$318	$275	$232	$189
$5,695	$5,765	$816	$737	$658	$579	$500	$421	$369	$326	$283	$240	$197
$5,765	$5,835	$831	$752	$673	$595	$516	$437	$377	$334	$291	$248	$205

TAX TABLE *D (Continued)

2022 Wage Bracket Method Tables for Manual Payroll Systems With Forms W-4 From 2019 or Earlier

MONTHLY Payroll Period

SINGLE Persons

MONTHLY SINGLE PERSONS

| If the Wage Amount (line 1a) is | | And the number of allowances is: | | | | | | | | | | |
At least	But less than	0	1	2	3	4	5	6	7	8	9	10
		The Tentative Withholding Amount is:										
$5,835	$5,905	$846	$768	$689	$610	$531	$452	$386	$343	$300	$257	$214
$5,905	$5,975	$862	$783	$704	$625	$546	$468	$394	$351	$308	$265	$222
$5,975	$6,045	$877	$798	$720	$641	$562	$483	$404	$360	$317	$274	$231
$6,045	$6,115	$893	$814	$735	$656	$577	$498	$420	$368	$325	$282	$239
$6,115	$6,185	$908	$829	$750	$672	$593	$514	$435	$376	$333	$290	$247
$6,185	$6,255	$923	$845	$766	$687	$608	$529	$450	$385	$342	$299	$256
$6,255	$6,325	$939	$860	$781	$702	$623	$545	$466	$393	$350	$307	$264
$6,325	$6,395	$954	$875	$797	$718	$639	$560	$481	$402	$359	$316	$273
$6,395	$6,465	$970	$891	$812	$733	$654	$575	$497	$418	$367	$324	$281
$6,465	$6,535	$985	$906	$827	$749	$670	$591	$512	$433	$375	$332	$289
$6,535	$6,605	$1,000	$922	$843	$764	$685	$606	$527	$449	$384	$341	$298
$6,605	$6,675	$1,016	$937	$858	$779	$700	$622	$543	$464	$392	$349	$306
$6,675	$6,745	$1,031	$952	$874	$795	$716	$637	$558	$479	$401	$358	$315
$6,745	$6,815	$1,047	$968	$889	$810	$731	$652	$574	$495	$416	$366	$323
$6,815	$6,885	$1,062	$983	$904	$826	$747	$668	$589	$510	$431	$374	$331
$6,885	$6,955	$1,077	$999	$920	$841	$762	$683	$604	$526	$447	$383	$340
$6,955	$7,025	$1,093	$1,014	$935	$856	$777	$699	$620	$541	$462	$391	$348
$7,025	$7,095	$1,108	$1,029	$951	$872	$793	$714	$635	$556	$478	$400	$357
$7,095	$7,165	$1,124	$1,045	$966	$887	$808	$729	$651	$572	$493	$414	$365
$7,165	$7,235	$1,139	$1,060	$981	$903	$824	$745	$666	$587	$508	$430	$373
$7,235	$7,305	$1,154	$1,076	$997	$918	$839	$760	$681	$603	$524	$445	$382
$7,305	$7,375	$1,170	$1,091	$1,012	$933	$854	$776	$697	$618	$539	$460	$390
$7,375	$7,445	$1,185	$1,106	$1,028	$949	$870	$791	$712	$633	$555	$476	$399
$7,445	$7,515	$1,201	$1,122	$1,043	$964	$885	$806	$728	$649	$570	$491	$412
$7,515	$7,585	$1,216	$1,137	$1,058	$980	$901	$822	$743	$664	$585	$507	$428
$7,585	$7,655	$1,231	$1,153	$1,074	$995	$916	$837	$758	$680	$601	$522	$443
$7,655	$7,725	$1,247	$1,168	$1,089	$1,010	$931	$853	$774	$695	$616	$537	$458
$7,725	$7,795	$1,262	$1,183	$1,105	$1,026	$947	$868	$789	$710	$632	$553	$474

TAX TABLE *D (Continued)

DAILY MARRIED PERSONS

2022 Wage Bracket Method Tables for Manual Payroll Systems
With Forms W-4 From 2019 or Earlier
DAILY Payroll Period — MARRIED Persons

And the number of allowances is: — The Tentative Withholding Amount is:

If the Wage Amount (line 1a) is — At least	But less than	0	1	2	3	4	5	6	7	8	9	10
$0	$50	$0.00	$0.00	$0.00	$0.00	$0.00	$0.00	$0.00	$0.00	$0.00	$0.00	$0.00
$50	$55	$0.30	$0.00	$0.00	$0.00	$0.00	$0.00	$0.00	$0.00	$0.00	$0.00	$0.00
$55	$60	$0.80	$0.00	$0.00	$0.00	$0.00	$0.00	$0.00	$0.00	$0.00	$0.00	$0.00
$60	$65	$1.30	$0.00	$0.00	$0.00	$0.00	$0.00	$0.00	$0.00	$0.00	$0.00	$0.00
$65	$70	$1.80	$0.10	$0.00	$0.00	$0.00	$0.00	$0.00	$0.00	$0.00	$0.00	$0.00
$70	$75	$2.30	$0.60	$0.00	$0.00	$0.00	$0.00	$0.00	$0.00	$0.00	$0.00	$0.00
$75	$80	$2.80	$1.10	$0.00	$0.00	$0.00	$0.00	$0.00	$0.00	$0.00	$0.00	$0.00
$80	$85	$3.30	$1.60	$0.00	$0.00	$0.00	$0.00	$0.00	$0.00	$0.00	$0.00	$0.00
$85	$90	$3.80	$2.10	$0.40	$0.00	$0.00	$0.00	$0.00	$0.00	$0.00	$0.00	$0.00
$90	$95	$4.30	$2.60	$0.90	$0.00	$0.00	$0.00	$0.00	$0.00	$0.00	$0.00	$0.00
$95	$100	$4.80	$3.10	$1.40	$0.00	$0.00	$0.00	$0.00	$0.00	$0.00	$0.00	$0.00
$100	$105	$5.30	$3.60	$1.90	$0.10	$0.00	$0.00	$0.00	$0.00	$0.00	$0.00	$0.00
$105	$110	$5.80	$4.10	$2.40	$0.80	$0.00	$0.00	$0.00	$0.00	$0.00	$0.00	$0.00
$110	$115	$6.30	$4.60	$2.90	$1.30	$0.00	$0.00	$0.00	$0.00	$0.00	$0.00	$0.00
$115	$120	$6.80	$5.10	$3.40	$1.80	$0.10	$0.00	$0.00	$0.00	$0.00	$0.00	$0.00
$120	$125	$7.30	$5.60	$3.90	$2.30	$0.60	$0.00	$0.00	$0.00	$0.00	$0.00	$0.00
$125	$130	$7.80	$6.10	$4.40	$2.80	$1.10	$0.00	$0.00	$0.00	$0.00	$0.00	$0.00
$130	$135	$8.30	$6.60	$4.90	$3.30	$1.60	$0.00	$0.00	$0.00	$0.00	$0.00	$0.00
$135	$140	$8.90	$7.10	$5.40	$3.80	$2.10	$0.40	$0.00	$0.00	$0.00	$0.00	$0.00
$140	$145	$9.50	$7.60	$5.90	$4.30	$2.60	$0.90	$0.00	$0.00	$0.00	$0.00	$0.00
$145	$150	$10.10	$8.10	$6.40	$4.80	$3.10	$1.40	$0.00	$0.00	$0.00	$0.00	$0.00
$150	$155	$10.70	$8.70	$6.90	$5.30	$3.60	$1.90	$0.10	$0.00	$0.00	$0.00	$0.00
$155	$160	$11.30	$9.30	$7.40	$5.80	$4.10	$2.40	$0.70	$0.00	$0.00	$0.00	$0.00
$160	$165	$11.90	$9.90	$8.00	$6.30	$4.60	$2.90	$1.20	$0.00	$0.00	$0.00	$0.00
$165	$170	$12.50	$10.50	$8.60	$6.80	$5.10	$3.40	$1.70	$0.00	$0.00	$0.00	$0.00
$170	$175	$13.10	$11.10	$9.20	$7.30	$5.60	$3.90	$2.20	$0.50	$0.00	$0.00	$0.00
$175	$180	$13.70	$11.70	$9.80	$7.80	$6.10	$4.40	$2.70	$1.00	$0.00	$0.00	$0.00
$180	$185	$14.30	$12.30	$10.40	$8.40	$6.60	$4.90	$3.20	$1.50	$0.00	$0.00	$0.00
$185	$190	$14.90	$12.90	$11.00	$9.00	$7.10	$5.40	$3.70	$2.00	$0.30	$0.00	$0.00
$190	$195	$15.50	$13.50	$11.60	$9.60	$7.60	$5.90	$4.20	$2.50	$0.80	$0.00	$0.00
$195	$200	$16.10	$14.10	$12.20	$10.20	$8.20	$6.40	$4.70	$3.00	$1.30	$0.00	$0.00
$200	$205	$16.70	$14.70	$12.80	$10.80	$8.80	$6.90	$5.20	$3.50	$1.80	$0.10	$0.00
$205	$210	$17.30	$15.30	$13.40	$11.40	$9.40	$7.40	$5.70	$4.00	$2.30	$0.60	$0.00
$210	$215	$17.90	$15.90	$14.00	$12.00	$10.00	$8.00	$6.20	$4.50	$2.80	$1.10	$0.00
$215	$220	$18.50	$16.50	$14.60	$12.60	$10.60	$8.60	$6.70	$5.00	$3.30	$1.60	$0.00
$220	$225	$19.10	$17.10	$15.20	$13.20	$11.20	$9.20	$7.30	$5.50	$3.80	$2.10	$0.40
$225	$230	$19.70	$17.70	$15.80	$13.80	$11.80	$9.80	$7.80	$6.00	$4.30	$2.60	$0.90
$230	$235	$20.30	$18.30	$16.40	$14.40	$12.40	$10.40	$8.40	$6.50	$4.80	$3.10	$1.40
$235	$240	$20.90	$18.90	$17.00	$15.00	$13.00	$11.00	$9.00	$7.00	$5.30	$3.60	$1.90
$240	$245	$21.50	$19.50	$17.60	$15.60	$13.60	$11.60	$9.60	$7.60	$5.80	$4.10	$2.40
$245	$250	$22.10	$20.10	$18.20	$16.20	$14.20	$12.20	$10.20	$8.20	$6.30	$4.60	$2.90
$250	$255	$22.70	$20.70	$18.80	$16.80	$14.80	$12.80	$10.80	$8.80	$6.90	$5.10	$3.40
$255	$260	$23.30	$21.30	$19.40	$17.40	$15.40	$13.40	$11.40	$9.40	$7.50	$5.60	$3.90
$260	$265	$23.90	$21.90	$20.00	$18.00	$16.00	$14.00	$12.00	$10.00	$8.00	$6.10	$4.40
$265	$270	$24.50	$22.50	$20.60	$18.60	$16.60	$14.60	$12.60	$10.60	$8.60	$6.70	$4.90
$270	$275	$25.10	$23.10	$21.20	$19.20	$17.20	$15.20	$13.20	$11.20	$9.20	$7.30	$5.40
$275	$280	$25.70	$23.70	$21.80	$19.80	$17.80	$15.80	$13.80	$11.80	$9.80	$7.90	$5.90
$280	$285	$26.30	$24.30	$22.40	$20.40	$18.40	$16.40	$14.40	$12.40	$10.40	$8.50	$6.40
$285	$290	$26.90	$24.90	$23.00	$21.00	$19.00	$17.00	$15.00	$13.00	$11.00	$9.10	$7.20
$290	$295	$27.50	$25.50	$23.60	$21.60	$19.60	$17.60	$15.60	$13.60	$11.60	$9.70	$7.70
$295	$300	$28.10	$26.10	$24.20	$22.20	$20.20	$18.20	$16.20	$14.20	$12.20	$10.30	$8.30
$300	$305	$28.70	$26.70	$24.80	$22.80	$20.80	$18.80	$16.80	$14.80	$12.80	$10.90	$8.90
$305	$310	$29.30	$27.30	$25.40	$23.40	$21.40	$19.40	$17.40	$15.40	$13.40	$11.50	$9.50
$310	$315	$29.90	$27.90	$26.00	$24.00	$22.00	$20.00	$18.00	$16.00	$14.00	$12.10	$10.10
$315	$320	$30.50	$28.50	$26.60	$24.60	$22.60	$20.60	$18.60	$16.60	$14.60	$12.70	$10.70
$320	$325	$31.10	$29.10	$27.20	$25.20	$23.20	$21.20	$19.20	$17.20	$15.20	$13.30	$11.30
$325	$330	$31.70	$29.70	$27.80	$25.80	$23.80	$21.80	$19.80	$17.80	$15.80	$13.90	$11.90
$330	$335	$32.30	$30.30	$28.40	$26.40	$24.40	$22.40	$20.40	$18.40	$16.40	$14.50	$12.50
$335	$340	$32.90	$30.90	$29.00	$27.00	$25.00	$23.00	$21.00	$19.00	$17.00	$15.10	$13.10
$340	$345	$33.50	$31.50	$29.60	$27.60	$25.60	$23.60	$21.60	$19.60	$17.60	$15.70	$13.70
$345	$350	$34.10	$32.10	$30.20	$28.20	$26.20	$24.20	$22.20	$20.20	$18.20	$16.30	$14.30
$350	$355	$34.70	$32.70	$30.80	$28.80	$26.80	$24.80	$22.80	$20.80	$18.80	$16.90	$14.90
$355	$360	$35.30	$33.30	$31.40	$29.40	$27.40	$25.40	$23.40	$21.40	$19.40	$17.50	$15.50
$360	$365	$35.90	$33.90	$32.00	$30.00	$28.00	$26.00	$24.00	$22.00	$20.00	$18.10	$16.10
$365	$370	$36.50	$34.50	$32.60	$30.60	$28.60	$26.60	$24.60	$22.60	$20.60	$18.70	$16.70
$370	$375	$37.20	$35.10	$33.20	$31.20	$29.20	$27.20	$25.20	$23.20	$21.20	$19.30	$17.30
$375	$380	$38.30	$35.70	$33.80	$31.80	$29.80	$27.80	$25.80	$23.80	$21.80	$19.90	$17.90
$380	$385	$39.40	$36.30	$34.40	$32.40	$30.40	$28.40	$26.40	$24.40	$22.40	$20.50	$18.50
$385	$390	$40.50	$36.90	$35.00	$33.00	$31.00	$29.00	$27.00	$25.00	$23.00	$21.10	$19.10
$390	$395	$41.60	$38.00	$35.60	$33.60	$31.60	$29.60	$27.60	$25.60	$23.60	$21.70	$19.70
$395	$400	$42.70	$39.10	$36.20	$34.20	$32.20	$30.20	$28.20	$26.20	$24.20	$22.30	$20.30
$400	$405	$43.80	$40.20	$36.80	$34.80	$32.80	$30.80	$28.80	$26.80	$24.80	$22.90	$20.90
$405	$410	$44.90	$41.30	$37.70	$35.40	$33.40	$31.40	$29.40	$27.40	$25.40	$23.50	$21.50
$410	$415	$46.00	$42.40	$38.80	$36.00	$34.00	$32.00	$30.00	$28.00	$26.00	$24.10	$22.10

TAX TABLE *D (Concluded)

DAILY SINGLE PERSONS

2022 Wage Bracket Method Tables for Manual Payroll Systems
With Forms W-4 From 2019 or Earlier

SINGLE Persons — DAILY Payroll Period

If the Wage Amount (line 1a) is — At least	But less than	_0_	_1_	_2_	_3_	_4_	_5_	_6_	_7_	_8_	_9_	_10_
		The Tentative Withholding Amount is:										
$0	$20	$0.00	$0.00	$0.00	$0.00	$0.00	$0.00	$0.00	$0.00	$0.00	$0.00	$0.00
$20	$25	$0.60	$0.00	$0.00	$0.00	$0.00	$0.00	$0.00	$0.00	$0.00	$0.00	$0.00
$25	$30	$1.10	$0.00	$0.00	$0.00	$0.00	$0.00	$0.00	$0.00	$0.00	$0.00	$0.00
$30	$35	$1.60	$0.00	$0.00	$0.00	$0.00	$0.00	$0.00	$0.00	$0.00	$0.00	$0.00
$35	$40	$2.10	$0.40	$0.00	$0.00	$0.00	$0.00	$0.00	$0.00	$0.00	$0.00	$0.00
$40	$45	$2.60	$0.90	$0.00	$0.00	$0.00	$0.00	$0.00	$0.00	$0.00	$0.00	$0.00
$45	$50	$3.10	$1.40	$0.00	$0.00	$0.00	$0.00	$0.00	$0.00	$0.00	$0.00	$0.00
$50	$55	$3.60	$1.90	$0.30	$0.00	$0.00	$0.00	$0.00	$0.00	$0.00	$0.00	$0.00
$55	$60	$4.10	$2.40	$0.80	$0.00	$0.00	$0.00	$0.00	$0.00	$0.00	$0.00	$0.00
$60	$65	$4.70	$2.90	$1.30	$0.00	$0.00	$0.00	$0.00	$0.00	$0.00	$0.00	$0.00
$65	$70	$5.30	$3.40	$1.80	$0.10	$0.00	$0.00	$0.00	$0.00	$0.00	$0.00	$0.00
$70	$75	$5.90	$3.90	$2.30	$0.60	$0.00	$0.00	$0.00	$0.00	$0.00	$0.00	$0.00
$75	$80	$6.50	$4.50	$2.80	$1.10	$0.00	$0.00	$0.00	$0.00	$0.00	$0.00	$0.00
$80	$85	$7.10	$5.10	$3.30	$1.60	$0.00	$0.00	$0.00	$0.00	$0.00	$0.00	$0.00
$85	$90	$7.70	$5.70	$3.80	$2.10	$0.50	$0.00	$0.00	$0.00	$0.00	$0.00	$0.00
$90	$95	$8.30	$6.30	$4.30	$2.60	$1.00	$0.00	$0.00	$0.00	$0.00	$0.00	$0.00
$95	$100	$8.90	$6.90	$4.90	$3.10	$1.50	$0.00	$0.00	$0.00	$0.00	$0.00	$0.00
$100	$105	$9.50	$7.50	$5.50	$3.60	$2.00	$0.50	$0.00	$0.00	$0.00	$0.00	$0.00
$105	$110	$10.10	$8.10	$6.10	$4.10	$2.50	$1.00	$0.00	$0.00	$0.00	$0.00	$0.00
$110	$115	$10.70	$8.70	$6.70	$4.70	$3.00	$1.50	$0.00	$0.00	$0.00	$0.00	$0.00
$115	$120	$11.30	$9.30	$7.30	$5.30	$3.50	$2.00	$0.20	$0.00	$0.00	$0.00	$0.00
$120	$125	$11.90	$9.90	$7.90	$5.90	$4.00	$2.50	$0.70	$0.00	$0.00	$0.00	$0.00
$125	$130	$12.50	$10.50	$8.50	$6.50	$4.60	$3.00	$1.20	$0.00	$0.00	$0.00	$0.00
$130	$135	$13.10	$11.10	$9.10	$7.10	$5.20	$3.50	$1.70	$0.00	$0.00	$0.00	$0.00
$135	$140	$13.70	$11.70	$9.70	$7.70	$5.80	$4.00	$2.20	$0.50	$0.00	$0.00	$0.00
$140	$145	$14.30	$12.30	$10.30	$8.30	$6.40	$4.50	$2.70	$1.00	$0.00	$0.00	$0.00
$145	$150	$14.90	$12.90	$10.90	$8.90	$7.00	$5.00	$3.20	$1.50	$0.00	$0.00	$0.00
$150	$155	$15.50	$13.50	$11.50	$9.50	$7.60	$5.60	$3.70	$2.00	$0.30	$0.00	$0.00
$155	$160	$16.10	$14.10	$12.10	$10.10	$8.20	$6.20	$4.20	$2.50	$0.80	$0.00	$0.00
$160	$165	$16.70	$14.70	$12.70	$10.70	$8.80	$6.80	$4.80	$3.00	$1.30	$0.00	$0.00
$165	$170	$17.30	$15.30	$13.30	$11.30	$9.40	$7.40	$5.40	$3.50	$1.80	$0.20	$0.00
$170	$175	$17.90	$15.90	$13.90	$11.90	$10.00	$8.00	$6.00	$4.00	$2.30	$0.70	$0.00
$175	$180	$18.50	$16.50	$14.50	$12.50	$10.60	$8.60	$6.60	$4.60	$2.80	$1.20	$0.00
$180	$185	$19.60	$17.10	$15.10	$13.10	$11.20	$9.20	$7.20	$5.20	$3.30	$1.70	$0.00
$185	$190	$20.70	$17.70	$15.70	$13.70	$11.80	$9.80	$7.80	$5.80	$3.80	$2.20	$0.50
$190	$195	$21.80	$18.30	$16.30	$14.30	$12.40	$10.40	$8.40	$6.40	$4.40	$2.70	$1.00
$195	$200	$22.90	$18.90	$16.90	$14.90	$13.00	$11.00	$9.00	$7.00	$5.00	$3.20	$1.50
$200	$205	$24.00	$19.50	$17.50	$15.50	$13.60	$11.60	$9.60	$7.60	$5.60	$3.70	$2.00
$205	$210	$25.10	$20.40	$18.10	$16.10	$14.20	$12.20	$10.20	$8.20	$6.20	$4.20	$2.50
$210	$215	$26.20	$21.50	$18.70	$16.70	$14.80	$12.80	$10.80	$8.80	$6.80	$4.80	$3.00
$215	$220	$27.30	$22.60	$19.30	$17.30	$15.40	$13.40	$11.40	$9.40	$7.40	$5.40	$3.50
$220	$225	$28.40	$23.70	$19.90	$17.90	$16.00	$14.00	$12.00	$10.00	$8.00	$6.00	$4.10
$225	$230	$29.50	$24.80	$20.50	$18.50	$16.60	$14.60	$12.60	$10.60	$8.60	$6.60	$4.70
$230	$235	$30.60	$25.90	$21.60	$19.10	$17.20	$15.20	$13.20	$11.20	$9.20	$7.20	$5.30
$235	$240	$31.70	$27.00	$22.70	$19.70	$17.80	$15.80	$13.80	$11.80	$9.80	$7.80	$5.90
$240	$245	$32.80	$28.10	$23.80	$20.30	$18.40	$16.40	$14.40	$12.40	$10.40	$8.40	$6.50
$245	$250	$33.90	$29.20	$24.90	$20.90	$19.00	$17.00	$15.00	$13.00	$11.00	$9.00	$7.10
$250	$255	$35.00	$30.30	$26.00	$21.50	$19.60	$17.60	$15.60	$13.60	$11.60	$9.60	$7.70
$255	$260	$36.10	$31.40	$27.10	$22.60	$20.20	$18.20	$16.20	$14.20	$12.20	$10.20	$8.30
$260	$265	$37.20	$32.50	$28.20	$23.70	$20.80	$18.80	$16.80	$14.80	$12.80	$10.80	$8.90
$265	$270	$38.30	$33.60	$29.30	$24.80	$21.40	$19.40	$17.40	$15.40	$13.40	$11.40	$9.50

2022 Wage Bracket Method Tables for Manual Payroll Systems
With Forms W-4 From 2019 or Earlier

SINGLE Persons — DAILY Payroll Period

If the Wage Amount (line 1a) is — At least	But less than	_0_	_1_	_2_	_3_	_4_	_5_	_6_	_7_	_8_	_9_	_10_
		The Tentative Withholding Amount is:										
$270	$275	$39.40	$35.80	$32.10	$28.50	$24.90	$21.20	$18.00	$16.00	$14.00	$12.00	$10.10
$275	$280	$40.50	$36.90	$33.20	$29.60	$26.00	$22.30	$18.70	$16.60	$14.60	$12.60	$10.70
$280	$285	$41.60	$38.00	$34.30	$30.70	$27.10	$23.40	$19.80	$17.20	$15.20	$13.20	$11.30
$285	$290	$42.70	$39.10	$35.40	$31.80	$28.20	$24.50	$20.90	$17.80	$15.80	$13.80	$11.90
$290	$295	$43.80	$40.20	$36.50	$32.90	$29.30	$25.60	$22.00	$18.40	$16.40	$14.40	$12.50
$295	$300	$44.90	$41.30	$37.60	$34.00	$30.40	$26.70	$23.10	$19.40	$17.00	$15.00	$13.10
$300	$305	$46.00	$42.40	$38.70	$35.10	$31.50	$27.80	$24.20	$20.50	$17.60	$15.60	$13.70
$305	$310	$47.10	$43.50	$39.80	$36.20	$32.60	$28.90	$25.30	$21.60	$18.20	$16.20	$14.30
$310	$315	$48.20	$44.60	$40.90	$37.30	$33.70	$30.00	$26.40	$22.70	$19.10	$16.80	$14.90
$315	$320	$49.30	$45.70	$42.00	$38.40	$34.80	$31.10	$27.50	$23.80	$20.20	$17.40	$15.50
$320	$325	$50.40	$46.80	$43.10	$39.50	$35.90	$32.20	$28.60	$24.90	$21.30	$18.00	$16.10
$325	$330	$51.50	$47.90	$44.20	$40.60	$37.00	$33.30	$29.70	$26.00	$22.40	$18.80	$16.70
$330	$335	$52.60	$49.00	$45.30	$41.70	$38.10	$34.40	$30.80	$27.10	$23.50	$19.90	$17.30
$335	$340	$53.70	$50.10	$46.40	$42.80	$39.20	$35.50	$31.90	$28.20	$24.60	$21.00	$17.90
$340	$345	$54.80	$51.20	$47.50	$43.90	$40.30	$36.60	$33.00	$29.30	$25.70	$22.10	$18.50
$345	$350	$55.90	$52.30	$48.60	$45.00	$41.40	$37.70	$34.10	$30.40	$26.80	$23.20	$19.50
$350	$355	$57.00	$53.40	$49.70	$46.10	$42.50	$38.80	$35.20	$31.50	$27.90	$24.30	$20.60
$355	$360	$58.10	$54.50	$50.80	$47.20	$43.60	$39.90	$36.30	$32.60	$29.00	$25.40	$21.70
$360	$365	$59.30	$55.60	$51.90	$48.30	$44.70	$41.00	$37.40	$33.70	$30.10	$26.50	$22.80
$365	$370	$60.50	$56.70	$53.00	$49.40	$45.80	$42.10	$38.50	$34.80	$31.20	$27.60	$23.90
$370	$375	$61.70	$57.80	$54.10	$50.50	$46.90	$43.20	$39.60	$35.90	$32.30	$28.70	$25.00
$375	$380	$62.90	$58.90	$55.20	$51.60	$48.00	$44.30	$40.70	$37.00	$33.40	$29.80	$26.10
$380	$385	$64.10	$60.10	$56.30	$52.70	$49.10	$45.40	$41.80	$38.10	$34.50	$30.90	$27.20
$385	$390	$65.30	$61.30	$57.40	$53.80	$50.20	$46.50	$42.90	$39.20	$35.60	$32.00	$28.30
$390	$395	$66.50	$62.50	$58.50	$54.90	$51.30	$47.60	$44.00	$40.30	$36.70	$33.10	$29.40

Check Figures

Chapter 2 Problems

2–1a. (c) $228.29
2–3a. (b) total gross earnings, $2,252.60
2–5a. (b) overtime pay, $11.52
2–7a. (b) total earnings, $1,252.40
2–9a. (c) gross earnings for the week, $472.64
2–11a. (b) gross pay, $683.90
2–13a. (b) overtime rate, $24.89
2–15a. gross pay, $729.00
2–17a. (d) total earnings, $608.46
2–19a. (c) total annual earnings, $43,250
2–21a. extra overtime pay, $33.93

Chapter 3 Problems

3–1a. total employees' FICA taxes, $457.89; $107.09
3–3a. (a) FICA taxes, $56.73; $13.27
3–5a. November 15 (Hanks), FICA taxes, $124.00; $105.13
3–7a. employees' taxes, $263.50; $61.65
3–9a. total employees' FICA taxes, $2,983.07; $741.16
3–11a. total taxes after adjustments—line 10, $21,771.83
3–13a. total taxes after adjustments—line 10, $12,008.76
3–15a. (b) last due date, April 3
3–17a. total OASDI taxes, $8,004.82

Chapter 4 Problems

4–1a. net pay, $192.80
4–3a. Lennon's tax, $47.16; $48.00
4–5a. total FIT, $485.84
4–7a. net pay, $667.85
4–9a. net pay, $50,255.87
4–11a. (c) take-home pay, $464.18
4–13a. Form W-3, box 2, Federal Income Tax Withheld $16,172.00
4–15a. Amoroso's amount to be withheld, $115.46
4–17a. Bower's amount to be withheld, $114.00

Chapter 5 Problems

5–1a. (c) total unemployment taxes, $6,663.60
5–3a. (b) net SUTA tax, $3,104.30
5–5a. (b) net FUTA, $528.60
5–7a. (b) $235.60
5–9a. (b) SUTA tax, $1,416.00
5–11a. (c) $957.60
5–13a. (a) voluntary = $1,190.00
5–15a. (b) tax rate = 5.5%
5–17a. Form 940, line 8, $474.60

Chapter 6 Problems

6–1a. federal tax levy, $517.10
6–3a. maximum to be deducted is $75.00
6–5a. (a) cash credit, $3,646.21
6–7a. Total $50 bills = 64
6–9a. cash credit, $10,773.00
6–11a. FUTA Taxes Payable debit, $98.75
6–13a. (d) Salary Expense debit, $1,196.00
6–15a. Vacation Benefits Expense debit, $740.00
6–17a. (c) 1. Total Liability, $3,019.40

Chapter 7, Appendix A and B Problems

See Net Paid Check Figures in Chapter 7, Appendix A and B margins

Glossary

This glossary includes terms from Appendices B and C. These appendices are available on the Bieg 2022 product Web site at www.cengage.com.

A

Annualizing Wages method of determining amount of income taxes to be withheld by multiplying the wages for one payroll period by the number of periods in the year, determining the annual amount of withholding required on the total wages, and dividing the annual withholding by the number of payroll periods.

Applicable Large Employers (ALEs) employers with 50 or more full-time employees during the previous year.

Application Form personnel record which gives the applicant an opportunity to provide complete information as to personal qualifications, training, and experience.

Average Indexed Monthly Earnings a worker's average monthly earnings, updated to reflect changes in wage levels.

B

Backup Withholding amount of income tax withheld by payers of taxable interest, dividends, and certain other payments made to payees who have failed to furnish the payers with correct identification numbers.

Biweekly every two weeks.

Business Expense cost of operating a business that is deductible by the employer for federal income tax purposes.

C

Change in Payroll Rate Form document that notifies the proper departments of a change in the employee's rate of remuneration.

Check-Off System withholding of union dues from employees' wages by the employer.

Commission stated percentage of revenue paid an employee who transacts a piece of business or performs a service.

Common-Law Relationship the state existing when the employer has the right to control both what work will be done and how it will be done.

Constructively Paid remunerations that are credited to the account of, or set apart for, an employee so that they may be drawn upon at any time, even though they are not actually possessed by the employee.

Continental System method of recording time on time cards in which the day is divided into one 24-hour period, with time running from 12 midnight to 12 midnight.

Contribution Report quarterly tax return filed with the state by the employer that provides a summary of the wages paid during the period and shows the computation of the tax or contribution.

Credit Reduction State states that have borrowed federal funds to pay state unemployment benefits and have failed to repay the loans within the allotted time period.

Currently Insured criterion used to determine eligibility for social security benefits; persons must have at least six quarters of coverage during the 13-quarter period ending with (1) the quarter in which they died or (2) the quarter in which they became entitled to old-age insurance benefits or most recently became entitled to disability benefits.

D

De Minimis Fringe Benefit a retirement plan that provides future benefits based solely on the amount paid by each employee and employer into the account, plus investment gains.

Defined Contribution Plan any property or service the value of which is so small that accounting for it would be unreasonable or impractical.

Dependency Allowance an additional weekly benefit paid to unemployed workers with dependents.

Disability Benefits payments to employees who are absent from their jobs because of illness, accident, or disease not arising out of their employment.

Discretionary Bonus a bonus not agreed on, announced, or promised before payment.

Dismissal Payments amounts paid by employers to workers who have been separated from employment; also known as *payments in lieu of notice*, *separation pay*, or *terminal leave pay*.

Disposal Earnings the earnings remaining after withholding for federal and state income taxes, FICA taxes, state unemployment and disability taxes, and deductions required for state employees' retirement systems.

Domestic Service services of a household nature performed in or about a private home of the person who employs the domestic.

E

Educational Assistance the expenses that an employer pays for an employee's education, such as tuition, fees, and payments for books, supplies, and equipment.

Electronic Funds Transfer System (EFTS) system whereby the employer transfers employees' net pays to employees' bank accounts with electronic equipment rather than issuing paychecks.

Electronic Paystubs paystub information made available through a secured Web site, kiosk, or interactive voice response system.

Employee any individual performing services for an employer in the legal relationship of employer and employee.

Employee History Record continuous record of the relationship between the employer and the employee.

Employee's Earnings Record payroll record for each employee that is used to provide complete information about the accumulated earnings of each employee.

Employer any person or organization who employs one or more individuals for the performance of services, unless such services or employment are specifically excepted by law.

Employment any service performed by employees for their employer, regardless of the citizenship or residence of either.

Enterprise Coverage applied to determine if employees of an enterprise are covered under the provisions of the FLSA. The test criteria are at least two employees engaged in interstate commerce and an annual gross sales volume of at least $500,000.

Executive Orders regulations issued by the federal government that ban, in employment on government contracts, discrimination based on race, color, religion, sex, or national origin.

Exempt Employees workers exempt from some, or all, of the FLSA requirements such as minimum wages, equal pay, and overtime pay.

Experience Rating method by which employer contribution payments may be adjusted because of a favorable employment record; also known as *merit rating*.

F

Fair Employment Practices laws that deal with discrimination on the basis of age, race, color, religion, gender, or national origin as a condition of employment.

Form I-9, Employment Eligibility Verification form that lists the documents an employee must furnish to the employer; they identify the employee and, if an alien, verify authorization to work in the United States.

Form W-2, Wage and Tax Statement form used by the employer to report the amount of wages paid each worker in the course of the trade or business of the employer.

Fully Insured criterion used to determine eligibility for most retirement and disability benefits; generally, a worker needs between 6 and 40 quarters of coverage.

G

Garnishment legal or equitable procedure by means of which a portion of the wages of any person must be withheld for payment of a debt.

Gross Earnings total regular earnings and total overtime earnings, also known as *gross pay*.

Gross-Up gross-up amount of supplemental payment so that after the appropriate payroll taxes are withheld, the net amount left is equal to the original intended payment.

Group Insurance life insurance program for employees at a low cost.

H

Hiring Notice form that is sent to the Payroll Department so that new employees are properly added to the payroll.

Hospital Insurance (HI) plan program of medical care that provides protection against costs of certain hospital and related services; also known as *Basic Medicare* or *Part A Medicare*.

Human Resources System those procedures and methods related to recruiting, selecting, orienting, training, and terminating personnel.

I

Income Tax levy on the earnings of most employees that is deducted from their gross pay.

Independent Contractors persons who follow an independent trade, business, or profession where services are offered to the public.

Indexing updating, or adjusting, a dollar amount over any particular time period (such as a calendar year) to reflect changes in wage levels that have occurred since a predetermined base time period.

Individual Employee Coverage applied to determine if the FLSA covers an employee. The test is that the employee either engages in interstate commerce or produces goods for such commerce.

Individual-Account Plan supplemental unemployment benefits plan in which the employers' contributions are paid into a separate trust for each employee.

Information Returns forms upon which an employer reports compensation paid to individuals who are not employees.

Interstate Employee an individual who works in more than one state.

Investigative Consumer Report study done by a consumer reporting agency on a job applicant or current employee concerning the individual's character, general reputation, and mode of living.

J

Journal Entries transactions recorded in the accounting system of a business.

L

Lookback Period the block of time, consisting of four quarters beginning July 1 of the second preceding year and ending June 30 of the prior year, used to determine if an employer is a monthly or a semiweekly depositor.

M

Medicaid program of medical assistance provided to aged and needy persons by means of a joint federal-state program.

Merit Rating *see* experience rating.

Monthly Depositor one who reported employment taxes of $50,000 or less for the four quarters in the lookback period.

N

Negative-Balance Employers those whose reserve accounts have been charged for more benefits paid out than contributions paid in to the fund.

Nondiscretionary Bonus a bonus normally based on hours worked, units produced, production efficiency, or work quality.

O

Overtime Premium method of calculating overtime pay by multiplying the total hours worked (including overtime hours) by the regular rate of pay and then multiplying the overtime hours by one-half the regular hourly rate.

P

Part-Year Employment another method of calculating the withholding of federal income tax from an employee's pay.

Partial Unemployment employment by the individual's regular employer on a reduced scale because of lack of work.

Partial Unemployment Notices forms completed by the employer and given to partially unemployed workers so that supplemental unemployment benefits may be obtained.

Payroll Accounting System those procedures and methods related to the disbursement of pay to employees.

Payroll Register multicolumn form used to assemble and summarize the data needed at the end of each payroll period. It lists all employees who earned remuneration, the amount of remuneration, the deductions, and the net amount paid.

Percentage Method method of determining amount of income taxes to be withheld using Percentage Method Withholding Tables provided by the IRS, which take into consideration length of payroll period, gross earnings, and filing status.

Person an entity defined by law as an individual, a trust or estate, a partnership, or a corporation.

Personal Allowance a deduction allowed in computing taxable income; also known as a *personal exemption* (used with Form W-4 from 2019 or earlier).

Piece-Rate System compensation plan under which workers are paid according to their output (units or pieces produced).

Pooled-Fund Laws unemployment insurance system wherein the cost of unemployment benefits is spread among all employers in a particular state.

Pooled-Fund Plan   supplemental unemployment benefits plan financed by employers' contributions into a general fund; also known as the *auto* or *Ford-type plan*.

Positive-Balance Employers   those who have built up a balance in their reserve accounts (contributions paid in less benefits charged).

Pre-Hire Inquiries   questions asked in the employment interview and on application forms, résumés of experience or education required of an applicant, and any kind of written testing.

Primary Insurance Amount (PIA)   a person's monthly retirement or disability benefit, which is the base upon which monthly benefits of the worker's family and survivors are computed.

Principal Activities   those tasks employees must perform for the employer.

Profit-Sharing Plans   compensation plans in which employer shares with employees a portion of the profits of the business.

Q

Quarter of Coverage   criterion used to determine if workers are fully insured, currently insured, or insured for disability benefits; the minimum amount of wages or self-employment income with which individuals must be credited in a calendar quarter if they are to receive credit toward being insured for that period.

Quarterly Averaging   method of determining the amount of income taxes to be withheld by estimating the employee's average wages for the calendar quarter, computing an average payment, and withholding an amount based on the average payment.

R

Reciprocal Agreement   arrangement entered into by two or more states whereby the resident of one state working in another state will not be subject to the withholding of income taxes by the state in which the person is employed if that state has entered into a similar agreement with the employee's resident state.

Reciprocal Arrangements   agreements between states to provide unemployment insurance coverage and payment of benefits to interstate workers.

Reference Inquiry Form   document used by the employer to investigate the

references given on the application blank by the job applicant.

Requisition for Personnel   document submitted by a department head to the Human Resources Department asking for additional or replacement employees.

Reserse-Ratio Formula   experience-rating plan used in most states, based on: Reserve Ratio = Contributions – Benefits Paid/Average Payroll

S

Safe Harbor Rule   rule that determines if an employer has satisfied the deposit obligations by (a) having no shortfall (under deposit) that exceeds the greater of $100 or 2 percent of the amount of employment taxes required to be deposited and (b) having deposited the shortfall on or before the shortfall make-up date.

Salary   remuneration paid on a monthly, biweekly, semimonthly, or yearly basis.

Self-Employment Income   the net earnings derived by individuals from a business or profession carried on as a sole proprietorship or as a partnership.

Semimonthly   twice a month.

Semiweekly Depositor   one who reported employment taxes of more than $50,000 for the four quarters in the lookback period.

Separation Report   report that provides a wage and employment record of the separated employee and the reason for leaving.

Shortfall   the excess of the amount of employment taxes required to be deposited over the amount deposited on or before the last date prescribed for the deposit.

Sick Pay   any payment made to individuals because of their personal injury or sickness that does not constitute wages.

Small Employers   employers with fewer than 50 full-time equivalent employees with average annual wages of less than $50,000.

Social Security Benefits   payments made under Title II of the Social Security Act to retired workers, their spouses, children and parents, as well as widows, widowers, and some divorced persons; also known as *OASDI benefits* and *Title II benefits*.

Special Withholding Allowance allowance claimed by employees so that wages which are below the level subject to the income tax will not be subject to withholding (used with Form W-4 from 2019 or earlier).

Standard Deduction   an amount of money used to reduce an individual's adjusted gross income in computing taxable income.

Status Report   initial statement filed by new employers with their state unemployment office, which determines their liability to make contributions into the state unemployment compensation fund.

Supplemental Unemployment Benefits (SUB)   private supplementation of state unemployment compensation benefits to employees during periods of layoff.

Supplemental Wage Payments   additional compensation such as vacation pay, bonuses, and commissions paid to employees.

Supplementary Medical Insurance Plan   program of voluntary medical care for aged and disabled persons designed to cover costs of doctors' services and other items and services not covered under the basic program; also known as *supplementary* or *voluntary Medicare* or *Part B Medicare*.

T

Taxable Wage Base   the maximum amount of wages during a calendar year that is subject to a particular tax, such as FICA.

Time Card   form on which employee's time worked is recorded manually by the worker or automatically by a time clock.

Time Sheet   form that indicates an employee's time of arrival and time of departure.

Tip   gift or gratuity given by a customer in recognition of service performed for him or her.

Tipped Employee   one engaged in an occupation in which tips of more than $30 a month are customarily and regularly received.

Title XII Advances   funds borrowed from the federal government by states that, due to financial difficulties, cannot pay their unemployment compensation benefits.

U

Unemployment Compensation Benefits payments made to workers who are temporarily unemployed.

Unemployment Insurance   a federal-state program that provides economic security for workers during periods of temporary unemployment.

V

Vesting the process of conveying to employees the right to share in a retirement fund in the event they are terminated before the normal retirement age.

Voluntary Contributions payments deliberately made by employers to their state funds in order to qualify for a lower unemployment compensation tax rate.

W

Wage remuneration paid on an hourly, weekly, or piece-work basis; total compensation paid to employees for services.

Wage and Tax Statements statements furnished by employers to their employees informing them of the wages paid during the calendar year and the amount of taxes withheld from those wages.

Wage Information Reports statements filed by the employer, usually with the quarterly contribution report, which list employee names, social security numbers, taxable wages, taxable tips, state in which worker was employed during the reported quarter, and employer's federal account number.

Wage Theft a term that refers to situations when employers do not pay employees in accordance with statutory or contract requirements.

Wage-Bracket Method method of determining amount of income taxes to be withheld by reading amount from tables provided by the IRS, which take into consideration length of payroll period, gross earnings, and filing status.

Wages remuneration paid on an hourly, weekly, or piece-work basis; total compensation paid to employees for services.

Worker's Compensation Insurance protection provided to employees and their dependents against losses due to injury or death incurred during employment.

Workweek fixed and regularly recurring period of 168 hours—7 consecutive 24-hour periods.

Index

A

ABC test, SUTA coverage, 5-4
Absences, 2-21
Account and payroll records, books of, 7-2
Accountable plan for traveling expenses, 4-6
Accounts comparison, partial chart of, illus., B-3, illus., B-25
Accounts used in recording payroll transactions, summary of, 6-29
Activities
    preliminary and postliminary, 2-20
    principal, 2-17
Additional withholding allowance, 4-37
Adjusting entry, 6-28
Adjustments, recording end-of-period, 6-28
ADP (Automatic Data Processing), 1-25
Affordable Care Act of 2010 (ACA), 1-12, 4-26
Age Discrimination in Employment Act of 1967 (ADEA), 1-7, 1-20
Agent-drivers, 3-3, 5-3
Agricultural Employees, Form 943, Employer's Annual Tax Return for, 3-20, illus., 4-30
Agricultural employers, 5-2
Agricultural occupations, 2-14
Agricultural workers, deposit requirements for employers of, 3-20
ALEs (applicable large employers), 1-13
Allowance values for 2021, table of, illus., 4-40
Allowances
    additional withholding, 4-37
    for dependents, 4-37
    other withholding, 4-37, 4-38
    personal, 4-37
    special withholding, 4-37
American Payroll Association (APA), 1-2
American Rescue Plan Act (ARPA), 3-10
Americans with Disabilities Act of 1990 (ADA), 1-7, 1-11
Americans working overseas, coverage of, 5-7
Annual FUTA return—Form 940, 5-21
Annual Reconciliation of Employer Wage Tax for Philadelphia, A-24, B-41
Annual statements, 4-34
Annualizing wages, def., 4-18
Annuities, distributions from, Form 1099-R, illus., 4-31
Annuity payments, withholding for, 4-14
APA code of ethics, illus., 1-3
Applicable large employers (ALEs)
    def., 1-13
    Form 1095-C, 1-13

Application for employment, 1-16, illus., 1-18, illus., 1-19
Application form, def., 1-17
Archer Medical Savings Accounts, 4-8
At-will employee, 1-22
ATIP (Attributed Tip Income Program), 3-7
ATM (automated teller machines), 6-18
Automated General Ledger Software, B-1, B-3, B-11, B-23, B-25, B-26, B-32
Automated payroll systems
    2022 percentage method tables for, illus., B-2, illus., B-24

B

Background checks, FCRA and, 1-17
Backup withholding, illus., 4-30
    def., 4-31, 4-32
Bad checks, 3-33
Badge systems, 2-22
Bankruptcy Act, Chapter 13 of, 6-10
Base of operations, location of, 5-5
BELO plan, 2-29
Benefit Cost Ratio (BCR), 5-13
Benefits, qualifying for, 5-7
Biometrics, timekeeping, 2-24
Biweekly, def., 2-4
Bonus
    discretionary, 2-4
    nondiscretionary, 2-4, 2-33
Book of original entry, A-7
Business expense, def., 6-22
Business tax credit, Form 8846, 3-6

C

Cafeteria plans, 4-7
Card-generated systems, 2-22
Cardless and badgeless systems, 2-22
Cares Act, 3-10
Cash, paying wages and salaries in, 6-15
Cell, A-2, A-7
Certificate of age, 2-15
Change in payroll rate, 1-22
    form, def., 1-22
Change in status form, illus., 1-22
Chart of accounts, partial, illus., 7-2, illus., A-7
Check-off system, def., 6-10
Check, paying wages and salaries by, 6-15
Checkpoints, A-5
Child-labor provisions violations, penalties of, 2-16
Child-labor restrictions, 2-13

Child support, 6-10
Circular E, Employer's Tax Guide, 4-4, 4-29
Civil Rights Act
    of 1964, 1-5
    of 1991, 1-7
Code of ethics, 1-2, 1-3
Commission, def., 2-32
Commission-drivers, 3-3, 5-3
Common-law relationship, def., 2-2
Common-law test, 3-2, 5-3
Compensation plans, contributions to deferred, 3-8
Compensatory time off, 2-10
Computerized time and attendance recording
    systems, 2-22
Constructively paid, def., 5-9
Consumer Credit Protection Act (CCPA), 6-10
Consumer Finance Protection Bureau (CFPB), 6-19
Consumer Price Index, 3-9
    and minimum wage, 2-5
Continental system, def., 2-22
Contribution rate, computing, 5-17
Contribution report, def., 5-30
Contributions
    to deferred compensation plans, 3-8
    pension and retirement, 6-14
    and withholdings, payroll taxes, 7-4
Control of operations, location of, 5-5
Convenience of the employer, 3-8
Copy and paste, Excel, A-2
Coronavirus Aid, Relief, and Economic Security
    (Cares) Act. See Cares Act
Corporation, employees of, 2-3
Credit reduction state, def., 5-10
Credit week, def., 5-30
Credits
    against FUTA tax, 5-10
    unemployment compensation taxes and, 5-9
Cumulative earnings, 7-11
Current payroll journal entries, illus., B-7, illus., B-30,
    illus., B-38

D

Davis-Bacon Act (1931), 1-9
De minimis, 2-20
    fringe benefit, def., 4-5
Deferred arrangements, 4-8
Deferred compensation plans, contributions to, 3-8
Defined contribution plan, def., 4-8
Denver Occupational Privilege Tax, 4-36
Department of Homeland Security, 1-10
Department of Labor
    child-labor restrictions, 2-13
    Employment Standards Administration homepage, 2-2
    illegal aliens, 2-5
    informational reports, 1-12

Dependents, allowances for, 4-37
Deposit requirements for
    employers of agricultural workers, 3-20
    employers of household employees, 3-20
    nonagricultural workers, 3-18
    state and local government employers, 3-20
Deposit rules, illus., 7-5, illus., A-12
Depositing taxes, 7-4
Depositor
    monthly, 3-18, 3-19
    semiweekly, 3-20
Deposits
    electronic, 3-20
    failure to make timely, 3-32
    procedures for making, 3-20
Direct sellers, statutory nonemployees, 2-3
Direction of operations, location of, 5-5
Director of corporation, 2-3
Disability benefits, def., 1-14
Disclosure requirements, ERISA, 1-12
Discretionary bonus, def., 2-4
Dismissal payments, def., 5-9
Disposable earnings, def., 6-10
Dividends and Distributions, Form 1099-DIV,
    illus., 4-30
Doctor's appointments, 2-20
Domestic service, def., 2-3
Domestics, 2-3
Drug testing, 1-20
Dumping, 5-21

E

E-verify, 1-10
Earnings statement (check stub) showing payroll
    deductions, illus., 6-16
Educational assistance
    def., 3-8
    payments for, 3-8
Electronic deposits, 3-20
Electronic Federal Tax Payment System (EFTPS),
    3-20, 5-28
Electronic filing Form W-2 and information
    returns, 4-32
Electronic filing of Form 941, 3-29
Electronic funds transfer (EFT), 4-33
Electronic funds transfer system (EFTS), def., 6-17
Electronic paystub, def., 6-19
Electronic transfer, paying wages and salaries by, 6-17
Employee(s), 3-2
    access of personnel files, 1-23
    at-will, 1-22
    contributions, 5-16, 6-7
    of a corporation, 2-3
    def., 2-2
    exempt, 2-10, 3-4

FICA (OASDI/HI) taxes and withholdings, 3-10, 6-7
Form 4070, Employee's Report of Tips to Employer, 3-5, illus., 3-7
Form SS-5, Employee's Application for a Social Security Card, 3-16
Form SS-8, Determination of Employee Work Status, 2-2
Form W-4, Employee's Withholding Allowance Certificate, 1-8, 4-10, 4-11, illus., 4-12, 4-37, 4-38, illus., 4-38
FUTA, 5-3
of the government, 3-3
history record, def., 1-21
hospital, 2-9
household, 3-3
list, illus., B-4, illus., B-27
penalties, 4-14
personnel data, illus., 7-3
receiving remedial education, 2-10
residence, location of, 5-6
in retail, 2-10
salaried nonexempt, 2-28
salaried with fluctuating workweek, 2-28
in service industries, 2-10
SUTA, 5-4
taxable payments to, illus., 4-3
terminating, 1-22
tipped, 2-6, 2-7, 2-9
work time, determining, 2-16
Employee list, illus., B-4, illus., B-27
Employee Retirement Income Security Act of 1974. *See* ERISA
Employee's earnings record, illus., 1-25, 6-5, illus., 6-6, 7-3, 7-41, A-8, illus., A-18
def., 1-24
Excel template, A-6
new, illus., A-19
Employees to be paid this pay period, illus., B-5, illus., B-12
Employer(s), 2-2
agricultural, 5-2
applicable large, 1-13
Circular E, Employer's Tax Guide, 4-4, 4-29
contributions, 5-16
convenience of, 3-8
def., 3-2
FICA (OASDI taxes), 3-12, 6-21
Form 940, Employer's Annual Federal Unemployment (FUTA) Tax Return, 5-21, illus., 5-22, 5-23, 7-20, A-23, B-40
Form 941, Employer's Quarterly Federal Tax Return, 3-17, illus., 3-17, 3-21, illus., 3-23, 3-24, illus., 3-24, 3-25, illus., 3-25, illus., 4-30, 7-19, A-23, B-40
Form 941-PR, Employer's Quarterly Federal Tax Return, 3-17

Form 941-SS, Employer's Quarterly Federal Tax Return, 3-17
Form 941-X, Adjusted Employer's Quarterly Federal Tax Return or Claim for Refund, 3-17, 3-29
Form 943, Employer's Annual Tax Return for Agricultural Employees, 3-17, 3-20, illus., 4-30
Form 944, Employer's Annual Federal Tax Return, 3-17, 3-29, illus., 4-30
Form 945, Annual Return of Withheld Federal Income Tax, 3-17
Form 8027, Employer's Annual Information Return of Tip Income and Allocated Tips, 3-6, illus., 4-30
Form UC-2, Employer's Report for Unemployment Compensation—Fourth Quarter, 7-20, A-23, B-40
FUTA, 5-2
household, 3-20, 5-2, 5-29
negative-balance, 5-17
new, 3-19
positive-balance, 5-17
Quarterly Contribution Return and Report of Wages, 4-34
returns they must complete, 4-29, *illus.,* 4-30
seasonal, 3-28
small, 1-13
successor, 3-12
SUTA, 5-3
unemployment compensation reports required of, 5-19
Employer contributions, 5-17
Employer-employee relationship, 4-2
Employer identification number (EIN), 3-14
application for, *Form SS-4,* illus., 3-15
Employer information report (EEO-I), 1-5
Employment
application for, 1-16, illus., 1-18, illus., 1-19
def., 3-2
exempt, illus., 3-2
family, 3-3
reciprocal arrangements, 5-6
transfers of, 5-6
Employment Eligibility Verification, Form I-9, 1-8
Employment Reference Release, 1-21
Employment tax returns, failure to file, 3-30
Employment taxes, failure to fully pay, 3-31
End-of-period adjustments, recording, 6-28, B-41
End-of-period payroll adjustments, recording, 7-22
End-of-year activities, 7-19, A-22, B-39
End-of-year payroll adjustments, recording, A-24, B-41
Enterprise coverage, def., 2-1
Equal Employment Opportunity, 1-5
Equal Employment Opportunity Commission (EEOC), 1-5
Equal Pay Act, 2-13
Equal Pay Law, 2-13

ERISA, 1-11
    disclosure requirements, 1-12
    Pension Benefit Guaranty Corporation, 1-12
    vesting, 1-12
Excel, getting to know, A-2
Excel screen, A-2
Excel template, A-5
    instructions for payroll project short version, A-1,
        A-6, A-19
Executive orders, def., 1-7
Exempt employees, 3-4
    def., 2-10
Exempt employment, illus., 3-2
Exempt payments, 3-8, illus., 4-6
Exempt status, indications of, illus., 2-12
Exemption status of workers under FLSA, illus., 2-10
Exemptions
    blue-collar workers, 2-13
    from FLSA requirements, 2-10
    from income tax withholding, 4-13
    salary basis, 2-12
    test of, 2-10
    white-collar workers, 2-10
Expatriates, 3-3
Experience rating, 5-17
    def., 5-11

F

Failure-to-comply penalties, 3-30
Failure-to-deposit penalty, EFTPS and, 3-21
Failure to file employment tax returns, 3-30
Failure to fully pay employment taxes, 3-31
Failure to furnish
    information returns, 3-32
    payee statements, 3-32
Failure to make timely deposits, 3-32
Failure-to-warn lawsuits, 1-20
Fair Credit Reporting Act (FCRA) of 1968, 1-17
Fair employment laws, 1-5
Fair employment practices, def., 1-5
Fair Labor Standards Act. See FLSA
Fair Minimum Wage Act of 2007, 2-4
False data, penalties of, 2-16
Families First Coronavirus Response Act (FFCRA), 3-10
Family and Medical Leave Act of 1993 (FMLA), 1-10
Family employment, 3-3
Family Support Act, 6-12
Federal Disability Insurance Trust Fund, 1-4
Federal False Information Act, 2-16
Federal income tax (FIT), 1-4, 6-7
    depositing withheld, 6-26
    withholding, 4-16, 4-39
Federal Income Tax Withholding Law, 4-2
    coverage under, 4-2
Federal Insurance Contributions Act. See FICA

Federal laws affecting the need for payroll and personnel
    records, other, 1-8, illus., 1-9
Federal Old-Age and Survivors' Trust Fund, 1-4
Federal payroll laws, summary of information required
    by, illus., 1-6
Federal Personal Responsibility and Work Opportunity
    Reconciliation Act of 1996 (PRWORA), 1-8
Federal Reserve Bank, ACH credit method and ACH
    debit method, 3-21
Federal salary requirements and overtime rules, 2-11
Federal tax levy, 6-12
Federal Unemployment Tax Act. See FUTA
Federal Wage and Hour Law, 1-3, 2-1
FICA, 1-4, 3-1
    contributions to deferred compensation plans, 3-8
    coverage under, 3-1
    educational assistance, 3-8
    employees' (OASDI/HI) taxes and withholdings,
        3-10, 6-6
    employer's (OASDI taxes), 3-12, 6-24
    exempt employees, 3-4
    exempt payments, 3-8
    family employment, 3-3
    Federal Disability Insurance Trust Fund, 1-4
    Federal Old-Age and Survivors' Trust Fund, 1-4
    government employees, 3-3
    Health Insurance Plan, 1-4
    household employee, 3-3
    independent contractors, 3-4
    international agreements, 3-3
    lookback period, 3-18
    meals and lodging, 3-8
    Medicare, 1-4
    occupations specifically covered by, 3-2
    returns required for social security purposes, 3-17
    Self-Employment Contribution Act (SECA), 1-4
    sick pay, 3-8
    tax rates, 3-9
    tax returns and deposits, major forms for preparing,
        illus., 3-17
    taxable wage base, 3-9
    taxable wages, 3-5
    tips, 3-5
    voluntary coverage, 3-4
FICA taxes, depositing withheld, 6-26
Final pay, 6-19
Fixed salary arrangement, 2-29
Flat 22 percent rate, 4-20
Flat 22 percent supplemental wage rate, 4-4
Flexible reporting, 4-4
Flexible-spending accounts, 4-8
FLSA of 1938, 1-3, 1-25, 2-1, 2-4
    agricultural occupations, 2-14
    areas not covered by, 2-16
    blue-collar workers, 2-13

certificate of age, 2-15
child-labor restrictions, 2-13
coverage, 2-1
employee, 2-2
employer, 2-2
enterprise coverage, 2-1
Equal Pay Act, 2-13
exempt employees, 2-10
exemption status of workers under, illus., 2-10
individual employee coverage, 2-2
minimum wage, 2-4
mom and pop stores, 2-2
nonfarm occupations, 2-13
overtime hours and overtime pay, 2-8
penalties, 2-15
piece-rate system and, 2-30
records used for timekeeping, 2-21
requirements, exemptions from, 2-10
salary basis, 2-12
test of exemption, 2-10
tips, 2-6
wages, 2-4
white-collar workers, 2-10
workweek, 2-8
FMLA leave, exception to FLSA salary pay requirement, 2-13
Form 668-D, Release of Levy/Release of Property from Levy, 6-13
Form 668-W, Notice of Levy on Wages, Salary and Other Income, 6-13
Form 940, Employer's Annual Federal Unemployment (FUTA) Tax Return, 5-21, illus., 5-22, illus., 5-22, 7-20
    amending the return, 5-26
    completing the return, 5-24, illus., 5-24
    electronic filing, 5-24
    filing the return, 5-26
    final return, 5-26
    Schedule A, multi-state employers, 5-26, illus., 5-27
Form 940V, payment voucher form, 5-28
Form 941, Employer's Quarterly Federal Tax Return
    Schedule B, Report of Tax Liability for Semiweekly Schedule Depositors, 3-22, illus., 3-27
Form 941, Employer's Quarterly Federal Tax Return, 3-17, illus., 3-17, 3-21, illus., 3-23, 3-24, illus., 3-24, 3-25, illus., 3-25, 4-29, illus., 4-30, 7-19, A-23
    completing the return, 3-22
    electronic filing of, 3-29
    filing, 3-28
    non-filers of, 3-29
    preparing, 3-21
    sources of information for completing, illus., 3-26
Form 941-PR, Employer's Quarterly Federal Tax Return, 3-17

Form 941-SS, Employer's Quarterly Federal Tax Return, 3-17
Form 941-V, Form 941 Payment Voucher, 3-17
Form 941-X, Adjusted Employer's Quarterly Federal Tax Return or Claim for Refund, 3-17, 3-29
Form 943, Employer's Annual Tax Return for Agricultural Employees, 3-17, 3-20, illus., 4-30
Form 944, Employer's Annual Federal Tax Return, 3-17, 3-29, illus., 4-30
Form 945, Annual Return of Withheld Federal Income Tax, 3-17, 3-22, illus., 4-30, 4-32
Form 1040, Individual Income Tax Return, 3-12
    Schedule C, Profit or Loss from Business, 3-14
    Schedule SE, Self-Employment Tax, 3-14
Form 1095-C, applicable large employers, 1-13
Form 1096, Annual Summary and Transmittal of U.S. Information Returns, 4-30, 7-21, A-24, B-41
Form 1099, 3-4
Form 1099-DIV, Dividends and Distributions, illus., 4-31
Form 1099-G, Certain Government Payments, illus., 4-31
Form 1099-INT, Interest Income, illus., 4-31
Form 1099-MISC, Miscellaneous Income, illus., illus., 4-30, 7-21, A-24, B-41
Form 1099-NEC, Nonemployee Compensation, illus., 4-30
    independent contractor payments, 4-32
Form 1099-PATR, Taxable Distributions Received From Cooperatives, illus., 4-30
Form 1099-R, Distributions From Pensions, Annuities, Retirement or Profit-Sharing Plans, IRAs, Insurance Contracts, etc., illus., 4-30
Form 4070, Employee's Report of Tips to Employer, 3-5, illus., 3-7
Form 4137, Social Security and Medicare Tax on Unreported Tip Income, 3-22
Form 4419, Application for Filing Information Returns Electronically (FIRE), 4-32
Form 5498, IRA Contribution Information, illus., 4-30
Form 5500, pension plan annual report, 1-12
Form 8027, Employer's Annual Information Return of Tip Income and Allocated Tips, 3-6, illus., 4-30
Form 8453-EMP, 4-29
Form 8655 (Reporting Agent Authorization), 5-26
Form 8846, business tax credit, 3-6
Form 8846, Credit for Employer Social Security and Medicare Taxes Paid on Certain Employee Tips, 3-7
Form 8879-EMP, 4-29
Form 9779, EFTPS Business Enrollment Form, 3-21
Form DE 9c, California Quarterly Contribution Return and Report of Wages, illus., 4-35
Form DE 88ALL, California Payroll Tax Deposit, illus., 4-34
Form I-9, Employment Eligibility Verification, def., 1-8

Form REV-1667, W-2 Transmittal, 7-21, A-24, B-41
Form SS-4, Application for Employer Identification Number, illus., 3-15
Form SS-5, Application for a Social Security Card, 3-16
Form SS-8, Determination of Employee Work Status, 2-2
Form UC-2, Employer's Report for Unemployment Compensation—Fourth Quarter, 7-20, A-23
  Part I, Pennsylvania Form, illus., 5-30
  Part II, Pennsylvania Form, illus., 5-31
Form W-2, Wage and Tax Statement, 3-6, 3-20, 4-23, 7-20, A-23, B-40
  and information returns, electronic filing, 4-32
  def., 1-24
  how to complete, illus., 4-24, 4-25
Form W-2c, Corrected Wage and Tax Statement, 4-26, illus., 4-27
Form W-3, Transmittal of Wage and Tax Statements, 4-28, illus., 4-28, 7-21, A-24, B-41
Form W-3c, Transmittal of Corrected Income and Tax Statements, 4-29
Form W-4, Employee's Withholding Allowance Certificate, 1-8, 4-10, 4-11, 4-38
  and withholding calculations, revised, 4-10
  changing, 4-13
  completing, 4-11
  electronic filing of, 4-13
  from 2019 or Earlier (Employee's Withholding Allowance Certificate), 4-37, 4-38, illus., 4-38
  from 2020 or Later (Employee's Withholding Certificate), 4-11
  invalid, 4-14
  procedures for submitting, illus., 4-14
  requested, 4-14
Form W-4P, 4-15
Form W-4S, Request for Federal Income Tax Withholding from Sick Pay, 4-15
Form W-4V, 4-15
Form W-7, Application for IRS Individual Taxpayer Identification Number (ITIN), 3-16
Formulas, entering into worksheet, A-3
401(k) plan, 4-9, 6-13
Fringe benefits, 4-3
  de minimis, 4-5
  nontaxable, 4-4
  withholding on, 4-4
Fundamental Payroll Certification, 1-2
FUTA, 1-4, 5-1
  coverage under, 5-2
  employees, 5-3
  employers, 5-2
  excluded coverage from, 5-3
  nontaxable wages for unemployment purposes, 5-8
  penalties, 5-29
  quarterly deposit form, 5-28

statutory employees, 5-3
  tax rate, 5-10
  taxable wages for unemployment purposes, 5-8
  wages, 5-7
FUTA tax, 6-21
  credits against, 5-10
  paying, 6-27

G

Garnishment
  def., 6-10
  of wages, 6-10
General journal report, illus., B-9, illus., B-31
General ledger, 7-2, A-7
  Excel template, A-5
  partial report, illus., B-32
  payroll taxes account, illus., A-18
  report, illus., B-10, illus., B-10
Government employees, 3-3
Government employers, deposit requirements for state and local, 3-20
Government insurance program, informational reports, 1-12
Government payments, withholding on, 4-15
Government savings bonds, purchase of, 6-8
Gross amount, 4-2
Gross earnings, def., 2-25
Gross income, 3-13
Gross payroll, 6-7
  and withholdings, recording, 6-7
Gross-up, def., 4-22
Gross-up supplemental, 4-22
Group insurance, 7-5
  def., 6-8

H

Health Care and Education Reconciliation Act, 1-12
Health insurance, 6-9
  Plan, 1-4
  program (HI), 3-1
Health savings accounts, 4-8
Help and how-to, Excel, A-2
Hiring notice, illus., 1-21
  def., 1-21
Hiring process, human resources department procedure, illus., 1-16
Hospital employees, 2-9
Hourly rates
  converting biweekly wage rates to, 2-27
  converting monthly salary rates to, 2-27
  converting semimonthly salary rates to, 2-27
  converting weekly wage rates to, 2-26
Household employee, 3-3
  deposit requirements for employers of, 3-20

Household employer, 5-2
    taxes, 5-29
Household Employment Taxes, Schedule H, 5-29
Human Resources Department, 1-15
    procedure in the hiring process, illus., 1-16
Human resources system
    and payroll accounting systems, 1-14
    def., 1-15

I

Idle time, 2-18
Illustrative case
    Brookins Company, 6-30
    full project, B-3
    Glo-Brite Company, A-13, B-1, B-23
    short project, B-25
Immigration Reform and Control Act of 1986 (IRCA), 1-8
Income
    gross, 3-13
    self-employment, 3-13
Income Tax Code of 1914, 4-2
Income Tax Reform Act of 1986, 4-2
Income tax withholding, 4-2
    exemption from, 4-13
Income tax withholding laws, 1-4
    coverage under federal, 4-2
Income taxes
    def., 1-4
    state and city, 6-7
    withholding local, 4-34, 4-36
Independent contractor payments, 4-31
    Form 1099-NEC Nonemployee Compensation,
        4-31
Independent contractor status, test for, illus., 3-5
Independent contractors, def., 3-4
Individual employee coverage, def., 2-2
Individual retirement accounts (IRAs), 4-9, 6-14
    distributions from, Form 1099-R, illus., 4-30
    Form 5498, illus., 4-30
    Roth, 4-10
Individual's distributive share, 3-13
Information, general, payroll project, 7-3
Information reports—SUTA, 5-29
Information required by major federal payroll laws,
    summary of, illus., 1-6
Information returns, 4-34
    def., 4-30
    electronic filing Form W-2 and, 4-32
    failure to furnish, 3-32
    major, illus., 4-30
Inpatriates, 3-3
Insurance
    group, 6-8, 7-5
    health, 6-9

Insurance contracts, distributions from, Form 1099-R,
    illus., 4-30
Interest Income, Form 1099-INT, illus., 4-30
International agreements, 3-3
Internet, timekeeping, 2-24
Interns, 2-4
Interstate commerce, 1-3
Interstate employee
    coverage of, 5-4
    def., 5-4
Interstate Reciprocal Coverage Arrangement, 5-6
Investigative consumer report, def., 1-17
IRA. *See* Individual retirement accounts
IRS, informational reports, 1-12
IVR (Interactive Voice Response), 2-24

J

Job descriptions, 1-16
Journal, 7-2, A-7
    Excel template, A-5
Journal entries
    def., 6-3
    for current payroll, illus., B-7, illus., B-30, illus., B-38
    for payroll taxes, illus., A-16, illus., B-8, illus., B-30

L

Labor cost accounts, Glo-Brite, illus., 7-6, illus., A-11
Labor costs, distribution of, 7-6
Labor distribution, illus., B-11, illus., B-33
Licensed real estate agents, statutory
    nonemployees, 2-3
Life-style discrimination law, 1-17
Living wage, 2-6
Lookback period
    def., 3-18
    for calendar year 2021, illus., 3-18

M

Makeup pay for military duty, 3-8
Mark-sense time card used in the timekeeper
    computerized system, illus., 2-23
Married persons—weekly payroll period, illus., 4-41
McNamara-O'Hara Service Contract Act (1965), 1-9
Meal periods, 2-18
Meals and lodging, 3-8
Medicare, 1-4, 3-1
Merit rating, def., 5-11
Military duty, makeup pay for, 3-8
Minimum wage, 1-3, 2-4
    paying less than, 2-5
    paying more than, 2-5
Misclassified workers, penalties of, 2-15
Misclassifying employees, 3-4
Mom and pop stores, FLSA and, 2-2

Monthly depositor, 3-18
  def., 3-19
Multi-state employers, Schedule A of Form 940, 5-26,
  illus., 5-27

N

National Automated Clearing House
  Association, 6-16
National Call Center, 2-1
National Directory of New Hires, 1-8
Navigation through worksheet, A-2
Negative-balance employers, def., 5-17
Net pay, 6-14
Ninety-eight percent rule. *See* Safe harbor rule
Nonaccountable plan for traveling expenses, 4-6
Nonagricultural workers (deposit requirements), 3-18
Nondiscretionary bonus, 2-33
  def., 2-4
Nonemployees, statutory employees, 4-2
Nonexempt employees, salaried, 2-28
Nonfarm occupations, 2-13
Nonpayroll reporting, 4-32
Nonprofits, 5-21
Nonresident aliens, withholding on, 4-14
Nontaxable fringe benefits, 4-4
Nontaxable wages for unemployment purposes, 5-8

O

Obamacare. *See* Affordable Care Act
Occupational Safety and Health Act (OSHA) (1970), 1-9
Occupations specifically covered by FICA, 3-2
Office of Child Support Enforcement (OCSE), 1-8, 6-12
Old-age, survivors, and disability insurance (OASDI), 3-1,
  3-9
One-day rule, 3-19
Operations
  location of base of, 5-5
  location of direction or control of, 5-5
Outsourcing payroll, 1-25
Overtime, 7-4
  different rates for different jobs, 2-26
  paid in advance, 2-26
Overtime earnings for pieceworkers, method A and
  method B, 2-31
Overtime hours and overtime pay, 2-8
  provisions, exceptions to, 2-9
Overtime pay, calculating, 2-25
Overtime premium, def., 2-25

P

Paid family leave plans, 1-11
Part-year employment, def., 4-18
Partial unemployment, def., 5-32
Partial unemployment notices, def., 5-32
Partnerships, 2-3

Patient Protection and Affordable Care Act, 1-12
Pay cards, 6-18
Pay equality for women, 1-20
Pay, final, 6-19
Paycheck, 1-25
  with stub showing current and year-to-date earnings
    and deductions, illus., 1-26
Payday, 7-4
Payee statements, failure to furnish, 3-32
Paying a living wage, 2-6
Payment voucher form, Form 940V, 5-28
Payments exempt from withholding, 4-6
Payments for educational assistance, 3-8
Payroll
  analyzing and journalizing, 6-1
  outsourcing, 1-25
  project, B-1, B-2
  report, illus., B-7, illus., B-29
Payroll accounting system, 1-1
  def., 1-23
  human resources and, 1-14
  procedures in, illus., 1-23
Payroll activities, major changes in laws concerning, 1-3
Payroll adjustments
  recording end-of-period, 7-22, B-41
  recording end-of-year, A-24
Payroll cash entries, general journal, illus., B-8, illus.,
  B-30
Payroll deductions
  earnings statement (check stub), illus., 6-16
  other, 6-8
Payroll Department, 1-15
Payroll entries, journalized, illus., A-16
Payroll Guide, 1-2
Payroll profession, 1-2
Payroll professional, 1-1
Payroll Professional Certification, 1-2
Payroll project, 7-1, A-1, B-1
  Excel template instructions for short version of,
    A-1, A-6
  short version, A-19, B-23
  start of, 7-6
Payroll rate, change in, 1-22
Payroll rate form, change in, 1-22
Payroll records
  books of account and, 7-2
  need for, 1-1
  other federal laws affecting the need for, 1-8,
    illus., 1-9
  other state laws affecting the need for, 1-13
Payroll register, illus., 1-24, 6-1, illus., 6-2, illus.,
  6-3, 7-2, A-8
  checkpoint error message, illus., A-16
  deductions section, illus., A-14
  def., 1-24

earnings section, illus., A-14
Excel template, A-5
proving the totals of, 6-3
taxable earnings and labor cost distribution,
    illus., A-15
using the information in, 6-4
Payroll Tax Deposit Coupon, 4-33
Payroll taxes, illus., A-11, illus., 7-5
    contributions and withholdings, 7-4, illus., 7-5
    entries to record wages and, 6-21, 6-23
    journal entry for, illus., A-17, illus., B-8, illus., B-30
    recording the deposit or payment of, 6-26
Payroll transactions, summary of accounts used in
    recording, 6-29
Paystub, electronic, 6-19
Penalties, 2-15, 4-28, 4-29
    employee, 4-14
    failure-to-comply, 3-30
    FUTA, 5-29
    SUTA, 5-32
*Pennsylvania Quarterly Reconciliation of Income Tax
    Withheld*, A-24
Pennsylvania state income tax, illus., A-24
Pension and retirement contributions, 6-14
Pension Benefit Guaranty Corporation, 1-12
Pension payments, withholding for, 4-14
Pension Protection Act of 2006, 6-14
Pensions, distributions from, Form 1099-R,
    illus., 4-30
Percentage method, 4-16
    def., 4-16, 4-39
    for Manual Systems with Forms W-4 from 2019 or
        Earlier, 4-39
    Tables for Manual Payroll Systems with Forms W-4
        from 2020 or Later, semimonthly payroll period,
        illus., 4-17
Periodic withholding returns, 4-33
Person
    def., 3-2
    self-employed, 3-13
    unemployed, 5-2
Personal allowance, def., 4-37
Personal computer-based systems, 2-22
Personal identification number (PIN), 3-21, 3-29,
    5-25, 6-18
Personnel data, illus., A-9
Personnel files, employee access of, 1-23
Personnel records
    need for, 1-1
    other federal laws affecting the need for, 1-8,
        illus., 1-9
    other state laws affecting the need for, 1-13
Personnel, requisition for, 1-16
Piece rate, 2-30

Piece-rate system, def., 2-30
Pooled-fund laws, def., 5-13
Portal-to-Portal Act, 2-20
Positive-balance employers, def., 5-17
Postliminary activities, 2-20
Pre-hire inquiries, def., 1-17
Preliminary activities, 2-20
Premiere Payroll Tax Research Library, 1-4
Pretax salary reductions, 4-7
Principal activities, def., 2-17
Printing, Excel template, A-6
Privately printed forms, 4-29
Profit-sharing plans
    def., 2-33
    distributions from, Form 1099-R, illus., 4-30
Project audit test, 7-69, 7-71, 7-73, 7-75, 7-77, A-26,
    A-27, A-28, B-43, B-45, B-47, B-49, B-51
Protected cell error message, illus., A-7
PTO (paid time off), 6-28
Publication 15-T, 4-10

Q

Quarterly averaging, def., 4-18
*Quarterly Contribution Return and Report of
    Wages*, 4-34
Quarterly deposit form, FUTA, 5-28

R

Railroad Retirement Tax Act, 5-4
Railroad Unemployment Insurance Act, 5-4
Rate(s)
    computing contribution, 5-17
    converting biweekly wage rates to hourly, 2-27
    converting monthly salary rates to hourly, 2-27
    converting semimonthly salary rates to
        hourly, 2-27
    converting weekly wage rates to hourly, 2-26
    table of decimal equivalents to convert into weekly,
        hourly, and hourly overtime salary, illus., 2-28
    tax, 3-9
Reciprocal agreement, def., 4-33
Reciprocal arrangements
    def., 5-6
    of employment, 5-6
Reconciliation returns, 4-34
Recording systems, computerized time and
    attendance, 2-22
Recordkeeping requirements, 1-5
Recordkeeping system, 1-23
Records, retention of, 5-32
Reference inquiry, 1-20
    form, def., 1-20
Reissued Statement, 4-26

Requisition for personnel, def., 1-16
Reserve-ratio formula, def., 5-17
Retail, employees in, 2-10
Retirement accounts, tax-deferred, 4-8
Retirement contributions, pension and, 6-14
Retirement plans, distributions from, Form 1099-R, illus., 4-30
Returns employers must complete, 4-29
Returns filed by employers, major, illus., 4-30
Returns, major information, illus., 4-30
Roth IRA, 4-10. *See also* Individual retirement accounts

S

Safe harbor rule, def., 3-19
Salaried employees with fluctuating workweek, 2-28
Salaried nonexempt employees, 2-28
Salaries
    computing wages and, 2-1
    def., 2-4
    methods of computing, 2-24
    methods of paying, 6-15
    paying by check, 6-15
    paying by electronic transfer, 6-17
    paying in cash, 6-15
Salary reductions, pretax, 4-7
Salesperson, 3-3, 5-3
Saving a workbook, A-4
Schedule A of Form 940, multi-state employers, 5-26, illus., 5-27
Schedule B, Form 941, Report of Tax Liability for Semiweekly Schedule Depositors, 3-22, illus., 3-27
Schedule C (Form 1040), Profit or Loss from Business, 3-14
Schedule H, Household Employment Taxes, 5-29
Schedule SE (Form 1040), Self-Employment Tax, 3-14
Seasonal employers, 3-28
Section 403(b) plan, 4-9
Section 457(b) plan, 4-9
Self-employed person, 3-13
Self-Employment Contributions Act (SECA), 1-4, 3-1, 3-13
Self-employment income
    def., 3-13
    reporting, 3-14
Self-employment OASDI/HI taxes, 3-13
Self-employment taxes, 3-4
Semimonthly, def., 2-4
Semiweekly depositor, 3-20
    def., 3-20
Semiweekly schedule depositors, report of tax liability for, illus., 3-27
Separation report, def., 5-32
Service industries, employees in, 2-10

Shortfall, def., 3-19
Sick pay, 3-8
    def., 3-8
    withholding from, 4-15
Simple plans, 4-9
Sleep time, 2-19
Small Business Health Options Program, 1-13
Small Business Job Protection Act, 2-7
Small employers, def., 1-13
Social Security Act of 1935, 1-4, 3-9, 5-1
Social Security Administration (SSA), 1-10, 3-8, 5-1, 6-12
Social Security Disability Insurance, 1-14
Social Security number (SSN), 1-10
    verifying, 3-17
Social Security Online, 3-8
Social security purposes, returns required for, 3-17
Social Security Tax Law, 4-2
Social Security taxes, 3-1
Society for Human Resource Management survey, 1-20
Special incentive plans, 2-32
Special period rule, 4-4
Special withholding allowance, def., 4-37
Spouse, FMLA definition of, 1-11
Standard deduction, def., 4-16, 4-39
State and city income taxes, 6-7
    paying, 6-27
State and local government employers, deposit requirements for, 3-20
State Directory of New Hire Reporting, 1-8
State disability benefit laws, 1-14
State Disbursement Unit, 6-12
State income tax
    returns and reports, 4-33, 4-34
    withholding, 4-32, 4-33
State laws affecting the need for payroll and personnel records, other, 1-13
State laws for minimum wage and overtime rules, 2-6
State Unemployment Compensation Laws (2021), summary of, illus., 5-13, illus., 5-14, illus. 5-15
State Unemployment Tax Act. *See* SUTA
States' minimum wage and maximum hours laws, 1-3
Status report, def., 5-30
Statutory employees, 2-3, 4-2, 5-3
Statutory nonemployees, 2-3, 4-2
Successor employer, 3-12
Summary of Your Rights Under the FCRA, 1-17
Supplemental Security Income (SSI), 1-14
Supplemental wage payments, def., 4-20
Supplemental wages paid separately from regular wages, 4-21, 4-22
    method A, 4-21, 4-22
    method B, 4-22
Supplemental wages paid with regular wages, 4-20, 4-21
Supplementary payroll sheet, illus., 6-15
SUTA, 1-4, 5-1

Americans working overseas, 5-7
computing the contribution rate, 5-17
contribution reports, 5-30
coverage under, 5-2
employee contributions, 5-16
employees, 5-4
employer contributions, 5-16
employers, 5-3
experience rating, 5-17
information reports, 5-29
interstate employee, 5-4
nonprofits, 5-21
partial unemployment notices, 5-32
penalties, 5-32
pooled-fund laws, 5-13
qualifying for benefits, 5-7
reciprocal arrangements, 5-6
separation reports, 5-32
status reports, 5-30
tax rates, 5-13
terminating liability, 5-20
voluntary contributions, 5-19
wage information reports, 5-30
wages, 5-9
SUTA Dumping Prevention Act, 5-21
SUTA taxes, 6-21
paying FUTA and, 6-27

T

Table for amount exempt for tax levy (single person),
    2021, illus., 6-13
Table of allowance values for 2021, illus., 4-40
Table of decimal equivalents to convert into weekly,
    hourly, and hourly overtime salary rates, illus., 2-28
Taking work home, 2-19
Tardiness, 2-21
Tax Cuts and Jobs Act (TCJA), 4-10, 4-11, 7-20
Tax-deferred retirement account information, illus., 4-9
Tax-deferred retirement accounts, 4-8
Tax-deferred retirement plans, 3-8
Tax levy, (single person) 2021 table for amount exempt
    for, illus., 6-13
Tax liability for semiweekly schedule depositors, report
    of, illus., 3-27
Tax Overhaul Bill of 2017, 1-13
Tax rates, 3-9
    FUTA, 5-10
    SUTA, 5-13
Tax Relief Act, 3-10
Taxable payments to employees, illus., 4-3
Taxable tips, 4-5
Taxable wage base, def., 3-9
Taxable wages, 3-5, 4-2
    for unemployment purposes, 5-8
    other types of, illus., 3-6

Taxable year, 3-14
Taxes
    and withholdings, employees' FICA (OASDI/HI), 3-10
    depositing, 7-4, illus., 7-5
    depositing withheld FICA, 6-25
    employee FICA, 6-5
    employer FICA, 6-21
    failure to fully pay employment, 3-31
    federal income, 6-7, 6-26
    FUTA, 6-21
    household employers, 5-29
    paying FUTA and SUTA, 6-26
    payroll, 6-21, 6-23, 6-26, 7-4, illus., 7-5, A-11
    self-employment OASDI/HI, 3-4, 3-13
    Social Security, 3-1
    state and city income, 6-7, 6-27
    SUTA, 6-21
    unemployment compensation, 5-1
    unemployment compensation credits and, 5-9
    withholding local income, 4-34, 4-36
Taxpayer identification number (TIN), 4-31
Terminating liability, 5-20
Testing applicants (EEOC), 1-20
Time and a half, 7-4, 7-11
Time card, illus., 2-23
    def., 2-22
    used in timekeeper computerized system,
        mark-sense, illus., 2-23
Time rate, 2-25
Time sheet, def., 2-21
Timekeeping, 7-4
    badge systems, 2-22
    biometrics, 2-24
    card-generated systems, 2-22
    cardless and badgeless systems, 2-22
    Internet, 2-24
    IVR, 2-24
    next generation, 2-23
    personal computer-based systems, 2-22
    records used for, 2-21
    touch-screen technology, 2-24
Tip retention violations, penalties of, 2-16
Tip(s), 3-5
    allocated, 4-5
    child support and, 6-12
    def., 2-6
    Form 8027, illus., 4-30
    taxable, 4-5
    withholding from, 4-5
Tipped employee, 2-9
    def., 2-6, 2-7
Title VII of the Civil Rights Act of 1964, 1-5
Title XII advances, def., 5-12
Touch-screen technology, timekeeping, 2-24
Training sessions, 2-19

Transfers of employment, 5-6
Travel time, 2-17
Traveling expenses, 4-6
    accountable plan, 4-6
    nonaccountable plan, 4-6
Traveling salesperson, 3-3, 5-3
2021
    Form W-4, Employee's Withholding Certificate, illus.,
        4-12
    Percentage Method Tables for Manual Payroll
        Systems With Forms W-4 From 2020 or Later,
        semimonthly payroll period, illus., 4-17
    Table for amount exempt for tax levy (single person),
        illus., 6-13
    Wage Bracket Method Tables for Manual Payroll
        Systems With Forms W-4
    From 2019 or Earlier, weekly payroll period,
        illus., 4-41
    From 2020 or Later, weekly payroll period,
        illus., 4-18

U

Unclaimed wages, 6-20
Unemployed persons, 5-2
Unemployment compensation program, 5-1
Unemployment compensation reports required of the
    employer, 5-21
Unemployment compensation taxes, 5-1
    and credits, 5-9
Unemployment purposes
    nontaxable wages for, 5-8
    taxable wages for, 5-8
Unemployment tax acts, 1-4
Uniform Unclaimed Property Act, 6-20
Uniformed Services Employment and Reemployment
    Rights Act (USERRA) of 1994, 1-11
Union dues, 6-10, 7-6
Unpaid leave, 1-10
U.S. Bureau of Labor Statistics, 3-4
U.S. Citizenship and Immigration Services (USCIS),
    1-8, 1-9
U.S. Department of Labor
    child-labor restrictions, 2-13
    Employment Standards Administration homepage,
        2-2
    illegal aliens, 2-5
    informational reports, 1-12
U. S. Office of Personnel Management, 2-8

V

Vacation pay, 4-20, 6-28
Vesting, def., 1-12
Vietnam Era Veterans' Readjustment Act (1974), 1-9
Violations, penalties for repeated, 2-16
Vocational Rehabilitation Act (1973), 1-9
Voluntary contributions, def., 5-19
Voluntary coverage, 3-4

W

W-2 Transmittal, Form REV-1667, 7-21, A-24
Wage and Hour Division of U.S. Department of Labor
    (DOL), 2-1
Wage and Hour Law, 2-13
Wage and hour provisions (willful violations), penalties
    of, 2-16
Wage and tax statements
    def., 4-23
    Form W-2, 1-24, 3-6, 3-20, 4-23, illus., 4-23,
        7-20, A-23
    Form W-2c, corrected, 4-26, illus., 4-27
    Form W-3, Transmittal of, 4-28, illus., 4-28,
        7-21, A-24
    Form W-3c, Transmittal of Corrected, 4-29
Wage-bracket method, 4-17, 4-39
    def., 4-16, 4-39, 4-39
Wage Bracket Method Tables for Manual Payroll Systems
    With Forms W-4
    From 2019 or Earlier, weekly payroll period,
        illus., 4-41
    From 2020 or Later, weekly payroll period,
        illus., 4-18
Wage information reports, def., 5-30
Wage tax coupon, Philadelphia, illus., 4-36
Wage theft, def., 2-15
Wages, 6-28
    and payroll taxes, entries to record, 6-21
    and salaries, computing, 2-1
    annualizing, 4-18
    def., 2-4, 4-2
    FUTA, 5-7
    garnishment of, 6-10
    methods of computing, 2-24
    methods of paying, 6-15
    other types of taxable, illus., 3-6
    paying by check, 6-15
    paying by electronic transfer, 6-17
    paying in cash, 6-15
    supplemental paid separately from regular,
        4-21, 4-22
    supplemental paid with regular, 4-20, 4-21
    supplemental payments, 4-20
    SUTA, 5-9
    taxable, 3-5, 4-2
    unclaimed, 6-20
Walsh-Healey Public Contracts Act (1936), 1-9
Withholding
    backup, illus., 4-30, 4-31, 4-32
    employees' FICA (OASDI/HI) taxes and, 3-10
    exemption from income tax, 4-13
    federal income tax, 4-16, 4-39
    other, 4-14
    other methods of, 4-18
    payments exempt from, 4-6
    payroll taxes—contributions and, 7-4, illus., 7-5
    recording gross payroll and, 6-7

Withholding agreements, additional and
    voluntary, 4-13
Withholding allowances, 4-37, 4-38
    additional, 4-37
    for dependents, 4-37
    other, 4-37
    personal, 4-37
    special, 4-37
Withholding for pension or annuity payments,
    4-14
Withholding from
    sick pay, 4-15
    tips, 4-5
Withholding laws, coverage under federal
    income tax, 4-2
Withholding local income taxes, 4-34, 4-36
Withholding on
    fringe benefits, 4-4
    government payments, 4-15
    nonresident aliens, 4-14
Withholding rate, 37 percent, 4-21
Withholding state income tax, 4-32, 4-33
Work
    location of, 5-5
    regular hours of, 7-3
Work-at-home individuals, 3-3

Work time
    absences, 2-21
    clothes-changing time and wash-up, 2-17
    doctor's appointments, 2-20
    fractional parts of an hour, 2-20
    idle time, 2-18
    meal periods, 2-18
    preliminary and postliminary activities, 2-20
    principal activities, 2-17
    rest periods and coffee breaks, 2-18
    sleep time, 2-19
    taking work home, 2-19
    tardiness, 2-21
    training sessions, 2-19
    travel time, 2-17
    waiting time, 2-18
Workbooks, A-2
Workers' compensation insurance
    def., 1-13
    expense, recording, 6-25
Workers' compensation laws, 1-13
Worksheet, navigation through, A-2
Worksheet tabs, illus., A-6
Workweek
    def., 2-8
    salaried employees with fluctuating, 2-28

2023
FEDERAL PAYROLL TAXES CALENDAR

The following calendar shows the due dates for various returns, reports, and statements that employers must file, as well as the due dates for monthly and quarterly deposits. The due dates for **semiweekly depositors** and those affected by the **$100,000 one-day rule** are presented in Chapter 3.

JANUARY

10.   **Form 4070.** Employees receiving cash tips in December of $20 or more must report them to their employer. (See Chapter 3.)

17.   **Form 1040-ES.** Final payment of 2022's estimated tax due by self-employed persons required to file declarations, unless Form 1040 is filed no later than February 1. Farmers and fishermen file declarations and pay estimated tax or file final returns for 2022 by March 1 instead of making estimated payments.

      Electronic transfer of FICA taxes and withheld federal income taxes for December due. (See Chapter 3.)

31.   **Form W-2.** Employer must furnish employees with copies of the Wage and Tax Statement, showing wages paid, federal income taxes withheld, and FICA taxes withheld during 2022. Employees terminated during 2023 may request that Form W-2 be furnished to them within 30 days of their last payment of wages or the date of their request, whichever is later.

      Form W-3, along with SSA copy of Form W-2 for each employee whether filed electronically or using paper forms. (See Chapter 4.)

      Form 940. Annual return and deposit or remittance of any undeposited tax due for 2022 under Federal Unemployment Tax Act. If tax deposits paid employer's tax liability in full, return may be delayed until February 10. (See Chapter 5.)

      Form 941. Quarterly return and remittance or deposit of undeposited FICA taxes and withheld income taxes for 4th calendar quarter of 2022. If timely deposits of tax have been made that pay employer's tax liability in full, return may be filed on or before February 10. (See Chapter 3.)

      Form 943. Annual return for agricultural employees, showing income taxes withheld as a result of voluntary withholding agreement and required FICA information for covered employees. (See Chapter 3.) Individuals (other than farmers or fishermen) may file final return for 2022 instead of filing estimate on January 17.

      Form 944. Annual return of FICA and withheld income taxes for employers who owe $1,000 or less in employment taxes per year.

      Form 945. Used to report income tax withheld during 2022 for nonpayroll items such as backup withholding and withholding on pensions, annuities, IRAs, gambling winnings, and payments of Indian gaming profits to tribal members. If timely deposits have been made, employers have until February 10 to file the return.

      Form 1099. All businesses give recipients an annual information statement for certain payments made in 2022 such as compensation to nonemployees, dividends, interest, prizes and awards, rents, royalties, etc.

FEBRUARY

10.   **Form 940.** Annual return due, provided timely deposits for 2022 satisfied employer's tax liability in full.

      Form 941. Quarterly return showing withheld income taxes and FICA taxes for 4th calendar quarter of 2022 due, provided timely deposits for that quarter satisfied employer's full tax liability. (See Chapter 3.)

      Form 4070. Employees receiving cash tips in January of $20 or more must report them to their employer.

15.   Electronic transfer of FICA taxes and withheld federal income taxes for January due.

      Form W-4. This is the expiration date for Form W-4 on which employees claim exemption from federal income tax withholding because they anticipate no federal income tax liability.

28.   **Forms 1099 and 1096.** Annual information returns due to report compensation of $600 or more paid to nonemployees (Form 1099-NEC must be filed prior to February 1), dividends in excess of $10, and compensation from which federal income taxes were not withheld and which was not reported on Form W-2. (See Chapter 4.) Last day for farmers and fishermen to file tax return for 2022 instead of filing estimate on January 17.

MARCH

10.   **Form 4070.** Employees receiving cash tips in February of $20 or more must report them to their employer.

15.   Electronic transfer of FICA taxes and withheld federal income taxes for February due.

31.   Electronic filing deadline for copy A of W-2G issued.

APRIL

10.   **Form 4070.** Employees receiving cash tips in March of $20 or more must report them to their employer.

17.   **Form 1040.** Final return and payment of individual's income tax for 2022 due.

      Electronic transfer of FICA taxes and withheld federal income taxes for March due.

      Form 1040-ES. Declaration and payment of 1st quarter estimated tax for 2023 by individuals other than farmers and fishermen.

MAY

1. **Form 941.** Quarterly return and remittance or deposit of undeposited FICA taxes and withheld income taxes of less than $2,500 for 1st calendar quarter of 2023. If timely deposits for the quarter have paid employer's tax liability in full, the return may be delayed until May 10.
   Electronic transfer of FUTA taxes due for the 1st calendar quarter of 2023 if liability exceeds $500. (See Chapter 5.)
   Status determination date for adjusting an employee's withholding to correspond to the employee's changed withholding status.
10. **Form 941.** Quarterly return showing wage and tax information for 1st calendar quarter of 2023, provided employer's timely deposits for that quarter satisfied the tax liability in full.
    Form 4070. Employees receiving cash tips in April of $20 or more must report them to their employer.
15. Electronic transfer of FICA taxes and withheld federal income taxes for April due.

JUNE

12. **Form 4070.** Employees receiving cash tips in May of $20 or more must report them to their employer.
15. Electronic transfer of FICA taxes and withheld federal income taxes for May due.
    Form 1040-ES. Payment of 2nd quarter estimated tax for 2023 due by individuals other than farmers and fishermen. If declaration is being filed for the 1st time, one-third of estimated tax must be paid.

JULY

10. **Form 4070.** Employees receiving cash tips in June of $20 or more must report them to their employer.
17. Electronic transfer of FICA taxes and withheld federal income taxes for June due.
31. **Form 941.** Quarterly return and remittance or deposit of undeposited FICA taxes and withheld income taxes of less than $2,500 for 2nd quarter of 2023. If timely deposits for the quarter have paid employer's tax liability in full, the return may be delayed until August 10.
    Electronic transfer of FUTA taxes for 2nd calendar quarter of 2023 if aggregate undeposited liability exceeds $500.

AUGUST

10. **Form 941.** Quarterly return showing wage and tax information for 2nd calendar quarter of 2023 due, provided employer's timely deposits for that quarter satisfied the tax liability in full.
    Form 4070. Employees receiving cash tips in July of $20 or more must report them to their employer.
15. Electronic transfer of FICA taxes and withheld federal income taxes for July due.

SEPTEMBER

11. **Form 4070.** Employees receiving cash tips in August of $20 or more must report them to their employer.
15. Electronic transfer of FICA taxes and withheld federal income taxes for August due.
    Form 1040-ES. Payment of 3rd quarter estimated tax for 2023 by individuals other than farmers and fishermen, or payment of 2nd one-third of the tax. If declaration is being filed for 1st time, one-half of the estimated tax must be paid.

OCTOBER

10. **Form 4070.** Employees receiving cash tips in September of $20 or more must report them to their employer.
16. Electronic transfer of FICA taxes and withheld federal income taxes for September due.
31. **Form 941.** Quarterly return and remittance or deposit of undeposited FICA taxes and withheld income taxes of less than $2,500 for 3rd calendar quarter of 2023. If timely deposits for the quarter have paid employer's tax liability in full, the return may be delayed until November 10.
    Electronic transfer of FUTA taxes for 3rd calendar quarter of 2023 if aggregate undeposited liability exceeds $500.

NOVEMBER

10. **Form 941.** Quarterly return showing wage and tax information for 3rd quarter of 2023 due, provided employer's timely deposits for that quarter satisfied the tax liability in full.
    Form 4070. Employees receiving cash tips in October of $20 or more must report them to their employer.
15. Electronic transfer of FICA taxes and withheld federal income taxes for October due.

DECEMBER

1. **Form W-4.** Employers should request amended withholding certificates from employees whose filing status changed during 2023. Status change is to be given effect at beginning of 2024.
11. **Form 4070.** Employees receiving cash tips in November of $20 or more must report them to their employer.
15. Electronic transfer of FICA taxes and withheld federal income taxes for November due.